# MEANY

Books by

# JOSEPH C. GOULDEN

MEANY     1972
THE SUPERLAWYERS     1972
THE MONEY GIVERS     1971
TRUTH IS THE FIRST CASUALTY     1969
MONOPOLY     1968
THE CURTIS CAPER     1965

# MEANY

## Joseph C. Goulden

ATHENEUM

New York

1972

FOR CARL D. BRANDT

# CONTENTS

|  |  |  |
|---|---|---:|
|  | *Prologue* | 3 |
| **I** | Mike Meany's Boy | 7 |
| **II** | The Man with the Monkey Wrench | 18 |
| **III** | The State Fed Presidency: The Plumber as Lobbyist | 38 |
| **IV** | Ascent into Boredom | 78 |
| **V** | The War Labor Board | 93 |
| **VI** | Birth of a Cold Warrior | 116 |
| **VII** | Outscowling John L. Lewis | 138 |
| **VIII** | At Peace and War with Harry Truman | 155 |
| **IX** | Labor United: A Hyphen for the AFL-CIO | 181 |
| **X** | I Like Ike . . . Sometimes | 207 |
| **XI** | "Hoffa's Too Rich for Our Blood" | 233 |
| **XII** | Meany versus Reuther: Round One | 263 |
| **XIII** | The Kennedy Years | 290 |
| **XIV** | Expansion at Home and Abroad | 324 |
| **XV** | All the Way with LBJ—to Vietnam, Too | 336 |
| **XVI** | Meany versus Reuther: Knockout | 371 |
| **XVII** | Nixon One: Tricked by Dick | 404 |
| **XVIII** | Nixon Two: The Battle of Bal Harbour | 430 |
|  | *Epilogue* | 463 |
|  | *Sources and Acknowledgments* | 468 |
|  | *Index* | 483 |

# MEANY

# PROLOGUE

*At seventy-seven he has the bulk and deliberate grace of an old lion. Time is eroding him. Lines cut deeply across his face, flaring downward from either side of a broad, stubby nose. The flesh hangs, in the beginning of an old man's wattle, from the pugnacious jaw. The two patches of hair—fringes, really—separated by a gaping bare stretch of freckled scalp, are wispy and silken white, tending, by midday, to go where they wish. Too much Florida sun from this year's midwinter vacation has burned the sides of his neck the purplish color of raw, cold steak.*

*We are sitting in the sunny southwest corner of the eighth floor of the AFL-CIO Building in Washington. Behind George Meany's right shoulder, beyond the American flag and the window, across verdant Lafayette Park and its splashing fountains and noontime strollers, is the White House. George Meany has been talking about Richard Nixon, the man who lives there, and suddenly his stubby index finger jabs at my tape recorder. After I turn it off he continues talking, saying something very uncomplimentary about a President of the United States, and then we drift on to a long-concluded dispute he had with another President, Franklin D. Roosevelt, over a New Deal program. I say something to the effect that few men in America have had the opportunity to joust with both Roosevelt and Nixon. Meany fingers his cigar, thrusts it into his mouth, slightly to the right of center where he likes to carry it, and puffs. He is thinking, and I have learned not to intrude when Meany is poking around in his memory. Finally he blurts, "Jeez, you know, there is a lot of history back there."*

DURING THE EARLY MONTHS of the Nixon Administration, when George Meany still spoke to its high officers with humor and tolerable civility, he had occasion to call a cabinet officer he knew on a first-name basis. Meany asked the officer about some minor problem that had crossed his mind.

"George," the man said, "what the hell has that got to do with labor?"

"Sonny boy," George Meany replied, "everything that happens today has to do with labor."

Indeed it does, as the Nixon Administration learned to its abrupt discomfort in 1971, when George Meany staged an audacious one-man revolt against the President's wage-price freeze. Meany's opposition was risky. He opposed the President on his own initiative, acting against what the polls showed to be the wishes of the vast majority of Americans, including the union members who are Meany's constituency. Inflation had America in a rebellious, ugly mood, the sort of kitchen-rooted discontent that tells a politician he must do something, *anything,* lest he be clubbed from office. When an Administration puts the aura of "national emergency" around a program, few public figures dare step up front to ask disparaging questions.

George Meany, president of the American Federation of Labor and Congress of Industrial Organizations, is not an inhibited man. With savage slashes of rhetoric he cleaved away the public relations camouflage to reveal Nixon's "new prosperity" for what it was: a program tilted against the American worker, one that froze his income but not his expenses, while giving lucrative tax bonanzas to business. The freeze ultimately failed, and the new prosperity did not materialize; whether its inherent flaws or Meany's opposition was responsible is a judgment that must be made eventually by the economic historians when they sort through the fiscal debris of the early 1970's.

The peculiar feature of the months-long confrontation was that, for all his power, Meany is an enigmatic figure even to the 14 million members of AFL-CIO unions who comprise his constituency. To rank-and-file unionists, Meany is a dour face with a cigar, seen occasionally on the television screens or in newspaper photographs; a gruff old Irishman who speckles his speech with the dem-and-dose Bronxisms of his youth; a hard-hat in a business suit. Meany's public anonymity is deliberate. An intensely private man, Meany maintains an impenetrable wall between his family life and his career as professional unionist. The trait developed soon after he became a business agent for the plumbers union, when the telephone and drop-in visitors constantly disrupted his home life. His wife declared, "Your office is there, my home is here. My home is my castle, and I am the queen here. If you want to work, do it at the office, not here, because I can't raise a family this way." Miss Virginia Tehas, a stately, elegant woman who has been Meany's administrative alter ego for more than three decades, can recollect only three weekend phone calls from him. "He works from nine to five and leaves it on the desk when he goes home," she says of Meany. The reticence extends to much of the affairs of the AFL-CIO and its 123 affiliated unions. To

Meany, "union business is union business," and discussable only in union councils; his is the secretiveness of an era when "management finks" spied on embryonic labor organizations.

Here a brief job description is in order. Meany is a labor leader, not a union leader. The AFL-CIO is a federation, each affiliate autonomous in its own affairs (save for violations of AFL-CIO constitutional strictures on corruption, discrimination, and communism). Meany has no trade union functions. He does not engage in collective bargaining, he does not arbitrate grievances, he cannot order a single American worker out on strike. But for organized labor as an entity, he is the political and legislative spokesman for each person whose union is affiliated with the AFL-CIO.

Lobbying, like spying, is a business best performed with as little public trace as possible. Meany wants legislation, not credit for legislation. Labor furnished the unseen muscle for much of the social legislation of the Kennedy-Johnson years, from Medicare through civil rights. "Let the politicians have the glory," Meany says frequently. "They'll feel better about us when we come ask them for something."

This biography is intended to breach labor's self-imposed privacy—to chart George Meany's progress from working plumber to the $90,000-a-year presidency of the AFL-CIO, and to show what uses he has made of the movement he controls. It is an unauthorized biography, one that has benefited from Meany's cooperation but was not subject to his control. When I first approached Meany in mid-1970 and told him I intended to write such a book, his attitude was benign noninterference. He did not desire such publicity, and he would neither help nor hinder my work. After several months, however, he developed a keen interest in the book, and thereafter gave me hours of taped interviews on his career and unrestricted access to records of the AFL-CIO executive council, as well as valuable introductions to persons within and without the labor movement who were involved in his career. More explicit identification of sources is found under Sources and Acknowledgments.

# I

## Mike Meany's Boy

ONE OF GEORGE MEANY'S first memories was hearing the word "organ-EYE-zation." He didn't understand what it meant, but when his father's visitors, sitting in the parlor eating sugar cake and drinking tea and black coffee those long Sunday afternoons, pronounced it in lilting Gaelic voices, "they did so in terms of reverence and in terms of something in which they had great faith." Meany gradually learned that the visitors—Irish-American, as was his father, with the same hard, work-flattened hands and reddish-brown hair that grayed early— were members of something called the plumbers union, which happened to be the same as the organ-EYE-zation. The young Meany, chunky of body even then, would scrunch down on the floor by his father to listen to the men talk about some new apprentice who "didn't know how to wipe a jernt" and argue about the internal politics of Local Two, of which his father was president. Then he would drift across the street and watch a farmer who had a cow barn and lot there do the evening milking, or he would sit on the front stoop and look out across the open fields for three quarters of a mile to see steamboats returning from festive Sunday excursions on Long Island Sound, puffing toward their piers beyond Hell Gate.

The Irish discovered the Bronx early, especially those Irish who earned their livelihood with hammer, saw, wrench, and brawn; strong men lured from the immigration piers, beginning around 1837, by the promise of construction jobs on the Harlem and Hudson River railroads, and the Croton Aqueduct. The Meany and Cullen families, as nearly as their children's children can reconstruct (neither clan cared much for preserving its own history), arrived in the United States around 1853, driven from their farms in central Ireland by the lingering starvation threat of the great potato famine of 1847–49. Michael Joseph Meany, born in 1864, grew into a husky, round-eyed man who was an accomplished plumber before his twentieth birthday. He married pretty, big-boned Anne Cullen in 1891 and they settled into a modest row house on 125th Street and Madison Avenue in Harlem.

William George Meany was born there August 16, 1894, the second of ten children, two of whom died in infancy. Neither Meany nor the family ever used the name William; his sisters, who adored him, called him Brother, as eventually did everyone else in the household. By 1899, his Harlem house overflowing with toddling youngsters, Mike Meany bought the Bronx home and entered a quasi-urban blue-collar haven.

Today, from the vantage point of the Triborough Bridge, the southern fringe of the Bronx is a pastiche of the very worst of contemporary big-city America, a grayish smear of run-down apartments, rag-tag factories with broken bottles on the roof, and trashy vacant lots. Tucked away under the bridge's north piers, hard by the stinking, slow-flowing East River, is a three-story red-brick house, one of six in a tight row—695 East 135th Street, near Southern Boulevard, a shabby place waiting the inevitable wrecker's ball—lost in a neighborhood that somehow went to ruin during the past half century. But at the turn of the century, and for a couple of decades beyond, when the Meany family lived at that address there, the Bronx was a different place altogether.

Edward J. Flynn, Meany's friend and contemporary (he was born in 1890), a shrewd Bronx politician who became Democratic National Chairman in the 1940's, recollected that people who settled in the Bronx "were mostly immigrants of a better type . . . men and women who wished to bring their families up in an atmosphere away from the activities of a large city. As a result, they became small homeowners." In the Bronx of Flynn's youth, "people got jobs the day after they got off the boat, worked hard, reared families that were never hungry, worshiped as they pleased, earned their simple pleasures."

The *North Side News,* a Bronx newspaper, boasted in 1901: "Nowhere else in the world perhaps can there be seen so large a proportion of boys and girls who are pronounced specimens of rugged health. . . . Not only are their little figures sturdy, but their complexions are clear, their eyes are bright, and their evident high spirits are indicative of cheerful dispositions. Their round cheeks, their good color and their neat appearance, show that they come from homes where they have all the comforts of life." Joseph A. Goulden, a Bronx insurance man and (briefly) a congressman, declaimed in 1895: "The healthfulness of this section, the charm of landscape, the historic interest of the territory, and the intelligence of the people are powerful attractions to those in search of a home."

Although the latter two statements carry the unmistakable scent of boosterism, the Bronx of Meany's boyhood *was* a comfortable place—especially in juxtaposition to the squalor of the Lower East Side, Chelsea, and Hell's Kitchen, where other immigrant Irish clustered. The Meanys moved to the Bronx in the midst of a boom that rushed its population from 88,000 in 1890 to 431,000 in 1910. Nonetheless, to George Meany the Bronx was a "series of small villages connected by a trolley line, at least thirty different villages"—his Port Morris neighborhood, Mott Haven, Casanova, Hunt's Point, West Farms, Fleetwood, High Bridge, Fordham, and Mount Hope. A few apartment houses were beginning to rise along the major avenues, yet farms and orchards stretched from the lower end of the borough north to Westchester County. Although the Meanys lived in a row house, Meany recalled that "most of the homes were little white clapboard houses with little gardens around them. It was strictly a rural area, by no means a poverty area." A legislative committee that studied tenement conditions reported in 1894 the average New York City dwelling housed 3.82 families. In the 23rd Ward, where the Meanys resided, the average was only 1.84 families; more than 60 percent of the homes there were one-family. The Bronx retained its small-town qualities well into the twentieth century. According to Meany, "you didn't see a great influx of poverty until people started to move up from the East Side. . . . They started to build these so-called row apartments—railroad flats—two apartments on one floor, one room right after the other, with one toilet on a floor for two families. They became slums very, very quickly." Nor was industry a problem. "Here and there, scattered in and around the homes in this area of the Bronx, were at least fifteen or eighteen piano factories [one in the same street as the Meany home]. Our German neighbors, and we had a lot of German neighbors, were all in the piano-making business. That was actually the only industrialization there was at all. Outside of that, it was all residential."

Rustic. An atmosphere in which George Meany and other neighborhood kids could stand for hours, watching a blacksmith at work—the odor of a hot shoe burning into a hoof and the ring of the smithy's hammer were vivid memories to Meany seven decades later. "We kids would go there and stand all day, if somebody didn't pull us away." Kid pranks. "The worst trouble George ever got into," in the opinion of one of his sisters, Mrs. Marie Tinsley, "was when he and some other boys smeared real smelly cheese on a radiator at school. When the pipes got hot, it made such a stink the teachers had to stop classes." But his sister remembered how serious George was about school: "With all the kids, our house was pretty chaotic in the evenings. But it didn't bother Brother. He would sit at the dining room table, with all of us running and whooping around him, and do his lessons. It was as if we didn't exist, when he had work to do. He could shut out the noise and concentrate."

In the winter evenings there was bobsledding. The hills were the local streets, and there'd be a tremendous crowd out. In the summer the boys swam and fished in the East River and the lower end of Long Island Sound, shouting excitedly at the sight of the Commonwealth & Puritan Line's Boston–New York steamer, which churned up mini-breakers they could ride to the beach. A recollection of another Meany contemporary, Bert Sack, was of "the horn of the fishmen on Friday, and the man who shouted 'I cash clothes' " as his horse-drawn cart clattered around Port Morris. There were German bands "playing Strauss waltzes and stirring marches, mostly out of tune," and back-yard serenaders. Along Willis and Southern avenues "the tenants would throw coins, sometimes wrapped in paper, down to them."

For a workingman's family like Meany's, the trolleys provided cheap and long-lasting entertainment. "All the trolley cars were wide open in the summertime, and it was quite a stunt in the summer evening to take a trolley ride. The woman would take two, three, four kids and pay for her fare—she didn't have to pay for the kids, they'd ride for free. You could go from one line to another and get a transfer and keep coming around all evening; you could ride a car from the lower end of New York to Hastings, at least ten miles above Yonkers, last on the line, for five cents."

And baseball, always baseball, from school through young manhood, when union business, courtship, and then marriage began to occupy his weekends. Meany was a good ballplayer; not good enough, according to him, even to think about the pros, but nonetheless skilled enough as a catcher to earn extra money on a loosely organized semipro circuit that staged games in the Bronx, upper Manhattan, and northern New Jersey. "Those were the Blue Law days when there was no professional baseball on Sundays, so semipro games, they really thrived." Meany played often on two fields in Harlem, both on Seventh Avenue, one at 137th Street, the other at 145th. "They had maybe four or five thousand seats, and admission was twenty-five cents, which wasn't too bad considering the top price in the Polo Grounds then was fifty cents. We used to play under the name of the Bronx Professionals, then maybe the following year we were the Osceolas or some other Indian name. One time I played a couple of years on a semipro team known as the Hoboken Stars; now, how they ever got that name I don't know. I used to catch, and play the outfield once in a while. I was a big, husky kid, and they just picked out the fattest kid in the crowd, and he'd be made the catcher."

Unlike the major leagues, the semipros had no color bar, hence Meany competed against such underground standouts as Cy Williams of the Lincoln Giants, "a big, skinny colored boy, about the best pitcher in baseball." When the major league season ended, "there'd be a tremendous rush for the next four or five weeks to these semipro parks; all these big league players would go on these semipro teams." Batting against Cy Williams a few times convinced Meany that plumbing held a more promising future for him than big league baseball. Thus, at age twenty-two, after six years of semipro ball, he hung up his glove.

Such is the boyhood that comes through the golden, softening filter of memory: a close-knit second-generation Irish-American family, blue-collar but comfortable; the children's lives centered around Public Schools 9 and 29, the priests and nuns of St. Luke's Parish, and the sprawling city park eventually laid out across the street from the home; the girls learning to make fruit preserves and sugar cake for the inevitable Sunday visitors; George and brothers John and Joe responsible for keeping the wood stack high; George earning $2 a week pocket money, at the age of twelve, by delivering "official entry cards"—fliers with race track and baseball results, and the next day's entries and starting pitchers—around neighborhood saloons.

Comfort, however, does not equate with security. A working family depended upon each week's paycheck; if one was missed, because of illness or bad weather, the household skimped. And steady work in the building trades, then as now, was relative. A man considered himself fortunate if he worked thirty-five weeks a year. Between 1904 and 1916, an average of 26.5 percent of the unionized building trades workers in New York were unemployed, compared with 19.8 percent in all occupations. As a professional union official during much of this period, Mike Meany was not as affected by seasonal layoffs as the average worker. The Meanys never went hungry but, as one of Mike Meany's daughters recollected, "there were times, and there were better times."

As he neared his sixteenth birthday, the age at which Bronx boys of the era left school, George Meany talked with his father about becoming a plumber. "He didn't want me to work at plumbing," Meany would recall, without further elaboration. His sister Marie had an explanation. "It was hard, dirty work. They worked like dogs, like all labor did. Father had come home from the job, dead tired and dirty, all his life; he wanted something better for Brother." And Mike Meany said no to his son.

George obeyed for a while. In June 1909, after graduating from P.S. 29, and one year in Morris High School, he found a job as a messenger for a Manhattan advertising agency (the firm that became Batton, Barton, Durstine and Osborn) and spent several unhappy months hustling packages along Madison Avenue and downtown to printing shops. There was vague talk about night school and a business degree. Meany nonetheless was determined to try plumbing, Mike Meany's opposition notwithstanding.

"Finally I got a job without him knowing it, from a foreman named William Duggan, one of the fellows who used to visit the house on Sunday. I followed him down to the trolley when he left, and asked him if he would put me to work. 'Sure, come on down tomorrow,' he said. So on Monday, October 3, 1910, I went to work as a plumber. So, that night, when I come home from work, of course he [Mike Meany] knew then that I was working as a plumber. He said, 'Now get yourself all cleaned up, and you get over to that vocational school, and you'll take plumbing three nights a week. As long as you are going to work at plumbing, you are going to learn something about it.'

"Now, I hadn't bargained on that at all, I hadn't even thought about that, going to school. I went over to the school in the heart of Harlem, 138th Street and Fifth Avenue, for three nights a week for two years."

The trade school curriculum was a blend of plumbing theory and practice, equivalent to college undergraduate engineering courses. The plumbing trade, when Meany entered it, was in a state of technological transition. Traditionally, the plumber had manufactured pipe on the work site, melting lead in a portable furnace and shaping it into the size fixtures needed, then fitting the joints together with melted solder. In the early twentieth century, however, he was beginning to work with precast iron pipe and fixtures, with ready-made brass joints that screwed together. Martin Segal, a plumbers union historian, wrote that the plumber "became a mechanic concerned with installation rather than with making or processing articles used in the plumbing system." The trade was revolutionized further beginning in 1889 with construction of the ten-story Tower Building, the first in New York to make use of the "steel skeleton," or skyscraper, technique. Segal commented, "The improvements and greater complexity of plumbing installations—particularly in the very large commercial and industrial buildings—called for an increasing practical knowledge of some aspects of hydraulics and pneumatics." The public now best knows the plumber as the man in overalls who unstops a sink or repairs a leaking faucet or installs a hot-water heater in the basement. The vast majority of the unionized plumbers in the Bronx, however, were heavy construction workers, and such was the work for which Meany was trained. To graduate, Meany and the other fledgling plumbers had to draw a detailed layout of the plumbing required for a major office building, from the connection with the main water main on the street to the smallest interior tap. Later, when he was AFL-CIO president, Meany would grump sarcastically at newspaper articles that called him "unlettered" or "unschooled." He once said, "My education might not have been formal, but I'd like to put some of those college professors through the plumbers' apprentice school. They talk about a plumber as if he was some kind of meat head. Well, it might not have been Shakespeare, but it wasn't any cup of tea, either."

After three years Meany took the examination to qualify as a journeyman plumber. He flunked. And, as he said ruefully, "it was on the level because my father was president of the union, and he had appointed the examining board. He was just as sore as hell. Not at the examining board that turned me down, but at me. And I had to wait six months and serve another six months as an apprentice." Meany passed the next examination and became a probationary member of the Manhattan-Bronx local of the United Association of Journeymen Plumbers, Gas Fitters, Steam Fitters and Steam Fitters Helpers of the United States and Canada—the plumbers union.*

Initially, Meany was not an enthusiastic unionist, despite his childhood indoctrination. In his words, "I didn't take much interest the first couple of years I was a member. No particular reason, I just didn't get excited about the union." He did attend Local 463's weekly meetings each Wednesday night in a 700-seat hall on 84th Street near Second Avenue in Yorkville. But so did everyone else, if for no other reason than that they had nothing else to do in the evenings. "It was a way of life. You'd see members there week after week, sitting right in the same place." Meany sat along with them, content to let the older men run the union. Sons might be brought into the plumbing trade—the workingman's legacy, the Irish called their form of nepotism—but their place was as clearly subordinate there as it was in the home.

So Meany kept his mouth shut, worked hard and obtained his full membership on January 10, 1917, when his probationary period ended. In the words of several men who labored alongside him, he became a first-rate plumber. William Dodd, a Bronx native who became secretary-treasurer of the United Association, first met Meany during construction of a hospital at Camp Upton, a World War I army base near Yaphank, Long Island. "He was a big, burly guy who could move faster than any of us," Dodd recalled. "He was methodical. He would lay out the work to be done, and not horse around until it was finished. We lived in a camp out at the work site—these were the days we didn't have autos, you know—and although we worked long hours we also got in some fun. We played a lot of baseball in the evenings—God, but George was a sight when he ran, as big a fellow as he was—and we played a game of pinochle or two. We sort of felt one another out, and became pretty close

---

* This much-inclusive title has contracted and expanded several times since Meany joined the union, finally stabilizing as the United Association of Journeymen and Apprentices of the Plumbing and Pipefitting Industry of the United States and Canada. Further references to the union will be the plumbers' shorthand for their organization—the United Association, or the plumbers union.

friends; not that we would visit each other's homes, but we knew where we stood. Later on, when I wanted office in the union, George helped me along."

To Meany, those working years are a blur of pipes and fixtures, where job blends into job. "You see a building when it is a skeleton, and the pipe is going in, and you don't always recognize it later, when it is finished. I worked all over midtown Manhattan, particularly in the Grand Central area." One project of which he was proud was the Commodore Hotel, which he used as a New York headquarters after moving to Washington. "That was a good piece of plumbing work. I know. I did it." Wartime work took him briefly to Rhode Island, where he helped construct a naval training station, and to Colonia, New Jersey, for a military hospital. He even went under the carpenters union jurisdiction for several months so he could work as a dock-builder in Port Newark, New Jersey. But the bulk of the work was within an hour's trolley ride of the Bronx, mostly for plumbing contractor Sam Minskoff. Meany became a foreman, and he earned a master plumber's license, so that he could look forward to a respectable, if not overly remunerative, blue-collar career—one plumber among a thousand in the Bronx, an anonymous young man with no life plan beyond the next week's paycheck and the Saturday night dance at one of the Irish social clubs in the neighborhood.

Then, suddenly, responsibility, and with it, maturation, both as unionist and as man.

During the winter of 1915–16 Mike Meany suffered a prolonged siege of pneumonia that permanently weakened his health; he continued to work, but at a reduced pace, and the doctors decided his heart was damaged. In early 1916 he died. The eldest son, John Meany, meanwhile, had enlisted in the 69th Regiment and gone to France. He was gassed, invalided home, and died within months. So in 1918, at age twenty-four, George Meany found himself the sole support for the entire family—six younger brothers and sisters, two barely of walking age; his mother; and his maternal grandfather, John Cullen, an octogenarian who spent his last years in the household.

"Brother had it all put on him," was his sister Mrs. Helen Fitzpatrick's account. "We were really too little to know what a responsibility he had shouldered, but suddenly Father and John were gone, and Brother was in charge at home." Meany felt simply, "There wasn't anyone else." And a year later he had further responsibility. At a church dance he met Eugenia McMahon, an Irish-American girl with coal black hair, flashing blue eyes and a zest for pungent comment. Two years George's junior, Eugenia operated an embroidery machine in a Bronx clothing factory and was a dedicated member of the International Ladies Garment Workers Union. Contrary to stubborn labor legend, they did *not* meet on a picket line. But because the ILGWU was still in the throes of organizing New York garment workers, Eugenia had been exposed to a more militant brand of unionism than her husband. After a courtship of little more than a year she and Meany married, on November 26, 1919, and set up housekeeping in a small Bronx apartment. Meany, meanwhile, continued to support his mother's household. He also began to take an active role in union business.

He did so at a time when the construction industry, employers and unions alike, was caught up in what a New York legislative committee called a "scandal of major proportions." The central figure was a semiliterate Canadian named Robert P. Brindell, a sometime dock worker who "became the most successful extortionist the building trades were ever to know," in the opinion of John Hutchinson, a student of labor corruption. Both Samuel Gompers, president of the American Federation of Labor, and William Hutcheson, head of the powerful Carpenters Union, wanted to meld all New York building tradesmen into a single bargaining council, and they seized upon Brindell as a man with enough muscle to do the job. Hutcheson first used Brindell to put down a rebellion by New York carpenters who did not accept his leadership, then set him upon richer game. Working through Carpenters Local 1456 —largest in the nation, with more than 5,000 members, and a power center in New York labor—Brindell forced all union business agents in the city into a building trades council, of which he became president. The ecumenical Brindell extorted vast sums from workers and employers alike, in the form of inflated "dues" from union members and "strike insurance" from contractors. Workers were forced to buy dues cards and gaudy souvenir brochures issued by Brindell, and he exacted monthly "assessments" from local unions. Contractors cooperated with his corrupt schemes so they could fix prices and freeze out competition. Appalled at the monster it had created, the AFL ejected Brindell's council in 1919, and moved to set up a rival building trades central organization. Brindell continued his group under the name of a "business agents association."

The plumbers union fought Brindell. "We recognized him for what he was—a crook—and we wanted nothing to do with him," Meany said. "He tried to boss internal union affairs. He demanded that business agents be elected for three-year terms, so he could control them. We told him to go to hell." Local 463 refused to pay the special assessments demanded by Brindell. Nonetheless, when a special legislative committee began probing Brindell's activities in the early 1920's, the plumbing industry—including the union—was caught up in the scandal. The key figure was James T. Hettrick, attorney for the plumber contractors association.

According to testimony at his conspiracy trial, Hettrick operated a

classic bid-rigging scheme. Hettrick received bids on all plumbing contracts, grossly inflated them, and decided, on the basis of a prearranged
split of the market, which company would submit a bogus "minimum"
bid. Hettrick took from one to three percent of the amount of the winning bid as his fee; another three percent was divided among other companies who had bid as a sort of consolation prize. Hettrick also coordinated a price-fixing agreement for plumbing supplies.

According to trial testimony, connivance of plumbers union officials
was essential to success of the scheme. Two ranking officials of Meany's
local—William L. Doran, the president, and William H. Chapman, a
business agent—threatened to withdraw workers from any contractor
who did not "cooperate" with Hettrick. Doran, Chapman, and Hettrick
were sentenced to three-year prison terms. Brindell, in a separate trial,
drew a term of five to ten years, for corruption which netted him an
estimated $1,000,000 per year. In all, 529 persons were indicted for
extortion or conspiracy in cases arising from what became known as the
"Brindell investigation," eighty-one of them union officials, the remainder employers or public officials (the latter chiefly building inspectors).
In the press the union officials were lumped together as the "Brindell
Ring." Meany, however, insisted that the Doran and Chapman cases had
no connection with Brindell. William Dodd, who was active in Meany's
local at the time, also asserted that Doran was "made a patsy" in the
probe. And Doran, after his release, once again became a local union
official. Few persons in New York labor, however, would defend the infamous Brindell. The selectivity of the prosecutions and of public opinion
—harsh on unions, sympathetic to the corrupt employers—infuriated
Meany. But he considered Brindell's systematized graft even more repugnant, since it siphoned dollars from the pockets of workingmen.
Meany was mad for another reason: Mike Meany had devoted his life
to professional unionism, and anything that damaged the name of the
plumbers union, however indirectly, hurt the Meany family as well.

In 1919, as rank-and-file disgust swelled against Brindellism, Meany
ran for a seat on his local's executive board, and he won. In September
1922, when a business agent's position opened in the local, Meany went
after it, and again won, thereupon becoming a professional union official.
Never again did he pick up a plumber's wrench for pay.

Why the change of career? Meany called it "just one of those things
that come naturally," rather than any loss of interest in plumbing. The
business agent pay was considerably better—$60 per week, plus $15 for
expenses, instead of the $49.50 he had earned as a plumbing foreman—
and the job was steady, not subject to the seasonal layoffs that plague
the building tradesman. According to Mrs. Anne Cassin, another of
Meany's sisters, "Brother realized he was too smart to spend the rest of

his life working with his hands, that he would not be happy. He wanted to do something in life other than be a workingman. Not that Brother— or any of us—look down on men who do physical labor. I suppose that every generation wants to pull itself a little bit above the last one. Goodness knows but that our father provided for us, and did his best, and we're proud of him. But George didn't have the mind that would let him remain the 'follower' in any situation.

"That's why, I think, that once he got interested in the way the union worked, he went right to the top."

# II

# The Man with the Monkey Wrench

UNIONS OF THOSE DAYS," George Meany said more than half a century after joining the plumbers union, "they were primitive, compared to the unions today. Actually, the big thing was your wages and your hours." Meany's description was acutely true of his own union, one that historian Martin Segal wrote had "always concentrated its main efforts on the 'nuts and bolts' of trade unionism—wages, benefits, apprenticeship and jurisdiction." The plumbers union, by the time Meany became a member, was decades beyond the travails of organization and employer recognition. The plumbers union organized early, tightly, and efficiently, and an admittedly key reason for its existence was to limit the number of men permitted to work in the trade. Local autonomy, disdain for the unorganized, economic self-interest—such were the features of the unionism in which Meany spent his formative years.

Meany's Bronx local—Local 463, for most of its existence—had a tempestuous history, but one more concerned with intraunion rivalries than conflicts with employers. The local grew from an old Knights of Labor plumbers union formed in Manhattan and the Bronx during the 1870's through hard, bitter strikes—"Local Two," in its early years. Several factors gradually broke employer resistance. Most contractors had worked as journeymen themselves, and there was scant economic or social difference between the boss and "the man in the overalls." Shops were small and tightly knit; a turn-of-the-century plumber seldom worked far away from his own home, and he was apt to attend the same parish church as his boss. And there was considerable economic pragmatism on both sides, as exemplified in a landmark agreement signed in

1886 between Local Two and the New York Master Plumbers Association, the employer group, a basic document under which the plumbing industry operated thereafter.

In return for a closed-shop agreement, Local Two pledged that its members would work for "none other but members in good standing" of the employer association. The contract provided for a boycott of any manufacturer or dealer who did not "properly protect the trade"—that is, who sold plumbing supplies directly to homeowners or general contractors, bypassing union members and employer association members. The pact had the effect of putting the New York plumbing industry off limits to independents, be they worker or boss. The union did not have to organize actively; if a man wanted to work as a plumber, he came to the union. To contractors, the barring of nonunion labor—men who might work at a lower scale—protected them from being underbid on jobs by competitors. The union assured them a steady flow of competent workers, at the same wages paid by builders throughout the metropolitan New York area. In return, commented William Haber, an early analyst of the building trades, the contractors "docilely accept whatever restrictions the union may impose."

With a membership of more than one thousand, representing about half the organized plumbers in the country, Local Two was able to dominate the United Association for several years after the national union was formed in 1889. Then things began to fall apart. Local Two's influence over the national union lessened as more and more plumbers joined the UA. Because of its high wages ($20 per week), Local Two had an initiation fee of $50, compared to $10 in other United Association locals. Out-of-town UA members, their initiation fees already paid, flocked to New York whenever they could, quite naturally, to get the higher salaries. Finally, in 1895, Local Two said it would no longer accept "traveling members" and declared New York off limits to outsiders; when the national union protested, the local withdrew from the UA.

In the following decade Local Two was in again-out again, its leaders trying alternately to start their own international union and to make peace with the United Association. Local autonomy soon became the overriding issue. Since Local Two predated the United Association and had won its own organizational fights, members felt they owed no loyalty to any national office or to plumbers in other cities. In 1902, for instance, Local Two delegates to the UA convention opposed national sickness and death benefits on grounds that such programs should be administered by the local unions. The UA countered by forming rival locals—480, in the Bronx, was the direct competitor of Local Two—and threatened to strike New York contractors' jobs in other cities if employers did not recognize them. Finally, in 1906, both sides recognized the futility—and expense—of continuing the fight, and Local Two came back into the United Association.*

The bitterness over the split had subsided by the time Meany was elected to union office, but autonomy remained a strong tradition in Local 463. So, too, was exclusivity, and especially as the union won premier wages for building tradesmen. The basic pay for New York plumbers increased threefold from 1903 to 1929, from $4.25 to $13.20 for an eight-hour day. Initiation fees increased even more rapidly. When David Holborn, also an early union business agent, joined Local Two in 1911, he paid a $55 initiation fee in installments from a salary of $2.75 a day. In 1924 the fee was $350; in 1927, $500. In Meany's own words, "My union was a closed union, closed in the fact that it didn't take in new members." Sons or other close relatives of members got the few openings.

The union also zealously sought out jobs. Of this, Meany said, "When we had industrial work crop up that we felt that we should do, we made an effort, if we had any weight, any pressure, to get that work for our contractors. We would not work directly. We wouldn't work for anyone but our own contractors. We didn't want [to organize] the people that were on the work, we merely wanted the work. So far, as the people that were on the work were concerned, for our part they could drop dead.

"We even went so far that we wouldn't take clearance cards. We shut the union to other union members of our own craft from other cities. I am not bragging about it. I am not proud of it. I am telling you that is what we did."

Because of the union's tight controls, the *United Association Journal* could boast of "the strength of our organization and the better feeling existing between us and the contractors." At the United Association's 1924 convention in Atlantic City, Meany pressed for a new bylaw requiring members' photos to be on their union cards so they could not "come over from the other side of the river for five cents' carfare" and take work from Local 463 members.

The key figure in building trades unionism was the business agent. He served as the daily buffer between contractor and worker, and his importance cannot be overstated. Meany described his own duties in bread-and-butter terms: "To visit the jobs as often as I could; to see to it that the terms of the contract were observed, and that the proper ratio of helpers to journeymen was followed; and that fellows kept their [union] cards up."

* Not, however, as Local Two, but as Local 498, based in Manhattan. In 1916 Local 498 merged with Local 480, becoming Local 463, which a few years later regained the old Local Two designation. Despite the name changes, "Local Two" had a continuous existence, but it bore another number when Meany joined and when he became a business agent.

Local 463's jurisdiction was split into four geographic regions, and the four business agents covered them in rotation. "We felt this kept any one guy from getting too close to a particular contractor or group of men," explained David Holborn. "The territory went way down into Manhattan, and even split four ways you had to hustle to get around it in a day, and to keep tabs on what was happening. George was a guy who liked to get an early start—to hit a big apartment job, say, just before the men started working; ride the elevator or hoist to the top floor, and walk his way down, talking with the men—you know, seeing what they are thinking, shoot the bull a little, see if any problems are developing. Since most of the plumbing contractors had come up through the ranks they knew the ropes, and you could generally count on them to go by the rules."

As a person employed directly by the union and hence not dependent upon the contractor's good will, the business agent could represent members more fearlessly than a shop steward, who would be subject to punitive work assignments or even discharge. Further, as working rules increased in number and intricacy, the unions needed an expert to enforce them; William Haber wrote during the 1920's that "one of the principal qualifications of the business agent is a knowledge of these rules."

The business agent had virtually boundless authority to stop work in the event of contract violations, for the speed of building operations made impossible the referral of all disputes to an arbitration board or union meeting. The work could be finished, and the dispute moot, before such formal proceedings were convened. But strikes have always been an inefficient and unpopular means of enforcing a contract; building tradesmen lose so much working time because of bad weather that they are reluctant to walk off their jobs when the sun is shining. Hence the business agent needed the negotiating skills to resolve disputes without stopping work. "George was good about this," said Holborn. "The bosses knew that he wouldn't horse around with them, and that he wouldn't raise a ruckus for the sake of hearing his own voice. So when he griped about something, they listened." Meany and the other plumbers business agents refused to bargain with any employer representative who did not have the authority to make agreements. In Meany's words, "We would say, 'the hell with sending superintendents. We want the guy there with power to act. We are not going to waste our time.' " Holborn says the working plumbers generally gave the business agents ample bargaining room. "The plumbers are more conservative [about strikes] than any union in the labor movement. They wanted no fights or troubles. They were never that advanced."

The union had the authority to inspect all the plumbing work done in a building, and to order substandard work removed. "In our business," Meany said, "if they cheated on the building code, they cheated on us. When they cheated on the building code, they cut the labor cost." Contracts required that a business agent be notified when inspection was to be done by the city building department. "This had the effect of keeping the building inspector fairly honest, you know what I mean. He couldn't okay a test which really didn't shape up if he knew we were there or would be there before the day was out. In our trade, this was awfully important, the standard of work. We fought over the building codes, we spent our money to defend building codes, to see that they [the building contractors] did not break them down, because when they did they cost us money."

Eugene Murray, one of Meany's successors as a Local 463 business agent, remembered him as being "really tough" on inspections. Before plaster went onto walls, for instance, pipes were sealed and pumped full of water under pressure to ensure that they did not leak. "The contractors would try to cut corners, they'd try to get close to the business agents and the building inspectors. But they couldn't shove George. If the work was no good, he'd say, 'Tear it out.' And under the contract that's what happened."

The United Association's position was that union-approved inspection was essential to good work; that hasty production "lowers the quality of the job and endangers the good name and skill of the craftsman." But employers frequently charged that business agents used inspections as a means of "making work," and that responsibility for quality should rest with the contractor, not the union. In one famous New York case, a Painters Union business agent forced the owner of the Ambassador Hotel to rip down a wall because the travertine marble did not suit his taste. As authority, he cited the painters' claimed jurisdiction over the work.

Especially galling to contractors was union use of "inspection" as a tactical weapon in jurisdictional quarrels with other crafts. The plumbers' arch foes were the steamfitters. After years of strident feuding the AFL in 1914 forced both factions into the same union, but rivalries persisted over the division of work. (The plumbers originally laid claim to any work involving lead pipe; the steamfitters, to that with iron pipe; their other differences are too complex for exploration here.) "For two or three years after I became a business agent," Meany said, "I had one duty, and that was to see what I could do to make it tough for the steamfitters local of [our] international because of jurisdictional disputes . . . at the local level. I think I had been re-elected three times before I realized that we had any problems in the world other than how to lick the steamfitters."

Meany's first test came shortly after his election as business agent, in a dispute over division of work at Consolidated Edison's Hell Gate Power House, being constructed at 134th Street and the East River. The steam-

fitters claimed jurisdiction over installation of certain pipes and connec-
tors linked to the boilers and the turbines. So did the plumbers. "The
plumbers refused to work unless the pipes set up by the steamfitters were
taken out and the work permitted to be done by the plumbers," a New
York legislative committee reported. The amount of work in dispute was
$60,000 of the power house's total cost of $30,000,000. Nonetheless
the plumbers struck the job after 99 percent of the work was finished,
and the entire project "remained at a standstill for seven months." The
legislative committee criticized the plumbers union for creating "an utterly hopeless and discouraging situation." It heard the plumbing contractor, Patrick F. Kinney, testify about meeting several union officers:
"They told me to forget it, they were never going to let any man go back
on that job. This is my finish after twenty-seven years as a plumbing
contractor." The plumbers stood firm even under the combined pressures
of the New York building trades council and the UA international president, John Coefield. And they won. When the strike finally ended, Dave
Holborn said, the union refused to approve any plumbing work in the
power house. "Meany said, 'Bust it down,' and out came thousands of
dollars of plaster, and the pipes." Meany said of the episode, "The piping was in a gray area between the plumbers and the steamfitters. The
contractor decided to give it all to the steamfitters, for some reason or
another, and we decided we wouldn't work on the job."

Consolidated Edison learned its lesson. Four years later it constructed
an identical power house at Fourteenth Street and the East River. "Due
to their experience in the first job," Meany said, "they allocated the work
half and half, without making a decision, and the job went through without a murmur."

In other disputes the plumbers frequently resorted to arbitration.
Many of the issues, standing alone, appear trivial. For instance, Local
463 fought furiously with the carpenters to win the right to install "medicine cabinets and other plumbing accessories . . . in connection with
the plumbing fixtures outside of bathrooms" at Columbia Medical Center; and with the tile layers union over the installation of bathroom fixtures in plastered walls at the Waldorf-Astoria Hotel. But each of these
cases that the business agents won via arbitration meant a permanent
expansion of the plumbers' jurisdiction vis-à-vis other unions. Meany
developed an encyclopedic memory for arbitration decisions. "The contractors, and the other business agents, came to realize that when George
started citing chapter and verse, he wasn't making it up, and that he
knew his precedents," was Holborn's recollection. "He was sort of a
walking library for the other business agents. He had all this stuff in his
head, and he could pull it out in a hurry when a beef came up on the
job."

Meany was also responsible for enforcing Local 463's own work rules, many of which were explicitly written to squeeze as many hours of work as possible out of each building project. Members couldn't ride bicycles from job to job. A helper was permitted on a job only if there were two journeymen working; if a single journeyman was working, and needed assistance, the extra man would have to be another journeyman, at half again a helper's pay. Plumbers wouldn't install pipe of less than two inches' diameter if it had been cut and threaded in a shop, insisting that this be done by hand at the job site. Building contractors fumed against such regulations but were powerless to change them.

The business agent derived considerable personal power through his ability to supply craftsmen for specific jobs. Building contractors retain no permanent work force; when they need men, they go to the union, which is to say, the business agent. "In our business," again according to Dave Holborn, "there were no steady jobs. There was a percentage [of men] that did work twelve months a year, but that is a very small amount. When a contractor had no work he didn't keep you. You kept moving. There was no such thing that we would get a minimum amount of time, weekly or monthly. We were never fortunate enough to get something that would give us a living wage the entire year. Oh, if you showed on the job, and the weather was bad, you might get minimum time of two hours or so, if the foreman took you off. But if you quit on your own, nothing." As a result, workmen eagerly sought the big construction projects that would guarantee them long-term employment.

For an ambitious man such power, if adroitly used, guaranteed tenure in office, for no dissident would dare challenge an officer who determined when and where—and if—he worked. Union bureaucracies, then as now, were self-perpetuating. The business agent had considerable subjective discretion in how strictly he enforced union rules. The Local 463 bylaws, for example, provided that a man more than three months in arrears was subject to suspension, which would knock him off the job. "But you wouldn't do that," said Meany. "You'd go over and say, 'Hey, go down on Saturday and pay up a couple of months' dues.'" Meany's contemporaries said he studiously avoided favoritism. In one instance a plumber asked Meany to give him a ride across town to a work site to which he had been assigned. Meany was driving to within a few blocks of the site but he refused the request. "If you ride up with me," he told the man, "everybody will say, 'Look at Meany, he's playing favorites and giving the best jobs to his friends.'" The plumber was irritated, but he didn't ride with Meany. From his father's experience, Meany knew that Local 463 elections were seldom fought on basic trade union issues, but on personalities. "In other words, this guy running the union was no damned good, and vice versa; it was the sort of thing that comes up in all human relationships." Meany decided early on to avoid intraunion politics whenever possible; "taking it down the middle" was the surest insurance of retaining his office.

Under the United Association constitution, business agents and other officers were responsible to their local memberships and ultimately to the national conventions, which established policy for the entire union. But as UA historian Martin Segal wrote, "the system also gave the officers considerable freedom to shape and execute policies." This freedom, and Local 463's insistence on autonomy, enabled Meany to win a protracted plumbers strike that, although it infuriated United Association officers, brought him his first national attention in the labor movement.

In the spring of 1927 Local 463 signed a contract guaranteeing members pay rates as high as those paid plumbers in any other borough of New York, and containing a no-strike promise. But Local One, based in Brooklyn, was unable to obtain a desired raise from $12 to $13.20 per day, and a forty-hour week rather than a forty-four. On April 1 some 3,200 journeymen and helpers in Local One struck the Brooklyn Master Plumbers Association. "The bosses said, 'Oh, this is outrageous, that is too much,' and of course some of the builders said, 'This will upset the whole pattern,' " Meany recalled. Meany saw no reason for the strikers to sit at home during spring months when they could be working. So he found plumbing jobs for the Brooklyn men in the Bronx and Manhattan. "After a couple of weeks," he said, "the Brooklyn plumbers had a very, very effective strike. Their jobs were completely shut down, and all their men were working elsewhere in New York—eighty percent of them, anyway. Our [Manhattan and Bronx] employers were not kicking, they needed the men.

"But Brooklyn was shut down tight as a drum. You see, you shut down the plumbers, or the electricians, or anything else, the other trades can only work up to a point. You can't bring your plaster up unless the plumbing is already in the walls. You can't plaster the walls if the walls have still got to go in. So the one trade automatically shuts the work down, not that day, but as the work proceeds." The other craft unions, following Meany's example, also began shuttling their idled men into Manhattan and the Bronx.

"They [Meany's latter-day critics] talk about picket lines. We never picketed in a strike. There's no reason to picket. You just went home, you didn't show up. The other trades on the job, they'd go on working as far as they could, but they could only work so long, so we didn't ask them to stay off. There was no question of nonunion replacements or anything like that. They [the contractors] couldn't bring strikebreakers in because that would *really* shut the building down. They say, 'Meany was never on a picket line.' Well, there was no *reason* to be on a picket line."

After several weeks, however, building financiers pressured the Manhattan Master Plumbers Association, the employer group, into closing their jobs to bring all work to a halt, in hopes of countering the union strategy. "They locked us out, in violation of our contract. We were not violating any contract, working with the Brooklyn plumbers, and if they thought we were, they had a very simple remedy: they shouldn't hire the Brooklyn plumbers." The net result, however, was a lockout of about 10,500 plumbers in the Bronx, Manhattan, and Queens, and a shutdown began spreading to the 200,000-odd construction workers in the New York area.

The Brooklyn negotiations got nowhere. Several contractors published advertisements asking Local One members to return to work at the "prevailing" (i.e., prestrike) wage. When there was no response, the Brooklyn Master Plumbers Association advertised for workers "to take the place of men now on strike" at $12 per day, with travel expenses for out-of-town applicants. The situation sent a tremor of alarm through Local 463, for it marked the first time in a quarter century that employers had been so intransigent. The New York *Times* commented that the advertisement for strikebreakers "means the employers have determined to ignore the union as an entity to be dealt with, either through the courts or through negotiations, at least until the present dispute is ended."

To Meany, it was obvious the employers felt the other building trades unions would pressure the Brooklyn plumbers into yielding and ending their strike. So Meany decided to try something which labor had never before done in New York: "After three weeks we went looking for a friendly judge. These were the days when labor injunctions were issued on *ex parte* testimony, generally on the grounds there would be irreparable damage done and so forth.

"So we looked around for a judge and we found one [Thomas Churchill, of Manhattan Supreme Court] that we felt from his background would be sympathetic. We knew where he came from, the heart of Manhattan, a working-class district. So we applied for a temporary restraining order to prevent the Master Plumbers Association from continuing the lockout, and he gave it to us, and we broke the lockout and went back to work.

"Now, there was a lot of comment at the time because the antilabor injunction was in the news. Labor was hurting, we were all yelling about injunctions. This was prior to passage of the Norris-La Guardia Act [which sharply limited injunctions in labor disputes] and in those days the use of injunctions to break strikes was widespread. There were some misgivings that a union would use this 'bad weapon' the other way."

Thomas Burke, secretary-treasurer of the United Association, was one of the persons who objected. "He told me, 'Oh, George, this is awful.' I said, 'I don't think this is awful, they locked us out illegally and we want to get back to work.' " When a formal hearing was heard weeks later on whether Judge Churchill's order should be made permanent, "we didn't even defend it. We didn't care. We got our men back to work."

The United Association hierarchy fumed for weeks over Meany's tactics. Secretary-treasurer Burke felt that Meany had "legitimized" the injunction and that contractors would benefit. Meany firmly disagreed. Throw the injunction back at the bosses, he said, and they'll stop using it against us. The long-range significance of the 1927 strike, from Meany's standpoint, was that it brought him attention as an innovative building trades unionist. And in a sector of labor more noted for conservatism than original thinking, this was no little achievement.

"A plumber with brains," someone called Meany at the time. "No," another man said, "all plumbers have brains. The difference is that Meany *uses* his."

Concurrent with his work as a plumbers business agent, Meany wore another hat which made him increasingly prominent in the convoluted internal politics of New York labor. After the Brindell scandals, the American Federation of Labor suspended the building trades council he had headed and created a new one. Meany had the proper credentials: he had spoken out against the Brindell faction in his own local, and in his campaign for business agent he had talked quite a bit about "clean unionism." The secretary's post, which he took in 1923, put him in the very power center of the New York construction industry.

In their early days the building trades unions suffered because one organization acting alone could not close down an entire project. Contracts expired at different dates. There were no uniform wage rates, since each union negotiated its own contract. Enough fraternal jealousies existed to make sympathetic general strikes difficult to sustain. Contractors played one union against another.

The union answer was the building trades council, an amalgamation of all unions working in the construction industry. The councils, in New York and other cities, were formed first as war agencies to aid unions in conducting strikes. But, as William Haber wrote, "the building trades council soon became an agency to preserve peace, to prevent violations of agreements, to settle disputes between the unions and to represent the unions on arbitration boards. Overshadowing the separate unions in importance, it has greatly restricted their power. For purposes of collective bargaining, and wage determination, the council unifies all the organizations." Haber said the council "provided an approximation to industrial unionism."

In New York, the building trades council had the authority to review any demands for increased wages or reduction of hours before they were presented to employers, even after their approval by the national union office. The council had to approve any strikes, a recognition that a walkout by one union eventually could affect all workers on a job.

The council office also brought Meany into proximity with men of national prominence within the labor movement: the irascible Daniel Tobin, a no-nonsense Irishman, equally adept (and quick) with his tongue and fists, who became president of the Teamsters Union when it was formed in 1903 and ruled it until 1953, to the repeated benefit of Meany; Joseph Ryan, of the International Longshoremen's Association, a hulking, hard-drinking man who spoke for Tammany Hall in New York labor ("The Central Trades and Labor Council is Tammany first and labor afterwards," Ryan once boasted); and William Hutcheson, president of the Carpenters Union, a blustering, bellowing bully, six feet three inches tall, 300 pounds, who dominated the AFL executive council through repeated use of a single-minded stratagem: if he didn't get his way on an issue, he and his carpenters would quit. Since his carpenters comprised about 40 percent of both the New York building trades council and the AFL's building trades department, Hutcheson's threats worked. Although Tobin and Hutcheson held no New York offices, the strength of their national unions gave them tacit control—if only by veto—of anything done by the New York building trades council. And each was a proponent, acknowledged or not, of business unionism, defined by Haber as the use of a union "as a business institution paying dividends in the form of higher wages, shorter hours, better working conditions and greater control over those factors which endanger the security of the job . . . embodying a philosophy which is essentially opportunistic." Such was Meany's mandate, both from the plumbers union and the building trades council.

In labor the power of the organization often determines the power of the individual. The plumbers, numerically, were a second-level organization. Meany's description of his career was a recitation of the inevitable—of someone who simply did his job, and stood for re-election, and spoke when he felt it was necessary. For instance, a vacancy occurred in 1932 on the executive board of the New York State Federation of Labor. "Our trade didn't have a member. Now, you weren't entitled to a member, but it was always an argument, if you were looking for a member, to say you didn't have one. I went over to the convention in Utica in August 1932. I was quite friendly with [John] Sullivan [the SFL president] and he sort of decided I'd make a good vice-president, and he sort of promoted me." But Meany claimed he neither consciously prepared himself for any office higher than business agent, nor really expected one. He denied any political skill. He denied the existence of any patron saint who guided him out of the obscurity of the plumbers union.

Why, then, George Meany?

Edward Maguire, long-time counsel for the Teamsters Union in New York, and later for the New York State Federation of Labor, perhaps gave some of the answer in his account of a first meeting with Meany. A dispute involving the Teamsters was to be heard before an arbitration panel.

"When I got downtown," Maguire said, "we were in such a hurry that we weren't even introduced to the members. I was immediately struck by a big, young, well-dressed guy. He asked some of the most penetrating questions, right to the point. He was so well-dressed I thought he was a boss.

" 'Who the hell is this millionaire who knows all these things?' I asked myself. After it was over I went over to thank him for helping bring out the essentials in the case, and found out he was a business agent for the plumbers union.

"George had a great faculty for reducing highly technical problems such as unemployment insurance—something that I don't understand fully to this date, and I'm a lawyer—to simplicity. This is indicative of the capacity of the guy."

Two other factors were important: the onset of the great depression, and the emergence of a vocal and highly-effective left-wing minority in labor, with particular strength in New York City. Caught up in a double crisis, New York labor was forced toward new leadership. George Meany was one of the new faces who happened to be available.

The depression staggered the New York construction industry. During the five years 1925–30, building in New York had averaged one billion dollars annually, nearly twenty percent of the total for the entire country. The swift evaporation of building funds, the precipitous drop in demands for apartment and office space, the halt of industrial expansion, the inability of builders to complete even those projects that were in progress, exploded on the building trades like a bombshell. By 1933, according to Albert F. Day, of the Building Trades Council of Greater New York, Long Island and Vicinity, more than eighty percent of the 200,000 construction workers in the area were jobless. "Most of them have been idle for the better part of the past three years," Day reported. "Many of them are now destitute, having been forced to sell their possessions or put their furniture in storage and double up with relatives and friends." In its 1932 contract negotiations, Local 463 for the first time in its history suffered a wage reduction—from the $13.20 daily rate of 1929 to $11.20.

The AFL's response to the economic misery of American workers was agonizingly slow. The AFL was tardy in realizing the severity of unemployment, in analyzing its causes, and in recommending solutions. The AFL spent the first several years of the depression quibbling over why the economy had gone sour, rather than trying to find ways to aid the suffering. The federation finally decided automation and mechanization were to blame; that industrialists, using technological innovations, were producing more goods with fewer men and earning profits disproportionate to wages. The solution: reduce the work day. How? By publishing, through a federal agency, data on wages, hours, and the distribution of national income. Arguing for creation of such a data bank in 1931, the AFL executive council said "it need only have authority to make facts public in order to render service and have effective influence." This was the AFL's sole "program" for ending the depression. And although the AFL formally endorsed the shorter work week, its moss-backed leaders fretted for eighteen months before endorsing Senator Hugo Black's bill (which failed) making the thirty-hour week mandatory.

The AFL's route toward endorsement of unemployment insurance was equally stumbling. It was on this issue that George Meany suddenly found himself years ahead of AFL "leadership." Initial impetus for the program came from the left-wing Conference for Progressive Labor Action (CPLA), which had been created in the 1920's to reform the AFL from within. Led by Louis Budenz, the long-time Communist party official, and A. J. Muste, the social activist, CPLA launched a campaign for unemployment insurance in June 1930, concentrating on the eastern states and particularly New York City, where street meetings, mass demonstrations, and lectures kept the issue before both the public and organized labor. Budenz asserted, "There is only one alternative to unemployment insurance: food riots." Helped by academic economists, CPLA drafted model state and federal unemployment insurance bills. Senator Robert F. Wagner (Dem., New York) introduced a federal bill in January 1931; its chief features (merit rating, employer financing with no worker contribution, and a federal subsidy for state administration) survived to become features of the unemployment insurance provision of the Social Security Act of 1935.

The AFL, however, wanted no such plan. Its leaders decried the prospect of members carrying "identification books," as required by the British insurance plan, and of becoming reliant upon a system that President William Green charged "demoralizes ambition, stultifies initiative, and blights hope." But the AFL's real fear was that insurance would harm unions by shifting worker loyalty to the government (which would administer the program) and to employers (who would finance it with a payroll tax). Green told a convention of the International Ladies Garment Workers Union in 1932 that "the AFL is not so much opposed to the principle as it is jealous of its own protection and its own life. We don't want to exchange our birthright for a mess of pottage. If we can develop some unemployment insurance plan that would guarantee the perpetuation of the movement, in my judgment the AFL would support it." And Victor Olander, an Illinois union official, told the 1931 AFL convention that insurance ought not to be promoted "with the cry, 'There are hungry men, there are hungry women, they must be fed!' Good God, that is the excuse for the oldest profession the world knows. Have we so far lost our virtue that we think of nothing else except bread . . . [and] employment?"

Meany shared labor's general antipathy toward government interference in worker-employer relations. "We were a little afraid of the law getting into the picture, on the theory you start to depend on the law to organize, the first thing you know you'll be controlled by the law. We were very skeptical on minimum wages. We just didn't see the minimum wage situation the way we saw it later. We saw these proposals as something that was going to hurt us, on the theory that if you had a minimum wage law that established a legal wage, it would virtually become the maximum wage. Now of course that never happened, but that was the general thinking, that was what you heard from labor."

During the first thirty years of the century the distrust was well placed, for most levels of government were cool, if not outright hostile, to organized labor. When the counsel for a New York legislative committee asked Gompers in 1922 whether he felt the courts should be empowered to review intraunion disputes he exclaimed, "God save labor from the courts."

Q. You have no faith in the courts?

A. Very little!

Unemployment insurance, however, was another matter. As a business agent Meany heard daily pleas for work from men he had known for years, men caught up in the failure of an economic system over which they had no control. He read all the material he could find on unemployment insurance and gradually decided this was one government program he could support. So, too, did Dan Tobin of the Teamsters, and Joe Ryan of the Longshoremen. At the 1931 AFL convention, Tobin berated the executive council for its opposition to insurance, and in doing so hit directly at President Green. Tobin told of visiting Indiana towns populated by members of Green's union, the mineworkers: "You can travel from village to village and from town to town and see starving men, children and mothers suffering from the loss of every kind of necessity, sickness predominating everywhere." With labor support, New York Governor Franklin D. Roosevelt had the governors of Connecticut, Massachusetts, New Jersey, Ohio, and Pennsylvania join him in appointing a commission to study unemployment insurance. Its report, issued in February 1932, urged establishing such a system, with compulsory participation by all employers.

The AFL reluctantly yielded, first at an executive council meeting in July 1932, then at its convention a few months later. (The left-wing CPLA interpreted the switch: "Business agents were unable to find jobs and to keep up wages for their members and some other way of satisfying them had to be found. . . . [S]o the 'die-hards' in the labor movement have had to retreat another step.") Green asked Louis D. Brandeis to help draft legislation for submission to Congress and the state legislatures. But the AFL hierarchy wasn't enthusiastic. John P. Frey, of the AFL metal trades department, wrote a friend after the convention that "a number of members were in rather strong opposition personally but did not care to state their position because of the popular movement which has developed in favor of this utterly impossible and visionary program."

It was against this backdrop of national labor foot dragging that Meany became directly concerned with winning an unemployment insurance program for New York. At the New York State Federation of Labor's 1933 convention, Elmer F. Andrews, the state commissioner of labor and industry, asked for labor's help in drafting a program. Meany met throughout the winter with a committee that included Professors Joseph P. Chamberlain of Columbia; Henry Fowler of the City College of New York; Herman Gray of New York University; Mary Dreier and Dr. John B. Andrews of the New York Permanent Conference on Unemployment Insurance; and Dr. Abraham Epstein of the American Association for Social Security. The experience, Meany's first close association with academicians, soured him on professors. "We didn't even get to the point of a bill because we spent the whole year wrangling among ourselves. These were all the big experts. They just spent a whole year meeting, but they couldn't agree with one another. Joe Chamberlain couldn't agree with Herman Gray, and John Andrews couldn't agree with anybody else."

The main division was over which of two approaches to take in writing a program. The Wisconsin legislature had already enacted a plan, to be effective in mid-1934, calling for creation of separate reserves by individual employers, who would run their own programs. The other format, the so-called Ohio plan, provided for a single, state-pooled fund, collected, administered, and disbursed solely by the state, with both the worker and the employer making contributions. Meany says he wanted the state-run plan. "The people who opposed us in the joint committee did not oppose us on the ground that our attitude was not the best one for organized labor, but that it would be easier to get a bill through the legislature if it called for company reserves." Mark Daly, Albany lobby-ist for the Associated Industries, the manufacturers' group in New York State, was willing to support the company reserve plan because he knew, as Meany stated, this "would tie each and every worker to his job; that while he is working there they would be building up a reserve fund that he could draw only from that company, and that if the worker went to another company that had no reserve, why, he would just have to be out of luck if he again got out of employment. . . ." In early 1934 Meany and Commissioner Andrews asked Governor Herbert L. Lehman, Roo-sevelt's successor, to support the state-run plan. Lehman "practically gave us to understand that he would sign an unemployment insurance bill if it passed." But labor couldn't get the bill through the Republican house in the 1934 legislative session.

Meany reported on his work to the 1934 state federation convention. In the printed record his speech survives as a straightforward, factual statement, an exploration of both approaches to insurance, and the pros and cons of each; an analysis, rather than a hand-wringing appeal. But in several thousand words Meany succeeded in reducing a highly complex subject to intelligible, nonlegalistic language that could be understood by an audience of workingmen. Meany said passage of a program was inevi-table. "So the question before us is not whether we are going to get unemployment insurance or not, but rather, what type are we going to get?" He asked approval of a resolution that "tells the major political parties that we do not want a mere statement from them in favor of unemployment insurance . . . but that they will favor unemployment insurance of the type . . . that we recommend, the type that will pro-tect . . . organized labor without tying the company union and the yel-low dog contract into it." And he urged the federation to support legisla-tive candidates who would vote for labor's plan. Dr. Abraham Epstein, who followed Meany on the program, said Meany's work had had na-tional significance. Only two weeks previously, Dr. Epstein said, the Massachusetts State Federation of Labor had used his arguments to get a state pool plan. "You have saved not only the New York [labor] move-ment," Dr. Epstein said, "but you have saved the movement in the coun-try."

Labor lawyer Edward Maguire, a Meany-watcher for four decades, called the 1934 convention speech "one of George's best, and one that came exactly at the right time. It really impressed the convention." That it did was important, for the speech came at the peak of Meany's cam-paign for the presidency of the state federation.

When Prohibition ended in 1933, the state legislature created an Al-coholic Beverage Commission to oversee the state's restored liquor in-dustry. Labor had a great interest in jobs in the brewing industry, so the brewery unions asked for representation on the ABC. Governor Lehman picked John Sullivan, the state federation president.

Selection of an interim president to serve from December 1, 1933, the date of Sullivan's resignation, until the August 1934 convention fell to the thirteen-member executive council. At the urging of fellow building tradesmen, Meany ran against Emanuel Koveleski, a member of the bartender and hotel employees union who was a first vice-president, and who had been on the executive council for almost a quarter of a century. Koveleski's longevity notwithstanding, simple arithmetic dictated a Meany victory. The council had six upstate members, six from New York City, and a swing member from suburban Westchester County who was friendly to Meany. But one of the New Yorkers decided to settle an old feud and voted against Meany, tilting the interim presidency to Koveleski by a seven-to-six vote.

Undeterred, Meany immediately began campaigning for the full term, looking toward the vote at the August convention. Meany said no philosophical issues were involved in the contest. "The issue was New York versus upstate, and to some extent building trades versus the miscellaneous trades. Another thing that was very definitely in my favor was that there were only two salaried officers in the federation. For years and years, as long as anyone could remember, back to Gompers' time, one of the salaried officers always came from New York, and one from upstate." Koveleski's election gave upstate both offices, for secretary-treasurer John O'Hanlon was from Troy. "Of course we harped on this, and I got the entire printing trades union in the city of New York pretty much on that argument, not on the trade argument, but on the geographical argument."

Meany's major problem was ensuring that his delegates could afford to make the trip to the convention, which was to be held in Buffalo, and would be eligible to vote when they got there. "Remember, this was at the depth of the depression. The first thing you had to do when you came to a convention was to have credentials. There's a ledger there, and if your dues are not paid up, you don't get in. We had a situation where a great many of the unions—not only the building trades, but other unions —were delinquent in their dues. They didn't know whether they'd be able to make the convention or not.

"So the first campaign, among the building trades in New York in particular, was to get the locals to pay up their dues. I wanted the New York building trades—hell, I needed them—and we succeeded.

"The next thing we done, we started to figure out how we were going to get these delegates to Buffalo. The unions didn't have any expense money. So we ran a Saturday afternoon party up in Throgs Neck, some sort of resort, a little beer garden, and we raised some money that way.

And we collected money from the business agents, ten dollars here, fifteen dollars there. I remember we got three hundred dollars, which was all the money in the world, from a fellow named Ed Smith, who was in the elevator constructors union.

"Then we got three buses to take the delegates, about a hundred and twenty people, from New York to Buffalo. We got a block of rooms in one of the cheapest hotels there. I think the whole operation cost about two thousand dollars. Buses were not expensive in those days."

But the operation did give rise to a *sotto voce* story occasionally heard in the anti-Meany faction of American labor: that he and building trades supporters transported carloads of "goons" to Buffalo and seized control of the convention. "That is, of course, absolute nonsense," was Meany's retort. "These were fellows who would normally go to the convention. They'd been doing it for years before, but they would not have made it this year because they didn't have the money."

By convention rules, the balloting for officers was held on Thursday morning of convention week. Of this official vote, Meany said, "It is a mere formality. It is bang-bang-bang over. The actual election is held in the unofficial caucus the night before, on Wednesday, conducted by someone designated by the president. Those who come to the caucus are expected to be bound by the results. They are free not to come."

Few holes developed in Meany's New York support. The bartenders union, of course, backed their colleague Koveleski, as did theatrical and stage employees, an allied union. But Meany more than compensated for these defections with the nigh-solid support of building trades members throughout the entire state, with the exception of Rochester, Koveleski's home city. ("I didn't even bother about Rochester.") As a last-gasp gesture, the Koveleski group had a Rochester plumber make the nominating speech. "This was to show that Meany doesn't have all the plumbers, here is a plumber against him, which is all right. But, hell, the thing was done in a very good spirit." Eight months of campaigning made Meany confident. "The thing had been so well canvassed that I sat down and wrote my figure of what votes I was going to get, and what votes he was going to get, and I done that the morning of the election, and I was only two votes out of the way. I said I would get 233 and he would get 185 votes. Instead of that, I got 235 and he got 183. That was how close the thing was figured out."

The next day—August 30, 1934—the convention formally ratified the caucus vote, electing Meany by acclamation. Not a hint of the contest appears in the formal convention record. "The idea back of it was that they didn't want internal fights to get into the press, really get into the open. Now, of course the press knew what was going on, but it didn't have the same effect as if you were meeting in a regular convention session. This idea was to put up a good front."

Koveleski complained to reporters after the election, "Tammany Hall has been seeking my defeat for a long time because I am a Republican" (although he denied receiving any GOP support in the contest). Meany in later years denied that politics affected his election, "in the sense that I had any sort of political following within labor." In fact, Meany's rise inevitably affected national labor politics. The AFL's traditional abstinence from national politics was nonsensical, and especially at a time of Democratic ascendancy. Dan Tobin had angrily resigned from the AFL executive council in 1928 because of President Green's refusal to permit a labor endorsement of Alfred Smith's candidacy for President (he quietly rejoined after the election) and almost did so again in 1932 to protest the Carpenters' William Hutcheson's campaigning for the detested Herbert Hoover. Now Franklin D. Roosevelt was in the White House, and uncomfortably (to Tobin) cozy with such AFL insurgents as the feisty John L. Lewis, of the United Mine Workers of America, and Sidney Hillman, of the Amalgamated Clothing Workers. Governor Lehman, a non-Tammany Democrat, also was listening to progressive unionists unobligated to the AFL and its city and state bodies. What Tobin realized, in essence, was that the largess Roosevelt and Lehman would spend in antidepression programs would far exceed local favors available through ward politicians; that power, when it exists, must be recognized; and that the pragmatic course for labor was to cooperate. Tobin was also increasingly unhappy with the quality of AFL leadership. "One by one," he had written in the Teamsters magazine in 1930, "those men of great minds who helped to make the labor movement what it is have been taken from us, and the pity of it is that we are finding it impossible to duplicate them."

But Meany's victory must not be oversimplified as a machination of labor politics. Meany was young (he celebrated his fortieth birthday exactly two weeks before his election) and he was considered a "forward thinker" by other unionists, and therefore a counterbalance to the emerging left wing of labor; yet as a Catholic and a building tradesman, he could be trusted to keep his progressivism on the safe side of radicalism. George Meany had learned his trade unionism in a reactionary atmosphere, from contemporaries and elders who put narrow self-interest above the welfare of labor (and society) as a whole. In comparison with the firebrands of the Committee for Progressive Labor Action, the slowly maturing socialism of David Dubinsky and other garment worker leaders, and the organizing zeal of the mercurial John L. Lewis, the George Meany of 1934 was a moderate. Yet he must be judged by another standard: against the attitudes of the national AFL leadership, and of the rank-and-file members of the state federation of labor. Compared with these men, Meany was a near-radical, but nonetheless one they chose to represent them in Albany at the peak of the economic and social reforms of the New Deal. George Meany, plumbers business agent, was about to become George Meany, lobbyist for state labor.

# III

## The State Fed Presidency:
## The Plumber as Lobbyist

I WORKED HARD but I was damn lucky, I was very lucky," George Meany said of his six years as president of the New York State Federation of Labor. "I came in at the depth of the depression. It is an amazing thing how the attitude of a state legislature toward labor could be influenced by a depression. During the so-called boom days in the twenties—the Coolidge and Hoover days—it was a rare thing to get two labor bills through the state legislature. But when labor was flat on its back it was a very odd thing [how things improved]. I suppose it was due to the fact that these people had to run for office and they knew that workers needed this sort of help.

"We got unemployment insurance, we wiped out the so-called yellow dog contract [which required workers to pledge, as a condition of employment, not to join a union]; we passed a companion bill to the Norris-La Guardia Act,* we set up a state labor relations board, we overhauled our workmen's compensation law. We put seventy-two new laws on the statute books in one year, 1935, out of 112 bills. But I had a governor who was without parallel in my book in the field of public service— Herbert Lehman. I don't think there could have been any comparison to that man. His approach was nonpolitical, and being nonpolitical was the most valued political asset [he] had because he worked [and] looked at

* The Norris-La Guardia Act, passed in 1932, provided that U.S. courts could not issue injunctions against the "normal and peaceful" activities connected with industrial disputes, and that injunctions could be granted only after open hearings. It declared the worker's right to self-organization and collective bargaining to be the public policy of the United States.

everything in a straightforward manner." (Public hyperbole is a bane of labor; Meany, however, made this particular statement during an interview ten years after Lehman's death.)

As president of the New York State Federation of Labor—largest in any state, comprising nearly a quarter of the total AFL membership—George Meany wore a variety of hats. During the annual three- or four-month legislative session, he was labor's chief lobbyist in Albany. Because of labor's greater dependence upon, and regulation by, government during the 1930's, Meany acted as the unions' chief negotiator with the city, state, and federal governments on issues ranging from welfare eligibility to pay scales for relief projects. As titular head of state labor he did what he could, with his limited powers over autonomous affiliated unions, to halt fratricidal strife. And as labor politician he tried to maneuver union votes to candidates friendly to labor. There were also interminable public relations chores—speeches to civic groups, the formalized banquetry endemic to labor, goodwill visits to city and central labor councils, and statements on public issues.

Meany at forty—bald now "all the way back," as a friend put it, and flecks of gray beginning to appear around his temples; the midafternoon roast beef sandwiches and the late-evening platters of corned beef and cabbage at Jack Dempsey's Restaurant on Broadway pushing his girth tighter and tighter against his vest; a growing reputation for gruffness, even with friends, when he was trying to think through a new problem; a confidence that to some people seemed to border on arrogance, for the distinction is thin indeed between standing-on-principle and bullheaded stubbornness; and a capacity for swift, total relaxation with building trades chums, on the Friday night train from Albany, or around the card table in the Central Trades and Labor Council office in lower Manhattan.

And, always, a firm separation of job and home. At Mrs. Meany's insistence, Meany refused to do any union business from his home; rank-and-file members and business agents who telephoned him in the evening were told brusquely, "Call me tomorrow downtown." The Meanys settled into a comfortable row house at 1626 Mayflower Avenue in the Bronx, and began their family: daughters Regina, born in 1923; Eileen, 1925; and Genevieve, 1930. Meany learned to play handball and golf, and set aside Saturday evenings for union socials—despite his girth and a weak ankle caused by a school football injury, he was a spry dancer—and enjoyed a middle-class Bronx life—a union man, but one who had thrown away his overalls. But his personal comfort as a union bureaucrat did not distract Meany from an immediate challenge: relieving the sting of the depression.

The summer of 1934 was a grim one for a nation now almost five years into the depression. On August 27—three days before Meany's election—New York City Welfare Commissioner William Hodson told a city council committee that one of every four New Yorkers received relief, 400,000 families, at a cost of $201 million annually, and that he expected the figure to rise to 500,000 families the next year. Nationally, 3.6 million Americans were on emergency relief rolls, 970,000 more in improvised works programs, another 180,000 in Civilian Conservation Corps camps. Newspaper headlines were a daily montage of industrial strife: one million persons staging a multistate strike of the textile industry; the San Francisco docks closed, and authorities resorting to "Red raids" to halt organizers; the Kentucky coal fields in turmoil; near civil war in Minneapolis, with sixty-eight persons, including two policemen, wounded when officers convoyed trucks through a picket line. A worried William Green cautioned against militants' demands for a general strike in a midsummer statement that such walkouts would "violate legitimate contracts and risk losing all economic gains achieved through years of sacrifice and effort." In other words, the AFL was going to play under the same old rules. On this particular issue, Meany agreed with Green, for preservation of the sanctity of contracts was a cardinal tenet for the building tradesmen. But it was also obvious to Meany that labor must swing to the left.

In September 1934, right after his election, Meany presented labor's legislative program to platform committees of the state Republican and Democratic parties. The Democrats endorsed six of eight planks, including employer-financed unemployment compensation; the GOP but two. The state federation executive council thereupon endorsed Governor Lehman for re-election, Meany calling his labor platform "the most important labor utterance in years." Most of Meany's campaign speeches and statements centered on unemployment insurance, but he tailored messages for specific audiences. To circumvent minimum wage laws, for instance, clothing and other manufacturers farmed out homework to women and children who earned ten to twelve cents hourly at piece rates. The 1933 legislature had passed a law bringing the homeworkers under wage-and-hour laws, but the Republican majority limited its jurisdiction to cities of 200,000 persons or more. The employers, of course, promptly moved their homework to the suburbs and small upstate towns. Meany argued to garment workers that Lehman and a Democratic legislature would halt this abuse.

Not that Lehman was in any real danger of defeat. His opponent was the arrogant and politically maladroit Robert Moses, a turncoat Democrat who had served in Governor Alfred Smith's cabinet and then became a Republican. Lehman transformed the election into a mini-referendum on the New Deal and overwhelmed Moses 2,202,000 to 1,394,000, carrying both upstate and metropolitan areas for the first time in New York history. More important, the Democrats won control of both houses of the legislature for the first time in two decades, 29 to 23 in the Senate, 77 to 73 in the Assembly.

Previously, according to Meany, tacit control of the legislature had been wielded by Associated Industries, the New York equivalent of a state manufacturers association. Mark Daly, AI's chief lobbyist, "was the kingpin of the city of Albany during the legislative session," in Meany's view. Joe McGinnies, the aged speaker of the Assembly, and John Knight, perennial president pro tem of the Senate, worked closely with Daly. "They owned the state of New York. Al Smith used to say that when they left Albany on weekends they took the state of New York with them, and they brought it back on Monday."

Physically and socially, Lehman and Meany were an odd couple—the shy, diminutive Jewish investment banker, who preferred subdued drawing-room conversation to the forced gregarity of politics, now in partnership with the strapping, blunt Bronx unionist, whose idea of genteel entertainment was pinochle or gin rummy. Somehow it worked, and Lehman and Meany developed what several of their mutual friends call a "true affection for one another." Lehman gave Meany both social and political access to the governor's mansion, and Meany learned to be comfortable in a tuxedo, to make polite table talk with Harvard and Yale men, and to develop a taste for a life style with trappings more elaborate than beer-garden picnics and boiled beef and potatoes. He also developed an unabashed admiration for Lehman as a man and legislative strategist. Lehman, in turn, so appreciated labor's friendship that he hobbled into the state federation's 1938 convention on crutches, an ankle-to-thigh cast supporting a knee smashed several days earlier in an auto accident.

In November and December 1934 Meany and Francis X. Sullivan, counsel for the state federation, met weekly with Charles Poletti, Lehman's chief legal adviser, to translate the Democratic platform promises into specific legislation. By the time the legislature convened on January 2, 1935, to hear Lehman's state-of-the-state message, the Democratic leadership was ready with a package of forty-four bills, all introduced within an hour of the governor's speech. Senate leader John J. Dunnigan appointed committee chairmen with instructions to report as many bills as possible the next day so they could be passed by the upper house the following week. Thirteen of the first eighteen labor bills introduced were in fact reported within twenty-four hours. The Republican Albany *Knickerbocker Press* was awed: "Never before has there been such a swift start toward action on legislation. . . . Democratic legislative leaders made it clear that they regard the 800,000 plurality which the Governor received in the last election as a clear mandate from the people to enact the proposals which he had advocated during his campaign and those which had been incorporated in the Democratic platform." A handful of dissident Democrats led by Manhattan Democratic Assemblyman George Kaminski tried to slow the rush of legislation but, as the *Knickerbocker Press* commented, "for any Democrat to oppose Lehman's program would mean political suicide, according to the legislative chiefs." Postmaster General James A. Farley, as titular head of the New York Democrats, deflated Kaminski "with nothing more than a few smiles and frowns," the *Knickerbocker Press* marveled.

The Republicans could do nothing more than hurl ineffectual jibes at the smoothly functioning Democratic machine. George R. Fearon, GOP leader in the Senate, said, "We don't act just as rubber stamps on bills sent up from the second floor [Lehman's office]. We don't take orders from a Huey Long or a Jim Farley." Senate leader Dunnigan replied: "You are the same old bunch of reactionaries. You are still the Old Guard, but you can't hold back the progressive program of these three Democratic governors [Smith, Roosevelt, and Lehman] any longer. That is why the people voted you out of power."

The only recovery measure the Republicans could muster—one vigorously promoted by GOP leaders Irving Ives, in the House, and Fearon, in the Senate—was spending $236 million in state funds to eliminate railroad grade crossings. New York railroads wanted this bill because they were under strong public pressure to get rid of the dangerous grade crossings; if it could be done at public expense, so much the better for the shareholders.

Meany's role was to keep labor pressure on Democratic representatives and senators, and to ensure they knew what the bills were about. With Dunnigan and Irwin Steingut, a liberal young Brooklyn lawyer who was elected speaker of the Assembly, he arranged public hearings on labor's bills for the first time in New York legislative history. The pattern was ritualized. Every night before a committee appearance, Meany would sit up until two or three o'clock with federation counsel Frank Sullivan, stuffing himself with recondite details and trying to anticipate any question the committee might conceivably ask. The next morning, labor leaders and rank and file would come into Albany on early trains and meet with Meany in the Ten Eyck Hotel or the state federation offices to hear details of the bills to be heard that day. Meany, Sullivan, and John O'Hanlon, the federation secretary-treasurer, would allocate time to speakers, and then lead a mass march to the hearing room. Meany testified on a total of 120 bills in three months, sometimes a dozen at one sitting.

The first major fight was over reform of the state workmen's compensation laws. Under the existing system, employers contracted with private insurance companies for policies covering their workers. But the depression had thrown eighteen insurance companies into bankruptcy, causing default on payments in some 6,000 cases where awards had already been made to victims and survivors. "These included all sorts of major cases—injuries, deaths, payments to widows," Meany said. "There was a great hue and cry because it hurt a great many people." The defaulted payments ranged up to $70,000 in death cases. The state federation wanted protection against future defaults.

The insurance industry took the position that no legislation whatsoever was needed, that the state should permit the companies to devise a voluntary guarantee system. Lobbyist Daly maintained many firms handled compensation policies more or less as a public service and made no money from them. He charged that involving the state in compensation insurance "exposes to political domination a business of eighty million dollars a year." He and James Beha, an insurance lobbyist who had been state insurance director in the 1920's, mobilized opposition throughout the state. On the day set for hearings, according to Meany, "the insurance companies ran a couple of special trains from Buffalo, and a couple of special trains from New York City, and they picked up people at the stations on the way." When Meany, Sullivan, and O'Hanlon arrived to testify, "this place was packed, and we were absolutely alone, everybody in the room was against us."

Based on the companies' past records, Lehman and Meany did not trust them to clean their own house. "It requires a major operation to correct the abuses being perpetrated by the private insurance companies," Meany testified. "We can't believe that the companies are sincere about being ready to take care of the situation. It is the duty of the state to see that the worker is protected." And Meany scoffed at the companies' claimed "public service" in handling compensation policies. Waving his arm at the galleries packed with insurance men, he said, "The private carriers say they don't make money on compensation insurance. Well, look at this turnout and the money behind it."

The public hearing was pro forma, because Meany and Lehman had already decided upon some shrewd legislative gamesmanship to jolt the insurance people into accepting a compromise acceptable to labor. "The threat we held over their heads was to put them out of the business, by creating an all-inclusive state fund," Meany says. Under this plan, the state would have collected premiums from employers and established a statewide compensation pool. Employers would have had no say whatsoever in its administration.

"We had no chance of passing that bill. We knew it, Lehman knew it, I knew it, but we pretended that we were going to pass it, and this really got them up in arms." Hence Meany devoted his testimony to recitation of case after case where workers and widows had been left penniless by collapsed companies. The insurance men, although they had a vast numerical majority at the hearing, were edgy at Lehman's demonstrated control of the legislature, and Meany's testimony had considerable emotional impact on legislators who might otherwise be friendly to the insurance industry.

"The hearing adjourned about six o'clock, and everybody trooped home. Lehman called a press conference at about eight o'clock and made a statement that he was going to pass his state fund, and that was all there was to it. [Lehman said] there was nothing that happened at the hearing other than that the insurance companies 'put a lot of bodies in there.'

"Well, by God, at nine o'clock the next morning Jim Beha was up in the executive office, pleading to see the committee, pleading to see Lehman. So the bluff worked. As a result of that, we compromised, but it was all to the good."

There were several weeks more of haggling over technicalities, but in the end Lehman and Meany obtained what they wanted: a one percent tax on compensation insurance premiums to pay off claims against the defunct companies, and immediate transfer of the full amount of awards to a newly created state board.

The unemployment insurance fight, next on labor's agenda, once again pitted Meany and Lehman against the insurance industry. This time, however, the contest had national significance. For twenty years various state legislatures had considered taxing employers to care for the jobless, but no state dared start a program alone for fear the tax would put its industries in a competitive disadvantage with other states. Federal entry into the field, via the 1935 Social Security Act, dashed this particular fear. The federal act did not directly establish a system of unemployment insurance, but it gave states and their industries an incentive to do so by imposing a federal tax on payrolls. If an employer was covered by a state unemployment insurance plan, he could deduct most of these payments from the federal tax. Employers in states without unemployment insurance laws had to pay the full federal tax; hence there was every inducement for speedy passage of state programs.

The federal bill was debated in Congress in the late winter and early spring of 1935, concurrently with the New York legislature's session. According to Meany, business opponents of UEI considered New York's decision crucial to the national debate over social security. The business lobbyists, once again marshaled by Mark Daly of the Associated Industries, maintained New York had no assurances neighboring states would adopt UEI even if the federal bill passed, and "they did not want the industries of New York to be burdened by taxes . . . that were not to be placed on other states." Meany called this argument hollow. "They didn't tell us the true reason they wanted New York State's unemployment insurance law defeated. They wanted to be able to go to Washington at the end of the session . . . and say to the congressmen and the senators . . . that New York State had turned down this great social reform and use that argument in opposition to the President's Social Security Act."

The Lehman administration made Meany the chief public spokesman for its bill. Meany seized the assignment with zest. He arranged for special buses and trains to bring hundreds of union members to Albany for a hearing on March 6, introduced dozens of them as witnesses in a packed Assembly chamber, and presented the major argument for the bill. Meany had done his homework. The committee chairman, Senator William T. Byrne, familiarly referred to him as "George" as he called witnesses, and gave him time to rebut hostile testimony.

Meany faced diverse adversaries: the employers, who were willing to yield enough to create their own unemployment plans, with no state role in collections, disbursements, or administration; and remnants of the militant Committee for Progressive Labor Action, which wanted a system that would begin paying benefits immediately.

The CPLA case was tough to answer. Why tarry while New Yorkers literally starved? CPLA witnesses asked; why settle for a UEI bill that would not bring immediate relief?

Meany and Lehman knew their slim legislative majority would never approve the CPLA plan. Besides, they feared it would not be self-supporting. As Elmer F. Andrews, the state industrial commissioner, testified, "It is obviously impossible to set up a system of unemployment insurance and immediately load it with the accumulated weight of existing unemployment." The Lehman-Meany plan was for graduated taxes on payrolls reaching three percent in 1938, to create an initial pool from which benefits would be paid beginning three years after the act became law.

Too, Meany wanted UEI to be an ongoing program, not simply an antidepression stopgap that would lapse as soon as the economy recovered. "At the present time there are eleven million people unemployed in this country, but I don't think that we should take the attitude that during good times there is no such thing as unemployment," he testified. "In the best of times we have this problem. . . . In 1923, the low record of unemployment, there were approximately two million people in the country without any source of income." Meany emphatically dismissed employer promises for voluntary action, or further studies. Their attitude, he said, "can be summed up in one . . . sentence: . . . 'Leave us alone, don't bother us, let us go along and let us handle our employees and work out our own plans. . . .'

"Their attitude is comparable to the attitude of the slave-owning states. 'Let us alone. Do what you want with the rest of the country.' We can't solve this gigantic unemployment problem by going along with any such attitude."

Meany noted that two weeks previously Senator Wagner had told a congressional committee "that he thought New York State should act immediately in order to give impetus to this movement throughout the entire country." For that reason, Meany said, the legislature should reject delaying amendments.

UEI faced formidable opponents. Bainbridge Colby, who had been Secretary of State under President Wilson, charged UEI would retard business recovery. Marion B. Folsom, an executive of Eastman Kodak (Meany was to encounter Folsom three decades later as President Eisenhower's Secretary of Health, Education, and Welfare) argued for the company plan. But UEI was an idea whose time had come. In a key Assembly vote on March 20 it passed 77 to 73; the final vote for passage was 102 to 42, with 24 Republicans joining the solid Democratic majority. The Senate stalled briefly, with Tammany Democrats threatening to kill UEI unless Lehman softened a reapportionment plan that would have cut Manhattan's legislative delegation. In the waning hours of the session, finally, Tammany yielded, UEI passed 30 to 16, again with several GOP votes. At the bill-signing ceremony Lehman called UEI "the most progressive and enlightened piece of social legislation enacted in this state in many decades." Lehman gave the ceremonial signing pen, and credit for the enactment, to George Meany.

The federal Social Security Act passed Congress four months later, in August, and within two years all states had UEI laws paralleling that of New York. For this reason, it would be easy to dismiss the significance of Meany's work, to call New York merely first among many; assuredly, social security ultimately would have come, regardless of the lobbying of a single state labor official. But the New York passage was important because it ruined the hopes of big business opponents to kill social security at the state level. New York's bill meant that employers in a major industrial state were to pass their payroll taxes back to workers in the form of UEI, and not pay them into the federal treasury. Other states could ignore New York at their own political and economic peril. Further, the New York passage demonstrated a grass-roots support for the New Deal that encouraged Congress to continue social legislation even in the face of such setbacks as the Supreme Court's invalidation of the National Industrial Recovery Act in the spring of 1935. A proud Meany told the state federation convention in late summer: "I feel that the passage of this law in the state of New York is responsible for the passage of the Social Security Act in our federal Congress."

The compensation reforms and UEI took the bulk of Meany's time during the 1935 session, but not at the expense of the remainder of the labor program. The Democratic majority, and Lehman's support, meant snap passage of most of the labor-supported legislation. The act outlawing yellow dog contracts, for example, passed on January 8, a week after the legislature convened. Manufacturers didn't even bother to testify against the bill restricting homework in the garment industry. "Apparently they don't dare show their heads," remarked Senator Byrne. The state federation submitted eighteen bills, sixteen of which were enacted exactly as written. (The defeated bills would have regulated employment agencies.) It endorsed 115 bills, 62 of which were enacted. Measures long anathema to the Republican-dominated legislature zipped methodically through both houses: a jury trial for persons accused of violating labor injunctions; a maximum work week of forty-eight hours for women, instead of the previous seventy-two hours (including overtime); an increase in the mandatory school age from fourteen to sixteen years; a five-day forty-hour week for all public employees, from state to village level; reduction of the permissible working hours for boys sixteen to eighteen years old from fifty-four to forty-eight hours; vacations for hourly workers on the New York City subway system.

By the time the legislature adjourned in early April the *State Federation Bulletin* could boast of "the most constructive and liberal annual session . . . ever held. . . . These enactments establish an achievement in social and industrial well-being for men, women and children that has no parallel in the legislative history of this or any other state on the American continent."

The 1935 session proved to be the pinnacle of Meany's career as labor lobbyist. Control of both houses returned to the Republicans in the 1936 elections, and the few victories labor won thereafter were fiercely fought. Meany's record in those years follows a discernible philosophical pattern: if social legislation benefited union members, he supported it; if it threatened to usurp what labor considered its own role in worker-employer relations, he opposed it. George Meany, labor progressive, could not (and did not try to) forget he was also George Meany, building trades unionist.

In 1937 Meany refused to support Lehman's request for a minimum wage for men, although he did endorse such protection for women. Meany testified that unions had never favored minimum wage legislation for men. "During their long-continued existence," Meany said, "these unions have established prevailing rates of wages by collective bargaining in their trades and industries and make them effective by their economic power." Meany's words sound coldly indifferent to underpaid workers whom labor did not attempt to organize and who were excluded from the protection of such unions as Meany's United Association. The traditional unionist attitude, which Meany accepted wholeheartedly, was that if government performed trade union functions, workers would lose their incentive to organize. Meany feared "that if you had a minimum wage law that established a legal wage, it would bring down your union wage. Now, of course, that never happened."

When government could help unions, however, Meany lobbied strenuously. In 1939, for instance, he testified for a bill requiring that demolition of buildings and other structures "shall be accomplished by taking them down story by story from the top story downward." Ostensibly a safety measure, the bill actually was intended to force contractors to use men, not the wrecking ball, in demolition work. Another Meany bill, also unsuccessful, would have required hiring of a "hall man" in all buildings where an automatic elevator put a man out of work—an attempt to do a favor for the newly organized Building Service Employees International Union. He opposed restrictions and taxation of unsightly billboards "because its effect would be to throw thousands of skilled mechanics . . . out of work and thus add to the army of unemployed." In 1939 Meany brought two trainloads of union members to Albany for hearings on implementation legislation for $300 million in slum clearance and low-cost housing. According to the *State Federation Bulletin,* the men "completely filled the two Senate galleries." The federation executive council noted in a resolution that the "carrying out of this program will employ thousands of building tradesmen throughout the state." *

As a Catholic Meany was caught up in a struggle between conservative and progressive wings of the Church over a measure supported by Lehman and labor: New York ratification of a constitutional amendment giving Congress the power to regulate working conditions and wages for persons less than sixteen years of age—the so-called child labor law. Most national church leaders supported the law. But the conservative New York State Catholic Welfare Committee feared the amendment would give Congress "the complete control of every activity of all young people in the nation," and claimed "harmful child labor is now practically nonexistent in the United States." Meany, however, lobbied for ratification, telling one legislative committee, "I do not think that there is anyone in this room who is in favor of children

---

* The New York lobbying paralleled national activity of the AFL. Joseph A. McInerney told the 1938 AFL convention that the Building and Construction Trades Department, of which he was president, "was very largely responsible for the enactment" of legislation providing $800 million for low-cost housing and slum leveling. "This vast authorization," McInerney said, "would provide thousands of jobs for the unemployed in the building trades."

working in the mills, canneries, workshops, or factories of America at the age of ten, eleven, twelve, or thirteen years. We who glory in the name of Americans must of necessity feel a sense of guilt when we contemplate a system which allows, *aye,* in many cases *compels* children of tender years to slave for long hours while their parents remain in the ranks of the army of unemployed." Ratification failed, and Meany blamed opposition by the Catholic bishops for the defeat.

Continuing opposition from the manufacturers' lobby on health and safety issues strengthened Meany's conviction that labor must be active politically to protect its own interests. The New York building trades unions could protect themselves because of tight organization and raw economic strength: contractors might detest unions, but reality demanded that they be accepted. But what Meany saw of big business in Albany left him with a deep contempt for corporations. Three decades later Meany still spoke bitterly of how business opposed a bill requiring installation of exhaust fans in work areas where abrasive grinding put harmful dust in the air. The state manufacturers' association, he said, resisted "on the theory that this was going to cost the manufacturer . . . five dollars to cover an area maybe half the size of this room"—a hotel dining hall.

Intensive as it was during the legislative sessions, lobbying consumed less than a third of Meany's calendar year. For three months at the beginning of each year Meany was a commuter, riding the New York Central's Monday morning "legislative special" to Albany, using the time to fraternize with New York politicians who were aboard, and returning to his home in the Bronx on Friday evening. Although he used the state federation office and its lone secretary in Albany, his "home" office was a cubbyhole in the Central Trades and Labor Council Building at 265 West 14th Street in New York. Meany never bothered to hire a New York secretary. He was not a man who cared to do his business on paper. His forte was the give and take of face-to-face negotiation, the business agent technique of persuasion and blunt talk. Too, the labor movement even at this late date retained the secretiveness of its founders, men so fearful of management spies they dared not reduce their plans and activities to writing. Despite his state-wide responsibilities, most of Meany's work was in Albany and New York, and could be conducted in person or by telephone. On the rare occasions when he wrote a letter he would compose a draft in longhand and persuade a secretary from one of the many union offices in the building to type it for him.

As a state federation official Meany had no direct responsibility to involve himself in the periodic disputes between unions and the municipal government, matters traditionally handled by the Central Trades and

Labor Council. But the council president, Joseph Ryan of the Long-shoremen, a Tammany Democrat, was barely on speaking terms with Mayor Fiorello La Guardia, who had been elected on a Fusion-Republican ticket over a Tammany candidate in 1933. During his decade in Congress La Guardia had consistently supported labor legislation, and as House sponsor his name was on the Norris-La Guardia Act, much treasured by labor, which severely curbed the use of injunctions in strikes. To Meany, La Guardia was a friend of labor and deserving of support. To Ryan, La Guardia was a Republican, and there the matter ended; Ryan wouldn't—*couldn't*—do business with such a man. But Ryan was pragmatic enough to realize unions can't operate in New York without speaking with the mayor, hence Meany became labor's liaison with La Guardia by default as much as by right.

The relationship was symbiotic—a friendly reception for labor at City Hall in return for as much labor support as Meany could muster at the polls. La Guardia had a standing arrangement with Meany. Once or twice weekly the mayor's chauffeured limousine would drop La Guardia on a corner in uptown Manhattan near Gracie Mansion, the mayor's residence, and Meany would meet him. "They'd ride downtown in George's old Ford automobile and talk about whatever business they had," said a Meany friend of the era. "A few blocks from City Hall La Guardia would meet his limousine and ride on to the office in style, with no one the wiser as to what he had been doing. People used to wonder how Meany and La Guardia got so many things worked out. People around City Hall would say, 'They never see one another in the office.' "

Meany liked La Guardia's direct style. In one dispute a Midwestern contractor installing signals in the subway system refused to employ union workers, to the chagrin of the electrical workers union. Meany and Harry Van Arsdale, the union president, complained to La Guardia. Morris S. Novik, a La Guardia aide at the time, recalled: "La Guardia agreed with them right away that union men should be doing the work. 'Wait right here,' he told them, and burst out of his office and got on the telephone. (La Guardia would never have a phone in his office; it distracted him.) He called the company president and made up some story about apparent irregularities in bidding on the job, and how the contract might have to be canceled unless the company accepted the union. The problem ended right there, within three or four minutes."

Overtime pay for snow removal crews; union-scale pay for painters and ironworkers who were city employees; licensing problems for laundry drivers—much of Meany's business with the city was the business agent routine he had done for the plumbers union. And Meany's rigidity on preserving labor's "rights," even when the employer was government, brought him into a unique confrontation during his first year as state federation president. "I am always amused," he said proudly, "when I hear some of my critics say, 'What does Meany know about labor? He never carried a picket sign, he never conducted a strike.' Well, I conducted a strike, and it was a big strike, and it was against a really formidable employer, which was the United States government."

The situation developed this way. By early 1935 President Roosevelt had decided that the "federal government must and shall quit this business of relief. . . . Work must be found for able-bodied and destitute workers." Roosevelt and Harry Hopkins, his relief administrator, wanted instead a vast program of more or less permanent public works, to substitute for the leaf raking and other makeshift emergency projects begun during the first months of the New Deal. Roosevelt asked Congress for a Work Relief Bill of almost five billion dollars for "useful" projects which promised an "ultimate return" to the Treasury of most of their cost, and "of a nature that a considerable proportion of the money spent will go into wages for labor." The House passed the bill swiftly but it fell into trouble in the Senate. With private construction at a virtual standstill, labor recognized that work relief would soon be the major employer for the building trades. How, then, could labor ensure that the government would pay workers standard union rates of pay?

Senator Pat McCarran (Dem., Nevada), a good friend of labor, introduced an amendment providing that workers receive the prevailing wage in their community—another way of saying the union rate. The amendment put the Roosevelt Administration in a quandary. It did not wish to damage wage-and-hour standards, especially at a time when national policy encouraged unionization. But neither did it want to set wages at a level competitive with private employers, for to do so would give workers no incentive to leave work-relief rolls. After hard debate the McCarran amendment failed, and fixing of pay rates was delegated to the President with the proviso they should accomplish the purposes of the act "without affecting adversely or otherwise tending to decrease prevailing wages." The rates were to be in the form of a "security wage," larger than the relief dole, but "at the same time not so large as to encourage the rejection of opportunities for private employment or the leaving of private employment to engage in government work." An executive order issued May 20, 1935, set schedules ranging from $10 to $94 monthly for various occupations, and decreed a maximum work period of eight hours per day, and 140 hours per month. The administrator in each state was authorized to specify the number of hours the employers had to work in return for their monthly security wage. But Harry Hopkins, acting under his broad powers as administrator of the program, immediately issued a directive that the maximum 140-hour month be standard.

To organized labor—and particularly the building trades—Hopkins' order was equated with a return to sweat-shop slavery. Figures for the plumbers union illustrate the money involved. The union rate for plumbers in New York City in 1935 was $1.50 per hour. Hopkins' "security wage" would have required plumbers to work 140 hours for $85— slightly more than 63 cents an hour.

The unions' case was strong on paper. Reality was a different matter. The WPA computed that since the beginning of the depression, few building trades craftsmen had worked enough to earn even the "security wage" of $85 monthly, their $1.50 hourly rate notwithstanding. The average monthly earning, according to one WPA calculation, was less than $50. Newspaper classified advertisements from the summer of 1935 tend to support the WPA argument, for plumbers begged for work for $6, $5.50, even $4.50 per day. ("Plumber, fitter, alterations, lead, anything; hustler. Wages $6" read one plea among a column of jobs-wanted ads from plumbers in the New York *American*.)

As administrator for New York City, Hopkins selected General Hugh Johnson, who had been thrown into bureaucratic limbo earlier in 1935 when the Supreme Court declared the National Industrial Recovery Act unconstitutional, thereby putting his National Recovery Administration out of business. A former cavalry officer, Johnson had helped run the draft and the war industries board during World War I; later he became a business associate and confidant of the financier Bernard Baruch. A thick-necked man with a square jaw and a perpetually florid face, Johnson was one of the more rambunctious characters in the New Deal— "colorful, vivid, and outspoken, with a command of racy, forthright language," in the tactful words of his friend Baruch. In other words, a perfect match for New York's roughneck building trades unionists should a brawl develop. Or so Hopkins thought.

Johnson didn't want a fight over the prevailing-wage issue, and the first thing he did upon arriving in New York in early July was to arrange a meeting with Meany and other labor leaders in the St. Regis Hotel. When the work-relief program began in 1933 the Central Trades and Labor Council had appointed Meany to a committee to monitor wages and other issues, and he was prepared. Hopkins had not attempted to put the security wage into effect anywhere else in the country. "They evidently felt there was going to be some resistance to it," Meany said. "Somehow or another they had the idea that if New York would accept the policy, then they would have no trouble in handling it in the other cities." Hence the St. Regis meeting was so important that Johnson brought along Edward F. McGrady, a former AFL Washington lobbyist turned FDR labor troubleshooter with the title of Assistant Secretary of Labor.

General Johnson's mood was conciliatory and confident, and he offered a compromise. "It was that everybody got $75 a month, everybody worked 130 hours a month, and this was going to be fair to everyone, so forth and so on, and it was explained to me in great detail," Meany recounted. "I sat listening, and Eddie McGrady said, 'George, you'll go along with that, won't you?' and I said, 'I will like hell. I will not go along with anything which requires members of our unions to work for below the prevailing scale of wages, which also happens to be the union scale.' " Meany also said he did not accept the argument that WPA was "made work." Meany continued: "At this point General Johnson hadn't said a word. He hit his fist down on the desk, and he said, 'Goddammit, I knew there was a catch here, I knew I was getting myself in for some trouble.' "

According to Meany, Hopkins had told Johnson the mission would be simple: "Go up to New York, and Ed McGrady can talk to George Meany, and you'll get everything straightened out." Meany said he convinced Johnson that Hopkins was wrong and Johnson thereafter was privately sympathetic to labor. But he quoted Johnson as telling him, "I've been given a job to do, and the job I've got to do according to the rules." Johnson did tell the press after the meeting he wanted some modifications in the security wage rules. "Labor doesn't like it, and I don't like it," he said. "It's going to give me a lot of headaches."

Meany proposed putting the WPA work under private contractors, rather than have the federal government act as employer. This procedure would have violated both the letter and spirit of Hopkins' security wage directive, but Hopkins was ready to bend the law if necessary. He told Johnson by phone: "You could do it and it wouldn't bother me. You got a tough job up there and I know now that we will have to break some of our rules and regulations up there because the thing has to be made to work." The private contractor idea proved unworkable, however, and after more talks the Central Trades and Labor Council met on July 13 to take a strike vote. The council said that "under no circumstances are any of our organizations to permit their members to work on relief projects at less than the prevailing rate. . . ." Instead, Meany said, union members would quit WPA jobs and return to the home relief rolls.

Johnson by now was very nervous, for he knew Meany was serious about the building trades quitting work. But Hopkins would not yield further, apparently because he feared that political repercussions might ensue if New Yorkers received union scale pay for what much of the country considered to be an elaborate version of the dole. The Administration was suddenly and acutely skitterish ("Roosevelt in Retreat," historian Arthur Schlesinger, Jr., called these 1935 months). It had been buffeted by a hostile Supreme Court. It was uncertain of how many Americans endorsed the "moral terrorism" of Senator Huey P. Long and

Father Charles E. Coughlin, the Michigan radio priest. It was aware how precarious its Senate margin would be if Southern conservatives were to follow their natural instincts and stop voting for progressive legislation. And it was torn from within by the debate over recovery-versus-reform. Of the congeries of existing and potential dangers, the building tradesmen seemed least dangerous, for no one in Washington felt a group as inherently conservative as AFL unions would strike the United States government.

The indomitable Johnson kept trying. On July 25 he got WPA to agree to boost the salary of skilled workers by ten percent over the security wage, as permitted by Hopkins' broad salary policy. There is sharply conflicting documentary evidence as to whether Johnson thought the increase would prevent a strike. WPA archives contain a telegram that Jacob Baker, the WPA assistant administrator, sent Hopkins aboard a Washington–Chicago train that day: "General Johnson felt it important that you should know that he got agreement of the unions in New York not to strike his jobs." New York newspapers of July 26 carried the same story. But the WPA files also contain a "personal and confidential" telegram from Johnson to Hopkins dated July 25 in which he warned that the "impending strike of skilled trades threatening to paralyze almost all projects will start Federal [WPA] in New York City off on August first in the worst possible atmosphere and in general condemnation." He complained of the "arbitrary and inflexible" attitudes of unnamed Hopkins subordinates and cited as an example the inability of WPA's Washington office to pay WPA workers weekly, rather than biweekly or monthly.

Meany hammered away. Hopkins had also ruled that at least 90 percent of the workers on any project should come from the relief rolls, and that only one member of a family could work on a project. Meany said building tradesmen who had succeeded in stretching out their savings over the long months of unemployment and "preferred deepest poverty to the dole" were unjustly penalized by this provision. The family limitation ignored the clannish character of the building trades, where a father and three sons might work side by side on a job. Meany's basic position was that the federal government was simply another employer, and not a relief agency, and that it could not make rules interfering with union practices. Contractors supported this position. "Requiring men to be on relief before they can get work is wrong," J. Lawrence DeNille, of the New York heating and piping contractors association, wrote Hopkins. "Attempts to construct buildings, highways, or any other improvements under inexperienced direction or supervision with relief subjects results only in waste, inefficiency, poor construction and unsafe structures."

By late summer the national implications of Meany's confrontation with the government were recognized. The New York *American* reported, "New York City . . . has been selected as a national area for a finish fight that will affect labor and work relief jobs throughout the country." Johnson's agony was intensified by the fact that many of the threatened projects were already under way: swimming pools, public school playgrounds, demolition of the Welfare Island penitentiary, slum clearance on the Lower East Side, planning for East River Drive. As overseer of more WPA spending than any other city or state official in the nation, Johnson had the opportunity to remake New York City; that the unions defied his conciliation attempts brought his cavalryman's temper forward at a gallop. "If they strike they go out of employment," Johnson said. He threatened to replace strikers. "I don't want to do it, but I'll have to. I hope, for their sake, they don't do it." Further, Johnson felt New York had received preferential treatment from the outset. Since the passage of the Work Relief Act "the whole WPA organization centered all their time and effort on New York," which in August was the only city "ready to start employing every jobless man on the relief rolls." Of 550,000 men then working on federal relief projects, 400,000 were in Civilian Conservation Corps camps, 100,000 on WPA rolls in New York, and only 50,000 elsewhere in the country. "What does this mean?" Johnson stormed. "It means that, in every aspect of this great national sharing, New York workers have been given so far the best of the deal that there isn't room for comparison."

The showdown came on August 8, when the WPA committee of the Central Trades and Labor Council, composed of representatives of some thirty unions, and chaired by Meany, voted to strike all WPA projects. With Meany's permission Johnson was permitted to enter the meeting after the vote and urge reconsideration. For ninety minutes he argued emotionally against a strike. Johnson's intended clincher was the reading of a speech he had prepared for national radio that evening if the strike began. The oration was a peculiar mixture of solid economic argument, which by itself could have had considerable impact upon rank-and-file members as well as the public, and of sheer political nonsense with which Johnson demolished his own credibility.

Johnson said the building trades workers' high hourly rate created a false illusion of riches; that regardless of their *hourly* salary, most earned a "starvation *monthly* salary. . . . The government says, 'We offer you six months' steady employment at a fixed salary of $93.50 per month. We will pay you, whether the work goes on or not, rain or shine, and we only ask you to work five eight-hour days a week, three weeks, or 120 hours a month.'

"Skilled building workers never had a better deal than that. Except for short stretches, and never over any five-year period, did these trades ever average $93.50 a month.*

"Before this federal work started there was almost no work in the building trades, and the average earnings were not half of that. What we now offer them is a full fifty percent increase in monthly earnings and against this they threaten strike.

"Every worker knows that thousands are working for almost anything they could get, and when they now talk about the government breaking down the hourly rate, they know that they let it break down in practice and what the government did through relief work was to come in and save it."

And then Johnson descended into howling nonsense. He claimed Communists were fanning the threatened strike. The Communists, he said, "have played upon the distress and resentment of victims of this depression until they have organized into disguised Communistic groups many misguided people. . . . They say this is class war and that lies and all are fair in war. Their aim is to pollute the AFL. They have never been able to do it. . . . They are not a majority, but they are strong enough to put American labor leaders on the spot. . . . If that strategy succeeds, and the AFL unions are made to appear as the spearhead in a Communistic strike, public support will depart from unionism, and the clock of the labor movement will be set back twenty years. . . . Don't do it, boys. Don't let yourself be used to foul your own nest and play a sucker's game."

Johnson called Meany and Joe Ryan "as good labor leaders as ever walked on shoe leather," and noted they acted as his "advisers" on labor matters. "They are on my staff [*sic*] to protect your interests. That puts Meany in a spot. But his duty is to his union. I told him the other day that I had no request to make of him that would interfere with him, and if he volunteered anything I would lose my great respect for him. It is his duty to support you, right or wrong." But labor's position, he maintained, was "so sickly that it couldn't get a night's lodging in a leper colony."

Hoots and shouts of derision interrupted Johnson as he read the speech. In mid-course he began shouting back and banging his heavy fist on the table, Meany matching him shout for shout. After the General finished the council promptly reaffirmed its strike vote.

Johnson's speech was either a naïve or a mendacious appraisal of New York labor. Communist organizers did keep WPA white-collar workers in ferment, and Communist functionaries did hold many positions, major and minor, in the WPA bureaucracy. But the building trades council was about as Bolshevik as the College of Cardinals. In fact, in

---

* Johnson's reference apparently was to the depression period, for construction workers averaged above $100 monthly throughout the 1920's.

the midst of the WPA dispute Meany refused to permit seating of a bricklayers union delegate at the state federation convention because of alleged Communist ties, and Joe Ryan used the incident to declare Central Trades and Labor Council policy: "We know something about the intentions and the practices of the Communists in boring from within and getting control of our movement. . . . We ask you to send that answer back so that they can hear it in Soviet Russia, that here is one of their tools that can't bore from within the labor movement. . . ."

Answering Johnson on a national radio broadcast August 9, Meany denied any Communist voice in the strike decision, and asserted the trades council had been fighting for years against the "Communist element that has crept into some of our unions. This campaign has been so successful that I am making the flat statement now that there is not even *one* known Communist in the delegate body of our central council." Meany pointed out the inconsistencies that riddled Johnson's speech:

"It seems that we are at once being charged with being agents of chiseling, grasping employers; the medium of a Communistic attack on the government; disturbers who are, without reason, trying to bring chaos and disorder into a situation now supposedly full of peace and contentment; and also the advocates of increased misery and suffering among the destitute.

"We merely say to our government, 'If you can afford to allot our people $60, $70, $40 or $50 per month we have absolutely no complaint. But we must firmly say to you that whatever you want to allot, do so at the legal standard in order that we may be able to maintain that which is dear to every union man—a standard rate of wage.' "

Working under a strike committee headed by Meany, the building tradesmen walked off their jobs, with Hearst's New York *American* screaming in the background, "AF OF L IS MISLED BY COMMUNISTS, JOHNSON LAYS WPA STRIKE TO REDS." President Roosevelt declared that strikers would not receive federal home relief funds, an order Meany denounced as "work or starve." And the war was on: the New York building tradesmen versus the federal government.

Just how many men struck, and with what effectiveness, is a truth that lies buried beneath the countering claims of a Meany–Johnson numbers game. According to public statements by Johnson and Edward McGrady, and also to private reports from Johnson to Hopkins, only about 15,000 of the 200,000-odd WPA workers belonged to building trades unions, and the highest number of strikers Johnson ever conceded was 1,157. Johnson also campaigned to hire replacement workers for the strikers, and claimed "10,000 new men" within a week. Johnson repeatedly told the press the strike had no effect whatsoever on WPA projects.

By Meany's version, which is understandably different, Johnson never understood the unions' strike strategy. Although the union members were a numerical minority, most of them worked as supervisors of unskilled crews. "We just pulled our people out, told them to stay at home, and of course when the other fellows got to the job they couldn't proceed, there was nothing they could do. This would happen four or five days in a row.

"The newspapers said the strike didn't mean anything, ninety percent of the people were working. Ninety percent of the people *were* there, but they weren't working, even though they were on the job.

"After about a week of this Johnson called me up and he said, 'Georgie Porgie'—he used to call me that—'your strike is a failure. They're coming in ninety percent.'

" 'But General, they're not working.' He didn't answer me on that."

Because workers were accomplishing little if anything, project managers began shutting down jobs. But Johnson had them reopened, ordering that anyone who reported for work be paid. Meany: "We promptly said to our 22,000 people, 'Report for work. If they ask you to do any work, that's different. But report.' They checked in, and this happened for three or four days, and then of course Johnson got wise and shut the whole thing down again."

Working through AFL President Green, Roosevelt and Hopkins tried to pressure Meany into compromise, complaining that his strike endangered the entire WPA program. The press joined in. Hearst columnist Arthur Brisbane, who did not care for WPA, opined nonetheless, "The President will decide whether he and our 'representative government' shall run the country and dispose of its funds, or turn that business over to organized labor." Editorially, the *American* called the strike a "mutiny." In continuing radio broadcasts Johnson depicted the strikers as selfish. "No strike in the world can coerce the federal government . . . to give one group more than its share at the expense of other groups," he said. "The federal government stepped in to keep people from starving. The Congress of that government decided to offer work for this purpose and to create the dole. Nobody has to take that work. But neither, under the law, was any choice given of work or dole. Only work. In other words, any man on the dole can refuse to work. But he can't refuse to work and also stay on the dole." Meany says Johnson's attacks did not diminish their mutual respect. "Johnson would call me sometimes in advance and say, 'I'm going to make a speech tonight, and I'm going to read something I'm going to say about you.' I'd say, 'Fine, General, that's all right with me.' "

By early September Hopkins realized that since the WPA was not about to break the strike, the best solution was to pacify the New Yorkers so the program could proceed. Hopkins was temperamentally unfit for a protracted war of attrition such as Meany was waging; compulsively impatient, he frequently brushed past fine points of the law in his eagerness to get things done. Meany, however, constituted a challenge to his authority and prestige, and Hopkins was not the sort of personality to be outmanuevered publicly by a former plumber. So his retreat, when it became essential, was on his own terms, and very quiet.

According to Meany, Johnson called him at home on a Friday evening in early September and said, "I got it straightened out, you are going to get your prevailing rate of wages." Johnson paused, then said, "One condition, one condition, and remember it."

"What is it?" Meany asked.

"You can't shout victory."

"I'm not interested in shouting victory," Meany replied. "All we want is our money."

Meany and James Barry of the pavers union, who had helped direct the strike, met Johnson and staff members the next morning in the WPA office. Johnson's surrender was total, and he invited Meany to spell out the settlement terms. Barry handed Johnson a list containing the number of hours each craft would work in return for the security wage—enough hours to bring them the prevailing wage, no more, no less. "That goes into effect Monday morning," Johnson said, and initialed the list.

Over the weekend union business agents quietly passed the word to strikers to return to their jobs. Nothing was said publicly, either by the building trades or the WPA. The following Saturday morning Meany was working at his office in the central trades council building. His recollection was that "all of a sudden there was a knock on the door, and in comes about ten newspapermen, a whole crowd, led by a little guy named Ray Towr. They hadn't seen me all week, all they knew was that the people were going back to work.

"Towr asked, 'George, what's the plumbers' hourly rate?' I told him. 'What's the electricians' hourly rate? Plasterers? Bricklayers?' He was writing them all down, and figuring against the number of hours that the men were having to work for their WPA wage.

"Towr looked up and said, 'Why, it's the prevailing rate of wages. That's what WPA is now paying.' "

Meany's New York victory set a national pattern: thereafter WPA guaranteed that skilled craftsmen received their regular union rate. Pockets of opposition occasionally developed, one of them, ironically, in upstate New York, and only a few months after the New York City settlement. Lester Herzog, WPA administrator for New York State (exclusive of New York City), yielded to pressures from local contractors and officials and tried to circumvent paying the prevailing wage. Meany complained directly to President Roosevelt, saying it was grossly unfair for upstate men to work 120 hours monthly for the same amount New York City craftsmen received for 60 to 70 hours. "I am sure that it is unnecessary for me to attempt to remind you of the keen concern with which the New York State Federation of Labor has always tried to safeguard and improve state laws calling for prevailing wages," Meany wrote the President. In short order both Roosevelt and James A. Farley told Hopkins to pacify Meany. Hopkins apparently was not eager for a return encounter with New York labor. On January 11, 1936, he telephoned R. C. Branion, the WPA field representative for New York, and instructed him to lean on Herzog. Hopkins' eagerness to settle is evident in the WPA's transcript of the conversation:

HOPKINS: I don't want to *talk* to him [Herzog], I want to *tell* him.

BRANION: He says that we will lose more support. . . .

HOPKINS: I don't care a damn what he says. I want it done immediately. . . . I want him to adjust those hours down to substantially what New York City has done. And I want it done . . . right away. . . . I think what ought to be done is that Herzog ought to send for Meany this afternoon, for Meany to come to Albany. And tell Meany to keep his mouth shut so Herzog can announce it. . . . I don't want him [Herzog] to get into a long-winded discussion about it. We want to get some good will on it. Let the New York *Times* yell its head off.

BRANION: They claim the unions don't really want it, but they have to make a noise about it.

HOPKINS: You discount that 100 percent.

The prevailing wage issue remained quiescent thereafter until 1939, when its revival by Congress threatened to breach Meany's friendship with Roosevelt and his support of the New Deal—a rapport that had commenced in 1936 with Meany's first direct involvement in national politics.

In early 1936 Postmaster General James A. Farley, President Roosevelt's chief political operative, telephoned Meany with a terse message: "The Boss wants me to talk with you." The President was already planning his re-election campaign, a task originally begun with a flush of confidence. National income had risen by about 50 percent since 1933, to $64.7 billion, while the number of jobless had been nearly halved, from a peak of 13 million to between 6 and 8 million. On January 30 FDR calculated he would win 325 electoral votes, the Republicans 206.* But nonetheless Roosevelt fretted. "We are facing a very formi-

* FDR missed. His actual margin was 523 to 8.

dable opposition on the part of a very powerful group among the extremely wealthy and the centralized industries," he wrote Ambassador Breckinridge Long in Rome on February 22. The renegade Democrat Al Smith vehemently opposed the New Deal, and threatened to siphon away Eastern Democratic votes to the Republicans. The Union party, Father Coughlin's personal creation, was a veritable conglomerate of crackpots aimed at a broad spectrum of zaniness: Coughlin was supposed to appeal to Irish Catholics and neo-Fascist ethnic groups in urban areas; Dr. Francis E. Townsend, the octogenarian share-the-wealther, had his old folks in the Far West and Michigan; and the party's presidential candidate, Representative William (Liberty Bill) Lemke, a populist Republican from North Dakota, was supposedly revered by the impoverished farmers throughout the Midwest because of his attempts to halt foreclosure sales.

In New York, Roosevelt's concern was the Socialist party, which in the 1935 municipal elections drew almost 200,000 votes. Norman Thomas, backed by young, adventurous militants who drove the moderate old guard from the party early in 1936, considered FDR "a good man in a bad party," whose state capitalism was a first step toward fascism. To support Roosevelt, Thomas stormed, "is to repeat the mistake of the German Social Democrats who voted for Hindenburg because they did not want Hitler." Thomas had no chance of carrying New York, but he was undeniably popular, and threatened to be a spoiler who could siphon away enough left-wing votes to throw the state to Republican Alfred M. Landon. The Socialists' antipathy to Tammany Hall further complicated the situation: even those left-wingers sympathetic to Roosevelt would hesitate to vote a ticket that would help the city Democratic machine. By late 1935, Meany says, it was "quite obvious" that although militant unions such as the ladies garment workers and the hatters would never vote Republican, they nonetheless "had a fetish about the Democratic party" because of Tammany Hall. "Franklin Roosevelt was a terrific politician and like all people in a real political frame of mind he wanted all the votes he could get . . . so Roosevelt come up with this idea that in order to ensure that he would carry New York State, he wanted another line on the ballot." Roosevelt had already talked with Sidney Hillman, head of the Amalgamated Clothing Workers, and David Dubinsky, of the ILGWU. Morris S. Novik, one of the breakaway Socialists supporting Roosevelt, and an aide to La Guardia, summarized, "He wanted to give them a place to go without going to the Democrats." Roosevelt's idea was for an American Labor party whose electors would be listed separately on the ballot, but who would cast their votes for him.

Meany was dubious when Farley first told him of the scheme. Meany accepted without question the philosophy of Samuel Gompers, the first AFL president, "that the American trade union movement should fit into the American system, which was basically a two-party system, and that our best interests would be served by being neutral politically." Nonpolitical did not mean neutrality in specific elections, but labor (in theory, at least) supported candidates on the basis of their records, not their party. Yet here was Roosevelt proposing not only that labor form a political party, but that Meany and other unionists go on the ballot as electors. When Farley presented the President's idea "we pooh-poohed it, we wouldn't have anything to do with it." Meany considered Dubinsky and Hillman "a minority in the labor movement"; although he accepted the fact that they had a perfect right to go their way [with a third party] he had no intention of joining.

But Farley managed to wear Meany down, if for no other reason than the astounding irony of the scheme. "Now here was the chairman of one of the two top parties throwing his influence behind the formation of a *third* party," Meany exclaimed. On that basis, Meany agreed to help with forming the American Labor party, but with the understanding his affiliation would not interfere with organized labor's "nonpartisan campaign committees" for Roosevelt and Vice-President John Nance Garner.

There was a final irony. "When they came to setting up the American Labor party," Meany said, "the legal staff of Tammany Hall done the work for them." The party held its organizational meeting on July 4, 1936, in a $10 per day room which Morris Novik rented at the Hotel New Yorker. Novik and Joseph E. Grill, an attorney related by marriage to one of Sidney Hillman's secretaries, did the leg work thereafter. Novik recalled, "We had to get petitions signed in each county in New York to get the American Labor party on the ballot, so we sent out a crew of six guys in a fifty-dollar flivver to all the remote counties." For contacts, Novik's crews used a New York State Federation of Labor mailing list provided by Meany. Using state federation letterheads, Meany also wrote letters of introduction to local labor leaders, explaining why he was endorsing such an unusual undertaking, and asking that they produce the number of signatures required in each locality to qualify the party for the ballot.

Meany made clear he thought of the ALP solely as a vehicle to ensure the re-election of Roosevelt, and not as a commitment to organize a permanent third party, either in New York or nationally. Once the petitions were gathered and filed with state election officials, and the ALP certified for the ballot, Meany directed Novik to destroy the lists of names so they could not be used as the nucleus for any new party. Novik protested. "In 1937 we have La Guardia; in 1938 we have Lehman," he said. "We could do the same thing for them." Meany refused to budge. Labor cannot become the property of any political party, he responded, in what came to be a recurring statement in ensuing years; it must remain independent to "reward its friends and punish its enemies"—Sam Gompers' old political guideline.

Nationally, the American Labor party was paralleled by Labor's League for Political Action, formed independently of the AFL by John L. Lewis, of the United Mine Workers of America, George L. Berry, of the Printing Pressmen's Union, and Sidney Hillman. William Green frowned on the political activism but a number of AFL craft unions contributed to the league, and Berry spoke optimistically of "the permanent establishment of a liberal party, if necessary, in the United States in 1940." Previously the Democratic National Committee had relied on a "labor division" headed by Dan Tobin of the Teamsters—useful chiefly as an ornament, because Tobin did not grasp the potential of a national political role for labor, and consequently contributed little to campaigns. Hillman, Lewis, and Berry, conversely, wanted to mobilize labor to protect an administration that had given it, among other things, the NRA and the Wagner Act. The labor contribution came to almost three quarters of a million dollars, two thirds of it from Lewis' mineworkers, and manpower as well.

Meany stumped New York State for the Roosevelt-Garner ticket, concentrating particularly on nominally Republican upstate building tradesmen. His message was simple bread-and-butter: the Roosevelt Administration, he said in a typical speech, "has fully justified faith in his promise to give the workers of this nation their rightful share in its wealth of production and to banish insecurity from their lives. . . . President Roosevelt has enlisted for the duration of the war against the evils in our economic and social systems, and the workers have joined the ranks and hail him as commander-in-chief."

Meany's position in the American Labor party helped the Democrats defuse an issue that could have frightened away Catholic construction workers: the depiction of David Dubinsky, an ALP elector, as an agent of Moscow. Dubinsky in fact had resigned from the Socialist party because he feared its leader, Norman Thomas, was "too close" to the Communists. Nevertheless the Republicans Red-baited him fiercely during the campaign. Senator James A. Reed of Missouri, for example, told one labor audience, "It was this same David Dubinsky who gathered funds for the Reds of Spain, where they are butchering nuns, priests, and ministers of the Gospel. Roosevelt led the Democratic party into the Communist slaughterhouse and there had it slaughtered." The Hearst papers bristled with demands that FDR strike Dubinsky from his roll of electors. Dubinsky retaliated vehemently: at one rally, speaking in his habitual third-personese, Dubinsky said the GOP called him a Communist "because his name is Dubinsky, because he spells it s-k-y, because

Trotsky is spelled s-k-y—that's the evidence that he's a Communist."
Hillman, similarly attacked, called the Hearst charges "the lowest kind
of political clowning." The Brooklyn *Eagle* was among newspapers in-
dignant at the Republican tactics: "The AFL's antagonism to anything
that smacks of Communism is well known." For this reason, perhaps,
the GOP criticisms, and those of the Hearst newspapers, excluded
Meany's name when listing ALP electors, content to point alarmedly at
such names as Max Zaritsky of the hatters union, Hillman, and Dubinsky.

Also among the ALP electors, to his chagrin, was Joe Ryan, the old
Tammany stalwart. "The Democrats let the American Labor party
choose seven of their forty-seven electors," Dubinsky said. "We wanted
strong labor representation, so, of course, someone added Joe Ryan to
our list. Ryan repudiated our endorsement. He publicly stated he did not
want to be an American Labor party elector. But it was too late—he was
on our ticket." *

The American Labor party mustered almost 300,000 votes for Roosevelt in New York—an unneeded cushion, in view of his landslide victory over Landon, but nonetheless a demonstration of labor's political
energy, and of Meany's willingness to assert his independence of old-line
building tradesmen. And, just as he promised, Meany had no further
dealings with the American Labor party (although, as lobbyist, he cultivated the votes of five legislators elected on its ticket). To Meany's
amusement, the ALP soon acquired many of the habits it had condemned when practiced by Tammany Hall. In 1937 the legislature was
considering a Lehman–La Guardia bill making some 35,000 New York
subway workers public employees. Meany and Michael J. Quill, head of
the Transport Workers Union, and by then an ALP leader, differed over
details of the bill, and Meany met with the ALP legislators to try to
resolve the dispute. "When we came to an agreement I said to one of the
ALP people, 'You will withdraw your opposition, won't you?' And he
came right back, 'Oh, I've got to call Alex'—meaning Alex Rose, head
of the ALP. When he said that, boy did I blow! 'Oh, you've got to call
Alex! And you are the guys who are criticizing the Democrats up here
because they've got to call Tammany Hall before they can vote.' That's
when I lost it with the labor party and Alex Rose." †

George Meany loved politics. He quickly grasped the root truth of the
game: that elections are decided by the actions of men who influence
bloc constituencies, not by the oratory one hears from a politician in

* The ALP electors were Meany, Ryan, Dubinsky, Hillman, Zaritsky, Arthur
R. Armstrong of the pressmen's union, and Michael Cashal of the Teamsters. For
technical reasons they were also listed as Democratic electors.

† When the ALP split later in the 1930's Rose headed the faction that became
the present New York Liberal party.

public. Power unused is power wasted, and Meany could influence, if not control outright, one of the larger pockets of votes in New York. Not for Meany the backslapping gregarity of the political clubhouse—he saw two positive values in politics: to keep friends in office, thereby making easier his work as state federation president; and to use campaigns as a medium for publicizing what he was accomplishing for the rank and file.

In 1937 Tammany Hall produced an amiable but undistinguished political lawyer named Jeremiah T. Mahoney as its candidate against Mayor La Guardia. Under normal circumstances Mahoney could have expected automatic endorsement by New York labor. He was close to Joe Ryan, and he was active in the Union Life Insurance Company, the creation of Matthew Woll, a photoengravers' union official who was in the tight inner circle that dominated the AFL executive council. But when the endorsement went before the central trades council Meany argued for La Guardia. "Why do I care that La Guardia calls himself a Republican?" Meany asked. "He's been a good mayor and we should support him." Joe Ryan, Mahoney's advocate, talked about the traditional friendship of the Democratic party and labor, and not much else; when the vote came, La Guardia won handily. An old-line New York unionist said: "Meany was good at getting to the heart of the coconut. Ryan didn't have Meany's reasoning power, especially that night. Ryan was a big old roughneck who was too fond of the bottle, and he didn't do well at all. He came away mad, too. He and George had always been friends, and they continued that way, but this was one that Joe Ryan decided to fight about." Ryan's chance came early.

Meany delegated Frank Sullivan, the state federation counsel, to form a labor committee for La Guardia. Sullivan, in turn, hired Bernard Tassler, a city hall reporter for the Long Island *Press* who had just been fired for activism in an American Newspaper Guild strike. In a speech at Cooper Union, one of the first of the campaign, Mahoney asserted he had the best labor record of any candidate, and deserved labor support. Tassler remembered, "Meany got mad as hell. He decided he wanted the AFL legislative department in Washington to get him La Guardia's record while in Congress. He phoned one of Green's people. He didn't think there was going to be anything to it: after all, he was head of an AFL state organization and was entitled to this sort of service as a matter of course. But the record didn't come. Meany pursued the matter. What happened was that Matthew Woll got to Green and said he and Ryan were for Mahoney. 'I don't want anything that would be helpful to La Guardia to be released to George Meany,' Woll told Green. By God, they *never* sent the record, we had to research it ourselves, from New York."

Both Woll and Ryan issued periodic statements implying the mass of labor supported Mahoney, and that Meany's endorsement was meaningless. But in another Cooper Union speech, Mahoney asked the question directly, "Why isn't labor supporting me?" and went on to repeat his claim of a better record than La Guardia's.

"This gave us a great big opening," Barney Tassler recollected. "I got the New York *Times* early that evening and was down at the office at 5:30 A.M. the next day, drafting a reply. It led off to the effect, 'Mr. Mahoney has asked the question, and he is entitled to a frank and full answer. Here it is.' And I went on to list the records of the two candidates. La Guardia looked a lot better. It was a very strong statement, since it put Meany against people like Ryan and Woll, and the labor reporters loved it. It stayed a big front-page story all day. The funny thing is that Meany had left town to attend the AFL convention in Denver and had given Frank Sullivan authority to run things. That same day he returned. Here he is, stepping off a train and finding his name on a statement that was dominating every front page in town. 'Did I say all this?' he asked. 'Good.' "

Urging union members to vote for La Guardia via the *State Federation Bulletin,* Meany promised, "We are delivering to the Mayor, the only candidate in whom we are interested, assurance of the votes of more than 600,000 members of the American Federation of Labor living in this city. This membership is the nucleus of a distinctly AFL vote which may be conservatively estimated at a million and a half, taking . . . relatives and friends . . . into consideration." Meany was confident "we have sufficient voting . . . to return him to City Hall for four more useful, constructive years." La Guardia won by 453,374 votes.

After his first election Meany never again was opposed for the state federation presidency. For all his innovation in politics and legislation, Meany paid careful respect to local unions' cherished autonomy. If asked, he would attempt to mediate disputes between rival unions, "but as far as trying to dictate to them what to do, never." He did not interfere with unions' internal affairs, even in instances of gross (and publicized) corruption.* He acquired a reputation as a unionist who kept his word and expected other men to do the same. After violence at a Long Island strike, the district attorney and police chief persuaded the union chief involved to limit his pickets to ten men. As soon as the officials left, the union leader called in 200 men, who brawled with non-strikers. When the man bragged to Meany how he had "outsmarted" the law, Meany cursed him to his face, and would never speak to him again. David Dubinsky, who did not care for Meany at first exposure, was

---

* For a detailed discussion of union ethical practices, see Chapter XI, "Hoffa's Too Rich for Our Blood."

among the New Yorkers who noticed a change in him during 1934-39. Dubinsky said that when Meany first took office, "he was a typical New Yorker. The state federation was conservative at the time, and the building trades dominated it. The progressive unions were 'strangers.' But Meany, he turned out to be different, and I think he surprised the building trades. Because he worked with unions such as the ILGWU on legislative and political matters, some of our progressivism rubbed off on him. He moved leftward, toward a liberal ideology." (Another New Yorker suggested that Dubinsky took more credit than he deserved for the "transformation" of Meany.) Charles (Zacha) Zimmerman, longtime vice-president of the ILGWU, noted, "As state fed president, George realized he had to represent all the unions, not just the plumbers. This made quite a change in him."

In mid-1939 the old prevailing wage issue revived when Congress drastically revised the Works Progress Administration. Among other restrictions, the new law required WPA employees to work a minimum of 130 hours monthly to qualify for pay, more than double the existing standards. The bill passed Congress on June 30; President Roosevelt said it would cause hardships but signed it anyway; otherwise WPA would have expired on July 1.

Labor, angered, considered the law a breach of faith by government, and fought it furiously for three weeks, with Meany in the forefront. The sequence was much the same as during Meany's encounter with General Hugh Johnson four years earlier: work stoppages by WPA crews, beginning after the July Fourth weekend; angry cross-volleys of statements, with New York City Welfare Commissioner William Hodson saying anyone who refused a WPA job would not receive home relief, and Meany denouncing him for his "zeal to cooperate with the Fascist-minded congressmen who would grind labor into the mire"; and attempts at mediation. WPA gave strikers a five-day deadline to return to work or be fired, and William Green warned of AFL reprisals against congressmen who had voted for the curbs. But Green was obviously chary of Meany's strike, urging instead that Congress reconvene and restore the old law. On July 15 Roosevelt invoked the prestige of his office to end labor's rebellion. "You cannot strike against the government," he told the AFL via a press conference. The President emphasized his words by authorizing the press to quote him directly, a rarity for a presidential news conference at the time. Two days later Green asked the strikers to return to work, and said the AFL would devote its energies to obtaining $300 million for housing construction and $500 million additional for WPA appropriations.

The dispute dominated the front pages of the New York newspapers for more than two weeks, yet Meany says the "struggle" contained a good deal of sham insofar as he and the state federation were concerned. Although New York labor opposed abandonment of the prevailing-wage principle, "by that time, nobody gave a damn. There was only one job of consequence going on in WPA [in New York City] and that was La Guardia Airport. Our people were working; the depression was practically over; nobody give a damn. We weren't interested in that work any more." Nonetheless Roosevelt's acceptance of legislation killing the prevailing wage—even though Congress almost certainly would have overridden any veto—irritated Meany. The government had made an agreement with him in 1935, and now had broken it. The New York *Times* quoted unnamed State Federation of Labor "leaders" after the strike— Meany, actually—who said Roosevelt's position "was endangering Democratic control of New York State politics."

Such was Meany's temper in early August when the New York State Federation of Labor gathered in Manhattan for the most spectacular convention ever staged by a state labor organization. The state fed had not met in New York City since 1896. "Over the years the state convention was sort of a break-up-the-summer for people in New York," Meany says. "They'd all want to go upstate, they'd take their families along, and stick in a vacation; they never wanted a convention in New York. I come up with the idea it was time we reversed it. We had the New York World's Fair in '39, and for one year we ought to let the upstate people come to New York."

The convention opened August 13 with a mammoth parade of union members up Fifth Avenue past a reviewing stand in front of the New York Public Library, 100,000 marchers by police estimate, 120,-000 by Meany's. AFL President Green and his two key vice-presidents, Dan Tobin of the Teamsters and Matthew Woll of the photoengravers, both New Yorkers, marched in the front rank with Meany; close behind them was the jaunty Mayor La Guardia, with the Air Line Pilots Association, one of the many unions in which he held membership. The marching began at 10:00 A.M. and lasted well into the evening, to Meany's delight. "It was a rather odd thing," he said. "They say Americans don't parade. Well, when we come up with this parade idea, the response was tremendous, amazing; *everybody* in the damned unions wanted to parade." Many of the members marched in work clothes—the white-clad painters, for instance, swinging brushes in a semblance of cadence. The New York *Times* counted 178 bands, many of which rode the subway back downtown after passing the reviewing stand so they could march again. Members of an ice cream workers union threw cups of ice cream from a float into the cheering crowd.

At midday Meany excused himself briefly from the reviewing stand and rode to the Battery with La Guardia to meet Roosevelt aboard the cruiser U.S.S. *Tuscaloosa,* on the first leg of a ten-day rest cruise. This was Meany's first private chat with the President, and it was a mixture of cordiality and candid talk about the prevailing wage. Meany complained mildly about imposition of the security wage, and the President promised to do what he could in the next session of Congress.* Roosevelt also told Meany of his fears the United States would soon be drawn into World War II. The meeting lasted less than half an hour, and was considered nothing more than a courtesy call by both parties. What did you talk about? the press asked La Guardia and Meany when they left. "The weather and fish," the Mayor replied.

When the convention formally opened the next day the *Tuscaloosa* was at sea, but Roosevelt was much on labor's mind. Among the dozens of routine resolutions was one submitted by the International Typographical Union urging labor endorsement of Roosevelt for a third term. Meany objected. "There can be no question as to President Roosevelt's record on most of the things that we are interested in, but I, for one, will not give a blank check endorsement of the New Deal policies," Meany said. The "so-called security wage . . . is in reality a starvation wage," he said. "And let the record be clear, let there be no misunderstanding: the security wage . . . is a New Deal policy dictated by the New Deal and put over by the New Deal." Then Meany blocked the third-term resolution with a parliamentary maneuver. He submitted a substitute resolution saying endorsement was a matter of "national politics, which, insofar as labor endorsement goes, lies wholly and solely in the hands of the parent body [the AFL] whose judgment must be supported and recognized by the State Federation of Labor."

Meany now says candidly: "I blocked that resolution because despite the fact that I was very friendly with Roosevelt, I had a fundamental opposition to anybody having a third term. . . . However, by the time 1940 rolled around, and we had our next convention, it was not an academic subject, because FDR had been nominated for a third time, against a guy named Willkie, and our problem was, did we back Roosevelt or Willkie? And of course we couldn't back Willkie, so we went with Roosevelt."

The convention re-elected Meany by acclamation, raised his salary to $10,000 a year (he had begun, in 1935, at $6,000, and had come up to $8,000 in 1938), and adjourned in an atmosphere of self-satisfaction. The parade had received national publicity—newsreels of the day loved such photogenic spectacles—and Meany's refusal to endorse Roosevelt was the sort of man-bites-dog story that delights the press. Meany was set to continue as state fed president the rest of his life. "I was very well

---

* WPA had so withered by 1940, as the nation prepared for war, that the issue became moot.

set and happy," he said as he looked back. "I had been quite successful in my legislative work, I had very close personal connections with Governor Lehman, our people were working. This was it, so far as I was concerned."

The American Federation of Labor, meanwhile, was preparing for a convention that portended to be not nearly so festive as the New York meeting. The AFL was in deepening trouble in 1939. The insurgent Congress of Industrial Organizations, now in its second year, had excited the imagination of workers and the public alike, and its blitzkrieg organizing drives threatened to displace the AFL as the dominant central labor organization in the United States. Few unionists loved the bellicose, egotistical John L. Lewis, the CIO's founding father, but none dared ignore him, or knew how far he could carry the internecine warfare that divided American labor. In July Lewis had hit directly at the building trades by forming a "United Construction Workers Organizing Committee," with no initiation fee, flat dues of $1.50 per month, and open to any workers "regardless of creed, color, nationality or classification of employment . . . in and around construction work." The AFL, stung by a threat to the core of its membership, decried the declaration of "relentless industrial warfare" and raids on "old, long-established unions," but fear was discernible beneath the truculent reply. Where would Lewis strike next? And how effectively? Sidney Hillman, another CIO founder, ranked high among Roosevelt's labor advisers. Everywhere the AFL looked it saw unfriendly faces, even in Congress. Among the bad news prepared for the 1939 convention were reports that unemployment remained above 10 million persons, despite seven years of intensive recovery measures; that Congress had killed "spend-and-lend" legislation for $2.3 billion in continued public works; and that labor could not win passage of another bill for $800 million in housing and slum clearance bonds. The latter failure, by estimate of the AFL's Building and Construction Trades Department, "resulted in the discharge of more than one million men and women." The loss of the prevailing wage, the department said, threatened to cut building trades wages 50 to 75 percent. ". . . [T]he bill had not been signed by the President an hour before contractors in New York, Cleveland and other cities demanded a reduction in the building trades wages," the department told the convention.

To affiliated unions, the prevailing wage defeat was symptomatic of the leadership failure in the AFL. As Meany stated, "There was resentment here and there because the AFL made no attempt to fight this new order, resentment on the part of individuals against Bill Green." In fairness to Green, the critics complained of a mediocrity of their own making. The AFL weaknesses were manifold—structural, philosophical and personal. And here some brief background is in order.

Samuel Gompers, the five-foot four-inch former cigar maker who was the principal architect of the AFL, devoted thirty-eight years to the federation, building it from a paper organization into the nation's trade union center. In the early days Gompers worked from an eight-by-ten-foot office "furnished" with a kitchen table and old vegetable crates for filing cabinets and chairs. Because the AFL was his personal creation, Gompers ran it as such. Unionists who looked beyond Gompers' latter-years' gregarious, beer-hall conviviality ("The general executive board has never had the pleasure of seeing Mr. Gompers sober," charged the AFL's rival, the Knights of Labor) found a man of single-minded stubbornness. Few men dared argue with Gompers when he lived. But when he died, in 1924, a clique of aspiring strong men on the executive council, in a burst of posthumous defiance, rejected Gompers' hand-picked successor, Matthew Woll. Instead, they deliberately sought out a subservient, plodding president, one unlikely to disturb the do-what-we-wish autonomy of the federated unions. The man they found—William Green, a one-time pit coal miner and Baptist Sunday school teacher—proved eminently bland, and therefore satisfactory. Green had worked his way up through the United Mine Workers hierarchy, with a four-year hiatus in the Ohio State Senate, to the AFL executive council. His docility was legendary. Francis Perkins, FDR's first Secretary of Labor, called Green "the mildest and most polite of men," sweet attributes, to be sure, but not necessarily useful to a labor leader. "Explore the mind of Bill Green?" the vitriol-tongued John Lewis once exclaimed. "I have done a lot of exploring of Bill's mind and I give you my word, there's nothing there." Lewis spoke these words in the 1940's, when his CIO was in bitter battle with Green. But presumably Lewis knew something about Green also in 1924, when he helped maneuver his election to the presidency, helped by William (Big Bill) Hutcheson, the hulking dictator of the Carpenters Union, and T. A. Rickert, a Machiavellian schemer who ran the United Garment Workers. A conservative newspaper in Richmond, Virginia, inadvertently paid Green damning tribute: "Labor is safe under his leadership, capital has nothing to fear during his regime, and the public is fortunate in having him as the responsible spokesman of a highly important group of citizens."

Having elected Green, the executive council proceeded to ignore him. Lewis and his cronies preferred to decide AFL business over a poker table in Washington's Hamilton Hotel the evening before the executive council held its quarterly meeting. Green would be handed an agenda, and the decisions, the next morning. A pompous man despite his ineffectuality, Green loved the position of figurehead, and his faculty for "strict neutrality"—his words—on almost any issue permitted the stronger heads of international unions to do as they pleased. Since conflict made enemies, Green avoided it; since he was driven by neither imagination nor an overwhelming ambition, he happily plodded through the years. By the late 1930's he had the well-fed, comfortable appearance of a small-town banker. "His pince-nez gave him dignity; the heavy gold watch chain gleaming across his paunch added to the proper air of solidity," wrote two contemporary observers, Bruce Minton and John Stuart. At times, according to a man who worked at the AFL during the 1930's, the high point of Green's day appeared to be his afternoon nap.

Ironically, Green was in trouble in 1939 because he was doing exactly what his original patrons had intended—nothing. So long as lassitude served John Lewis' purposes, he supported Green. But when opposition by the building trades prevented the AFL from taking full advantage of the organizing opportunities under the National Labor Relations Act, Lewis turned on Green with Welsh fury. Hired for passivity, attacked for passivity, the hapless Green sought only to please, but couldn't. Restless men such as Dan Tobin of the Teamsters were disgusted with the AFL's lack of lobbying skill. Tobin said labor's plight was such that even friendly Congressmen criticized the "weakness of our legislative representatives."

The AFL's second ranking officer, Frank Morrison, was seventy-nine years old in 1939, and had been secretary-treasurer since 1896. Morrison spoke often and fondly of the "good old days" under Sam Gompers; he wore high, stiff collars throughout the 1930's, and did his AFL business in about as modern a style. An AFL staff member who worked under Morrison recollected, "Mr. Morrison used slow, tedious accounting methods which kept the office roaring along at the gait of a snail. He was supercautious. He counted every dollar three times before letting it out of his hand. After about three days of watching him I was going very batty. He was a good old man, but he had definitely been around too long." This man continued: "Mr. Morrison didn't realize that unions were changing. He thought he was still dealing with the semiliterate workers of the 1890's. For instance, he always insisted that his letters be double-spaced. 'Our people don't read too well,' he would say, 'it's a little easier on them my way.' He insisted that the letters begin with a full restatement of the communiqué to which he was responding, and he ticked off his answers in the form of numerical points." People around the AFL had true affection for Morrison, but as his health and effectiveness gradually slipped away it was apparent he must be replaced. Hutcheson and Tobin, by reliable authority, would have swept away Green as well, but declined to do so for fear of starting a bloody internecine brawl within the federation that could drive unhappy losers into the embrace of the detested Lewis and his CIO. However, by the late summer of 1939 the decision was made: Morrison must go.

As a replacement, Hutcheson and Tobin picked another AFL staff member, and quietly began informing other executive council members they would present him at the convention. Green agreed. Then, suddenly, trouble. The intended successor was discovered to have been taking favors from employers and could not explain away what he had done. The man remained in his job for several more years, but his chances for promotion were dead. So when the AFL convention got under way in Cincinnati in October 1939, Tobin and Hutcheson did not have a successor for Morrison.

When Meany boarded a Baltimore & Ohio Railroad sleeper for the overnight ride to Cincinnati he was aware of the stresses in the AFL, but he had no desire to get involved in them. He did carry one minor embarrassment with him. Harry Price, the president of a small local of marble-cutters in the bricklayers union, had persuaded his members to pass a resolution asking the retirement of Green, and his replacement by Meany. "This came completely out of the blue," Meany said. "Price sent out a press release, and one or two of the papers printed a little bit about it." Price's brother was a first vice-president of the bricklayers union, a most important AFL affiliate, and a close Meany friend; apparently some union leaders read between the lines and found a dump-Green move—something Meany flatly declared did not exist.

"Now, I knew that a lot of people in the labor movement had seen it [the resolution] and I was embarrassed, very very much embarrassed. To begin with, the idea of me taking Bill Green's place was completely ridiculous." Meany was what labor called a "one-lunger" at an AFL convention; that is, he had only one vote, even though the New York State Federation of Labor had more than one million members. Voting at AFL conventions is based upon dues-paying membership of affiliated international unions, one vote per one hundred members. The largest bloc in 1939 was Dan Tobin's Teamsters, with 3,500 votes, trailed by Hutcheson's Carpenters, with 3,000, and the machinists, with 1,900. (The plumbers were tenth of the 89 unions present, with 400 votes.) The state and city labor groups were allocated only one vote because their membership was represented at conventions by the international unions.

Meany maintained he had "no political following, no political power, nothing like that, and no interest, really, in the politics of the AFL." He checked into the convention hall the first morning to obtain his credentials and listen to the welcoming speeches but thereafter stayed away, except for several meetings of a committee of which he was a member. "I didn't even stop at the headquarters hotel, the Netherlands Plaza. I stopped at the old Stinton, an old-fashioned hotel down the street. . . . I didn't want to be in any way prominent, to give any ideas that I was after Bill Green's job.

"I remember seeing the head of my own international union, John Coefield, who was also a member of the executive council. He said, 'Well, I see you are a candidate for something.' And I said, 'Oh, John, that is just nonsense.' He said, 'Well, I thought it was, too.' It was. Here was a guy with one vote, with no political backing at all, going to challenge the head of the AFL?" And, Meany added, unless the powers in the AFL *wanted* him as president, his New York record, sterling though it might be, "wouldn't be very much help in the politics of the AFL. The politics of the AFL was the executive council—Dan Tobin, Bill Hutcheson, T. A. Rickert, of the United Garment Workers, John Coefield, a few more, people who could raise a finger during a roll call and say, 'I vote 600,000 members.'"

The convention had opened on Monday. Returning from dinner on Thursday evening, Meany and a group of friends walked past the Netherlands Plaza. Someone called to Meany that Harry Bates, the head of the bricklayers union, "is looking for you, is very anxious to talk with you." Curious, Meany went up into the lobby.

"There was the usual gang standing around, and some fellow said Bates had gone up to bed. This was about nine-thirty or so. As I stepped away and started to go over to the stairway to walk down to the street, Dan Tobin came along. 'George, I want to talk to you.' He took me down to the end of the lobby, and I'll never forget it. We stood by the cigar stand, which was closed, and he said—he was very brusque—'Old Morrison has got to retire. He's fumbling all around; he doesn't know what he is doing. He can't see any more'—all this sort of thing. 'We want you to take his place.' Just like that!

"Now, I knew enough about politics to know that this was the word from the real top gang. Dan Tobin was in the hierarchy, there was no question about it. 'Dan, I don't know, I hadn't even thought about it.'"

Tobin mentioned that the secretary-treasurer's job paid $10,000 a year. "So I said, 'That's good, Dan, I get ten thousand now, and I'm quite happy.'"

Meany was too surprised to make a decision, and asked for time to think about the offer. But he did make one stipulation: "'Before we go any further,'" he told Tobin, "'if you are thinking about putting me as a candidate against Frank Morrison, just forget about it. I will not be a candidate for Morrison's job. I'm no damned fool to run against a fellow who's held the job for forty-four years, and to run just because he happens to be seventy-nine years of age.'" "Well," Tobin said, "He'll get out, we'll give him a pension."

Meany went to his room and telephoned his wife. "She wasn't in the least bit enthusiastic, because it meant moving from New York to Washington. I finally said, 'Well, you know, this *is* a promotion. There's no question about it. The second biggest job in the labor movement. This is my life, you know.' And she said, 'Well, whatever you do is all right with me, you make your decision.' " Meany did more checking, and he got discouraging answers: his New York friends said he was "better off" as state federation president. "But the more I thought about it, the more I felt it was something I just couldn't say no to. It wasn't a question of salary, but of promotion."

On Sunday he went to Crosley Field with Tobin and Bates and watched Charlie Keller, Joe DiMaggio, and Bill Dickey hit home runs as the New York Yankees beat the Reds 7–3 for their third straight World Series victory. The temperature was sweltering for October—the mid-80's by midafternoon, the public address announcer said—and Meany had trouble keeping his mind on baseball, even his beloved Bronx Bombers. But before the game ended he reached his decision. Back at the hotel he took Bates aside and told him he would accept the secretary-treasurer position under two conditions: that Morrison would step aside voluntarily; and that John Coefield, the plumbers union president, would consent. "You see," Meany explained, "this was a case of shifting from a one-lunger to the mainstream; I had to come into this Washington scene as a member of the plumbers, not as a president of the state federation. There had been a very bitter internal fight in the building trades for several years which found my international president on one side, and Harry Bates and Dan Tobin on the other. This would have to be cleared up." Meany apparently feared the promotion could offend Coefield. "I was not close to him, I had never held an office in my international union, I had never been a delegate to a [AFL] convention from my international union. My background was local and with the state organization." To Meany's relief, Coefield, at a breakfast meeting the next day, said he was pleased.

Coefield, however, did pass on some disquieting news. As yet no one had dared tell Morrison what was happening. Meany quoted Coefield: "The reason they haven't talked to him is that he will tell them to go to hell." Coefield, who was close to Morrison, volunteered to break the bad news to the old man. According to what Coefield told Meany later, Morrison was stunned. "Who have they got for this job? Who are they going to put in my place?" he demanded. Meany, he was told. "George Meany would never run against me for this job," Morrison exclaimed.

"You are right," Coefield said gently. "He won't. But if you're not in the picture, Frank, I think he would be all right." Morrison then realized what Coefield was trying to tell him, and after a few minutes' more pained protests he agreed to "retire."

Coefield also informed Morrison the convention would vote him the lifetime title of secretary emeritus and a pension. "There was no provision at all for his retirement," Meany recollected. "We didn't think in terms of pensions in those days; workers didn't have them either." Morrison went along with the arrangement, although there were indications he did not agree a man should necessarily retire just because he was seventy-nine years old. He told the convention the next day: "Some feel that when officers reach that age they should give way to younger men. Of course, my education has been that men should carry on their work as trade unionists, as craftsmen, so long as they are able to perform the work to be done." Morrison noted he had been secretary-treasurer since 1896. "So far as my general health is concerned, it is the same now as it has been for many years," he stated. He did admit to eye trouble but denied that "I was incapacitated" as had been reported in labor circles the preceding winter.

But the decision had been made and on October 12, 1939—Columbus Day—the convention formally ratified it. Coefield, in the nominating speech, introduced Meany as "a young man who I think has made more progress in the last few years in the position that he holds than any other labor representative I know of. . . . He is a man of very fine habits, a clean-living young man who is not addicted to the bad habits that some people are. He lives a perfectly clean and honorable life. . . . George Meany—an honest plumber."

On rolled the seconding speeches—from John Possehl of the engineers union, Joe Ryan of the longshoremen, Joseph A. Mullaney of the asbestos workers. When Tobin's time came he complained mildly that seconding speeches are "something of a nuisance," then proceeded to make the longest of all. And Tobin's address explained both why he and the executive council tapped Meany, and what they expected of him in Washington.

"Most of you," Tobin said, "know how the State Federation of Labor in New York was run for many years. Men who were officers of the federation were devoting their time principally to providing political jobs for themselves. When we got George Meany in there he changed all this, and he has done many things, but he has cleaned up a bad situation and he worked for the labor movement of New York and not for George Meany."

Tobin said Green needed an officer "who will be helpful and assume responsibilities of office. He does not need just a bookkeeper. You can hire bookkeepers as secretaries for thirty dollars a week. The president wants a man who is able to take his place, engage in the work of the federation, one who is able to take the platform in his absence, explain-

ing the work and the position of this federation.* One of the criticisms
that men in responsible positions in Washington have made of this federation . . . in recent years and of the executive council has been the
weakness of our legislative representatives." The legislative service
Meany could provide "in the absence or in the inability of our president," Tobin said, "will be more than sufficient to recompense the federation for his entire salary. He is fearless, he cares nothing about who the
governmental officer is who disagrees with him." Tobin quoted Meany's
tart comments on President Roosevelt at the August convention of the
New York federation.

The convention elected Meany by acclamation, and he responded with
a brief and modest acceptance speech. He said the AFL's record "on
behalf of the working people of this country . . . is without parallel
in the history of the world." He praised Gompers, Green, and Morrison.
He pledged to "do my utmost to carry on . . . to do all in my power to
make this organization even a better federation, to make it a better instrumentality for the welfare and advancement of the workers of our
great nation."

In talks later with friends, when the speculation turned to "How did
you do it?" Meany would reply, "I think that parade we had did it."
There was also speculation about Meany's future. In all the talk and
conjecture, however, no one hit upon what actually was to come: that
George Meany, despite the "promotion," was about to commence the
most frustrating, disappointing years of his life, and that within less than
a year he would be ready to return to the New York unions.

* William Green wanted no such thing, as we shall see.

# IV

## Ascent into Boredom

I N 1940 the American Federation of Labor was headquartered in a nondescript seven-story office building on the northeast corner of Massachusetts Avenue and Ninth Street, N.W., on the fringe of downtown Washington; a sleepy place where an acoustical quirk carried even a whisper for two or three floors up a stairwell, and where the lazy whoosh-whoosh of overhead wooden fans occasionally brought a faint stir of life to American labor.

George Meany came to Washington with high expectations but with little direct authority. The secretary-treasurer, then as now, had no policy-making authority. He was the federation's chief administrative officer, a high-titled clerk/bookkeeper who had to depend upon the good graces of the president—or external forces—if he wished to do more than sign checks, collect dues, and write routine correspondence. The external forces upon which Meany depended were Dan Tobin and Harry Bates, who recruited him for the job. He was soon disappointed.

When Meany came into the AFL, according to Boris Shishkin, who worked there for more than three decades, the immediate effect "was a pretty thorough rejuvenation of the whole place." Shishkin, a voluble, rotund man whose avocation was writing gloomily romantic poetry in his native Russian, joined the AFL staff in 1933 to do liaison with the National Recovery Administration, then moved into research and lobbying. Thirty years younger than Green, Shishkin fretted at the drone's pace of the AFL, and especially at the fixed opinions and procedures of both Green and Frank Morrison. "When Meany was New York state fed president," Shishkin said, "he would come down to Washington and ask our research department for all sorts of information that would help him on his legislative problems. Not many state presidents did that, and Meany impressed me as a man who meant business." So when Meany came to Washington, Shishkin naturally gravitated toward him.

"The sad thing," Shishkin said, "is that he just didn't work out with Green. Meany moved a little too fast for Green, and friction developed quickly. This had the effect of encouraging Meany to push stronger, for he is that sort of person. The conflict was not so much on substance but on the manner in which things were done. Meany wanted to make the AFL more responsive to current conditions; Green liked things the way they were." Staff members like Shishkin were caught in the middle; those who agreed with Meany's activism nonetheless owed Green an institutional loyalty, and there were worried hours of talk about the "fight between the sixth floor [Meany's office] and the seventh floor [Green's office]." At AFL conventions Green frequently reassured himself, in keynote speeches, of the wisdom of conservatism. The philosophy developed by the AFL, he said in 1940, "suits every changing need of our national life, a philosophy we could apply equally well during the period of war and adversity as we can during the days of peace and normal activities. . . . We are not seeking a new philosophy; we are endeavoring to guard faithfully the [old] philosophy." And lauding the AFL again the next year, Green declared, "Its principles seem to deserve the classification of eternal." So, too, did its operating procedures, when Meany came into the federation.

One early clash came when Meany decided to revamp *The American Federationist,* the AFL's monthly magazine, then edited by Florence Thorne, a sweet, sixtyish spinster who was Green's administrative assistant and alter ego. Miss Thorne, according to her contemporaries, viewed the *Federationist* as an ersatz *Atlantic Monthly.* Shishkin, a respecter of intellectualism, described the content as "excellent think pieces, but not the kind of thing that would interest the rank and file. After all, this was a *labor* magazine." Any union member whose local paid the AFL per capita tax automatically received a subscription. According to Shishkin, "the magazine was so blasted thick it scared readers away. One large electrical workers' local in Camden, New Jersey, had a trailer truck drive up to the office monthly and unload bale after bale of the *Federationist.* A couple of days later another truck would haul them away for scrap. Nobody ever stopped to think what was happening, what the membership thought of the magazine." Meany took home a stack of back issues, spread them on the dining room table, and did several evenings' work with a ruler and a pencil. He found that the costs of soliciting and printing advertising far exceeded the revenues produced. Worse yet, many of the ads came from what he called "the biggest labor-hating corporations in the country."

According to Bernard Tassler, who followed Meany to Washington as a researcher and publicist, Meany took his figures to one of the first executive council meetings he attended as secretary-treasurer and proposed a drastic overhaul of the magazine. "Meany called it a 'stale old magazine that gathers dust,' and said 'nobody reads it.'" Meany also attacked Green's policy of accepting corporate ads. Green was vulnerable. Recently the *Federationist* had run an advertisement from the open-shop General Electric Company, even though GE had forced its workers into a company union and was having labor troubles when the issue appeared. When an AFL local complained, Green replied that acceptance of the ad did not imply endorsement of GE's labor policies.* Tassler said, "Green would justify the ads on the grounds that such-and-such a firm was not 'antilabor,' they were 'just not organized.'" Meany said dropping the ads, which lost money, would enable him to cut the per-copy cost from fourteen to five and one-half cents. Green objected, but Meany prevailed, and the executive council endorsed his reforms. Green was angered but remained silent. Miss Thorne groused privately for months, for she considered the *Federationist* editorship a signal honor for a woman. But according to Shishkin, "Meany definitely streamlined the magazine and made it easier to read."

Barney Tassler emphasized that although Meany and Green disagreed on many specific issues, "there was never any acrimony in their relationship. Oh, they'd get cool occasionally, but they never tried to knife one another. It was more a matter of going their own ways, and not agreeing; the one an activist, the other conservative and standpat. Meany didn't take work *away* from Green; he simply did things that never occurred to Green."

Meany's greatest disappointment was that Green would not permit him to act as the AFL's chief lobbyist in Congress. Green zealously guarded his position as the spokesman for the federation, an honor he did not intend to share with anyone. "Now, I had the idea from Tobin when I came here," Meany related, "that I was going to be used, not only for the secretary's job, but also for legislative work. I found out that this was not true, that the only way I could do legislative work would be on assignment from President Green. He carried it all himself. In all the years I was secretary-treasurer I think I appeared before committees on behalf of President Green only half a dozen times.

"Oh, in some cases where he'd be out of town he would ask me to go over and testify, but he kept it [lobbying] as his prerogative, and he had

---

* Green was equally oblivious to problems in other media. He once made a speech on a radio program sponsored by *Collier's* magazine, whose printing company had just locked out members of the ITU, and which was on the AFL blacklist for unfair labor practices at the time of his appearance.

every right to do it, that was his job. But Tobin had expected Green to use me on legislative work, because of my experience in New York."

There is circumstantial—but no direct—evidence that Green feared Meany would use the secretary's job as a springboard to the presidency, and consequently gave him as little important work as possible. The ease with which Tobin and Hutcheson dictated Meany's succession to Frank Morrison reminded Green of the reality of their power. Green could not prevent Meany from making administrative reforms clearly within the jurisdiction of the secretary-treasurer. And he cheerfully dispatched Meany to speak at uncounted union conventions and state and city labor body gatherings, dreary, mind-grinding fetes of self-adulation whose primary purpose is to provide labor leaders a forum from which to reassure themselves of their importance and efficacy. Persons close to Meany in those years insist that the quasi-quarantine imposed by Green was unnecessary; that Meany did not covet the AFL presidency. "For several years," one man said, "George was dazzled by the reality of being secretary-treasurer. This was far higher than he had ever dreamed of going in labor. George had a keen sense of loyalty; going after the boss's job, even when he disagreed with the boss, wasn't his style."

Meany also feared his Catholicism would prevent him from rising higher in the labor movement. Meany decried religious prejudice, but he also felt that having a Catholic as president would handicap the AFL because of deep-rooted public biases. The AFL executive council had a strong Masonic strain, and there was considerable (if quiet) pushing and pulling among Masons and Catholics. Tobin, a Catholic, and Hutcheson, a Mason, even had an informal agreement that new council members would be alternately Mason and Catholic. "This isn't something Mr. Meany would bring up in idle conversation," a long-time associate said, "but you knew it was on his mind."

After one year in Washington, Meany thought seriously about returning to New York and the relative freedom of the state federation presidency. His wife, after agreeing to the change of jobs, refused to leave the Bronx for Washington. During his first months in Washington he lived in the Shoreham Hotel, then took an apartment in the Broadmoor. His eldest daughter, Regina, lived with him while attending Catholic University, and helped with the housekeeping. He did not like the strain of living away from home, and of riding a plane or train to New York each weekend. But Mrs. Meany wouldn't budge. Friends got the idea she felt "George will forget this Washington lark" in a few years and come back to New York labor. She clung to the notion for eight years. Not until 1948 did she consent to move to Washington.

Meany was so unhappy by mid-1940—both with his job and his prolonged family separation—that he talked about resigning. His hand-picked successor in New York, Thomas Lyons, had died after only a few months in office, and the state presidency was his for the asking. Stay on for at least another year, some friends told him, let's see what happens. But in early 1941, Meany's restlessness and his problem of finding meaningful work were suddenly and irrevocably resolved by the chilling awareness that America was on the brink of World War II.

The defense boom, beginning in mid-1940, brought both prosperity and dangerous strains to American labor. Eight years of intensive recovery by the Roosevelt Administration had contained but not overcome unemployment. Now, however, the trend suddenly reversed. Between April 1940 and Pearl Harbor, nonfarm employment shot from thirty-five million to more than forty-one million, and wage rates increased by nearly twenty percent. In the durable goods industries basic to defense work, average weekly earnings went from $29.88 to $38.62 during the period. But the boom contained hidden perils for organized labor.

From the beginning of the national emergency, labor's position was stated clearly and frequently: labor would cooperate wholeheartedly in transforming America into an "arsenal of democracy," as President Roosevelt wanted, but not at the expense of gains painfully won during the New Deal. In a Labor Day speech in Syracuse Meany promised vigorous opposition to "those who would use the present situation to their own selfish advantage. Labor today as in the past is prepared to make whatever sacrifices are necessary in order that we may help our government preserve and protect this nation and its free institutions. But labor is determined that the gains made by labor . . . shall be maintained and preserved. These rights and guarantees are our most priceless possessions. . . . Surely it is not intelligent to throw them overboard just at the time when we are getting ready to defend them." Labor's position was that the gush of new defense workers enjoyed high wages and good working conditions because of past union activities, and hence they should not reap these benefits without union membership. Management, however, saw the defense boom as an opportunity to curb unionization. The surfeit of new jobs and the high salaries possible under cost-plus contracts diminished the immediate, tangible values of union membership. The war gave business the chance to drape a cloak of patriotism around antiunion activity; to insist that "labor peace" was essential to labor production; and to attack mandatory union membership (the so-called closed shop) as undemocratic and un-American.

As a result, 1941 was one of the more turbulent years in labor history, with strikes in virtually every industry. At one time or another during the year, 8.4 percent of the nation's industrial workers were on strike—4,288 disputes involving more than two million persons; twice the disputes and four times the participants of 1940. Anticipating the troubles, Roosevelt in March 1941 had created the tripartite National Defense Mediation Board, with four representatives each from labor, management, and the public. The board could use either mediation or voluntary arbitration to try to solve disputes in defense industries. But at the insistence of both business and labor, Roosevelt did not give the board authority to enforce its decisions. The unions would not submit to control by a governmental body, even one on which they were represented. Management did not trust any panel created by the Roosevelt Administration to give it fair treatment. Voluntary cooperation proved too tenuous an incentive, and the board came to naught. Indeed, labor accepted the board only as an alternative to various proposals for antistrike laws then proliferating in Congress. In a June 1941 speech to a building industry congress in New York, Meany attacked one bill that would require a 25-day "cooling-off" period before a strike. If Congress could require men to work for one minute, Meany said, "then Congress obviously has the power to compel them, by the same method, to work indefinitely without their consent. And that is slavery!"

As chairman of the National Defense Mediation Board, Roosevelt selected William H. Davis, a New York patent attorney. Roosevelt permitted the AFL and CIO to share the labor seats by naming two members each. Green chose himself and Meany; Philip Murray, president of the CIO, brought along Thomas Kennedy, of the United Mine Workers. The public and management groups included such figures as Eugene Meyer, publisher of the Washington *Post;* Gerard Swope, of General Electric; and Charles Wyzanski, then a prominent Boston attorney, later a U.S. district court judge and Ford Foundation trustee.

The board spent three months haggling over organization and procedures (as late as June members hadn't even agreed on whether to hire a public relations man) and managed to resolve only a handful of minor cases. Its ineptness was made all the more conspicuous by the magnitude of its failures. At the North American Aviation Company in Ingleside, California, a key aircraft producer, a jurisdictional dispute between AFL and CIO unions erupted into a walkout that was not ended until the War Department seized the plant. Likewise, the Navy Department took control of the Federal Shipbuilding and Dry Dock Company in Kearny, New Jersey, when the board could not settle a union shop dispute.

Further, according to Meany, the CIO unions used the board "as an instrument in their organizing campaign." The scheme worked this way. When CIO and AFL unions competed to organize workers in the same plant, the CIO would issue a "strike threat," often in a form no more substantial than a press release. The mediation board, to avoid a "strike," would immediately certify the case as within its jurisdiction, and begin talks. Likely as not, Meany said, the CIO would be numerically weaker in the plant than the AFL; nonetheless, the certification order was de facto recognition of the CIO as the bargaining agent. The AFL union, unwilling to make premature strike threats, would find itself "technically out of the picture," in Meany's words. Meany bitterly denounced the CIO stratagem in September 1941, saying the AFL could not remain on the board if the practice continued. Murray and James B. Carey, the CIO secretary-treasurer, entered general denials but did not make any concrete promises.

The board's most nagging headache, however—one that eventually proved fatal to it—was John L. Lewis, of the United Mine Workers of America. And here a tight capsule of events is necessary for perspective.

Lewis felt that formation of the CIO had made him America's foremost labor leader, and that his political support of the President entitled him to veritable "partner" status with the Roosevelt Administration. Lewis frequently said, to Roosevelt's irritation, that labor had "re-elected the President," and could put its kingmaker's power behind another candidate if FDR didn't do its bidding. Roosevelt in fact was obligated to Lewis, for as James A. Wechsler, an early Lewis biographer, wrote, "If Roosevelt had been forced to rely on the flabby minds and stodgy spirits of the AFL craft unionists, he would have had puny resources with which to wage the New Deal struggle." But FDR's obligation did not equate to abdication of presidential responsibility to Lewis —to Lewis' apparent chagrin. During a White House meeting in 1939, when the two men were still on speaking terms, Lewis suggested to FDR that as the "two most prominent men in the nation" they would make an invincible ticket in 1940. Roosevelt, no stranger to egotisms, replied sweetly, "Which place will you take, John?" Lewis' friendship deteriorated rapidly into hate when Roosevelt did not give him the attention he felt he deserved. During the struggle between the Steel Workers Organizing Committee, which he headed as CIO president, and the Little Steel companies for organization of the steel industry, Roosevelt denounced violence on both sides by declaring a "plague o' both your houses." The enraged Lewis rejoined, "It ill behooves one who has supped at labor's table and been sheltered in labor's house to curse with equal fervor and fine impartiality both labor and its adversaries when they become locked in deadly embrace."

Lewis opposed a third term ("Mr. Roosevelt made depression and unemployment a chronic fact in American life") and he gave the CIO a him-or-me choice in a dramatic 1940 election eve speech in which he endorsed Republican Wendell Willkie: If Roosevelt were re-elected, something he felt only labor support could bring about, Lewis would interpret the outcome as a personal "vote of no confidence" and quit as president of the CIO. When FDR won, Lewis kept his word and resigned soon after the election, to be replaced as CIO president by another miner, Philip Murray. Lewis withdrew into a brooding isolation, filling his days with black, storming rages against Roosevelt and his erstwhile CIO allies. He even wreaked brutal revenge upon Murray, convening a kangaroo court of miner allies and expelling him from the UMWA on grounds of disloyalty for accepting the CIO presidency. Labor people wondered among themselves whether the erratic Lewis this time had wandered beyond the limits of sanity. The AFL enjoyed the torment of its old foe. Philip Pearl, the AFL director of public relations, gibed at Lewis in columns distributed by the AFL Weekly News Service: "Behind sound-proofed walls and bulletproof windows sits the loneliest man in America, deserted by his former friends and supporters, ridiculed by every newspaper in the country, the leader of a vanishing army. . . . John L. Lewis is through. He may hide himself away in his office and cut himself off from contact with the outside world but he cannot dodge his fate." And Meany said the CIO had tired of "the bitter taste of domineering dictatorship," and was glad to be rid of Lewis.

In the autumn of 1941, however, Lewis found an issue that gave him the opportunity to settle, with one dramatic confrontation, a host of outstanding grievances: against FDR, against the rest of labor, against American business. The issue was whether the UMWA was to have a closed-shop agreement in the so-called captive coal mines; that is, the mines owned and operated by the steel companies for their own supplies. A dramatic strike victory would bolster Lewis' dwindling prestige by demonstrating to rank-and-file workers that at least one union leader remained willing to wield the bludgeon in fights with management and was not dazzled by Roosevelt's "arsenal of democracy" speeches. Lewis was in a good strategic position to be tough, too. Closing the mines would eventually close the steel mills and hamper attempts by the detested Roosevelt to aid the detested British. If John L. Lewis could not force the United States into isolationism by the ballot box, by God, he could do it by shutting off the furnaces of America's defense industries.

In October 1941 the closed-shop issue went before the National Defense Mediation Board, which was reluctant to act. In rapid sequence, Lewis called a strike; Roosevelt declared that world security was being endangered by "the selfish obstructionism of a small but dangerous minority of labor leaders"; antistrike legislation advanced rapidly through Congress; the United States Steel Corporation, in desperation, reopened the talks, putting the case back before the NDMB; and Lewis put his miners back to work. To his chagrin, however, the board refused to order the closed shop. The vote was nine to two, with AFL members Green and Meany voting with management and public members, and with only the CIO members siding with Lewis. Meany strongly favored the closed shop, of course, and he abhorred voting against a fellow unionist, even Lewis. But what Lewis was demanding ran counter to a principle Meany considered basic to trade unionism: the closed shop was something to be won by collective bargaining, not by edict of a governmental agency.

The decision, in effect, killed the National Defense Mediation Board. The CIO members angrily withdrew, and the board never met again. Lewis' miners struck once more, and Roosevelt put the closed-shop issue before a special arbitration panel composed of Lewis, Myron Taylor, president of United States Steel, the largest captive-mine owner, and Dr. John Steelman, of the U. S. Conciliation Service, a closed-shop advocate. The ruling, made public December 7, 1941, gave Lewis the closed-shop status he wanted.

It also established a dangerous precedent, and one certainly not overlooked by Lewis: that he could defy, with impunity, the President, public opinion, the mainstream of organized labor, and labor-management arbitration machinery based upon the principle of voluntarism.

On the Wednesday before Pearl Harbor, in an overwhelming vote reflecting an antilabor tide of public opinion, the House of Representatives approved 252 to 136 the first piece of avowedly antiunion legislation since the Wagner Act. The bill, aimed directly at John Lewis and indirectly at all American labor, would have banned all strikes at defense plants involving the closed shop or stemming from jurisdictional disputes, and *any* strike not approved in a government-supervised election after a thirty-day cooling-off period—in sum, an abnegation of collective bargaining. From the narrow viewpoint of self-preservation, therefore, the Japanese attack on December 7 was a reprieve for labor. In the exuberant post-Pearl Harbor gush of national unity, labor foes in Congress suspended their drive for restrictive legislation to permit Roosevelt time to tool up machinery to control the wartime economy. On December 15 Roosevelt called a conference of labor and management with the desired aim of reaching a "unanimous agreement to prevent the interruption of production by labor disputes during the period of the war." Roosevelt wrote, "I do not expect that there will be any hesitation on the part of either labor or industry gladly to accept this basic condition of the nation's safety. Production simply cannot be halted." Roosevelt left it to the conference "to decide what form the machinery will take," but made clear he wanted a means by which "disputes may amicably and finally be settled," with "appropriate guarantees for both labor and management." He suggested a tribunal for defense industries "whose decisions will be binding on all parties."

The conference convened on December 17 in a Treasury Department

Building meeting room for five days of intensive debate. FDR carefully apportioned labor invitations to all factions of the divided movement— Green, Meany, and Matthew Woll for the AFL; Murray and Julius Emspak for the CIO; and the redoubtable Lewis for the UMWA. Although he was by many years the junior labor representative, Meany's knack for bargaining soon established him as the chief union spokesman. Meany could not match Lewis' acerbic sarcasm (when management demanded the open shop, Lewis retorted, "I have heard this open shop talk before. The open shop is a harlot with a wig and artificial limbs, and her bones rattle. But how much production will she give us?"). But Meany found the chairman, Senator Elmer Thomas (Dem., Utah), eager to make the conference a success, and therefore receptive to suggestions for compromise.

"We agreed immediately there should be no strikes and no lockouts," Meany said. "We agreed also that labor disputes should be settled by a board set up by the President." But there bargaining snagged for three days, with management insistent on keeping the closed/open shop issue away from any new board, and maintaining the status quo for the duration of the war. The management position would have halted union organizing drives, hence labor would not accept it. Nor would management back away, even after an all-night caucus that didn't end until 5 A.M. the fourth day.

Green was ready to break off the conference at this point and ask the President to order the labor plan into effect. But Roosevelt declined to talk to the labor members, saying it would be "unwise and inadvisable" for him to meet privately with either side. Then Meany had an idea that broke the impasse: he proposed that Senator Thomas write the President that all parties had agreed to three points—no strikes or lockouts; creation of a war labor board; and referral of all grievances to the board for resolution—and that management had proposed a fourth point, that the open shop question not be subject to board action. Thomas did as Meany suggested, and Roosevelt (properly alerted) seized upon the opening. With lavish praise for the conferees' diligence and patriotism, he accepted the no lockout-no strike pledge, and created the proposed War Labor Board. But Roosevelt said absolutely nothing about the closed shop, a silence that labor correctly accepted as a victory. By not *excluding* the open shop issue from the board's jurisdiction, Roosevelt tacitly made it a subject for resolution. Next, he indirectly committed the government to support of union security and a form of the closed shop by naming three avowedly prolabor figures as public members—Wayne Morse, former law professor at the University of Oregon and a mediator in the maritime and labor industries, and later United States senator from Oregon; Frank P. Graham, the liberal educator who became president of the University of North Carolina and United States senator; Davis, who had been chairman of the defunct National Defense Mediation Board; and Dr. George Taylor, professor of labor relations at the Wharton School of the University of Pennsylvania.

Conspicuously absent from the board was John L. Lewis, an omission he felt was a deliberate slight by the White House, and also notice that Roosevelt no longer considered him a major labor figure. Also galling were reports which drifted to Lewis of talks between Phil Murray, James Carey, the CIO secretary-treasurer, and various AFL people "looking to collaboration for the war effort." Lewis was suddenly frightened that the AFL and CIO might merge behind his back, leaving him totally out of the labor mainstream. He withdrew to brood, and to plot a way to restore some of his fast-fading prestige. Exactly what Lewis did, and with whose cooperation, is a truth that cannot be established with certainty even after three decades. But Meany, who claimed to have been an innocent bystander, was almost toppled in the process.

One fact is certain—and also most peculiar: Lewis chose as his chief collaborator William Hutcheson of the Carpenters Union. The alliance was one of convenience only, for the men hated one another. At the 1935 AFL convention, as Lewis argued for industrial unionism in a floor speech, Hutcheson repeatedly interrupted him with cries of "point of order, point of order." Lewis paused and muttered he thought the objections were "pretty small potatoes." The gigantic Hutcheson arose, saying he had been raised on "small potatoes," and called Lewis a bastard. Lewis' fist shot out in a straight-armed jab, with all his heavy-shouldered power behind it, and connected with Hutcheson's jaw. Hutcheson fell backwards across a table, which collapsed beneath his weight. Lewis straightened his tie and hair, relit his cigar, and proceeded to the podium while Hutcheson went to wash away his blood.*

Now, in January 1942, Lewis needed Hutcheson's support for an audacious undertaking. He proposed to bring the AFL and CIO back together. William Green would be retired at his full salary of $20,000 a year for life. Phil Murray would be made secretary-treasurer at $18,000 a year. George Meany would become president of the merged organization at $20,000. Lewis would take no office, and he promised Hutcheson he would dismantle the United Construction Workers Organizing Committee, which had been fighting the AFL building trades unions and the Teamsters in many cities. Lewis apparently felt that Meany would be so grateful for the promotion he would obey any orders

---

* "You shouldn't have done that, John," Bill Green told Lewis on the platform. "But he called me a dirty name," replied Lewis. "Oh, I didn't know that," said the ever-diplomatic Green.

given him, and that Lewis' old CIO enemies would be swallowed up in the large, merged organization. By most accounts, Hutcheson began recruiting support for the plan among members of the AFL executive council, which was to meet in Washington on Saturday, January 17.

Just before the council meeting ended, according to Meany, Hutcheson casually read a letter from Lewis, addressed to Green, proposing a resumption of the unity talks, and predicting they would succeed "under conditions existing at present." Lewis chose his words carefully, and put much of his meaning between the lines. "It is obvious that *if accouplement could be achieved, with unified and competent leadership,*" he wrote, "the results would be advantageous and in the public interest." (Emphasis added.) "Accouplement" is the "act of coupling or state of being coupled"; Lewis used this word rather than "merger" because the AFL considered the CIO a splinter group unfit to return as an equal. Lewis did not mention his proposed shuffling of officers in the letter, but the phrase "competent leadership" was an obvious dig at Green and Murray. Lewis also gave copies of the letter to the press, and accounts of his proposed "accouplement"—sans his slate of officers—appeared in newspapers of Sunday, January 18. The stories quoted an AFL spokesman as saying no action was taken on Lewis' idea, but that Green said, "Our peace committee stands ready to meet with a committee from the CIO at any time." On Monday, January 19, in a story without a trace of attribution (other than "it became known last night"), A. H. Raskin, the New York *Times'* labor reporter, made the following points:

—Lewis and "leaders of the AFL are so confident of unity . . . that already they have reached an understanding on officers to head a unified labor movement." Raskin detailed the Green-Murray-Meany shuffle.

—The AFL executive council "informally agreed to a proposed slate" at the Saturday meeting after "unofficial conversations had been carried on for nearly a week" by Lewis and Dan Tobin.

—The principal obstacle to the proposal "is that Mr. Murray has not been consulted on any part of the scheme."

Raskin (and apparently his unnamed sources) were optimistic about an early merger. Raskin wrote:

> The pressure of public opinion, the urgency of the war situation, and the desire of the rank and file of both organizations for a cessation of hostilities, were regarded as factors likely to triumph over the personal and jurisdictional obstacles that have kept the warring factions apart for six years.

When the proposed slate of officers was brought up at Saturday's meeting . . . Mr. Green was reported to have demurred at the thought of stepping aside, but he finally agreed "in the national interest" . . .

Mr. Meany's acceptability to Mr. Lewis is based largely on his stand in support of the union shop in the controversy between the United Mine Workers and the operators of the captive coal mines and in the recent labor-industry conference sponsored by President Roosevelt. Unlike Mr. Lewis, Mr. Meany has been a consistent supporter of the President.

The episode was still embarrassing to Meany when he discussed it three decades later. He denied any involvement in the Lewis scheme; the Raskin version, while interesting reading, "just isn't what happened," he said. Meany insisted he knew nothing of the plan until Hutcheson read Lewis' letter to the executive council. In fact, he maintained, "I had never spoken to Lewis," other than perfunctory greetings at the meetings that resulted in formation of the War Labor Board. "But that was a great big group thing and I had no personal connection with him." The attitude of the executive council, Meany related, was, "Well, let's see what develops. We took no action on it, there was nothing definite."

Whatever the facts of the Lewis plan, the incident sent a tremor through the CIO and the sensitive White House. Murray, who had gone South for a brief vacation, first learned of the proposal from a Sunday newspaper he bought on the train in North Carolina. By the time he arrived in New York and read Raskin's further account, he was furious. "No one has the right to trade me for a job," Murray said. "Jobs are not sufficiently alluring where principles are concerned. . . . My manhood requires a little reciprocity—and, by God, despite this feeble frame of mine, I will fight any living man to maintain my manhood." Any "agreements" reached by Lewis would not be binding on the CIO, Murray warned, and he advised Lewis to work within established channels if he wanted labor unity. Green and Tobin also issued denials that "an understanding of any sort" had been reached by the executive council and CIO officers. "No peace proposal or slate of officers was agreed on, formally or informally, by the executive council," Green said. "The subject was not even presented or discussed. . . ."

Roosevelt was also alarmed, for he feared the Lewis machinations could drive the AFL and CIO further apart, and disrupt the labor harmony he had been cultivating in the interest of national defense. Administration agents spent many hours trying to find out who and what were involved in the plot. Mrs. Anna Rosenberg, a New Yorker who advised Roosevelt on labor, told him in a memo: "David Dubinsky, Hutcheson and Matt Woll negotiated this Lewis business. Then Lewis, without telling them, jumped the gun and gave out the newspaper stories. Murray, of course, had no idea of it. He is furious. But it is Dubinsky who is really behind the thing." Gardner Jackson, the Undersecretary of Agriculture, an economist with good labor sources, told Roosevelt a slightly different version in a personal-and-confidential letter:

> The AFL executive council discussion on the proposal did take place but John [Lewis] jumped the gun with his publication of the letter. Those definitely in the play were Matt Woll, Dan Tobin, and George Meany, along with John and Bill Hutchinson [sic].
>
> Phil Murray, Jim Carey and some of their people had been carrying on informal talks in good faith with some of the AFL people looking to collaboration for the war effort. John got wind of these as well as the results of the Gallup Poll * and decided to make the play to cut Phil's throat.

Jackson's letter was misleading, for it lumped together separate events: the public talks about AFL and CIO cooperation in the war; and the secret plotting by Lewis and Hutcheson. Tobin, Meany, and Woll— by Meany's account—were involved in the first, not the second. Tobin, indeed, was Roosevelt's strongest friend in the AFL, and not a man to cooperate in what the White House called a "scheme by isolationist enemies"—meaning Lewis and Hutcheson—to "undermine the President's standing with organized labor." Roosevelt called Murray to the White House to pledge support in any showdown with Lewis. Roosevelt said merger was no longer essential because the AFL and the CIO intended to work together on the War Labor Board. He added that peace negotiations might cause so much intrigue, with various union officers maneuvering for high positions, that production could be hurt. According to another Raskin story, this one on January 20, Roosevelt told Murray "an investigation by his aides had convinced him of the accuracy of the main points" of the *Times'* account of the intrigue. Roosevelt supposedly did not "suspect Mr. Meany of any ill will," toward him or the Administration, but he "did question the motives of those who drafted the proposed slate." Raskin also wrote that "circles close to proponents of the Meany slate" regretted FDR's opposition. Raskin said these "circles" were genuinely interested in peace, personalities were not a factor, and they had no intention of permitting Lewis back into the AFL as a dominant figure, or to harm Roosevelt. The next day the White House said Roosevelt "repudiated" Raskin's statement that he was convinced of the accuracy of the original *Times* story. To underline his statement that he

---

* The Gallup organization (the American Institute of Public Opinion) published a poll January 18 of AFL and CIO leaders and members in 82 industrial centers. It found that 87 percent of the leaders and 71 percent of the rank and file would "like to see the AFL and CIO join in one organization."

considered merger a dead issue, Roosevelt named a "labor cabinet" of three persons each from the AFL and CIO, and said it would "provide sufficient unity" for the war. (Named were Green, Meany, and Tobin; and Murray, R. J. Thomas, of the United Auto Workers, and Julius Emspak, of an electrical workers union.) Roosevelt told Green he wanted the committee "sufficiently small to make this a real 'round table' talk." The labor cabinet met irregularly until Roosevelt's death, at least once and sometimes twice weekly during its first year, then at longer intervals. Emspak was not impressed with it. He called creation of the committee "a political move, because, obviously . . . he [Roosevelt] needed as much unity in the country as possible. If members of the labor unions were at each other's throats . . . it was obviously not a good situation." Emspak called the committee a "sounding board for Roosevelt," with no specific functions.*

The Lewis controversy had several sour aftermaths. It deepened the chasm between the AFL and the CIO, with leaders of both factions wary of talking about unity for fear they would be accused of plotting against other officers of their organizations. It made Lewis even more the outcast of American labor, and contributed to the rogue's role he was to play throughout the rest of the war, to the outrage of almost everyone in the country save his faithful miners. And Meany's involvement, however unwitting and unwilling, rekindled Green's old suspicions. A congenital activist, Meany now could reach for new assignments and authority only at the risk of appearing to be shoving past Green. A man close to Meany during those years said, "George cut back. He didn't want to, but he did. He couldn't risk getting into a wrestling match with Bill Green. Sure, he [Meany] was the stronger of the two, and he had his supporters. But if it ever came to a showdown, the executive council wasn't about to fire the AFL president publicly. And that's the way Green would have made them do it, too, with a guaranteed splash." This man continued, "But the more you think about the idea—replacing Green with George—the better it sounds. In retrospect, it should have been done, whether George and Green liked it or not."

* The labor cabinet did afford Roosevelt the opportunity to clear labor appointees with both factions. At an early meeting the AFL vetoed the appointment of a young United Auto Workers officer named Walter Reuther to head the Labor Production Section of the Office of Production Management. Green told the President that Reuther was "unacceptable to the AFL," and Roosevelt appointed someone else.

# V

# The War Labor Board

*Was ever an infant less tender and mild*
*Than this, F. D. Roosevelt's most terrible child?*
*Not a moment of peace has it had in its life,*
*It was nurtured in discord and weaned upon strife;*
*Indeed, like Minerva's, its birth was aberrant,*
*For it sprang, armor-clad, from the brain of its parent.*
                    —Anonymous staff member's view of the
                       National War Labor Board, *circa* 1944

THE WAR LABOR BOARD was part of a panoply of agencies created by President Roosevelt and Congress to regulate the wartime economy. Its jurisdiction and authority ebbed and flowed during its four-year life. Initially a "voluntary" board, with labor and management members bound only by their words to try to enforce decisions, it eventually came under strong White House control, bound in fact if not in law to carry out policies set by Roosevelt and his economic advisers. Because of its tripartite nature, the board spent an inordinate amount of time bickering. But as was noted by Dr. George Taylor, a public member, the crises "came to a head in the board room, instead of at the workplace where they would have interfered with maximum production and the prosecution of the war."

Although there were a considerable number of strikes during World War II—from Pearl Harbor to V-J Day, 14,731 work stoppages lasting a day or longer involving 6½ million workers—labor economist Florence Peterson noted "most of them were of short duration and a large portion of the time lost [almost 40 percent] was concentrated in the coal mining industry." According to an AFL analysis Meany quoted with pride, "the man-days lost due to strikes came to only 11/100ths of one percent of the time worked. We were not 100 percent perfect. Only 99 and 89/100ths percent perfect. Who in America that had any part in the war effort can honestly say that he did better than labor with a record, so far as the no-strike pledge is concerned, of 99 and 89/100ths percent?" According to Bureau of Labor Statistics figures, only .05 percent of the available working time was lost to strikes in 1942; .15 in 1943; .09 in 1944, and .47 in 1945.

The picture of Meany contained in the voluminous records of debate within the War Labor Board is that of a business agent in action: dogmatic on what he considered to be matters of principle; quick to complain, and loudly, at any hint of a breach of promise, be it by the Roosevelt Administration or other board members; ready to quit when he felt the board was about to go beyond its authority, to the disadvantage of labor; impatient with theoretical argument; briskly direct in dealing with specific cases; and frequently given to sudden, savage sarcasm. (During discussion of a Teamsters dispute Meany interrupted employer member Robert Black. "Bob," he said, "you are talking through your hat." "Mr. Chairman," Black protested, "even if I am talking through my hat, I think I have a right to talk." "All right," said Meany, "continue to talk through your hat.")

Chairman William Davis, a New York lawyer before the war, admired Meany's negotiating style. When arguments became wordy, "I could say to him, 'Now George, you've made your speech, is it all right if I go ahead with consideration of the subject before us?' Then he'd say 'yes' and then he would talk sense. There was a lot of tactics in George's behavior, proper timing and all that. George was pretty good at that, so if he came out with anything that looked like a conciliatory move, it meant a great deal. A lot of what he was saying was for the sake of its effect on his AFL constituents." Wayne Morse detected a distinct shift in Meany's bargaining style after the first few months. "Meany had no industrial background, nor any particular philosophy. He was a self-educated man who dealt in practicalities, not in philosophies or concepts. A business agent in the construction trades must be a hard, tough bargainer to be successful. Well, Meany realized early he was sitting down with men who would not be scared, and within six months he learned the interests of labor would be much better served by the WLB than by the hard-nosed procedures he had followed in New York. Meany accepted my thesis that you can't have substantive rights save in terms of procedural rights. I've argued this in many forums, from law schools through collective bargaining sessions. ['Let me determine the procedures, and I'll determine your substantive rights.' I kept hammering away—'This board must establish procedures,' I would say.] Meany realized what I was talking about, and at times he out-Morsed Morse on the subject."

Once it obtained jurisdiction over a dispute the board would hold public hearings and receive briefs from both parties, then retire into executive session to make its decisions. Morse, Taylor, and Frank Graham, because of their legal and academic backgrounds, wrote most of the opinions. The labor and employer members protected their constituencies, and did what they could to enforce decisions. "George was tough," Wayne Morse related. "He would never criticize a union publicly, or even in the executive sessions. But he would take some local labor leader and just shake the pants off him because he didn't follow the decisions. Meany could pick up the phone and order the guy to Washington, and lay down the law to him. If a local was recalcitrant about following an order, a word to George would suffice. He would seldom tell us exactly what he had done, but the results spoke for themselves."

Dr. George Taylor, the vice chairman, who had distinguished dual careers for forty years as academician (at the University of Pennsylvania) and labor mediator, called the board "a great invention because it didn't throw collective bargaining out the window," even during the pressures of war. The board spent its life in precarious balance, and could have been tilted out of existence at any time had either labor or management refused to abide by a decision. The public members, according to Taylor, had the responsibility of not "throwing our votes to the extreme position of either side; that would have broken it up in no time. Our job was to come up with a proposal, one side would vote with you for, and the other wouldn't withdraw. Those are the parameters in which we worked." Dr. Taylor concedes labor's acceptance of the board, and its continuation on it even when outvoted, was a lesser-of-the-evils choice. "Our threat always was, 'You had better go along with us, or else Congress will move in on you.' If Congress moved in, especially in the early days of the war, ye gads!"

Meany's first task on the board—one he accomplished at its maiden meeting—was to make plain that although the unions had signed a no-strike pledge for the duration of the war, labor was not going to be shoved around. Both the AFL and the CIO suspected management would attempt to play them against one another for bargaining advantage, and business was already chortling to itself about the opportunities afforded by the WLB. The National Association of Manufacturers, in a bulletin distributed soon after the board was established, exulted, "An offer not to strike or to postpone a strike, often an important factor in gaining concessions from an employer, should no longer carry weight as a bargaining device." At the board's first meeting employer member E. J. McMillan casually suggested that the board end a Teamsters strike at a Washington state apple orchard "in the spirit of the emergency." Meany cut McMillan short with one terse question: "Isn't it well," he asked, "to find out what the case is all about before we take any action?" He said labor members had no intention of making the WLB "a strike-breaking agency," and would act in cases only after both sides had a chance to be heard.

In its first substantive decision, on the closed-shop issue, labor managed to obtain what it wanted, albeit in somewhat disguised fashion. Public opinion polls showed that only ten percent of the people sided with labor on the closed shop, hence Dr. Taylor and Morse wanted to dispose of the matter as discreetly as possible. Their solution was a "maintenance of membership" plan, which required new workers to join the union within fifteen days or lose their jobs. Labor made what Taylor called "pro forma protests," but willingly accepted the plan. Management members, however, became most unhappy. They had pushed for an "elective plan," under which workers could quit unions, even though the union shop had been established in previous contracts. If all members withdrew from the unions, Meany asked, "Who, in God's name, would be responsible for the execution of the contract?"

The maintenance-of-membership decision made the employers acutely aware the WLB was at most a mixed blessing. It also threw the board into its first name-calling debate. The National Association of Manufacturers, angry that the WLB was not to be as useful to business as anticipated, lashed out at it in full-page advertisements in Washington newspapers, calling it destructive of private enterprise and criticizing the maintenance-of-membership decision. The NAM also charged the closed shop was hurting war production.

The advertisement so angered Morse that he suggested the WLB consider dissolving itself. He called the employer representatives "mouthpieces" for the NAM and the Chamber of Commerce of the United States. Meany joined in his attack, calling the closed-shop issue "hollow," and demanding of the employer group: "Just where has it become troublesome? Has there been any stoppage of work over this question? Where is the impasse?" Only in the "minds of the people" in business, Meany answered his own question. What management really wanted, Meany said, was "stopping all union activity for the period of the war." He turned on Roger Lapham, a San Francisco shipping executive who was the leader of the employer group on the board. If the union shop issue had caused any trouble within the board, Meany said, "it lays on the industry side of the table. Let me make one more statement or request to my friend Roger: Will you get the NAM to make some more statements and print some more advertisements as a personal favor to me?"

The WLB record states at this point: "Mr. Roger Lapham's response was not recorded at his request."

Meany was also blunt in his first confrontation with the CIO members, in a case involving the Spicer Manufacturing Company, an Ohio auto parts firm. Spicer wanted to use assembly line workers, rather than AFL building craftsmen, to construct a plant addition. When the AFL men protested, they "were escorted off the job," according to Meany, in violation of the no-lockout pledge. A labor board panel recommended a full hearing to determine who should do the work, but Spicer management meanwhile gave it to the CIO workers. William S. Knudsen, director of the Office of Production Management (OPM), asked the full board to issue a back-to-work order—that is, override its earlier decision—so the AFL men could continue assignments elsewhere in the plant.

Meany sounded incredulous when Morse presented Knudsen's proposal. "We are going to back up Knudsen?" he asked. "If you think it will do this board some good to get a slap in the face, go ahead and do that. If you do, as far as I am concerned, I won't sit here at ten o'clock in the morning. Our panel makes a decision that keeps the work in abeyance and then this employer comes in and violates that decision and puts the CIO on this work, and then you are going to tell my men what to do out there." Meany suggested it would be "very simple for the CIO automobile workers to stay in the automobile field and stay out of construction work."

Morse argued that keeping the work going was paramount. "I am very practical about that," Meany said, "and I think I know something about how building trades mechanics think. There is one thing I can't visualize: I couldn't visualize myself working on a job with a nonunion man doing part of my work, nor could I visualize myself working with a CIO man doing a portion of my work." If the CIO claim had any merit, Meany said, he might accept Knudsen's idea. "But it is just as I said to Mr. McMillan a minute ago, that if I claimed his watch, that would perhaps be a controversy. But I can't see him submitting it to arbitration or to anybody else to settle it." ("I think the analogy is wrong," interjected George Taylor. "While you're squabbling as to who gets the watch, there's a Jap and a Nazi ready to swat you on the head.")

Davis lectured Meany. "Here your AFL organization has made the most solemn pledge to the country that there won't be any strikes and that if one of the organizations struck, that the other organizations would cross their picket lines. Now, that has gone out under the signature of William Green, and I think it is a very disastrous thing to depart from, and [it is] going to take a lot of explaining." When R. J. Thomas of the UAW offered to compromise and split the work, Meany said, "We don't think your people should have the right even to go into the building. That is our attitude." After almost an hour's more debate Meany finally agreed to let the CIO men remain, as Knudsen wished, pending a full hearing.

He had made his point—and the AFL also eventually won the case.

Overriding his complaints in individual cases, however, was Meany's irritation with the board's procedural snags and the resultant delays. George Taylor, also discouraged, lamented in April that "we have been pretty wasteful of time." Meany said the board should handle cases as rapidly as possible "and not spend all our time trying to work out a perfect system." He said, "We weren't set up here as an over-all agency to determine policy. We were set up to handle labor disputes. If the workers of the country are going to get the idea that we are not going to settle labor disputes, they are going to go back to the old method"—that is, strikes. Several weeks later Meany again told the board that labor's patience was wearing thin. Labor made the no-strike pledge in the belief the WLB would protect workers' interests, he said. "So we have people pounding the devil out of the people sitting on this board and saying, 'Here we are, we want our conditions rectified. We are working under conditions that are distasteful to us.' " Meany complained, "There are too many ways open to delay and delay a case." Management's attitude, he charged, was "Well, let the thing boil. Let the pot boil. It won't do the union any good. They will lose members in the meantime."

Arguing for expedited procedures, Meany urged, "I think we should try to hustle these cases up, even taking a gamble we may do something that isn't right. We get a wild-eyed business agent coming into our [AFL] office yelling his head off about the terrible conditions, and all we say is two things, 'We agree, and there is the War Labor Board.' " *

The War Labor Board's original mandate said nothing about wage controls. Inevitably, however, it began to consider the fairness of wages in settling disputes, first on its own initiative, in a case decided April 15, over vehement labor objections; next, under what the majority considered to be an implicit directive in a Roosevelt message to Congress on April 27.

The April 15 ruling, in a case involving the International Harvester Company, said labor could not expect to receive raises throughout the war "which will enable it to keep pace with increases in costs of living." The labor members, who were outvoted, said controlling wage levels was none of the board's business; that such questions should be settled through collective bargaining. Roosevelt's message to Congress, how-

---

* Meany did advise other members not to fret about one form of criticism: that of the press. He referred specifically to the Washington Merry-Go-Round column, then written by Drew Pearson and Robert S. Allen. "When I came to Washington I learned very soon that that was one column that you couldn't go by, anything that they printed there. I think that if they were paid on the basis of the veracity of the statements they made, and find something deducted from their pay when they were wrong, that they would both be bankrupt long ago."

ever, pointed up growing concern within the Administration over runaway inflation. Roosevelt laid out a seven-point program for stabilizing the cost of living, including price controls, rationing of scarce goods, and wage "stabilization." If the cost of living could be checked, Roosevelt said, "wages in general can and should be kept at existing scales." However, he did not specifically ask for a wage freeze. Roosevelt added that the "existing machinery for labor disputes will, of course, continue to give due consideration to inequalities and the elimination of substandards of living."

The board fell into immediate disagreement over how much authority the President expected it to exert over wages. Meany insisted the President did not intend for the WLB to "become a wage control board." Taylor disagreed. He said he "read into [FDR's] order that this board has a responsibility to meet in effectuating a wage stabilization."

"I think you're nuts," Meany replied. "I don't think he said anything of the kind. I am a little bit prejudiced, perhaps, in my reasoning. I talked to the President on four different occasions on what he meant before he made that speech to Congress, and I am of the opinion that he agrees with me." Meany said he was ready to face any responsibility requested by the President. "But I am not touched with the germ of bureaucracy even though I am a government official of some sort. I am not looking for more worlds to conquer, nor more territory for this board, even though the public members may be." ("All right, George," said Davis, "get off your high horse.") Meany said he felt collective bargaining—not laws or government edicts—would stabilize wages. The board's job, he said, "is not to go out and meet disputes before they become disputes, and become a wage control board, but to solve disputes."

Stringent controls were impractical, Meany said. "There are a lot of things we could do. We could perhaps wage this war on the basis of complete perfection. We could stop every normal activity of our citizens and place them all in the service of the state, but we haven't done that. We haven't stopped people from going to race tracks. We haven't stopped baseball." The board should concentrate on disposing of existing business, not look for more work. The labor members lost. In a split vote, the board decided upon a broad interpretation of Roosevelt's stabilization message. Price controls were impossible without some sort of wage controls, the majority said. A report by the four public members said flatly that "for the duration of the war, organized labor is expected to forgo its quest for an increasing share of the national income. . . . Labor was called upon [by FDR in his April 17 speech] to assume a sacrifice. . . . The time has arrived when 'sacrifice' stops connoting hard conditions in the distant future and begins to mean the assumption of tough obligations now in a war-ridden world." If wages began a "hopeless pursuit of prices which have gotten out of control, the task of stabilizing our domestic economy may well be impossible of achievement."

But how could the board call a fair halt to the wage spiral? As William Davis put it, "You can't stabilize around a moving thing, so you've got to fix a point in time." George Taylor hit upon a solution. "Our research showed that for some period of time prior to May 1941, wages and prices had been together, with no marked deviation in their trend. Once defense preparations began, however, you no longer had any normal market. By 1942, the wage movement was on, but it hadn't run its course. Some wages were up only ten percent, others more than fifteen percent, some none at all." The cost-of-living index, meanwhile, was found to have increased fifteen percent. Therefore the public members recommended that pay raises, as a general rule, be held to fifteen percent above the level existing in May 1941, and limited increases to those "necessary to iron out inequalities and eliminate substandards of living."

The board majority developed the fifteen percent rule in settling a contract dispute between the United Steel Workers of America and five small steel companies, and it was thereafter known as the Little Steel Formula (LSF). The board adopted the LSF, eight votes to four, over heated labor objections, the UAW's R. J. Thomas calling it a "lot of economic or academic hooey," and challenging whether fifteen percent was high enough. In its bargaining the United Steel Workers had asked for a $1 per day raise; the board majority allowed forty-four cents, although it conceded a larger increase might be justified. Meany found this reasoning highly inconsistent. As an alternative, he proposed giving the steelworkers the full dollar—forty-four cents in cash, fifty-six cents in war bonds "that would not be negotiable or spendable until after the war to prevent the money being used to start an inflationary spiral." The savings "might help the producers of consumer goods by setting up a reservoir of purchasing power that can start us going after the war," Meany said.

The employer representatives welcomed the Little Steel Formula. Roger Lapham said, "When you get to war you have to be tough, and Washington hasn't learned to be tough. As far as we are concerned, we can be tough." Meany retorted, "The country will never know we are at war until we are tough with the workers and freeze their wages. That is just what you mean, Roger, isn't it?"

Despite his strong opposition to the LSF during the WLB debate, and a vote against it (LSF carried, eight to four) Meany told the 1943 AFL convention the formula "was based on what I would say is some reason, some justice." His chief objection was that "it was too rigid [and] would perhaps prevent us from doing justice in a certain case." The labor left-wing criticized the LSF as a "sellout," and called it the "Little Steal Formula."

Although Meany did not recognize it at the time, adoption of the Little Steel Formula meant the beginning of the end of the War Labor Board's status as a voluntary, independent agency. The strains of war made inevitable the appointment of an economic czar to assume over-all direction of the plethora of economic boards, agencies, and commissions that sprang up in Washington. One major weakness of the WLB, for instance, was its lack of control over wage increases voluntarily granted by employers. At Roosevelt's request, Congress on October 2 authorized the Executive to issue a general order stabilizing wages and prices effective, so far as practical, at levels of September 15, 1942. The WLB had to approve any raises past those levels, and only when "necessary to correct maladjustments or inequalities, eliminate substandards of living, or to aid in the effective prosecution of the war." A few days later Roosevelt issued Executive Order 9520 which, as Meany said, "completely changed the nature of the War Labor Board. It now became another governmental war agency created by executive order and assigned a job to do. The unique quality of voluntary regulation was considerably altered; only the structure remained unchanged." The order created an Office of Economic Stabilization to take over-all charge of the control program.

Roosevelt had considered setting up the entire control machinery by executive order, but was advised against it by Supreme Court Justice James F. Byrnes. A conservative Democrat who had served in both the House and the Senate, Byrnes continued to give Roosevelt quiet political and economic advice even from the bench. Byrnes told Roosevelt he should submit the matter to Congress if he wanted it to succeed. The regulation of wages and prices was so controversial, it touched so many people so directly, that enforcement would be difficult without congressional authorization. It would be tough enough with it. Roosevelt agreed. On October 3, the day after the act became law, Byrnes resigned from the Supreme Court at Roosevelt's request to become director of economic stabilization. Roosevelt wanted him to referee the "increasing number of jurisdictional conflicts that came from the new agencies. 'I'll issue an executive order giving you power to settle them, and I'll let it be known that your decision is my decision,'" Byrnes quoted Roosevelt as saying.

Thereafter Byrnes acted as Roosevelt's buffer and resident bastard on economic matters. By his account it was a "bitter struggle" with congressmen, labor leaders, farmers, businessmen, and spokesmen for groups of all kinds who wanted exemptions from controls. Whenever possible, they would go directly to the President, hence Byrnes' utility. "The President was good at taking them on. After listening sympathetically, he would say, 'You know, Justice Byrnes is temperamental on this subject. I do not want to talk with him about it but you should go over and see him.' " Consequently, Byrnes said, "it was a job in which I made many acquaintances and no friends."

Meany was among the persons deceived by Roosevelt's sympathetic clucks and near-doubletalk—briefly, at least. Soon after the new stabilization program began, Byrnes told Meany that if the WLB granted a wage increase, and the Office of Economic Stabilization refused a balancing price increase, the wage increase was dead. Meany felt such an interpretation endangered the WLB's "integrity," and he complained to Roosevelt during a meeting of the joint AFL and CIO labor cabinet at the White House. Reporting on the conversation later to WLB colleagues, Meany quoted Roosevelt as saying, "The War Labor Board's decision is to be final." To Davis, who had raised the question, Meany said, "You know, Bill, when I want to get something definite I have a way of getting it definite, and I got it by the question-and-answer method. When the conversation was all over, I said, 'Now, Mr. President, do I understand this right?' and we went through it, and I understood it perfectly, and so did everybody else in the room. Everybody left there satisfied that the War Labor Board was the final tribunal in wage questions, that Byrnes and [Leon] Henderson [another economic official] were not possessed with veto power over the actions of the War Labor Board."

His careful questioning notwithstanding, Meany soon learned Roosevelt had not been totally candid: although WLB orders might be "final," and not subject to change or veto, they could not become "effective" until Byrnes settled the accompanying price issue. The labor members complained; there was talk within the AFL executive council of withdrawing from the WLB, now that it was no longer voluntary. But labor stayed. Meany later explained labor's threats to quit as strategic maneuvers that should not be taken at face value. "This was a place where we felt we had the Administration on the defensive, and we tried to keep them on the defensive because they had broken their word." Meany insisted that "as far as taking the big step of advocating withdrawal, it never entered our minds." By remaining on the board, labor could argue individual cases, and by its very presence serve as a check on the Administration.

According to Byrnes, the October 1942 order did not succeed in halting inflation. Between October 1942 and April 1943 the cost-of-living index increased 4.3 percent. "The effort to hold the line on wages and prices should have started with the beginning of the war," Byrnes wrote later. "Because we entered the fight late, it was always an uphill battle. I became tired of saying, 'I'm sorry, but it can't be done.' "

During the early months of 1943 labor became increasingly restive as prices outstepped wages. Workers were becoming so outraged, Meany said, that price controls were going to come "through vigilante committees . . . going right into those grocery stores, taking the law into their own hands." The no-strike pledge showed signs of strain. The aircraft industry was especially critical. Unable to win WLB approval of raises it had negotiated with management, the International Association of Machinists threatened progressive "plant-at-a-time general meetings" that would remain in session until members received more money. The specter of work stoppages had haunted the West Coast aircraft industry since 1940. Although strikes had cost minimal time, jittery procurement officers had recommended putting the plants under direct military control to ensure continued production. Meany thought the Roosevelt Administration was already moving toward tacit control of the plants. He charged that Byrnes and Ben Cohen of the White House staff were "deciding these wages" through dictation to the board's public members. "This is no longer a democratic board," Meany declared.

"For the record I say it isn't true, and it is an irresponsible statement," retorted Davis. "I tell you it is a slander which you ought not to indulge in, the assertion that Mr. Byrnes told the board what to do and the implication that the public members of the board haven't got the guts to do what they think is right." Chimed in Taylor: "You must withdraw that about anybody controlling the vote of one public member."

Meany asserted the government was attempting to provoke a strike that would justify an army takeover of the aircraft industry. "There is no question," he said. "That is the cold naked fact. I didn't think I would live to see a fascist government in this country, but this case is going to bring a fascist government. To say that these workers are a lot of traitors, to say that 100,000 or more workers are un-American and unpatriotic because they think they have a rotten, raw deal from this board just doesn't make sense." Meany said the WLB had lost all prestige with workers. "We are just completely out. We don't influence them one iota because of our membership on this board."

The public members contended the aircraft industry wages had increased by seventeen to eighteen percent since the war began, beyond the Little Steel Formula bounds, and hence no further raises were justified. "Maybe you'll send the statisticians out there to produce airplanes, or maybe you'll send Ben Cohen out there," Meany said. "There is no use of us sitting here and grinding out reams and reams of paper about this situation. Put yourself in the position of the average aircraft worker. He has for the last ten months been kicked around and kidded and told that he is going to get a raise. And who has stopped him from getting a raise? The government!"

After days of heated argument labor lost. The only concession it could extract from the full board was a quasi-promise to bend the fifteen-percent limit of the Little Steel Formula to keep pace with price increases. The board agreed that "if the cost of living continued to rise, the formula would have to be readjusted in justice to the wage earners of this country." But Davis was not prepared to abandon the Little Steel Formula altogether, saying he felt it would be "indiscreet for the board to attempt to change the national policy in that regard."

Meany replied, "I am sure the housewives out on the Pacific Coast will understand your remarks perfectly, Bill. I think they will be perfectly satisfied, Bill, with your remarks."

After the heated aircraft case—one that could have disrupted the most vital of the war industries had a strike occurred—Roosevelt gave controls the final turn. In a "hold-the-line" order issued on April 8, 1943, he directed the establishment of wage and price ceilings, based on levels of September 5, 1942, where possible. On wages, the order left a number of loopholes, but in general it forbade the War Labor Board to approve any increases beyond the Little Steel Formula.

Meany considered the directive (Executive Order 9328) a gross breach of faith by the Roosevelt Administration, especially since it countermanded the board's intention, stated only two weeks previously, of going beyond the LSF when warranted by specific cases. Further, Roosevelt kept the order so secret "that not even the members of the War Labor Board were accorded the courtesy of being informed that a change of wage policy was about to occur. . . . [They] were made aware of this development by newspaper reporters." Meany said he had met with the President on April 1 to discuss food prices. "The President gave no intimation that he was going to superimpose his policy on the War Labor Board. There was nothing like that at all." So far as he was concerned, Meany said, "The board stopped functioning on the eighth of April." Van Bittner, on the board for the CIO at the time, agreed. "I wonder where they got this from?" he said of the order. "That sounds like Goering stuff to me."

Since most organized workers had already won the increases due them under the LSF, the net effect of the new order was to freeze their wages for the duration. There were other handicaps for unions. As the AFL executive council stated in late 1943, "organization of workers is effectively hobbled since the wage rates of newly organized workers cannot be raised above the minimum or nonunion rate, which represents the bottom of the wage bracket."

Thereafter Meany did not take the War Labor Board seriously, although labor retained its seats and continued to attend meetings so as to have as much voice as possible in individual cases. As employer member Roger Lapham quipped, "We started off being generals. Then we got down to colonels, and now I think we are down to captains." Meany's attendance record, always spotty, became even worse; for weeks at a time he did not appear, relying upon an alternate, Robert Watt.

Meany's disgust was evident in the few appearances he made immediately after the hold-the-line order. He refused "to just sit here and be kidded for another month or two and keep on telling our people 'hold your horses and don't do anything.' I am not going to go along with that sort of a policy." Already, he said, strike threats were pouring in from AFL unions denied pay raises. He demanded a workable policy, not hopeful theory. "I am an active trade unionist," he said, "and I am not sitting back and taking an academic viewpoint of the trade union movement as yet." Any honest answer he gave unions inquiring about wages would be bound to precipitate strikes, for he would have to say, "This board can do nothing for you."

When he did attend meetings, however, Meany behaved with the outspoken bluntness other members had come to expect of him. "There were days when George acted like a plumbers' business agent," in the opinion of Wayne Morse. The public members were never certain just how seriously they should take labor's threats to quit the board, and Meany did his best to sustain their uncertainty. Archetypical were his tactics in a case involving the Cuneo Press, a large Chicago printing firm, owned by R. R. Donnelly & Sons.

Typographical unions had tried for years to organize Cuneo, which printed yellow-page sections for Bell Telephone System companies and magazines for several large publishers, including Time Inc. According to labor, Cuneo locked out workers who were trying to organize the company, and continued operations with other employees. Meany thought he had won a promise from the board that the organizers would be put back to work pending a full hearing; nonetheless, the board issued an order that effectively killed the strike. Meany came to the next board meeting in a rage. Complaining of "this trick you people pulled off here last night," he declared: "Mr. labor-hating, Jew-baiting, Catholic-hating Donnelly wins a case if this is decided, and after I get a definite promise that I get a hearing on it. The worst rotten scabby employer in America gets the services of this board *sub rosa*." Meany read a telegram in which he told the Chicago union, in effect, to ignore the War Labor Board—the first time labor had refused to enforce a board order. Meany's telegram said the back-to-work order was given "in spite of official promise of authorized board representative to your officials that such action would not be taken without a full hearing to all unions concerned. . . . These commitments have been disregarded evidently to render service to America's number-one labor-hating employer, R. R. Donnelly & Sons. In our judgment we believe that your organizations are fully justified in insisting that the assurance given to your representatives be carried out fully by the War Labor Board before you are asked to carry out any orders of the board." Meany and Matthew Woll signed the telegram.

"You ought to take an awfully long walk before you send that," Morse told Meany.

"I am going to take a walk to the telephone," Meany replied. "You ought to take a little more time studying a case before you make motions."

Davis pleaded with Meany. "I call your attention to the fact that this is the first occasion on which a member of this board has repudiated the majority action of the board."

"Right," snapped Meany.

"I regret very deeply to see that come from the side of labor," Davis said. "If God hasn't struck you blind, George, you must know what is going on in this country today." Destroying the War Labor Board, Davis said, would be the "worst service for labor that any labor leader in America ever did."

Morse said, "I think George Meany knows just as well as anyone else that if he sends that wire he has struck at the very heart of this board." Both he and Davis denied any breach of promise.

Meany said he realized the gravity of what he and Woll were threatening to do. "I am an old-fashioned sort of fellow, you see. I don't need a deed or a contract with my name signed to it. When I give my word I keep it, and I expect people to deal with me that way. When you take an authorized representative of this board and he has given me his word . . . and you say he is just an agent, it doesn't mean anything, then you are striking at the integrity of this board, and not me."

When Morse argued the board's order protected the men's right to an eventual hearing, Meany said, "If you do that, you have less sense than I thought you had." "I will say this," broke in Davis, "I say that any member of this board who is not prepared to support a majority decision, however wrong it is, should not remain a member of the board."

"The President appointed me, and if he wants me to resign, I'll get off; that's perfectly all right," Meany said. "Do you want the resignations? You will get them right here and now."

Davis repeated his theme that destroying the board would bring anti-union sentiment down on labor. "If you do this," he told Meany, "it is an act of treason against your own people."

"Oh, hell," replied Meany. "We were accused of treason before, right in this room." After more argument he scooped up the telegram and started to walk out of the room, saying, "All right, I will go and send this." Davis called him back, and the public members caucused briefly. Davis then told Meany the board would rescind its order and recall the union organizers for further hearings.

"Thank you, gentlemen," Meany said, and left.

Concurrent with Roosevelt's flow of orders, the board was losing even more credibility with labor because of its inability to cope with John L. Lewis. In early 1943 Lewis repudiated the board's jurisdiction and during six months of in-and-out strikes forced the Roosevelt Administration to capitulate to his contract demands at terms far better than those won by other unions.

Lewis had considerable justification for pique, for miners' working conditions declined perhaps more than those of any American workers during the first two years of the war. (In company-owned stores, for instance, potatoes went from forty-five cents to seventy-five cents a peck during a single two-month period early in 1943, immediately preceding his strike.) Lewis' concept of the board's shortcomings was markedly parallel to that of Meany: government had entered into a "contract" with labor in creating the War Labor Board, and then changed it without labor's consent. The Little Steel Formula was no longer a voluntary, flexible standard, but a law, and Lewis could not correct inequities in miners' pay inside the board. Dr. George Taylor felt there was "much substance to his [Lewis'] argument," but nonetheless "an argument like that is pretty hard to get across to the public." Angry though Meany was, he stayed on the board; the equally angry Lewis went his own way.

There was also considerable opportunism in Lewis' manuevering. He sensed the growing restiveness of workers bound by the AFL and CIO no-strike pledge, and the record suggests he retained visions of grasping again the leadership of American labor. Another factor was his unabated hatred of Roosevelt—which by now was fully reciprocated. John Brophy, a long-time mine union official, and later a key figure in the CIO, wrote privately in 1943 that the Lewis matter "is not just a simple trade union dispute, but a conspiracy on the part of America Firsters, composed of certain business, financial and political interests. John L. is part of this combination. . . . That is the reason he can get away with so much. . . . The stakes are the capture of the federal government at the next general election. To attain this it is necessary to undermine and discredit the Roosevelt-New Deal Administration at every turn. The miners, confused and bedeviled, know nothing of this and refuse to believe it is anything more than a labor dispute and that John L. is fighting their cause solely." The Roosevelt Administration countered with its own protective plotting. In early January 1943 Meany learned of a

White House scenario—written by Ben Cohen—that called for seizure of the mines by the government and their operation by army troops if necessary to break the anticipated Lewis strike. Meany said Roosevelt's April hold-the-line order "was drawn in order to drive another nail in the coffin of this man [Lewis]."

Through public speeches and the *UMWA Journal* Lewis hammered at Roosevelt's economic policies (calling anti-inflation a "code word" for cutting wages) and deriding labor participation on the War Labor Board. Come, follow me again, Lewis said time after time, evoking memories of his creation of the CIO: "It has been up to the United Mine Workers to break any new ground for other unions and industry to follow," he declared. "We are glad to render that service and will be glad to do it again—in the interest of the flag and the country." In early 1943 Lewis demanded wage, benefit, and other increases amounting to about forty percent, and said he intended to ignore the WLB in his negotiations. "Under its arbitrary and miserably stupid formula," he said, "it chains labor to the wheels of industry without compensation for increased costs, while other agencies of government reward and fatten industry by charging its increased costs to the public purse. Assuredly labor, despite its present weak and vacillating leadership, cannot long tolerate such economically paradoxical and socially unjust treatment. When the mineworkers' children cry for bread, they cannot be satisfied with a 'Little Steel Formula.' When illness strikes the mineworkers' families, they cannot be cured with an anti-inflation dissertation. . . ."

Ignoring direct pleas from Roosevelt not to strike, and refusing WLB attempts at negotiation, Lewis on April 27, 1943, launched the first great strike of World War II, one that was to sputter on until November, his miners alternately returning to work under government seizures, then leaving again at key bargaining junctures. The War Labor Board—and particularly the labor members—saw Lewis as a many-faceted problem. Meany feared Lewis' defiance of the WLB's ostensibly voluntary machinery would bring Congress crashing down on all of organized labor with punitive legislation, and that any special Administration treatment of Lewis would be an affront to other unions which remained faithful to the no-strike pledge. When the Roosevelt Administration, through Labor Secretary Frances Perkins, talked of creating a special commission to deal with the mine strike, Meany proposed a WLB resolution saying that if and when this occurred "the resignation of all members of this board is in his [Roosevelt's] hands." If Mrs. Perkins created such a commission, Meany said, Lewis would "have won all his points. He would have destroyed the usefulness of the board and would have gotten special treatment, which he has been looking for." When Interior Secretary Harold Ickes, put in charge of the seized mines by Roosevelt, tried to bargain with the strikers, Davis, Meany and Wayne Morse appealed to Roosevelt. In an acrimonious White House meeting they traded shouted insults and recriminations with Ickes, saying he was fatally undercutting the board's authority by ignoring its policy of not negotiating with strikers until they returned to work. Ickes replied that the board's insistence on formalities was prolonging the strike, because he had managed to bring the parties to within a few cents of one another. At this meeting, in May, Roosevelt sided with the War Labor Board and directed Ickes to halt his negotiations.

Lewis further complicated the situation on May 17 by suddenly asking the AFL executive council to take the mineworkers back. He sent along a check for $60,000 as "payment on account" of per capita taxes, and a letter talking at great length about the virtues of "unification." But in later meetings Lewis made clear he would not disband two UMWA units —the all-inclusive District 50, which claimed jurisdiction over any American who did not work in a coal mine, and his construction organizing committee, which competed directly with AFL affiliates. Lewis said he "accepts the AFL as it now exists, and expects the AFL to accept the UMWA as it now exists." Jurisdictional problems could be solved after his re-entry, Lewis said.

Lewis' old friend Bill Hutcheson argued his case to the executive council, with Meany and Dan Tobin vociferously opposing him. Meany demanded that Lewis must agree to drop all organizational work "not directly connected with the digging of coal" before readmission to the AFL. The executive council sent the question to the 1943 convention without recommendation. During floor debate, however, Green finally came around to Lewis' side, saying, "Well, it is my opinion that the years have mellowed his judgment. He has admitted he is wrong." Green said the AFL must "rise above the mire of hate and suspicions and passion." The convention approved a resolution calling for negotiations with Lewis, and a committee met periodically with him as his strike continued.

The Roosevelt Administration, meanwhile, was falling back upon the weapon of public opinion to try to break Lewis. This campaign, despite an intensity bordering on hysteria, also failed. The WLB participated. In formal statements, it accused Lewis of putting himself "above and beyond the laws which apply to all other citizens of the United States" and of giving "aid and comfort to our enemies." The Mediterranean edition of Stars and Stripes, the servicemen's newspaper, declared, "Speaking for the American soldier, John L. Lewis, damn your coal-black soul." In a memo written in midsummer, even such a prolabor figure as Wayne Morse advocated a government propaganda campaign against Lewis, employing the Office of War Information and other agencies. Morse said enforcement of WLB decisions "depends upon their acceptance by public opinion." He was convinced "that if Lewis persists in challenging the government with threats of work stoppage and actual work stoppage, his program can be beaten only by the pressure of public opinion upon the mineworkers." Morse called for "an intensive and sustained program of publicity calling attention to the great damage caused to the war effort by Lewis' programs." If such a campaign "is properly handled," Morse said, "it is very doubtful if the mineworkers would continue to follow for very long the Lewis program."

Lewis argued throughout the confrontation that he knew exactly how much coal was above ground, and how long the supplies would last, and that the defense effort was in no way endangered by the strike (a contention verified in large part by postwar governmental reports). Frank Waldrop, editor of the Washington *Times-Herald,* was on a New York-Washington train during the strike when he spotted Lewis sitting in a compartment, vest open, smoking a cigar and drinking bourbon. After some conversation Waldrop asked Lewis, "What the hell is this strike all about?" Lewis replied, "All the coal the country can use is out of the ground. I'm just giving the men some time off." But general press hysteria was such that the general public expected the lights to dim and the furnaces to grow cold at any moment. To the wartime public, the bombastic Lewis personified labor—a man "willing to let our boys die" to win his strike. Regardless of the merits of what Lewis sought, his strike was a strategic failure, for it provoked an antilabor backlash that was to plague unions for a full decade. The average American could not understand the justice of such Lewis demands as portal-to-portal pay.* The public equated a mine train ride with a streetcar ride, and asked, as did a St. Louis editorial writer, "Why should *any* American be paid for riding to and from his job?"

The coal strike dragged into early fall, and Roosevelt finally threw up his hands and ordered Ickes to settle it and forget the War Labor Board. Ickes did, and in short order, by giving Lewis considerably more money than the board recommended, and juggling overtime and fringe benefits so that the miners' weekly pay increased from $45.50 to $56.74. Ickes then put the contract before the WLB as a *fait accompli* and asked its approval. Meany was outraged: acceptance of the contract, he said, meant admission that the no-strike pledge was dead; no longer would other unions be restrained from quitting work to win contract disputes. But Davis and Taylor submitted that the dispute was a daily reminder of

---

* Miners traveled as long as forty-five minutes after going underground to reach their work places. Lewis wanted them to be paid from the time they entered the mine to the time they emerged. The owners wanted to pay them only for the actual time they spent mining.

the board's impotence, and that the sooner it ended the better. They prevailed, and Meany and labor grudgingly voted to settle, Wayne Morse voting a solitary no.

Lewis' "victory" at the expense of the War Labor Board also marked the death of his attempt to re-enter the AFL. In January 1944 the executive council voted to invite the UMWA to return "with the jurisdiction they had when they left," which meant dismembering both District 50 and the construction organizing committee. Lewis, unsatisfied, demanded a simple yes or no vote on readmission, with no conditions, which the executive council refused to do; whereupon Lewis accused the executive council of acting "with characteristic servility to the Roosevelt Administration" and of colluding with "New Deal politicians" to keep the UMWA outside the AFL. Instead of facing the issue head on, Lewis said, the council members "have constantly muttered and mumbled and indulged in fearsome incantations over the fallacious and hoary question of jurisdictional rights. It is an amazing exhibition of base hypocrisy approximating moral turpitude." Lewis demanded the return of his $60,000. Once again the AFL closed the books on John L. Lewis.

By mid-1943 Meany was so aggrieved with the deterioration of the War Labor Board's authority, and with Roosevelt's economic policies in general, that he began criticizing the Administration publicly. The AFL permitted him to do so to make plain, both to rank and file and to the White House, that cooperating with a program did not necessarily equate with endorsing a program. In a radio broadcast in May 1943 Meany called Roosevelt's price stabilization program a complete failure. He claimed an AFL survey found food price increases of 75 to 87 percent in selected cities since the war began, and put the blame squarely on the Administration. (An AFL press release accompanying the speech called it "the bluntest attack ever publicly voiced by any high official of the AFL or CIO against any breakdown on the part of this Administration.") And on May 29, in another radio speech, Meany said the economic stabilization program faced "complete collapse" because of the lack of cost-of-living controls. He warned that "sheer desperation" would force workers to strike to protest "the stupid unrealistic governmental policy which freezes their wages by arbitrary edicts on the one hand and which, on the other hand, permits the prices of food to rise to unconscionable heights."

Inside the board itself, Meany once more resorted to threats of resignation to pressure Judge Fred Vinson, Byrnes' successor as economic czar, to permit pay increases to iron out inequities in worker pay. Unless the WLB had some flexibility, Meany said, "I'm not going to make a damn fool out of myself by telling my own executive committee something which is not true." If the WLB regained some discretionary authority, Meany said, he could convince the AFL to remain on the board. If the AFL left, he said, "of course, you can always get some traitors. You can always go out and pick up someone. . . . Some officials of fairly good standing in the AFL will say, 'All right, as long as there is a War Labor Board and the President wants to appoint me, I will sit on it.' " But Meany warned such a "traitor" could not prevent strikes by AFL unions. The Administration yielded to the extent of permitting pay increases "to correct substandards of living," but it would not alter the fifteen percent limit set by the Little Steel Formula.

So Meany tried another tack. The language of the original Little Steel Formula, and the various clarifying and modifying orders issued by the WLB and the Administration, specifically said the formula would be fair only if the cost of living stabilized. The cost-of-living index, then as now, was compiled by the Bureau of Labor Statistics, the research arm of the Department of Labor. In October 1943, largely at Meany's urging, the War Labor Board appointed a Committee on the Cost of Living, with Davis as chairman and Meany and R. J. Thomas of the United Auto Workers as labor members. Meany and Thomas, working with their respective research staffs, issued a report in January sharply challenging the accuracy of the cost-of-living index as measured by the Bureau of Labor Statistics. The BLS claimed the index was 123.5, on a scale on which 1940 was 100. Meany and Thomas claimed the actual figure was nearer 145.

Davis, in turn, had his own set of experts poke over the figures. They agreed there were defects in the BLS index, and made the "crude guess" the error was 5½ points, rather than the 20-odd claimed by Meany and Thomas. The board majority rejected a labor demand that the Little Steel Formula be re-evaluated, and stuck to the fifteen percent figure.

Now thoroughly angry, Meany went after the BLS. "We took newspaper advertisements of the large supermarkets and compared them with advertisements of three and four years back, of the same things. We used these to show the percentage price increase of food. We brought these figures into the War Labor Board, and we got an agreement the Bureau of Labor Statistics should be looked into, that we [the labor members] should go to the Bureau and find out if they wouldn't refine their procedures to get a more realistic result. For instance, they ignored completely what we call the 'mobility cost' of labor. During the war thousands of mechanics in the cities where there was was not much war work going on had to pick up and go all over the country. This meant additional expense for travel. It meant the expense of maintaining themselves on the job and also of sending money back home. These expenses were not reflected in the cost-of-living statistics at all."

Meany took a delegation to A. Ford Hinrichs, chief of BLS, and asked for a cost-of-living index tailored for war workers, rather than the general populace. "He took a very bureaucratic stand. He said, 'No, this is the way we do it, and we're doing it now the way we did it five years ago because this is the way you compare the cost of living.' " According to Mrs. A. J. Wickens, a long-time BLS official who was at the meeting, Hinrichs confused Meany with a highly technical explanation of the workings of the index. She recalled: "Presently Mr. Meany got exasperated, and you could see his color rising in his face, as it does when he gets annoyed, and he hammered on the table and said, 'See here, Doctor, what we need to get this steel wage policy opened again is ten more points on this index. Are you going to help us, or aren't you?' "

Mrs. Wickens continued: "Hinrichs, instead of saying bluntly, 'Hell, no, you know we can't rig these figures!' gave him a long sort of academic answer about reliability in the bureau and such, and Meany got mad."

Meany's version of the meeting was substantially different. He stated that when Davis tried to explain why the old index did not accurately reflect expenses of war workers, Hinrichs broke in to demand, "Just how are you going to use these figures?" Meany said he told Hinrichs: "Now, wait a minute. You are a statistician. We are asking you to make certain assessments, we want you to come up with the truth. Now, how we use it is none of your business." Both versions are the same on one point: the meeting ended with both sides angry and accusing one another of bad faith. Hinrichs absolutely refused to change BLS procedures.

Several weeks later the BLS hosted its annual meeting of labor research officials, normally a dry session given over to arcane discussion of the nuances of statistical analysis. Meany asked for permission to speak. What he said was a bombshell, and a well-publicized one, for advance texts went to the press. Meany exhaustively documented defects in BLS procedures, drawing upon research both of labor and of the prestigious American Statistical Association (which said the BLS index was "not satisfactory" for measuring wartime living expenses). Meany charged the BLS with conspiring with the Office of Price Administration to produce a falsely favorable picture of Roosevelt's anti-inflation program. He said the BLS kept figures only on items strictly controlled by OPA and ignored a host of out-of-pocket expenses unavoidable to war workers. For instance, workers who ate lunch in cafés and canteens, rather than at home, spent an extra $2.10 per week, a sum that did not appear in the BLS index. Meany said, "There are sharp indications that, the price control policy of the government having failed to keep living costs down, the Administration decided the next best thing to do was to keep down the cost-of-living index. In this policy the Bureau of Labor Statistics obse-

quiously acquiesced. We are led to the inescapable conclusion that the
bureau has become identified with an effort to freeze wages, to the extent
that it is no longer a free agency of statistical research." The bureau,
Meany said, had "identified itself with the objectives of a specific political administration." He called Ford Hinrichs "a bureaucratic monkey on
a stick who moves up and down in conformity with the dictates of administration wage policy."

On and on Meany rolled, for more than an hour of factual analysis
and billingsgate. The BLS officials present listened to him in stunned
silence, for the BLS heretofore had managed to avoid being drawn into
public debates. Mrs. Wickens called Meany's attack on Hinrichs "exag-
gerated and scurrilous." The repercussions were immediate. Roosevelt
complained to Green that Meany's criticisms were "undermining the anti-
inflation program by destroying public confidence in OPA and the BLS,"
and demanded that he be muzzled. Green agreed, and he ordered Meany
not to make any more speeches criticizing the Administration without
advance clearance. Green was also furious that Meany received so much
attention for the speech, and his office went to great pains to disassociate
the AFL from the criticisms. Florence Thorne, Green's administrative
assistant, spread a story with friends in the Labor Department that
Meany had never even seen the critical report supposedly coauthored by
him and the UAW's R. J. Thomas. The Green-Thorne version, as related
by Mrs. Wickens, was: "Meany was mad. His name was on a report. He
honestly thought the index understated the rise. But he was out on a
limb. His own people didn't agree with what he had done, and they
hadn't seen it, and he hadn't seen it, but at this point in time they
couldn't admit it publicly. So he attacked." Both from the existing record
and Meany's statements, however, this version is wrong. Meany knew
what he was doing when he attacked the Bureau of Labor Statistics, and
he would not back down, even when disciplined by Green. But Green's
reaction to Meany's speech offered further evidence of the strained relations in the AFL hierarchy.

The War Labor Board began winding down its activities immediately
after V-J Day and went out of existence at the end of 1945 (although
some of its functions were transferred to the new National Wage Stabilization Board). In its final report the board toted up its four-year record:
20,800 disputes handled, involving 12.5 million workers; and more than
463,000 nondisputed wage agreements processed, covering another 26
million persons. The board managed this case load with a peak staff, in
Washington and in the field, of 2,613 persons.

To George Taylor, the fact that unions survived the war with their
basic rights undiminished was proof of the board's success, an assess-

ment accepted by Meany. "Meany was never fooled for a minute," Taylor said. "He knew business was in a union-destroying mind when the war began, and that they would use Congress—and the war—to crush labor. Sure, labor had a friendly White House. But labor also had the good sense to scramble around and protect itself. Labor was on thin ice from 1940 on; Meany knew it, and he knew how heavy he could walk, and when he should back away." Total union membership increased from 8,900,000 in 1940 to 14,800,000 at V-J Day, and industrial wages went up by an average of about one third (uncomfortably behind the cost-of-living index rise of forty percent). Labor's over-all scorecard is unbalanced. On the negative side, labor was forced to forget about enforcement of several cherished laws. Strictures on child labor, for example, were tacitly ignored during the war, as were many safety rules. But Meany has pointed out another gain which, although not obvious to the general public at the time, had enormous long-term significance.

"I remember the time," Meany said, "when it was unheard of to think about having a paid vacation for an industrial worker or for a building trades or construction worker. We said, 'Well, that's all right for a fellow who is a steady employee, a white-collar worker. He is in an office; that is part of your practice there.' But we [the building trades] didn't even talk about it."

In applying the Little Steel Formula, however, the War Labor Board held that noncash fringe benefits were not subject to the fifteen percent limitation; that the "fringes were not inflationary," in Meany's words. "They were sort of money that you get down the road. As a result, union after union, in order to bring something out of negotiations that would look attractive to their membership, turned to health and welfare plans, and they became widespread."

Nonetheless, his experience on the War Labor Board reinforced Meany's trade-unionist conviction that government was a poor substitute for collective bargaining. Summarizing the board's record in *The American Federationist* in April 1946, he wrote: "There is a moral in this story of 'wage stabilization' by government that should appeal equally to American business and to American labor—keep politicians out of the field of labor relations."

# VI

## Birth of a Cold Warrior

I N N O V E M B E R 1 9 4 3, in one of a series of *Saturday Evening Post* articles on "some of the more responsible labor leaders . . . who are on the way up," Washington business journalist Merlyn S. Pitzele called Meany the "heir apparent" at the American Federation of Labor, and wrote, "Compared to bumbling Bill Green, he's a Sandow." Such public comparisons, even when he agreed with them, embarrassed Meany. Favorable press attention made Green all the more suspicious of him, a supposed subordinate, and caused him to curb even further Meany's freedom of operations. Meany studiously avoided criticizing Green, even in private conversations with friends and with staff members he trusted. But his frustration was so overwhelming that anyone who watched him realized that Meany must find an outlet for his energies lest he, in the words of a close associate, "go quietly batty trying to get along with Bill Green."

The War Labor Board consumed much of Meany's time, yet he made no pretense of attending meetings regularly, sending instead an alternate, Robert J. Watt, and appearing personally only when major policy decisions were to be made, or when he had a special interest in a case. Roosevelt's "labor cabinet" gradually diminished in importance as the war wore on and the union leaders realized that the President really was not paying as much attention to them as he pretended. The White House manipulations of the War Labor Board made Meany keenly distrustful of Roosevelt.

Meany's problem thus became one of finding an area in which Green had no interest and pre-empting it. He found such an opening in international affairs—the beginning of an involvement of marked significance not only to his personal career, but to the entire American labor movement. The attitudes Meany developed during the early 1940's, in the midst of World War II, remained intact in the succeeding quarter century, to form the core of "labor foreign policy" in the 1970's.

The AFL's concern with foreign affairs in its first half century was largely ceremonial. Conventions regularly passed windy resolutions commenting on almost any issue that happened to be in the headlines, and the AFL and the British Trades Union Congress dutifully exchanged "fraternal delegates" at their annual meetings. The ritual was stylized: the "fraternal delegate" made a speech which was occasionally audible above the convention hubbub, and he received a gift watch, which he accepted with gratitude and further platitudes. The AFL helped form the International Labor Organization (ILO), an adjunct of the League of Nations responsible for creating model codes for workers around the world. The ILO's record was mixed: in Western nations with strong unions, its codes were adopted. In Africa, Asia, and elsewhere, they were ignored. The AFL also had *pro forma* contacts with the Confederación General de Trabajadores (Mexican Federation of Labor, or CGT) and a handful of other Latin labor groups affiliated with the ILO.

As war and fascism swept down upon Europe in the 1930's the AFL mirrored the concurrent isolationist and pacifist moods of America— opposed to aggression in principle, but too caught up in domestic problems to give other than passing attention to world affairs. The AFL did collect funds to aid refugees, mostly exiled labor officials, and it passed resolutions urging "intensification of our efforts in behalf of the persecuted and oppressed minorities in Germany" (the language of the 1938 convention). But even though the AFL was willing to support a boycott of German goods, it opposed any acts by the United States government, such as a blockade of German shipping, which might increase the possibility of American involvement in the war. Even after the fighting began in 1939 the executive council urged that "our government shall pursue a judicious policy, exercising care and caution and a firm determination to avoid involvement in European conflicts or in European wars." The 1939 convention, while deploring war, declared, "As for our own country, we demand that it stay out of the European conflict, maintaining neutrality in spirit and in act." After the Nazi invasion of Holland and Belgium in the spring of 1940 the executive council said that although "we are shocked by what is going on in Europe . . . we do not see how the cause of democracy could be furthered by our involvement in a foreign war. . . . Our function as a nation should be and must be to safeguard and maintain peace and democracy *in the Western Continent* by maintaining strict neutrality regardless of our sympathy and feelings towards the victims of totalitarian aggression in Europe." However, the AFL did support FDR's aid to the British beginning in mid-1940, and after Pearl Harbor it pledged unstinting support to the war effort.

Nelson Cruikshank, who worked closely with Meany beginning in the 1930's as an AFL staff member, said, "George was not an internationalist when he came in; he was a parochial New Yorker. But Green didn't give a damn about international affairs. There was a vacuum, so George filled it." Meany's previous experience in foreign affairs was understandably limited. In April 1933, three months after Hitler came to power in Germany, he had helped form a New York group called "The German Labor Chest" to support labor leaders forced to flee Nazism. A companion labor organization based in New York worked for a boycott of German-made goods. The stimulus for both groups came from the heavily Jewish International Ladies Garment Workers Union. But Meany was busy enough—first, through the New York central labor council, then through the State Federation of Labor—to satisfy David Dubinsky, the ILGWU president and a foreign affairs activist. "George had a lot of problems, getting the New York state fed to support what was essentially a Jewish relief operation," Dubinsky said. "Regardless of what you hear today, Jewish labor leaders weren't universally loved by the AFL inner circle in those days."

Meany went into foreign affairs with his customary thoroughness. If he must deal with foreign labor leaders, he wanted to speak to them in their own language. So he enrolled in a night-school Spanish course. Reading Spanish proved easy; but wrapping his thick Bronx accent around the sibilants and trills of a Latin language produced frustrating splutterings that defied hours of intensive practice. But Meany's personal secretary—Virginia Tehas, a young, Texas-born woman he had recruited from the AFL stenographic pool—helped him along, and within two years Meany was tolerably fluent in Spanish. An old New York acquaintance, Nelson Rockefeller, was in Washington as an Assistant Secretary of State for Latin America, and he arranged for Meany to meet with visiting Latins. At Meany's initiative, the AFL began publishing a Spanish-language newsletter, *Noticiario Obrero Norteamericano,* for distribution in Latin America. Miss Tehas edited the newsletter, a clipsheet of U.S. labor news. "This was our operation all the way," Meany said. "Green never even knew the thing was published." Meany also went deep into records of AFL conventions and executive council meetings and found a plethora of resolutions on international affairs, papers with language so grandiose of purpose, so sweeping in aim, that they justified almost any program he cared to develop. Meany's interests gradually crystallized in four broad areas:

—To help the government use labor specialists in both covert and overt roles to assist the war effort. The AFL cooperated openly with the Office of Strategic Services, predecessor to the Central Intelligence

Agency, during World War II. Officially, the AFL's foreign activities in the cold war period and beyond were conducted independently of U.S. intelligence agencies, and Meany steadfastly denied any connections, formal or otherwise, with the CIA. But the AFL was a conspicuously muscular participant in European unionism in the immediate postwar period, helping crush pro-Communist labor groups and providing the cash and manpower to create unions friendly to the United States and its policies. This work was done through the AFL's international affairs division and the AFL-financed Free Trade Union Committee (FTUC), directed by Jay Lovestone, formerly head of the Communist party in the United States and later an anti-Communist of bare-fanged ferocity. Competent witnesses who worked both for and with Lovestone stated that CIA funds helped finance the AFL programs that he directed.

—To lead unrelenting AFL opposition to the Soviet Union and the Communist movement it spearheaded through the 1940's. The AFL accepted wartime cooperation with the Soviet Union as a pragmatic military necessity, but it did not give even lip service to the notion of wanting a lasting friendship. As the war ended, the AFL, chiefly through Meany, became the first national organization of any stature to denounce Soviet activities in East European nations seized from the Germans, and to declare that the United States should gird for battle with "another form of totalitarianism."

—To ensure AFL recognition as the only spokesman for American workers in international labor organizations. Complex domestic and world union politics were involved in this decision. On one level, the AFL wanted to deny to the rival CIO any recognition as a coequal labor federation; on another, it sought to outmaneuver the Soviet Union and its allies, who were attempting to forge a "labor international" as an instrument of global power politics.

—To muster labor support for an end to American isolationism. The AFL, largely at Meany's urging, was an early and strong buttress of the foreign aid program, into which it dovetailed many of its own international activities. Meany summarized the reason for labor's backing of the Marshall Plan and subsequent aid programs in one terse word: "self-interest." He elaborated, in a 1947 speech: "Enlightened self-interest, if you will, but self-interest nonetheless—that is the basic reason for helping these countries of Europe to recover economically. It is far better, far wiser, far more practical, in our judgment, to make moderate sacrifices today in order to avoid being compelled to make sacrifices a thousand times as great tomorrow. That is just plain common sense."

The sole function of the AFL "international program," when Meany first looked at it, was reprinting pamphlets containing the rhetoric-bloated resolutions on foreign policy passed by annual conventions. Mat-

thew Woll, a vice-president, ran the "program," through a languid standing committee on international relations. (The acerbic James B. Carey
of the CIO remarked, "The AFL considered Matty Woll an expert on
foreign affairs because he was born in Luxembourg.") Labor's most active foreign program, in fact, was run under the auspices of David Dubinsky's ILGWU, which teemed with anti-Fascist European refugees
with the contacts and conspiratorial flair essential to underground work.
The ILGWU had begun a program in the 1930's to spirit democratic
and socialist labor leaders from the Axis countries. After the war started,
the union became a veritable recruiting hall for the Office of Strategic
Services. One such early recruit was an extraordinary Italian-born Socialist, Serafino Romualdi, who in his youth had been beaten and jailed
for anti-Mussolini activities, and who once hid in a well to escape a firing
squad. Romualdi eventually got to New York and went to work for Dubinsky. Early in the war Romualdi, with labor financing, went to Latin
America to organize an anti-Fascist underground among the many anti-
Mussolini Italians there. He later shifted to Italy as a member of the
OSS's labor relations division,* helping to re-establish unions crushed by
the war.

The ILGWU supplied more than a score of such operatives, some on
its own payroll, others working directly for the OSS. Directing this network, as head of the ILGWU international relations department, was
Jay Lovestone, a deliberately mysterious man who for some four decades was one of the more controversial (and least known) figures in
American labor. A short, stocky-framed man with a slightly lopsided
face and errant gray hair, Lovestone was long credited—or blamed—for
Meany's hard-line anticommunism. To the left, Lovestone was an arch-
reactionary hobgoblin who kept American labor fighting the cold war
long after the rest of the world (and most Americans) had declared an
armistice and opted for peaceful, if guarded, coexistence. To the moder-
ates and right within labor, Lovestone was "Meany's secretary of state,"
a man whose activities were considered all the more important because
no one outside Meany's immediate circle knew exactly what he did.
Which was the way Lovestone preferred it.

Lovestone was long wed to mystery and conspiracy. Born in Lithuania
in 1898 (as Jacob Liebstein), he came to New York City at the age of
ten, embraced socialism in his teens, was graduated from the City College of New York with an accounting degree, and in 1919 became one of
the founders of the American Communist party. For more than a decade
Lovestone worked in the party's highest echelons, editing *The Communist,* the party's theoretical journal, and serving as general secretary, the
ranking office. Lovestone lost his trappings of power—and very nearly

* Romualdi's OSS affiliation was no secret; his overseas mailing address even
included an OSS designation.

his life—in a brutal showdown with Stalin during the 1928 congress of the Communist International in Moscow. The dispute had a convoluted genesis involving intraparty quarrels over personalities and policies in both the Soviet Union and the United States. In the end, Lovestone's gravest error, to Stalin, was his support of Nikolai Bukharin, soon thereafter expelled from the Soviet party for doctrinal heresy. Lovestone refused to repudiate Bukharin, and Stalin stripped away his party offices. For several anxious weeks Lovestone feared he would never leave Russia alive, Stalin telling him in one frightfully tense meeting, "There is plenty of room in Russian cemeteries." Finally Lovestone obtained an exit visa and conspicuously purchased a railroad ticket for Poland, knowing full well he faced arrest at the frontier. Several days in advance of his scheduled departure he managed to procure an airline ticket* and flew to Germany. The Soviet secret police were none the wiser until he was safe.

For the next several years Lovestone remained a Communist, although a vigorously anti-Stalin one. His adherents—Lovestoneites, in intraparty language—alternately sought readmission to and/or control of the American Communist party, but gradually dwindled away. With his insider's expertise in communism, Lovestone next became a consultant to labor leaders fighting Communist elements within their unions. His first client was Homer Martin, beleaguered president of the United Auto Workers, who was being opposed by a Communist-supported slate. "Martin was not the best man for the UAW by any means, but he was better than any Communist party member or Communist agent," asserted Lovestone. Dubinsky, with whom Lovestone was friendly and had done work, sent him to Detroit to organize opposition to the Communist-tainted slate. At Dubinsky's suggestion, Lovestone talked with Walter Reuther, gaining stature within the UAW, and whom Dubinsky considered a good prospect for the presidency. "I gave Reuther a twenty-point program," Lovestone said, "and we met in the lobby of the Woodward Hotel in Detroit to talk about it. He said he would accept ninety-five percent of it. 'Fair enough,' I said, 'but it depends on what the other five percent is.' He objected to provisions for a fight against communism and subversion. He told me, 'I will do it, but I won't put it on paper—I don't want to be a Red-baiter.' That was all there was to it; I was through with him." Reuther supported R. J. Thomas, who won over Martin. But as Lovestone stated, "Because I worked so hard for Homer Martin, Reuther never had much use for me." Lovestone eventually went to work for Dubinsky full time, directing the ILGWU's international affairs program.

Meany and Lovestone met in the mid-1930's, and Lovestone candidly admitted, "It wasn't love at first sight on George's part. Here I was, the

---

* By one account, Lovestone swapped his train ticket with an airline passenger who was never seen again after reaching the Polish border.

former head of the Communist party, now working in the labor movement. Hell, George was anti-Communist when I was still running the party, that's how much of a gap there was. Dubinsky vouched for me, but for a good many years I don't think George really trusted me." "When I first started seeing Lovestone around labor meetings," Meany said, "he was a reporter for the *Jewish Daily Forward*. He was having a hell of a tough time. The Communists hated him, and the anti-Communists wanted no part of him. Me, I wouldn't be seen on the same side of the street with him. But Dubinsky worked with him about five years, and then told me, 'The son of a bitch is OK, he's been converted.' On Dubinsky's say-so, I accepted him. We got along fine. It does gripe the hell out of me for people to say 'Jay Lovestone runs labor foreign policy,' and that 'Lovestone makes Meany anti-Communist.' Hell, I was fighting the Commies when Lovestone was running the Communist party."

Meany detested the Communists. They were anathema to him as a trade unionist and a Catholic. The New York building trades, which were tightly organized decades before the Communists became a political force in America, were never troubled by them. But Meany, a state fed president, saw firsthand the Communist attempts to dominate weaker craft unions and their manipulation of many of the new CIO constituent unions. Meany said American workers should recognize Soviet labor "for what it is—a government-controlled, government-fostered, and government-dominated labor front that denies to the workers of Soviet Russia the basic human freedoms that American workers hold are prerequisite to a free trade union." This tenet is crucial to understanding Meany's unflinching anticommunism. A nation is not free unless its trade unions are free—such is Meany's litmus test, and Communist regimes fail it.

A compulsive brainpicker, Meany questioned Lovestone incessantly about Communist strategies, both in the United States and abroad. "I know the Communist movement better than they, the Communists, do themselves," Lovestone stated. "There is a tremendous advantage, you know, in having had an association with the founder. I knew Lenin at first hand." On one subject Lovestone offered Meany the special warmth of reassurance. As did Meany, he felt the U. S.-Soviet alliance would end abruptly when peace came, and that Moscow would attempt to seize what territory it could in the postwar turmoil. So what can we do about it? Meany finally asked. Lovestone argued roughly as follows: The Communists would attempt to substitute a central "labor international" for the autonomous national unions of the world, and use labor as a key element of conquest by subversion. Pro-Communist unions, for example, could stage general strikes to weaken democratic governments. If acceptance of a Communist regime was the price demanded for labor peace, the public would acquiesce. Communist unions could be a negative force retarding industrial recovery. Lovestone suggested that the AFL do two things: go into liberated countries immediately to restore free trade unions, offering leadership, guidance, and money; and sabotage at any cost the inevitable Soviet attempt to create a puppet "labor international" and strive for a confederation of democratic unions from non-Communist countries. Communism was now a world movement, Lovestone said, one incapable of containment by isolated national labor federations which could be picked off, one by one.

At Meany's behest, Lovestone wrote a resolution for the 1944 AFL convention creating a Free Trade Union Committee to be the AFL's foreign operations arm. The FTUC was authorized to raise one million dollars to "assure prompt practical assistance to the workers of the liberated countries in Europe and Asia as well as to the workers of South and Central America in their efforts to organize free democratic trade unions." Green took the chairmanship but was never active in FTUC work. Meany, Dubinsky, and Woll, who comprised the total membership, ran things, with Lovestone as executive secretary, based in an ILGWU office in New York.

Because of his background, Lovestone said it was important that the committee bore what he called "the kosher stamp of Matty Woll." One building tradesman on the AFL executive council grumped about the wisdom of hiring "one of Dubinsky's Jew Communists" to run a program that many council members did not really want. But, as Lovestone stated, "Woll was a good Catholic, intelligent, a force in the executive council, and they trusted him to keep an eye on me." The FTUC picked up many of the ILGWU's agents abroad, and became labor's liaison with the Office of Strategic Services. Lovestone also began planning for the immediate postwar period, for he realized the AFL must be in a position to act quickly when the war ended and the Communists moved to fill any political vacuums that existed.

One phase of the battle, in fact, was already under way, a dispute with the British Trades Union Congress that simmered out of public view for three years during the war, threatening not only the AFL's long-time relations with British labor, but also relations between the governments of the United States, Great Britain, and the Soviet Union. The AFL, after much hesitation about association with Socialist unions, in the mid-1930's had summoned the courage to join the International Federation of Trade Unions, based in Paris. In 1939 the AFL succeeded in blocking affiliation of the Central Council of Trade Unions of the USSR on grounds the Russian unions were agents of the state. The war shattered the IFTU, which became a paper organization in impecunious exile in London.

In May 1942 Walter Citrine, secretary-general of the British Trades

Union Congress, told the AFL executive council the British public was in "a high state of almost unreasoning admiration" for the Soviets, in the belief they had saved Britain from invasion. He felt close association with the Soviets was inevitable, and that it could best be controlled if channeled through an Anglo-American-Soviet labor alliance run by the BTUC. Collaboration with the Soviets did not mean an "endorsement of communism," Citrine said, nor was it likely that either the American or British unions could "learn so much from Soviet Russia." According to executive council minutes, however, Citrine did make a strong argument for an attempt at coexistence. He

> suggested we might let it be a little one way traffic for a time, and let the Russians learn from us. He stated that he felt certain the Russian delegation who were in Great Britain had opened their eyes when they saw the standard of life and he suggested that if they come to the United States he would imagine they would think it was Mecca.

Green, responding, denounced the prewar Soviet alliance with Hitler and the subsequent flip-flops of U.S. Communist policy. While the AFI could understand how British proximity to the war made workers there warmer to the Soviets, Green said, "We could not explain to our people how and why we would join with Soviet Russia." He said, "We have a different situation here, a different state of mind, and a different psychology; therefore, it would be difficult to explain to our workers why we would join with Soviet Russia after we have repeatedly declared in conventions over and over again that we would not and could not cooperate with them or have anything to do with them." The AFL also asked Citrine to keep away from the CIO. Citrine declined, saying he "felt compelled" to ask the CIO to join the proposed alliance, noting it had served on the now-defunct IFTU. The executive council told Citrine it was "deeply disappointed." So, too, was he, but the AFL would not yield, even to pleas from the White House and the British government (via the United States Embassy in London).

Reporting back to the AFL in January 1943, Citrine said the AFL's attitude had offended both British labor and the Soviet Union. He told of the "very delicate task" of explaining to the Soviets "that you are not willing to associate with them. . . . It was very plain from the communications we received that they were very deeply aggrieved about their exclusion, very deeply aggrieved." Citrine said British workers could not understand the AFL's attempted blackball of the CIO either. "With the slightest encouragement," he said, "the preponderance of membership [of British unions] . . . would be found demanding that we associate with the CIO." Citrine said the AFL's attitude baffled him. "If you can sit side by side on committees under your President or under your government departments with CIO representatives," he said, "it should be possible to find an arrangement whereby we can sit side by side in this international phase of the war effort. We had hoped you would listen to our appeal just as much as you would listen to your own government." The British unions and government, he said, were in an "embarrassing position."

But the AFL would not move. Dan Tobin claimed the British did not understand how deeply American unionists detested Communists because of their "attempted destruction of the American labor movement for over eighteen or nineteen years." The CIO role was also a goad to the AFL.

The British went ahead with their conference, which, because of war conditions, did not actually begin until February 1945. The AFL declined its formal invitation. The CIO, the United Mine Workers of America, and the railway brotherhoods, all outside the AFL, accepted, as did, of course, the Soviet Union and many of its bloc nations. The meeting resulted in formation of the World Federation of Trade Unions, which demanded recognition as spokesman for "world labor" at the founding conference of the United Nations in San Francisco later in the year.

During the thirty-odd months of negotiations with Citrine, the AFL remained virtually silent, saying little publicly of its opposition to the "Anglo-American-Soviet" alliance. Roosevelt had asked a moratorium on criticisms of the Soviet Union, so as not to harm the war effort, and the AFL complied. By April 1945, however, Germany was on the obvious brink of defeat, and the Soviet Union and the West were deep into their political maneuverings over the postwar make-up of the world. The AFL, fearing it was about to be shoved aside by the WFTU, decided to set the record straight on why it was boycotting the WFTU. Meany was spokesman, via a speech to the New York Central Trades and Labor Council on April 5, a bare month before the German capitulation.

The speech was important because it was tantamount to a first public declaration of the cold war by the AFL. Meany bluntly refused any suggestions of postwar cooperation with the Soviet Union or the nations it was swiftly converting into satellite states. "We see no virtue in groveling in the dust of a false unity which would simply replace one form of totalitarianism with another," he said. "We do not propose to be a party to the rigging of international labor machinery to be used as a medium of infiltration or the chocolate coating of any ideology among people who would choke if they knew the consequences of what they were swallowing." Meany attacked the make-up of Soviet trade unions, calling them "creatures of the state" without the essential freedoms of speech, press, assemblage, and worship. He declared: "What common ground for discussion could we find in cooperating with those who pretend to speak for government but in reality represent the government itself? What could we talk about? The latest innovations being used by the secret police to ensnare those who think in opposition to the group in power? Or, perhaps, bigger and better concentration camps for political prisoners?"

Meany said it was "obvious" that the British–Soviet-sponsored conference "was primarily . . . part of a struggle to secure world political power in the postwar world." He found the WFTU an odd combination of British imperialism and Soviet communism. Fifteen of the thirty-five countries represented were British dominions and colonies, seven* of which had no bona fide labor movements; according to Meany, the British government recruited "leaders" and flew them to the London conference to "bolster up British representation." Under the weighed voting system, Meany said, the "so-called Soviet trade unions" would have twenty-seven million votes, the British only six million. Meany also had harsh words for the CIO: "We did not picket the White House to protest lend-lease aid to Britain. We did not carry signs in 1940 reading 'The Yanks are not coming.' We did not accuse President Roosevelt of being a warmonger or of aiding Britain in carrying on an imperialistic war. We did not accuse him of taking bread out of the mouths of America's workers to make bullets. . . ."

Meany's attack on the British and Soviets so staggered the White House, according to his aides, that the Administration invoked "voluntary" censorship and persuaded the New York newspapers not to publish an account of the speech, lest U.S. relations with the two Allies be harmed. Whether the White House did any such thing is unconfirmable; whatever the reason, no stories on the speech appeared in the press, although it amounted to a major policy declaration by the AFL. A month later, after V-E Day, Meany made basically the same talk before the Chicago Federation of Labor, this time with considerable publicity. And in September Meany attacked the British unions to their face, at a convention in Blackpool, England, of the BTUC. Meany charged that the BTUC's friendship with the CIO had delayed American labor unity, and then hit at the Soviet unions as "instruments of the state . . . and of its ruling dictatorial political." Delegates shuffled their feet loudly in protest and some shouted "Shame! Shame!" as the chairman tried to restore order. (The Russian delegate demanded equal time to reply, but the British refused.)

The World Federation of Trade Unions proved to be exactly what the AFL had warned: an instrument of Soviet foreign policy, totally subser-

---

* Sierra Leone, Northern Rhodesia, Gambia, Cyprus, Jamaica, the Gold Coast, and British Guiana.

vient to Moscow. A French Communist labor leader, Louis Saillant, was elected secretary-general, and he dutifully followed directives of the Cominform (a resurrected successor to the old Comintern, the Communist International, which Stalin had disbanded during the war). Saillant's election made the CIO immediately suspicious of what it was getting into. James B. Carey, the CIO secretary-treasurer, called Saillant "an untrustworthy political bastard, not fit to serve in any capacity in the labor movement." Besides, Carey said, "he's pompous and walks like a pigeon in a park." John Brophy, another CIO official, refused to accept a WFTU vice-presidency. Brophy said he told CIO president Phil Murray that Saillant "was an agent of the Soviet delegation . . . whether he was a party member or not, I don't know; I could sense he was an agent of theirs, who would follow very vigorously the Soviet line they wanted." When Murray sent Brophy a letter ordering him to take the vice-presidency for one year, Brophy said he replied, "You might as well be in the Communist party as be in that sort of organization. I'm not going. Here's your damned letter, and that's the end of it."

The CIO was also offended by an attempt by Saillant, at an early WFTU council meeting in Moscow, to order its maritime unions to strike to support a WFTU blockade of Franco Spain. James Carey responded that not even the CIO, much less the WFTU, could call a strike by a constituent union, a decision entirely within the province of individual members. The matter died there. Despite all its doubts, however, the CIO stayed within the WFTU, attempting coexistence with the Soviets at the time of the cold war's deepest frost.

The AFL, during all these maneuverings, was conducting its foreign programs independent of any international organization. Lovestone put together a team of foreign specialists with varied talents and backgrounds.* His chief operative in Europe was Irving Brown, an intense, energetic man who had been a union organizer in Michigan before the war, and who first became associated with Lovestone in the Martin-Thomas contest for the UAW presidency. During the war Brown was a labor adviser to the War Production Board. In Germany, Lovestone relied upon Henry Rutz, a Socialist and university graduate who specialized in worker education while with the Milwaukee Typographical Union. Fluent in German, Rutz had gone to Europe initially with the American Military Government. In the Far East, the AFL recruited Richard L.-G. Deverall, another education specialist who had worked

* Formally, these representatives were associated variously with the AFL international affairs department, after its founding in 1947; with the ILGWU; and with the Free Trade Union Committee. All, however, answered to Lovestone, who in turn took his orders from Meany and, to lesser degrees, from Dubinsky and Matt Woll.

for the UAW and then as the founding secretary of the Detroit chapter of the Association of Catholic Trade Unionists. Immediately after the war Deverall served as a labor adviser to General Douglas MacArthur, helping re-establish unions in Japan. Serafino Romualdi, fresh from the OSS, took Latin America.

In France, which the AFL considered the most important battleground, Irving Brown found the Confédération Générale du Travail (the General Confederation of Labor, or CGT) under tacit Communist control. Because of their Resistance record, according to Brown, the Communists were able to appeal to the "masses as their only savior." Conversely, what survived of the old-line non-Communist CGT leadership carried the taint of collaboration with the Pétain government. To succeed in France, Brown would have to unseat a leadership accepted by the vast majority of workers.

Brown made a hurried survey of the available talent and decided to put the AFL's money (and prestige) behind an anti-Communist faction called Force Ouvrière, led by Robert Bethereau, a Resistance veteran who was willing to attempt to unite opposition forces. Even if Bethereau could not capture the CGT personally, he felt he could encourage Léon Jouhaux, an aging Socialist who had led the federation before the war, to slough off Communist ties and take the position. Brown's first strategy was to help the Force Ouvrière oust the Communists through direct vote at the CGT convention in April 1946. He failed miserably, because the Communists had so consolidated their strength that they ran the election machinery. So Brown changed his course. Next he set out to create a new labor central as an umbrella for non-Communist unions willing to leave the CGT.

Brown was not entirely happy about doing so, for "dual unionism" is a cardinal sin in the labor movement. In essence, he was doing with the French unions what the CIO had done in American labor, and he wrote Matthew Woll, "it is not a nice way of doing business." But Brown called the situation in France "desperate" and said "the stakes are high, and are worth the fight for free trade unionism." He asked that financing be discreet because he was "working with opposition rather than with official unions," and he wanted "neither the AFL nor the comrades in the CGT . . . [to] be open to justifiable criticism." One group Brown used as a front was the Jewish Labor Committee in New York, which acted as a conduit to get AFL money to the FO, ostensibly for Jewish relief, actually for organization. By late 1947 the AFL was committed to sending the FO $5,000 every three weeks. The ILGWU also made contributions.

By the account of one insider, Lovestone and Brown had another source of funding which, for security reasons, was never mentioned even in intra-AFL correspondence: the Central Intelligence Agency. According to Thomas W. Braden, who ran the CIA's division of international organization activities during the postwar years, the funding began in 1947, when the CGT "led a strike in Paris which came very near to paralyzing the French government. A takeover of the French government was feared." Lovestone and Brown chose this strike as an opportune time for the Force Ouvrière to break away from the CGT and form a new anti-Communist labor federation. But the crisis put them in an intolerable financial strain, one that couldn't be solved by either the AFL or the ILGWU.

According to Braden, "When they [Lovestone and Brown] ran out of money, they appealed to the CIA. Thus began the secret subsidy of free trade unions which soon spread to Italy. Without that subsidy, present history might have gone very differently." The CGT general strike, called to try to keep France from participating in the Marshall Plan, failed. But Brown did succeed in reducing CGT membership from six million to three million, 800,000 of whom affiliated with Force Ouvrière. Included were members of key transportation and communications unions, which the Communists had never been able to control.

"Braden is a damned liar," Meany retorted. "I didn't even know there was a CIA until 1955, when I met Allen Dulles. That was my first contact with it. If Irving Brown had been working for the CIA, he would not have been working for us the next day. I am dogmatic on this point. We use our own money—those are the orders. Certainly Brown might have exchanged information with the United States intelligence people. He's a citizen, he should do so, if it would help his country. But as far as us working for the CIA—it just never happened, period. And that is straight and the truth."

After managing to split the CGT, the AFL openly acknowledged its support of FO, and its reasons for doing so. In a 1951 speech to the Catholic Labor Alliance in Chicago, for instance, Meany said Force Ouvrière existed "primarily due to our efforts." He credited FO with preventing the Communists "from destroying the economic life of France and thereby opening up the gates of chaos and Communist revolution in that pivotal country." Meany was more explicit in a 1964 speech to the Bond Club of New York. "We played a major part in keeping the Communists from taking over [in France and Italy]," he said. "We financed a split in the Communist-controlled union in France. I say we financed this split—we paid for it. We sent them American trade union money; we set up their offices; we sent them supplies and everything else so we could weaken the Communist front."

AFL contributions to the Free Trade Union Committee were minuscule during these years, ranging from $6,200 in 1947 to a high of

$32,400 in 1949. The ILGWU paid Lovestone's salary (less than $15,000 a year) and office expenses, and many individual unions made contributions. But the labor funding did not begin to cover the "nearly two million dollars annually" that Thomas Braden estimated Lovestone was paying to non-Communist unions in France and Italy alone. The balance came from the CIA, both in ongoing, permanent subsidies and in cash for specific emergency projects. One souvenir Braden retained from his CIA days (he left the agency in 1954 to become a journalist) was a yellowing receipt, "Received from Warren G. Haskins, $15,000" and signed "Norris A. Grambo." Stated Braden: "I was Warren G. Haskins. Norris A. Grambo was Irving Brown. The $15,000 was from the vaults of the CIA. It was my idea to give the $15,000 to Irving Brown. He needed it to pay off his strong-arm squads in [French] Mediterranean ports, so that American supplies could be unloaded against the opposition of Communist dockworkers." The supplies, Braden noted, were Marshall Plan goods intended to save France from economic collapse.

CIA funds also went to the Far East, sometimes through intermediaries, sometimes directly through Richard Deverall, Lovestone's representative there. Deverall, who retired from the AFL after a near-fatal illness in the 1960's, talked candidly about the process. "Many times I was in Lovestone's office in New York, one of those he got from Dubinsky, and a man would come in with a stack of crisp new hundred-dollar bills. Lovestone would sign a receipt for them. Sometimes he would ask me to take money to Washington for him, if I happened to be going there within the next few days, and I would pass it on to whomever he directed. Most of it, however, went to support me in the field. I don't think Meany knew where Lovestone was getting the money. Of course, it's all pretty much common knowledge now, and I don't see anything wrong with it." Deverall said that when he first joined Lovestone's staff, he did not know the source of the new hundred-dollar bills but later "satisfied myself" they came from the CIA.

The problems the AFL found in Germany and Italy were considerably different from those in France, as were the end results of its efforts. In Italy, the AFL financed opposition to Giuseppe Di Vittorio, Communist president of the Confederazione Generale Italiana del Lavoro (the Italian General Federation of Labor, or CGIL). Brown was never able to put together a viable opposition, for under AFL policy he could not work with church-connected unions. Nonetheless, Meany asserted the splinter groups the AFL encouraged were "sufficiently strong to make it impossible for the Communists to inflict paralyzing general strikes on the Italian people." Critics claim the AFL left Italian labor so fragmented the nation's economy was endangered. They maintain a strong central labor federation would have helped Italy escape the political chaos that resulted in the succession of swinging-door governments since 1945.

The AFL's work in Germany was complicated by opposition—and naïveté, in Lovestone's opinion—on the part of the American Military Government. A Communist clique in the AMG's manpower division (headed by George Wheeler, who later defected to Czechoslovakia) tried to block formation of any trade unions the Communists could not control, and to make others subservient to the Soviet-influenced World Federation of Trade Unions. Henry Rutz and Irving Brown fought daily bureaucratic battles with the military; at one juncture, the AFL had to appeal all the way to Secretary of State James F. Byrnes to force the military to give the German unions some of the typewriters, autos, printing presses, and office equipment that had been seized from the Nazis. Rutz told the 1946 AFL convention that when U.S. occupation forces entered Germany they found anti-Nazi worker committees already formed and asking recognition. Most were trade unionists of pre-Hitler days, "the fortunate ones who had not been liquidated," as Rutz put it. Of one group of fourteen men Rutz met in Frankfort, eight had been in concentration camps. Yet Rutz and Brown had to work for nearly three years to persuade the military government that unions should be encouraged.

Under one military rule, union officials would have to be elected in single factories, from among workers actually on the job. The military government argued this procedure would make the new unions "completely democratic and representative of the actual work force." But as Brown noted in reports to Lovestone and Meany, no former union officials were working in the factories, for they had all been blacklisted by the Nazis; hence "the most experienced trade unionists" would be excluded. The rule, Brown said, would "give an advantage to Communists in gaining control of the local plant organizations." In the absence of experienced leadership and advice it would not be "difficult for a small Communist nucleus to take control." The Soviets, meanwhile, were busily organizing mass, party-run unions in their occupation sector. Lovestone, Woll, and Dubinsky made several trips to Germany to argue the issue with General Lucius D. Clay, head of U.S. occupation forces, who at most "considered the unions as a sort of necessary evil," in the words of a subsequent AFL report. Meany, meanwhile, did higher-level arguing in Washington, with President Harry Truman, Byrnes, and the War Department. Eventually the AFL obtained the working freedom it desired for the Germans.

The AFL's main objective in Germany was to persuade unions to band together in a single federation. In prewar Germany, Socialist, Catholic, and Protestant unions had separate federations. "If they had kept divided that way," Meany said, "the Communists would have walked all over them." Meany made two visits to Germany to advocate the single federation. When Joe Keenan reported that German labor officials could not function on the 1,100-calorie-per-day diet prescribed by occupation forces, Meany arranged for shipments of special CARE packages. The German unionists adopted the single federation concept, and also succeeded in establishing strong unions in the steel and coal industries. In doing so, Meany asserted, the unions "have weakened the hold of the Ruhr magnates and cartels on the economic life of Germany."

The World Federation of Trade Unions, meanwhile, continued to have problems. The CIO, at its 1949 convention, moved to eliminate eleven unions charged with being Communist-dominated, and organized new unions to replace them. Officials of the ousted unions, charged President Phil Murray, had followed a policy of "harassment, of opposition, and of obstructionism" in adherence to Communist programs, a "small but noisy clique" which the CIO did not need. The domestic purge coincided with a sudden shift to the right in the CIO's foreign policy, and a testier attitude toward "coexistence" with the Soviets. The climax came at a January 1949 meeting of the WFTU executive bureau. When CIO representatives tried to present arguments in favor of the Marshall Plan, they were heckled and booed by Louis Saillant, the WFTU head, and other Communist delegates. Giuseppe Di Vittorio, the Communist Italian labor chieftain, lashed out at both the CIO and the British, calling the Marshall Plan "a political and military pact which is being used to enslave a certain number of countries to the world domination of capitalist interests." Arthur Deakin, of the British Trades Union Congress, branded Di Vittorio's charges "completely repulsive to all those who give value to the truth." Two days later the CIO, the British, and the Dutch withdrew from the WFTU, claiming it was dominated by the Cominform, and citing a WFTU principle of noninterference by governments with affiliated labor federations.

Richard Deverall, who was watching the WFTU from the vantage point of the Far East, noted that although the WFTU split was "generally ascribed to the anti-Marshall Plan activities" of WFTU affiliates in Europe, "this is only a partial explanation." For the British, Dutch, and French, Deverall stated, the split related directly to a Communist-run youth conference that met in Calcutta, India, in January and February 1948 and "ordered guerrilla uprisings" throughout Asia and the Indian subcontinent. Deverall gave the following analysis in a subsequent report to Meany:

The French, the British, and the Dutch colonies (or semi-colonies) were at once affected; indeed, the richest source of dollars in the British Empire—Malaya—was stricken in June 1948 by a civil war which cut down the lush profits which Britain had exacted from the area. By the end of 1948 the new governments of Asia were not only bitter at the guerrilla activities of the Communists and their unions, but the British and other leading powers had apparently decided to break the WFTU before it broke them in Asia and Africa. During 1949, as Communist prestige dropped throughout Africa, the British and American trade union centers (and their governments) took the decisive steps splitting the WFTU in a transparent transfer of the cold war to the "labor front." The subsequent split of the WFTU . . . in 1949 and launching of the [ICFTU] marked a new development not only in trade union evolution but in the policies of the respective governments.

The International Confederation of Free Trade Unions (ICFTU) was the AFL's answer to the WFTU, after the CIO-British-Dutch breakaway of 1949. The AFL's independence in international affairs, while giving it freedom of action, at the same time posed many problems. The AFL wanted a way to give international legitimacy to the trade unions it was underwriting in Europe and elsewhere. The AFL wanted protective international coloration for some of the solely American activities it was conducting abroad. Finally, the AFL wanted a world-wide labor group with which to wage propaganda battle with the now-avowedly Communist WFTU.

In the spring of 1949 the AFL began talks with Vincent Tewson and Arthur Deakin, leaders of the British Trades Union Congress, about forming a new international federation. Tewson and Deakin demanded one condition that the AFL initially would not swallow: the CIO must be a full partner in any new group. Green especially was unhappy at this demand. But after a series of meetings with the British and CIO leaders the AFL slowly changed its position. The CIO's vigorous purge of Communist-tainted unions, then being completed, was one factor, for it convinced the AFL the CIO "had sobered up" on the Soviet issue, as one AFL man put it. The United States government exerted its own pressures. It needed labor support in implementing the foreign aid program, and close liaison with foreign unions was essential.

Meany went to Europe twice in 1949 for conferences which created the International Confederation of Free Trade Unions—to Geneva, in June, for a preliminary meeting; then to London, in late November and early December, for the formal constitutional session. He succeeded in putting across the AFL's major bargaining point: the ICFTU should not be the creature of any single nation; its headquarters should be in a small country; and the top officers should not be citizens of a "great power" nation. (Although the AFL trusted the then-British leadership, it did not wish to risk a repetition of the WFTU experience.) A Dutch railway union official, J. H. Oldenbroek, was elected the first general secretary, and headquarters were set up in Brussels.

The stated purpose of the ICFTU, as expressed in an AFL executive council paper, was to "coordinate and assist on a world scale the efforts of the working people of all lands to protect and promote their economic interests, social security and well-being." Further, the AFL stated, "Through devotion to democratic ideals and the mighty cohesive force of international labor solidarity, the ICFTU can play the decisive role in fostering and preserving world peace." Richard Deverall used more candid language in describing ICFTU goals, in a paper written after he had served on its staff for several years as an AFL representative. From its very founding, Deverall stated in an analysis written for Meany:

> The British government has financed in one way or another
> —or let the Americans finance—the activities of the ICFTU in
> order to (a) use ICFTU unions to choke off rebellious Communist
> and/or vigorously national unions in the colonies; and (b) develop
> ICFTU unions in areas where they did not exist in order to divert
> nationalist aspirations into activities which were non-political.
>
> I have found British sources frank in noting that ICFTU unions
> are "useful" in diverting the attention of many persons to internal
> struggles on the economic front and the suppressing for a longer
> period the development of nationalist demands for independence
> and freedom.*

In a speech in May 1945 Meany declared that the workers of America, through the AFL, "have earned the right, both before and during the war, to examine with a critical eye any actions that are taken or contemplated by our government in an effort to insure this nation and all peace-loving nations against the diabolical destruction of modern war." The labor-government relationship during the cold war years was symbiotic. Labor supported the over-all foreign policy of the Truman Administration—containment of Soviet expansion; the democratization of Germany; an activist United States role in the United Nations; the foreign aid program, first as a relief operation, then as a vast economic rebuilding plan. Government, in turn, ensured that AFL men had seats on advisory committees throughout the executive branch, and that labor had veto power over selection of labor attachés detailed to United States embassies. In the latter instance, the Truman Administration had to please both Lovestone and Michael Ross, the head of international affairs for

---

* For other reasons, the AFL was never entirely happy with the ICFTU, and later withdrew, first from its substantive programs, then from membership altogether. See Chapter XII, "Meany versus Reuther: Round One."

the CIO. But Lovestone was so confident of his ability to name attachés that when one of his foreign operatives complained he was ready to leave AFL service, Lovestone promptly told him, "Would you consider working in the State Department in the North African section? If you are interested, let me know and I will begin to push the thing."

Meany's special interest was the foreign aid program. Secretary of State George C. Marshall, in his famed June 1947 Harvard speech, called for U.S. financing of European recovery. President Truman named Averell Harriman, then the Secretary of Commerce, to head an advisory committee to translate Marshall's idea into a practical plan. Harriman had met Meany in Albany during the New Deal when he was a deputy regional administrator for the National Recovery Administration. Harriman asked Meany to serve on the council, with the specific task of recommending how labor foreign activities could be worked into the aid program. Meany and James Carey, on the council for the CIO, proposed a labor section for the program, to give technical assistance to European unions. Harriman bought their idea, which was included in the Marshall Plan legislation when it went to Congress. Meany and other AFL officers stumped the country for the remainder of 1947, asking labor and public support for the Marshall Plan.

"We know that the program will cost us billions of dollars," Meany said. "We know that it means postponing the day when there will be sufficient goods to satisfy all the demands of our own people—that it means continued high taxes on our wages; that it means further pressure on the already high cost of living here in America." But unless France, Italy, and other non-Communist countries received help, he said, "they will fall into the Russian basket. Nothing helps the Communist cause more effectively than hunger and misery and economic chaos." After spending four hundred billion dollars to win World War II, Meany asked, "would it not be bitterly stupid to throw away the victory, because we refused to spend five percent more? . . . If we do nothing, if we make the tragic choice of saving some money and letting Western Europe work out its own salvation unaided by America, it is but a matter of time . . . before we will find a new neighbor on the Atlantic shore— Joseph Stalin's brutal, Fascist dictatorship."

When Harriman went to Paris to run overseas operations of the Economic Cooperation Administration (first of the many names for the agency conducting the aid program) he asked both the AFL and CIO to put labor representatives into his office. Boris Shishkin went for the AFL; Clint Golden, of the United Steel Workers, for the CIO. Thereafter American labor had both policy and operational roles in the aid program.

Critics of AFL programs in France, Germany, and elsewhere have questioned the "legitimacy" of American union leaders deciding, on their own initiative, whether a foreign union was "good" or "bad," and should be supported or crushed. Sidney Lens, for instance, noted David Dubinsky's claim that "had it not been for the extensive educational activities of the Free Trade Union Committee . . . the Communists . . . might by now [1949] have seized control of the reviving trade unions." Lens agreed such an outcome "might have been unfortunate," but he commented, "it is odd that Dubinsky never asked himself whether the German workers had a right to make their own choice without 'educational activities' from the outside. Had the help been given to *all* union leaders, or even to all non-Communist leaders, it is possible that a different movement might have evolved." And, as Henry W. Berger wrote, AFL involvement in the labor affairs of other nations "paralleled the very practices of the Communists that the AFL daily condemned." The Swedish Federation of Labor complained in 1955 that "Brown's maniac anti-Communist attitude is a valuable asset to communism. When it comes to a consistent and effective fight against the dictatorship ideology of communism, Irving Brown has nothing at all to teach—and everything to learn from others." The Socialist unionists of Europe, once the immediate dangers of Soviet expansion waned, wanted a relaxation of tensions. The AFL policy, as expressed by Meany and executed by Lovestone, however, was consistent: So long as the Soviet Union has no free labor movement, American labor cannot be a friend of Moscow.

Lovestone commanded loyalty of his field subordinates by ensuring that anyone he hired shared his hard-line views. Yet persons who watched world labor at first hand—rather than from offices in Washington and New York, as did Lovestone—did not always share Lovestone's certitude about AFL policy. Richard Deverall, who frequently disagreed with Lovestone, complained at length of the labor attaché system the AFL helped develop after the war. Both U.S. and British attachés, he wrote, "generally act as if they are branch offices" of the International Confederation of Free Trade Unions. Although the attachés conducted "legitimate labor information activities," Deverall stated their work was marked also by "(a) the use of a trade union card . . . in order to secure information which would normally be regarded as the fruit of espionage; (b) the use of trade union member attachés and/or government funds in supporting or even buying up trade union centers so that they follow policies formulated not by trade unions but by a government . . . and (c) . . . in selling government policy and finding it impossible or difficult to represent an independent trade union point of view." According to Deverall, "Classic examples of such activities can be found in . . . Japan, where corrupt elements within the right-wing labor movement are given trips to America purely because they express pro-

American sentiments to the labor attachés; or in the Philippines, where the U. S. Embassy has from the beginning supported a strange collection of gangsters, gamblers and parasites in the [Philippine central labor federation] because they can be controlled and are subordinate to British-American policies. . . ."

The foreign policy goals of the AFL, however, were pragmatic; if fostering anti-Communist unions required collaborating with conservative —even reactionary—allies, so be it. Meany maintained that the stakes were too high to gamble on foreign labor leaders who "might" be able to work successfully with the Soviets. Time and again Meany responded to critics by pointing to Czechoslovakia, where the Communist coup of 1948 had as a key element control of the labor movement. "They [the Communists] don't turn the members into Communists," Meany stated. "They get the machinery, that is all they want. They had less than fifteen percent in the Parliament; they did not have a newspaper; they did not own any industries. But they got control of the trade union movement in a country where freedom is valued as high as in this country." Meany continued: "They tied up the city of Prague for twenty-four hours. No telephone, no bus, no radio, no hospital service, no milk, no mail service or anything else. Then they went to the politicians in charge and they said, 'Have we proved that we have the workers of this city with us—that we control the workers?' They wanted in and they got in. They only wanted one position, minister of internal security. . . . Within seven days they had the entire country. Masaryk and Beneš were dead. . . ."

Green never interfered with Meany's foreign work. Meany abided by strict bureaucratic protocol. He reported fully to Green on activities of the Free Trade Union Committee. He ensured that Green had right of first refusal on appointments to labor advisory committees in the State Department and other agencies. He sent draft copies of resolutions and other material to Green in advance of executive council meetings. But foreign affairs was one field in which Green was content to let Meany have his head. Judging from accounts of contemporaries, Green did not think foreign work was all that important. He felt that once the war ended Meany's interests would return to more traditional trade union channels. In the 1940's, then well into his seventies, Green may have been too tired to care. And George Meany's occupancy of the field was so all-encompassing there really was not room for anyone else. Hence international activities stands as the first AFL program that bore the exclusive brand of George Meany.

# VII

## Outscowling John L. Lewis

T HE POSTWAR PERIOD held all the ingredients of disaster for American labor. Both business and the unions came out of the war in feistily belligerent moods, sleeves rolled up to resume the organizational and other conflicts that the national emergency had thrust into limbo. The wartime "harmony" of the AFL and the CIO rapidly dissolved, to be replaced by a hopelessly convoluted series of Machiavellian, back-stabbing plots that pitted unionist against bitter unionist. Caught in the economic backlash of seemingly endless "labor troubles," the press's catchword, the public increasingly blamed unions for denying it the expected comforts of peace. Several times during 1946 more than 2,000,000 workers were on strike simultaneously. Disputes cost some 116,000,000 workdays, compared with only 8,721,079 in 1944—three times as many as in any other year in history, even during the turbulence of industrial organization during the 1930's. Congress transformed public disgust into punitive legislation, reversing a decade-long trend of public policy encouraging unionization. And the strife started a chain reaction that in the end gave two major boosts to George Meany's career: the final crushing of John L. Lewis, establishing Meany as *de facto* leader of the AFL (although he was to wait five more years for the mantle of the presidency); and the serious entry of the AFL into national politics, under Meany's guidance.

The AFL's overriding concern, as the war drew to a close, was maintaining the high earnings made possible by the premium overtime pay and full employment of defense work. Meany's deep involvement in pay issues on the War Labor Board made him the logical spokesman for the AFL on reconversion problems, and he developed the federation's stand in a loose series of speeches beginning in the fall of 1944. Meany wanted pay hikes before the war ended so that workers would not suffer when defense spending subsided. The increased wages, he said, would maintain the purchasing power essential for a full-employment, full-production economy. As he declared in November 1944, "Increased purchasing power in the hands of the consumer is a good thing for the manufacturer, the merchant, and the banker, just as it is a good thing for the workingman." In other speeches he asked, variously, for the thirty-hour week and increased unemployment compensation to help absorb returning veterans into the job market. Meany would not accept the business assumption (as stated by a National Association of Manufacturers' spokesman during a 1945 radio debate) that a full year would be required to restore full peacetime employment. "I think a national thirty-day week may be the thing to carry us over that," Meany retorted. "You may not be allowed a year by the unemployed to work this problem out."

The unions, in sum, were primed to regain the economic ground they felt workers had sacrificed during four years of restraint under the no-strike pledge and the Little Steel Formula. Labor served notice, through statements of both the AFL and the CIO, that it thought wartime controls had discriminated against workers, and that it intended to obtain not only a larger share of the expected postwar prosperity, but also compensation for alleged past deprivations as well. Not that labor was impecunious: the increase in weekly earnings, the full employment of wartime, and the scarcity of consumer goods forced Americans to build an unprecedently hefty nest egg of $136.4 billion in savings and government bonds at the end of 1945—money that citizens were eager to spend. But as labor economist Florence Peterson noted, the end of the war threatened to make this prosperity transitory: "With the elimination of overtime in night shifts, and the downgrading from high-wage war jobs, workers experienced substantial reductions in their take-home pay, although prices and costs of living were rapidly rising."

Meany also wanted labor brought out from under government controls as peace came. Bolder now as William Green grew older, he succeeded in overriding Green in setting AFL strategy for the postwar period. Green came to the August 10, 1945, executive council meeting with a draft statement to be issued upon the imminent Japanese surrender. It contained a no-strike pledge for six months after the end of the war. William Hutcheson of the Carpenters Union objected, saying, "We have been anxiously awaiting the time when we could get back to our old system of contractual relations with the employer. . . ." Meany agreed, saying he was "unalterably opposed to a no-strike pledge." Making one, Meany said, "would not represent our entire membership. We have been begging the War Labor Board and the President to prepare for this very day and we have been ignored from the start on this question." As a trade unionist, Meany wanted the WLB abolished as soon as possible; he was willing to rely upon collective bargaining to protect workers. "A group of men [is] sitting there trying to find ways and means of carrying these controls over into peacetime, and if we give them a no-strike pledge, we will have them trying to get legislation to make it law," he said. The council deleted the pledge. So far as labor was concerned, the no-strike pledge ended with the war.

Business, meanwhile, saw postwar conversion as an opportune time to brake union activity. One factor was an anticipated high unemployment rate as the armed forces mustered out the twelve-odd million men still in uniform on V-J Day. The Truman Administration, a few days after the fighting stopped, estimated eight million jobless by the spring (a fear that never materialized; the highest unemployment level in the year ending August 1946 was slightly more than three million persons). Reinforcing business' hard-line attitude were the so-called "carry-back" provisions of the tax laws that permitted corporations that lost money after the war to get returns on earlier excess profits taxes. In fact, commented *Fortune* magazine, tax and other circumstances made "strikes fairly cheap, in the short-range view, for some corporations." *Fortune* continued:

> The excess profits tax was in force until December 31, 1945; in the first eight months of the year the big war contractors had already made about as much money as they could hope to clear for the whole year; in some cases it was actually more profitable, in terms of the 1945 balance sheet, to shut down toward the end of the year rather than pay higher wages in advance of price relief.

The National Association of Manufacturers in late 1945 meetings pledged a to-the-finish fight against "excessive" labor demands, even if lengthy strikes resulted. An NAM group also began planning legislation that would blunt the organizational weapons given labor by the Wagner Act of a decade before. Accentuating management uneasiness were innovative demands by labor: Walter Reuther of the United Auto Workers, for instance, wanted access to corporate books to determine "ability to pay." And Communist infiltration in the CIO raised the specter of labor taking the wrong side in the Cold War.

The first wave of strikes began in the fall of 1945 and by New Year's Day more than 900,000 workers were on picket lines: 175,000 of Walter Reuther's autoworkers, followed shortly by 700,000 steelworkers; 263,000 packing-house workers; 200,000 electrical workers; 50,000 phone company workers. The strikes were endurance contests, not slugging matches, and they lacked the violence of earlier critical labor disputes. But as labor historian Foster Rhea Dulles noted, as strike piled upon strike, "the tremendous implications of the nationwide organization of industrial workers that had taken place since 1933 were borne home with dramatic force. Here was an entirely new challenge to the national economy. It was not the threat of violence, sabotage, industrial warfare in the old sense, but of a paralysis of economic life through peaceful but far more effective work-stoppages on a nationwide scale."

The vast majority of these strikes involved CIO unions, whose leaders had considerable trouble retaining loyalty of the rank-and-file members. The United Auto Workers, for example, had to strike 113 days before winning an 18½ cent raise from General Motors. The AFL leadership, concurrently, was boasting loudly that during the first six months after the war its affiliates secured pay increases ranging from ten to twenty-plus percent for 2,500,000 workers (one third of its membership), with only about 100,000 members forced to strike. James Y. Newton wrote in the Washington *Star,* "It is no secret that many CIO rank-and-file members as well as lesser leaders are wondering why they should have to pay so high a price to gain reasonable wage settlements." With strikes raging in four major industries in the autumn of 1945, the CIO struggled for its very existence, with strike benefit funds exhausted and fratricidal fights among leaders of key unions.

It was an appropriate time for the AFL and John L. Lewis to resume their friendship with the unabashed intention of cutting the CIO's throat by luring away disaffected unions. Despite his wartime troubles, Lewis' name remained synonymous with militant, effective leadership with hordes of rank-and-file members, especially in the CIO. Indeed, during the GM strike, several UAW locals petitioned Lewis to take them into the UMWA. And despite their many harsh exchanges since 1938, Lewis and most of the AFL leadership were on common ground in wanting labor unity. Not all trusted Lewis; Meany, for one, would have preferred to work around him. But a majority on the AFL executive council felt that if Lewis came back into the AFL, most of the CIO unions would rapidly follow, regardless of the CIO leaders' wishes. By November 1945 the AFL, through executive council members, had made more or less serious feelers on reaffiliation to the United Auto Workers, the United Steel Workers, and the rubber workers, collectively about two million members, roughly one third the CIO strength. Lewis and Bill Green tossed hints to one another for months that rapprochement was in order. "As concentrated capital is the chief asset of the corporations," Green said, "united economic strength is the chief asset of the workers of the nation." And Lewis wrote in *Collier's,* "There is no labor movement. Labor's temple is a Tower of Babel. Instead of a single authoritative voice, we have a confusion of tongues." Roosevelt's death gave Lewis a face-saving opening: he had always blamed the split on "politicians [who] continue disunity by a persistent intensification of interlabor differences." Now that Roosevelt was gone, Lewis could say, as he did, that he and the AFL could start with a fresh slate. And that they did, with Lewis rejoining the AFL (and the executive council) in January 1946, with freshets of praise to and from all parties involved.

Lewis came back as a victor, too. The AFL backed away from its earlier condition that he agree to curb organizational work of the UMWA's catch-all District 50 that conflicted with AFL unions. Instead, jurisdictional claims were to be settled "subject to ordinary AFL procedures," which meant talk but no decisions. To Green's irritation much of the press speculated that Lewis would soon accede to the presidency. He called these stories "false, without any foundation whatever," and declared, in words he was to repeat frequently during the next eighteen months as the shadow of John L. Lewis loomed ever larger over his rounded shoulders, "I am going to continue as president of the AFL." But Lewis never got around to his primary mission of bringing CIO unions back into the AFL family. No sooner had he settled into his executive council chair than his miners were in angry confrontation with President Truman. This Lewis strike, and an overlapping dispute involving two rail unions, were the final exasperation for a strike-weary nation. As President Truman wrote in his memoirs, these conflicts "eclipsed all preceding ones in their direct effect on the public." In the rail case, eighteen of the twenty railroad brotherhood unions accepted an arbitrator's recommended settlement, but Truman had to threaten to draft members of the remaining unions into the armed forces to keep the trains moving. Public opinion solidly supported the President. The coal strike followed the classic John L. Lewis pattern: bombastic, insulting rhetoric ("Truman doubts the legality of our demands? What does Truman know about legality?"); walkouts ended by government seizure (in this instance, after forty days); supposed settlement, then sudden renewal. This time, however, Lewis overreached himself, with both the President and the public. During the strike the nation exhausted its coal stockpiles in a month, forcing closing of factories, curtailing of trains and "dimouts" and "brownouts" to conserve fuel. Truman forced a settlement in May by seizing the mines. In November, however, Lewis claimed a technical violation of his contract, and took his miners out again, for the eighth time in five years. The thoroughly angered Truman had government attorneys obtain an injunction ordering the miners back to work. When Lewis flouted it, the judge fined the United Mine Workers of America $3,500,000* and Lewis $10,000 personally.

If only a few reactionary business elements opposed unions in prin-

---

* An appeals court reduced the UMWA fine to $700,000 when the miners returned to work.

ciple, nonetheless the American people felt—as the hostile newspapers constantly told them—that labor power had outstepped labor responsibility. Lost in the turmoil over "labor strife" were some rather basic economic figures. According to government studies, industry could have increased wages by twenty-four percent immediately after the war and still earned profits far beyond the prewar rates. During 1946, corporate profits hit $12.5 billion—their highest point in history, and twenty percent above the best boom year of the war. Throughout late 1945 and 1946 Truman tried desperately to coax meaningful wage and price controls from Congress. He did not succeed. The demise of the Office of Price Administration in the spring of 1946 sent prices soaring. The index on basic commodities was up twenty-five percent in two weeks; milk went from sixteen to twenty cents a quart; veal cutlets, when they could be found, from fifty to ninety-five cents a pound.

Black markets for scarce items such as autos, beef, and nylons; rent gougers for scarce housing, shortages of autos and other consumer goods; strike after strike after strike—America's economic problems were many, and aggravating. Four front-page headlines for the January 22, 1945, New York *Times* show the stuff of which public opinion was shaped during these trying months:

**FRENZIED DEMAND FOR NEW CARS SWAMPS KAISER EXHIBITION HERE**
**CITY FACES MILK SUPPLY CUT AS STEEL STRIKE OFFSHOOT**
**CONSIDER SEIZURE OF PACKING PLANTS**
**SNYDER\* ASKS ACTION TO BAR AN "ECONOMIC PEARL HARBOR"**

By election time 1946 the country's mood was sour—toward labor, toward the Truman Administration, toward any identifiable person or institution that disturbed the anticipated but unfound comforts of peacetime. The Republicans lumped America's discontent into a two-word slogan, "Had Enough?" and won control of both houses of Congress for the first time since 1930.

Austere; pedantic; publicly snippish with senatorial inferiors, supposed or otherwise ("I think the Senator is talking tommyrot!"); "driven by the gnawings of a masochistic Puritan conscience" (in Richard Rovere's phrase), Robert A. Taft was the Senate's foremost exponent of conservatism almost from the day he took his seat there in 1939. In 1947, as Senate Majority Leader, he finally got a chance to do something positive for his business friends. He put his full prestige behind the Taft-Hartley Act (coauthored with Representative Fred Hartley, a New

\* John W. Snyder, Truman economic adviser.

Jersey Republican) and said, with an unsmiling face, that its reasons "may be simply stated: to restore justice and equality in labor relations; to correct the abuses of discretion and procedure of the National Labor Relations Board; and to eliminate special privileges conferred on labor union officials by law and administrative regulation." Just as somberly, he also consistently denied he was motivated by "any hysteria or because of any prejudice against unions." Perhaps not, but to labor, the Taft-Hartley Act was a declaration of war.

The draft of the bill was so ponderously complicated that few union leaders, much less laymen, understood it fully. The act was to provide a full generation of work for battalions of government bureaucrats and labor law specialists. The act's main thrust was to bar a host of "unfair labor practices" by unions, just as its proponents said the Wagner Act had barred "unfair" practices of management. Included were the closed shop, jurisdictional strikes, and secondary boycotts.* It restored the use of the injunction to stop strikes, although only on motion of the government, not employers. It permitted wide government intervention in union affairs on the theory (repugnant to labor leaders) that rank-and-file members needed protection from their officers as much as from employers. It required unions to file their constitutions, bylaws, and extensive financial reports with the Secretary of Labor. Each officer of a national or international union was compelled to file an affidavit he was not a member of or in sympathy with any Communist organization. It prohibited labor groups from making any contributions or expenditures in connection with national elections or primaries. On and on rolled the act, for page after restrictive page, an amalgam, in its final form, of more than one hundred antilabor bills that eager conservatives added to the original Taft-Hartley version.

The AFL cranked up the most vigorous lobbying campaign in its half-century history to attempt to defeat Taft-Hartley in Congress. It assessed each member fifteen cents to raise a war chest of almost one million dollars to finance radio and newspaper advertisements. A fifteen-minute denunciation of Taft-Hartley was aired twice weekly for six weeks over 635 radio stations. And Meany's increasing stature in the AFL was reflected in his designation as chief spokesman in the campaign.

Meany's rhetoric was blistering, against both the Republican party and the businessmen supporting the legislation. Speaking to a labor rally in Madison Square Garden in June, he called Taft-Hartley "only one phase of an all-out war against the common people of America. Just as Hitler struck down labor unions as one of the first steps in his plan to enslave the people of Germany, so today we see the profit-greedy indus-

---

* In simplest form, a secondary boycott occurs when a union that is striking Company A persuades other unions to strike Company B with which Company A does business.

trialists here attempting to destroy workers' organizations as the first step in their plan to control the economic life of America." And from the New York State Federation of Labor the next month he drew standing applause when he declared: "To those employers who feel that the Taft-Hartley law is going to enable them to dictate at will the terms and conditions of employment without regard to the welfare and desires of their employees, we say 'Come on, let's go—if you want industrial warfare, we accept the challenge.' " Meany repeatedly denied that the Republican win of Congress "constituted a mandate to clamp handcuffs and a strait-jacket on the American wage earner." Instead, he said, it was a "mandate to eliminate bureaucracy . . . a protest against high prices and administrative failures in price control . . . a protest against the very bureaucracy and regimentation that this legislation would bring about." And he warned the Republicans that passage of the bill would force the AFL into Congressional politics:

> The American wage earner has been told over and over again down through the years that the Republican party was the party of privilege, or profit, the party of Wall Street and the big corporations. The American worker has hesitated to believe these charges because he was convinced that this was the one country in the world where the class struggle could not be a national political issue. But when we scrutinize the origin of this vicious antilabor proposal, when we hear the paid spokesmen for big business strongly urging its passage on the air, when we see the large corporations using the power that comes with a swollen treasury proposing its restrictions through full-page advertisements in our daily press, when we see and hear all these things and then in addition hear the official spokesmen from the Republican membership in the House of Representatives, not only endorsing this bill but boasting of their ability to enact it into law, we wonder if the class struggle is about to shift from the economic to the political field.
>
> For nearly three quarters of a century, the AFL has maintained itself as a strictly nonpartisan organization representing workers as workers, not as pawns in a political game. I am sure that our organization desires to continue as such. In the face of the political aspects of this proposal to destroy trade unionism, the question arises as to whether or not we will be compelled by force of circumstances to revise our basic position in order to protect the future of the wage earners of our country who in themselves constitute the vast national wealth of which Americans so often boast.

Again, in speeches over the ABC, CBS, and NBC radio networks in April and May, Meany challenged the Republicans to prove their claim of a "mandate" to move against labor. The CIO waged an equally bitter fight, Philip Murray castigating Taft-Hartley as a bill "conceived in sin," and calling its promoters "diabolical men who, seething with hatred, designed . . . this ugly measure for the purpose of imposing their wrath upon the millions of organized and unorganized workers throughout the United States."

Labor lost. Taft-Hartley passed both houses overwhelmingly. President Truman vetoed the act, saying it would "contribute neither to industrial peace nor to economic stability and progress," and that it contained "seeds of discord which would plague this nation for years to come." But Congress would not be swayed. It swiftly overrode his veto, and Taft-Hartley became law.

In a speech to the California State Federation of Labor in August, shortly after passage of Taft-Hartley, Meany once more attacked the act, but acknowledged defeat and pledged compliance with it as the law of the land. But obedience to the law, Meany said, did not diminish labor's right to continue to fight for justice, a right not abridged by the passage of an unfair and unjust law.

The AFL's immediate problem was the anti-Communist affidavit required of union officers by Taft-Hartley. Soon after passage of Taft-Hartley, Robert N. Denham, general counsel of the National Labor Relations Board, ruled the affidavits would be required not only of union officers, but also of officers of federations with which the unions were affiliated. If the chain of affidavits was broken at any point, even by a single officer, from union local to national federation, none of the affiliated organizations could use NLRB machinery in representation elections or in pressing unfair labor practice cases against employers. Denham's ruling, in effect, gave any one of the fifteen AFL officers—Green, Meany, and the thirteen vice-presidents who comprised the executive council—a veto power affecting the entire federation. And John L. Lewis chose to exercise his veto, to the dismay of much of the federation hierarchy.

The majority of the AFL executive council, by this point, looked at Lewis through eyes glazed by both fear and awe. Lewis made no secret of his ambition to succeed Green and unify all of American labor into the AFL. Given a choice, few wanted Lewis as president. But as Victor Riesel, the labor journalist, wrote in mid-1947, many of the AFL leaders "are frightened men who see their own organizations being undermined by legislative curbs. They fear self-destruction as a result of civil war in their own ranks. They hear the bell tolling for them in a future depression. So they turn to Lewis to do for them, with his phrase-making and ability to outmaneuver his enemies, what he has done for the miners." At one point, in late 1946, the Meany council members privately agreed that Lewis should replace Green, although no formal vote was taken. Green, however, would not agree to step aside voluntarily, saying he intended to stay in office as long as his health permitted. When the executive council approved a pension plan permitting officers to retire at age sixty-five (Green by then was seventy-three) a journalist asked Green if this would clear the way for Lewis' succession. Visibly annoyed, Green replied, "As far as I know it's fantastic. Somebody's dream."

Unfortunately for his ambitions, Lewis never won over Dan Tobin of the Teamsters. Tobin distrusted Lewis to the point of obsession; he detested him as "erratic" and "egomanic"; the "rule of chaos" was one of the kinder phrases Tobin used about Lewis. Tobin feared Lewis wanted control of the AFL not to benefit workers, but to use as a battering ram against his many enemies. Tobin felt Lewis' long-nourished political ambitions still retained a flicker of life. In one private conversation during 1947 Tobin remarked, "Sure, John wants to be president, but not only of the AFL. John has bigger things in mind, and he'll rub our asses in the mud to get them." Finally, Tobin never fully forgave Lewis for starting the CIO. For Meany's purposes, Tobin's opposition was important because the craggy old teamster, representing more than a tenth of the AFL strength, could veto Lewis' election as president. Meany shared Tobin's distaste for Lewis, and he said at one point during the period, "If he goes in, I go back to New York. I'd rather be a plumber than a member of any circus that John Lewis ran." And Lewis' behavior within the council (James Wechsler once wrote he "inspires physical fear as well as mental servility in those around him") caused second thoughts among his supporters almost every time he spoke. During a jurisdictional hearing before the council, Tobin called Walter Cenerazzo, the Watch Workers Union president, a "secessionist" because he formerly was with the Jewelry Workers Union, the other party to the dispute. Cenerazzo replied that if he was a secessionist, Lewis also deserved the name, because he had been in and out of the AFL. Lewis arose with a growl, clutched his lapels with both hands, and boomed across the room, "How old are you, son?" "Thirty-seven," replied the stocky, muscular Cenerazzo. "I would have no reluctance in crossing that table and belting you one," said the sixty-seven-year-old Lewis.

The Taft-Hartley Communist disclaimer oath gave Tobin and Meany an issue through which they could force the council to take a formal stand on Lewis. The council members, if anything, were even more anti-Communist than the Republican congressmen who drafted the oath. Publicly, they groused about the oath as a "matter of principle," for no similar requirement was imposed on management. Labor objected that union officers were being unfairly singled out as potentially "un-

American." In private, however, they were more pragmatic, for they thought the oath would hamstring CIO unions with Communists and sympathizers in their upper ranks. Tobin publicly directed all Teamster officials to sign the oath. "We are pleased to have the government take this stand now. But it is our opinion the government is too late; the Communists are already entrenched in some unions." And when the executive council gathered at the Drake Hotel in Chicago in September 1947 Green confidently predicted members would grudgingly sign the oath.

Lewis rebelled. He railed against the oath, and called other council members "cowards and weaklings" for even considering signing it. He said he was convinced that foes of labor had thrown down the gauntlet to the unions, and that the challenge must be met. Labor could not acquiesce to Taft-Hartley and fight Taft-Hartley at the same time; signing the oath, he said, meant surrender of bargaining ground. When a council member said weaker unions might suffer in a protracted fight, Lewis stormed, "Let the weak fall. Do you think you can fight a battle against this slave law without some casualties? If you do, you are crazy." Unions had stored away funds in their treasuries for use on a rainy day, Lewis said, "and now the deluge has arrived." He said Taft-Hartley, and the oath, "make second-class citizens out of every man around the council table" and every man he represented. Lewis began the battle in the council singlehandedly; by the end of the first day he had the support of William Hutcheson of the Carpenters. (Hutcheson was in one of his recurring sulks over a jurisdictional dispute, this time with a council decision giving the stagehands union control over jobs he claimed for the carpenters.) The council ultimately decided to defer the question until its September convention in San Francisco, because of reports the full NLRB intended to overrule counsel Denham's ruling. In intervening weeks the AFL metal trades and building trades departments, representing half the AFL membership, called upon Lewis to sign, saying "cool judgment and wise action should dictate our course, and not our emotions"; Tobin said that unless Lewis yielded, "apparently there is no answer except that we [the Teamsters] withdraw from the AFL"; a host of smaller unions also talked of withdrawing; and Lewis leaked a claim of "overwhelming support of the AFL convention" in his opposition to the oath.

On the eve of the convention the NLRB partially yielded, saying that nonsigning by federation officers would not affect affiliated unions. However, because the AFL contained some 1,300 "federal unions" (that is, local unions it chartered directly, rather than through affiliated national or international unions), AFL officials still had to sign the oath. The ruling represented a partial victory for Lewis, for it showed that the

NLRB could be pressured. Federation officers still faced the dilemma of whether they should sign to protect the federal unions.

Meany and Tobin, after several talks in Washington, decided upon an open-ended strategy towards Lewis. In hopes of keeping him within the AFL, they looked for a means of giving him a face-saving way of backing away from a confrontation with the executive council. But if Lewis refused a compromise, they intended to force a showdown with him at the convention. They reasoned that Lewis "would keep pushing" until other federation officers completely capitulated to him—as had happened in the United Mine Workers—and he could run the AFL as a personal fiefdom. Lewis' flouting of majority decisions by the council offended their sense of order. So, too, did Lewis' arrogance. "It is unsafe to criticize the UMWA," Lewis had stormed at one council meeting. "It is unsafe to criticize the president of the UMWA." Meany set about mapping a strategy to follow in dealing with Lewis.

First Lovestone tried to interest Lewis in a compromise plan that would have kept the fight off the convention floor. The AFL would sign the oath, but under public protest, and vow to challenge its legality in the courts. "The main AFL delegation was at the Saint Francis Hotel," recalled Lovestone. "Not Lewis. He was too egomaniacal, too conceited, to associate with other union leaders, so he stayed at the Palace, which was considerably more ostentatious, and hence to John's liking." Lovestone outlined the compromise to Lewis. "I had every reason to think he was going to accept. He kept saying, 'That looks all right, that makes sense, I could buy it.' But he did not say specifically he *would* accept it." At the Commonwealth Club the Friday night of the convention Lewis made remarks on the oath so ambiguous that Lovestone said, "I knew that was the swan song." Lovestone passed on a warning to Meany that he had best ready himself for battle.

The showdown came on a resolution from the executive council (approved over Lewis' objections) amending the AFL constitution to strip the title of vice-president from council members, leaving the president and secretary-treasurer as the only persons required to sign the oath. Meany, Tobin, and Green knew they had enough votes for overwhelming approval of the compromise; however, Lewis kept his own counsel, and would tell no one whether he intended to fight it on the floor. After it was read, Thomas Kennedy, a UMWA vice-president, made a relatively mild opposing speech, complaining that engineers, doctors, and lawyers were not required to file similar disclaimers. So, too, did Anthony Turco, of the minute Seattle newsboys' union.

Green asked if anyone else cared to speak. All eyes in the hall swung to Lewis, who sat impassively amidst the miners' delegation. Green repeated his call twice more; just as he prepared to bang his gavel and order the vote, Lewis slowly rose to his feet and asked recognition. Bristling black eyebrows drawn into a scowl, fists tightly clenched at his sides, Lewis strode down the center aisle "like a dirge," a buzzing rising from the hushed audience behind him, increasing in volume as he reached the stage. Lewis did not hurry. He walked across the front of the auditorium to steps at the side, paraded the rostrum and then, hands gripping the sides of the lectern, stood a long moment staring "silent and menacing" at the audience. "No actor ever made a more studied or prolonged entrance," commented labor journalist Nat Damien. Lewis' first sentence, when it came, had the echoing, commanding resonance of an organ chord:

" 'Thou shalt not muzzle the ox that treadeth out the corn.' " He let the words settle into the air, then continued, his voice sometimes fading to a whisper, then roaring rapidly up the volume scales to the rumble of a storm. "So runs the Scripture," Lewis said. "But the Congress of the United States designated fifteen million workers in this country, organized into one form or another of unions, as being cattle that treadeth out the economic corn of our country and the Congress placed an economic muzzle on each of you. What are you going to do about it? Oh, I see. You are going to change our constitution. God help us!"

And on he rolled for fifty-six minutes, denouncing the executive council, the Congress, the details of the act. Green sat to the side, staring morosely at the floor. Meany, behind him on the platform, hurriedly scribbled notes.

Lewis had harsh words for Taft-Hartley ("the first ugly savage thrust of fascism in America") but even harsher ones for the executive council. "The welkin is filled with the outcries and the lamentations of our great leaders of labor in this country calling upon high heaven to witness that all indeed is lost unless they can grovel on their bellies and come under this infamous act. . . . At last we come to the fatal and unhappy day when men who purport to lead the mighty host within the American Federation of Labor cry aloud and say, 'There is nothing else for us to do—nothing else for us to do.'

"I will tell you what you should do at least once in your lives—you should do your duty by your membership.

"Is it true that the leaders of our movement are to be the first of our mighty hosts of eight million members to put their tails between their legs and run like cravens before the threat of . . . Taft-Hartley? I am reminded of the Biblical parable, 'Lions led by asses.' " Lewis said he cringed at labor's plight, at the thought of "that mighty host trying to advance across the plains of America, led and flanked and having their thinking done for them by intellectually fat and stately asses."

The saving loophole in Taft-Hartley, Lewis argued, was that the oath was optional. If labor declined to sign, he said, "the act would have been discredited, there would have been no cases filed before the [National Labor Relations] board, and its only functions would have been functions solely in the interests of the employer"—which the American people would not have long tolerated. Accepting the oath, he said, only invited further trouble.

"You are humbling yourself in abasement before the return of government by injunction. . . . If you grovel enough in this convention, you will probably have more to grovel for next January and March, because when the Congress and the enemies of labor find out how easy you are, they will give you more to grovel for."

Miner delegates and scattered voices from the galleries shouted, "Pour it on, John!" as Lewis carried his peroration toward a climax. If the resolution passed, he said, "I will not be a candidate for re-election to this debased board. Perhaps that makes no difference; perhaps you will say, 'John Lewis is trying to hold a gun to the head of this convention.'

"That is not true. I don't think anyone can hold a gun to the head of this convention. I am simply telling you what I think of principle, so that you can make your decision with full knowledge of what it means.

"As far as that is concerned, on this particular issue I don't think that the federation has a head. I think its neck has just grown up and haired over."

By the time Lewis finished, the delegates were torn between shame and anger—shame, because many realized the weaknesses of the AFL leadership; and anger, because of the vehemence of the attack. "For a couple of very long minutes," stated a man who worked for the AFL at the time, "I thought John's speech had carried the convention."

"Delegates and fellow belly-crawlers," Dan Tobin began his reply, and the audience came to its feet with a roar of laughter and applause. "I want to say to the previous speaker that the Brotherhood of Teamsters never crawled in their lives. When the miners were there on their bellies, we tried to lift them up." Tobin carefully answered Lewis' charges about the wisdom of the AFL strategy, saying, "I don't think we should take this issue half so seriously as the representatives of the United Mine Workers make out," and arguing that the 286,000 members of AFL federal unions "need our help." Tobin said, "Personally, I'm happy to have a chance to say by affidavit, 'I'm not a Communist.' " But Tobin did not attack Lewis directly.

Meany began in much the same fashion, saying the convention faced a "very practical problem," and that "I don't think we are going to solve it by impugning the integrity of men who feel that they can best represent their membership by complying with the law of the land." Meany gave a long, technical explanation of the constitutional change, and how the executive council would function under it. And he did not think the small federal unions should be used as "shock troops" against Taft-Hartley when larger international unions declined battle. "Whether you like it or not . . . the Taft-Hartley law is on the statute books. . . . We know that it is a bad law, but it was placed on the statute books by our repre-sentatives under the American democratic system, and the only way that it is going to be changed is by our representatives under that system."

Then Meany made a difficult decision, one unprecedented in an AFL convention. He proceeded to fling Lewis' insults back into his face. "Lewis liked to talk loud because no one would ever slug it out with him. Well, I thought I'd just give him a big mouthful of his own medicine, and see what happened."

Meany began by tracing various stratagems the Communists used in their "attempted destruction of the AFL"—the dual unionism of the Trade Union Unity League during the 1920's, through the "boring from within" of the early 1930's. Finally, he said, "We remember 1935, when they [the Communists] cast aside all other activities because they found a national home. They went into the CIO. They are there today.

"The president of the United Mine Workers stated not so very long ago that Phil Murray was the prisoner of the Communists. I agree. Who walked out and left him prisoner?

". . . Of course, the president of the United Mine Workers has up-held the position of the United Mine Workers in regard to communism. With his right hand from 1935 to 1940 he upheld the position of the United Mine Workers in uncompromising resistance to communism; but with his left hand he made fellowship with Harry Bridges [president of the CIO International Longshoremen's and Warehousemen's Union]; Lewis Merrill [recently retired president of the CIO office and profes-sional workers]; Michael Quill [head of the CIO Transport Workers Union]; Julius Emspak [secretary of the CIO electrical workers union]; and all the other stinking America haters who love Moscow.

"So, I am prepared to sign a non-Communist affidavit. I am prepared to go a step further and sign an affidavit that I was never a comrade to the comrades."

During Meany's rebuttal, Victor Riesel sat at a delegates' table in the rear of the convention hall. When Meany reached the words "comrade to the comrades," Riesel recollected, "I felt a trembling hand on my shoul-der. It was Lewis, shaking with rage, steadying himself on what he ap-parently believed was an AFL delegate." When Meany finished Lewis rushed to a floor microphone and demanded a "correction" of the rec-ord. But as he began speaking, trying to explain his relationship with Bridges, Quill, and the other leftists, Meany broke in, "Point of order, that's not a correction." But Green permitted Lewis to continue. Chest heaving angrily, his hair in disarray, his eloquence for once dulled, Lewis admitted, "Of course, Communists came into the CIO." But so what? he asked. AFL unions even then were planning raids which would steal away CIO affiliates with Communist members. "In the light of that," Lewis said, "I ask now who is willing to become the 'comrade of comrades'?"

Meany rejoined, "Whatever action this convention takes, this delegate will go along with it. He won't pick up his bat and ball and go home."

Green didn't even bother with a roll-call vote on the constitutional amendment. Barely one hundred of the thousand delegates shouted "no" along with Lewis, even William Hutcheson abandoning him.

"It was an incredible performance," stated Boris Shishkin. "Lewis was absolutely crushed. He came back into the hall the next day for some sort of routine business, but that was it—George had finished him in the AFL. Lewis had been beaten, publicly and decisively, on an issue he had dramatized. George talked back to him, which had never been done before, and Lewis couldn't take it. It was the old story about belling the cat. Well, the AFL had sat for years, with nobody daring to take on Lewis publicly, because they were afraid of him, literally afraid of him; Lewis had a tongue like a butcher's knife, and he could chop a man to little pieces in public, and enjoyed doing so. So here was Meany, this building tradesman from New York, not a Shakespearean actor by any means, knocking the stuffing out of Lewis with facts, facts, facts, and setting him up for that one knockout punch, 'comrade of the comrades.' "

The confrontation also resolved any doubts as to who would be Green's successor. "George 'elected himself' in San Francisco," Jay Lovestone remarked. "Thereafter it was a matter of time."

Several weeks after the convention ended, a friend in the United Mine Workers sought out Jay Lovestone and asked him to relay a proposition to the AFL: "Tell Meany there is a way to keep Lewis in the federation. John wants to be chairman of Labor's League for Political Education (the AFL political wing created at the 1947 convention)." Lovestone took the message to Meany, who laughed. "This job would have given Lewis recognition throughout the country, the sort of stature his ego demanded. He would have poured all kinds of money into the league and built it into something bigger than the AFL. I said, 'Hell, no.' That was the end of it."

The rejection stung Lewis. A few days later, K. C. Adams, editor of Lewis' *United Mine Workers Journal,* called labor reporters to his office and with much levity showed them a two-and-one-half-by-four-inch white card bearing scrawled words by Lewis:

> *Green—A. F. of L.*
> *We disaffiliate.*
> *Lewis.*

Then Adams handed the card to William Thomas, one of the janitors of the UMWA Building, and told him, in the reporters' presence, "Run this over to Bill Green's office." Green was in New York, and did not actually see Lewis' card for several days. But his absence did not lessen the sting of the insult. The AFL, with irrevocable finality, never again considered John L. Lewis when speaking of "labor unity."

# VIII

## At Peace and War with Harry Truman

O N T H E D A Y that Congress overrode President Truman's veto
of Taft-Hartley," said Joseph D. Keenan, the ruddy Chicagoan who was to become the AFL's first full-time politician, "I was
walking down the street in Paris when I ran into James Carey and Ambroise Croizat, the Communist minister of labor in France. Croizat lit
into me: 'This labor movement you brag about is finished—finished—
finished. Your capitalist government is crushing the workers and their
unions and you can't do anything about it.' " Keenan continued, "I tried
to make the point that this was not the case, that we swing back and
forth from election to election. But we *had* taken a licking."

Keenan, at that time the AFL's representative in Germany, returned
to the United States later in 1947 for the AFL convention, and during
stopovers in New York, Washington, and Chicago he found an unprecedented labor interest in politics. "Everybody was talking about Taft-
Hartley and what they were going to do in '48 to defeat the people responsible for its passage. By the time I got out to San Francisco for the
convention, there must have been sixty resolutions on politics, asking
various sorts of things from the AFL."

As a onetime lobbyist, George Meany was foremost among the AFL
officials who were appalled by the sorry political plight of labor revealed
in the Taft-Hartley vote. With Republicans firmly in control of Congress
after the 1946 mid-term debacle, the AFL had not expected to beat Taft-
Hartley in a straight floor vote. But President Truman promised early in
the debate he would veto any unduly harsh version of Taft-Hartley. Yet
as was lamented later by James L. McDevitt, Keenan's contemporary as
an AFL labor pol, "labor's estate in Congress had fallen so low that we

could not even muster the necessary one-third vote to sustain a veto."
Labor received twenty-five of ninety-six votes in the Senate; eighty-three
of 435 in the House. As McDevitt complained, "Both Truman and Roosevelt had been faced with a hostile coalition majority [of Republicans
and conservative Democrats, mostly Southern] since 1938. But not until
after the disastrous 1946 election were they unable to muster a one-third
vote needed to sustain a veto of a vicious bill. Labor had sat on the
sidelines not only in 1946 but for more than twenty years previous. Obviously, inaction gained nothing. Our enemies had neither respect nor
mercy for us." Preoccupied with economic issues, unions long felt they
should shun political action. This notion, McDevitt said, was "based on
a fallacy that the unions have a choice. They have no more choice than a
man in ten feet of water has a choice of swimming or not. You can't
organize unions and negotiate contracts for better pay if the legislative
bodies enact laws which make unions and their actions illegal. You can't
enact workmen's compensation laws if the legislators don't like the idea.
Favorable laws are written by favorable legislators. The first step in lobbying is to elect favorable legislators."

Before 1947 the AFL did minimal direct political work. The education department issued dull brochures on voting records of congressional
and other candidates to guide the rank and file in following Sam Gompers' old dictum, "Reward our friends and punish our enemies." The
executive council periodically set up an ad hoc "nonpartisan campaign
committee"—Green, Meany, and whoever else felt energetic, and Democratic—but as a body never endorsed even such a labor friend as Franklin D. Roosevelt. "You must realize," stated Keenan, "there was a strong
Republican presence on the council—Bill Hutcheson, for example, and
Lewis, when he was in the federation. Except for 1936 Lewis always was
a Republican. Although the Democrats had a majority, both on the
council and in the membership, there were enough Republicans to create
a standoff."

The Congress of Industrial Organizations, meanwhile, through its Political Action Committee, created in 1943, became the *de facto* labor
wing of the Democratic party. PAC helped Roosevelt with funds and
manpower in 1944, and aggressively campaigned against antilabor congressmen. PAC incited virulent conservative animosity, particularly
when Roosevelt, in considering his 1944 running mate, reportedly said
to political advisers, "Clear it with Sidney" (meaning Sidney Hillman,
the PAC chairman). Republican candidates skillfully exploited the presence of Communists in the CIO to Red-bait labor in the 1946 campaign,
somberly warning the populace, "Keep Stalin out of Washington."

The AFL entered active politics both to defend itself against labor
animosity in Congress and to offset the CIO's increasing power within
the Democratic party. Leading the way were Meany, David Dubinsky,

and George H. Harrison, of the railway clerks union. Their strategy was to sell a new program in an old wrapping. Realizing that the hidebound old bulls of the executive council must be led slowly, if they were to be moved at all, but also feeling the strong rush of rank-and-file sentiment for action, the activists put together a political program under the guise of an expanded "educational" effort. To council colleagues Meany cited a study of the 1946 election that showed more than forty million eligible voters did not bother to go to the polls. "We are convinced that a substantial portion of those were trade unionists and the members of trade unionists' families," Meany said. Give them the facts, show them they have a personal interest in electing a prolabor Congress, and the unions could protect themselves in Congress, he said. Meany was determined not to put the AFL into partnership with the Democratic party. He was equally determined, however, to heed what he called "the tremendous demand from within our ranks that we take protective action at the polls."

On Meany's recommendation, the 1947 convention created Labor's League for Political Education (LLPE) and in boiler-plate language from past statements authorized it to inform workers of the "economic and political philosophies" of the AFL, and of the views and voting record of candidates. The new feature, a significant one that required considerable suasion by Meany, was the hiring of a permanent political staff, with authority to raise money from affiliated unions.

At a late December conference in Washington at which LLPE was formally organized, Meany declared the league was "by no means a departure from the old political philosophy of the AFL, of 'defeating your enemies and rewarding your friends.' " Instead, he said, it was an "attempt to give effect to that philosophy in line with present conditions. . . . We have got to make our people politically conscious; develop them politically in their own self-interest, not for the purpose of attempting to run the country but for the purpose of protecting themselves."

Another factor, according to Meany, was the Republican party's formal alliance with the antiunion forces responsible for Taft-Hartley. The Republican National Committee printed a draft version of the bill in full-page newspaper advertisements and "had the audacity to offer free mats to any business organization which cared to republish it as a newspaper advertisement." Meany met a Wall Street executive in a bar one evening while having a drink with a newspaperman after a speech. "My name must have rung a bell somewhere. He said, 'Oh, you are the labor guy.' 'Yes, that's me.' He said, 'Well, come the first of the year you fellows will be put in your place. There is going to be a very simple rule. The people that put the money into business in this country are going to make the rules.' "

The league's first business was hiring a director, and the AFL executive council went through a disappointing succession of prospects. Former Senator Robert La Follette declined the appointment. Former Senator Burton K. Wheeler haggled over the offered fee of $15,000 and finally agreed to accept the directorship for $20,000 a year. Then Dubinsky and Max Zaritksy, of the Hat, Cap and Millinery Workers Union, objected loudly: despite an early friendship with the railway unions, Wheeler's labor record was so poor that virtually every union in Montana opposed him in 1946, when he was defeated. Before the war, he was an archisolationist, even lending his senatorial mail frank to George Sylvester Viereck, later convicted of being a German agent. When Dubinsky and Zaritsky threatened to make their objections public the executive council persuaded Wheeler to announce he could not devote full time, as the job required, and decline the appointment. Former Senator James Mead of New York, a long-time Meany friend, also declined the job. Eventually Meany got around to Keenan, who had left his AFL international representative's post and returned to his prewar job as secretary of the Chicago Federation of Labor. An electrical worker by trade, Keenan was also a street-wise politician who had made labor a key member in Chicago's powerful Democratic organization. "Meany had no sooner asked me to take a leave to be Midwest director of the league than he called again and said they were having a devil of a time finding a full-time director, and could I take it. By the time I got to Washington, in the late winter, Meany had things in motion—he had found office space, hired help, and had contribution books printed. George spent one half his time getting the thing going, he and George Harrison. The rest, they were so-so, they were on the committee but they kept away from things. Bill Green never said a word; he was content to let George do it.

"Actually we had only a small force of people, not more than five or so, for the entire campaign. But there was a lot of enthusiasm, especially among the rank and file, and what we did was to give ammunition to the local groups, the state and local bodies."

Keenan had to oversee three separate campaigns simultaneously: the campaign for friendly congressional candidates; the campaign for state legislative candidates opposed to right-to-work laws, which were permitted by Taft-Hartley, and which many states had already passed; and the campaign for the re-election of President Truman.

LLPE stressed local union activity. As James McDevitt once explained, "While the power of the trade union movement lies in the national and international unions, they are not adapted to political action. An international union parallels the industry in which its members have collective bargaining contracts. It does not parallel political institutions. Even a union of half a million members has very little effect since its members are scattered thinly throughout the ninety-seven million potential voters. . . . Thus the league had to be organized to parallel the election districts. . . . The most pressing problems facing the league when it was first formed was to get more union members registered. In some communities surveys showed that less than one half of the members were even registered to vote. . . ." Also, surveys found that union members resented being told by their leaders how they should vote, but were appreciative of factual information on voting records. As McDevitt said, the problem was to persuade members and officers to vote on the record without leaving them "feeling they are being blindly instructed."

"You had some peculiar things at the state and local level in those days," Joe Keenan said. "Politicians wanted your support, but not so that they got tied up with you very closely. Some of the state federation presidents were reluctant to get into campaigns. One of them told me, out in Minnesota: 'My job in the labor movement is to pass legislation. I can't pass legislation in the session and then be out campaigning against the party in power.' We had that to overcome. Now George, of course, he could just cite his New York record as a reason for getting into politics, because the New York State Federation, when he was president, had made no bones about the fact that it tried to get friends elected to Albany. George gave the state federation presidents an argument that was pretty hard to answer."

In the congressional races, according to Meany, a politician's stand on the "nefarious" Taft-Hartley Act was "the sole test used by Labor's League for Political Education in determining support or opposition to an incumbent running for re-election." Although LLPE compiled right-or-wrong voting records on twelve issues, including European recovery and housing and tax measures, "no matter how many favorable votes a congressman had on other issues, an unfavorable vote on the Taft-Hartley Act disqualifies him from receiving LLPE support."

In the presidential race, the AFL's interest in politics fit snugly into a campaign format drafted by Clark M. Clifford, then a White House special counsel, months before the election. To win, Clifford wrote Truman in a forty-three-page strategy memo, he had to hold together the "unhappy alliance of Southern conservatives, Western progressives, and big-city labor." Success, he said, depended upon Truman's ability "to lead enough members of these three misfit groups to the polls." Clifford counseled:

It is dangerous to assume that labor has nowhere else to go in 1948. *Labor can stay home.* . . . The labor group has always been politically inactive during prosperity. When they are well fed they are not interested. They will probably be well fed in 1948.

Labor leaders should be invited to the White House to flatter them—but to talk on *general* issues. To invite advice on specifics, and then not follow it, is to court trouble. . . .

Any enthusiasm the AFL had for Truman stemmed directly from the fact that he was the only alternative to New York Governor Thomas E. Dewey, the Republican candidate. Truman's threatened draft of rail strikers into military service, his contempt proceedings against John L. Lewis and the coal miners, his coterie of conservative domestic advisers, caused labor to regard him warily. Mindful of labor's uneasiness, Truman chose a Labor Day rally in Cadillac Square in Detroit to launch his campaign. Speaking to more than one hundred thousand union members massed in the square, Truman used scare language:

> If, in this next election, you get a Congress and an administration friendly to labor, you have much to hope for. If you get an administration and Congress unfriendly to labor, you have much to fear, and you had better look out. . . .
>
> If the congressional elements that made the Taft-Hartley Law are allowed to remain in power, and if these elements are further encouraged by the election of a Republican president, you men of labor can expect to be hit by a steady barrage of body blows. And, if you stay at home, as you did in 1946, and keep these reactionaries in power, you will deserve every blow you get. . . .
>
> If you place the government of this country under the control of those who hate labor, whom can you blame if measures are thereafter adopted to destroy the powers, prestige, and earning power of labor? . . . You are fighting for the whole future of the labor movement. We are in a hard, tough fight against shrewd and rich opponents. They know they can't count on your vote. Their only hope is that you won't vote at all. . . .

As Truman wrote in his memoirs, the Cadillac Square theme "set the pace for the campaign speeches that were to follow." Again and again, in his "give 'em hell" campaign, Truman warned workers and farmers that if they "did not get out and help me win this fight . . . the Republicans would soon be giving [them] the little end of the stick again. I . . . warned . . . that if they were fools enough to accept the little end again, they deserved it."

Even though it recognized the consequences of a Republican victory, the AFL executive council was unwilling to take the final political step of an outright endorsement of Truman. William Green opposed endorsement when the question arose at the council's August meeting in Chicago. In oblique reference to the council's Republican members, Green said a unified AFL was paramount in the election. "If any attempt is made to endorse a candidate for president or to endorse any political party," he said, "it would mean a divided vote and would mean a divided AFL and serious injury might be done." George Harrison, arguing for endorsement, said many Republican unionists would not split their ticket by voting for Truman unless the AFL endorsed him. An endorsement, he said "would mean a lot more votes [for Truman] by those people." Meany, too, was cool toward endorsement, for he said it would exceed the bounds set by the convention in the resolution establishing Labor's League for Political Education. The LLPE, he said, has confined itself to working for repeal of Taft-Hartley, defeat of congressmen who supported it, and election of those who opposed it. The council then agreed informally to adhere to its previous policy of not endorsing a presidential candidate* but not to publicize the decision. One member pointed out that Joe Keenan had already prepared a report by Labor's League containing an endorsement of Truman. Green and Meany said that if this was so, Keenan "did not consult them about it." They said they would see to it that the endorsement was taken out of the report.

The record suggests Meany was not telling the council the total truth about links between Labor's League and Truman. As Keenan stated, "Although the resolution creating the League only mentioned Congress and Taft-Hartley, we worked closely with the Truman campaign as well, getting labor people into the picture. Things looked awfully bleak when we started. But we could see a change coming by mid-September, when the President started drawing crowds; he was outdrawing Dewey two to one." Keenan traveled several days on Truman's campaign train, helping arrange labor crowds for the whistle-stop appearances.

"The beauty of working for Meany," Keenan said, "was that he left you alone. He hired you, and gave you the job, and as long as you reported to him you were okay. You didn't have him pulling you back—he was always pushing you forward.

"During the 1948 campaign I began working closely with Jack Kroll, my counterpart at the CIO. It made good sense. Here we were, trying to get labor votes in a state—why work at cross-purposes? There were some pretty loud growls in the executive council, because to some of these guys working with the CIO was a form of treason. I know Meany got some of these kicks, but he never said a word to me, he let me go on working with Kroll. I agreed with Meany there was no trade union reason for the split."

In a series of radio speeches in the fall—financed by LLPE, not the AFL directly—Meany stressed the voting record theme, telling his

---

* The AFL had not formally endorsed a presidential nominee since Samuel Gompers supported the third-party candidacy of Senator Robert La Follette in 1924.

unionist audience (and whoever else happened to be listening) that the Republicans were hostile to workers. Get to the polls, he said, and use your head when you do. In one speech Meany sought to deflate the third-party candidacy of former Vice-President Henry A. Wallace, who was appealing for labor votes. Meany warned unionists about being caught up in a Communist-supported united front: "Is there a Communist fifth column operating in this country today? Do you know whether or not that fifth column has entered a presidential candidate in this election campaign? Is it entirely possible, in the event of a disastrous depression, that the Communists could gain millions of converts in this country?" Meany continued: "These are not 'scare' questions. They are serious questions that every thinking American must face."

Fortunately for labor, the U.S. Supreme Court ruled in midsummer that Taft-Hartley bans on spending union funds for political purposes did not restrict union publications from commenting upon candidates and political issues. "The regular union publications and the labor press immediately became labor's main tool in educating our members and the public as to the issues and the prolabor candidates in the campaign," Meany said. "It was fair enough. Should we leave it to the newspaper publishers, to the owners of radio stations, or possibly to the politicians themselves to inform our members?"

When the campaign began, Meany said, "None of us were too hopeful of electing a decent Congress." Most public opinion polls and political journalists forecast a Republican landslide. The nation, to its collective surprise, woke up on November 4 with Truman still in the White House and with the Democrats in control of Congress. What the AFL identified as "prolabor" representations increased from twenty-five to forty-four in the Senate, from 83 to 209 in the House. "Reactionary congressmen had suffered their worst defeat since 1932," Meany said.

How important was labor's role in the campaign? In Meany's opinion, labor "was undoubtedly given too much credit for this victory. We heard it said so often that labor had won that I'm afraid a lot of us were convinced we had done it alone. Probably it was as much general dissatisfaction with the Eightieth Congress as anything else that did the trick." In terms of money, the LLPE's first-year record was mixed. Because of bans on spending union funds directly for political purposes, the league was forced to create two separate funds: an educational fund, which could draw upon union resources; and a political fund, which was to be supported by voluntary contributions, hopefully of $1 from each of the AFL's seven million members. Response was desultory. Instead of raising the "$7,000,000 labor boss slush fund" feared by alarmed Republican orators, the political fund attracted only $360,000 in donations— around five percent of the quota. The largest amount the league spent in any state was $18,000, in Illinois, spread over more than a score of candidates and campaign groups. At the same time, many international unions freed staff members for full-time political activity, and distributed hundreds of thousands of pro-Democratic fliers and "records" of candidates—expenses not reflected in the LLPE financial report. Several outside observers did credit labor's work on congressional races with helping mobilize the pro-Truman vote. *Newsweek,* in its postelection analysis, cited labor's help for such "lesser fry" as Senators Hubert H. Humphrey of Minnesota, Matthew M. Neely of West Virginia, James E. Murray of Montana, Paul Douglas of Illinois, and Lester C. Hunt of Wyoming.

Immediately after the election the AFL made plans to demand a *quid pro quo* from the Truman Administration. At the December executive council meeting, George Harrison said the AFL "has every good reason to feel that it has the right to call upon [the] Administration for a square deal." With 120 new members in the House, he said, "we have a lot of people who are pledged to repeal the Taft-Hartley Act." At Meany's suggestion, a committee was dispatched to discuss repeal plans with Secretary of Labor James Tobin. In his State of the Union message Truman asked for outright repeal and House and Senate committees responded so enthusiastically that the AFL predicted Taft-Hartley was on its way to the scrap heap. The Republican-Southern Democrat coalition regrouped however, and by April had regained the offensive. Instead of winning repeal, labor barely prevented a strengthening of Taft-Hartley. Meany took the defeat philosophically. "Some complained that our friends had let us down," he said. "Actually none let us down, and quite a few who had previously voted for Taft-Hartley switched over to our side. Still, we were five votes short of a majority in the Senate and fourteen in the House.* However, that was a sensational change from the Eightieth Congress, when we could not muster in either house even the one-third vote needed to sustain a presidential veto."

Still, Meany was so disappointed that at a Liberal party function in New York in May 1949 he spoke with unaccustomed warmth about the idea of creating a third party. "It is quite evident to me," Meany said, "that the present Tweedledee and Tweedledum two-party system and its virtues have been greatly overrated." Meany did not think it "would be a catastrophe if the two-party system were weakened by a third party assuming a stature that would give it a balance of power." Meany noted that the AFL's political activism had raised the question of how far labor would go—"Will this trend bring us to the point where labor will be ready to sponsor and maintain a national party of its own?" Answering himself, he said, no, "as of now," but that "labor will go as far down this

* Based upon the key votes during the parliamentary maneuvering over repeal.

road as time and events prove it necessary for us to go to carry out our basic purpose."

In other areas, however, the liberalized Congress was much kinder to labor programs. President Truman had tried unsuccessfully for three years to persuade Congress to increase the forty-cent-an-hour minimum wage. Labor gave high priority to the issue in 1949, and Congress boosted the minimum to seventy-five cents, and provided time and a half for overtime for about 1,500,000 workers involved in production of goods for interstate commerce. Acting on a bill that William Green said "was drafted by the AFL," Congress in 1950 extended the Social Security program to 9,700,000 more workers, including the self-employed, regularly employed farm and domestic workers, outside salesmen, federal civilian employees, and Americans working abroad. Monthly benefits increased an average 77½ percent (a man and wife who formerly received $38.25 got $75 under the new law). And at both the federal and state level, the AFL succeeded in broadening unemployment compensation laws.

To Meany's keen disappointment, support for LLPE evaporated rapidly following the election, especially when the "labor Congress" did not bury Taft-Hartley. Financial support was niggardly, both from international unions and rank and file. A plea for $1 contributions from each of the AFL's seven million members in 1949 produced less than $500,000. In June 1950—an election year—LLPE funding was so haphazard that the meager Washington staff was halved. The chief "educational" organ, *The League Reporter,* was cut from weekly to semimonthly publication; voting records of congressmen were mimeographed rather than printed. The LLPE told friendly congressmen it could no longer pay for radio broadcasts in their home districts. And Meany found that a "somewhat shocking" percentage of the AFL members who registered during union drives never made it to the polls. According to Joe Keenan, "Were it not for Meany's influence, the league would have been voted out of existence."

But Meany kept trying, even though he met a continuous string of disappointments. Immediately after the 1948 election, he and Keenan began plotting the defeat of Senator Taft, who faced re-election in 1950. Keenan said, "Meany and I went out to Ohio, and sat down with the officers of the federation, with the political leaders, and we asked them if they would not try to get us a candidate of the stature of Taft. This whole organization was interested in that one state, and we wanted to carry the fight there." Labor's first choice was Murray Lincoln, insurance and farm labor official. "We spent two months with Lincoln, and we got him to the point where he was ready to accept, and go for the Democratic nomination. Dave Dubinsky was even ready to guarantee his pension rights if his organization put him out." Then a veteran Democratic politician named Joseph Ferguson, then state auditor, entered the race, and the AFL reluctantly abandoned its efforts to pick the candidate. "We had to be satisfied with the result of the primary," Keenan said. "None of us were happy." Taft swamped Ferguson, running well even in labor districts.

Keenan said labor learned a lesson in Ohio. "It taught us that we should let no political organization just give us a candidate and tell us we can take it or leave it. Again, hindsight is better than foresight. Probably if we had sat out the Ohio election and used the money in some other places, we might have saved a few senators who lost by a narrow margin." After the election labor counted 183 "friends" in the House (compared with 209 before) and 38 in the Senate (compared with 44).

The Ohio campaign reinforced Taft's enmity toward labor, to the alarm of more conservative elements in the AFL. On December 14, five weeks after the election, Taft called in W. C. Hushing, the AFL's chief lobbyist, and outlined a series of Taft-Hartley amendments he was considering. One of them, Hushing reported to the executive council, was an "elimination of loopholes of committees which claim to be 'educational' or 'nonpolitical' but which actually influence elections." Hushing said Taft wrote the amendment with the intention of killing LLPE and the CIO's Political Action Committee. Were the AFL to revive Taft-Hartley repeal, Hushing said, amendments well might be enacted "making the law more distasteful." Hushing cautioned, "For this reason, I suggest that we rest our oars. . . ." Other council members were ready to cut LLPE to a skeleton and keep out of Taft's sight for a year. Meany and George Harrison, however, argued them down, Harrison saying that midterm slumps could be expected, and that LLPE "had a large influence" in minimizing losses.

Nonetheless, the fact that Meany and Harrison were continually on the defensive with LLPE in the executive council sorely restricted their freedom. So, too, did the fact that Meany was asking the council to make a rather basic policy change.

Traditionally, the international unions affiliated with the AFL ran their own organizational campaigns, signing workers who held jobs in their various jurisdictions. The AFL maintained its own organizing staff, but for rather tightly defined duties. The AFL staff assisted the smaller international unions. It helped resolve the frequent jurisdictional disputes. And it organized workers in areas not claimed by any international unions, by enlisting them in "federal" unions chartered directly by the AFL. The process was expensive (by 1950, according to Meany, the AFL spent about half its $4,000,000 income on organizing) and after Taft-Hartley it was grossly ineffective. With a staff of 191 full-time organizers, the AFL during 1950 managed to charter only 170 federal unions, 58 of which were suspended or disbanded before the year ended. Meany lamented to the executive council at its January 1951 meeting, "For the last year, these 191 organizers averaged less than one charter for the year."

To Meany, the question was whether the AFL should continue to sink its money in the organizers, or improve the public climate for unions through political activity and "educational programs." At his insistence, the AFL in mid-1950 hired Frank Edwards, then an unknown announcer on an Indianapolis station, for nightly news broadcasts. Sixty percent of the expense was met by the AFL, the remainder by LLPE. A political liberal and a commentator who blended hard news and biting opinion, Edwards proved quickly popular. Within six months his program was heard over a network of 176 stations, mostly affiliates of the Mutual Broadcasting System, and had attracted an audience estimated at seven million persons.

Yet the program was expensive, costing the AFL around $35,000 a month, LLPE about $25,000. In early 1951 the league, financially exhausted, put the entire cost on the AFL, and the AFL was hard pressed to pay for the program. Meany told the executive council the AFL was running a deficit of about $32,000 a month because of higher salary expenses and legal fees resulting from Taft-Hartley actions. The question, he said, was whether the AFL would obtain more long-term benefits from the organizing staff or the political education program. Personally, Meany opted for the latter. Unions were spending "millions of dollars for legal assistance, and the only way we are going to get relief is when we have some influence in Washington, but today in Washington we have absolutely no influence with the Administration or with Congress. We cannot organize a new union today unless the employer is willing to let us organize, and if not he will fight every step of the way. The National Labor Relations Board is full of these cases."

Meany thought the AFL was wasting much of the $1,860,000 a year it spent on organizers. He cited specifically $400,000 for an organizational campaign among insurance agents, with minimal results. The AFL received far more for the $700,000-plus it spent on Edwards' radio program and LLPE, he maintained. With reluctant council approval, Meany received permission to cut the organizing staff by twenty-five persons between May and August, down to 159. An increase from three to four cents in the per capita tax levied on affiliated unions put the AFL back into the black.

Concurrently, the AFL grappled with a problem that seemed to make a mockery of Meany's dictum that electing "friends" would make labor's lot easier: the economic controls program of the Korean War, and a resultant blood feud with the Truman Administration.

\* \* \*

The Korean War taught the AFL that politics did not guarantee favored treatment—or even equitable treatment—for labor by the Truman Administration. When the war began in June 1950 the AFL was campaigning actively to re-elect a Democratic Congress, and President Truman was most happy with its attempts to unseat Senator Taft in Ohio. However, within six months Truman totally alienated his erstwhile labor friends, plunging White House-AFL relations to their lowest depths since the pre-Roosevelt years. The issue was labor participation in the war economic stabilization program, which Meany and other AFL leaders charged was stacked with antiunion businessmen.

Formally, the AFL's position on controls paralleled that of World War II. It accepted wage restraints as a wartime necessity, but demanded balancing price controls and machinery for resolving pay inequities. It preferred voluntary programs, but recognized (in the words of the September convention) that "positive controls will be necessary to avoid the greatest danger of the defense program, the danger of inflation." And it called for "full-scale participation by the nation's workers and their unions in the administration of the defense program." In August Meany made a qualified offer of a no-strike pledge similar to that of World War II. Speaking to the annual convention of the New York State Federation of Labor, he said, "I haven't any doubt at all that labor will give a no-strike pledge when the time comes. But how about a 'no excess profits, no excess profiteering' pledge from the United States Chamber of Commerce and the National Association of Manufacturers? How about a pledge from the Tafts, the Martins, the Hollands, and the Wherrys [all right-wing congressmen] to lay off their war against labor while this country is in danger?"

The Truman Administration, however, fumbled away chances for labor cooperation. After the first frightening weeks of war, when U.S. forces repelled North Korea's lightning offense, the Administration tarried on controls, apparently believing the fighting would end without significant impact on the economy. Truman accepted a toothless "defense production act" passed by Congress which contained meaningless, unenforceable price controls. Joseph D. Keenan, who left Labor's League for Political Education early in the war to accept a stabilization post, said Truman botched inflation controls by announcing several months in advance that he intended a price freeze. "Of course, the obvious happened. Inflation went into a spiral, because everyone kicked up prices before the effective date. We were never able to correct it." By mid-August food prices were up nine percent above the level of June 24, when the fighting began, and were 13.3 percent above the year-ago level. In a White House meeting with Truman that month, Green and Meany asked that wages be permitted to rise to catch up with prices before any freeze became effective, saying a wage increase would be easier than any attempted roll-back of prices. Meany repeated the offer of a no-strike pledge, again asking, however, for a "no excess profits" pledge from business.

The rout of General Douglas MacArthur's forces by the Chinese Communists in late November dashed Truman's quick-victory euphoria, and "the complacent attitude of the previous months had to be abandoned," in William Green's later words. On December 16 Truman declared a national emergency and created a full-blown war controls bureaucracy. He named Charles E. Wilson, president of the General Electric Company, to direct a new Office of Defense Mobilization (ODM), with wide authority to "direct" the war economy. ODM's major component was an Economic Stabilization Agency, headed by Eric Johnston, head of the Motion Picture Association of America and a former president of the U. S. Chamber of Commerce. Under Johnston were a Wage Stabilization Board headed by Cyrus S. Ching, director of the U. S. Mediation and Conciliation Service; and an Office of Price Stabilization, run by Michael V. DiSalle, former mayor of Toledo, Ohio (and later Ohio governor).

Wilson was undisputed boss. An associate once said of him, "He's a great team man—so long as he can be captain." Gruff and combative, Wilson had lifted himself from boyhood poverty in Hell's Kitchen through mail-order engineering courses, and he had the self-made man's contempt for lesser humans, particularly those who relied upon labor unions for protection. Wilson once declaimed that most people who fail to get what they want "don't want it badly enough to do the hard work—there just ain't no golden chariot that will take you there." General Electric, where he spent his working life (becoming president in 1939 for $175,000 a year) was notoriously antiunion. American business, stated broadly, by 1950 had settled into two camps. One faction, of which General Motors was the prime mover, accepted, even welcomed unions in the interest of labor peace, and as an adjunct to management in worker discipline. The rules were orderly: once labor won a point in collective bargaining, management accepted it. Conversely, the hard-line group, centered around General Electric, considered each contract negotiation an opportunity to reverse labor gains of previous years. The GE strategy of attrition was based on the hope that management eventually would catch labor in a weak period, because of recession or member discontent, and throw the unions for a loss.

Meany first met Wilson during World War II, when Wilson was a deputy to Donald Nelson, chairman of the War Production Board. He considered him a "loud mouth" and a poor tactician, a businessman who used his government office "to try to shove people around." Meany and other labor people in wartime programs were not unhappy when Wilson quit in a huff during a minor bureaucratic squabble in 1944 and returned to GE. Meany was much surprised when Truman suddenly summoned Wilson to Washington in December 1950 and made him, in effect, an economic czar. Answerable only to Truman, Wilson had the final word on production, manpower, wages, prices, transportation, and defense buying. To labor's dismay, Wilson picked as his two top assistants men who were outspokenly antiunion: Sidney Weinberg, a senior partner in the Wall Street investment house of Goldman, Sachs, and also a GE board member; and retired General Lucius Clay, board chairman of Continental Can Company. During World War II Clay had been the War Department's most relentless advocate of a wholesale manpower draft for defense industry, and he had sabotaged the AFL's attempts to restore West German unions when the war ended.

As Meany complained, Wilson put businessmen "in every key spot in the defense machinery—the owner of a restaurant chain regulating restaurant prices; the president of a steel company in charge of the metals branch of the Office of Price Stabilization; the former president of the National Lumber Manufacturing Association as director of the wood products division of the National Production Administration and so on right down the line through every division of every agency in the defense program." ("The Kuomintang," the CIO's James Carey called the Wilson bloc.) Further, Wilson seemed to look for opportunities to irritate labor. At his first press conference, he said he was not considering appointing any labor people to top policy posts because he wanted "technicians, not pressure groups." Wilson did concede that "from time to time I will naturally consult with labor and other interested parties."

In Joe Keenan's opinion, Truman suffered from bad advice on labor and economic matters, especially from John Steelman, a burly, jovial Southerner with a knack for glad-handing. Steelman carried the title of Assistant to the President, but in fact was *de facto* Secretary of Labor. A native of Arkansas, Steelman studied economics at Harvard and Vanderbilt, and was teaching at a women's college in Alabama when, in 1934, Secretary of Labor Frances Perkins called him to Washington. A skilled bureaucrat, Steelman soon became head of the Federal Conciliation Service, and Truman brought him into the White House in 1946. Conservative by nature, Steelman constantly sought to shove Truman toward the middle of the road, away from such liberal advisers as Clark M. Clifford. To Steelman the Republican-conservative Democratic coalition was a political fact, and he continually told Truman to get along with it as best he could, even if labor's feelings were hurt in the process. When Clark Clifford left the White House in early 1950 to enter law practice, labor lost its last high-level friend in the Administration, and Steelman and Treasury Secretary John W. Snyder, another conservative, thereafter set policy toward unions. "Anna Rosenberg was still around," said Keenan, "but she rode any horse that came along; she was supposed to be labor's friend, but you couldn't trust her to stay on your side." Nor did Truman feel truly comfortable with labor leaders; as labor journalist Claire Neikind wrote, he "likes to swap jokes with them but seems to have little comprehension of, and less interest in, their viewpoint."

The onset of war, meanwhile, put the AFL and CIO back into cautious alliance. The executive council in July authorized Charles J. Mac-Gowan of the AFL boilermakers union to meet with Allan Haywood of the United Steel Workers to see if there was any hope for formal unity. To his surprise, MacGowan discovered CIO president Philip Murray had invited John L. Lewis to the talks, even though the AFL executive council had specifically said it wanted nothing more to do with the mineworkers. According to MacGowan, Murray was "still strongly convinced that if Lewis was not invited in, he might undertake a counteroffensive of some type which would at least impair the negotiations . . . if not actually destroy them. . . ." The AFL withdrew.

Almost immediately, however, the AFL and CIO were brought back into cautious alliance through the good offices of Eli L. Oliver, a quiet Minnesotan who had been active for three decades as labor academician, politician, negotiator, and administrator. Oliver's main endeavor in 1950 was bargaining representative for rail and transit workers, through the Labor Bureau of the Middle West, a consulting firm. Oliver related, "I had been with the War Production Board throughout the Second World War, when the AFL and CIO were fighting quite bitterly. It was necessary to have AFL and CIO people in parallel positions throughout the board to get any work done. Whenever a job required a single man, I almost always took one from an unaffiliated railroad union, because they weren't lined up with either group, and could get cooperation. This caused us all sorts of administrative headaches, as you can imagine.

"During the first phase of the Korean War I was on the National Security Resources Board, working with Stuart Symington [formerly Secretary of the Air Force; later senator from Missouri]. I thought this might be the opportunity to knock down some of the barriers between the AFL and CIO, and make the board's work a lot less complicated in the process. I went to George with the idea of a United Labor Policy Committee, which would formulate policy for the AFL and CIO and enable them to speak with a single voice in the defense program.

"George listened to me, and he was immediately very much taken with the idea and said the AFL would go along with me. At the CIO, the top people were also for it, with the exception of Arthur Goldberg [counsel for the CIO]. My own feeling was that Goldberg felt he was a pretty big toad in that puddle; that if it got any bigger, he might not have such a resonant croak. Finally I had to go to Phil Murray to put it across. We put the United Labor Policy Committee [ULPC] together in rather loose fashion, but it definitely served a purpose, and got some of these people talking civilly to one another again."

The ULPC argued for two principles: that wage stabilization could not succeed unless accompanied by an over-all system of anti-inflation controls; and that wage stabilization should supplement, not substitute for, collective bargaining. Each time, as Green complained, the ULPC "found its recommendations ignored, or positively rejected." Some of the officials, he said, were "actually hostile to organized labor, and were willing to take direct steps to make certain that organized labor would not be allowed to contribute to the defense effort."

Labor's grievances crystallized during attempts by the Wage Stabilization Board to fix a limit on pay increases. From the end of World War II through 1950, wages and prices had increased at almost identical paces. The consumer price index rose 33.67 percent (from an index of 128.6 to 171.9) while gross weekly earnings of manufacturing production workers went up 33.65 percent (from $44.39 to $59.33.). In early February, with prices eight to ten percent above their year-ago levels, the stabilization board debated limiting wages. Labor wanted a twelve-percent limit over levels existing on January 15, 1950, including fringe benefits. According to Meany, at midday on February 15 the public and management members agreed on nine percent, including fringe benefits, outvoting labor six to three. In midafternoon, however, General Motors asked that the limit be set at ten percent, an amount needed to cover a contract it had just settled with the United Auto Workers. By Meany's version, "The three public members . . . received their orders from Mr. Wilson, and then sold the idea to the industry members. . . . Charles Wilson* of General Motors Corporation didn't want his organization to be the immediate battleground over that formula. He felt that one percent would cover his problem. And it was raised up from nine to ten percent between twelve o'clock noon and nine o'clock that evening, during a period in which there was no meeting of the board and in which the labor members were not present. That was not a democratically functioning board."

The labor members caucused and voted to walk off the board, saying that until prices were under control, the margin for wage increases should be wider. The ULPC charged, "The price stabilization program is a cynical hoax on the American people." It noted statements by economic stabilizer Johnston and price stabilizer DiSalle that "nothing they

---

* The General Motors' Wilson was Charles E. "Engine Charlie" Wilson, no relation to the stabilization czar, General Electric's Charles E. "Electric Charlie" Wilson.

can or will do under the Defense Production Act will stop the cost of living from rising another six percent by next summer." The ULPC, summarizing its case, declared: "Wages are frozen. Nothing else in the economy has been frozen." Walter Lippmann, for one, sympathized with labor. "What has made the labor leaders so furiously angry," he wrote in the New York *Herald Tribune,* "is the realization that prices are not being frozen but that they are going to be held personally responsible for freezing the wages of union workers. . . . They see themselves assigned the job of stabilizing union labor—and being pilloried before the public if they do not prevent strikes and wage increases—while nobody is in fact stabilizing the cost of living in the 200,000 stores where wage earners and others go shopping."

Under prodding by Truman, who was disturbed at the public disintegration of his controls program, Wilson agreed to talk with the labor people. One grievance had been his unwillingness to have a labor adviser in his office. Wilson said he would not take any assistant who had not completely severed union ties, "as I have done with my association with GE." But as Meany pointed out, Wilson still drew $60,000 annually in retirement from GE, as well as munificent stock dividends, and his two advisers from business, Weinberg and General Clay, retained their private jobs, Clay at $100,000 per year. So, too, did five other high functionaries in Wilson's office. Somewhat chagrined, Wilson sent the ULPC a letter asking for an adviser—"dated the fifteenth, postmarked the sixteenth, and signed with the rubber stamp of Wilson's signature," Meany said sarcastically. The showdown meeting came on February 27, "the business agent against the boss," in Meany's words, and during an hour or so of yelling both men reverted to their boyhood vernacular—Wilson in the tough language of Hell's Kitchen ("Now look here, dammit . . ."), and Meany coming back in Bronxese ("The trouble with you is . . ."). James Carey finally asked, "Are you trying to tell us that you think no labor leader can be a good public servant?" "That's exactly what I think," Wilson replied. With a final flurry of shouts the labor delegation gathered up its papers and left.

What to do next? Arthur Goldberg, long-time CIO lawyer serving the ULPC as a special counsel, cautioned discretion, saying labor should not further embarrass the Administration. Stay around awhile, he and other CIO representatives said; we can bargain our way out of this bind. But Meany was in no mood for compromise. "We're not 'partners' in this Administration," he said. "They've shoved us around, they've treated us shabby, and we don't have to take this nonsense." By unanimous vote the ULPC voted to withdraw all labor representatives from the economic controls program.

Unfortunately for Wilson's cause, a few days after labor's break the

CIO electrical workers union put its hands on two very indiscreet "confidential newsletters" GE had distributed to upper-echelon management as a guide to labor negotiations. Dated February 12 and 19, the letters said, among other things, that there was "only one way" to settle the problem of escalator clauses, namely, "by ruling [them] out"; that pension and insurance programs were "troublesome," and should be kept out of contracts whenever possible; that the Walsh-Healy and Bacon-Davis acts, which require minimum wage standards for all government work, "are no longer necessary in the least"; that payment of time and a half for overtime work presents "an inflation and taxation difficulty"; and that labor officials should not be appointed to government posts because of their "lifelong careers of interfering with production; they are not very useful . . . in the gentle art of increasing [it]." Labor thought it more than coincidence that the stabilization board's February 15 order had covered many of the points of the "GE Manifesto"—barring escalator clauses in contracts, for example, and curbing nonwage fringe benefits such as pension plans and insurance contributions. To labor, the letters were proof positive that business (i.e., Wilson) was using the defense stabilization program to crush unions. And labor went on the attack. In a network radio interview Meany charged that Wilson "hasn't taken into consideration anything but the interests of big business." Meany said he did not think business wanted a tripartite panel such as the War Labor Board. "They've got their man and their men in this entire defense setup and I don't think they want any equality for labor. They're doing too well as it is." Denying any personal animosity toward Wilson, a statement that must not be taken at face value, Meany declared, "It's quite obvious that we can't get along with the Charlie Wilson that we've had for the past month or two running this defense mobilization program. . . . [T]hat means in the final analysis that he either changes his approach to take into consideration someone else in the country outside of big business or that he's replaced by someone who can think in terms of . . . all of the people in the country." To the Academy of Political Science, Meany made the strongest antibusiness speech of his career, one that had the unfamiliar refrain of class warfare: Meany charged that businessmen were in the stabilization program for a single reason: "greater profits."

The history of modern American business discloses that time after time it has had to be rescued from crises brought about by its own insensate greed. In this defense program—to date—it shows no perceptible change.

The rush of corporation executives to get aboard the gravy train in the defense mobilization setup in Washington during the last eight months is a picture of American business at its greedy worst.

I, for one, reject as hypocritical blather the notion that all the businessmen who have attached themselves to government positions in the defense agencies are motivated by a high degree of patriotism and a keen sense of devotion to the general good. It is interesting to note that they are all in positions where they can take good care of their particular industry including, of course, their own particular business.

. . . Since the Communist invasion of Korea . . . business has manifested its patriotism by raising its prices sky high. . . . While the government was appealing to business to hold the line voluntarily and avoid the necessity for controls, businessmen plunged into an orgy of speculation, hoarding, and war-scare luxury production that was bound to break the line.

Although Meany did not mention Wilson by name in this speech he had barbed comments for the strong-willed GE executive and his domination of the stabilization program: "No person should be allowed to veto democratic solution of labor-management problems during the crisis. If any executive in the defense program cannot adjust his personality to democratic methods, then he should be allowed to resign."

On the surface, Truman's first reaction to the labor revolt was bland indifference. He flew to his vacation retreat in Key West, Florida, leaving peace talks in the hands of a special assistant, Charles S. Murphy. When Truman returned to Washington, in mid-March, he called in a delegation from the United Labor Policy Committee for a chat. For half an hour the President exuded generalities, reciting at length his "friendship for labor" and the "necessity for national unity during emergency." Truman talked about the "reality" of putting a manufacturing executive over the defense program, "because, basically, the problem is production." And he said he would create a broad-based defense advisory committee including labor members. But never did Truman promise the top-level representation in Wilson's program that labor had sought.

Meany squirmed uneasily, for he felt Truman was either uninformed or was attempting to gloss over a bad situation. However, Green and Murray, the titular leaders of the delegation, said nothing. Finally, as Truman was pushing his chair back from the table, a signal he considered the conference at an end, Meany spoke up.

"That won't do, Mr. President," he said. "That doesn't take care of it. I don't think you know the story, Mr. President, and I think you ought to have it. The trouble is, there's not enough responsibility in the agencies themselves, they're run by business." And Meany proceeded to tick off labor's grievances with Wilson, citing his antagonistic attitude and his selection of underlings. By one account, blood rushed to Truman's face, and he bit his tongue in silent anger, for Meany, in effect, was lecturing the President of the United States. When Meany finished, the President frigidly bade the delegation farewell.

Meany's blunt language dismayed Green and Murray, and they left the White House in uncomfortable silence. You either ruined us forever, or you attracted Truman's attention, someone said to Meany. And the evidence suggests that Meany indeed "attracted the President's attention." On April 7, Truman partially met labor's demand for a voice in policy making by creating a seventeen-man Advisory Board on Mobilization Policy, with four representatives each from labor, industry, agriculture, and the public, and Wilson as chairman. The significance of the committee was indicated by the New York *Times,* which noted: "The new national board will advise the President—not Mr. Wilson—and will meet with him once a month. Although Mr. Wilson's executive authority is untouched, labor and the other economic groups will now have an official channel for going over his head to Mr. Truman should the occasion arise."

The advisory board's first recommendation, given to the President on April 17, was for a new eighteen-member Wage Stabilization Board, tripartite in composition, with authority to make recommendations, and, where both parties agreed, to make binding decisions in disputes affecting the national defense. On April 21 Truman accepted the recommendation. As labor wished, he directed that it be "administered in such a way as to preserve collective bargaining between labor and management." As chairman of the new board Truman picked Dr. George Taylor of the University of Pennsylvania, Meany's colleague on the War Labor Board.

The United Labor Policy Committee accepted the changes as a labor victory. On April 30 the ULPC stated that "a significant change of attitudes has taken place in Washington . . . since labor representatives withdrew from defense posts." As a result, the committee anticipated "that substantive progress can now be made." The ULPC cautioned the Administration against assuming labor "is now satisfied with all defense policies or programs," claiming that "the cards are still stacked against the consuming public," and calling for "more vigorous price regulations." Nonetheless the import was clear: labor's withdrawal and Meany's blunt talk to President Truman had forced a drastic revision of the stabilization program. Truman forced Wilson to accept George H. Harrison as one of his assistants, and other labor men went into top positions through the war bureaucracy. Wilson knew he was licked. Beginning in May the new board approved increases in the packing house, auto, and shipyard industries surpassing his old ten percent guideline.

Wilson eventually quit when the board granted a fifteen percent increase in the steel industry and a union shop.

The AFL and CIO, thrust toward one another by adversity, split again soon after labor made peace with the Truman Administration. The decision was the AFL's, and the stated reason and the true reason were not the same. On August 28, 1951, to the surprise of the CIO, Green issued a statement saying, in effect, the United Labor Policy Committee had served its purpose and could be discontinued because labor had won representation on both policy and operational levels of war agencies. Green emphasized the ULPC "was established on a temporary basis. Its operations never were and never could be regarded as a satisfactory substitute for organic unity of the free American trade union movement."

Actually, the AFL was mad because of what Meany called the "double-crossing tactics of the CIO delegation" at a conference of the International Confederation of Free Trade Unions in Milan, Italy, earlier in 1951. Although the AFL felt the CIO had agreed to a joint position on all major issues, the CIO voted for Sir Vincent Tewson, a British trade union official, as president of the ICFTU. The AFL did not want the presidency to be held by any of the major powers.

At an executive council meeting just before Green's announcement, Meany said that since the Korean War emergency had subsided, "We should re-examine our relationship with the CIO in the light of what has happened." There was a "mistaken idea outside the labor movement that the breach between the AFL and CIO has been healed," he said. On Meany's motion, the council voted to "discontinue our affiliation" with the ULPC. "This was the first time in the history of matrimony that divorce proceedings had been instituted because the marriage was too successful," Reuther told Green.

Eli L. Oliver, who was responsible for founding the ULPC, felt keen disappointment when it disintegrated. "At one of its mass meetings in 1951," he said, "Phil Murray and Bill Green embraced on the stage. Everybody there got the impression we were breaking down some of the high barriers and that unity was in sight. The attitude of some of the CIO people was responsible. The CIO top leadership had progressed from the local to the national level only through ingenuity and skill in factional fighting, within their own organizations as well as within the CIO. You must remember that both Reuther and Jim Carey were survivors of some rather bitter internecine battles. When they got into the United Labor Policy Committee, their early conduct was moderately cooperative, but it wasn't long before they lapsed into factional tactics again. They seized on the fact that Bill Green was resentful of the AFL leadership passing out of his hands; they played upon it. Meany finally found it necessary to take a firm position, and call things to a halt, because Bill Green was being unduly influenced. It should have been a merger. Reuther, Carey, and Goldberg were responsible for the committee's not maturing into unity."

William Green's health failed rapidly during the late 1940's, and he spent long weeks away from his office, preferring the restful quiet of his small cottage in the mining town of Coshocton, Ohio. His absence put Meany in an ambiguous situation. Meany had the responsibility for running the American Federation of Labor but not the actual authority. Respectful of protocol, and unwilling "to shove a dying man out of the way," in the words of an associate, Meany was more discreet than ever in his dealings with the executive council. Green's spirits revived briefly during the wage stabilization fight with President Truman ("This is the greatest day of my life," he exulted in February 1951, when labor walked off the defense agencies). But before the year ended Green was virtually immobile, unable to pay more than cursory attention to federation business. "That was a pretty hectic year for George," recollected Boris Shishkin. "He was doing the administrative work, and also trying to get the federation through a political campaign."

Meany's chief concern in 1952 was maneuvering the AFL into a position where it could be persuaded to give formal endorsement to the Democratic candidate for President. All spring he argued that "business interests" and "big business"—his euphemisms for Republicans—were not content with a "subservient Congress." Additionally, he said, "They want a President in the White House who subscribes to the theory that prosperity comes only from the top—that if the large corporations are allowed to increase their already swollen profits, then more and more will trickle down for the benefit of the people as a whole." Meany said labor could find "little inspiration or encouragement from the mildewed mumblings of those who failed the nation so miserably in the early crucial years of the great depression."

Meany's strategy called for scrupulous, if formalistic, adherence to the principle that labor endorsed a candidate on the basis of his labor attitudes, not his party. His first step was to persuade the executive council to hold the AFL convention after the nominating conventions, but before the election. Meany made lengthy presentations to the platform committees of both parties. Speaking for the AFL, he asked for repeal of Taft-Hartley, enactment of a strong anti-inflation program, and for strengthening the defense of the free world against Communist aggression. Other points included pledges on federal aid to education, more low-cost housing, liberalization of Social Security to include Medicare insurance, a $1-per-hour minimum wage, and a federal fair employment practices law. Just as labor anticipated, the Republican convention rejected or ignored most of its platform, then nominated General Dwight D. Eisenhower. At the Democratic convention labor fared better. Meany led a labor coalition that managed to dissuade Vice-President Alben W. Barkley, President Truman's favorite for successor, from seeking the nomination. Labor told Barkley he was too old, and he withdrew. Then Meany threw AFL support behind Governor Adlai E. Stevenson of Illinois, who won handily over Senator Estes Kefauver.

Stevenson's victory, and the Democratic platform, made obvious whom labor would support, but Meany carefully avoided making any formal commitment until both candidates had a chance to address the AFL convention. At the AFL convention Stevenson endorsed outright repeal of Taft-Hartley. Eisenhower, however, would endorse only unspecified amendments, saying, "I have talked about the Taft-Hartley Act with both industry and labor people. I know how the law might be used to break unions. That must be changed. America wants no law licensing union busting, and neither do I." Whereupon the convention overwhelmingly endorsed Stevenson.

Labor's campaign for Stevenson was vigorous but futile. Labor's League for Political Action, acting as the front group for labor campaigning, once again found the rank and file unenthused about cash contributions. Indeed, LLPE's reported spending in 1952 was $10,017 less than the $259,275 reported as Republican contributions by four families alone—the Rockefellers, Mellons, duPonts, and Pews. Despite the overwhelming Eisenhower victory, however, labor's political work—registration drives, radio speeches by Meany and other officials, and doorbell-ringing campaigns—did help the Democrats preserve control of Congress, with 47 senators and 213 representatives.

That Green was a sick, failing man was obvious to everyone at the September convention. Weak though he was, however, Green insisted on presiding and making several long speeches, and attending committee meetings and conferences. "It was a sad thing," said Boris Shishkin. "Green was so near the end of the road, and he seemed to realize it. He didn't want to turn loose." After adjournment Green returned to Washington briefly, then called in Meany and said, "I'm tired, and I think I'll go home a few days and rest."

Back in Coshocton, where he was born and had worked as an open-pit miner, Green entered the hospital for a two-day checkup that showed him suffering from exhaustion and a failing heart. His physician ordered him to bed. Eisenhower's victory upset Green. Then, on November 9, another shock: Philip Murray died suddenly, of a heart attack, at age sixty-six. Despite their union differences the two old miners had respected and liked one another personally, and Green felt the death keenly. He did not try to go to Murray's funeral, and he telephoned Meany to say, "It doesn't look like I'm going to be back in the office for a while; you have authority to do whatever needs to be done. Good luck." The night of November 20 Green suffered a severe heart attack; midafternoon the next day, he died.

Meany had been in New York that day—at Green's request—for a meeting with President Eisenhower and was en route back to Washington on the train when his secretary, Virginia Tehas, phoned and notified him of Green's death. Meany mused to a close friend years later, "I sat down, and closed my eyes, and said a prayer for Bill. I had known the day was coming, but I was back in Washington before I really realized what it meant."

The executive council gathered in Coshocton on November 24 for Green's funeral. Under the AFL constitution Meany automatically became acting president. Although the press speculated briefly about competition for the presidency—George H. Harrison of the railway clerks and Dan Tobin of the Teamsters were two of the names mentioned—Meany's election was a virtual certainty. Old-timers on the council persuaded Tobin to try for the presidency. Then president emeritus of the Teamsters, Tobin had served on the council since 1917, and his friends thought he deserved the presidency until the next convention, in the fall of 1953. "Dan scouted around and managed to get six votes," Meany said. "But he needed seven, and he couldn't find that last one. When he realized he couldn't win, he let the whole thing slide. Old Dan knew how to count, and he wasn't going to be beaten in a council vote just for the sake of making the race."

At ten-thirty in the morning on November 25, the council convened again, this time in its conference room on the seventh floor of the AFL Building in Washington. Crepe shrouded both Green's portrait and chair, which remained vacant. Meany, who knew he would be nominated for president, asked Matthew Woll to preside. The council stood a moment in silent homage to Green, appointed a committee to write a memorial resolution for presentation to his family, and then got down to business.

As a gesture of respect, W. C. McFetridge put Tobin into nomination and asked that he serve until the next convention. Tobin, realizing he had no chance of beating Meany, said he was honored, but he declined to run. "I am getting old," he said. "Of course, it would be quite an honor to my children and my grandchildren if I was for a few months president of this federation for history to write, but sensibility and decency and courage for this labor movement means more than honor." Tobin said he could not accept the presidency, even if elected, "because of my age and my health." Then Tobin nominated Meany, beginning by recounting how he had persuaded him to become secretary-treasurer at the 1939 convention in Cincinnati. Tobin noted that Meany had been performing the job of both president and secretary-treasurer for a year, and quite well. The vote was unanimous. George Meany, at age fifty-six, was president of the American Federation of Labor. At his request, the council then named William Schnitzler, a hulking bakery union official from New Jersey, as secretary-treasurer.

The AFL constitution does not contain an oath of office, so Matt Woll, after declaring Meany president, simply gave him the floor. After thanking the council for the vote and pledging to "do the very best I can in this job," Meany mused about himself, what he brought to the presidency, and what he intended to do with it: "I have no other interest in life outside of my family and this federation. I have no investments. I have nothing outside of what the federation gives me. I have no grudges. . . .

"I relish this job just for one thing alone. I was born in this movement. My father was a trade unionist. He was a vice-president of the plumbers union in 1902 and he was local business agent in my union back in those days. He had a great interest in it. I learned a great deal about the trade union movement and to me this is the greatest honor that could possibly come to me in my lifetime. I do not relish the work in the sense of the time it will take but I am prepared to give it all of my time and give it the very best that I have in me.

". . . I say to you that I am in this job not as a building trades mechanic, not as a plumber, but as an American trade unionist. There is a job to be done. I hope to be able to do that job, and I expect and depend on the cooperation of each and every member of this council here."

# Labor United:
# A Hyphen for the AFL-CIO

I
N LATE 1952 George Meany found trouble in almost every direction he looked. President Eisenhower's election meant labor could no longer use a friendly White House as a buffer against the conservative coalition controlling the nominally Democratic Congress. Labor had fought the Republicans, bitterly and openly, and it had lost, and now it could face the consequences from an antiunion, probusiness Administration. AFL and CIO unions dissipated whatever organizational energies they had in dreary, money-consuming feuds, which the general public dismissed as petty jealousy, and which aided few workers. The stench of corruption from a key AFL union, the International Longshoremen's Association, exposed beginning late in the year by a New York investigative commission, sickened even labor's friends.

To Meany, unity with the CIO transcended every other issue. "The idea of putting all unions into a national trade union center is just as basic to the trade union movement as going into a shop and saying we think everybody in this shop ought to join the union. It's a question of presenting a solid front on labor problems. No union, no matter how big it is, has the authority of a national trade union center, nor commands the respect a center does." At a press conference immediately after his election, Meany announced the reactivation of a "committee on organic unity" and said he was ready to open talks with whomever the CIO elected to replace Philip Murray.

Previously, by Meany's analysis, the "barrier of personality" had prevented merger. The public issue involved in the original split was the refusal of the AFL executive council to carry out the mandate of the 1934 convention to organize in the rubber, steel, cement, and auto industries. "The council done absolutely nothing," Meany said. "Arthur Wharton, of the machinists union, was typical. He said, 'Organize anywhere you want to, but don't you dare touch a machinist.' That was awfully stupid, but it was a way of life in those days." John L. Lewis and other advocates of industrial unionism fumed for three years, then formed the Committee on Industrial Organization, within the AFL. The executive council ordered the committee disbanded, Lewis refused, and in 1937 its member unions withdrew from the AFL and became the Congress of Industrial Organizations. But Meany never accepted the thesis that industrial-versus-craft organizing was at the core of the dispute.

"The real reason the CIO was formed was John Lewis' desire to control the labor movement politically," Meany said. "Lewis was thinking of bigger things than organizing. Frankly, I think John was dreaming of being the leader who led the working class to the control of society. He was that ambitious." Meany also felt President Roosevelt encouraged the schism in 1936 as a means of going over the head of the conservative AFL executive council to obtain rank-and-file labor support. "There was absolutely no trade union reason for the split," Meany said. "It was strictly personality."

And Meany blamed lingering animosities for souring peace talks until he and Reuther were suddenly thrust to the fronts of their respective organizations. "The strong people on the AFL side and the strong people on the CIO side who were on those unity committees were the people who were engaged in the original split. They were no longer around. Neither Reuther or me had been involved in the split, so we didn't have that problem. It was a lot easier also because the CIO fellows knew me, because of our contacts during the War Labor Board days and the wage stabilization during the Korean War. My contacts with the CIO in those years were not adversary contacts; they were contacts of cooperation."

Green considered the CIO renegades who should return as repentants. In speeches he referred to "my erring fellow workers" and invited them to "come back into the house of labor, happily furnished, beautifully decorated, and occupy the rooms we have kept for you." Meany said, "Bill Green had done nothing for five years but go around making speeches denouncing the group which was tearing us apart. He would always wind up that they should 'come back home.' This wasn't convincing anybody. So I didn't have any of these disadvantages. In fact, I remember one of the early meetings of the unity committee, one of the CIO fellows said, 'Hell, we don't have to talk about who's going to be president, it's going to be that fellow right there,' pointing to me."

Paradoxically, labor "peace" was made the easier by turmoil within the CIO. The contestants for the presidency were Walter Reuther, of the United Auto Workers, and Allan S. Haywood, executive vice-president of the CIO, who had strong sentimental identification with Murray. Reuther, then forty-five years old, carried a hard-earned reputation for dynamism. A stocky redhead with constantly alert eyes, son of a German-born Socialist brewery worker, Reuther literally came off the auto production line to power in the UAW. He was a director of the sit-down strikes that broke General Motors' resistance to unionism. He survived a bloody public beating by Ford security guards and a shotgun assassination attempt (whether by union rivals, Communists, employers, or the underworld was never established) that permanently crippled his left arm. Reuther won the UAW presidency in 1946 in a vote that split the union almost 50–50, but by 1952 he had consolidated his hold on it. Allan Haywood, then sixty-four, an English-born coal miner, was a stand-in candidate for David J. McDonald, the newly elected president of the United Steel Workers, second only to the UAW in CIO membership. Murray had headed the CIO and USW simultaneously, and McDonald felt he deserved both offices as well. A vain, strutting popinjay with the silver locks and self-important mannerisms of a movie idol, McDonald detested Reuther as a usurping upstart. According to Reuther, "McDonald used Haywood to try to put a caretaker in charge of the CIO on the basis that at the next convention he [McDonald] would take over." Haywood was a good substitute candidate. A gregarious man with an impenetrable Yorkshire accent, he stressed he could be a "full-time president" since he would not be running an international union in addition to the CIO. Reuther's abrasiveness had offended many CIO unions. Reuther supporters, however, maintained that he would be a more vigorous and attractive spokesman for the CIO than the down-to-earth Haywood, and that his youth would revitalize the organization. Reuther won, by holding support of all the larger unions except McDonald's steelworkers. On the basis of claimed membership-strength balloting, Reuther received 3,078,181 votes; Haywood, 2,613,103.*

McDonald was so embittered at the outcome that he declined to free his steelworker delegation to cast the traditional unanimous vote for convention winners. And after Reuther's election a majority of the convention voted to change the constitution to make the president's actions subject to review each two months by an executive committee of principal officers of affiliated unions and CIO vice-presidents. The CIO was not about to give Reuther the free-wheeling authority of a John L. Lewis or a Philip Murray.

---

* The roll call embarrassed the CIO, because many unions claimed more members than they actually had. By mutual agreement, Haywood and Reuther boosted voting strength of all affiliates to match the claimed figures.

In his acceptance speech, Reuther endorsed unity, but also used some ambiguous language that left uncertain what role he or Meany might play in a merger movement. At no time, he said, would "a vested right in an office be the smallest obstacle in the way of achieving a united labor movement." Meany, when he called soon after Reuther's election to offer congratulations, found the CIO president noncommittal. Later, talking with reporters after presiding over his first CIO executive committee meeting, Reuther said the CIO was in no hurry. He did not intend to name a unity committee until January or February and CIO leaders wanted to "think through" the question before acting. However, the CIO executive committee did authorize Reuther to talk with Meany. They had a casual conversation at a dinner given by the International Confederation of Free Trade Unions in early December, and agreed to talk more formally in January, after Reuther recuperated from planned gall bladder surgery. Hence they did not get down to business until early 1953, over sandwiches in Reuther's suite in the Statler Hotel in Washington.

Meany said of the session, "I don't think he had preconceived ideas about unity. I think at the time he was paying lip service to his instructions, by meeting with me. I explained to him that I wasn't going to have any great number of meetings unless there was some chance of success. I made a proposal that if we really wanted to get unity, the first thing we should try to do was to stop the open warfare between the AFL and the CIO. There were areas where relations were good, but there were a certain number of organizations which were raiding, on our side and theirs. I said, 'Let's see if we can create an atmosphere which would be conducive to unity by ending the raiding.' He was responsive to that. I suggested that as a first step, we should try to find out just how much raiding there was, and how much movement on either side we gained in terms of membership. I felt we should get this information and see if we could go from there to a no-raid pact. He agreed to that."

Although Meany wanted unity, he also made plain he did not intend to waste time in fruitless bickering. "I was going to find out if there was a definite possibility of unity; if so, I was going to work very hard at it; if not, I was going to come back and tell them [the executive council] that we would go about our business, and the CIO would go about their business." Meany tried to make plain to outsiders that the process would be long and probably painful. To the National Press Club, on December 11, he said that as a "two-dollar bettor, I'd say the odds are not in favor of unity. Let's say eight to five. . . ." Neither he nor Reuther "can pick up a union and say you go over there" and merge; that neither "owns these unions. Each AFL and CIO union is autonomous, and proud, and has officials interested in keeping their jobs."

The negotiations got off to a fitful start. As a personal assistant Meany recruited George Brown, a professor of economics at Johns Hopkins University, a friend from War Labor Board days. Meany assigned Brown to analyze National Labor Relations Board records on cross raids between AFL and CIO unions. And in several forums Meany and Reuther made clear that the differences between the two organizations were real. On Taft-Hartley revisions, for instance, Reuther became alarmed that Meany would strike a deal with the Republican-conservative coalition for changes helping craft unions and hurting industrial unions. Meany in fact did ask the House Labor and Education Committee to leave intact the right of a craft union to carve away craftsmen from a broad, industrial-type bargaining unit. Reuther, speaking to the same forum a few days later, angrily charged that the NLRB was leaning over backward under Taft-Hartley to favor craft severance, at the expense of CIO unions. Reuther brought the differences to a head in a March speech to the United Auto Workers convention, one that both the labor and the daily press interpreted as demanding four "conditions" for unity: maintenance of the industrial union structure; establishment of "rational machinery" to settle jurisdictional disputes; elimination of racial and religious discrimination in all affiliated unions; and expulsion of racketeering elements as well as Communists.

The speech irritated Meany. His understanding was that the exploratory talks were not to go into specifics of any merger agreement; hence he felt Reuther had bent, if not broken altogether, his word. Although Meany claimed to be "still hopeful" about the merger, "the odds are against it," he said in response to Reuther. And in a backhanded retort to Reuther's precondition on Communists, he thanked the CIO for solving the AFL's problem "because the Communists disappeared overnight into the CIO when it was formed. John L. Lewis took them into his bosom and kept them there." Testifying to the Senate Labor Committee on Taft-Hartley a few days later, Meany professed to be worried that Communists were trying to get back into the CIO. "I'm afraid they might succeed now that Mr. Murray is dead," he said. Meany referred specifically to a 10,000-member New York local of a department store union, part of a left-wing union the CIO had expelled in 1950 when its officers took the Fifth Amendment when questioned about Communist activity. In readmitting the local to the CIO's Retail, Wholesale and Department Store Union, Reuther maintained the officers had disavowed communism and the union was now clean. Nonetheless Meany's speech stung him.

Concurrently, Reuther had troubles within his own camp, from the irascible David McDonald, still smoldering over Allan Haywood's loss of the CIO presidency. In his autobiography McDonald was candid about his feelings toward Reuther. "I didn't like Reuther, and I presume he felt the same way about me. His patronizing attitude and tendency to lecture those of us among the unwashed were difficult for me to swallow, and I considered his absentee stewardship of the CIO ineffective." In midspring stories cropped up in the press that McDonald was considering leading the United Steel Workers out of the CIO. The stories contained enough detail to have the ring of truth, and they bore trustworthy bylines. Nonetheless McDonald went before the UAW convention to make pained protestations of innocence. The United Steel Workers, he said, had "invested" $15,672,732.59 in the CIO since the USW's founding in July 1938. "In view of this, would we idly cast away such an investment? Of course not. We would no sooner cast away an investment like that than would the General Motors Corporation cast away its investment in the Cadillac plants. . . .

"Now there have been stories around that I, Dave McDonald, have been meeting with representatives of the American Federation of Labor, and I want to tell you here and now that those stories are absolutely true: I have been.

"As a matter of fact, just Wednesday of last week, I went into a famous fish house in New York City and lo and behold a fellow said, 'Dave, I have a table for you over here.' I had a little conversation with him. Do you know who that fellow was? He was business agent for the Waiters Union in New York City. Since I have been in town I have been meeting with representatives of the AFL. I had a conversation with a couple of bartenders here. . . . But that is as far as my meetings have gone."

McDonald's denial was something less than the truth. McDonald, in fact, had sought out Jay Lovestone, as a trusted member of Meany's inner circle, and discussed with him the possibility of the USW coming back into the AFL unilaterally. Lovestone was all for it. Lovestone said he told Meany, "George, if you have a merger, you will have trouble. Get them one by one—then you'll have no problem with a merger." Meany knew what was happening. Because of "the personality clash between McDonald and Reuther," Meany said, he realized the CIO "was about to disintegrate." Meany stated: "I don't want them to fall into my lap, because I think if the CIO disintegrates, it's going to be bad for labor, it's going to be bad for everybody to have a national trade union center sort of fall apart. It wouldn't even work to the interest in the long run of the unions in the AFL to pick them all up. If this would be the way they were assimilated, this could be the way they leave, too. I wasn't interested in that."

But Meany recognized that Reuther and the other CIO leaders had one legitimate condition for merger: that the AFL expunge its ranks of corrupt unionists, just as the CIO had thrown out Communists and their adherents. To do so required that Meany breach the time-honored autonomy of affiliated unions.

The longshoremen's union for half a century—that is, since its founding—was a recognized but untouched labor scandal. Employers, union bosses, and politicians alike exploited the unskilled, illiterate Irish and Italian immigrants who worked the piers of New York's West Side and Brooklyn—low-paying arduous work no one else would touch. The corruption was staggering in scope and visibility. Men were hired through the "shapeup," the arbitrary selection of men by a hiring boss from a group huddled on a pier. Gangster-controlled ILA locals kept work forces inflated so that hiring bosses could command kickbacks from men put on jobs. Compulsory "six-for-five" loan sharking and forced "charitable contributions" further drained members. Insurgents were brutally eliminated. In 1937–39 a young longshoreman named Pete Panto won about a thousand supporters from six Brooklyn ILA locals controlled by Albert Anastasia, the head executioner for Murder, Inc., the Mafia's enforcement arm. Panto disappeared; his body turned up a year later in a lime pit in Ohio. Other locals were dominated by such mob figures as Anthony ("Tony Cheese") Marchitto and Anthony ("Tony Bender") Stroller, an associate of Lucky Luciano. Steamship and stevedore companies paid ILA bosses handsomely for "labor peace."

Joe Ryan worked in this atmosphere all his life. A product of the West Side's tough Chelsea district, Ryan went to the docks at age twelve. He listened and worked uncomplainingly in the existing system, and in 1926 he became president of the ILA. A strapping, solidly built redhead with a longshoreman's physique and an Irishman's quick tongue, Ryan on the surface was the epitome of the family man and strong union leader. He liked good food and well-tailored suits; he was an Elk and an enthusiastic golfer. A devout Catholic, he found much time for the Holy Name Society. He was a vice-president of the New York Central Trades and Labor Council. Faithful to Tammany Hall, Ryan funneled ILA funds—money from employers—to state and city politicians in New York and New Jersey. The Joseph P. Ryan Association, created solely to caress Ryan's ego at an annual banquet, had as sponsors and guests at its annual affair virtually every major political figure in the area—Governors Smith, Roosevelt, and Dewey of New York; and Mayors Walker and Impellitteri of New York and Hague of Jersey City. In fact, Joe Ryan had only two defects: drink and corruption.

As New York state fed president, Meany kept his distance from Ryan. He overrode Ryan and Tammany Hall to put labor behind Fiorello La Guardia in the 1933 and 1937 mayoralty races, and he managed to keep both La Guardia and Lehman from being caught up in the self-adulation

—and gangster guest list—of Ryan's annual banquets. Yet Meany never lifted a hand against recognized ILA corruption, either as state federation president or as AFL secretary-treasurer. He asserted he was not in a position to invade the principle of autonomy enunciated by Gompers in 1888, that "the federation has no powers except those which are authorized and conceded by the organizations which compose it. . . . The AFL has no power to enforce its judgment. . . ." The AFL, through convention resolutions and executive council, time and again said corruption was a matter for police authorities and international unions.

But Joe Ryan's ILA, when Meany became president, was a cesspool which the AFL could ignore at its own peril. ILA corruption came under increasing attack in the postwar period, from returning veterans tired of the old shapeup/graft system, and from New York merchants drained by the extra costs of thievery and ILA racketeering. A New York State Crime Commission, appointed by Governor Thomas E. Dewey, spent much of 1951 and 1952 amassing evidence on ILA affairs. It traced hundreds of thousands of dollars in kickback money paid by employers to Ryan and other ILA officials. Ryan admitted taking some money but claimed it was for "political and anti-Communist" activities. His bank records, however, revealed the money to have gone for golf club dues, Caribbean cruises, expensive clothes, and personal insurance premiums.

In discussing Ryan's case years later, Meany tried to give the old longshoreman the benefit of whatever doubts he could find. "Now, Joe Ryan, in his day," Meany said, "was an outstanding labor leader, one of the best. But he had this personal problem—liquor." Meany continued, "He would go on these benders. He would start drinking at the Hotel New Yorker, and three or four days later he'd be down in these joints on the waterfront, quite literally right in the gutter. They'd go down there and find him, and dry him out, and put him in the hospital, and get him off it. For a while this is something that happened every year or eighteen months, then it got to be twice a year, and then almost every month.

"The gangsters and the hoodlums, of course, they were able to move right in around him and take over the union. The poor guy who depended on dock work for his livelihood, he couldn't get regular work. There was also the loan sharking and kickbacks to hiring bosses, a real mess."

The New York State Crime Commission's initial report, issued in August 1952, called the ILA crook-dominated, and the AFL shot back that the investigation was a "biased and dangerous invasion." Throughout the fall, however, the commission continued to amass evidence, concluding that Ryan even used his position on the New York State Pardons Board to put ex-convicts into business agent and other positions in the ILA locals. One witness said the ILA preferred that thugs be hired:

"The worse record you had, the easier it was to get a job." The Washington *Evening Star* commented on December 11, less than a month after Meany's election, ". . . If this sort of 'union autonomy' continues unchecked, the AFL cannot escape a share of the blame for the type of lawless unionism it has bred on the New York docks. . . . The AFL, for its own protection if nothing else, should join eagerly in the move to restore law and order on the New York waterfront."

Meany did not care for journalistic pressures. When a *Newsweek* interviewer asked in early January 1953 why the AFL didn't move against the ILA, he testily replied, "It might just as well be asked why the American Bankers Association doesn't act on charges of embezzlement against officials of member banks. Punishment for crime is provided for in the laws governing all citizens. . . ." And in a National Press Club speech he said, "It isn't a case of the union using gangsters; it's a case of the gangsters using the union."

The criticisms of the AFL carried an implication that touched Meany to the quick: that he "accepted" corruption as an inescapable concomitant of unionism. Meany frequently pointed with pride to his Local 463 in New York—a union where members attending weekly meetings were given mimeographed sheets listing every cent of expenditures, from paper towels, drinking cups, and postage stamps to officers' salaries and expenses. "The honest plumber," columnist Westbrook Pegler called Meany during the 1930's, when he wrote about corruption elsewhere in New York unionism. Meany demanded strait-laced deportment of subordinates in Washington. While secretary-treasurer, Meany discovered an AFL functionary was taking numbers bets from other employees. Nelson Cruikshank, of the AFL staff, said, "When he came back from lunch there was Meany sitting at his desk. Meany said, 'You've got half an hour to get your papers out of here. Here is your check.' Meany stayed right there and conducted him out of the building." Another employee was arrested for drunk driving in Miami Beach during an AFL convention; a woman staff member was with him. Meany, outraged, said he wanted to see neither at out-of-town AFL functions again: "They are an affront to the organization."

One past association did cause Meany fleeting embarrassment. Beginning in the 1920's he was a friend and sometime golfing companion of Joe Fay, head of the powerful operating engineers union in the New York metropolitan area. "Joe was a pretty nice guy except when he was drunk," Meany said. In 1945 a jury convicted Fay and an officer of the hod carriers union of taking at least $368,000 from contractors on an aqueduct project. Fay was sentenced to 8½ years in prison. From his cell in Sing Sing Fay tried to persuade old political and labor friends to win him freedom. One person approached was Meany, who had known Fay, his mother, and his brothers "for twenty years or so." Meany saw Fay twice, first in 1949, again the next year; each visit lasted about twenty minutes. Not wishing the trips to be charged against Fay's monthly quota of visitors, Meany made the visits with another friend, State Senator William F. Condon, a Yonkers Republican, who as a state official could enter Sing Sing at will. According to Meany, "the only thing Fay talked about was how he could get out of prison—through a pardon or commutation or something like that. I gave him no encouragement on that." The visits became known in October 1953, when an investigation of the prison showed Condon's name on Fay's list of visitors. The disclosure caused a twelve-hour ripple in the press, and Meany heard jibes thereafter about "your Sing Sing buddy." The public, however, accepted Meany's declaration that he did not condone what Fay had done, and visited him from loyalty to the family.

Meany brought the Ryan case before the executive council at a special meeting in January 1953. Meany wrote Ryan that the state hearing record indicated "that these workers in the Port of New York are being exploited in every possible way. . . . Your relationship with the [AFL] demands that democratic ideals and clean and wholesome free trade unionism must be immediately restored within your organization and all semblance of crime, dishonesty and racketeering be forthwith eliminated." Speaking in the name of the executive council, Meany demanded the reform of the shapeup hiring system and the firing of officers with criminal records and persons revealed to have taken bribes.

Meany recited the AFL's traditional policy of autonomy, but he added a new codicil: "The exercise of autonomy . . . presupposes the maintenance of minimum standards of trade union decency."

The dispatch with which Meany moved against the ILA surprised some AFL staff members long accustomed to Green's deliberate pace. Nelson Cruikshank, for example, noted, "Meany hadn't yet run the gantlet of a convention election. So in a way this was his trial period . . . and he moved in on Joe Ryan. Now, here was a man in his own constituency, in a sense, in his own state, a powerful international president, moving in on him before he had ever been elected by a convention. The people in the AFL who had been ashamed of what was going on in New York took new hope; here was a real leader, not afraid to do something."

The issue, Meany said, was whether an AFL union "could use autonomy as a shield for people who are corrupt. . . . It was a tough question, but we had a tough situation. However, there was no division at all within the executive council; none whatsoever, there was no politics at all in the sense of some opposing moving on Ryan. Everyone was concerned about the problem, because the facts had been brought out rather forcibly. . . ." Officers of other unions concerned about the ILA situation "weren't willing to act on their own, to criticize another union; they wanted the executive council, the AFL, to take the lead, and that is what we done."

Meany, for the council, ordered Ryan to report by April 30 what he was doing to cleanse the union. A New York grand jury, in the meanwhile, indicted Ryan for misuse of $11,390 of union funds—an assessment bond at a golf club; for insurance premiums, silk shirts, real estate taxes, even funeral expenses for a sister-in-law. Ryan's response to the executive council was defensive. He claimed that longshoremen rank and file favored shapeup hiring. He defended acceptance of gifts ("Thanksgiving turkeys, bottles of liquor, or simple cash presents") as "commonplace" for officials of AFL unions but agreed to halt the practice. He opposed criminals holding union office but warned against blanket condemnations. "The AFL should not throw men and organizations to the wolves to justify journalistic hatchet men or ambitious politicians who seek to ride to power on the back of some outstanding labor leader," Ryan said. "Yesterday the howling mob were after some other labor leaders whose names are undoubtedly fresh in your minds. Today it is Joseph P. Ryan. . . . The ILA and Joseph P. Ryan represent today a good case in which to apply the great principles of justice, law, and equality for all."

Ryan's answer did not satisfy Meany. The ILA could abolish the shapeup without waiting for new employer negotiations, he said. Meany also saw no action against union bribe-takers or underworld figures in the ILA, nor any implementation of the internal "reforms" pledged by Ryan.

An investigative subcommittee chaired by Senator Charles W. Tobey (Rep., New Hampshire) prodded Meany to move faster. At hearings in May Meany testified that neither he nor the executive council had the power to expel the ILA; that such action could come only from the convention. Tobey said that would be too long a delay. "Don't you think you ought to amend the constitution—"

Meany interrupted. "We'll amend the constitution as we think it should be amended. And we will not ask you. We'll decide—you won't —what should be done about waterfront unions."

Piqued, Tobey shouted, "We've decided. We'll pass legislation that will put the hooks in this situation." When Tobey put criminal records of ILA officers into the hearing record, Meany, his voice rising, interjected, "If a member of Congress is accused, does the Congress kick him out? They wait until he is convicted."

Meany worked hard to avoid the final step of expulsion, gradually tightening pressure on Ryan. "We called the ILA in, and said, 'You people got to change this situation.' They made promises off and on over the months, and the fact is they did nothing." In August the executive council voted to recommend suspension by the September convention. Meany hoped expulsion could be avoided. "Bear in mind that there are 60,000 members of the ILA involved," he said. "They have a traditional adherence to the AFL. The ILA . . . has been a part of the AFL for more than sixty years. We have to think of their welfare. These 60,000 are not the guilty ones." His efforts were to no avail, and at the convention Meany submitted a formal resolution asking for expulsion. "The ILA," he declared, "has permitted gangsters, racketeers, and thugs to fasten themselves to the body of its organizations, infecting it with corruption and destroying its integrity, its effectiveness and its trade-union character. . . . For such, there is no place in the American Federation of Labor."

Ryan pleaded to the convention for further time, arguing that the crime commission findings were "triple-plated hearsay" from "notorious pro-Communist spokesmen." Ryan was wasting his time; one reporter described him as a "weary and broken figure" who made "his fruitless plea in a gravel-throated voice." The convention heard him in icy silence, then voted 72,362 to 765 for ouster. The federation chartered a new union, the International Brotherhood of Longshoremen, and authorized the executive council to spend $200,000 to organize old ILA members into a new waterfront union.

The campaign failed, although the dock unions were substantially cleansed of corrupt elements in the process. The National Labor Relations Board gave the AFL only one week to prepare for the first election, held amidst a strike in December 1953. The ILA won, 9,060 votes to 7,568, but there was so much violence at the polls that the NLRB ordered a new election for May 1954. Again a loss, this time by 263 votes after several thousand challenged ILA ballots were discarded. Friends of the insurgent longshoremen sharply criticized the AFL's organizing prowess. Mrs. Mary Vorse, editor of *The Masses,* a leftist publication supporting dock reforms, called the loss "completely inexcusable" and put much of the blame on Meany. "There were no big mass meetings. The longshoremen were never addressed by higher union officials. Free time on television was refused by the AFL press department. George Meany seems to have treated the drive as a local matter." During the campaign Edward R. Murrow spent an hour talking with Meany on his famed "See It Now" television program. Despite the opportunity to publicize the vote, Mrs. Vorse complained that Meany "made but one fleeting reference to the waterfront drive . . . he spent all his time showing [Murrow] cups and presents that he'd gotten from the ICFTU." Meany said the AFL deliberately remained in the background. "This was an internal union thing," he said. "We didn't want it to look like it was a

Washington-versus-the-leadership sort of thing; we wanted the opposition to look local. So we kept the hell out of the way."

The executive council, however, blamed the loss on the "combined opposition of underworld forces . . . and the New York Shipping Association." The employers, the council said, were quite happy to continue sweetheart contracts negotiated by the ILA.

By the third dock union election, held in 1956, Meany had internal problems. The Teamsters were encountering trouble from Senate investigators* and apparently thought the time opportune to find new allies outside the AFL-CIO. Early in the year James R. Hoffa, a rising power in the Teamsters, offered to lend the ILA $400,000 for organizational purposes. Meany complained to Dave Beck, who had replaced Dan Tobin as Teamster president in late 1952. Meany noted that the Teamsters had supported the expulsion of the ILA "because of corrupt influence." He continued, "To what extent the accord mentioned might make the Teamsters . . . an ally with the corrupt influence that still seems to dominate the ILA is a matter of concern. . . ." If Hoffa made the loan, Meany told Beck, he intended to ask the executive council to suspend the Teamsters from the AFL-CIO. Hoffa withdrew the offer. Another dissident, Joseph Curran, of the National Maritime Union, announced his support of the ILA a few hours before the election. Meany exploded, for Curran was a member of the AFL-CIO ethical practices committee, establishment of which the CIO had insisted upon as a condition of merger. Meany wrote Curran: "You wrote to me and transmitted the contents of your letter to the newspapers of New York City in the early evening of October 15 FOR ONE PURPOSE—AND ONLY ONE PURPOSE—TO ASSIST THE OLD ILA GANG TO RETAIN THEIR CONTROL OVER THE LONGSHOREMEN OF THE NEW YORK AREA. . . . [Meany's emphasis.] Under these circumstances, I have serious doubts as to any effective contribution you could make as a member of the ethical practices committee." The IBL lost this time by a three-to-two margin, and the AFL abandoned the campaign.

"We spent over a million dollars, we did a real tough, hard organizing campaign," Meany said. "The problem was we were trying to go against an old tradition, to persuade fellows to vote against their own union. The younger fellows they did this, because they knew what the gangsters were doing; the old ones, they wouldn't. They'd say, 'What the hell, we've always been with the ILA, we can't go against our own union.' "

The 1959 federation convention approved the readmission of the ILA to its ranks. Seventy-five persons had been barred from office in the union, either for criminal activity or taking money from employers, and Ryan's successor, Captain William Bradley, had substantially improved

* See Chapter X.

contract terms. The average wage of $2,469 in 1954 had been boosted to $4,108; the ILA had a seniority system, a dental and medical clinic, paid holidays for the first time, and workable grievance machinery. "We did some good when we kicked them out and we are now ready to take them back," Meany said.

The merger talks, concurrently, proceeded with fits and starts. After resolving the brief flurry on preconditions, the negotiators hit another snag on exchanges of internal information. The AFL merely gave the CIO copies of its convention proceedings, which contained detailed membership lists, by international unions, and financial statements. James Carey, the CIO secretary-treasurer, produced a copy of the CIO constitution, a booklet containing jurisdiction claims of each organization, and a financial statement. But Meany reported to the executive council that Carey would not give the AFL membership figures, only what he called "voting membership"—the admittedly inflated claims used in the Reuther-Haywood election. The "voting membership" was 5,692,000. However, Meany said, dividing dues income by the per capita tax revealed a true dues-paying membership of 3,900,000. Reuther would not confirm this figure, Meany said, on the grounds the information "might be of some advantage to the employer."

In midsummer the report on cross-raiding between AFL and CIO unions was completed. "It turned out pretty much as I expected, that the real purpose of the raiding was to sort of keep the fight alive; in other words, fighting with other unions made good copy when they got to conventions. . . . We got some astonishing figures out of this thing, showing, number one, that the unions who raided were the unions who were in turn raided. . . ."

During the years 1951–1953 AFL affiliates filed 790 representation petitions with the NLRB covering 213,144 workers for whom the CIO was the recognized bargaining agent; CIO affiliates, 936 petitions covering 357,783 workers in AFL unions. Two of the three petitions were unsuccessful, workers voting to stay with their old bargaining unit. The AFL won away 44,000 members from the CIO, while the CIO, in its successful elections, took 40,755 former AFL members, a "margin" for the AFL of 3,245. However, in the same elections 4,446 workers voted to withdraw all union affiliation. From the AFL's standpoint, Meany said, "more people went nonunion than actually those represented by the net gain of affiliation."

Based on reports from presidents of international unions, Meany said raids cost from $10 to $40 per member. "At a ten-dollar figure, which is surely a minimum figure, these representation cases which brought about a switch of seven-tenths of one percent of the people involved cost the

AFL and the CIO affiliates $11,418,000." Hence, Meany said, each of the 4,124 workers who changed affiliation cost the AFL and CIO an average of $2,768.

Intra-AFL raids were even sillier. During the three years AFL affiliates filed 1,025 NLRB petitions against other AFL unions—fifty percent more than attempted raids against CIO unions. Seven of ten of the raids failed; only 17,558 of 84,000 workers switched affiliation. "Insofar as the AFL is concerned," Meany said, "this 17,558 membership switch merely meant that there was no addition to the membership of the AFL —it merely meant that they went from one union to another." On the basis of a $10 cost, this cost the AFL affiliates $1,685,000. The four most aggressive raiders were, in turn, most frequently raided. One union spent $54,000 in 148 raids, and gained only 42 members, at an average cost of $1,309; another, in more than 400 cases, won 5,228 members while losing 3,307, for a net gain of 1,921, at a cost of $160 each.

In June Meany and Reuther agreed on the principle—but not the specific details—of a no-raiding pact. The main point was that when a labor union was the duly certified or recognized bargaining agent for workers, rival unions were to stay away. A shift in allegiance from the AFL to the CIO, or vice versa, would not be sanctioned. If members of a local had "valid and compelling" reasons for changing over, the unions involved would try to work out an agreement. There was recent precedent for such a pact. The United Auto Workers and the International Association of Machinists, an AFL union, in fact had worked under one since 1949. And the IAM president, A. J. Hayes, helped get the AFL-CIO agreement over a few rough bumps. Early in the negotiations, Hayes said, he told Reuther the only possible way to bring about a merger "was to freeze the jurisdictions as they were then and to offer to assist the unions with parallel or conflicting jurisdictions to work out their differences. Pending the time that this was done, the new federation would protect the established jurisdictions and bargaining rights of every union, even though they might be in conflict." Hayes's approach, in essence, was the core of the June agreement.

Two months later Meany asked the AFL executive council to approve a final version of the pact for submission to the September convention. He stressed the pact would be voluntary and not binding on any union that chose not to sign. Since the council had approved a first draft earlier in the year, Meany did not expect any trouble with it. Then, unexpectedly, came a bombshell, one that could have shattered the merger talks. John L. Lewis, David J. McDonald, and Dave Beck, the new president of the Teamsters Union, began plotting a rival federation to both the AFL and the CIO. The instigator, appropriately, was Meany's old adversary Lewis. Here we take a few steps backward for perspective:

The unhappy McDonald, still casting around for a way to topple the detested Reuther, in midsummer tentatively sounded out Lewis for an alliance. Since Meany would not take the United Steel Workers into the AFL unilaterally, McDonald envisioned joining forces with the United Mine Workers. The alliance was a natural. The UMWA had financed the USW's creation, and despite the long feud between Lewis and Phil Murray, there was considerable friendship between the upper echelons of the organizations. Lewis feared further isolation from labor. Meany flatly barred the UMWA from entering a merged AFL-CIO as long as Lewis ran the union. "Good Lord, he's the fellow who split the AFL," Meany exclaimed to one interviewer. "He's the fellow who tried to split the CIO after he got tired of that. He's the fellow who came back to the AFL in 1947 and tried to split again. He says every once in a while that there can be no unity without the miners. That's baloney."

To the delight of Lewis and McDonald, in midsummer a third dissident joined their talks on creating a new labor federation. Dave Beck in late 1952 had succeeded Daniel J. Tobin as president of the International Brotherhood of Teamsters (Tobin, however, remained on the AFL executive council). A vigorous, somewhat loud-mouthed man, Beck had great dreams for the IBT. He set a goal of doubling the IBT's 1.4 million membership within the decade, and he maintained his jurisdiction logically extended to every industry requiring transportation. Beck saw the no-raid pact as a deterrent to his ambitions, and ignored it. To Reuther's dismay, in June he lured away ten locals with 10,000 members of the CIO Brewery Workers Union. Reuther angrily said the "law of the jungle" should not settle jurisdictional disputes, and he said he hoped "leaders of the AFL . . . will give serious consideration to the harm caused by these raids." Beck did not recognize Meany's authority to limit the Teamsters' jurisdiction.

Beck, Lewis, and McDonald held several carefully publicized luncheons in Washington restaurants, they put their names on a single letterhead in corresponding with congressmen, and they leaked enough of their scheme to the labor press to goad Meany. The gist of their plan was that if Lewis was not brought into the unity negotiations, they would organize a "Committee for Labor Unity," and open its membership to any unions interested—AFL, CIO, or independent. Years later McDonald said "I really have no idea" whether Lewis or Beck would have carried through on what he called the "Lew-Mc-Beck" plan. "Our purpose was to try and move the CIO and AFL leadership off dead center, and that we accomplished."

The intrigue, predictably, attracted the attention of William Hutcheson of the Carpenters Union, a man addicted to behind-the-scenes plotting. Hutcheson, too, disliked the no-raiding agreement. The Carpenters were succeeding in wooing away members of the CIO International Woodworkers of America in the Pacific Northwest, and Hutcheson did not wish to stop. Hutcheson had become president emeritus of the union in 1952, but still kept a tight rein on his successor, his son, Maurice Hutcheson.* To Hutcheson fell the task of sabotaging Meany's no-raid plan.

When Meany put a draft of the no-raid pact before the executive council in August, William Hutcheson immediately objected, in language, however, that concealed his true reasons for doing so. Because of jurisdictional disputes within the building trades, Hutcheson said, "it would be a ridiculous arrangement to enter into an agreement like this until we are able to settle our own controversies." If the council recommended convention approval, Hutcheson said, he "will have to resign from this council because [I] cannot sign it." The AFL should be able to "get understanding within our own family before making agreements with a 'dual' organization," Hutcheson said.

The threat of resignation, and the dramatic exit, were time-worn stratagems for Hutcheson. In four earlier disputes the Carpenters Union had in fact withdrawn from the AFL (in 1910, 1913, 1921, and 1929) only to return when the council backed down on whatever was at issue. Having established the credibility of his threats, Hutcheson thereafter had only to mutter "I'll resign if you do this" to frighten the council into submission. According to David Dubinsky, "Green or someone else would always say, 'Now, Bill, don't talk like that; we can work out this matter,' and he'd stay on, and get his way. He was a big bully." The Carpenters had large enough membership—600,000 in 1953—to make the council blink at the thought of losing the per capita revenue.

Meany, temporizing, stressed that only signatory unions would be bound by the pact. As Hutcheson well knew, he said, another council committee was working on building trades jurisdictional disputes. Meany admitted the building trades problem was "critical," and that its organizations were "going to be destroyed by outside unions" unless a solution was found. Nonetheless, he did not see why the AFL had to wait for an intraraiding pact before signing the CIO agreement. For the first time since the CIO broke away in 1936, he said, unity was being discussed in a "reasonable way." Merger was needed. "The proof of that is the situation in which we find ourselves in now, in which the Congress is dominated by big financial interests," Meany said. If the no-raid pact was not approved, "it means the end of the unity talks with the CIO."

A few minutes before the luncheon recess, Hutcheson moved that the council instruct Meany to break off negotiations with the CIO. No one

* The Hutchesons, father and son, ran the Carpenters Union from 1915 until Maurice's retirement, at age seventy-four, in February 1972.

sided with him. The old carpenter arose—a pathetic figure, his bluster eroded by age and the sudden realization he could not bluff Meany—and shuffled to the door. He turned and said, *"Au revoir,"* and was gone.

"Let me go talk to him, George," suggested Matthew Woll. "I can get him down again. He'll come back." "Hell, no," Meany replied. "We start that, and he'll run it in the ground." Meany adjourned the council for lunch. When members gathered at 2:00 P.M. to resume, Maurice Hutcheson was waiting at the door, with a letter from his father to Meany. It announced the Carpenters' withdrawal from the AFL and William Hutcheson's resignation from the executive council. Meany read it and rapped his gavel on the table. "All right," he said, "first vice-president Hutcheson has resigned." He motioned to Matthew Woll, who as second vice-president occupied the next seat down the table. "Matty, you move up one, and the rest of you fellows, too." David Dubinsky said, "It was stunning. George never blinked when Hutcheson left. God, but that removed any doubt about what kind of president he was going to be. Sixty thousand dollars in per capita tax walked out the door, and he didn't flinch."

At Dan Tobin's behest, and over Meany's objection, the council then elected David Beck, the Teamster president, to the vacant seat. Meany argued he did "not think it is a wise policy" to have two men from the same international union on the thirteen-member board; as a consolation, the council did agree to enlarge its membership to fifteen. (Meany said he did not object to Beck personally.)

The withdrawal sent the Building and Construction Trades Department into turmoil, for the Carpenters were their largest affiliate. Richard Gray, the department chairman, stormed privately, "Meany is wrecking the goddamned organization. You can't run a labor federation without the Carpenters." Meany sent curtly formal letters to Gray and heads of the state and local building trades councils, noting the Carpenters' decision, and citing the constitutional provision that unions not affiliated with the AFL could not belong to subordinate councils. Meany directed that the Carpenters be dropped from membership. To the Carpenters, ouster at the local level was deadly, because it automatically excluded them from industry-wide bargaining units. "The defection of the Carpenters is not going to hurt our organization very much," Meany said. "We didn't like to see it happen, but we're still stronger than ever before in our history."

After a closer look at an alliance with Lewis, McDonald, and Beck, Hutcheson apparently thought better of it. Meany was not surprised. "John L. Lewis has no effect these days other than to stir up a little wind now and then." William Hutcheson sued for peace. Not in person, however, for he was too vain a man to admit he was beaten. Son Maurice drew the task of asking for readmission. "George and I talked it out, and we agreed it would be best if we came back in," Maurice Hutcheson said. "There were no hard feelings when it was over; a lot of guys you don't agree with on every point, but you got to work with them the best you can." In less than a month the Carpenters humbly re-entered the AFL. At the AFL convention in September Meany had the council expanded by two seats, and Maurice Hutcheson was elected to fill one of them. The Carpenters union executive board, angered at William Hutcheson's actions, ordered him to take no further part in union affairs. He died later in the fall at age seventy-nine.

At their fall conventions both the AFL and the CIO approved the no-raid agreement. There were scattered dissenters. James Carey, the CIO secretary-treasurer, had reservations, saying his United Electrical Workers had been raided "by twenty different AFL unions." Many AFL building trades unions were also dubious. In the end, however, agreement was unanimous in both organizations. (McDonald demonstrated his continuing disdain for Reuther by pointedly standing to one side of the auditorium, chatting with a friend, during Reuther's re-election.) And Reuther, in his keynote speech, made plain he was ready for peace—but not at the price of any compromises with his principles as a trade unionist. Reuther began by again implying that he realized Meany would receive the top position in a merged movement. "For too long there have been vested interests standing in the way of . . . organic unity," he said. "Always there was the question of prestige and position and power. I can assure you for the CIO we are not going to be looking for jobs." Reuther continued:

> We don't care who leads the new labor movement providing it can be put together solidly and provided it is for the purpose of advancing the basic working interests of the American working groups. We broke away from the AFL in the old days not because we wanted to divide the labor movement, but because the AFL would not accommodate itself to the changing times and the new problems. If they have learned their lesson, and I hope they have . . . I have respect for people like George Meany; I think he is a solid trade unionist—and if the AFL will go into this meeting in that way we can build a united labor movement.

Then, a cause for CIO complaint. Meany had his pact, but he could not persuade some key AFL unions to sign it. Dave Beck said the Teamsters preferred to negotiate unilaterally with unions with which they had jurisdictional problems (the old system, which had never worked). Beck claimed to have lost 50,000 members in raids by both the AFL and CIO. Maurice Hutcheson continued the Carpenters' opposition, calling the no-raid rule "foolish." The CIO executive board in March 1954 unhappily noted that 98 percent of the CIO unions had signed, and only 46 of 111 AFL affiliates. The CIO needled Meany. "The CIO trusts that the leadership of every section of the American labor movement will meet their responsibilities in this matter so that unity discussions can be pursued." Meany promptly wrote Reuther that there had been no understanding a minimum number of signatures was required to make the pact take effect. He noted the agreement would affect only signatory unions, so that signers would be free to take any action desired against nonsigners. In June, somewhat reluctantly, and still lacking the big steel and textile workers unions himself, Reuther signed an agreement with Meany, formally declaring the pact in effect.

The haggling over the no-raid pact and the constant danger of sabotage by recalcitrant unions disturbed Meany. If the AFL and CIO had to labor over each point, consummation would require years. "We decided we wouldn't live long enough to do it by that method," Meany said. So at the unity committee's next meeting, on October 15 in the Mayflower Hotel in Washington, Meany decided to cut away some of the procedural underbrush.

Reuther opened with a long recitation of the "trade union principles" he expected to govern the merger organization. It was a gloomy day; Hurricane Hazel was bearing down on Washington, and no one—not even Reuther's associates—wanted to spend the afternoon listening to him. Meany brusquely broke into Reuther's monologue, and compressed the issue into four terse sentences:

"We can go after unity the long way or the short way. The short way is to merge into one trade union center which will protect the integrity of all affiliates. The long way is to solve all of our problems before merging. Which will it be?"

The CIO accepted.

A few days later, at the United Steel Workers convention, David Mc-Donald fell into line. Arthur J. Goldberg, long-time counsel for the CIO, said, "Dave realized the membership wasn't with him on the question of leaving the CIO. Hell, to the men in the mills, the CIO and the USW were synonymous." But McDonald did draw prolonged applause for his complaints about the way Reuther ran the CIO. McDonald said I. W. Abel, the USW secretary-treasurer, had trouble getting into the CIO building in Washington because "he didn't have an appointment." The USW, McDonald noted, paid the CIO $200,000 monthly. The convention also heard, with foot-stomping approval, a letter from John L. Lewis, denouncing Reuther (although not by name). "You are unfortunate," Lewis wrote, "in your affiliation with a federated group, dominated by intellectual inebriates and in frantic pursuit of butterflies of their delusions." McDonald, who had been serving on the CIO unity committee despite his hostility to Reuther, said the job could be accomplished in a "few weeks."

As Meany said, "We got really into the guts of the merger question, by agreeing that we would proceed to negotiate terms of the merger on the basic principle that would protect the integrity of every single union on both sides. Now this dispelled the fear of a great many of the CIO unions that they would be gobbled up."

In February 1955 the AFL invited the CIO negotiators to Miami Beach for talks immediately after the AFL executive council's winter meeting. The meetings were at the plush Roney-Plaza Hotel (a location that caused the austere Reuther great discomfort; Goldberg says he "would have preferred that the meeting be held almost anywhere else in the United States"). According to Goldberg, there was little apparent progress for most of the first day. Then, late in the afternoon, "the fog of semantics and varying viewpoints suddenly lifted." At 4:30 P.M. Goldberg and J. Albert Woll, AFL counsel (and Matthew Woll's son), were instructed to put the thoughts of the participants into a draft agreement. They finished it late the night of February 8, and the unity committee gave approval the next morning in less than an hour. While staff members scurried to the nearest mimeograph machine, a half mile away, the AFL and CIO men "participated in the most cordial social meeting that the two branches of organized labor had seen in eighteen years," in Goldberg's words. Meany sat down at an elegant grand piano in the corner of the conference room and played a medley of Irish songs. The group was too excited to wait for the mimeographed copies. Goldberg said, "The press was called in, and in the form of two somewhat bedraggled carbon copies, the historic merger agreement was made public."

The document restated the AFL and CIO intention to merge, and listed seven governing principles:

—that each affiliated union retain its charter and become an affiliate of the merged federation;

—that "the integrity of each affiliated union . . . be maintained and preserved," and no raids to be permitted;

—that unions keep the same organizing jurisdiction as they previously held;

—that in the case of "conflicting and duplicating" organizations and jurisdictions, affiliates be encouraged to eliminate them "through the process of agreement, merger, or other means";

—that "the merged federation shall be based upon a constitutional recognition that both craft and industrial unions are appropriate, equal and necessary as methods of trade union organization";

—that "the merged federation shall constitutionally recognize the

right of all workers, without regard to race, creed, color or national origin, to share in the full benefits of trade union organization in the merged federation. The merged federation shall establish appropriate internal machinery to bring about, at the earliest possible date, the effective implementation of this principle of non-discrimination";
—that "the merged federation shall constitutionally affirm its determination to protect the American trade union movement from any and all corrupt influence and from the undermining efforts of Communist agencies and all others who are opposed to the basic principles of our democracy and of free and democratic trade unionism."

The next step was to work out practical details of merging two organizations into one. As expected, Reuther readily agreed that Meany and William Schnitzler continue in the top two positions. AFL tradition had been for the president and secretary-treasurer to work full-time for the federation, not their international unions. The CIO presidents, conversely, had continued as presidents of their unions (Lewis, the miners; Murray, the steelworkers; Reuther, the autoworkers). John Brophy, a long-time Reuther associate, said it was obvious the president of the merged AFL-CIO "had to be a full-time operator. Walter recognized his power resided in his national union, so it was easy for him to get that issue out of the way. It also made it easier for George Meany to work strongly for unity on a reasonable basis, to avoid any fencing or going through a lot of make-believe motions, to find out what position he would hold in the merger. So the presidency or secretaryship was not an issue from the start. That removed a personality problem . . . that was highly important in any merger."

The difference in internal structures of the two federations was more of a problem. In Meany's opinion, the fact that each CIO officer also ran a major union meant "it was not a solid structure." Headquarters staff people held their jobs "because they were sponsored by a union. Their tenure depended on that union, not on the national CIO. For instance, Jack Kroll, who was their political director, was a member of the Amalgamated Clothing Workers. He did not work for the CIO, he would not go with the CIO. They had a legislative representative in Washington, and he was answerable only to Reuther. This was true in a great many of their departments, and out in the states. When they formed a state organization they parceled out the top officers to the major unions in the state. Our state federations of labor grew from the ground up. But when the CIO started operating they found out that they needed state organizations, and they didn't have the time to wait for them to develop, so they were sort of imposed on the states from the top. The CIO executive board would meet, and say, 'We have to set up a federation in a state; who has members there?' The state conventions were dominated by people who were employed by the various national unions, not the local unions."

In the merger, all headquarters staff personnel were to be employed directly by the AFL-CIO. An Industrial Union Department (IUD) was created, with Reuther as chairman. The CIO had anticipated that only CIO unions would affiliate with the IUD. However, immediately after the merger many AFL craft and other unions rushed to join, apparently intending to seize control. Meany intervened and served as credentials chairman at the IUD's first meeting, limiting each union's representation to its industrial-type membership. The resulting balance prevented the AFL unions from dominating the IUD, but ensured it would not become the "little CIO" that some of Reuther's supporters desired.

Thereafter, according to Meany, "the only real dispute . . . was the structure. Reuther wanted a structure where all power rested in the national trade union center. We wanted the so-called 'loose AFL structure' in which everybody had autonomy, everybody had guarantees. For instance, it was always possible in the AFL years for a union to go over to Capitol Hill and take a directly opposite position from the AFL itself." On Reuther's motion, the proposed constitution provided for a new "general board," composed of executive council members and heads of affiliated international unions. The board was to meet annually to "decide all policy questions referred to it by the executive officers and the executive council."

Meany objected strenuously to Reuther's plan. Meany said Reuther demanded "that there be full power at the top, that the general board . . . have power to do anything they want, to assign jurisdictions, to tell unions who they could organize and could not organize. This was a structure that didn't fit into our plans at all, and we didn't give one inch on it." At an August meeting he listed a host of objections. The executive council would "have a power so great that never at any time will a convention be able to upset [any] decision." The "power of arbitrary decision" would be concentrated "in the hands of a mere handful of men who can perpetuate themselves in office by the support of their affiliated unions." There were three hours of what Meany called "good hard discussion." "Then McDonald turned around and said, 'Well, I'm not going to sit here all day arguing. I think the AFL fellows are right.' He sort of tipped the scales, and that ended that."

In his own executive council, paradoxically, Meany was criticized by members who thought the merged federation would invade their autonomy. Woodruff Randolph, president of the 100,000-member International Typographical Union, quoted the old Chinese proverb, "The big fish eat the little fish, and the little fish eat mud." Randolph said, "We want to keep that from happening in the labor movement." Arguing for strictures on the AFL-CIO's powers, Randolph said it was not the "objective or purpose" of the federation "to exercise authority over the internal affairs of affiliates." Matthew Woll rebutted that in actuality "Randolph wants a completely weak federation without any authority at all."

Meany and Reuther, in midsummer, had agreed to put the constitution before their respective conventions in New York in December for approval, then convene a joint merger convention. But as late as October Meany still faced internal opposition. Dave Beck of the Teamsters said his union had "thirty-five or forty lawyers" studying the constitution, and that the Teamsters would not approve it until they completely understood it. Meany told Beck, "You are complicating things." It should be "quite obvious," he said, "that if there is to be a constitution approved to satisfy all the lawyers of the different groups, there never would be a merger." William Schnitzler said bringing in a plethora of outside lawyers "will tear the constitution apart." Meany asked Beck to be patient; if the constitution proved to have flaws, amendments could be made after the merger. Beck grudgingly agreed.

Thus was the stage set for the premerger conventions. The AFL, meeting at the Statler Hotel in New York on December 1, acted first. The convention was the AFL's seventy-fourth, and last, and it was all business. Labor reporter Stanley Levey observed, "There was no mood of history in the making, and there was scarcely a glance at the past." Randolph, the only verbal opponent, rehashed his old arguments about autonomy, which Meany patiently rebutted. Once the unanimous vote was recorded, Levey noted, "no demonstration followed, no confetti flew, and the convention droned its way to adjournment for lunch." In his valedictory Meany acknowledged the "misgivings" of many delegates, including executive council members "that something new is about to happen and they are not sure just what it is." He said, "I may be—well, to use the vernacular of New York—I may be a chump. But I don't have any misgivings about it. . . . I haven't the slightest doubt that there will be trying moments, that some of the old rivalries will spring up inside the new organization. But I am certain we can overcome any and all differences we face."

The CIO, meeting at the Manhattan Center on West 34th Street, provided more excitement. Michael J. Quill, president of the 90,000-member Transport Workers Union, wanted a seat on the executive council. Hell, no, not that damned Commie, Meany said, in approximately those words; he had watched "Red Mike" for more than two decades, and considered him a ranting fool—and also a blasphemous one. When the

Association of Catholic Trade Unionists combated Communists in the TWU in the late 1930's, Quill glibly conferred honorary TWU membership on Jesus Christ, and said that were He on earth He "would follow the party line." Quill's closest associate in the TWU for years had been John Santo, an avowed Soviet agent. "That guy's not coming on any executive council I sit on," Meany told Reuther. Quill thought he deserved the seat, and Meany's blackball infuriated him. Quill knew he could not block the merger, but he took some kicks at Meany's shins anyway. "Why in the name of God Almighty are we giving this movement away?" Quill shouted in quavery Gaelic tenor. "George Meany doesn't see eye to eye with us on industrial organization; George Meany and the people around him do not see eye to eye with us on the question of organizing the unorganized. There are powerful leaders in the AFL who do not see eye to eye with us in equality between us and the minority groups . . . and our Negro brothers. George Meany does not see eye to eye with the CIO on domestic policy or on foreign policy. George Meany is only slightly to the left of Senator Knowland [the right-wing California Republican]." Quill rumbled on for half an hour: "black day . . . tragic liquidation . . . sacrifice of honor for expediency." When he finished, the convention delivered him the ultimate contempt of icy silence. Reuther replied, "I say to Mike in all good spirit, 'Mike, you have broken with some of your former colleagues in the party, but somehow the tactics linger on.'" Quill and CIO industrial councils from Springfield, Illinois, and Wilkes-Barre, Pennsylvania, cast the only opposing votes.

After a weekend respite, the delegates reconvened on Monday, December 5, in the Seventy-First Regiment Armory, Park Avenue and Thirty-fourth Street, under gigantic banners brandishing the formidable and unwieldy title, "American Federation of Labor and Congress of Industrial Organizations." "There was quite a bit of discussion on the name," Meany said. "Some of the fellows said, 'They were part of the American Federation of Labor, they should come back into the name they left.'" Various combinations of the two names were discussed; at one time, according to Jay Lovestone, "the United American Federation of Labor" was favored. "I made the decision," said Meany, "sitting right there without consulting anybody. There was no sense in arguing over this, it was complete nonsense. I said, 'We've got two names, let's put them together.' There could have been a good case made for retaining the old name, but it would have hurt a lot of people's feelings." When Meany announced the name, a newspaperman exclaimed, "Gee, the editors on the copy desk won't like that; it's too long." "I said, 'You mean the editors over at the Washington *Post-Times-Herald?*'"

Meany and Reuther, to symbolize the unity, jointly swung a massive gavel to open the session. Meany, customarily poker-faced in public, beamed, and he and Reuther exchanged endless variations of hand-shakes and embraces for the photographers and lauded one another and the future of the merged labor movement. Differences were thrust under the carpet. "Everything approved at that first convention had all been done in advance," Meany said. "We went through the formalities of ap-proving a constitution and resolutions. But there was a sort of gentle-men's agreement that whatever differences we had, we weren't going to register them." For instance, the all-black Brotherhood of Sleeping Car Porters was unhappy about the amalgamation into the AFL-CIO of two independent railroad unions* that barred Negroes from membership. Meany persuaded the president, A. Philip Randolph, not to speak out, and promised the racial barriers would be stricken before the unions were admitted. Randolph and another black, Willard S. Townsend, pres-ident of the CIO United Transport Service Employees, were slated for the AFL-CIO executive committee. (In neither the AFL nor the CIO had any black ever attained the rank of vice-president.) Meany said their election was the first specific implementation of the no-discrimination pledges in the new AFL-CIO constitution.

In their formal speeches both Reuther and Meany talked grandly of the future. Reuther set a goal of doubling the membership, to thirty mil-lion workers, during the next decade. Meany proclaimed the merger would enable labor to "make a better and more vital contribution to the community as a whole and to the welfare and security of our nation." The moment was among the happiest in Meany's life.

So, too, was it in Walter Reuther's. As biographers William J. Eaton and Frank Cormier have noted, his three-year tenure as CIO president "had been, in many ways, a disappointment to Reuther. He never re-ceived the esteem accorded his predecessor by CIO colleagues, and he was plagued by McDonald's hostility as well." Jack Barbash, the labor scholar at the University of Wisconsin, felt the growth of industrial un-ionism diminished the importance of Reuther's office. "When the na-tional unions began to stand on their own, the tutelage of the CIO dimin-ished," Barbash wrote. "Walter Reuther's accession . . . marked the end of the period of CIO protectorship." Hence Reuther saw the merger as an opportunity for personal as well as trade union gain. As Cormier and Eaton wrote, "With the formation of the AFL-CIO, Reuther had every reason to expect that he would be in line to succeed George Meany, after a reasonable interval, and thus enhance his influence within the labor movement and in the conduct of national affairs."

The merger survived; Walter Reuther's expectations did not.

* The Brotherhood of Railroad Trainmen and the Brotherhood of Locomotive Firemen and Engineers.

# I Like Ike . . . Sometimes

SEVERAL DAYS after the 1952 elections, Sherman Adams, appointments secretary to the President-elect, invited George Meany to New York for a chat with General Eisenhower "about the general labor situation." Meany had said some rather biting things about Eisenhower during the campaign. Although he praised Ike as a man of "great personal charm" and a "military genius," he said, "It is as a civilian that he is seeking the highest civilian office in the land . . . there is little evidence available that General Eisenhower possesses any intimate knowledge of, or experience with, the great domestic problems facing our nation." Eisenhower's public embrace of Senator Robert A. Taft, Meany said, "came as a shock" to American workers, as did his friendship with "such notable reactionaries" as Senators McCarthy, Jenner, and Bricker. With this campaign oratory in the back of his mind, Meany was curious about what reception he could expect from Eisenhower.

Surprisingly, Eisenhower was most conciliatory. Regardless of labor's stand in the election, he said, he wanted to "work with everyone." Meany, with customary candor, replied he "personally had no regrets on the stand that we took," but that he was ready to cooperate with Eisenhower.

After the amenities, Eisenhower asked for suggestions on a Secretary of Labor, saying he wanted "to get someone who is not in labor's hate book." Meany said labor "had no 'hate book.'" He told Eisenhower that when he appointed a Secretary of Commerce, he would "look a little beyond the point of trying to find somebody who is not ⟨in⟩ business' 'hate book,'" and hoped he would do the same with a Secretary of Labor. Meany would not object to a CIO appointee. If the job was closed to a labor man, Eisenhower "should give us an employer, because the fellow who knows our problem best next to ourselves is the fellow we work for." Meany would not propose any specific individuals; he did ask that Ike "not give us a politician or a college professor."

The friendly tone of the meeting pleased Meany, and Ike's choice of a Secretary of Labor, announced later in the month, was a further gesture of conciliation. He picked Martin P. Durkin, a Chicagoan who was president of Meany's old United Association of Journeymen and Apprentices of the Plumbing and Pipefitting Industry of the United States and Canada—the plumbers union. Meany and Durkin had met in the 1920's at the United Association conventions and were friendly, if not personally close, in their dealings in later years. Meany, however, said he had nothing to do with the appointment, jesting to a friend, "If Ike tried to make friends with me, he got somebody from the wrong side of the United Association—Durkin was a steamfitter when he was on the job, not a plumber."

In his memoirs Ike wrote that since a businessman traditionally headed the Commerce Department, "I thought that as a counterbalance the Labor Department should be headed by one actually experienced in the labor movement." Eisenhower kept his intention to pick a union man secret until the announcement because if it became known "violent criticism would make it almost impossible to get anyone to agree to serve in the post." Eisenhower and Durkin had problems defining what the President would expect of him. Ike said Durkin could "no longer owe personal allegiance to labor" and that once decisions were made he must abide by them. According to Ike, Durkin worried whether he would have any future in labor after serving in a Republican cabinet. Senator Robert A. Taft called the Durkin appointment "incredible" and an "affront" to union members who had crossed party lines to vote for Ike. Taft felt that Richard J. Gray, head of the AFL Building and Construction Trades Department, should have the job. Gray and the Carpenters' Maurice Hutcheson had headed a "labor committee for Ike" run by the Republican National Committee, and Gray had an audience with Eisenhower immediately after the election. (By one account, Attorney General Herbert Brownell, Ike's chief recruiter, vetoed Gray because of his persistent attempts to free Joseph Fay, onetime power in the Operating Engineers Union, then imprisoned in New York for extortion.)

Labor's first priority in the new Congress was repeal of Taft-Hartley. In their talk, according to Meany, Eisenhower repeated that "certain things" in Taft-Hartley were "unfair" and should be changed. He referred specifically to a section that provided for the disenfranchisement of strikers in representation elections. In practice, employers were provoking strikes when contracts expired, then hiring nonunion workers who would petition the NLRB for a decertification election and vote out the union. Eisenhower asked Meany "to talk to Senator Taft about amendments, making the Taft-Hartley Law, as he put it, a fair law for both labor and management."

Previously, the AFL position had been for outright repeal, rather than amendments. After the talk with Eisenhower, however, Meany was prepared to bargain for what he could get. He was optimistic about Taft. "In a good many of the things that we were interested in—not all—he [Taft] was one hundred percent with us," Meany said. For instance, Taft agreed the building trades should have a so-called pre-hire contract, permitting a union shop on construction jobs without a representation election. At Durkin's confirmation hearings, Taft agreed that Taft-Hartley was difficult to apply to the building trades and that most of its provisions were written with mass industry in mind. When the act was passed, Taft said, "I never thought it was intended to apply to the building trades on the local level. It has been so applied." Eisenhower, in his State of the Union message, instructed Durkin to appoint a fifteen-member committee—five men each from management, labor, and the public—to discuss Taft-Hartley revisions. The actual work fell to a subcommittee composed of Meany; Cyrus Ching, head of the Federal Mediation and Conciliation Service; and Harry Moses, a coal operator. Meany told the subcommittee that because of Taft-Hartley, organizing activities of the AFL's federal unions "has dwindled to absolutely nothing, despite increased expenditures." From 1934 to 1946, he said, the AFL averaged 344 new local unions each year, with a staff of 140 to 160 organizers; in 1953, with 175 organizers, the AFL chartered only 34 local unions. Meany noted this was at a time of high corporate profits and employment, factors favoring unionization. Had economic conditions been worse, he said, organizing would have stopped altogether. Employers used Taft-Hartley to delay elections, knowing that the NLRB required an average of 450 days to hear an unfair labor practice case. Meany complained management drained unions in time and legal expenses. "We have had demonstrated to us . . . that if an employer . . . is willing to spend the money and willing to make his plant or shop a battleground for the antiunion forces in this nation, he can do it. The machinery is there under Taft-Hartley in most cases."

In short order the subcommittee worked out an agenda of twenty items for discussion, with Ching choosing the order in which they would be discussed. Ching made enfranchisement of strikers number one. Meany said, "He felt wisely that this would be a good starting place for the committee, give them something they could agree on rather than get into something over which there would be a wrangle." Twelve of the fifteen members—all but two business and one public member—agreed disenfranchisement should be scrapped, and Durkin, who was presiding, asked for a vote. Meany insisted on having a vote putting the committee majority on record. Otherwise, he said, "You have no recommendation from this committee of any kind; you just have individual opinions." The employer representatives protested and asked for an overnight recess so they could caucus. The next day the employer members refused to vote. They were unwilling "to submerge our individual views in majority votes of a committee whose members represent diverse interests"; they maintained that to recommend specific legislation would make them assume a "legislative function" they did not wish. Meany scoffed at the excuse. "Is that such a terrible thing to happen to you people?" he said. "My Lord, you should be used to it by now. . . . The National Association of Manufacturers has been on the wrong side of every public issue for fifty years, according to the record." The next day business quit the panel.

The experience disgusted Meany, for he felt Eisenhower was sincere in appointing the committee. "They [the business members] sabotaged that committee, that effort by the President of the United States to reach labor-management agreement. . . . That just about set the tone of the attitude of the employers, of the people who feel they have labor over a barrel, and that they are going to use their advantage to the fullest degree." A few months later, testifying before the Senate Labor Committee on Taft-Hartley amendments, Meany warned business that punitive legislation against one sector of the economy was a dangerous precedent for others. "The minute you start to take away the rights of a worker on the grounds of paramount public interest," he said, "you raise the question that if the industry is so important that individual rights should be suppressed, the public should own that industry. Once you take away one person's rights to protect another person's rights or to protect the state, you'd invite fascism. And it should be remembered that Mussolini handed out the castor oil treatment indiscriminately, both to workers and to employers."

Dubious about winning any changes, Meany nonetheless continued meetings with Taft and Durkin throughout the spring. Durkin discovered early on he had no real status in Ike's cabinet of "eight millionaires and a plumber." The Administration cut his budget by nineteen percent, chiefly by firing 600 investigators and other employees in the Labor Department's Wage and Hour Division. The White House would not clear three men he wanted as assistant secretaries. But he kept working, and with Meany, Taft, and other Administration figures, hammered out a set of nineteen amendments, most of them acceptable to labor. One of them would have repealed the especially hated Section 14b, which permitted states to pass right-to-work laws barring the union shop. By Durkin's account, he discussed the nineteen amendments with Eisenhower, who approved them for submission to Congress. Before this could be done, however, Senator Taft, who had been stricken with cancer in late spring, died. Eisenhower told Durkin to hold back the amendments for a few weeks. In the interim, Administration opponents of the amendments leaked them to the *Wall Street Journal,* evoking enormous counterpressures from business. According to Durkin, Eisenhower assured him as late as August 15 that he personally "agreed with me" on the amendments. A few days later, however, Durkin was told the Administration would not support them.

By Eisenhower's account, Durkin completely misunderstood the situation—and also his role in the cabinet. Since no final decision had been "reached and announced" on amendments, continued discussion within the Administration was completely proper—"even if I had," as Eisenhower admitted, "inadvertently misled him in some particulars." Durkin irritated Ike by saying constantly his duty as labor secretary was to "participate in collective bargaining," and that he felt at a disadvantage in conferences because "he was but one man representing labor, while everyone else present was either a capitalist or a member of the professions."

Ike also complained that Durkin "seemed to carry a bit of a chip on his shoulder," and worried unduly about his future. If 14b was not repealed, Durkin told Ike, he would be disowned by his union and no job would exist for him when the time came for him to end his governmental tour of duty. In July, Durkin's plumbers union *Journal* denounced the Administration in an editorial entitled "Pattern of Plunder," criticizing Eisenhower for "giving away" off-shore oil, boosting interest rates, killing public housing, and failing to act on Taft-Hartley. Durkin, rebutting in the next issue, said that if he wasn't satisfied with the Administration's labor policies, he would resign. Durkin met with Eisenhower in late August and confirmed that the package of amendments would not be submitted. He resigned two weeks later.

Durkin had kept Meany informed of the machinations within the Administration on Taft-Hartley, and he began speaking out publicly after his resignation became effective on September 10. Durkin blamed Vice-President Richard M. Nixon and Commerce Secretary Sinclair Weeks for leading the campaign that killed the amendments. On "Meet the Press," Meany said Durkin would not have quit if it were merely a "White House clerk" who broke faith with him on Taft-Hartley. "I think Durkin felt the President of the United States broke an agreement with him—otherwise he would not have resigned. I believe Durkin felt he had an agreement because he said so—and he is a very truthful man."

Eisenhower declined an invitation to speak to the AFL convention, which gathered a week after Durkin's resignation in St. Louis. As a peace emissary he sent Nixon. The convention gave the Vice-President polite introductory applause, then sat back to listen to what he had to say.

Nixon confirmed Durkin's story that a draft presidential message had been written on Taft-Hartley amendments, and that he was instrumental in delaying its submission to Congress because of Senator Taft's death. When Nixon said the break between the President and Durkin resulted from a "misunderstanding," the convention erupted into a derisive horse-laugh. The outburst flustered Nixon, but he bore on—only to be thrown off stride again when the delegates vigorously applauded his declaration that the Eisenhower Administration "deserved to lose" if it pandered to a "greedy few to the detriment of the many." Nixon tried vainly to evoke applause for the President, but none was there. "I don't believe that any man in America, no man in the world today, is better qualified to lead the free world over the forces that would destroy us, to lead us to victory without war, than Dwight Eisenhower," he declared. The *AFL News-Reporter,* the AFL's official organ, said, "Nixon paused. No applause came, and he added another sentence: 'I trust him, and I think the American people indicated they trust him, by the overwhelming vote they gave him in the last election.' " Nixon paused again momentarily, heard only silence, and moved on to other territory.

Senator Wayne Morse, following Nixon on the convention program, called Nixon's explanation "confession by avoidance." The *AFL News-Reporter,* in a postconvention editorial entitled "Death of a Salesman," said, "The wave of mocking laughter which greeted that imposture was a complete answer to the brash young man who holds the office of vice-president." An accompanying cartoon depicted a crest-fallen Nixon standing before Ike's desk, carrying a briefcase labeled "alibi." Ike was reading a newspaper headline, "AFL Convention Mocks Ike-Nixon Alibi on T-H."

"When that program was ditched," Meany said later, "when that was broken, it was broken by the Eisenhower forces. They themselves have reached a point that even the President of the United States, who indicates that he wants to do something with this law, is not strong enough to stand up for his point of view against the people who now have control of this Administration in Washington. . . . Even the President does not seem to be able to control the reactionary forces who feel that this is their day. . . ."

As secretary-treasurer, Meany had groused because William Green would not permit him to lobby in Congress. As president, to his continuing chagrin, he found he had no time for the day-to-day work on Capitol

Hill essential to effective legislative work—the immersion in details of bills, the cajoling and backslapping, the trade-offs and plotting, that are a part of congressional life. Nor was he satisfied with W. C. Hushing, long the AFL's chief legislative man under Green. Meany's secretary-treasurer, William Schnitzler, had no legislative experience, hence he could not be used as a lobbyist. (In fact, Meany soon concluded, Schnitzler could not do much of anything; within a year, he was quietly shoved to the side and given only ceremonial functions. Schnitzler was to remain as secretary-treasurer for 1969, ignoring frequent hints from Meany that he retire. Despite his office Schnitzler was never considered part of Meany's inner circle.)

So Meany looked around labor for his own lobbyist—and found him in the person of Andrew J. Biemiller. Biemiller, who is not afflicted with modesty, said, "Meany used to tell me that if he picked a child to train as a lobbyist, and brought him all the way through, he couldn't have found anyone with a background better than I had." For more than two decades he was labor's chief emissary to Congress. Biemiller is a hulking, big-boned man who had an early background in both academic and practical unionism. A Socialist Quaker, he found common ground with Meany in his zest for lobbying. "At the University of Pennsylvania, I specialized in the British trade union movement, and for a long time I knew more about their unions than the American unions." He worked with the Milwaukee Federation of Trade Councils as a general organizer, served two terms in the Wisconsin legislature as a Socialist-Progressive, and was a deputy to Joseph D. Keenan on the War Production Board in Washington during the early 1940's. "When I was elected to Congress as a Socialist in 1944," Biemiller said, "I was billed as some kind of radical—I wasn't, really—and the House leadership wanted to stick me off somewhere out of sight. They decided on the House Naval Affairs Committee, which is just the thing for a guy from Wisconsin—we got a lot of navy yards out there, you know. But it turned out to be a fantastically good break. I was put on a subcommittee of which Lyndon Johnson was chairman and Margaret Chase Smith was the other member. Those were the kind of contacts it's good to have." Biemiller was defeated in 1950, worked in the Department of the Interior for two years, and ran (and lost) again in 1952. Meany called him over for a talk. "Meany told me, 'You are one of the few AFL guys who has got on with the CIO. I am determined to merge the CIO and the AFL, and I need some people who can talk to both sides.'" Biemiller accepted a post, ostensibly as assistant to W. C. Hushing, actually as chief lobbyist.

"George was so busy the first few years, with the merger and the ethical practices stuff," Biemiller said, "that he pretty well turned Congress over to me. Now, on major testimony on things like Taft-Hartley, it was obviously to our advantage to have Meany appear and present statements. Also, he wanted to know what was happening in Congress—any bill affecting labor, he wanted a continuing report on it, and also the differences in the various proposals on Social Security and that kind of thing. But the day-to-day stuff, he left me on my own, and he gave me the old rules he had used in New York: 'Don't beg or demean yourself in asking for votes; don't threaten; and don't assume you are always right, and congressmen always wrong.' "

After Durkin's resignation labor realized it could not get acceptable Taft-Hartley amendments through Congress. Indeed, when the Administration bill finally emerged from committee in the 1954 session, according to Biemiller, "it contained some goodies for us, but also some bad stuff we couldn't take; we had to kill it." Senator William Knowland (Rep., California), the majority leader, was determined to push the bill through with the assistance of conservative Southern Democrats. With Taft-Hartley "a holy issue" for labor, in Biemiller's words, Lyndon Johnson, as minority leader, began scheming with Biemiller for a way to defeat the Administration bill. Senate liberals were bent upon their own substitutes, including an amendment by Senators Irving Ives and Herbert Lehman, both of New York, tacking a Fair Employment Practices Commission onto the National Labor Relations Board to end job discrimination. The FEPC was as anathema to conservatives as Taft-Hartley was to labor. Biemiller related:

"At about seven-thirty one morning Johnson called me at home and said he had mousetrapped Knowland into a unanimous consent agreement to bring the bill to the floor with three hours' general debate, one hour on each amendment, and then a vote. Johnson told me, 'Get every liberal senator you can to get on the floor and talk five minutes about Ives-Lehman, and to show a great interest in passing the bill.' Well, I got the speeches, and later that day Johnson told me, 'You have scared the hell out of the Southerners; now they aren't going to vote for Taft-Hartley, because they don't want FEPC; we'll get it recommitted.'

"For tactical reasons—to conceal what was going on—we wanted the motion to recommit to come from a Southerner, but Jim Murray [a Nevada Democrat] was handling it. Johnson and I worked it out where I could persuade Murray to get out of the way and let Lister Hill [Dem., Alabama] make the motion, but without bringing Johnson into it. I talked to Murray, and explained the South would be more likely to go along if one of their men made the motion, and he said, 'That sounds like a good idea, let me see if I can sell it to Lyndon.'

"A little later I was sitting in the gallery, and Murray got Johnson off to the side, and Lyndon looked up and saw me and gave me a great big slow wink. Ten minutes later Lister Hill moved to recommit, and we had won."

The vote, 50 to 42 for recommittal, ended a seventeen-month fight over Taft-Hartley, and Meany was happy with the stalemate, calling it "a blow to those who sought to wipe out federal protection of labor's basic rights."

Meany was not without friends in the Eisenhower Administration. Nelson Rockefeller, his old New York friend, came to Washington as Undersecretary of Health, Education, and Welfare. Mrs. Oveta Culp Hobby, the Houston newspaper publisher, was HEW Secretary, and Nelson Cruikshank, the AFL social security director, immediately had problems with her. Cruikshank visited Mrs. Hobby in March with William Schnitzler and Boris Shishkin and reported later in a memo to Meany she had a "very superior and patronizing attitude. Her feeling, quite clearly, was 'We have found where the real power centers in the United States are. Labor cannot swing an election. We will get along with the American Medical Association and the big pharmaceutical houses, etc. . . .' She evidenced a remarkable ignorance of the American labor movement when, at the close of the conference, she asked Secretary Schnitzler if his office was located here in Washington." Cruikshank continued.

"She didn't know the slightest thing about the Social Security Administration, and the first thing she did was to start firing everyone in sight, on the grounds they were Democratic and no good. Well, she was wrong; this particular agency was nonpolitical, and the director, Arthur Altmeyer, was really the father of Social Security. When Rockefeller was appointed Mrs. Hobby's deputy, I asked Meany for an introduction. 'You must have known him,' I told George, 'and I'm going to have to deal with him a lot.'

"George got the appointment, and as we were riding over he said to me, 'We're not just going over there to chat; what do we want out of this guy?' I explained the Social Security staff had always been nonpolitical, and that we should try to save Wilbur Cohen,* who was next in line after Altmeyer. Anyway, after Rockefeller greeted us, he said, 'Well, you didn't come over here just to reminisce. What do you want?' George came right at him: 'To retain the nonpolitical integrity of this technical Social Security staff. We've never asked for a job or a bit of patronage in Social Security, and we never want to. But we do want to protect the career people.' Rockefeller said Mrs. Hobby made the decisions, but he would 'see what he could do.' The result was that not another one of them was fired."

In the 1954 mid-term elections the AFL had many concrete economic complaints—but also the task of overcoming the continuing personal popularity of President Eisenhower. Labor had complained so vigor-

* Secretary of HEW in the Johnson Administration.

ously—and futilely—against Taft-Hartley that Meany decided the time had come to move on to other targets. "We came to the conclusion that when you got down to the rank and file, the members didn't really give a damn about Taft-Hartley; they'd heard the union leaders yell about it so long they wanted us to shut up," said a man in Meany's inner circle at the time. The 1954 issue was unemployment. The post-Korea cuts in defense spending and Administration tampering with interest rates touched off a furiously accelerating recession which saw 3 million persons (4.9 percent of the work force) jobless in January 1954, 3.6 million a month later. Eisenhower, according to his memoirs, was determined not to be pushed into pump-priming spending programs. The AFL, among other groups, tried. The AFL executive council, in February, called for construction of 600,000 low-cost housing units over three years, rather than the timid 105,000 Ike asked of Congress. The *AFL News-Reporter* also complained of the "Republican policy [of giving] tax relief to corporations and coupon clippers while handing out crumbs to the rest of the country." In midsummer Meany called for election of a "more liberal Congress that will approve the progressive legislative programs of the AFL for the benefit of all the American people." Months in advance of any political endorsements by the AFL annual convention, the *News-Reporter* began running highly laudatory "profiles" of favored Democratic senatorial candidates—Alben Barkley of Kentucky, Pat McNamara of Michigan, Richard L. Neuberger of Oregon, Guy Gillette of Iowa, Paul Douglas of Illinois. "George was so much in charge by this time," said one of his assistants, "that he decided it was silly to wait until the fall; if you want to win elections, you get the word out early."

By autumn unemployment was tapering off, save for scattered hard-core knots in Ohio, Pennsylvania and Michigan. The Republican National Committee, sensing it could reverse the normal mid-term losses, persuaded Eisenhower to campaign vigorously in marginal states. For labor, the countering break was an offhand remark on unemployment by Secretary of Defense Charles E. ("Engine Charlie") Wilson. Speaking at a press conference in Detroit, quite possibly the most rabid labor city in the world, Wilson was asked about the jobless. "I've got a lot of sympathy for people when a sudden change catches them," Wilson replied, "but I've always liked bird dogs better than kennel-fed dogs myself. You know, one who'll go out and hunt for food, rather than sit on his fanny and yell." Democratic and labor orators fell upon Wilson with whoops; he apologized for his "inept remarks" and "bringing up those bird dogs at the same time I was talking about people." Meany said Wilson's comment was "what you could expect from a businessman in a position of responsibility in government." Meany also accused James P. Mitchell, Durkin's successor as Secretary of Labor, of "deliberately prostituting his office" for votes "by such cheap and tawdry methods" as painting a "rosy but inaccurate picture of the unemployment situation." (As if to show that one shouldn't take political oratory too seriously, Meany a week later permitted Mitchell to write a guest column for the *News-Reporter.*)

The campaign was a relative success for labor. Democrats took control of the Senate, 48 to 47 (Wayne Morse was in the independent phase of his transition from Republican to Democrat); and of the House 232 to 203. Labor's League for Political Education counted 23 more "friends" in the House, four more in the Senate; 18 of its 30 endorsed Senate candidates won; 152 of 282 in the House. But Meany cautioned that the conservative coalition still dominated Congress.

And, again, labor's political action proved an unconvertible currency. One failure suffices to illustrate Meany's frustration. At the outset of the session the AFL made federal aid for school construction its chief legislative goal. "You looked around the country and saw kids crammed into classrooms that went way back before the war," Meany said. By Administration estimate, the nation needed 300,000 more classrooms. Eisenhower submitted a bill for $8 billion in loans and direct grants over three years. The AFL counterproposal was considerably more grandiose—$22 billion in one form—but the conservative coalition blocked action on any bill whatsoever.

By the 1956 election, the merger had meshed the old AFL and CIO political wings together into a single Committee on Political Education (COPE), run by Jack Kroll, formerly of the CIO's PAC, and James McDevitt, director of the AFL's LLPE. Several things irked Meany during the pre-campaign maneuverings. Democratic leaders "talked about labor as if it belonged to them," Meany complained to one staff member. Representative John McCormack (Dem., Massachusetts), presiding over platform hearings at the Democratic convention in Chicago, brusquely cut off Meany without giving him a full chance to develop labor's position on civil rights legislation. Immediately after the convention, nominee Adlai E. Stevenson wrote Meany asking him to send a labor representative to regional campaign meetings. "Now, on the basis of that letter, we are now a branch of the Democratic party," Meany complained. "That is *his* interpretation. I am not prepared to admit we are a branch of the Democratic or Republican party."

Two weeks after the convention the AFL-CIO executive council met at Unity House, the ILGWU's resort in the Pocono Mountains, to consider political endorsements. Members from the former CIO unions, especially Reuther, were enthusiastic about Stevenson. Reuther had helped blunt an attempt by former President Truman to turn the convention to W. Averell Harriman, and he had already put the UAW behind Stevenson's candidacy.

To Reuther's astonishment Meany opened the discussion by declaring flatly, "My thought is that we should not endorse any political candidate this year." Reuther replied that lack of an endorsement would be interpreted—correctly, in his opinion—as pro-Republican. Stevenson "deserved" endorsement, Reuther said. "As far as neutralism is concerned," Meany said, "I am not neutral. I am against both parties." Meany felt the AFL made a mistake in endorsing the Democratic candidate in 1952, although he favored doing so at the time. "I have no apologies to make," Meany said. "The only explanation is that I am four years older and I know what has happened since 1952. I was one of the leading figures in getting the endorsement of Adlai Stevenson in the 1952 [AFL] convention. I do not take that same position today because, as I say, I have had four years' experience since then." Meany cited the continued Dixiecrat control of key congressional committees, McCormack's cavalier behavior at the platform hearings, and how Stevenson apparently took labor support for granted. Meany had also tried to persuade House Speaker Sam Rayburn (Dem., Texas) to pledge the Democratic party to abandon the traditional system of appointing congressional committees and chairmen on the basis of seniority. Rayburn refused. As a result, Meany said, even if the Democrats won the election, "we will have the same antilabor groups controlling the committees as we have today, if they happen to live." Meany did not agree with Reuther's statement that nonendorsement would be pro-Republican:

"My opinion is the Republican party stinks, and the Democratic party is almost as bad. I think we would be in a stronger position if we told both parties we did not care for them as parties but that we would pick out individuals as we liked them and give them support for the House and Senate. . . .

"I can see the sentiment is that we have to play a part as a political machine on a national basis. All right. We played a part in New Deal days. Our state agencies endorsed Roosevelt. The AFL did not endorse Roosevelt, and I don't think it weakened our position one iota. I have, in carrying out the traditional policy of the AFL, opposed the Democratic organization and went along with the Fusion and Republican candidates in New York, and we were successful, and when it was over we had the greater respect from the Democrats than we ever had before. If we are in the pockets of the Democrats, we are not important."

Meany lost. The first vote, on the question of whether to endorse any candidates, was fourteen to eight affirmative. All negative votes came from former AFL unions. Then, on a show of hands, the council voted to endorse Stevenson and Senator Estes Kefauver, his running mate. Meany and five other members, all former AFL, abstained. Meany said he would pass the recommendation on to the AFL-CIO general board composed of presidents of all affiliated unions, which had made formal endorsements for the federation. In the interest of harmony, he said, he would take no action "that will indicate I am in disagreement" with the majority decision.

Meany said nothing publicly of the split in the executive council, although his opposition to endorsement leaked to the press immediately. In his major campaign speeches Meany urged that union members study carefully the two parties' records. He also emphasized the "freedom of all union members to vote in accordance with the dictates of their consciences"—a roundabout way of answering Republican charges that "labor bosses" could control rank-and-file vote. Meany also endorsed Stevenson personally, after a September meeting in Washington. "Of course I'm going to support Mr. Stevenson," he said to newsmen who asked about his stand in the executive council.

The Committee on Political Education, in its campaign literature, attacked the "Republican Administration," rather than Eisenhower directly, and hit at its probusiness bias. But COPE did suggest voters should "take more seriously into account this year the qualifications of the candidates for Vice-President." COPE noted that President Eisenhower had suffered a massive heart attack less than a year previously and said:

> If President Eisenhower is re-elected and does not survive another four years in the White House, Richard Nixon would become President. His record as a representative and senator . . . shows that Nixon voted consistently against measures supported by labor. . . . He has shown ultrapartisanship in political campaigns. He obviously lacks the breadth of view and understanding to be the President of all the American people.

The Stevenson endorsement irked Meany because it nullified the former AFL's nonpartisanship. To his embarrassment, labor could not claim it endorsed "the man, not the party." He felt Reuther was too closely identifying labor with the Democratic party, to labor's disadvantage. Vice-President Nixon, for instance, constantly told Republican campaign workers that Reuther, not Stevenson, was "the man to beat." Nixon called Reuther "the smartest labor leader in America" and said he had the "big money" and union-paid political operatives capable of winning a Democratic victory. Meany did not equate Eisenhower with the Republican party. Further, organized labor prospered during the first Eisenhower Administration. Average weekly earnings of manufacturing workers increased twenty percent from 1953 to 1956. The consumer price index rose less than one percent between 1952 and 1955, contrasted with fifty percent between 1945 and 1952. Man-hours lost to strikes were sixty percent less than in 1949–52. Ike's 41,000 mile interstate highway program, commenced with $2 billion in federal spending in 1955, provided scores of thousands of jobs for construction workers. The President called it "the biggest peacetime construction project of any description ever undertaken by the United States or any other country." The failure of labor to achieve its legislative goals was more the fault of the Congress—Democratically controlled—than of Eisenhower. Meany was not satisfied with labor's accomplishments, yet he could declare to the AFL's final convention in 1955, "American labor has never had it so good" (though not because of the Republicans, Meany footnoted a year later, during the campaign). After a brief coolness because of the Durkin resignation, Meany and Eisenhower developed a cordial, if not close, relationship. Ike's second Secretary of Labor, James P. Mitchell, had been an industrial relations expert for the army during World War II; Meany knew him casually through the War Labor Board, and respected him for being both knowledgeable and sympathetic about organized labor's problems. Eisenhower dedicated the AFL-CIO's sparkling eight-floor headquarters building, across verdant Lafayette Park from the White House, and he got into the habit of calling Meany for chats on the phone, or to invite him to come to his private quarters late in the afternoon for general conversation and a drink. When the contractor remodeling the President's Gettysburg farm had a problem with building tradesmen, Eisenhower politely asked Meany if he could do anything about it. (Meany did; with two phone calls, the work resumed.)

As Terry Catchpole, the conservative political journalist, noted, "For the ability to get as much as it could for its members, from whichever party is in power, the AFL in 1956 substituted a dependence on—a servitude to—the Democratic Party. The CIO concept of political action had won out and the more moderate policy of the AFL was shoved aside. It made no difference whether the Democrats needed labor more than labor needed the Democrats: labor had cast its lot and the AFL-CIO's political policy was affirmed and set in motion."

By his own definition, during the 1950's George Meany was second only to Vice-President Richard M. Nixon as "the most rabid anti-Communist . . . in America." Meany was consistently suspicious of the Soviet Union, and hostile toward any détente that would "justify the crimes against humanity committed by these people [the Soviets] against the millions that they have enslaved." When Sir Winston Churchill spoke favorably of coexistence in 1953, Meany rejoined, "We do not want appeasement even if it is accompanied by a long cigar instead of an umbrella." A few days before Eisenhower's "Spirit of Geneva" summit conference with the Soviets, Meany warned, "Just because Molotov puts on a ten-gallon hat and visits some museum and has lunch with Barney

Baruch does not mean that Russia is suddenly converted to the ways of peace. . . . Just because Khrushchev gets tight and slaps somebody on the back does not mean that he has suddenly become a democrat, with a small 'd' or a large 'D.' "

A common theme ran through the dozens of foreign affairs speeches Meany made during the decade. The Soviet Union and the Communist nations oppress free labor. "We have never swallowed the theory . . . that while Russia was governed by a dictatorial system, it was after all a dictatorship of the proletariat . . . which would discriminate in favor of those who toil. As the most total expression of all tyranny, communism has, in our eyes, always been an ultra-reactionary movement . . . making the free trade unions its first and foremost target." The West must deal with the Soviets from a position of strength: During the defense cuts of the post-Korea period Meany warned of the "deadly drift into defeatism that has swung the free world far off course." Unless the Soviets changed their basic goals, pacts with them would be delusionary and hypocritical: "The only acceptable assurance from Soviet Russia of peaceful intentions towards the free world is complete renunciation of aggression."

Concurrently, Meany criticized France, Britain, and other European powers for clinging to colonial possessions. In June 1954 he, Walter Reuther, and John L. Lewis sent a strong telegram to French President Vincent Auriol asking that the siege of Tunisia be lifted. "We believe that the repression of Tunisian workers gives comfort to the unyielding enemy of free trade unions, the Soviet Union. . . . We are distressed at the stubborn colonialist policies still pursued by several democratic countries to the detriment of free trade unionism." Henri Bonnet, the French ambassador in Washington, tried to defend his country's policies in a series of meetings with Meany. The climactic salesmanship came during a dinner party at which a foreign ministry expert expounded at length on why the Tunisians were much better off under the French than they would be if they were independent. When the long discourse ended, the expert asked, "Now, Mr. Meany, do you have any questions?"

"Just one," Meany responded. "When are you fellows going to stop kicking the Tunisians around?"

As a supporter of the foreign aid program, Meany demanded a voice in its administration and also in the conduct of overseas labor programs. The Administration initially was cool. In March 1954 Eisenhower made Meany a member of a public advisory board to Harold Stassen, head of the Foreign Operations Administration, the aid agency. The board, however, did not meet until December. The "sudden activation" puzzled Meany and he checked into what FOA had been doing the past year. What he found prompted his abrupt resignation, in a cool letter to Stassen. Meany noted that national policy, as expressed by Congress in creating the aid program, was to "encourage the efforts of other free countries in the strengthening of free labor unions." Since aid's beginning, he said, the AFL had insisted on a "carefully and strongly developed labor program" within FOA.

This the FOA has not done. On the contrary, virtually the entire labor program of the agency has been dismantled and most of the key labor officers have been discharged. The agency's reports to the public and to Congress have given no notice of the many problems concerning labor in the development of the program or of the need to meet such problems. The evidence at every hand indicates that the FOA is unresponsive to the need for either consultation or participation of labor in its work.

Meany said he could not "in good conscience" continue membership on the public advisory board so long as labor was being ignored. After several private meetings with Eisenhower, Meany and Stassen made peace. Stassen appointed Meany's nominee, John J. Meskimen, of the railway clerks union, as director of labor affairs for FOA. He put together a special labor advisory committee chaired by Meany. And Stassen came to the 1954 AFL convention to make public amends, declaring, in an oratorical peace offering, he wanted the "active cooperation of the trade unions in the United States." The FOA authorized 75 overseas positions for labor people—13 in Europe, 24 in the Near East, 16 in the Far East, 22 in Latin America. The AFL agreed to fund training courses for foreign labor leaders and to escort them on tours of the United States to show off working conditions and standards of living.

Through the Labor Department's trade union advisory committee, Meany maintained that labor experience was of "primary importance" for labor attachés posted abroad. He wanted the unions to run a joint attaché-training program. He felt the Departments of Defense and State, the United States Information Agency, and the FOA "should receive their advice on labor matters from the Department of Labor, and should rely on the Department of Labor for operations carried out in the labor field. They should not establish 'departments of labor' within their agencies. . . ." But others in government were not sanguine about labor's efficacy as an ally in foreign work. At one meeting, in September 1954, Walter Bedell Smith, undersecretary to John Foster Dulles, ticked off good and bad points about involving labor in the attaché program. Smith admitted union professionals had "technical qualifications," but relying upon them was "bad because the unions' policies are not always the same as those of the government and their nominees may frequently be torn by divided loyalties." Smith agreed to give "prime consideration" to union nominees for attaché posts but would not promise anything further than that.

The Central Intelligence Agency also displayed a keen interest in the labor attaché and other union programs. Secretary of Labor Mitchell in December 1954 created a "working group on overseas labor matters" drawn from his department, the Pentagon, the FOA, and the CIA. Allen Dulles, the director of Central Intelligence, on December 28, 1954, designated Cord Meyer, Jr., as the CIA's representative on the working group. When the United Nations, at AFL-CIO insistence in 1958, established a committee to investigate forced labor, Allen Dulles agreed with Mitchell "it would be most advantageous to our mutual interests to coordinate our efforts" in its work. Dulles named James E. White, a CIA functionary, to do liaison with the Department of Labor official concerned. Dulles pledged that White "will have available to him the results of regular and systematic analysis of all pertinent materials known to this agency."

Meany was no armchair anti-Communist. The AFL's most spectacular foreign venture during the 1950's—one run in conjunction with the CIA—was toppling a freely elected Guatemalan government. After the overthrow of the long-time dictator Jorge Ubico in 1944, presidents Juan José Arévalo and Jacobo Arbenz relied upon newly recognized labor unions to maintain themselves in office. In one instance, in 1949, armed unionists fought alongside loyalist soldiers to defeat an attempted military coup. Arévalo and Arbenz instituted Guatemala's first, if modest, labor code: recognition of unions, a minimum wage, an eight-hour day, labor courts to hear worker-employer disputes, a rudimentary social security system. Arbenz collaborated with Communists, appointing them to key administrative positions, especially in agrarian reform and trade union matters, but not to his cabinet. Victor Manuel Gutierrez, an elected Communist member of the Chamber of Deputies, ran the Confederación General de Trabajadores de Guatemala (CGTG), and was a leading exponent of land reform.

In 1953 Arbenz commenced an ambitious land reform program aimed at vast holdings of the United Fruit Company (UFCO), the dominant employer in the country. Arbenz expropriated more than 400,000 acres of United Fruit lands and offered compensation in 25-year bonds at the company's assessed valuation.

The Eisenhower Administration considered the Arbenz government a Communist bridgehead on the continent, and set out to destroy it. One of the persons approached by the CIA as a potential rallying point for Arbenz opponents was General Miguel Ydígoras Fuentes, a respected military man who later was to become president. According to Ydígoras Fuentes, one of the things asked of him by the CIA (in addition to restoration of United Fruit's privileged status) was that he "destroy the railroad workers labor union." He refused. The AFL, meanwhile, funded the National Union of Free Workers of Guatemala (the UNTL, by its Spanish initials), in cooperation with the Organización Regional Internacional de Trabajadores (ORIT), the ICFTU affiliate for Latin America. Arbenz threw the UNTL leaders out of the country. They found refuge in Mexico with Serafino Romualdi, the AFL's man for Latin America.

In February 1954, during the psychological buildup for Arbenz's overthrow, Meany directed an extraordinary public letter to the Guatemalan president. He viewed "with profound apprehension the extensive subversive activities of the Guatemalan section of the world Communist party in your country." The AFL was "deeply distressed at the open attempt of the Communists to subvert [Guatemala's] democratic constitution in the interest of a foreign power that is brutally totalitarian and seeks to make your nation a mere pawn in the international Communist drive for world domination and dictatorship." Meany opined that "were it not for the continuous government support of the Communists' control of the organized labor movement, many workers' groups would be willing and anxious to break the shackles of Communist domination." Meany concluded that he was "looking forward to an early reply." He did not receive one, of course, but in ensuing months Romualdi put the exiled UNTL leadership at the disposal of the CIA-financed "liberation army" of Carlos Castillo Armas. Rubén Villatoro, the UNTL president, wrote anti-Arbenz articles for *The American Federationist*. In June 1954 Castillo Armas toppled Arbenz. Romualdi scurried to Guatemala City to persuade the new military government to permit labor unions to continue to operate, and Meany announced that the AFL "rejoices over the downfall of the Communist-controlled regime in Guatemala. . . ." He hoped the new government would "restore as quickly as possible absolute respect for civil liberties and human rights and will preserve the social gains codified in the Guatemalan labor and agrarian legislation." He pledged AFL support of the "difficult task of reorganization" of Guatemalan labor.

Serafino Romualdi spent July and August in Guatemala, trying to advise Castillo Armas on labor matters. In his memoirs Romualdi expressed surprise at the Pandora's box of labor repression that he and the AFL had helped open. He asserted the Guatemalan people were firmly behind Castillo Armas and "a strong wave of anti-Communism was sweeping the country"—so much so, in fact, that "this wave of anti-Communism threatened to sweep away the labor movement itself." Within a few months Castillo Armas dissolved unions representing workers on United Fruit plantations; employees of UFCO's subsidiary, the International Railway of Central America; and teachers. In 1956 the regime amended the labor code so drastically that, as Romualdi lamented, it became "much more difficult for a trade union to operate and exist." Authorities dismissed activist trade unionists as "agitators." Agricultural workers, in Romualdi's words, "were brought back to conditions of servitude if not actual slavery."

Other labor leaders immediately recognized the Guatemalan venture for what it was: a desire by the Eisenhower Administration "to give aid and comfort to the United Fruit Company which was doing all it could to set aside . . . some of the decent legislation that has been passed down there recently," as O. A. Knight, president of the Oil Workers Union, told the CIO executive board a few days after the coup. "We have been supporting the wrong people," said Emil Mazey, the UAW secretary-treasurer.

Guatemalan labor more than a decade later had not recovered from the Castillo Armas strictures—a situation for which Meany and the AFL must share the blame. The consequences of the Arbenz regime, had it continued in power, and its leftist drift accelerated, are a matter of conjecture. The consequences of its overthrow—the continued misery of the Guatemalan people, the political anarchy and terrorism of the left and right—are a matter of current history.

The election of Sir Vincent Tewson, the British trade union leader, as president of the ICFTU in 1951 so annoyed Meany that the AFL boycotted the ICFTU for the next two years. In July 1953 Meany set out to do battle with Tewson, at the ICFTU congress in Stockholm. Meany timed his trip so he could spend several days in London en route, jibing at Tewson on his home court. Joseph Stalin had died on March 4, and Meany knew Tewson intended to try to push the ICFTU into a conciliatory attitude toward the new Soviet leadership. Meany received the British press in a suite at the Claridge Hotel, and the reporters did not know quite what to make of him. "Beneath his navy blue jacket Mr. Meany wore a mustard-coloured waistcoat with one pocket full of wrapped cigars," observed the London *Express. The News Chronicle* was impressed by Meany's salary of 8,500 pounds a year.* Although Meany did not attack Tewson by name, he dashed any notions the AFL wanted friendship with the new Moscow regime. "If the Russians want peace,"

---

* *The Daily Herald* was more impressed with Walter Reuther, in town at the same time, calling him "the outstanding young man of the American Labour Movement" and "the human dynamo of the American trade unions." The Manchester *Guardian* noted that Reuther ("who speaks more like an academic person than a union boss") met reporters in the "discreet (and dry) Gothic committee rooms of the House of Commons" rather than "in a suite at Claridge's to the accompaniment of tumblers of iced whiskey."

he said, "let them throw open their slave labor camps and free those whose only crime is expressing their opinions."

In Stockholm Meany disagreed with almost every substantive point urged by Tewson in his major address. "No one in the hall can have failed to notice the contrast" in the two speeches, the *Times* of London said. A sampling:

> TEWSON: We welcome any manifestations of a change in the attitude of the new leaders of Soviet Russia which may ease long-standing tensions.
>
> MEANY: Moscow may change its tactics, but it has not changed to the slightest degree its basic aim of world domination.
>
> TEWSON: The present time is a time for caution. . . .
>
> MEANY: This is no time for backsliding under the pretext of caution.
>
> TEWSON: We must be careful not to jeopardize our means of defense, but neither should we countenance any sabotage, whether by word or deed, that may wreck the value of any talks that can take place.
>
> MEANY: No dictator in history has ever been converted to a policy of reason or human decency by appeasement.

Meany achieved his main purpose at the congress. Deserted even by many of his fellow British unionists, Tewson did not run for re-election. Meany pushed through changes in the ICFTU structure, enlarging the executive board from twelve to twenty-five members, both to increase the power of newcomers and to make room for Histradrut, the Israeli labor organization, with half a million members; and to eliminate the requirement that the president be elected from the general board. The latter qualified for election Omer Becu, a Belgian transit union official who had spent World War II in exile in the United States, and who was a close friend of both Lovestone and Dave Dubinsky. Becu shared Meany's hard-nose attitude toward the Soviets, rejecting outright any visits or conferences with their union leaders. "I don't want anything to do with the Soviet trade unions unless they are completely free agents," he said on a U.S. visit during his presidency. "They want to conquer us by charm. It is obvious they are seeking a new kind of popular front." As Philip Pearl, the AFL press man, wrote in the *AFL News-Reporter,* Meany "won a long, drawn-out fight to transform the ICFTU from a dormant debating society into an active and militant organization."

After Stockholm, Meany went on to Germany, France, and Italy. In Rome he received more publicity than any visiting American in several years, according to the *News-Reporter*'s correspondent, a resident journalist. "Here was no evasive, wary newsmaker, giving a beat-around-the-bush speech, but a dynamic hard-hitting representative of nine million Americans who spoke straight from the shoulder, giving quick, clear replies to the questions put to him."

At the 1955 ICFTU congress, again in Stockholm, Meany staged a major coup for United States foreign policy by persuading the West German Trade Union Federation to support a resolution backing rearming of West Germany. President Eisenhower wanted German rearmament as part of the preparation for the imminent Four Power conferences in Geneva with the Soviets; support of German labor was considered a key part of the maneuver. Meany's old nemesis Tewson argued against the resolution, fearing it would disturb the Geneva conference. Meany answered, "It is only from positions of strength that the forces of peace and freedom can advance their cause." The convention also denied reception of a Yugoslav trade union delegation because of its "Communist character." The United States delegation completed its overhaul of the ICFTU internal structure, in hopes of making it "a more effective instrument in combating communism," in Meany's words. The ICFTU was to hire a director of organizations, with three assistants, to encourage development of unions, especially in underdeveloped areas. The AFL would discontinue its unilateral field work in western Europe. Irving Brown, one of Jay Lovestone's original operatives, would move over to the ICFTU staff.

Meany's hopes of a strong ICFTU proved premature. The ICFTU's permanent secretary general, J. H. Oldenbroek, a Dutch railway unionist, was the major problem, in the AFL's opinion. "Oldenbroek wouldn't carry out the policies set by the ICFTU congresses or directors," said Boris Shishkin. "He was also pretty much of a bust as an administrator. He liked to disappear on these long 'inspection trips' without telling anyone an itinerary. But since he was an old railroad man, he'd always stay at some hotel near the station. Hell, his office would call all over Europe, trying to find him at some railroad hotel."

Meany had a secondary motive for strengthening the ICFTU. Conceivably it could mesh together the disparate foreign policy philosophies of the AFL and CIO, which were in the last stages of merger by mid-1955. During the merger negotiations Reuther frequently spoke apprehensively of the incendiary implications of Meany's foreign policy obiter dicta. In one private conversation Meany bitterly resented the implication he had ever favored "preventive war," an assurance Reuther accepted. Meany had no intention of changing his foreign attitudes simply to please Reuther or to make the merger possible. But a strengthened ICFTU would enable him to put the authority of world labor behind his foreign policy.

A strong defense preparedness program contained obvious economic benefits for American labor—as AFL publications constantly reminded rank-and-file workers. The *AFL News-Reporter* during a six-month period in 1955 had articles and photo displays on: the *Nautilus* nuclear submarine, "a 100 percent AFL operation," involving organized mechanics, pipefitters, office employees, boilermakers, painters, carpenters, teamsters, molders, and electrical workers; the Falcon, "latest miracle missile of the air force built by members of International Association of Machinists Lodge 933 at Hughes Aircraft"; and a naval amphibious assault exercise at Camp Pendleton, California, utilizing "equipment made by union members for the armed force." The Soviets berated Meany constantly as a warmonger and accomplice of "the American war machine." *Tass* called him "one of the trade union leaders who are faithful serfs of American imperialism . . . upholding the State Department in its aggressive policies . . . a confidence man of American capitalism."

Meany ignored his critics. Asked by one interviewer if his "far-flung international activities" did not take him away "from the actual business of trade unionism," Meany replied, "We have a stake in peace. It's the sons of workers who pay the price of war. It's the workers themselves who pay the taxes we shoot away when we have a war. When we build free trade unions, throughout the world, we're building peace. We don't get any membership across the sea. But we're investing in ourselves when we rebuild the trade unions Hitler and Stalin and Malenkov wiped out. We know that the way to save West Europe from communism is to keep the free trade unions strong."    Despite his self-assurance and justifications, however, Meany's hard-line foreign policy opinions had a unique capacity to make "sparks fly [and] hackles rise," and cause "a good deal of anguished squirming on the part of his well-wishers," in the words of the New York *Post*. "Equally troublesome," the *Post* continued, "is the impression Meany at times gives of regarding himself and the AFL as virtually the sole repository of moral rectitude in international affairs." So long as Meany dominated the AFL, he said what he wished about foreign affairs, a subject in which most unionists had a massive disinterest. But in a merged AFL-CIO, Meany's bellicosity was too controversial to be accepted in silence.

Reflecting on Dwight Eisenhower more than a decade after his presidency ended, Meany gave him qualified high marks. "Eisenhower, he was no reactionary. In fact, I think you get in down deep enough on a personal basis, he was a pretty liberal guy. But he was in the control of the reactionary machinery of the Republican party, he had absolutely no knowledge of government, he came in as an amateur. I think considering all the circumstances, he made a pretty good President. We made progress, legislatively and otherwise, while Eisenhower was President. Some of our great improvements in social security came while he was President —setting up a real live Department of Health, Education, and Welfare, for example."

Labor's strategy was to map out a series of attainable goals so as to improve social security in stair-step fashion. Operational responsibility fell upon Nelson Cruikshank, director of the department of social security. Immediately after the merger, Meany asked Cruikshank for ideas on legislation the AFL-CIO could obtain in a single session of Congress. Meany wanted a success to demonstrate to the rank and file the value of a merged labor organization. Cruikshank hit upon the idea of benefits for permanently and totally disabled persons, regardless of whether they had reached retirement age. "We consciously made the decision that this would be the first thing on which the united labor movement would work . . . because we thought it was attainable," Cruikshank said. Congress agreed to a bill providing payments for persons past the age of fifty years who were totally disabled—a program that proved so inexpensive Congress a few years later removed the age limit. For labor, however, the victory set a valuable precedent, legislatively and psychologically. "This was the first time we beat the American Medical Association at anything," Cruikshank said. "They were saying they didn't want the government touching the medical profession at any point—they wanted it where a doctor, not the government, would have to say whether a guy was disabled. Well, we won, and this gave us confidence to go after something bigger." The next target was health insurance for older persons—the Medicare program.

Medicare is acutely illustrative of two long-time features of labor's legislative activities: its relative impotence in formulating a program and pushing it to passage, even when friendly majorities control Congress; and its veto power over unacceptable proposals. Labor won several key preliminary skirmishes on Medicare during the Eisenhower years. Voters implicitly endorsed Medicare in the 1960 presidential election, when John F. Kennedy made the program a campaign issue. Full victory was not to come, however, until 1965, after the Lyndon Johnson landslide victory over Barry Goldwater.

Although Meany retained over-all responsibility for labor's efforts on behalf of Medicare, he "was not [so] immediately involved . . . as some people thought he might have been," in Cruikshank's words. But, Cruikshank added, "This should not be interpreted as disinterest. This is Meany's nature—to leave department heads alone." Early in the Medicare planning, Cruikshank urged Meany to hold staff meetings to discuss strategy. "Finally he agreed to do it once a month, and after the first two months I realized it was a mistake, because he didn't know what a staff meeting was for. It's like you can't blame the Hottentots for not liking symphony orchestras; they just don't know there is such a thing. And Mr. Meany doesn't know there is such a thing as a staff meeting, where there's a give and take and an exchange of ideas. It isn't the way he was brought up." Cruikshank saw similarities between Meany the AFL-CIO president and Meany the plumbers' business agent—both doing business out of their hat, with minimal recourse to paperwork and formal planning. Even as state federation president, Cruikshank noted, Meany had sufficed with a single secretary and one-room office. "He doesn't see why anybody needs anything more than that." Not everyone on the staff understood Meany's *modus operandi*. When economist Stanley Ruttenberg resigned from the AFL-CIO staff, according to Cruikshank, "Mr. Meany said to him a very significantly revealing thing: 'Stan, I don't see why you aren't happy on your job. I never bothered you.' And that is exactly what Ruttenberg didn't like. He wanted *more* communication. But this was Meany's idea of good support." Cruikshank was satisfied. Meany permitted him to form a special Medicare committee drawing upon other AFL-CIO departments—public relations, education, legislative. "If I needed a pamphlet or a radio program, or people to go into the field and stir up grass-roots support, I got it, because when I spoke I was acting for Meany. At one time we had thirty to forty people in the field. You could never do that without Meany sitting there and putting his blessing on it."

During the Eisenhower years the AFL-CIO's main concern was preventing passage of a weak Medicare program that would pre-empt chances for truly beneficial legislation. Labor's chief adversary was John A. Perkins, Undersecretary of Health, Education, and Welfare in 1957–58, who had been a member of the New York law firm that represented the Rockefeller family. Cruikshank called Perkins "very opinionated, dictatorial, aristocratic, and overbearing, always proud of his Harvard connections." And Perkins was also a political novice, a defect the AFL-CIO was quick to exploit.

Labor wanted a Medicare program grafted onto the existing Social Security system. The Eisenhower Administration proposed a plan for underwriting health insurance through private companies. After some internal debate, the AFL-CIO offered to support the Administration if it would include capital grants and loans to establish group-practice medical centers. Because of tremendous pressures generated by the AMA lobby, even liberal congressmen leaned toward the Eisenhower plan as a compromise that would satisfy citizen demand for Medicare without unduly offending the medical profession. The Administration was noncommittal on compromising, and finally Perkins admitted he was not seriously negotiating. Cruikshank quoted him: "I might just as well tell you. We found that we can pass our bill without your support." Eisenhower was to unveil the plan on national television, and then introduce Secretary Oveta Culp Hobby, who would explain it. "With Eisenhower's backing, nothing will stop it," Perkins told Cruikshank.

Perkins' statement made Cruikshank "pretty sore," and he told Andrew Biemiller, the AFL-CIO lobbyist, what was happening. "First, Biemiller said, 'I guess that's it.' Then he said, 'Wait a minute. I have a recollection that Sam Rayburn hates Mrs. Hobby's guts because she's a renegade Democrat from Texas, and he has said that sometime he was going to get her.' " Biemiller talked with Rayburn, who delighted in the opportunity to settle his old grievance. Biemiller told Cruikshank afterward: "Don't worry about the Administration passing their bill. There's only one thing now. If any congressman calls you and asks how we stand on that bill, remember the word is just to say, 'Well, follow the leadership. We have no position.' Andy passed the word down, 'Follow Mr. Sam. We have no position.' And Mr. Sam put the word out that this was one that he was personally interested in, and he wanted to kill it and kill it hard." The resultant vote, in Cruikshank's words, was "the most curious combination of right-wing reactionaries and left-wing liberals that you ever saw." A few days later Cruikshank encountered Perkins and could not resist a jibe. "Whatever happened to your bill? I saw your TV show." Cruikshank related:

" 'Gee, you know, that's a funny thing,' he said. 'Did you see the lineup on that vote?'

"I said, 'Yes, I saw it, a very curious thing.'

"He said, 'What do you think happened?'

"I was then very angry and I said, 'Well, I'll tell you, come around someday and I'll give you a lesson free. But next time don't be so sure that you can pass a bill without our help.' "

Such legislative gamesmanship, however amusing to Rayburn, Biemiller and Cruikshank, blurs a central fact of the Medicare struggle: Labor could block the Eisenhower bill, but could not push over one on its own initiative. Labor began work on Medicare in 1957. In the 1958 elections, a severe economic slump enabled the Democrats to strengthen their control of Congress substantially—63 to 34 in the Senate, 283 to 153 in the House. Senators John Kennedy, Stuart Symington, and Hubert Humphrey, all leading contenders for the Democratic presidential nomination, picked up the Medicare issue. So, too, in cautious fashion, did Arthur Flemming, who had succeeded Mrs. Hobby as HEW Secretary. But labor could not put together a coalition strong enough to move Medicare through Congress. Dr. Edward Annis, the chief AMA spokesman, astutely chose not to debate the issue, but to claim that Medicare was the creation of "labor puppets" in Congress, thereby capitalizing on public revulsion with the then-current revelations of corruption in the Teamsters union and elsewhere. In the end, as the Eisenhower Administration closed, the AFL-CIO had to content itself with beating down a limited Medicare plan agreed upon by the Administration and Representative Wilbur Mills (Dem., Arkansas), who through his position as chairman of the House Ways and Means Committee could start or stop any legislation requiring taxation. Because the AFL-CIO would not accept a compromise, the AMA turned vehemently on Meany, saying he had waged "a reckless campaign of rule or ruin and the public be damned." But *The Reporter,* in a more charitable evaluation of the AFL-CIO's position, said it had drawn "overwhelming support to the thesis that medical care has become a basic human right." Although Meany was disappointed at the slow pace of Medicare, he was satisfied that the essential groundwork had been done when President Eisenhower went out of office. He had every reason to expect final success from the Kennedy Administration.

In early afternoon of January 19, 1961, Eisenhower's last full day as President, Meany received a phone call from the White House. It was Ike. "What are you doing?" the President asked. "Why don't you drop over for a few moments?" The "few moments" turned into almost two hours of conversation, two aging men in a gush of comradeship that said, in effect, whatever their past differences, they were going to miss one another.

# XI

# "Hoffa's Too Rich for Our Blood"

I N EARLY JANUARY 1957 George Meany sat in a crowded dining room in the Senate Office Building and, during a two-hour lunch, heard a staggering story from Robert F. Kennedy, counsel for a select Senate subcommittee. Dave Beck, president of the International Brotherhood of Teamsters, largest union in the AFL-CIO and perhaps the most powerful in the nation, was a crook. Beck had stolen from his own union and taken money from employers. The sums totaled hundreds of thousands of dollars. Beck used the union treasury virtually as a private bank account for profitable real estate transactions, for silk shirts, golf balls, love seats, football tickets, even five dozen diapers he gave to friends. Kennedy told Meany the select committee, headed by Senator John McClellan (Dem., Arkansas) would open hearings on the Beck material within a month. "It's going to be rough, Mr. Meany," Kennedy said. "The evidence is here, and there's no way Beck can answer it."

Kennedy's story jolted Meany. Despite their reputation for rough-and-tumble unionism, the Teamsters, to the public, ranked far above the gangster-infested International Longshoremen's Association. Action against the ILA, run by mob figures, was considerably different from action against the IBT, run by Beck, a frequent White House guest who ranked high in the civic hierarchy of his native Seattle, Washington (which only a few years earlier named him Man of the Year). Because Beck was a prominent member of the executive council, the AFL-CIO was sure to suffer publicly.

Kennedy told Meany he recognized the investigation would cause problems for the AFL-CIO; nonetheless, he said, it had to be done. Kennedy had reason to be nervous about Meany's reaction. A few days earlier J. Albert Woll, counsel for both the AFL-CIO and the Teamsters, and Einar Mohn, Beck's executive assistant, had come to Kennedy's office "grim and angry." Woll and Mohn knew Kennedy and Carmine Bellino, a committee accountant, had obtained bales of records detailing Beck's finances from Nathan Shefferman, a Chicago labor relations specialist. By Kennedy's account, Woll and Mohn were angry: "Who did I think I was, who did the committee think they were? They would not tolerate what we had been doing. I must be out of my mind. If I stopped right now, though they would still be annoyed with me, I would be far better off than if I tried to continue with this silly business." Woll's credentials with the AFL-CIO were such that Kennedy wondered whether the federation would try to undercut the investigation.

Meany swiftly resolved Kennedy's question at the luncheon meeting. "All that he asked from us at that meeting, or any time," Kennedy said, "was that we be fair. Never did he ask us not to conduct an investigation, or to call a particular witness. He never attempted to bring any pressure."

For Meany the McClellan hearings were the first test of the ethical practices section of the new AFL-CIO constitution. Throughout the merger talks the CIO had insisted the AFL-CIO have the authority to move against corrupt unions and their officials. The CIO argument was a simplistic equation: "We kicked out our Communists, now you kick out your crooks." Meany often muttered that the CIO "was completely overstating the situation," but his experience with the International Longshoremen's Association convinced him the AFL-CIO did in fact need certain police authority over affiliated unions. "Although none of us would—or will now—say this for the record," an AFL-CIO staff man said more than a decade later, "our action against the ILA was morally sound, but constitutionally dubious. Meany got the council to go against the ILA because the ILA was in the wrong, but he really stretched precedent to do it." The AFL-CIO constitution resolved any legal questions. It said one purpose of the merged federation was to protect the labor movement "from any and all corrupt influences." It empowered the executive council to investigate unions suspected of corrupt activities, to make recommendations or give directions to unions involved, and to suspend affiliates that would not reform. A committee on ethical practices was provided to assist the executive council "in carrying out the constitutional determination of the federation to keep the federation free of any taint of corruption."

The provisions were a drastic departure from past practices of both the AFL and the CIO; where corruption was involved, autonomy for affiliated unions no longer existed. There was die-hard opposition from old AFL unions. A. J. Hayes, long the head of the International Association of Machinists, stated the ethical practices committee was opposed by Dave Beck as well as Richard Gray and James Brownlow, chairmen of the AFL building and construction trades and metal trades departments, respectively. Hayes said, "Each of these people will deny that they opposed these things, and yet actually in any considerations or discussions of the matter, they *did* oppose them."

When the Senate investigation began, Andrew J. Biemiller, the AFL-CIO lobbyist, said Meany was dubious of McClellan's motives, even though he agreed corruption existed. "Meany thought McClellan was an antilabor nut, and not a very effective senator, either." Meany and Biemiller talked with McClellan after the Kennedy luncheon and "found him impossible," in Biemiller's words. "But he had a hell of a lot of nasty material, so we had to walk carefully with him. You don't mess around with people who can kill you."

Meany saw three reasons for labor leaders to be worried about union corruption:

"We were concerned, number one, because we knew that this trend had developed . . . that seemed to have its roots in the idea—which I categorically reject—that the American worker doesn't care what happens to the money he puts in his trade union as long as he gets a good fat pay envelope. I don't believe that. So this concern was to the future effectiveness of the trade union movement.

"Number two, it was our concern as American citizens. We know that . . . no one segment of the population can long continue to exploit another segment . . . and continue to advance at the expense of the others. . . .

"And, then, very, very frankly, we were concerned on the question of public opinion—what the public might think of us if this corruption were to become some sort of a creeping paralysis fastening itself on the trade union movement. We know that we cannot ignore public opinion. But despite all this, our number one concern was maintaining the effectiveness of [the] trade union movement. . . ."

At an executive council meeting on January 28 Meany presented a resolution pledging AFL-CIO cooperation with McClellan. Teamster witnesses were already appearing before the committee for questioning about gangsters in the union. Beck, who had declined a request to appear voluntarily before McClellan, glowered as Meany discussed the meaning of the resolution.

"This means that all officials of the AFL-CIO and its affiliates should freely and without reservation answer all relevant questions asked by proper law enforcement agencies, legislative committees, and other public bodies seeking fairly and objectively to keep the labor movement free from corruption."

Meany presented a resolution recognizing that "any person is entitled, in the exercise of his individual conscience, to the protections afforded by the Fifth Amendment and [we] reaffirm our conviction that this historical right must not be abridged." But the use of the Fifth Amendment had special significance for a labor leader, the resolution continued.

> It is the policy of the AFL-CIO . . . that if a trade union official decides to invoke the Fifth Amendment, for his personal protection and to avoid scrutiny by proper legislative committees, law enforcement agencies, or other public bodies into alleged corruption on his part, he has no right to continue to hold office in his union.
>
> Otherwise it becomes possible for a union official who may be guilty of corruption to create an impression that the trade union movement sanctions the use of the Fifth Amendment not as a matter of individual conscience, but as a shield against proper scrutiny into corrupt influences in the labor movement.

Beck angrily attacked the resolution, screaming and bouncing in his seat for more than half an hour. "I have no use for racketeers," he thundered, "but I will be goddamned if I am going to be a party under any conditions with interfering with men's constitutional rights. . . . The Teamsters Union does not for one second intend to be maneuvered without at least protest and militant action and fighting in the courts and through every other avenue that we can travel, to fail to stop committees of investigation that in our opinion are not the authorized committees to conduct the investigations." Some of the Teamster officials who had already been brought before the committee, Beck said, "I have known for years and years, and I am not walking away from them. I will never walk away from them. You could get ten thousand friends when the going is smooth. When you need them is when it is tough."

Beck's demand for loyalty did not impress Meany. "Dave," he said, "do you advise this executive council to take the position that any individual official in the trade union movement would have the full backing of the AFL-CIO and would not be subject to discipline if he took the Fifth Amendment?"

"Yes," replied Beck.

"What would be the public reaction to the AFL-CIO?" asked Meany.

"I am not concerned with the public reaction," Beck said.

Meany disagreed. "We have an allegiance to the fellow who works for a living. If the AFL-CIO follows the proposal of your organization and equivocates on this question, we will get legislation that will hurt every one of our members and hurt every one of our unions. You don't know the legislation you will get. You will be under government control. . . . You can't have fifteen million people in an organization and say

. . . 'We are above the law.' "

Meany said the Teamsters' attitude toward the McClellan committee was responsible for the question being before the executive council. Einar Mohn, Beck's aide, had telegraphed Teamster vice-presidents that if the committee asked questions about their affairs, they should refuse to answer and that they could plead the Fifth Amendment without fear of punitive action by the union. "It is something, Dave, we can't avoid," Meany said. "We can't walk away from it."

Harry Bates of the bricklayers union, one of Meany's closest friends on the council, agreed with Beck. "I will go down before the Senate and the Department of Justice or any goddamn one of them can come into my office and I will let them see every one of the records . . . [but] if Dave Beck wants to take advantage of the Fifth Amendment, let him do so."

J. Albert Woll, the AFL-CIO counsel, who had also been advising Beck, was dubious about the resolution. "The moment that groups begin . . . to penalize a person when he exercises a constitutional right . . . the day will come in America when no man can any longer afford to take a constitutional right. . . ."

"How do we protect this labor movement?" Meany asked. "How do we protect the members? They are the people who own this movement." Meany took the offensive in the ensuing debate.

WOLL:     It may be, George, we can get something short of that. . . .
MEANY:    Do you think there is anybody in this country who reads the paper who doesn't feel that the Teamsters took this [Fifth Amendment] action to protect some corruption?
WOLL:     I say this, the Teamsters did not.
MEANY:    I didn't say they did, but don't you think the impression must be that—
BECK:     Are we going to be condemned for what people think, whether we are guilty or not guilty?
MEANY:    I am not condemning you. I am trying to get a statement to protect this labor movement.
BECK:     Not at the expense of the Teamsters, are you?
MEANY:    Has the union no obligation to protect the money of its members?
BECK:     Certainly it has.
MEANY:    What do you do after a fellow refuses to answer a question of personal corruption?
BECK:     You go to court on it.
MEANY:    The union doesn't do anything to protect its members' money?
BECK:     Certainly it does.

MEANY:  What do you do, then?

BECK:   Our members are all bonded, to start with.

MEANY:  Never mind the bond. What do you do?

BECK:   We certainly do not convict the Secretary—

MEANY:  I didn't ask you that. What do you do?

BECK:   Now, let me finish. I listened to you—

MEANY:  And I have listened to you for forty minutes. The question is a question of corruption, indicated corruption with union funds, and the fellow says, "I take the Fifth Amendment." All right, what do you do then to find out if he did? What do you do?

BECK:   As an individual or as a union?

MEANY:  As the president of the Teamsters. Do you do anything?

BECK:   Why, certainly we do.

MEANY:  What do you do, tell me.

BECK:   Certainly we do.

MEANY:  All right, what do you do?

BECK:   We proceed to refer the matter to our local union to go into the subject matter. It is their money, not ours.

MEANY:  I see. Have you had any of those cases?

BECK:   Yes, we have had a hundred of them.

MEANY:  I have heard that before.

Meany began to summarize. "I tell you gentlemen here today that if you evade this question, which is what our attorney wants you to do, and what Dave wants you to do—"

Woll interrupted. "I don't want that, George. I don't want that."

"We have a responsibility to the workers of America," Meany continued. "Right," chimed in Reuther. "Fifteen million of them," Meany said, "and I say to you that if you evade this question as it now is presented to the general public as the AFL-CIO then all bars are down, you will get legislation that will really hamstring your unions and will . . . hurt our membership. . . . Now, these things are giving the trade union movement a black eye. I am not trying to butt into the business of any international union. I am trying to lay down a policy for the AFL-CIO.

"What do we think of this? Should an official be protected by the trade union movement in an attempt to hide something that is corrupt on the surface? Do we sit back and say, 'Well, he is a good guy' until the courts convict him, or do we have a further obligation to protect our members' money?"

Meany pressed the resolution to a vote, and it passed 22 to 1, Beck casting the sole dissent.

Beck avoided his committee appearance for more than two months, first claiming his health would not permit him to travel to Washington to testify, then taking winter cruises to the West Indies and Europe. "I did not believe he would ever come back to this country," Kennedy stated. "On the assurances of Albert Woll, I had not subpoenaed Beck. Now that he was out of the United States, we had no power to subpoena him." In his absence, the committee used documents and Teamster witnesses to amass a damning case against Beck. The key points Kennedy summarized as follows:

—Beck took at least $370,000 from the Western Conference of Teamsters,* which he headed. When the Internal Revenue Service and the Senate committee began investigations, Beck desperately began looking for ways to return the money. He borrowed $200,000 from the Fruehauf Trailer Company, one of the country's major truckers. To repay Fruehauf, Beck sold his Seattle home to the Teamsters union for $163,-000, but continued living in it rent-free.

—Beck gave Nathan Shefferman, a Chicago labor consultant (for Sears, Roebuck & Company among other major employers), some $85,000 in Teamster funds to pay for personal purchases for himself, his family, and his friends.

—Beck used $150,000 in Teamster funds to improve his Seattle house (including a heated swimming pool) and an adjacent home for his son.

—Beck had a host of side business deals with employers and their representatives. Beck got Fruehauf to give his son, Dave Beck, Jr., $41,000 for toy trucks which Beck, Jr. marketed to Teamster locals around the country. According to Kennedy, Beck told the locals: "Buy or you'll answer to me." Beck also installed his son as president of a beer distributing company which Kennedy said "granted unusual favors to the Anheuser-Busch Company," the St. Louis brewer.

Beck finally went before the McClellan committee on March 26; his demeanor, wrote columnist Murray Kempton, was "the hollow empty geniality that is the shabby cloak left over from the days when he was taken seriously as a man of affairs. . . ." As Kennedy had anticipated, Beck took the Fifth Amendment, refusing to answer more than ninety questions. Senator Henry Jackson (Dem., Washington) slipped from the hearing room and phoned Meany, who said tersely, "That's the end of Dave Beck." Meany immediately issued orders for a special meeting of the executive council, to be convened three days later. (Asked afterward by a reporter about when he decided to call the meeting, Meany said, "About ten seconds after I was told that he had taken the Fifth Amendment.")

With Beck invited but absent, Meany convened the council on March

* For administrative purposes, the International Brotherhood of Teamsters is divided into six regional conferences.

29. For the record, he outlined the issues: McClellan had charged Beck with taking more than $300,000 in Teamster funds between 1949 and early 1953. When asked to explain, Beck pleaded the Fifth Amendment more than ninety times. McClellan accused him of showing "flagrant disregard and disrespect for honest and reputable unionism and for the best interests and welfare of the laboring people of this country."

Meany called Beck's conduct "pretty disgusting." He went through the testimony elicited from Nathan Shefferman and Teamster officials. "The union even paid eight dollars for the repair of Beck's false teeth when he dropped them in New York. It paid for diapers; it paid for cars for the girl friend of Brewster's* horse trainer. . . . It is the most astounding record I have ever seen in all of my experience." Meany read the AFL-CIO constitutional provision on ethical practices and said, "The Constitution applies to all unions. It does not make any difference how large the union is or how small it is. I am going to suggest action." He proposed that the council file charges against Beck for "conduct detrimental to the trade union movement"; that pending disposition of the charge, Beck be suspended from the council; and that the council investigate evidence that the Teamsters union "is under corrupt influence."

Walter Reuther, Jacob Potofsky of the Amalgamated Clothing Workers, and Dave Dubinsky immediately supported the resolution (Dubinsky was also upset at Beck's absence). But Harry Bates urged moderation. Give the Teamsters a chance to take action, he said. Bates warned the AFL-CIO could get into deep trouble. "Let me tell you what is liable to come out of this," Bates said. "You are going to have four, five, or six organizations in the building trades that are tied up with an ironclad agreement to do millions of dollars worth of highway construction work in this country—they are going to stand by Dave Beck unless he is convicted by his union against charges at some kind of trial." Once that happened, Bates said, the "segment of the building trades that is not in that close conclave" would have to decide whether to continue contractual and other cooperation with the Teamsters or to follow the dictate of the AFL-CIO. Bates' implication was that some of the building trades unions would choose the Teamsters and bolt the AFL-CIO if necessary. But Meany's resolution passed, and the council called Beck to appear on May 20.

Beck, his pride stung, tried to fight back, but found his union support melting beneath his feet. He tried to launch a million-dollar campaign to counter the unfavorable publicity the union was receiving, but John F. English, the IBT secretary-treasurer, refused to sign the checks. Straw effigies labeled "Beck the Fink" and "Beck the Thief" were hanged by

---

* Frank Brewster, Beck's close associate, was chairman of the Western Conference of Teamsters.

rank-and-file members, and numerous locals passed resolutions asking for his ouster as IBT president. When the Teamsters general board—still under Beck's control, but slipping fast—protested that Beck's suspension left the union without representation on the AFL-CIO executive council, Meany responded curtly to Beck: "I wish to point out that membership on the executive council is a personal matter. Members . . . do not sit on the council as representatives of any particular union but are required to act in the interests of the general membership of the entire trade union movement. The action of the council in suspending you as a member is based on your personal actions and not on any actions taken by the Teamsters Brotherhood as such." Meany did agree to let Beck come before the executive council to plead for reinstatement.

For Beck, the session (on May 20) was a disaster. Meany, standing only a few feet away from the president of the AFL-CIO's largest union, denounced him as a common thief. "By the time George finished chewing his ass," an executive council member recollected, "Beck wished he hadn't even bothered to come. His face got the color of a piece of meat that had been left out in the sun. Jesus, I thought the guy would fall over."

Meany was direct. "This is not an ordinary case," he said. "This is not just a local trade union official being charged with dishonesty. . . . This is not a local roughneck of some kind, hiding behind the Fifth Amendment rather than making an explanation of his activities. This is the head of the largest union in our federation. . . .

"If there is no substance to these charges, I can only say that Dave has certainly gone out of his way to make it appear that there is, running off to Europe, ducking a subpoena, members of his close family [Dave, Jr.] having to run away from subpoenas. . . .

"This is not a case of a local secretary dipping into the funds because of trouble. This is the case of a very, very wealthy individual spending every waking moment, if you can credit the testimony, to find some way to use his union as an instrumentality for his own personal profit. . . ."

One case that particularly disgusted Meany—and that he detailed to the council—involved Beck's profiting on a memorial fund honoring one of his best friends, at the expense of the widow. Teamsters throughout the country contributed more than $70,000 to the fund for the benefit of the widow and children of Ray Leheney, who had been public relations director of the Western Conference. Beck and an associate, Don Hedlund, received $71,000 from the Teamsters union, funds the bookkeeper thought was to purchase mortgages for the union. They held the mortgages six months, receiving payments which reduced their value by $11,000. Then Beck, acting as trustee for the Leheney memorial fund, used the $71,000 to buy the mortgages from himself and Hedlund at the par value of $71,000. According to Kennedy, "Beck and Hedlund then paid the union what the mortgages were actually worth, which was around $60,000, and pocketed the difference of $11,000. Hedlund and Beck split an $11,000 profit, which they had made first by defrauding the Teamsters, and then the widow of one of Beck's closest pals."

"Dave," Meany concluded, "you have the charges in front of you. I am quite sure that the council feels, and I know I feel as a trade unionist, that in trying to do our job of advancing this movement we are entitled to an answer."

Beck's rambling answer, in effect, was that his counsel had advised him not to respond to the charges "because private affairs are intertwined with the whole situation." Beck could not resist boasting briefly of his business acumen, as if to imply that the McClellan committee had confused his "private" activities with union deals.

"I have made plenty of money," Beck said. "I have never made any secret of that. I have made as high as $200,000 on private real estate deals so far removed from the Teamsters union there is not even any comparison of them. I have done it over and over again, with deals ranging in profit from $60,000 to $200,000." But Beck said he preferred to answer any charges in a court of law, with the right of cross-examination, and under rules of evidence. "With that preliminary statement I desire to say no more at this time," Beck said. "I have been in the trade union movement as long as most of us here. . . . I think I understand pretty well all of the implications involved in it. . . . In this business, if you can't take it, you had better get out of it."

Although not expecting anything to come of it, Beck handed Meany a legal brief challenging the legality of his suspension from the executive council. Beck maintained the suspension did not result from misconduct or malfeasance as an officer of the AFL-CIO. Since some of the incidents cited before the McClellan committee occurred during 1949–53, before he became a council member, or the AFL-CIO constitution was written, action based upon them would be ex post facto. Beck called his suspension a "nullity" and left.

"It is pretty sad when that is all the explanation you get in these things," Meany said. He recollected that Beck "used to make a speech— 'If anyone wants to make a quick buck, he had better get out of the Teamsters, because I will kick them to hell out as soon as I hear about it.' You could hear him bellowing all over the place.

"I don't see what Dave wants to be in the labor movement for. He is a millionaire, he has a genius for making money. Why does he want to be in the labor movement? He doesn't need the labor movement; if he is so good in making money, why doesn't he get into the financial business and let the trade union movement alone?"

What, then, should be done about Beck? Meany felt the executive council had the power to suspend, but not to remove, him from membership, that such drastic action could be taken only by a convention. George Harrison of the railway clerks disagreed, noting a constitutional provision that the executive council was "authorized and empowered to take such action . . . as may be necessary . . . to endorse the provisions contained in this constitution." Several members, including Dubinsky and Reuther, argued against being overly legalistic and technical. That the incidents predated the AFL-CIO constitution was irrelevant, Dubinsky said. "The constitution of honesty against crookedness has operated ever since Adam and Eve."

Meany then rewrote the resolution so as to drop Beck from the council and strip his title as AFL-CIO vice-president. He agreed that technicalities were secondary. "The big question is what we must do at this particular point from the standpoint of public relations," he said. "Suppose he were to sue us and say that we haven't got a right to remove him. If that went into a court of law and he got a decision . . . we would put him back. But in the meantime we would get the value of at least showing the public how we feel."

The vote to expel Beck was unanimous. Then Meany offered a unique approach to choosing a successor. He said a "very high-powered set of publicity people" employed by the Teamsters was depicting the Beck case as "an attack on the Teamsters union, not against him as an individual." Meany suggested electing John F. English, the Teamsters secretary-treasurer, to the council replacing Beck. A tall, crusty Bostonian, the sixty-seven-year-old English had long been a respected figure in the AFL. English drove a coal wagon in his youth, joining the Teamsters at age fifteen and becoming a business agent six years later. His closest ally was Meany's old friend Dan Tobin, and Meany considered him "the old guard's last friend" in the Teamsters. Besides, English cared not a damn for Beck and was too tough a man to be bullied. He had regularly fed Meany information about Beck's attempts to stave off the AFL-CIO action, and he readily accepted Meany's invitation to join the council. In an emotional, table-pounding speech after his election, English said he was confident the Teamsters could take care of themselves, and that Beck was finished and would be voted out at the Teamsters convention in the fall. "We have a little dirty linen that we must wash," he said. "Nobody wants to be a stool pigeon, nobody wants to be a detective." English said that, even before the suspension, "I had told Mr. Beck that I wouldn't work under him or with him. We were providing ways and means to get rid of him." English pledged, "We will start brand new again and it won't take us long, and we will be back in good with the people throughout the country. We are sorry this happened. We know that it has injured you in every way, and it has injured us, but it is just one of those things that had to happen."

Unfortunately for Meany, English was just as devoted to James R. Hoffa as he was opposed to Dave Beck. And the McClellan committee and the AFL-CIO were already well on the way toward establishing that Hoffa's corruption was worse even than that of Beck.* "English talked out of both sides of his face," Meany said. "Originally, he came in here and told us how awful Dave Beck was, what a crook and so forth, and how they were going to get rid of him and clean up the Teamsters. But to English, Hoffa could do no wrong." By English's account, Meany tried to use him as an AFL-CIO agent within the Teamsters. "They called me over and told me what to do. I told him, 'Nothing doing. If you put me on this job and think you are going to run me, you are crazy. I'm no tool of the AFL-CIO.' " After Beck's disgrace, Hoffa moved swiftly to seize command of the Teamsters' general board, aiming toward election as president at the fall convention. Senate disclosures of his own corruption did not delay Hoffa nor dissuade the board majority from siding with him. At Hoffa's bidding, the Teamsters' board reaffirmed the "right" of any Teamster official to use the Fifth Amendment. Meany was infuriated. According to English, "Meany says, 'You have got to get rid of Hoffa. You can beat him.' I said, 'I don't care if I can beat him or not. I am going to be with him. . . . He's not going to get out. He is going in.' "

During several months of intensive legal maneuvering Meany tried to force Hoffa and other Teamsters before the ethical practices committee to answer questions. Hoffa flatly refused. Through his attorneys he offered various reasons: the AFL-CIO constitution did not dilute the principle of autonomy; the Teamsters could not move against any union official who was under official investigation lest his case be prejudiced; the Teamsters could not talk about charges of corruption without the assurance the AFL-CIO hearing record would not be subpoenaed by Congress or law enforcement agencies; all corruption charged was at the local level and did not involve the international union.

Hoffa sauntered into Meany's office one day in midsummer apparently confident he could force him to back down. Meany was frigidly formal. "This was the only time that Hoffa and I ever talked about it face to face," Meany said. "I laid it out to him straight and clear: he was going to have to come in and sit down before the executive council and answer questions. Under the constitution, any officer or member can bring up charges, and I was willing to do it. Oh, but he was confident. They [Hoffa and the Teamsters officers with him] threw around a lot of fig-

---

* Hoffa's affairs are too tangled for unraveling here. He eventually went to jail for bribing a juror.

ures about how big and powerful they were, that they were twelve percent of the federation membership, and that sort of stuff. I told Hoffa, right to his face, that if they didn't care to abide by the constitution, I was going to move that they be expelled, period. Well, he almost fell out of his chair, he was so surprised. He thought he could bluster and tell us to go to hell, and we'd go away."

Hoffa told Meany, among other things, the AFL-CIO should not supplant law enforcement agencies and courts. "Well, we can't depend upon the law," Meany replied. "We know something about district attorneys, we know something about political influence. . . . I say, you can do any damned thing the local law enforcement people, or the federal law enforcement people, let you get away with." Meany disliked particularly two Hoffa deals which resulted in federal investigations but no indictments: his "borrowing" of $25,000 from a local union through an accountant, a loan that was never repaid; and the investment of a $400,-000 interest-free loan from a Detroit local in Florida land. "Some of the lots were a little wet," Meany commented. That Hoffa was not indicted Meany found irrelevant. "As far as we are concerned, we had an interest there, because we don't think we can have a trade union movement where we tolerate the stealing of the members' money by any method.

"If they steal it and we don't know about it, that's one thing. But if they steal it, and we do, that's another."

Hoffa, defending, tried to throw dirt at Meany. James P. Kelly, a McClellan committee investigator who worked closely with Robert Kennedy, received a call from a former New York police inspector who had become a private investigator. They met at a New York luncheonette.

"————started right in on Meany," Kelly said. "He said he had 'done some checking' and had some information he wanted to pass on to me. It was nothing. For example, he found out that Meany owned a share of Merkle Press [a Washington printing house that does considerable work for the AFL-CIO]. Big deal. So does Larry Spivak [the TV personality of "Meet the Press"]. I heard him out and then said, '————, why are you giving me this? Is it because you are trying to put us onto Meany so we'll leave Hoffa alone? I'll bet Hoffa hired you.'

"He jumped so hard his chair slid back. 'How did you know that?' he asked me. He was shook, but I had him—strictly on a guess—and he admitted it. I went ahead and took the information—it was absolutely nothing—and reported that night to Kennedy. He didn't even wait to hear what————had. 'We don't want anything to do with Meany,' Kennedy said. 'Let him alone.' "

At the September executive council meeting Meany was ready to press charges. John English pleaded for a delay, asking the council not to act until the Teamsters convention, due to start shortly. English claimed to have fought not only Beck but also the Teamsters general board and attorneys. "And it is pretty damned tough!" he said. English said the convention was sure to reject Beck, even if he ran for re-election. (He did not run.) The new leadership, he said, would be much better. "Jimmy Hoffa and [Frank] Brewster and those fellows did a wonderful job for this organization. They got wonderful conditions. You ought to read some of the contracts and agreements and welfare plans that these fellows got for us. . . . It is all right to say we should get rid of this fellow and that fellow, but what is going to happen to our organization?"

English urged, "Give us one year and I will guarantee . . . that our organization will be running along as good as it has ever run and for all the errors and mistakes we have made we will try to make up for them.

"What can I do? Even my own people don't want me to go. What can I do? Can I walk out and leave them? If I were fifteen years younger, I promise you this thing never would have happened, but I am only one man. Don't crucify the organization for a lot of fellows who have done things they shouldn't do. Give us one year. . . ."

Some council members had flickers of misgiving about punitive action. Joseph Beirne, of the Communications Workers of America, worried about the precedent. What if McClellan made the CWA account for interunion loans during strikes? Beirne mentioned specifically $25,000 the United Steel Workers gave the CWA during a 1955 strike of Southern Bell Telephone Company. The money was accounted for, Beirne said, but "if you demanded to know where it was spent I'd be up the creek without a paddle." Beirne worried that the council would "find ourselves offering up the sacrificial lamb to the wolves of the public."

Meany, however, wanted no delay. "There is no question that there were elements, and possibly are elements, with strong underworld connections that have access and companionship even with high officials of the Teamsters Union," he said. "If that was allowed to go unchecked on the ground that we had to wait until the law acted; if there were no action taken by the trade union movement itself to try to eliminate those conditions, I am quite sure you all can realize the amount of criticism that we would be subjected to by the press and the public. . . .

"Furthermore, if that were to go on unchecked would it remain in the condition that it has reached at the present time or would it get worse? . . . Well, our experience indicates that in those things they are never content. . . . They want other unions. The experience in Chicago in the late twenties and thirties* is an example of that. They just moved in and went from place to place in the union tightening the grip all the time.

"So we [can] sit back and say that we deplore all of these things,

* The underworld seized control of scores of Chicago unions during the 1920's and 1930's, and used them as a vehicle for extortion and other shakedowns.

these things are all matters for law, that stealing of union money, while we don't like it we expect someone else should do something about it and not us . . . and we should not take any action until such time as the law has acted. Then . . . we can say that that individual is no longer desirable.

"Now, it is my opinion that we can't afford to do that. I don't want to throw any union out of the AFL-CIO. . . . I have no illusions about what it will mean if the Teamsters are expelled from the AFL-CIO. I know it is going to mean a good deal of trouble." He foresaw other unions saying the AFL-CIO needed the Teamsters union more than vice versa. "I have never seen the union yet that was so big and powerful that the existence of the rest of the trade union movement depended on that one union. . . .

"Each union has to make its own decisions, but when we think in terms of this constitution we think in terms of trade union morality. And if a union is fighting for its life and it has got to spend its money in a way that will enable it to live—and we know what that means—well, that is not coming before the ethical practices committee—not by my say-so— and I am quite sure the ethical practices committee wouldn't want to have anything to do with that sort of case.

"If a trade union official has to sit before a committee of the United States Senate or any other place and has to say, 'Well, I don't know what happened to that money I used in that case; it was sent out there to try to help us win.' . . . I am sure we are not going to be greatly concerned because he is not able to spread out in detail on the record where the money went in an industrial dispute."

The only concession Meany would make was to delay final action until after the Teamsters convention. The council voted a resolution noting that the Teamsters had agreed to present the charges to the convention and that the AFL-CIO's ethical practices committee had demanded reforms, and asking that Teamster officers report back to the AFL-CIO within one month what they intended to do about the situation.

The Teamster convention, held in Miami the following week, was completely dominated by Hoffa. The hapless Beck presided, but Hoffa stood in the wings, wigwagging his hands to signal his supporters how to vote and when to demonstrate. As promised, the AFL-CIO report was presented, but hooting, jeering delegates interrupted the reading and voted to expunge it from the record. Although Hoffa and John English knew that continued Teamster membership in the AFL-CIO could depend upon compliance with the executive council resolution, it was not even presented. Hoffa, overwhelmingly elected, claimed total innocence of all charges. Although he professed to value affiliation with the AFL-CIO, he said the Teamsters might "tell the AFL-CIO to go to hell" unless they got better treatment. The convention voted the disgraced Beck a $50,000 annual pension and adjourned.

Hoffa, Einar Mohn, and eight vice-presidents returned to the executive council on October 24 to report on the convention. Mohn did the talking. He asked for a year to start various reforms. Meany was unimpressed. He got Hoffa to admit the executive council resolution was not read to the convention. "I never thought of it until right now," Mohn said. "I am not going to offer any alibi. I have nothing to say except it was an oversight."

Meany complained about the Teamster officers' permitting the ethical practices committee report to be stricken from the record. "I think there was a responsibility on the part of the Teamsters to present this matter in a proper way to the convention. None of these matters was presented to the convention. . . . You went through a *pro forma* reading of it and then expunged it from the record." No attention was given to individual cases, he said.

"I think that is correct," Mohn replied.

Later, when the Teamsters had withdrawn, Meany summarized what had happened to date. The attitude of Teamster leaders, he said, was that the "AFL-CIO was trying to destroy the union," and that the "AFL-CIO could go to hell."

When the AFL-CIO constitution was written, Meany said, "We hadn't the slightest idea of the corruption that was going to be spread in the newspapers of the country within a year or two of our [merger] convention." The council could not compromise, he said; the Teamsters had even promoted men who faced serious charges. "So I think we have come to the point where this labor movement has got to say whether or not we meant it when we wrote that constitution, and when we said that we wanted to keep this movement free from corrupt influences."

Meany recommended that the Teamsters be suspended from the AFL-CIO pending removal of Beck, Hoffa, Brewster, and Sidney Brennan* and cleansing of the union under a special committee appointed by the executive council.

Two old AFL members, William C. Doherty of the Letter Carriers and Harry Bates of the Bricklayers, told Meany to slow down. "Let's investigate more thoroughly," said Bates; if the council delayed, the issue might become moot. "I understand Hoffa is on the way out." Bates said suspension would create a "terrible situation" for the almost two million Teamster rank and file.

"If you put it off until your next meeting and don't act," Meany retorted, "you might as well forget your constitution. The whole country is looking in. And what is this idea of giving them more time after they spit

---

* A Teamster vice-president who figured prominently in the McClellan testimony.

in your face for five months?"

Beirne, supporting Meany, wanted a change of wording in the resolution so that no individuals were named. He said a "Hoffa ultimatum" would be a "bad policy." So the resolution was changed to call upon the Teamsters to bar from offices persons criticized in the ethical practices report.

Meany called the Teamsters back into the room and told them the council would recommend that the Teamsters be expelled from the federation by the AFL-CIO convention in December. "Thank you, gentlemen," Mohn said, and they walked out.

The Teamsters, now realizing that Meany was dead earnest about a purge, spent the next weeks in furious internal debate over what to do. A minority faction on the Teamster board wanted Hoffa to step down—if only for a year or two—so the union could remain within the AFL-CIO. Hoffa refused to do so, but he did entertain the notion he could strike a private compromise with Meany that would avoid expulsion. One intermediary was Patrick E. Gorman, of the Meatcutters and Butcher Workmen, who was working with the Teamsters in organizing in Chicago and the Midwest. At the behest of Teamster friends, Gorman talked with Meany "about the possibility of settling this matter without taking this drastic action" (of explusion). Gorman said Meany was "most cooperative."

"The first proposal that came was that the meeting had to be a secret meeting," Meany said. "It had to be so secret that he [Hoffa] could walk away and say that he never met me and that I could walk away and say I never met him. Well, I refused to accept that sort of arrangement. . . . Gorman said at this time, 'I don't blame you. Let's forget it. I tried to do what I could and we didn't succeed.'" On November 12, Gorman relayed another message: Would Meany meet Hoffa in New York or Washington? "It doesn't have to be a secret meeting," Gorman told Meany. "He just requested that you do not notify the press." Meany replied, "Well, that's easy. I am not in the habit of notifying the press who I am going to meet or where I am going, and the press is not in the habit of asking me where I am going each day and who I am going to meet." Through Gorman, Hoffa agreed to meet Meany at 11:00 A.M. November 19 at the AFL-CIO regional office in the Commodore Hotel in New York. "He never came," Meany said.

According to one man in the Teamster hierarchy at the time, "Hoffa was running on a mixture of bluff and fear. He had the idea some of the building trades people would get together and call off Meany. But when he realized Meany wouldn't be shoved down, he said, 'The hell with it.' A handful of people on the board tried to persuade Jimmy to withdraw from the presidency until things blew over, or at least to go talk to

Meany. 'Screw that old bastard,' he said. I really think Jimmy didn't want to get in the same room with Meany. Jimmy didn't scare easy, but he wasn't used to dealing with a rock like Meany."

The negotiations continued right up to the eve of the AFL-CIO convention, which was to open on Thursday, December 5, in Atlantic City. To complicate an already involved situation, Hoffa was on trial in New York the same week for alleged wiretapping of phones of Teamster officials in Detroit who had been called to testify before grand juries and the McClellan committee.* Early in the week "some other good friends came with direct messages from Brother Hoffa." Meany was told Hoffa would fly to Atlantic City Tuesday night. "He didn't arrive. Wednesday morning they came and said, 'Well, he couldn't charter an airplane.' " Next, Hoffa was to come Wednesday night by auto. "Well, then, he couldn't do that. Something else happened. All of this went on and on, and each time when the arrangements were made to meet, he didn't meet."

Late Wednesday afternoon Gorman talked with Hoffa "in a sort of last, desperate effort to do something." He reported to Meany that "Hoffa wanted to get down," but that he could not leave New York "because his lawyer advised him against it." That was at 5:30 P.M. At 9:30 he couldn't come because the judge forbade it. At 10:40 P.M. Meany got a call from the Teamster board, meeting in New York. "They said they had him [Hoffa] on the phone and that a car was ready, and that he would get down as soon as he could, and he had to get back, of course. Well, I just couldn't see at that time how I could wait up until three o'clock in the morning and be responsible for him coming down here on this errand, not knowing just what he had in mind except, as I say, through all this the indication was that he wanted to resign and get out of the way.

"So I said to this group, 'Ask the board of the Teamsters . . . if they can't get a commitment from him and let them bring it to the convention.' This fellow said, 'No, no, we can't try that, because he might repudiate us. We don't trust him.' " Meany kept staff members in his hotel room until 2:30 A.M., expecting either a call or visit from Hoffa. None came, and Meany said he was going to bed. But within an hour Meany called his son-in-law, Robert Mayer, at the convention as an AFL-CIO attorney, and Virginia Tehas, and asked them to return. "We sat listening to him until dawn," Miss Tehas said. "He did not display any self-doubt about the wisdom or right of what he was doing, nor any fears of a possible failure, even though if he *had* failed, it could have cost him the presidency." Although Meany seemed confident the convention would vote with him, he did not take any advance headcount of delegates. "George doesn't politic that way," Miss Tehas said.

* The jury deadlocked; Hoffa was acquitted in a second trial.

The convention decision on expulsion was foreordained, but the Teamsters went down fighting. Einar Mohn made a veiled threat about the consequences to other unions. "Nothing can change the dependence that the local unions . . . [in the AFL-CIO] will continue to have on Teamster locals throughout the country." John English, his voice shaking with anguish and anger, invoked the ghost of old Dan Tobin to remind delegates of labor's debts to the Teamsters. English pleaded for a year of grace. Beck and other crooks were out of the union, he said, and Jimmy Hoffa was not the ogre McClellan depicted him to be. "Jimmy Hoffa has done more for our international union than anybody connected with it, including myself," English cried. "How in the hell can we kick him out? Oh, it makes my blood run cold. I am coming near to the end of my days. I never thought I would see this. . . . The Teamsters will get along. Those in the AFL-CIO who are still friends of ours we will look out for, but the rest can all go straight to hell."

Teamster supporters droned on for more than two hours: Sol Hoffmann, of the upholsterers union; Joseph McCurdy, of the United Garment Workers; Edward Carlough, of the powerful sheet metal workers; Woodruff Randolph, of the typographical union; George Lynch, of the Pattern Makers; Pat Gorman of the butchers. Alex Rose of the hatters union presented a report recommending that the convention vote expulsion, as the executive council recommended; no one else cared—or dared—to take the floor to demand the ouster of the AFL-CIO's largest union. The summation, from Meany, was brief and to the point: the convention knew the evidence, now it must decide whether the law should be applied. "I perhaps look at the constitution differently than the delegate who votes for it and then walks away," Meany said. "I feel that I have an obligation to live up to it, and this is what I am trying to do." Meany concluded by affirming that he was "for the Teamsters and for the Teamster members," and pledging that the expulsion would not launch trade union warfare. "There is no attempt of any sort and no plan at all for a war with the Teamsters, and we hope that it will never come," he said. "But we have got to give these members a chance. We have got to free them from this dictatorship."

The vote was 10,548,598 to 2,266,497 for expulsion. Unions voting with the Teamsters included the bricklayers, carpenters, and hod carriers, mainstays of the building trades; Gorman's meatcutters, an old CIO union; and the metalworkers and typographers. The building and construction trades and maritime departments, reflecting the majority of their member unions, also voted against expulsion.

Hoffa said in his memoir that the expulsion left him "bitterly disappointed [and] . . . hurt, personally, to think that fellow unionists would so readily turn on me." Hoffa also charged elsewhere that "labor has been silenced, silenced if you please, by a George Meany out of fear of a subpoena and going back into the history of George Meany from New York [*sic*]. . . . Too long have they been intimidated; coerced; too long have they been away from the bargaining table." And in his memoir Hoffa said:

There is a possibility that the AFL-CIO was panicked by the crescendo of criticism directed at American labor by [Robert] Kennedy and the McClellan committee and wished to separate itself from what was the avowed immediate target, the Teamsters. But there's also the possibility that Kennedy whispered in the ear of an influential labor leader in the hierarchy of the AFL-CIO, suggesting that he would be wise, politically, to initiate and promote the movement for expulsion of the Teamsters. Some mighty large unions were not really investigated by Kennedy, and that fact is surely significant.

Through intermediaries, Hoffa tried several times to bring the Teamsters back into the AFL-CIO, only to be beaten down each time by Meany. Hoffa would not approach Meany directly, however. "Meany knows where to find me," he told one interviewer. "I'm not asking him anything. I have nothing to say to Meany." Michael Quill, of the Transport Workers Union, submitted a resolution to the executive council in October 1961 asking Teamster reaffiliation. Taking back the Teamsters with Hoffa "would amount to consigning the future of our members to underworld control," Meany replied. The motion received some support, however. Joseph Curran of the National Maritime Union, a frequent Meany adversary, said he needed Teamster help in New York organizing; that he saw no justification for expelling "people who hadn't been convicted." A. Philip Randolph of the Sleeping Car Porters felt "no man is beyond redemption." William L. McFetridge, of the Building Service Employees, said that unless the AFL-CIO "cleaned out all of our international unions" the council "could not oppose the readmittance of the Teamsters." In McFetridge's opinion, "many of the things said about the Teamsters could be said about other AFL-CIO affiliates." David J. McDonald, of the steelworkers, wanted Hoffa back for selfish reasons: he had a working arrangement with the Teamsters on a Canadian venture, and thought them useful. Besides, McDonald philosophized, "bankers don't condemn one another when they are caught embezzling."

"We would never lower our standards to match the standards of the business community or the marketplace," Meany replied.

Beaten in the executive council (of which he was not a member), Quill took his reinstatement motion to the convention floor in 1961 and charged the council members with being "an army of hypocrites." Quill attacked Meany: "His Holiness, Pope John XXIII, is changing Vatican precedent. He visits the prisons and hospitals. . . . The first time I ever heard of any labor leader making a pilgrimage to a jail was yourself, Mr. Meany, to comfort a convicted racketeer in Sing Sing many years ago. . . . You have amongst yourselves on the executive council a man who is already convicted of a crime* . . . but a man who hasn't been convicted, Hoffa, you keep out." A host of speakers beat down Quill. "Hoffa," declared Paul Hall of the Seafarers, "is a fink from his very heart. He always has been and always will be."

No further serious effort was made to bring the Teamsters back. Joseph Curran lamented to a Teamster convention during the 1960's that he could not get a vote on a reinstatement motion in the executive council—even when he made his own second. "Every time," Curran said, "I get the same thing. They don't leave the room because it is too small an audience to leave. There are only twenty-nine of them, but they sit there and freeze. And after I get through, President Meany moves on to the next point of business."

Meany and Hoffa had no direct contacts after the expulsion, although they exchanged frequent and bitter public insults via the press and speeches. Deriding Meany before a group of transportation executives in 1963, Hoffa said, "When you're old and decrepit on top of being stupid, you're in trouble. Someday the man is going to come to the door and tell you you're out of business. He's blocking us now, but he can't live forever." Hoffa also told a *Life* interviewer, "Meany's forgotten he's a labor man. But what the hell, he's never conducted a strike in his life." Hoffa admired Walter Reuther's style ("a hard worker, a smart fella, he knows his business") and often spoke glowingly of him in the next breath after deriding Meany. Meany considered Hoffa an outlaw, and demanded that AFL-CIO affiliates treat him as such. At his behest, the executive council in 1958 instructed affiliates to cancel working agreements with the Teamsters; to continue them, it said, would "constitute a fraud on all workers who look to a clean and decent trade union for the improvement of their standards and conditions." Meany also threatened to pull AFL-CIO conventions and executive council meetings out of the Americana Hotel in Miami Beach if it permitted the Teamsters to hold a meeting there just before a federation event. Both Hoffa and the hotel management groused, but the Teamsters relocated to the equally plush Eden Roc, three miles down Collins Avenue. Meany told anyone who asked the conditions under which the Teamsters could come back into the AFL-CIO: "While Jimmy Hoffa's president they're not agonna' come back. Jimmy Hoffa is not a trade unionist. He has his roots somewhere else. And, frankly, we can't afford him. He's too rich for our

* Maurice Hutcheson of the Carpenters Union.

blood. . . . As far as I am concerned the Teamsters are just as good as anyone else; . . . it's the leadership."

The ouster of the Teamsters touched off wide speculation—and concern among more timid executive council members—that Hoffa would start open warfare on the AFL-CIO, akin to that which the CIO waged after the split of 1937. For all his bluster about national strikes and organizing drives, however, Hoffa did not make any spectacular membership gains. The Teamster strength was 1,600,000 in 1957; fifteen years later, it was 1,755,025, according to Labor Department statistics. Meany felt the aura of corruption around Hoffa, well-publicized during his many trials during the 1960's, would prevent any ground swell of new Teamster members. AFL-CIO affiliates beat back many attempted Teamster raids by distributing a twenty-four-page brochure containing some of the more lurid McClellan disclosures.

But at the same time the AFL-CIO did not make any serious attempt to win away dissident Teamsters. (One critic on the executive council who asked anonymity said, "Meany thought it was foolish to stir up trouble; besides, if we had started a fight with Hoffa, we might have gotten our asses kicked off.")

Joseph Beirne, whose Communications Workers of America lost several thousand members to the Teamsters in raids, in 1961 proposed chartering an umbrella local for any Teamsters who wanted to leave Hoffa. Meany acknowledged that Hoffa ignored jurisdictions of AFL-CIO unions and took new members where he found them, regardless of where they worked. But he opposed any organizational battle. Any dissident Teamster officers who opposed Hoffa publicly were apt to be replaced by men "with long criminal records," Meany said. The council voted to leave to Meany's discretion which breakaway Teamsters should receive AFL-CIO charters. When the question went to the convention floor a few days later, Al Hartnett, of the International Union of Electrical Workers, complained about the lack of competition to the Teamsters in organizing. So, too, did Walter Reuther (although Reuther did not mention the Teamsters by name). The irascible Paul Hall replied that contesting the Teamsters required more "than getting up on the floor and doing a lot of talking. . . . Many of the guys who made wonderful speeches in the past about purity, I myself looked for them to sprout wings on their backs at any moment. But in the great New York fights [with the Teamsters] we have had as high as twelve or twenty-four or thirty-six men wiped out in one fight and dozens go to the hospital. Many of these people who made such glorious speeches on the floor . . . were conspicuous by their absence." Meany advised against any open confrontations with the Teamsters. Even if new AFL-CIO unions picked off Teamster locals, he said, the drivers would be "sacrificed" because they could not deliver goods in cities controlled by Hoffa forces.

Meany felt that younger members who "know what Hoffa is, and hate him," would eventually win control of the Teamsters. "We've had some situations where we tried to give these younger fellows a boost along. In Philadelphia, for instance, this bunch took off after Ray Cohen [head of Local 107] who was one of Hoffa's buddies, and who was every bit as crooked as he was. We put some AFL-CIO organizers up there, to help them, and we told these organizers, 'Now don't get out front, you help and you put out money, but don't take it over openly.' But it got all messed up, and Hoffa realized what was happening. He came up yelling, 'The AFL-CIO is trying to take over your union, are you going to let them do that to you?' We had wanted this to be a bunch of 'dissident Teamsters' because they might have won, but it all blew up."

After Hoffa went to prison in 1967 for jury tampering, Hoffa had a correct if not too cordial relationship with Frank Fitzsimmons, his hand-picked successor. Fitzsimmons joined Meany and Leonard Woodcock of the United Auto Workers in attacks on President Nixon's economic policies, and Teamster lobbyists helped push a national health insurance plan in Congress. The détente ended abruptly in December 1971, when Hoffa was paroled from federal prison. Meany felt the Nixon Administration released Hoffa for political reasons. He thought Hoffa's pension arrangement abominable. Several weeks after Hoffa's release Meany sat in the privacy of his office and mused about the future of the Teamsters and the AFL-CIO:

"Now that Hoffa is out of jail, I don't want anything to do with the Teamsters. He'll be running it; he may never go near there, because of the parole board watching him, but there's always the telephone. And Fitzsimmons. Fitzsimmons was never an elected member of the executive board of the Teamsters, or anything else, except one little local union. When Hoffa realized he was finally going to jail . . . he pulled Fitzsimmons up and created an office of vice-president and gave it to him. There was language that if the president died or couldn't serve for any other reason, the executive vice-president would automatically become president. So that's how you have Fitzsimmons. He couldn't stand up to Hoffa. If the parole board would let them, Fitzsimmons would step down in a minute and let Hoffa have it again.

"These pension deals, now, they are corrupt, and I don't care if the Teamster executive board did approve them. Look at Mrs. Hoffa, now, she's sick, at death's door they say, and they give her $40,000 or more a year as head of the women's division. She doesn't do any work. His kid [James Hoffa, Jr.] is probably an outstanding young lawyer, but what does he do for the labor movement to deserve $40,000 a year? I think Hoffa's $1,200,000 pension deal is also corrupt. He doesn't deserve it, he stole from his own union. Now, I could go into my executive council and tell them to give Mrs. Meany $40,000 a year, and she would do what she could for the labor movement. That would be stealing and corrupt, no matter how 'legal' and 'official' it was, because she wouldn't do anything, and I know she wouldn't. So far as I am concerned, I don't want anything to do with them."

Because of the Teamsters' size and the audacity of the corruption, the Beck-Hoffa cases dominated public consciousness. Simultaneously, Meany went after a handful of smaller unions that ran afoul of the AFL-CIO ethical practices code or the McClellan committee, or both. Meany's handling of the cases varied: expulsion; probation, under an AFL-CIO monitor, until reforms were made; purges of officers responsible for wrongdoing. John Hutchinson, a leading academic authority on corruption in labor-management relations, credited Meany's moral authority for ridding the AFL-CIO of tainted unions. Since the corruption was confined almost exclusively to old AFL unions, Hutchinson wrote, "the chief disciplinarian had to come from the AFL." Meany had the "support, and often the urging," of powerful men within the merged AFL-CIO. Nonetheless, Hutchinson concluded:

> . . . the particular policies adopted by the AFL-CIO towards corruption were not specified by circumstance; a number of alternatives have always been available; in particular, the policy of expulsion has clearly commanded something less than the enthusiasm of its ultimate supporters. It is difficult to avoid the impression that, whatever the pattern of influences at work, the firmness of federation policy, and the remarkable absence of organized opposition to it, owe much to the inflexibility of Meany and to the respect he commands in all quarters of the federation. Indeed it is questionable whether, in the absence of such manifest personal influence, the federation could have survived the adoption of its own draconian measures.

Unfortunately for the union officers involved, some of the corruption cases offended Meany's personal moral code as well as the law. Such was the misfortune of James Cross, president of the Bakery and Confectionary International Union of America, with 160,000 members, the union which William Schnitzler had headed before becoming AFL-CIO secretary-treasurer. In March 1957 the bakers' secretary-treasurer, Curtis Sims, brought Meany photostats of checks and other documents showing wide misuse of union funds by Cross and George Stuart, a vice-president. For instance, they purchased two Cadillacs for $6,500 each with funds taken from the bakers' treasury for "organizing expenses." When Sims protested, Cross rammed through amendments to the union constitution effectively barring any investigation of officers' activities. Hence Sims's trip to Meany, who knew all parties involved personally. "They were one happy family a few years ago. They taught me some crazy poker game and I didn't have a very happy experience." In rapid-fire order, Meany started an AFL-CIO investigation; Cross convened a bakers' board meeting which cleared him and Stuart, then fired Sims; and Sims took his material first to Meany, then to the receptive McClellan committee.

Dirt was found in many corners. According to testimony, Cross borrowed $96,770 from a baker employer; used union funds to buy air conditioners, luggage, camera supplies, Christmas gifts, and candy; and ran the union with a dictatorially iron hand, contrary to the AFL-CIO ethical code. To Meany's dismay, Cross had also spent more than $10,000 supporting the travels and good times of a lithe young brunette who had been arrested for residing in a house of ill fame.

When the executive council debated what to do about Cross, Meany got to the crux of things. "Now," he said, "I have no argument about Cross getting tied up with women. That's been going on for a long time. But I have an argument about paying that as part of the union's expenses. That is what I don't like about it. Let him have all the fun he wants. I am not preaching that anybody is an angel or I am . . . but goddamn it, you don't charge that as a legitimate union expense!"

Cross claimed the woman was an "organizer," and that she met him in such diverse places as New York, Ottumwa, Iowa, Miami Beach, and Denver to discuss union business. Asked by the McClellan committee what she did for Cross, she replied, "I don't know how you could really call it employment." She pleaded the Fifth Amendment when asked, "What was Mr. Cross paying you for?"

Meany was also angered by the alleged kidnaping and pistol whipping of dissident baker officers by Cross and cronies. This occurred at a wild San Francisco convention during which all semblances of democratic procedures were stricken from the constitution. According to testimony, Cross, Stuart, and two other men doing the beatings were roaring drunk. Meany cross-examined Cross with blunt tenacity during the executive council hearing. After listening to effusive denials for an hour, Meany exclaimed, "Oh, come on, Jim."

"I am not coming on," Cross said.

"Don't press your point too much," Meany said.

"Mr. Meany, I resent being called a drunken bum."

"I didn't say you were a drunken bum," Meany replied. "I said you got drunk."

Cross denied being drunk at the San Francisco convention and demanded of Meany, "Did you ever see me drunk?"

"Yes," Meany replied. "At a hotel in St. Louis in December of 1953, and you went through the lobby with your fists closed and you said, 'Where is that dirty son of a bitch? I will show him.' You were drunk. You came up to me and wanted me to help you find the fellow."

Herman Winter, president emeritus of the bakers and a long-time executive council member, warned Meany to keep out of the Cross-Sims rivalry, saying the situation was infused with personal rancor. He also implied, without saying so directly, that William Schnitzler might well be toppled if Meany got too deep into the bakers union. "I hate like hell to get into that because if I do I have to inject that fellow sitting up beside you, George," Winter said, gesturing at Schnitzler. "If something has to happen to Sims you are going to go a lot further than you think you are. I am not kidding you."

"What do you mean?" asked Meany.

"There will be other charges," Winter said. He did not elaborate, and nothing further was said of Schnitzler. The executive council, at Meany's initiative, directed the bakers to bar from office the persons responsible for the abuses turned up by the McClellan and ethical practices committee. The bakers did make some internal reforms, but Cross refused to step down. Meany suspended the union in November 1957. A group of so-called clean bakers claiming to represent 150 of the union's 250 locals appeared at the AFL-CIO convention the next month and asked that a new competitive union be chartered. Arthur Goldberg, representing the AFL-CIO, tried to bargain a settlement with Cross, and at one point Cross had agreed to withdraw from the presidency and accept a business agent's job. A draft resolution incorporating this agreement was printed and readied for distribution. Meany saw it, exploded, and ordered Goldberg to retrieve each of the more than 2,000 copies which had already reached the convention hall. "That was one of the maddest times I've ever seen for Mr. Meany," recollected Virginia Tehas, his personal secretary for more than thirty years. Meany told the convention he did not like performing executioner work, but "we have a job to do and it is a disagreeable job. I don't like it, but we wrote a constitution. . . . We determined to try to keep this organization what it is intended to be, an instrumentality to serve workers, not . . . to build up the personal affluence of an individual to make him a big shot in the community or make him an expert on finance. . . . This is a workers' organization, and I don't know anything else but this business. Let's keep it that way." The convention voted by a seven-to-one margin to expel the bakers unless they complied with the clean-up directive by March 15, 1958. Cross refused, and left the AFL-CIO with acid language for Meany. Cross accused Meany of abetting "dual unionism," and "acting out of his own personal hatred for one man." Cross said, "If the government keeps going, and the AFL-CIO leaders keep staying as dumb as they are, there is liable to be more unions outside the AFL-CIO than there is inside." He signed an alliance with Hoffa and vowed to keep fighting.

But the "clean bakers," with a new AFL-CIO charter, won away the bulk of Cross's membership. Cross enjoyed himself to the end. In 1958 Robert Kennedy by coincidence flew to Florida on the same commercial flight as Cross. "At the airport he was met by a red-haired woman who drove off with him in a flashy automobile. I checked the license plate. It was owned by a Washington, D.C., rental agency, and all the bills for the car were being paid by the rank-and-file members of James Cross's ousted Bakers Union." In 1962 Cross and other officers were convicted of embezzling union funds, and Meany brought all the bakery workers back into a merged organization.

The United Textile Workers of America got into trouble through a rather grievous error. Two of its officers lied to Meany in requesting a loan from the old AFL in 1952, when he was still secretary-treasurer. The officers, Anthony Valente, the president, and Lloyd Klenert, secretary-treasurer, claimed to need $100,000 to wean a dissident group away from the CIO Textile Workers Union of America. The request surprised Meany, for the raid had been in progress only a few weeks. He demanded a financial statement from Klenert, examined it, and declared it a phony. In a confrontation, Valente and Klenert admitted the report was a "complete fabrication," but claimed they were trying to conceal the UTWA's assets from the rival CIO union. Just how a report given to Meany could have reached the CIO was a question left unanswered. Despite the AFL's antipathy toward probes of affiliated unions, Meany persuaded William Green and the executive council to appoint an investigative committee.

The two sides did not get along. When the hearing started, Valente objected to a stenographer taking a formal record. "We are not on trial," he said, "we are not going to have cross-examination. I think this is a family matter. . . . Our counsel objects to it."

"Your counsel objects to it? Well, so far as I am concerned," Meany said, "that is the end of the meeting."

Valente retreated, and Meany compiled a record rich with instances of financial cross-dealing between Valente, Klenert, and the UTWA. They bought and sold real estate, and could not explain some unusual organizing expenses. But they insisted it was necessary to "fuzz up" the records in the event the CIO staged a cross-raid and won control of the UTWA. Meany did not find this explanation plausible.

"You think as a board and as officers running this union that you had a right to hide the organization's money to protect your own particular future interests in case of a split of some kind?" Meany asked.

"We were protecting the organization, Brother Meany," replied the UTWA lawyer, Joseph Jacobs.

"All I can say is you are going to have a great opportunity from now on to protect . . . because God knows it will need protection," Meany said. "Okay, let's go."

The AFL executive council heard Meany's report, refused to act on its own, and referred the matter to the UTWA board, which also declined to move. In 1957 when the McClellan committee revived the investigation, Meany was in a position to act, although Valente and Klenert claimed the incident was five years old and thus outside the executive council's jurisdiction. The McClellan committee also developed evidence the $100,000 loan, ostensibly for organizing, actually went to buy homes in suburban Washington for Valente and Klenert. The council called for reform upon pain of expulsion, and Valente and Klenert agreed to resign. Peter McGavin, Meany's executive assistant, became UTWA monitor. In resigning, however, Klenert would receive a pension of $100 weekly for twenty years. But nothing was said about his returning some $30,000 he had taken from the union in hotel-bill "paid outs," in cash, and for COD packages. "These people," Meany said of the textile workers, "are the poorest paid people in America. They are in a depressed industry." And yet, he said, there was the "spectacle" of Klenert using $3,100 in union funds to buy a grand piano. "This is a sample of the trade union morality that is built up in the minds of fellows who have worked for the union." Under threat of expulsion the union canceled the pension. Peter McGavin remained as monitor until February 1960, Meany insisting on (and receiving) the purge of all tainted officers.

In 1955 Meany heard rumors of wrongdoing in the welfare funds of the Laundry Workers International Union. He sent Nelson Cruikshank, the director of the AFL department of social security, to investigate. Cruikshank said, "There was a lot of business about shuffling funds and so forth. It was a mess, and I came back and gave him a report." A few days later Meany called Cruikshank to his office. "He looked at me and said, 'It's pretty bad, isn't it?' Now, this is one guy talking to another— not a president to a convention, but a man puzzled by his problems. He said, 'What do you think I ought to do?' It struck me as kind of funny, yet in a way it wasn't. 'It's very easy for me to say what you ought to do, but I don't have to meet the bills of this organization, I don't have to account for the per capita tax you lose. I could very easily say, on moral grounds, "Throw them out." But you are the man who has the responsibility.'

"He looked at me in the most earnest way, and he said, 'On the per capita tax and all that, I have never lost a wink of sleep. That isn't a consideration. The good name of this organization is the only consideration I have.' This wasn't a guy talking in public, making a speech for public relations. This was a guy talking who was disturbed about the dirt. I don't think that George thought I would ever repeat what he said. But I have seen the true picture of George Meany—a man of tremendous moral convictions."

Another man who worked closely with Meany during the late 1950's, when he was preoccupied with corruption, said the policing of tainted unions was a mixed blessing. "No doubt about it," this man said, "the job had to be done, because the McClellan committee could have killed the labor movement had we not acted. At the same time, George wasted a lot of energy playing cop. What the hell else did labor do besides defend itself?"

After the McClellan committee had been at work for almost two years, Meany professed to be surprised at the extent of labor-management corruption:

> We thought we knew a few things about trade union corruption, but we didn't know the half of it, one-tenth of it, or the one-hundredth part of it. We didn't know, for instance, that we had unions where a criminal record was almost a prerequisite to holding office under the national union. We didn't know that we had top trade union leaders who made it a practice to secretly borrow the funds of their union. We didn't know that there were top trade union leaders who used the funds for phony real estate deals in which the victims of the fraud were their own members. And we didn't know that there were trade union leaders who charged to the union treasury such items as speed boats, perfume, silk stockings, brassieres, color TV, refrigerators, and every thing else under the sun. We didn't know about those things.

After Congress passed the Landrum-Griffin Act in 1959* the AFL-CIO ethical practices committee became dormant. Meany felt the purges of the 1950's had effectively ended racketeering within AFL-CIO affiliates. Also, since passage of Landrum-Griffin implied Congress thought labor could not police itself, Meany could wash his hands of an unpleasant task. The AFL-CIO therefore turned its back on several smelly situations. In 1963 Maurice Hutcheson, the president of the Carpenters Union, was convicted of bribing an Indiana state official to obtain advance information on highway routes. The case did not involve union funds, and an appeals court later reversed the conviction. In the interim, however, Hutcheson pled the Fifth Amendment when the McClellan

* See Chapter XIII, "The Kennedy Years."

committee asked him whether he used union money to try to fix the bribery case. He was convicted of contempt of Congress and sentenced to six months in jail. Meany joined other labor officials in petitioning the U.S. District Court in Washington to reduce the sentence to probation. Meany called him a "man of character . . . [and] an able, devoted, and conscientious representative of the American trade union movement. . . ." The court put Hutcheson on two years' probation and fined him $500, and President Johnson later pardoned him. Despite Hutcheson's use of the Fifth Amendment—the plea that resulted in so much trouble for Dave Beck—the AFL-CIO took no action against him.

# XII

# Meany versus Reuther:
# Round One

*In February 1955, immediately after the merger agreement, Meany's staff compiled a sampling of newspaper editorial comment for the AFL News-Reporter. The working file, still in Meany's office, contains a Washington Post editorial that speculated on Walter Reuther's role. Someone drew pencil marks through two sentences: "Presumably he will become one of the twenty-seven vice-presidents in the new organization. It may well be that Mr. Reuther will ultimately succeed Mr. Meany." The de-Reutherized version is what appeared in the News-Reporter.*

ONE AFTERNOON in January 1956, soon after the AFL-CIO merger was consummated, Walter Reuther came to George Meany's office on routine business just as another visitor was leaving. Meany introduced Reuther to the man, a longshoremen's leader from New Orleans. The dockworkers were preparing for another representational vote between the old International Longshoremen's Association and the AFL-CIO's opposing International Brotherhood of Longshoremen. The New Orleans man controlled a key bloc of votes, and Meany tried to persuade him to vote for the IBL. He refused. The ILA, he explained, despite its many troubles, commanded the deep loyalty of members, who considered it almost a family. Meany replied he understood, and he would probably make the same decision were he in the unionist's position.

Reuther was incredulous when Meany told him of the conversation. He said Meany could have lured the man away with "a few of the proper promises," and ticked off a few. "But, Walter," Meany replied, "I couldn't deliver that sort of thing, and you know it."

"That's no matter," Reuther said. "In a situation like that, the ends justify the means."

Meany abruptly changed the subject. Later, when Reuther had left, Meany told Virginia Tehas what had happened. He was furious. "I wonder if he runs the UAW like that?" Meany asked.

"Meany never trusted Reuther after that episode," Miss Tehas related later. "Reuther made a very bad mistake. Mr. Meany most definitely saw him as a successor. He was young and smart and had a good following in the trade union movement. But Reuther constantly overstepped himself, from the very beginning. After thirty days it was obvious Mr. Meany would never step down and let Reuther have the presidency. He didn't trust him to run it."

For the AFL-CIO, merger did not equate with peace though both parties went into the marriage with apparent honorable intentions. Meany offered Victor Reuther, Walter's brother, a position as his executive assistant to ensure that the CIO unions knew what happened in his office on a daily basis. Victor declined, preferring to continue as director of international affairs for the UAW. Meany agreed to Reuther's suggestion that John W. (Jack) Livingston, a long-time UAW lieutenant, head the AFL-CIO department of organization—which by CIO interpretation was to be the number three position. Meany also put the AFL staff on notice that he wanted the merger to work and that he would not tolerate backbiting and obstructionism. Anyone who did not wish to work with CIO newcomers could find a new job.

Harmony, however, never happened. The organization squandered much of its energies in the 1950's dealing with the corruption problem—purging tainted unions and resisting restrictive legislation. Almost as much effort was wasted on the internal battles. Reuther and Meany, for separate reasons, in the first years managed to avoid a direct confrontation that could have split the AFL-CIO. Nonetheless, their mutual distrust—one felt keenly by their subordinates and followers—weakened the AFL-CIO from the very first days of its existence. "Unity did not so much resolve the differences as paper them over," one close associate of Reuther said.

Meany versus Reuther—a confrontation that deflected the flow of American labor for more than a decade. The differences were real, and they were personal as well as philosophical. Power struggles can be useful mechanisms if they improve the way institutions go about their business. But the Meany-Reuther feud was a battle matched in its ferocity only by its essential stupidity, one in which positions solidified, rather than changed.

Because of his industrial union background, Reuther saw the merged AFL-CIO as a potential vehicle for mass organization. Now that American labor was "one big family," save for the United Mine Workers and a handful of small unions, the AFL-CIO could get on with its obligation of providing a union haven for every worker in the nation. Whether he joined the plumbers or the autoworkers was essentially irrelevant; bring him into "one big union." Reuther also appreciated public relations. Dramatize issues to win support for your position; labor must use audacious salesmanship to penetrate public apathy. Reuther frequently used the General Motors sitdown strike of 1937 as an illustration of the boldness he expected of American labor. To the public Reuther was the extrovert—a man of soaring (if somewhat long-winded) rhetoric and a passion for grandiose ideas; the sort of leader who, by setting unreachable goals, persuades society to go part of the way with him, at least. Because Reuther recognized the value of good press relations—after all, he once said, what the hell is the value of an idea if one keeps it inside his briefcase?—he made himself easily available to newsmen. Reporters liked Reuther. Colorful, young, a man glib with both striking quotes and ideas, Reuther at the time of the merger was perhaps the best-known labor leader in the country. (To Richard Nixon, campaigning in 1956, Reuther was also "the smartest labor leader in America.")

The extroverted Reuther, the one known to the public, was one person. There was also the introverted Reuther—a man with an intense need for personal privacy. Reuther loathed the backslapping barroom camaraderie endemic to organized labor. Many in the CIO thought him snobbish, a leader too aloof to pause after a convention session for a glass of beer and a cigar. Why waste the time? Reuther would reply impatiently. There's so much to be done.

To Meany, however, the AFL-CIO was but a lineal extension of the old AFL—a federation of autonomous unions, each with the right to organize workers in its own jurisdiction, and nowhere else, and at its own pace. Meany was a strict constructionist. He would invade the autonomy of affiliated unions that were corrupt. He would referee jurisdictional squabbles. But matters of basic unionism—organizing and collective bargaining—were none of the AFL-CIO's business, and Meany intended to keep the AFL-CIO out of them.

Meany distrusted the press. From his early days in New York he considered the newspapers to be tools of big business and hostile to organized labor. The building trades unions won their fights at the collective bargaining table, not on the front pages of the newspapers. Meany kept himself aloof from most newsmen; a reporter who was not "for" labor was an enemy, and to be avoided. Covering Meany could be a frustrating assignment. When a newsman disturbed him late one evening soon after he arrived in Washington, Meany became piqued and obtained an unlisted phone number. Thereafter he would not take calls after office hours. Joseph A. Loftus, the long-time Washington labor reporter for the New York *Times,* said, "Every Secretary of Labor was in the phone book, but not George Meany. If you wanted to know where the AFL stood on a subject, you had to wait until morning. You could occasionally see Meany when he was secretary-treasurer, but when he became president he got high and mighty for a guy who needs the press. He was brusque, and arrogant, and completely inaccessible, unless you happened to be friendly to him." Meany finally reached the point where he would not see Loftus at all, to the bewilderment of the *Times* bureau. James Reston, the *Times* Washington correspondent, met Meany on a plane and during a chat asked, "What is the matter with you and Joe Loftus?" According to what Reston told Loftus, Meany "muttered something about an international story." Loftus said, "I don't know what he was talking about." Later Loftus learned an explanation more logical to him: "I am a Roman Catholic, and divorced and remarried. Meany is more Catholic than the Pope. He has no idea of being a bigot because he bears no discrimination towards blacks and Jews, but a Catholic had better be a good Catholic, and a family man. Since I wasn't, I was blacklisted. Meany was only hurting himself, of course." David Jones, another *Times* labor reporter, fell into disfavor also. Jones was assigned the Washington labor beat during a strike of the *Times* by the American Newspaper Guild. Jones, who was not a union member, continued working. Albert J. Zack, Meany's public relations director, said, "Meany cut Jones dead. Any man who would work during a strike was not welcome in his office. He would have nothing to do with Jones thereafter, and Jones never got a private interview." Meany, conversely, complained frequently "we have a lot of people who are covering the labor beat who are not good reporters." Meany was especially hostile to A. H. Raskin, who as labor specialist for the New York *Times* could affect public opinion toward unions perhaps more than any other journalist. "Abe Raskin's problem is not that he is not intelligent, but he doesn't want to be a reporter," Meany once complained. "He wants to be someone who maneuvers policy and who gets the labor movement to do the things that he thinks they should do." Meany's contempt for Raskin was frequently voiced within earshot of the writer's colleagues. Raskin once wrote that Meany tried to make a "doormat" of secretaries of labor. "What a rotten, dirty, lousy, stinking thing to do!" Meany said of Raskin.

A feud between a public figure and the press is an event of transitory importance. Meany's attitude, however, meant that organized labor spoke to the public in grunts and crusty snippets of sentences. Thus grew the image of Meany: a mule-headed plumber who had not entertained a new idea since he left the Bronx; a cold warrior even more fierce in his anticommunism than John Foster Dulles; a trade unionist moldy with the outdated philosophies of Gompers and Green.

Meany's health was another factor. He injured his ankle in a boyhood sports accident, and it never recovered properly. Meany was forced to wear high-topped shoes for support. As he grew older, the ankle weakened, altering his gait. This, in turn, put stress on his left hip, and caused a gradual deterioration of the socket. By the time of the merger the condition was so bad that Meany occasionally had to use a cane to walk comfortably. The constant irritation of the pain affected Meany's public behavior. Instinctively reserved with strangers, Meany became more than ever a person bent upon preserving his privacy. "George had so damned many fights going in the fifties," in the opinion of a friend, "that he couldn't let himself relax unless he was with guys he really knew." The McClellan hearings and the business-directed drives for antilabor legislation made Meany distrustful of anyone whose loyalties were not proven.

The differences extended to life styles as well. Once he could afford it, Meany managed well the transition from trencherman of corned beef and cabbage to gourmet of fine French foods and wines. Meany relished the amenities of office—the leisurely midwinter executive council meeting spread over a week in luxury Miami Beach hotels, with ample time for golf and the beach; first-class cabins and captain's table privileges when he sailed abroad; four-star restaurants and hotels on the Continent. (C. L. Sulzberger, who lunched with Meany in Paris in November 1951, wrote in his diary, "I must say that although Mr. and Mrs. Meany still talk like a plumber and his wife, they look and dress more like big business. She was wearing a mink cape.") Although Meany was not lavishly paid in comparison with presidents of big international unions (he earned $35,000 his first year as president; the Teamsters' Dave Beck, $70,000), an AFL-CIO expense account covered his travel and other out-of-pocket expenses, a substantial tax-free addition to his income.

Reuther, however, made a veritable fetish of avoiding ostentation. Luxurious living, Reuther argued, isolated professional unionists from the rank and file. Labor leaders should not use workers' dues to finance "vacations"—i.e., the Miami Beach meetings—beyond the reach of the workers themselves. At one of his first executive council meetings Reuther asked other members, in effect, if they wished to "wallow in luxury like a bunch of capitalists?" The taciturn Harry Bates, for whom two sentences was a major speech, looked up and said, "Yeah." David Dubinsky, another devotee of comfortable living, at the same meeting said that soon after his election as a business agent for the ILGWU he went to a greasy-spoon delicatessen for a favorite dish. As Dubinsky tells it, an ILGWU member saw him through the window and came in to protest: "So we don't pay you enough that you got to eat in a cheap place like this?" Many council members, including some of Reuther's friends, thought the "sackcloth and ashes bit" was a publicity gimmick. Even James Carey, secretary-treasurer of the old CIO, was occasionally amused:

"For one meeting, I reserved a sitting room in the Roney Plaza Hotel [in Miami Beach] with a bedroom attached for Reuther, so we could hold our meetings in comfortable circumstances. Reuther took one look at this elaborate room and said, 'I'm not going to sleep there.' I told him, 'Okay, Walter, take my room,' and I gave him a single. I had already signed Walter into the big room, and the newspapermen came up to look for him to talk about something or other. I told them, 'Hell, he's down the hall in a linen closet squeezing oranges.'

"I didn't think they would take me seriously, but off they went, and somebody asked Reuther about the oranges. Damned if he didn't send his wife out to buy him some oranges—a half-million dollars worth of publicity.

"Another time we were set for the Americana Hotel. Now this is a place that either you like or you don't. The first time I saw that big fountain in the lobby I thought the water came flushing down from the toilet. Reuther refused to stay there and said he had got a motel room. The way he described it, you'd think it was fifteen miles out in the country, behind a gas pump. Then he named it. 'Walter,' I said, 'that's right up against the Americana, and the rates are higher.'

"But Reuther was right about most of this stuff. Hell, it was pretty basic. For example, he didn't think it proper for the AFL-CIO ethical practices code to be adopted by a committee meeting in the Roulette Room of the Monte Carlo Hotel in Miami Beach."

Meany's directness and rough speech in council meetings appalled some of the CIO newcomers. Meany seldom philosophized about an issue. He would bargain and compromise, and attempt to strike a common ground between disputants. But once a decision was reached, he could pound the loser into submission. Meany prided himself on keeping his word, and he bristled indignantly at any implication he had broken a promise or acted deviously in private meetings. To some of the CIO people Meany was a thin-skinned bull, a man capable of spectacular (and predictable) explosions when goaded. One constant adversary was Jim Carey—mischievous to his friends, malevolent to his enemies. Carey admitted his wit could be provocative. "Many people," he said, "thought I should have been in the needle trades." Meany, however, did not think much of Carey's tactics. At a council meeting in February 1957 Meany brought up a jurisdictional dispute involving alleged raiding by Carey's electrical workers against the Sheet Metal Workers International Association at an upstate New York plant. Carey had resisted Meany's proposed settlement, and some of his private comments drifted back to Meany. When Carey charged Meany with unfair actions in the dispute, Meany interrupted with a boom. "I don't want to talk to you about these things, and I don't care who knows it in this council," Meany said. "I am so fed up with the vicious, slimy, foul-mouthed, obscene presentations and the things you say about people that I have known for years. I just can't take it, Jimmy, I can't take it."

Carey interjected, "I haven't had a chance to talk with you about this matter."

"You bet your life you haven't, and you are not going to get a chance," Meany said. Carey charged the jurisdictions committee had "rubber-stamped a decision that was already rendered" by Meany.

"That is not true," said William Doherty, a subcommittee member. "That is not fair."

"That is not true," echoed Meany. "You are making wild charges."

"Mr. Chairman," began Carey, "that is the opinion—"

Meany cut him off. "All right, I would like to hear from brothers [L. S.] Buckmaster and Doherty, and I would like to know if they accept the charge of being rubber stamps."

The debate quietened, but continued for half an hour or so.

The episode was not an isolated one. On another occasion Meany got into a cold exchange of insults with Joseph Curran, of the Maritime Union. "Liar!" Meany finally exclaimed. "If you were fifteen years younger," yelled Curran, a burly former seaman, "I'd climb over this table and beat the hell out of you." "Come the hell on," Meany said. Other members stopped the row short of fisticuffs; one commented later to labor journalist Lester Velie, "It's a lucky thing he [Curran] didn't get over that table; Meany would have been there first."

Meany resented any attempts—real or imagined—by Reuther to usurp his authority. "For the first few years," one of Meany's then-insiders said, "George didn't take Walter too seriously. He knew he could butt him down in a vote, so what the hell—you have a majority, you use it." At the 1959 winter executive council meeting, however, Meany decided Reuther had shoved far enough, and slapped him down —brutally and publicly. Even the site selection was classic oneupmanship. The previous year, unhappily yielding to Reuther's demands for "austerity" during a recession, the council agreed not to hold the winter meeting in Miami Beach, the customary site. Meany, however, quietly arranged for Governor Luis Muñoz Marín of Puerto Rico to invite the council to equally sunny Puerto Rico, to Reuther's annoyance.

Meany was fighting a bad head cold and was a day late arriving for the meeting. "Reuther couldn't live for the day that was not given over to work," said Jim Carey. "He had some unfinished business for the economic policy committee, so he called a session. He was just being attentive about his work." Meany's friends, however, thought otherwise when Reuther moved into the president's chair. Reuther proposed a mass march of jobless persons on Washington to dramatize "labor's rage" over President Eisenhower's economic policies, which he blamed for the 4.7 million unemployed. (At a press conference the next day Eisenhower ridiculed Reuther by noting that the concern was expressed on the "sunny beaches" of Puerto Rico, far from jobless centers. "Mr. President," Reuther responded by press release, "I have spent no time on the sunny beaches of Puerto Rico nor have I been with you and your many big business friends on the golf course, the duck blinds, and the quail hunts.") The economic policy committee approved Reuther's planned march, although senior AFL people fumed. William Schnitzler and George Harrison met Meany at the airport to report on the meeting. According to Carey, "They got him steamed up about Reuther trying to 'take over.' They did this to make themselves look good, and all they did was make George Meany look stupid. By the time he got to the hotel and opened the meeting, he was mad." Meany was also on edge because of a resolution Carey and William Doherty had prepared for council consideration calling for compulsory retirement at age sixty-five for AFL-CIO employees so they could "enjoy many years of recreation and dignified leisure." Meany, whose sixty-fifth birthday was only six months distant, suspected mischief in the resolution (although Carey said it would not apply to him and Schnitzler, both elected officers).

Meany opened the meeting with a rush. First, he argued down Reuther's planned mass march. Any such demonstration, he said, would attract Communists and other radicals, and "we want no damned part of it." Bridling, Reuther threatened to resign. The debate raged for more than two hours. At one point Reuther—who normally sat two seats away from Meany, next to Schnitzler—switched chairs with Carey, so he could speak with George Harrison, who was partially deaf. Carey, now sitting literally at Meany's elbow, joined the argument, denying that Reuther was "trying to take over the meeting."

"Don't you get into this!" Meany shouted to Carey. He made a veiled reference to a jurisdictional fight between AFL and CIO unions at a fabricating shop in New York, the implication being (to Carey, at least) that if he did not shut up, Carey's electrical workers would lose. One word led to another. Carey said, "Finally, Meany called me a 'bastard' and said he didn't want me sitting there. He told me to get the hell down to the end of the table where I belonged. That busted up the meeting.

"We all agreed to have breakfast at eight o'clock the next morning to see if we could start again. I got with Walter and May Reuther and we walked around the streets of San Juan, Reuther telling me I shouldn't try to land one on Meany. 'He's too old and crippled,' Walter said. 'There's nothing wrong with his tongue muscle,' I said."

Carey said he told Reuther he was worried because "we were having conflicts at the level that could make or break the labor movement, and over issues that we thought had been pretty thoroughly agreed upon. Reuther was anxious to preserve unity—in my opinion, he was over-anxious." Reuther persuaded Carey to help him find a compromise on the jobless demonstration.

"It was an extremely pleasant breakfast," Carey said. "Harry Bates was talking about how well they worked out jurisdictional disputes in 1910, and Schnitzler was talking about how well the roulette wheel worked at this casino he had visited the night before. God, it was awful. I didn't have the heart to tell Schnitzler you could have a motor twenty-five miles away that would stop the wheel on thirteen. And Meany started talking about 'democratic processes.' He told this story that although his father ran Local Two with an 'iron hand' and appointed all the committees, 'I didn't pass the apprenticeship test.' I said, 'George, that doesn't indicate Local Two was democratic—that means you couldn't wipe a joint.' "

After an hour of barbed bantering the sides got down to bargaining. "We wrangled, and then proceeded to write a script covering things over," Carey said. "Meany would say he didn't want Reuther to resign, and Reuther would make a conciliatory reply. We followed the script beautifully—didn't miss a line." Meany had wanted a legislative conference of union officers on the unemployment question. He agreed to accept a mass meeting of both union officials and jobless rank and file—but in a national guard armory in Washington, where the attendees could be controlled, rather than on the streets, as Reuther wished. A Meany friend said of the meeting, "George could have rubbed his face in the floor. He let him save some dignity." Lee Cohn, labor reporter for the Washington *Evening Star,* called the meeting "one victory after another" for Meany.

The personal antagonisms, the pushing and shoving by allies and subordinates, two previous decades of distrust—all these factors contributed to the explosive atmosphere in which the AFL-CIO spent its first years. Unsurprisingly, the rancor slopped over into two substantive areas: international labor policies and programs, and jurisdictional disputes between affiliated unions.

On December 13, 1955, a week after the merger convention, Meany addressed the annual social justice award luncheon in New York of the National Religion and Labor Foundation, an august gathering of American liberals including Mrs. Eleanor Roosevelt. The occasion was Meany's first foreign policy pronouncement as president of merged labor, and many in the audience were curious as to whether the CIO détente had softened his opposition to coexistence with the Soviets. It had not. The speech was vintage Meany. He lectured the "many people in our country who call themselves liberals" for being "stone silent about the Soviet concentration camps . . . [and] the Communist imperialist destruction of the national independence and democratic rights of hundreds of millions of people in Europe and Asia." Meany also warned liberals "against developing a certain type of McCarthyism on their own . . . [and to] shun like the plague the role of being anti-anti-Communist. . . . Only by refusing to be thus entrapped can liberals shed every vestige of subconscious and conscious regard for communism as a movement with which they have something in common." And Meany commented on Indian Prime Minister Jawaharlal Nehru, who had just escorted Soviet leaders Nikita Khrushchev and Nikolai Bulganin on a tour of his country. "No country, no people, no movement, can stand aloof and be neutral in this struggle," Meany said. "Nehru and Tito are not neutral. They are aides and allies of communism in fact and in effect, if not in diplomatic verbiage."

The speech contained nothing new, for Meany had attacked the "double standards" of American liberals repeatedly in the past, and he had never found anything praiseworthy in Nehru. But its timing was significant for two reasons. It offended persons such as Reuther who had hoped the merger would herald a new alliance of liberals and labor. Meany's "strictures against liberals seemed to leave many in his audience somewhat stunned," the New York *Times* reported the next day. Eleanor Roosevelt wrote in her newspaper column it was a "sad mistake" to say Nehru was Communist because he wanted his country neutral. "There was a certain lack of recognition in this speech also that leadership requires an acceptance of one's own shortcomings and a constant effort to improve at home." It was the focal point for the first public dispute between Meany and Reuther and, in turn, for an acid executive council debate.

Reuther, who followed Meany on the program, said nothing to indicate his disagreement. (His speech was a call for the United States to earn the right to lead the free world by a readiness to end "its own ugly and immoral practices in race relations.") In February, however, Reuther revived the Meany speech on the eve of a trip to India. According to Meany, "Walter gave a press conference which makes it emphatically clear that he disagrees with me—which is perfectly all right." But Reuther's choice of a forum irked Meany. "I don't think it is too good to bring it up before the public. I think if he disagrees with me, he should have brought it up before the [AFL-CIO] international committee or in the executive council. He did not do that. However, in this press release he makes the point I was just expressing my personal opinion and not a matter of policy."

Immediately after the press conference, Meany said, a person on Reuther's staff asked the Voice of America "to send this recording to all their outlets throughout the world, and send their recording to their [ICFTU] affiliates. . . . The fellow in charge of this Voice of America program said he didn't like to send out something over the Voice of America that would show a controversy between two top officials of the AFL-CIO. [Then] he called up Phil Pearl [the AFL-CIO public relations director] and told him of this request. . . . The Voice fellow said, 'I wanted to give you my opinion. I don't think it is a good thing.' Phil said, 'I happen to agree with your reaction, but it's your business; you handle it the way you like.'

"The next thing, Victor [Reuther] calls Phil Pearl and says, 'What the hell are you doing, trying to prevent Walter's speech from going overseas?' Phil told him 'This man called me up and he gave me his opinion and I told him it was his business.'

"The next thing is, Victor writes to the government official in charge of the program and complains about this employee of the Voice of America making a decision to keep this material from going over the air. They finally decided two days later they would ship it to India. Anyway, it got all over Europe, and it was the only thing in Walter's press conference which seemed to attract any attention, those few lines about having a dispute with the president of the AFL-CIO."

In New Delhi, Reuther disagreed totally with Meany's appraisal of Nehru, calling him "truly one of the great statesmen of the world." The Associated Press account of the talk said many knowledgeable Indians believed one of Reuther's main objectives was "to heal the wounds caused by Meany's speech." The episode put Meany on the brink of fury, for Reuther claimed "he is speaking for all of labor." (Richard Deverall of the AFL-CIO international affairs department, analyzing Reuther's Indian statements from the perspective of his Asian experiences, reported to Meany and Jay Lovestone that they reflected "a subconscious approval of the basic idea and premises of communism, but a conscious rejection of the 'excesses' of the system; an almost pathological anti-American attitude; extreme naïveté and a juvenile mentality.") At the next executive council meeting, on May 1, 1956, Meany berated Reuther on Nehru and other grievances.

"I am not used to working in this sort of atmosphere," Meany said. "I don't think your brother should interfere with our staff people. . . . I don't know just what your brother Victor is supposed to do, Walter, according to your instructions, but I do not think his job is to . . . scold representatives of our departments. . . . This is more than one incident. I do not think he is a business agent for your organization in dealing with the AFL-CIO."

Another irritant was a remark by Reuther, in explaining a delay in approving membership applications for the industrial union department (IUD), that "we are going to keep this department clean." Meany said, "The inference is that 'there is some uncleanliness around and we are going to keep it out of the IUD.' I thought that [remark] was unfortunate. I do not want to interfere with the IUD, but the thought occurs that . . . if the IUD wouldn't take those unions in on the ground that they are not clean, that those unions . . . should not belong to the AFL-CIO. . . . Those who feel they are not clean enough should bring the matter to the executive council and present their case."

Meany was also peeved that Reuther's economic policy committee was "working on some sort of power basis or patronage basis"; that Meany was being ignored "despite the fact [that] under the constitution these committees work under the president and cooperate with him." Meany accused Reuther of excluding building and construction trades department personnel from the committee, despite their long-term interest in economic policy. And, finally, he discussed a dispute with James Carey over the amount of money the CIO should pay into the merged organization. Meany said an auditor's report suggested the CIO should pay as much as $500,000 additional to the $1,238,000 agreed upon earlier, based upon its assets at the time of merger. Carey argued the $500,000 should go directly to the industrial union department.

Reuther, rebutting after Meany spoke for almost an hour, began with the $500,000 issue. "What bothers me about this situation," he said, "is not the arithmetic, but how the problem has come up. Why didn't George Meany talk to us about it? If people want to make the merger work, they have to learn to work with people. And to raise, in this kind of meeting, these issues, is not the way to work with people. You should try to raise the thing with me first and try to work it out, face to face and man to man. . . . What disturbs me essentially is that George Meany takes stories from staff members who seem to make a career out of making things go wrong—he takes his stories and has a grievance and brings it up here."

Reuther continued: "I want to make the merger work. But how do you make it work? Are the old AFL staff still part of the AFL staff or are they part of this merger? I can tell you many of them conduct themselves in that way—that the CIO part of the family are not part of the family. I don't know if we have a probation period to go through before we are considered part of the family. And they keep feeding George the stuff they think will advance this narrow point of view of theirs. . . .

"I think George Meany's speech in New York was unfortunate. I disagreed with it then and could have answered it, but I didn't and kept it under the bushel for many months, hoping it would be forgotten. . . . I did not say a word about this until I went to India. The question was raised, and I answered it. I suppose I still have a right as a free citizen, as a democratic trade unionist, to express my point of view. . . . When I was asked the question, 'Do you agree with Mr. Meany's characterization of the Indian government and its leadership?' I said, 'Mr. Meany has a perfect right to express his point of view, and I respect his point of view but I disagree with it.' I said I was asked an honest question and was going to give an honest answer. . . . I didn't go to India and say, 'George Meany speaks for himself and I speak for the labor movement.' "

Reuther was angered that "staff people whom we are paying to help build this union are making a career out of trying to create division and doubt. . . . I don't care how much these evil geniuses work overtime on it; I am not going to get into a personal fight with George Meany. When these people feed the dopesters, I can go out and feed other dopesters with my side of the story. But I have not done that. I am not going to let some little staff guy who doesn't represent one worker in America, snarl up this whole organization."

Meany flatly denied discrimination against CIO staff people. "That is absolutely false. There is no ground for that whatsoever."

A continuing irritant to the CIO faction in the early merger years was Jay Lovestone. The cross-hatred of Reuther and Lovestone dated to the UAW factional fights of the 1930's, when Lovestone campaigned against a presidential candidate Reuther supported. The UAW clash alone was sufficient to make Lovestone permanently *persona non grata* with Reuther. "Meany should have retired Jay at the time of merger on a gentlemen's agreement basis," one of Reuther's friends felt. "You just don't keep people's blood enemies in the next office." To Reuther, Lovestone compounded his unacceptability through the advocacy of foreign policy views the CIO faction considered not only unwise but absolutely dangerous. Lovestone thought both Walter and Victor Reuther were naïve about world affairs. "I am not against him because his name is Reuther," Lovestone once said. "I am against him because he does things that are bad—policy-wise."

During the merger negotiations Reuther refused to accept Lovestone as head of the AFL-CIO international affairs department. Meany was equally adamant against firing Lovestone. "Walter Reuther was determined to liquidate the Free Trade Union Committee," Lovestone said. "In that determination was also the feeling . . . that if I could be liquidated in the process, he would not object." As a compromise, it was agreed Lovestone would continue as director of the FTUC, supported by but outside the formal AFL-CIO structure. The international affairs department would be run by George Brown, a personal assistant to Meany. "Walter Reuther would have walked out had George Meany proposed me," Lovestone said. Lovestone would work in the FTUC office in New York, not in the AFL-CIO headquarters building.

To Reuther's distress, however, Lovestone was "isolated" in theory but not in fact. Lovestone wrote foreign policy statements for the executive council. The FTUC, with AFL-CIO funds, ran labor's foreign programs. Lovestone made no attempt to conceal his contempt for Reuther—"Sir Walter" was one gibing name that got back to Reuther. The sniping was as intense in the other direction. James Carey, who hones his bon mots to a fine point, maintained, "Meany won Lovestone from Dubinsky in a gin rummy game. Why the hell should AFL-CIO foreign policy be determined by the fact that Lovestone didn't sell enough subscriptions to the *Daily Worker* in 1929 and got kicked out of the party?" Carey called Lovestone a "fibbergibbet—essentially a gossip."

To the CIO faction, Lovestone was known as "half cloak-and-suiter, half cloak-and-dagger"—a reference to Lovestone's dual backgrounds. The CIO people, specifically, Reuther and Carey, had two aims: to strip Lovestone of influence over AFL-CIO international affairs; and to put AFL-CIO foreign programs under the International Confederation of Free Trade Unions.

Lovestone resisted. He did not think the ICFTU was competent to run any programs. In mid-1956 he complained to Richard Deverall, then in Brussels at ICFTU headquarters as an AFL-CIO emissary, that from Secretary General Vincent Tewson down, "the ICFTU bureaucracy is dead. Its carcass is irritating to the nostrils and a pain for the international labor movement." He felt the "cheap group of semiskilled bandits" running the ICFTU was deliberately affronting the AFL-CIO, appeasing Communist and neutralist nations. Lovestone was infuriated with the ICFTU's record immediately following the Soviet invasion of Hungary in 1956. With AFL-CIO help, the ICFTU raised a special Hungarian fund of $850,000—yet, according to Lovestone, spent only $2,000 of it. ". . . [I]f it were not for the Free Trade Union Committee, AFL-CIO—yes, our office, Room 209—the Hungarian question in the United Nations would be dead long ago; the Kadar* credentials would not have been withheld; no watchdog United Nations committee would have been set up; no report on Hungary would have been issued

* The Soviets installed Janos Kadar as head of the Hungarian government after crushing the revolt. The UN refused to accredit his government during debate on what action to take during the crisis.

by the UN. . . . The ICFTU spent not one ruble on the Hungarian hearings in the UN. . . ." When the AFL-CIO wrote a draft program for strengthening the ICFTU, Sir Vincent Tewson—"the Knighted Nut," in Lovestone's words—stalled so long Meany decided to withdraw it. Nor did former CIO people fit well into Lovestone's operations. Against Lovestone's wishes, David Dubinsky convinced Meany of the political wisdom of letting the CIO put representatives on the international and ICFTU staffs. One selection, made by David McDonald of the United Steel Workers, was Charles Millard, who headed the USW in Canada. Millard was made ICFTU director of organization for all of Latin America. The appointment distressed Lovestone, who felt McDonald was foisting Millard off on the ICFTU because of incompetence. Serafino Romualdi, in Latin America for the AFL-CIO, found a rather basic defect in Millard: he did not speak a word of Spanish. "As far as Latin America was concerned," Romualdi lamented, "he remained obdurate in his belief that the area's geography, culture, history, ethnic make-up, economic development, and labor movement were really no different from Canada." Millard tried to take control of the ORIT, the ICFTU regional affiliate Meany and Romualdi had created in Latin America, and to bar it from taking money from Lovestone's Free Trade Union Committee. Meany, infuriated, stopped Millard cold. When the ICFTU lagged in helping unionists in North African states emerging from French colonialism, Meany set about raising a special half-million dollar AFL-CIO fund outside the framework of the ICFTU.

Reuther, in turn, felt much of Lovestone's work was silly. At an executive council meeting in August 1957, Meany presented a draft resolution—written by Lovestone—discussing the current power struggle in the Soviet hierarchy. The statement was four pages, single-spaced, and detailed. Reuther didn't think the council should waste time with it. "I am sitting here representing my union as a trade unionist," he said. "I am not sent here to participate in the exercise of semantics of dialectical materialism. . . . I think that . . . we ought to say to the author . . . that it should be published in an appropriate magazine with his name on top of it. This is *his* evaluation of what is going on in the internal struggle for power in the Soviet Union." Reuther thought the council should stop fretting over machinations in the Kremlin and concern itself with current economic conditions in the United States. What would he reply, Reuther asked rhetorically, if a UAW member—"a man working three days a week in a General Motors plant"—should ask of him, "When did you know what is going on in the presidium of the Soviet Union bureaucracy? Why are you concerned about these little details and machinations?" Reuther continued: "I don't know what the internal power play is in the Soviet bureaucracy. I don't know really where Bulganin fits in in terms of Zhukov and how many notches Zhukov came up in the power struggle. . . . I want to fight them, but I will be damned if I want to try to analyze the internal manipulations."

Emil Rieve, of the CIO faction, interjected, "Maybe this ought to be published in the *Daily Worker* so Communists could read it and argue and debate about whether or not it is a fact."

The council agreed, without formal vote, to refer Lovestone's statement to Meany for review before it was released. The document, pared to about half the original length, ultimately was released as an AFL-CIO statement.

Reuther pressed the Lovestone issue to a showdown at the executive council meeting immediately prior to the 1957 convention. Reuther had Meany at a tactical disadvantage, for the same convention was to deal with the Teamster corruption question. According to Lovestone, "Meany feared he could not get the two-thirds vote required to expel the Teamsters. He was wrong—he had enough AFL votes without the CIO at all. But he wasn't certain." (An outside observer at the convention agreed with Lovestone's analysis. J. Ernest Wilkins, a Labor Department official in the foreign field, reported to Secretary James Mitchell after the convention: "President Meany needed support in his fight against corruption and racketeering while the leading industrial trade unions and, in particular, the UAW, needed support in their efforts to come to an agreement with the building and metal trades on jurisdictional conflicts.")

The result was a series of trade-offs. Meany would not fire Lovestone and Irving Brown, the AFL-CIO European representative, as demanded by Reuther. However, he did agree to bring Lovestone into the AFL-CIO international affairs department, with the title of "director of international publications." Michael Ross, an old CIO unionist with whom Lovestone was friendly, was made director of the department. The AFL-CIO agreed to switch a $50,000 African scholarship project to the ICFTU.

The decisions were widely interpreted—both within and without the AFL-CIO—as a setdown for Lovestone. But as Lovestone noted, the changes were more of form than of substance. The formal announcement said nothing about dissolution of the FTUC, and Lovestone quietly passed word to his foreign representatives that it could be reactivated at any time. In fact, Lovestone commented, the "committee" for some time had consisted only of him and Meany, with Schnitzler and David Dubinsky as cosigners of checks. "As you know," Lovestone wrote Richard Deverall, "I have been buried many times and had my carcass picked at. There will be many a vulture forced down before getting at me. I take a special delight in strangling vultures before they get to me. That is one of the reasons for my office in Washington."

In conversations with Deverall and other staff members, Meany made plain his discomfort over surrendering AFL-CIO programs to the ICFTU. The ICFTU, he said, was more interested in sham activity than accomplishment, and its career bureaucrats would knife the AFL-CIO at each opportunity. Deverall sent Meany and Lovestone a steady flow of reports on the intraoffice rivalries in Brussels; he complained frequently that his mail from Washington was opened, and he suspected that his phone was tapped. Deverall maintained, variously, that the ICFTU general secretary, Sir Vincent Tewson, a British unionist, was "interested only in maintaining himself in office and maintaining a façade of activity." The "actual boss" of the ICFTU, Deverall said, was Jay Krane, a former CIO unionist, who was the ICFTU's ranking career bureaucrat. Deverall said Krane "cannot work organizationally but only through intrigue [and] conspiracy." The "negative ideology of the top leaders of the ICFTU is unable to win over the loyalty of top trade union leaders in Asia, Africa, and Latin America, not to mention . . . Europe and the United States," Deverall said. The few comments Deverall made on substantive ICFTU programs were negative. The ICFTU resented the AFL-CIO's making direct grants to foreign labor centers. In 1958, according to Deverall, Jay Krane invited Tom Mboya, of the Kenya Federation of Labor, to Paris for an ICFTU board meeting. Meany considered Mboya one of the more promising African nationalist politicians and had supported Kenyan labor for several years, currently with a $35,000 grant for a labor building. The aid distressed Krane. Deverall said that when Krane learned of it, he refused to meet Mboya at the airport, to make him a hotel reservation, or to pay his plane fare, even though Mboya had come to Paris as an invited guest. "Krane told him [Mboya] that the ICFTU insisted that the AFL give the money to the ICFTU, and the ICFTU would decide what to do with the $35,000, not the Kenya Federation of Labor. Tom told Krane to go to hell . . . and he accepted the AFL* gift on behalf of the Kenya Federation of Labor without going through the ICFTU." Thereafter, Deverall said, ICFTU people spread the rumor among other Africans that "Mboya is on the payroll of George Meany and receives a thousand dollars each month from George Meany."

The net effect of Deverall's reports—voluminous documents of ten to twenty pages weekly, single-spaced—was to sour Meany on the practicality of channeling AFL-CIO programs through any international organization it could not control. In the late 1950's, when Meany needed Reuther's support in completing the merger and in policing corrupt unions, he pragmatically gave lip service to cooperation with the ICFTU. But according to Deverall, Meany was never so naïve that he thought

---

* That Deverall and other staff members did not feel "merged" was evidenced by their repeated use of the old name AFL in correspondence and reports, rather than the full AFL-CIO.

the ICFTU was the answer." In talks with Deverall and Lovestone Meany frequently spoke of ignoring the ICFTU and taking the AFL-CIO its separate way in international affairs, a route he ultimately was to choose.

Reuther, concurrently, could not understand Meany's unflinching opposition to détente with the Soviets, even when President Eisenhower tried to better relations as a matter of high national policy. When Soviet Deputy Premier Anastas Mikoyan visited the United States in 1959, he took a walk through downtown Washington early one Sunday and eventually found himself at the AFL-CIO Building, a block from the White House across Lafayette Park. Mikoyan told the guide he would like to see the inside of the building. A reporter in the entourage let a State Department official use his car telephone to ask Meany if he would open the building for the Soviet. "Hell, no," Meany replied. "I don't want him on the premises." Mikoyan had to content himself with standing with his nose pressed against the plate glass front window. Reuther, however, joined with three other AFL-CIO vice-presidents in inviting Mikoyan to luncheon at the International Union of Electrical Workers building across from the Soviet Embassy. Meany snapped that he could not understand Americans who "feel that they can meet the Soviet challenge at the conference table." The Reuther-Mikoyan encounter was testy, with Reuther criticizing the Soviet intervention in Hungary and actions in Berlin. And Reuther fended off Meany's criticisms, saying that he "thought it wise to tell . . . Mikoyan to his face" what Americans felt about "safeguarding the rights of free Berlin and securing a Germany united in freedom and democracy." Senator John Sherman Cooper (Rep., Kentucky) agreed, saying Reuther performed a "major service for peace."

The dispute revived several months later on a higher level when President Eisenhower invited Soviet Premier Khrushchev to the United States. The AFL-CIO convention would be meeting in San Francisco while Khrushchev was in that city. Eisenhower, through intermediaries, sounded Meany on the possibility of inviting Khrushchev to address the convention, or to meet with the executive council. Meany replied that Eisenhower had the right to invite anyone he wished to the United States, but that "the AFL-CIO has an equal right to decide who it would greet as a guest." Meany said, "We weren't going to play any gag about Khrushchev being the head of a 'labor government.' "

Reuther, however, offered to host a "labor dinner" for Khrushchev, and began rounding up support to undercut Meany. Countering, Meany asked the executive council to vote yes or no on whether it wished to invite Khrushchev to any AFL-CIO functions. Debate was spirited. Reuther said labor should help Eisenhower in his bridge-building attempts, and that "hidebound" attitudes were hurting national policy. Reuther noted that the prestigious Economic Club of New York, the veritable core of American capitalism, intended to host Khrushchev, and that he would be seeing such men as David Sarnoff and Alfred P. Sloan, board chairmen of RCA and General Motors, respectively. Surely labor could meet with Khrushchev without offending its anti-Communist credentials, he said. Reuther suggested the executive council join him in hosting the Khrushchev dinner. "That didn't get him any votes," commented Lovestone. The council voted 22 to 3 not to associate with Khrushchev, Reuther picking up the support only of James Carey and O. A. Knight, president of the Oil Workers Union.

Reuther went ahead with the dinner under his own auspices, joined by half a dozen other labor leaders. Emil Rieve, who voted against Reuther in the executive council, attended, saying that although he thought it would be wrong for the executive council to entertain Khrushchev, "If I want to have dinner with him, that's my business." The dinner made front-page news around the world, with Khrushchev and Reuther exchanging insults and arguing whether Russian or American workers had the better life. At the end Reuther slapped a booklet containing UAW wage scales on the table before Khrushchev and demanded, "How can he say these people are wage slaves exploited by capitalism?" (When Khrushchev met President Kennedy two years later in Vienna, he commented, "We hung the likes of Reuther in 1917.")

Meany and Lovestone actively tried to counter any public impression that Reuther acted for American labor in meeting with Khrushchev. Lovestone arranged for Anna Kethley, a Hungarian trade unionist in exile, to speak to the convention the day following the dinner. She told of the oppression of labor in Soviet-dominated states. The next day, Admiral Arleigh Burke, the chairman of the Joint Chiefs of Staff and an old Meany friend, spoke about the continuing dangers of Soviet military might. The speeches received minimal press attention, compared with the Reuther dinner, but Meany wanted the formal convention on record as anti-Soviet. Another plan aborted. Meany asked Henry Cabot Lodge, the UN ambassador and Khrushchev's escort, to dine with him, Dubinsky, Lovestone, and other AFL-CIO officers as a subtle endorsement for the AFL-CIO's boycott of the premier. Lodge agreed. On Saturday night, however, Lovestone received a call from Lodge's secretary, who said he had the grippe and must cancel. Lovestone said, "I called Lodge on Sunday, when we didn't have to mess with secretaries, and asked, 'Cabot, what the hell is this?' He was embarrassed and apologetic. I'm working under orders,' he said. 'General Eisenhower does not want to risk offending Khrushchev.' " Lovestone thought that despite the initial gush of favorable publicity, Reuther lost stature in the episode. "I don't think Walter knew he got screwed until he was eight months pregnant," Lovestone commented.

\* \* \*

The foreign policy disputes, however heated or publicized, did not affect the working American directly. Whether Jay Lovestone or the ICFTU signed a scholarship check for an African unionist was a matter of profound insignificance to the factory worker in Ohio or the painter in New Jersey. What did matter to the rank-and-file workers—and especially those outside unions—was how the AFL-CIO went about its primary reason for existing: leading American labor. In this area the cleavage between Meany and Reuther—on means, rather than ends—struck to the very core of the AFL-CIO. Involved were the overlapping areas of jurisdiction, organizing, and mergers of state and local labor federations.

Reuther went into the merger with the apparent expectation of civility between the old AFL and CIO unions, now that they pledged allegiance to the same parent. To his quick and pained dismay, Reuther found he had erred.

In February 1956, barely a month after the merger, he came to the executive council in a rage. A building trades union had posted a picket line at a Packard Motor Company plant in Detroit, claiming it, not the UAW, should have jurisdiction over new construction inside the factory. The dispute was one the building trades and UAW had encountered— and settled case by case—countless times in the past two decades. But Reuther said the old AFL union was telling him, "Now we are together, you are going to be treated just like another building trades organization."

Reuther was livid. Striding in a tight arc alongside the conference table, he declared, "I tell you very frankly, I did not come into the merged organization to be subjected to injustices that building tradesmen have inflicted upon each other for years." He asked whether the executive council would "act responsibly" or "whether we are going to look the other way and say, 'It's too goddamned bad that people act irresponsibly, but we are not going to interfere with their right to do that.'" Reuther said he realized the AFL-CIO had agreed to solve the jurisdiction problem as rapidly as possible after the merger. In the meantime, he said, the old CIO unions should not be harassed. "It is important that this executive council faces up to its obligation," he said. Meany interrupted, somewhat testily. "This body has not refused to meet its obligations."

"George, I would suggest you let me conclude," Reuther said.

The issue, Reuther said, was whether the old AFL unions really wanted a merged organization. "I did not agree to become a part of this united labor movement to dissipate my time and energy in this kind of endless and senseless controversy," he said. "I have more important things to do than this. I am unwilling to go through this every goddamn time we have sixty-six people involved in a controversy.

"You couldn't appease Hitler, and you can't appease anyone when they hold a gun to your head and say, 'Give us everything or else. . . .' " Reuther said the UAW did not intend to be frightened into submission by the building trades picket line. "I have never slugged a guy in my life, never intend to; but by Christ I will not yield!" he said. "I will never appease guys who use strong-arm tactics, whether they be inside the labor movement or Pinkerton men or company men, whoever it is."

Meany agreed with Reuther the picket line should not have been posted. He said he could try to resolve the argument by calling in the parties for talks, and he counseled patience.

To Reuther's frequently expressed distress, however, the jurisdiction question dragged on for some five years. The executive council and various special committees haggled over the problem in seemingly endless futility. At times Reuther wondered whether he should remain within the AFL-CIO. "I got the feeling," one of his associates said, "that the only reason Walter stayed in was because there was no place else to go. Hell, who was there? Jimmy Hoffa and John L. Lewis. Meany looked pretty good by comparison." Meany agreed the cross-fighting was nonsensical, and he continually told Reuther that procedures would be devised to stop it. Give me time, Meany said again and again. Meany stalled because he was in a political bind. Many old AFL unions followed him only reluctantly in his moves against corrupt unions ("George used a whole bank account of points when he went after the Teamsters," one building trades president said), and Meany was cautious about how far and how fast he could carry his supporters. To another inside observer, "George acted as if he was afraid that if he pushed too hard, the whole thing would have blown up. It well might've, too." Meany had a majority, of course, but he wanted a solid consensus; if a compromise was necessary "to keep the hyphen in the AFL-CIO," as he put it, he would compromise. Hence Meany let the jurisdiction question slide, giving priority to corruption, a problem much more visible to the general public.

Meany did not ignore the jurisdictions problem altogether, for its existence caused him continuing problems with Reuther. Meany tried a variety of approaches: conciliation, appeals to common sense, cajolery —even shame, in a speech to the building and construction department convention in 1957 at Atlantic City. If the building trades unions had their hearts set on fighting, Meany said, why not pick on people outside the labor movement? He suggested a list of targets:

The right-to-work people are still pretty much alive. Old Fred Hartley* is doing business down in Washington, getting additional

* The former congressman, coauthor of the Taft-Hartley Act, who started the National Right-to-Work Committee after leaving office.

funds. He is pretty well financed. He had a good machine and they are working. . . . There will be an opportunity to fight there. . . .

How about a little fight with Brown & Root [the Houston-based world-wide construction company]? What jurisdiction has Brown & Root got? Who gave it to them? They brag about the fact that they are nonunion. They seem to be doing all right. They just finished a job at Seadrift, Texas. You boys from that great big state should know about it—Union Carbide and Carbon Company, Seadrift, Texas, a one-hundred-million-dollar job.

The estimates are that private industrial and public utility construction are up fifty-five percent in dollar volume since 1954. Is building trades employment in this field up fifty-five percent? Maybe a little fight can be developed there.

A new Esso plant in Baton Rouge has a thousand men working year round on maintenance, repair, and relocation. They belong to a union. It is not a former CIO union or a former AFL union. Those thousand men belong to an independent union. How about starting a little fight there?

The building tradesmen listened to Meany in sullen silence as he ridiculed their designs on former CIO unionists who did construction work in industrial plants:

Is anyone here going to turn over members they have organized for twenty years at the point of a gun? Are they [the CIO] going to be compelled to turn them over? You fellows know that isn't going to happen. So how are we going to solve this problem? By a trade union war, by fighting until the last drop of blood is gone? I have had enough experience to know that we can't gain anything by that sort of practice. The only ones who gain are the enemies of labor.

But the building trades were in no mood to negotiate, and Meany's position was weakened further by their refusal to accept merger. The opposition centered around Richard Gray, chairman of the building and construction trades department (BCTD).

Gray, a Republican and a conservative, thought alliance with the CIO was foolish. In April 1956 Gray instructed BCTD-affiliated unions "to use every facility at their command to postpone merger of AFL-CIO state and local central bodies until such time as a satisfactory written understanding on jurisdiction is reached between the Building and Construction Trades [department] and the Industrial Union Department and until such agreement is approved by the AFL-CIO and/or by AFL-CIO convention action." Meany asked Gray to withdraw the letter. Gray refused in a letter listing more than a dozen jurisdictional disputes that had been referred to Meany without decision. "The inference," Meany told the executive council, "is that I did not do anything about these cases, and that is completely and absolutely untrue." Each went to an assistant for study and conciliation, he said. "This boils down to a personal attack on me," Meany said of Gray's letter. "I don't know why, because we have been friends for many, many years. Evidently he is looking for someone to blame his troubles on, and that someone happens to be me." George Harrison agreed. "It is rebellion and nothing else," he said.

Meany struggled with Gray for more than a year. "Gray never stopped for one single minute," Meany said. "He kept feeding resolutions [opposing merger] to state federation conventions, and so on. He went there and addressed the building trades groups and just never gave up on this idea. I don't know what his idea was. The only thing I can think of is that he felt that by pushing this thing and embarrassing us and delaying these mergers, that in some way someone was going to come to him and ask him to stop and say they would give them this, that, and the other thing." Meany, however, would not yield. "The more he puts this opposition in," he told the executive council in December 1957, "the more determined I am not to give in to him under any circumstances. He has gone right on and I suppose he will continue."

As his agents in bringing about the local and state mergers Meany chose Peter McGavin, formerly an organizer for AFL maritime unions, and R. J. Thomas, Reuther's long-time ally in the UAW. "The problem was," McGavin said, "that these fellows had been fighting one another at the local level for so long that they didn't even want to come into the same room together. So we would go between the two sides, trying to find some points of agreement." The process was especially difficult in states where the AFL and CIO were of nigh-equal strength. "Since the AFL was taking the top jobs on the national level, the AFL unions felt they should get them at the state and local federations, too," McGavin said. In Michigan, the Teamsters tried to retain some influence in the prospective merged federation by transferring key officers to old AFL unions. One Teamster official, for instance, appeared with a Painters Union card, and the AFL refused to drop him from its negotiating committee, despite McGavin's protests against a "subterfuge."

Meany finally became so frustrated that he had to obtain authority from the executive council to revoke the charters of any central bodies that had not merged, and to take "such action as may be necessary" to effect mergers. Reuther did not favor such drastic action, preferring further negotiations. "It is of no value to force people together with a shotgun," Reuther said. But Meany said some of the barriers in the states "are almost trivial, really silly," and could be overcome only by authoritative action.

Meany first used his authority in Michigan, where he revoked charters of both the Michigan Federation of Labor, the old AFL group, and the Michigan Industrial Union Council, of the CIO. He called a special convention with McGavin and Thomas as presiding officers, and pushed through the merger. Gus Scholle, former president of the CIO council, was elected state president, a recognition of the CIO's dominance in the state. Meany also had to revoke charters in New Jersey, putting all union assets in the hands of McGavin and Thomas. New Jersey was the last state to complete mergers—in September 1961, almost five years after the "founding" of the AFL-CIO.

Meany's choice of priorities, pragmatic though it might have been, stifled AFL-CIO organizing. Jack Livingston, the director of organization, estimated there were 26 million "organizable unorganized" workers in the nation at the time of merger. Yet the AFL-CIO could reach few of them, he claimed. "There is hardly an area of organizational potential but what the question of jurisdiction exists in one form or another." Although the AFL-CIO could identify targets, "the actual process of organizing will seldom progress beyond the planning stage until the jurisdictional obstacles are removed in some manner. Organizationally speaking, jurisdiction is the most troublesome spot in the foreseeable future." Livingston ticked off some of the more glaring overlaps: the carpenters, upholsterers, furniture makers, and woodworkers all had claims in the furniture industry. Two chemical unions competed at the vast duPont works in Delaware; four unions claimed parts of the garment trades, complicating organizing in Southern textile mills. Livingston could not resolve the conflicts through direct meetings with the unions. When two unions competed for workers in the same plant, AFL-CIO policy was to remain neutral. Consequently, Livingston said, despite the vast number of unorganized, "It is sometimes difficult for us to find important projects to work on." Meany suggested adding thirty-five or forty organizers to the staff of 275, preferably in the white-collar field. Since the staff averaged fifty-three years of age, Meany opined, "Try some younger fellows."

During the next four years the AFL-CIO gained about 800,000 new members in representation elections. Nonetheless, according to Livingston, while the AFL-CIO had "undoubtedly maintained our numerical strength [it had] suffered a loss in our relative position" from forty percent of American workers to thirty-nine percent. Only seventeen percent of the white-collar workers were in unions. Livingston lamented, "There are about as many unorganized, organizable white-collar workers in the United States as there are AFL-CIO members today." Livingston blamed a host of factors: "the worst antilabor drive in twenty years" by business, commenced shortly after the merger; the 1955–57 recession; "exploitation and distortion of the McClellan committee disclosures." The AFL-CIO won only fifty-five percent of collective bargaining elections before the National Labor Relations Board. Meany, however, put most of the blame on labor itself. In 1959, with the corruption cases apparently ended, he turned his full energies to the jurisdictional issue. Speaking to an AFL-CIO organizing conference that year, Meany declared, "I feel that the greatest obstacle now to organization we might find right in our own ranks, in the kind of interunion rivalry that not only expends the workers' money in a wasteful way but actually prevents organizing and plays into the hands of the employer who is opposed to organization." ("Amen!" echoed Livingston.) Meany had yet another reason for finding a solution: Reuther had decided to throw down the gauntlet on jurisdictions.

Speaking to the 1959 convention, Reuther derided the absurdity of existing procedures. "We have seen unions come before the executive council arguing and haggling over three members—not unorganized workers, but organized workers—when the two unions involved had 300,000 people . . . in their jurisdiction which they hadn't organized," he said. "We have seen unions haggling over ten members when the two unions involved . . . had a million workers within the proper areas of the jurisdiction who were unorganized." Reuther envisioned three responsibilities for labor: to advance the objectives of collective bargaining; to make progress on the legislative fronts; and to move forward in organizing "the millions of unorganized workers." He declared, "On each of these fronts we have been on the defensive."

The 1959 convention produced an interim plan—the so-called Miami Agreement—but one without enforcement teeth, and the jurisdictional squabbles continued unabated. Reuther decided a voluntary plan would not suffice. Either the AFL-CIO would exert its authority or he would get out and take whatever old CIO unions he could with him. Reuther spent the months preceding the 1961 convention in a round of caucuses with the industrial unions, drafting a lengthy case-by-case indictment for presentation to Meany. "Walter was very definitely trying to split us," Meany said. "I wouldn't give him a chance. I wouldn't let him . . . although he tried. He kept his caucuses going. The grievances were all nonsense, the old jurisdictional stuff. . . ."

For hour after dreary hour, during months of executive council and committee meetings, the arguments droned on—the steelworkers versus the carpenters at a General Motors plant in Baltimore; the pipefitters and the steelworkers at a paper products plant in Eureka, California; various building trades unions versus the oil and chemical workers at refineries and chemical plants in Ohio, Arkansas, and Houston, Texas. Incredibly, the jurisdictional dispute reached to the very table around which the executive council met in the AFL-CIO Building. Morris Pizer, of the furniture workers union, commented offhandedly during one discussion that his men assembled the council table while carpenters "stood by." C. J. Haggerty, who had succeeded Gray as head of the building and construction trades department, retorted Pizer was wrong: that the carpenters assembled the table while the furniture workers "stood by." "When we got into this remarkable bit of trivia," remarked an old CIO man, "I wondered what the hell I was doing in the labor movement—much less the AFL-CIO."

Reuther served notice he wanted the jurisdiction question resolved one way or another at the 1961 convention. Speaking to an IUD conference a few days before the convention opened, Reuther said the continued feuds threatened to destroy the AFL-CIO. "We merged," he said, "but we did not unite." Meany astutely put the jurisdictions committee under the leadership of A. J. Hayes, of the International Association of Machinists, whose union had enjoyed marked success in resolving jurisdiction disputes with both the UAW and the building trades. The showdown came at an executive council meeting that began at 12:30 P.M. on December 12 and continued, with one recess, until 3:40 A.M. the next morning.

The Hayes report went further than any previous format for jurisdictional disputes, providing for an impartial umpire who could make final and binding decisions, enforceable in the courts. William Schnitzler, the AFL-CIO secretary-treasurer, leading off the debate, said he could not support the report because many affiliates would not accept the binding arbitration. Based upon past acceptance of the no-raiding and other jurisdiction plans, Schnitzler said, "there are a minimum of forty affiliates who would be compelled as a condition of membership within the AFL-CIO to accept a plan to which they could not agree."

Meany also had misgivings about parts of the plan. A union that lost an umpire's decision would not be entitled to a review. Meany believed "that this is contrary to the concept of settling disputes within the organization." Meany was also disturbed that the Hayes committee did not give all affiliates the chance to present their views, although it had met for two and one half years.

Reuther said he was "worried about the future of the movement unless we can come to agreement." He was willing to make changes in procedures "but not . . . on the principles." Carey worried what would happen to the federation if it did not accept the report. The current extension of the no-raiding agreement expired on December 31, less than three weeks away, and old CIO unions were wary of letting the issue drag. Realizing sentiment was against the Hayes plan as submitted, Meany asked for a recess. When the meeting reconvened after dinner, he offered a compromise. Arbitrator rulings would be subject to review by the executive council, and no union would be compelled to accept them. However, if a union did not comply with a decision, it could no longer use the no-raiding agreement as a shield against other unions; the AFL-CIO was authorized to assist the raided union; no member union could go to the aid of the noncomplying union; and the noncompliance would be publicized. Cumbersome though it was, Meany said, this procedure would give the president's office enough muscle to settle most disputes.

Reuther didn't like the compromise. "He tried to sabotage it; he went off on one of his quirks," Meany said. "Come on, let's get out of here," Reuther said when Meany finished, and stood and began gathering his papers together. There was a long silence. Would enough CIO members follow Reuther out of the room to split the federation? Joseph Beirne of the Communications Workers of America broke the tension. "Oh, sit down, Walter," he said, "we're not through. We've got work to do." Lacking support for a walkout, Reuther returned to his seat.

The council haggled over Meany's compromise until well after midnight, with the chief opposition coming from the building trades. Dissent was brisk. Peter Schoemann of the plumbers union said that by using outside professional arbitrators, the AFL-CIO lost its concept of a "free movement." Harry Bates of the bricklayers feared the plan would cost his union seven or eight thousand jobs in the oil, chemical, steel, and other industries. George Harrison of the railway clerks objected to "rigidity." Meany kept tinkering with the language, attempting to meet the objections. Finally, he had a draft he thought was satisfactory. Reuther accepted it. But he asked, "What's the use? It doesn't matter what you do—the building trades won't buy it anyway." "Let's see," replied Meany, and called the roll of the building trades. Each accepted. The AFL-CIO finally had a workable jurisdiction plan.

The outcome was significant for another reason not apparent at the time: by healing the old CIO unions' major grievance, they were no longer a power base from which Reuther could hope to contest Meany. The climactic confrontation was years distant, but its outcome was foreordained in 1961. Put most simply, Meany had systematically beaten down Reuther, and his rule of the AFL-CIO could not be shaken.

# The Kennedy Years

W HEN THE DEMOCRATIC NATIONAL CONVEN-
tion gathered in Los Angeles in July 1960, George Meany
was honor bound to be silent on his personal choice of a candidate,
for the AFL-CIO would make no formal endorsement until after
both parties had picked their nominees. John F. Kennedy came to the
convention a heavy favorite. But Senators Lyndon Johnson and Stuart
Symington and former Governor Adlai Stevenson held enough strength
to make the outcome uncertain. Hence discretion demanded that Meany
slough off reporters who wanted to know the AFL-CIO's position.
Meany simply grunted at questioners who flocked around him at the
Ambassador Hotel, the convention headquarters.

Standing behind him, beaming broadly, was Mrs. Meany, resplendent
in a straw skimmer emblazoned with a KENNEDY FOR PRESIDENT ribbon.
What does your husband think of that hat? someone asked her. "He
absolutely loves it," she said, "and he told me to save it so I could wear
it again in 1964."

An old man, a tiring man, a man in constant nigh-agony from his
aching hip socket, now deteriorated so badly that each step, each movement in his chair, sent pain surging through his body. At times, late in
the afternoon of a day that had been particularly bad, his face would
suddenly pale and the beads of sweat would spring to his upper lip. He
walked with a cane, and wobbily. Frequently, pain would drive him from
his bed in the predawn hours. Rolling off the bed quietly so as not to
disturb his wife, herself ailing with arthritis, he would don an old flannel
robe and slip away to his electric organ, hoping the concentration of

learning the chords of a new Irish tune would distract him. AFL-CIO staff people traveling with Meany who stayed in adjoining hotel rooms became used to seeing a band of light beneath his door until two, three, four o'clock in the morning, as he read in a chair, agony keeping him from bed. Then, at six-thirty, a spirited rap on the door: "What the hell, you going to sleep all day? I've already been down for coffee; let's get going!"

And, among those who did not know of the pain, the growing reputation of public grump. Concentration shielded Meany's mind from awareness of pain; it also shielded him from awareness of outsiders. The stories got around: the new file clerk who was asked for the "erlwukkers" papers. She did not know whether the words were proper names or Gaelic, and was afraid to ask; after many minutes of frustration—and a growl from the inner office—she cried. Then somebody said be quiet, silly, and get Mr. Meany the oil workers union file. And the reporters, the professionals of the death watch, searching for signs of when Meany-versus-Reuther would come to a denouement, and "The Old Man" would step aside—or be buried—and let "The Redhead" have the job. *Mr. Meany, do you have anything to say on* . . . Hrrrrrmph, it's all in the executive council statement we passed out in Chicago last meeting, I don't have nothing to add to it. . . . *Mr. Meany, how about the presidential speech of* . . . Nah, we didn't take any action on that. . . . *Mr. Meany, would you tell us* . . . Nothing new, absolutely nothing new. . . .

Too pained now for golf, but the gargantuan appetite continued, and the massive paunch slid from beneath the waistcoat; in profile, even the cigar seemed to sag. "American labor, like Meany, is walking on a crutch," someone wrote in late 1959. And there were internal criticisms from persons whose voices carried more weight inside labor than that of Reuther because they were untainted with personal animosity. Joseph Beirne of the Communications Workers of America was bitingly candid in speeches to his 1960 and 1961 conventions. Labor should stop playing "tiddlywinks with little problems while the big ones wait outside the door to eat us alive." Meany, Reuther, and David McDonald "are aware of the nature of the big problems but as an organization, the AFL-CIO never quite gets around to doing much about them. . . . Will labor grow in America, or do we face a long period of downhill loss of leadership, real or relative, and a loss of influence at the place of work and in the community as a whole? *New challenges require new leaders.* . . ." Enough! cried Beirne, enough! "The leadership of the AFL-CIO has become neutralized under the dead-weight pressure of retrogression and bitter . . . jurisdictional disputes." Executive council meetings "are consumed, endlessly and without decision, in a process of backbiting and infighting which, if it doesn't stop, will reduce the AFL-CIO to complete impotence. . . . The truly important problems—organizing, legislation, economic growth, political action, social welfare, automation, play second fiddle to the internal squabbles." John Herling, the journalist who watched labor as a dispassionate friend for three decades, asked, "Where is the new burst of organization, where is the crusade? . . . Labor's prima donnas are still fighting, jealous of each other's headlines . . . memories of past suspicions live on rancorously in the big double bed. . . ."

Meany slowly became an isolated man—so scornful of critics that only rarely would anyone in his inner circle differ with him, upon pain of being denounced as a "Reutherite." Nelson Cruikshank, who left the AFL-CIO to run a Medicare lobby financed by labor, was distressed at what he saw. "George found himself surrounded by yes-men, by guys who thought the way to get along with him was to toady to him. They were wrong: they should have argued with him, for he respects people who do. But by the early 1960's all he heard was people who agreed with him, and told him only what they thought he wanted to hear." Another staff person said, "Once you could get to Meany, you could be assured your ideas would receive a fair hearing. The hard part was getting past Virginia Tehas, who had her own ideas on what Meany should be doing. Offend her, and you were dead." And nepotism. Son-in-law Robert Mayer was the first relative to appear in the office, as a staff lawyer. Then came son-in-law Ernest Lee, who after leaving the Marine Corps as a major joined the international affairs department as a deputy to Jay Lovestone. And, finally, son-in-law John Lutz, in the union label department. An outsider once said jestingly to Meany: "When are your grandkids going on the payroll?" Meany didn't laugh.

Meany's private life was just that—private. Friends such as James Suffridge of the retail clerks union learned to keep away from union business on the golf course or at the card table. On weekends Meany's life revolved around his thirteen grandchildren ("Pop-Pop," they called him), and he kept a closet of toys in his Bethesda home for them. He read little. The newspapers, the news magazines, union journals, government economic reports—but no serious nonfiction or novels. (During the eighteen months I interviewed Meany I asked occasionally what he was reading: he mentioned only one book, Joseph Lash's *Eleanor and Franklin.*) One unexpected talent he discovered during the 1960's was art. The family gave him a dot-painting kit for Christmas one year, and after several by-the-numbers works he tried with a blank canvas. His style was starkly primitive—a sort of Bronxian Grandma Moses—and he filled his living room with landscapes and sea scenes. "When I was in apprentice school I had to do line drawings of plumbing layouts," he said. "Painting isn't that much different." Meany initialed his works "GM," and a visitor asked, "George, where did you get all these Grandma Moses paintings?" He beamed and said nothing. (But he did growl when newspaper writers marveled at how his "stubby plumber's fingers" could handle an art brush. "So why the hell do they watch my hands? Why don't they just talk about the painting and let it go at that?")

But painting is a solitary recreation, and George Meany was a solitary man—one isolated, through a combination of circumstances, from fresh ideas and fresh people, and at a time of the great emotional fervor of the 1960's.

But, from the new President, the young President, Jack Kennedy, a clutching for regenerated vigor through catharsis; the White House suddenly held not by a contemporary but by a son figure, and an Irish-Catholic son figure. A son figure who was tough and respectful—always Mr. Meany, never George—and sympathetic without being sycophantic, the blackball many ebullient Democratic politicians unknowingly cast against themselves through overeager panting infatuation with labor. Jack Kennedy. A President labor could love.

That it could do so was a miracle of Kennedyesque politics, for organized labor, and particularly the AFL-CIO, could have easily detested Jack Kennedy. The Kennedys, John and Robert, worked in tandem on the McClellan committee investigation of corruption in labor-management relations—a probe that Meany supported, for reasons of both conscience and common sense, but one that nonetheless before it ended made him shout private imprecations at the "Arkansas banker-hillbilly" running it and denounce the committee as "little more than a vehicle of reactionary elements seeking to discredit the American labor movement." The Landrum-Griffin Act, which was to late 1950's labor what Taft-Hartley was to late 1940's labor, easily could have been the Landrum-Kennedy Act, for much of it was the handiwork of the senior senator from Massachusetts. Yet his name went on no major legislation; he was frequently absent on key votes ("I think the Senate will pass a minimum wage increase if we can just get Sonny Boy back from the cricks and hollers long enough to report it out of his committee," Senator Joseph Clark complained of Kennedy in May 1960, when he was scouring West Virginia for primary votes); and he was economic light-years wealthier than the average AFL-CIO member.

From the day John Kennedy entered Congress he served on the House and Senate labor committees, successively, and his vote satisfied the litmus test of loyalty demanded by the AFL-CIO ("right" on twenty-five of twenty-six issues between 1947 and 1958, as measured by COPE).

Yet the Kennedy brothers, despite mutterings to the contrary from labor backbenchers, kept the McClellan committee focused on individuals and unions Meany recognized as corrupt. His major complaint, expressed late in the probe, was that it virtually ignored business culpability in labor-management corruption. Meany was satisfied that Kennedy had the perspective to avoid turning the probe into a witch hunt. "You've got to remember," one of Meany's inner circle said of the investigation, "that the McClellan committee provided the documentary evidence that enabled George to get rid of a hell of a lot of our black hats." Kennedy's lack of legislative achievement Meany dismissed as irrelevant, the result of Congress' lassitude under the Johnson-Rayburn leadership. Kennedy possessed an attribute Meany cherished in a legislator: he would listen. Meany had known Kennedy casually when he first came to the House, but formed no opinion of him until well into his Senate years.

"The outstanding impression I got of him then was that he wanted to know everything there was to know about a subject," Meany said. "Now, we didn't always agree with him. In fact, there were cases where we felt that he was taking a wrong approach and we sat down with him. After discussions we found, however, that he was very easy to get along with; that if you had a good case, if you had an argument against what he had in a bill, the minute he saw that argument he would go along with you."

The 1958 elections proved an uncomfortable success for the Democratic party, for they put labor's friends in near-control of Congress at a time when the nation clamored for labor-reform legislation. Seventy percent of the congressional candidates endorsed by the AFL-CIO won. The Senate shifted from a 50–46 Democratic margin to 64–34; the House, from 231–200 to 283–153. Concurrently, the McClellan hearings had generated public pressure for laws to curb future Hoffas and Becks. Would the Democrats be "responsible" and pass needed legislation? "America teeters on the precipice of a labor-bossed Congress," Postmaster General Arthur Summerfield told the National Association of Manufacturers a month after the election. "Americans will watch with fascinated interest these next two years as the minions of the rampaging political combine move to reward their masters." The Democratic leadership decided early in the session legislation would be passed; the only issue, in the minds of Senate Majority Leader Lyndon Johnson and House Speaker Sam Rayburn, was the exact content.

Kennedy's idea, based upon his experience with the McClellan committee, was to require unions to make basic financial data public so it would be available to rank-and-file members. The Hoffa-Beck manipulations of Teamster funds, for instance, could be found in union books, but buried so deeply they were inaccessible to anyone lacking subpoena power. So, too, were details of pension and welfare fund operations, reservoirs of cash frequently tapped by corrupt union officers. Kennedy began writing legislation in 1957, in his capacity as chairman of the subcommittee on legislation of the Senate Labor Committee. His first bill had cleared the Senate only to die in the House.

The AFL-CIO's reaction was ambivalent from the beginning, due to divisions in the executive council rather than any indecisiveness on the part of Meany. "There was some feeling that we should react to this idea of legislation as insulting to us as citizens," Meany said. "But the opinion . . . which finally prevailed was that we had to recognize the fact that . . . while we couldn't be considered responsible for everything they had done, these people [the union officers exposed as corrupt by the McClellan committee] were part of the trade union movement . . . and the best approach would be for us to say that we felt that this corruption should be eliminated." Meany abhorred government interference in internal union matters, but he recognized the limitations of the AFL-CIO's police power. Expulsion did not shake Hoffa's hold on the Teamsters. The AFL-CIO did not have the resources—or the desire—to conduct a continuing watch of affiliated unions. Hence Meany grudgingly decided that full reporting of union finances was necessary.

"But, on the other hand," he said, "while we were willing to cooperate in writing legislation that would stop corruption, or make it more difficult, we would not agree to legislation that would have the entire labor movement punished . . . because of the sins of a few."

Meany went into the session in a suspicious mood, wary of legislative trickery by Johnson and Rayburn. Political reality dictated that he attempt to maintain friendly relations with them, and he sent Andrew Biemiller to a convention of the Texas Federation of Labor to declare "how great Johnson and Rayburn were." (Biemiller was "greeted with complete and total silence from the thousand labor delegates," *The Texas Observer* reported; Texas labor had watched Johnson too long, and too closely, to be swayed by a messenger from Washington.) At a labor-sponsored unemployment rally in March Johnson pledged, "I won't let them pass any antilabor legislation." Let's go along with him, Meany told his staff, but let's also wait and see.

As hearings opened on the original Kennedy bill, Meany was in a sour, truculent mood, still unconvinced of the wisdom of "government meddling" in the affairs of private organizations. The cluster of academicians helping Kennedy did not impress Meany. When Kennedy suggested diplomatically that labor should be kindly disposed toward reform legislation written by its friends, labor's enemies being such a horrid alternative, Meany exclaimed, "My only comment, Senator, is 'God save us from our friends.' " Kennedy replied, "I say that too, Mr. Meany." But

Meany finally came around to support of the Kennedy bill—essentially, a requirement that unions file exhaustive financial data with the Secretary of Labor.

McClellan, however, felt the Kennedy bill unduly soft, and he offered a so-called "bill of rights" amendment intended to guarantee rank-and-file members full participation in union elections and other business. Much of McClellan's amendment rang with plausibility. Members would have the right to comment adversely on officers without facing expulsion for factionalism. They could caucus without being charged with dual unionism. Disciplinary actions had to be based upon written charges, with ample time for defense. But unions looked warily at two other sections. One permitted members to sue their unions or officers before exhausting internal remedies. Most union constitutions provided that members who did so could be expelled. Courts generally upheld such actions on the grounds that unions, as private organizations, should be encouraged to settle their internal disputes. The other section authorized the Attorney General or the Secretary of Labor to file suits on behalf of private plaintiffs whose rights were violated and to obtain injunctions.

Meany at first seemed amenable to accepting the bill of rights. He and Andrew Biemiller met with McClellan in February 1959 and said they did not "see anything so terrible about the statement of basic rights or other features of the bill," according to Alan K. MacAdams, who wrote an exhaustive academic study of Landrum-Griffin. Internal labor politics, however, quickly forced Meany to reverse himself. The Teamsters, who wanted no bill whatsoever, accused Meany of "going soft" and "finking for that goddamned McClellan" (according to intelligence picked up by AFL-CIO lobbyists). The bill of rights was also opposed, for varying reasons, by the United Steel Workers, the International Association of Machinists, and the Communications Workers of America, all large unions susceptible to internal strife. The USW's David J. McDonald, for instance, felt particularly vulnerable. A few years earlier, an unknown and ill-financed millhand named Donald C. Rarick won thirty-five percent of the vote in a race against him for the presidency. Meany had pushed the building trades unions to the limit of their patience with his insistence on settlement of the jurisdiction and merger questions. They had gone along with him, growling unhappily but moving on expulsion of the Teamsters. Now could he offend them once more, and again on autonomy? The "bill of rights," attractive on the surface, contained a vast potential for mischief. Meany believed unions must maintain internal discipline during collective bargaining and other crucial periods. A union "ought not to be required by law to allow company agents who have wormed their way into membership to have free access to the courts or administrative bodies for disruptive proceedings," Meany argued.

(John L. Lewis was more vivid in his opposition: "You cannot place a cast-iron chastity belt around the waist of sixteen million union members.")

Several days after McClellan thought he had Meany's agreement to the bill of rights, Monroe Freedman, McClellan's legal adviser, visited Thomas Harris, the AFL-CIO general counsel, to work out the details. Freedman found, to his surprise, there was "no common ground at all" between labor and McClellan. "This unexpected turn of events closed further discussion with the AFL-CIO," reported MacAdams.

Labor was so sure the bill of rights amendment would be defeated that its lobbyists relaxed—and promptly fell victim to what labor politician Joe Keenan, lobbying that year for the AFL-CIO, called a "double cross" by Lyndon Johnson. "Johnson was responsible for the amendment passing," Keenan said. "The night of the vote he let Jim Murray [a Nevada Democratic senator] go home, saying nothing else was going to happen. Paul Douglas was off in Canada, and Hubert Humphrey was out in California, campaigning. There was a motion to table, and Johnson could have delayed it until the next day—we would have had those three votes for sure—but he let it go that night, and labor lost." The vote was a tie, 45 to 45, forcing Vice-President Nixon, presiding over the Senate, to cast the deciding vote, upholding the bill of rights amendment. Some observers interpreted the Johnson ploy as intended to embarrass Nixon ("A lie!" Johnson said to *Newsweek* when asked about this theory). But Joe Keenan had a more direct explanation:

"Johnson didn't give a damn for labor in those days. The Texas State Federation of Labor backed his opponent [Coke Stevenson] in that famous eighty-seven-vote election in 1948, and he never forgot it. I was traveling with him once, in the 1964 campaign, and he got in his cups one night and started talking about it—talking about seeing one of the Texas fed officers coming out of a private club in Houston or Dallas, with his arm thrown around the shoulder of Stevenson. He never forgot that. Of course, he turned around all right after 1960, and I think he made a fine president. But he gave us trouble in the 1950's. Johnson and Rayburn were completely out of touch with the Democratic party. We never could get them to push the Democratic platform. It got worse and worse."

Whatever Johnson's motives, the maneuver dashed any chances he had of labor support for the Democratic presidential nomination. "Meany had never cared a damn for Johnson, he thought he was too much a schemer, a trickster," said Andrew J. Biemiller. "Landrum-Griffin finished him as far as we were concerned." The final Senate version passed 90 to 1. "Lying Down Johnson" someone at the AFL-CIO called Johnson. Meany laughed. A few weeks after the Landrum-Griffin passage, Johnson sent a dear-friend form letter to a constituent who had asked about the bill. "Throughout my public life," Johnson said, "I have favored strong, effective regulatory legislation to protect Americans from improper labor practices, having voted for the Vinson Bill, the Smith-Connally Act [both wartime antilabor bills], and the Taft-Hartley Act." Johnson stressed he had voted to override presidential vetoes "to make these measures law." To clinch his case he enclosed an analysis of the Landrum-Griffin Act written by Senator Barry Goldwater (Rep., Arizona).

In the House, meanwhile, both the Democratic leadership and pro-labor congressmen realized some legislation would be necessary ("There's got to be a bill," said Sam Rayburn) to appease public opinion. Meany, however, was in no mood to compromise, even though several friendly congressmen tried to steer him toward what Representative Richard Bolling (Dem., Missouri) called "as good a bill as possible." The Senate bill, already anathema to labor, picked up several smelly incrustations from Representative Phil Landrum, a Georgia Dixiecrat: bans on so-called "hot cargo" contracts, under which union members may refuse to work with nonunion material, and on organizational picketing, where a union pickets in hopes of inducing a majority of employees to sign cards.

Bolling and Representatives Lee Metcalf (Dem., Montana) and Morris Udall (Dem., Arizona) tried to bargain with Meany, telling him the mood of Congress was such that legislation was inevitable. "Cut your losses and get out!" Udall told him at one point. Meany exploded. "I would rather go down fighting with my friends than buy any such mess as is being put together over here," one of the congressmen in the meeting quoted Meany as saying. At another meeting in Rayburn's office the Speaker suggested Meany should "explain the facts of life" to the unions and tell them why the bill would pass. "I can't go back to my people and tell them a thing like that!" Meany exclaimed. "I can't support antilabor provisions."

Robert Kennedy, distressed at the possibility the AFL-CIO would block passage of any bill whatsoever, appeared on Jack Paar's "Tonight Show" and made a moving plea for public support of reform legislation. He provoked a flood of mail to congressmen. Two weeks later President Eisenhower also went on television to ask for passage of Landrum-Griffin. The National Association of Manufacturers, the United States Chamber of Commerce, and other business groups assisted Ike with a well-coordinated publicity campaign. When action moved to the House floor, labor rallied behind a substitute measure offered by Representative John Shelley (Dem., California), a Teamster who had formerly headed the central labor council in San Francisco. The Shelley bill lost decisively; Landrum-Griffin passed 229 to 201. In the conference committee Kennedy and other labor friends managed to soften some of Landrum's strictures. The construction and garment industries were removed from the ban on hot-cargo agreements. The building trades were permitted to enter into contracts with employers before any workers were hired. Kennedy retained the original curbs on racketeering, and Theodore Sorensen said that the "final version was on balance closer" to his bill than that produced by the House. Nonetheless, Kennedy "thought it politic that it not bear his name," according to Sorensen.

How did the AFL-CIO manage to maneuver itself into a position where it would not accept pragmatic advice even from its friends? Meany's attitude baffled Dick Bolling for years, but he finally concluded, "Mr. Meany has a lot of people to keep happy on his executive council. This was one instance where there was a true conflict of opinions, and he went with the majority." Alan MacAdams, in his academic study, felt that "an intelligent course of action would have been for the AFL-CIO to continue to differentiate itself clearly from the Teamsters union, the public whipping boy of 1959. . . . It appears that President Meany found himself under attack and thus became preoccupied with demonstrating that he was a good union man fighting the good fight against labor's enemies. Perhaps with a greater degree of planning he could have avoided being placed in this position." Meany also felt threatened, MacAdams concluded, because of "the inability of the labor movement to trust in the Democratic political leadership."

For Kennedy's purpose, the important point was that he emerged from Landrum-Griffin as a continued friend of the AFL-CIO. Kennedy recognized that he needed labor support to win the Democratic nomination; nonetheless, he was not impressed with all its leaders. According to Theodore Sorensen, "Some, he remarked to me on a trip, had grown flabby through long years in power and were out of touch or out of tune with their members. Some were sterile in their thinking and relied on subordinates and attorneys. . . ." But Kennedy carefully kept such reservations to himself. The negotiations over Landrum-Griffin brought him into increasingly frequent contact with Meany; in 1959 they began talking politics, Kennedy the supplicant, willing to stand on his record, unfailingly courteous to the older man. Kennedy, Meany said, was good at "keeping in touch—just calling me up to say hello." Campaigning in San Francisco in 1959, purposely coincident with the AFL-CIO convention, Kennedy joined Meany for a festive breakfast, and was warmly introduced to dozens of national and state labor leaders.

"I don't recall anybody in our setup making any speeches or passing any resolutions about John Kennedy, but by the time 1960 rolled around, I could say quite safely that he was practically the unanimous choice of our people," Meany said. "It just seemed to be one of those things that just sort of came about and everybody knew it." Although other prospects were "acceptable" to labor, "there just wasn't anyone that was against him at that time. I am . . . speaking of the top trade union leaders who sit on our council." Of the several hundred labor delegates to the Democratic convention, "practically all of them were for Senator Kennedy," Meany said. "I was among those who had been exposed to the Kennedy charm and wit and personality, and I was really enthusiastically for him."

In labor caucuses before the convention opened, Meany and Reuther firmed up support for Kennedy among the 250 labor people who were delegates, both because of genuine enthusiasm for his candidacy and for fear Lyndon Johnson would win the nomination in his last-day lunge. Johnson talked with Meany for some two hours before the convention opened, implying that since he was the "man who controlled labor legislation," labor should be either for him or neutral. Johnson ticked off a list of items on which he would guarantee fast action: an increased minimum wage, medical care, school construction. Meany responded that Johnson had a very nice package—so nice, in fact, that he should have passed it months before the convention, in view of his "control" of the Senate. Meany also said he did not like to be threatened, and that labor intended to stay with Kennedy. The atmosphere was testy by the time the meeting ended.

In talks with Kennedy before the nomination, Meany had suggested Senator Henry Jackson (Dem., Washington) as a running mate. But because of Jackson's relative youth and inexperience (he was forty-eight years old, and in his first term), Meany did not push too hard for him. Reuther, meanwhile, lobbied vigorously for Hubert Humphrey. But no one in labor was prepared for the shock of midafternoon July 14 when Kennedy began passing the word he wanted Johnson. "Mr. Meany," Kennedy told Meany by phone, "I've got to have him to do anything at all in the South, and it will balance the Catholic thing." Meany told Kennedy he thought Johnson's labor record was "horrible." He promised not to try to block the nomination with a floor fight, but added, "That doesn't mean I am going to act happy about it." Meany tried to convene a hasty AFL-CIO caucus to go on record in advance with a statement saying labor would prefer another nominee. Before he could bring everyone together, however, Johnson's nomination was a *fait accompli*. When the council finally caucused, in the evening, Meany asked for a policy statement condemning the Johnson selection. Reuther and Arthur Goldberg, attending as UAW counsel, advised otherwise. According to Jack Conway, Reuther's administrator, "Reuther did the job. . . . Walter prevailed in blocking the council from issuing a statement of condemnation. And all it required was two and a half hours of plain goddamn hard work. What he did, in effect, was beat Meany down. And once he'd beat Meany down, that council never does anything that Meany doesn't want to do."

The next afternoon Meany was relaxing at the Ambassador Hotel swimming pool when former New York governor Averell Harriman, an old friend, strolled up and said hopefully, "It's a great ticket." "I'm glad *you* think so," Meany replied without turning his head.

The AFL-CIO general board—composed of presidents of affiliated unions—had been scheduled to meet in Chicago on August 17 to consider endorsing candidates. Seething over the Johnson nomination, Meany postponed the meeting and did not discourage speculation that if the Republicans nominated Governor Nelson Rockefeller at their convention later in July, he would recommend that the AFL-CIO endorse him or remain neutral. He said labor intended to watch closely Johnson's performance in the postconvention congressional session. The Republican selection of Richard Nixon ended whatever thoughts Meany might have had about not endorsing Kennedy. When the executive council gathered in Chicago a few days before the general board meeting, Meany recommended endorsement of the Kennedy-Johnson ticket. He noted the "widespread feeling that the labor movement must take a stand in this coming election." Meany recognized that Johnson's selection displeased many labor people. Nonetheless, "We have never had 100 percent support for any one course, and it would be a mistake to expect it now. . . . We must give leadership to our membership." A. Philip Randolph of the Brotherhood of Sleeping Car Porters did not want to endorse either Kennedy or Nixon, saying neither party platform went far enough on civil rights. He was talked down by a solid council majority, ranging the political spectrum from Reuther and Jim Carey to Peter Schoemann of the plumbers union.

Meany made radio broadcasts for Kennedy and appeared at a score of labor meetings in the fall. More important than oratory was quiet work performed by the AFL-CIO months before the election: COPE ran voter registration drives in fourteen states. Kennedy won all but two of them. The AFL-CIO created and financed a front group called "Senior Citizens for Kennedy," which brought Medicare supporters into the campaign; it aimed at nominally Republican old folks who were told a Kennedy victory could mean free medical care.

And no one was happier at the election results than Mrs. Meany. She had worn her Kennedy bonnet home from the convention, Meany recollected. "She took this hat and put it in a paper bag and put it in the attic and said, 'I'm going to have that for the convention in 1964.' I think she became more political at that time than at any time in her life."

* * *

"Labor and management will both be making a mistake if they believe that the Kennedy Administration is going to be prolabor," Secretary of Labor Arthur J. Goldberg warned early in 1961. Indeed, through selective use of evidence, one could build a record that Kennedy was antilabor. His wage-price guidelines of 3.2 percent—set in hopes of preventing a rejuvenated economy from touching off inflation—imposed a tacit limitation on collective bargaining. Kennedy jawboned unions repeatedly to be modest in their bargaining demands. He told the 1961 AFL-CIO convention, for instance, that "those of you who are in the areas of wage negotiations recognize the desirability of . . . maintaining stable prices." Kennedy intervened (in the person of Goldberg) in labor-management disputes ("ranging from toilets at General Motors to musicians at the Metropolitan Opera," in Theodore Sorensen's words) with unprecedented vigor and frequency. Goldberg direly forecast that "labor won't tolerate politicians meddling in negotiations"; Kennedy ignored him. Kennedy flatly opposed the shorter work week, which Meany wanted. Kennedy attacked the Flight Engineers Union by name at a press conference; a commission he appointed voided the engineers' classic featherbedding requirement for four men, rather than the necessary three, in the cockpits of airline jets. And Kennedy reluctantly but determinedly persuaded Congress to pass the first compulsory arbitration law in the nation's peacetime history when protracted rail negotiations failed in 1963.

Any of these actions would have brought labor crashing down upon a Republican President with pained oratory and threats of political reprisal. Labor tolerated, even applauded, Kennedy's intervention in union-management relations because its leaders trusted him. The rapport was political and emotional. Labor accepted the thrust of Kennedy's domestic programs—stimulating the economy, increasing social benefits, checking inflation—as intrinsically proworker. Further, Kennedy was equally firm with business. In 1962 the United Steel Workers accepted a contract with no general pay increase and boosts of less than three percent in fringe benefits as a result of strong presidential pressures to hold down inflation. When United States Steel attempted a price increase a few days later, Kennedy threw the considerable weight of his office into the fray and forced a backdown. Wage increases from 1961 to 1963 were the lowest of any comparable period since V-J Day; so, too, however, were working days lost because of strikes (despite the widely publicized rail, airline, and missile base construction controversies). With almost three million more persons on the work rolls in 1963 than in 1961, average and total national income soared.

But more important, labor felt at home in the White House for the first time since the New Deal. When the President wished to talk with

Meany, he would telephone directly, not through a secretary. Kennedy invited Meany to the White House for social fetes and private tête-à-têtes; he put Meany on the incorporating board of the Communications Satellite Corporation, and he followed his advice on most labor appointees throughout the government. At Meany's suggestion, Kennedy created a twenty-one-member Presidential Advisory Committee on Labor-Management Policy, tripartite, with representatives from labor, management, and the public. Kennedy saw the committee as an "equalizer" that would gather an informed consensus on economic matters without labeling his Administration either probusiness or prolabor. At the committee's initial meeting, in the Cabinet Room on March 21, Kennedy said its purpose "is to give direction to the general movement of wages and prices so that the general welfare of this country can be served." In the past, he said, "general exhortations from the White House" had not worked.

On the highest appointment open to labor influence, that of a Secretary of Labor, Kennedy did not heed Meany. The month after the election Meany went to Kennedy's Georgetown residence with a list of five men, all elected union officials, of the "type he considered appropriate" for the job. Included were Joseph Keenan, now secretary-treasurer of the International Brotherhood of Electrical Workers; George Harrison of the railway clerks; Joseph Beirne of the communication workers; James Suffridge of the retail clerks; and A. J. Hayes of the machinists. Kennedy declined. He told Meany that the public would not tolerate a professional unionist administering the Landrum-Griffin Act, which labor had fought so vigorously. He said he intended to choose Arthur J. Goldberg, now general counsel of the United Steel Workers. Goldberg was close to the unions, but not *of* the unions, and hence should be an acceptable compromise.

The choice did not please Meany. He considered Goldberg egocentric and somewhat of a bore, and overly enraptured with Walter Reuther, his long-time friend. For these reasons and others, Meany had refused to make Goldberg general counsel of the AFL-CIO after the merger, although Goldberg asked for the job ("We got Albert Woll; why should we go to this other feller?" Meany asked). Some of Goldberg's disappointed comments filtered back to Meany and irritated him. But he told Kennedy, if Goldberg is your man, we won't object; the building tradesmen don't particularly like him, but I'll see to it they don't make any opposing statements. (When Kennedy appointed Goldberg to the Supreme Court in 1962, Meany did not object to the White House's choice of W. Willard Wirtz as successor. Wirtz, a member of Adlai Stevenson's old law firm, had served briefly on the War Labor Board as a public member and was Goldberg's undersecretary.)

Intellectually, Kennedy felt more rapport with Walter Reuther, but he took care to maintain friendly relations with both men. For Reuther, a long hour on the beach with Jacqueline at Hyannis Port, the week after her husband's nomination; for Meany, an advance briefing on the Cuban missile crisis, so that the voice of organized labor would support the Administration. When a choice had to be made, Kennedy deferred to Meany's rank. Meany blackballed Reuther's appointment as a member of the United States delegation to the United Nations because the request did not come through the AFL-CIO. And he would not clear the appointment of Reuther's close personal aide, Jack Conway, as Undersecretary of Labor to Willard Wirtz—again, because Reuther did not check with the AFL-CIO before recommending Conway. "If Walter had spent five minutes on the telephone," Meany told Reuther biographers Frank Cormier and William Eaton, "Conway could have become undersecretary."

Labor reciprocated Kennedy's hospitality by amassing grass-roots support for much of his domestic program. The most pressing problem, when the Administration began, was unemployment, with 5½ million persons out of jobs, generally attributed to the slow (three percent) rate of economic growth during the last three years of the Eisenhower Administration. The AFL-CIO organized a series of regional conferences in early 1961 to demonstrate citizen concern for Kennedy measures that would bring immediate relief to the jobless: a temporary thirteen-week supplement to unemployment benefits, costing $800 million; aid for children of unemployed workers, $200 million; aid to distressed regions, through the Area Redevelopment Act, $400 million to one thousand counties; increased Social Security payment to encourage early retirement; increased minimum wages and broadened coverage, $175 million; emergency relief to feed-grain farmers; and a homebuilding and slum-clearance program, an estimated 420,000 jobs for construction workers. With the aid of labor lobbyists, each of these seven measures was passed and signed into law by the end of June, 161 days after Kennedy proposed them in his first State of the Union message. For his part, Meany muted anticipated labor criticisms when Kennedy put through an investment tax credit for business, something the President convinced him was necessary to stimulate the economy.

One Kennedy gesture that particularly delighted Meany was an invitation to travel with the President during his 1963 trip to Berlin and Ireland. Meany learned of Kennedy's plans to visit Berlin from the newspapers. During a White House visit, "I said to him casually, 'Say, I'm going to be in Berlin the same day you are. I'll be at the ILO meeting and I'll have to go up there from Geneva.' " Meany told Kennedy he would speak to German building tradesmen and added, "I'm quite sure that they would like for you to talk to them." Kennedy asked Meany to meet him in Wiesbaden and fly to Berlin on Air Force One, and have the German union send him an invitation. Meany relayed the message to the Germans. "About three days later they wired me that they had got a very prompt reply which said the President couldn't possibly be there. He couldn't possibly fit it into his schedule and so forth. So the next time I was over to the White House I mentioned this to the President and he said, 'Well, that's funny. I didn't even see the invitation.' Which, of course, we understood. 'I'll find ten minutes or so to go there,' he said to me."

Meany met Kennedy in Wiesbaden as planned, attended a civic reception with him, and then flew on to Berlin. The building workers were meeting about 150 yards from Brandenburg Gate, in a hall built with donations from the Benjamin Franklin Society of the United States. "On the entrance wall of this building was a saying by Franklin that struck me very forcibly," Meany said. "The gist of it was that Franklin said he hoped that he could see a world where a philosopher could go any place in the world and find freedom and therefore could say, 'This is my home. This is where I belong, where freedom is.'

"Well, anyway, before the President got there I had taken a little slip of paper and copied this quotation from the wall and gave it to the President as we were walking in. He stuck it in his pocket; I don't think he looked at it again. But when he opened his address he quoted from it. It was the most effective talk I think I ever heard on the question of freedom. And he related it to workers—to workers' unions—the fact that where workers could get together and form unions and use the unions to improve their conditions, that this was one of the essentials of freedom."

Meany continued with the presidential entourage to the Berlin Wall, where Kennedy made his famed *"Ich bin ein Berliner"* speech, and then on to Ireland. Meany beamed as Kennedy introduced him to Irish villagers as "another Irishman who made good in America"—"a gesture not forgotten by Meany back in Washington," as Theodore Sorensen recorded.

Meany and American labor shared another problem with the Kennedy Administration even more painful than the economy—the civil rights revolution. Labor's record in discrimination the first half of the century reflected the bigotries and race hatreds, covert and overt, of all of American society. Although the old AFL had an antidiscrimination clause in its constitution, unions flouted it without penalty or censure. When an Urban League officer asked the AFL in 1944 to create a "committee on minority group programs" to "examine thoroughly all problems of discrimination," William Green rejected the idea as "impractical and inadvisable." As late as 1947 the AFL would not support a fair employment practices commission. The convention resolved, "It is our belief that, while protection of nondiscriminatory employment is needed, especially during the difficult years that lie ahead, compulsory regulation of free and voluntary associations of workers is inimical to the basic right of freedom of association. Government activities interfering in the self-government of labor organizations must not be permitted." "When I became secretary of the American Federation of Labor on January 1, 1940," Meany said, "there were twenty-three national unions of the AFL that had a color bar in their constitution. This was a way of life. For instance, the machinists had a color bar, and you ask, Well, why? . . . I asked a machinist one time, and he said, 'Well, the best explanation I can give you is that our union was founded in a railroad round-house in Atlanta, Georgia, in the year 1869 by ten men. I can't give you any better explanation than that.' "

In citing labor's early record Meany did not apologize for it. "There was a built-in prejudice, built-in discrimination in this whole nation for the last hundred years. When I came to Washington thirty years ago, no Negro would walk into a downtown Washington hotel, no Negro could walk into a downtown Washington movie theater. . . . This was just thirty years ago, and this was at a time when Franklin Roosevelt had been president eight years—this was the seat and the model for discrimination against the blacks' rights in this city. This pattern extended all over the country, not just in the South."

Meany did not accept segregation as right or necessary. Local 463 of the plumbers union, when he was an apprentice, barred blacks from membership—and most other persons as well. "It wasn't so much that we discriminated against Negroes. Hell, we played ball with them in the semipro leagues, and got along fine. But we kept most everybody out of the union. We wouldn't even take a transfer card from a plumber who belonged to a Jersey local." Local 463's territory extended into Harlem, which Meany said "had a tremendous Negro population" during the 1920's, when he worked as a business agent. Nonetheless blacks did not waste their time trying for a plumbers' card. "We never had a Negro applicant," Meany said. "Oh, there were Negro shops, but they were in a class with other nonunion shops. We didn't bother them and they didn't bother us." Although Meany's trade was segregated, the construction projects where he worked were not. "I never worked on a building as a boy where there weren't plenty of Negroes, but they were not in my trade . . . they were in the plasterers, the bricklayers, the laborers." Meany's attitude toward race in the years before he was AFL president paralleled that of many Americans: prejudice was a subject that seldom crossed his mind; when it did, he satisfied his own conscience, and did not actively seek to change the attitudes of other persons. And on occasion he did more.

In May 1946 Meany was keynote speaker at an AFL organizing conference in Asheville, North Carolina, attended by officers of scores of Southern state and local labor councils. AFL and CIO unions were competing to organize textile and other workers, and Meany spent most of the 7,000-word speech castigating "devoted followers of Moscow" on the CIO executive board. Then he interjected two paragraphs:

> Let there be no pussyfooting on the race issue. The American Federation of Labor is determined to bring into the fold of real free trade unionism all American workers of the South—white and black, gentile and Jew, Protestant and Catholic. The American Federation of Labor has consistently opposed racial and religious prejudice in all its conventions for long years past. It stands on the same solid convictions today—in the South, in the North, and in every other area of our country.
>
> Our federation gave its complete and full support to a war which was waged victoriously to eliminate the theory of superiority of one race over another. It stands today on the same principles and ideals —principles and ideals for which it was opposed to Hitler and his vicious racial theories from the very beginning.

At an AFL convention in the mid-1940's in Houston, Meany received a distressed phone call from A. Philip Randolph, president of the Brotherhood of Sleeping Car Porters. Randolph said he and a vice-president, Milton P. Webster, could not even get into the headquarters at Rice Hotel to obtain their convention credentials. "The functionaries of the Rice Hotel are not easy to convince that a colored gentleman has even a right to make use of the front entrance to the hotel, to say nothing of entering upon the sacred precincts of the passenger elevators," Randolph said. Meany went downstairs, marched Randolph and Webster into the manager's office, and told him, "These two gentlemen are here as members of the American Federation of Labor. They are going to attend our convention, and stay in the Rice Hotel, or else the convention is pulling out of the Rice Hotel, beginning about two minutes from now. The choice is yours. Now, what do you say?" The management apologized and yielded. (But even though Randolph, Webster, and other black delegates gained admittance, some functions remained segregated. Negroes were shunted off to a special "colored entertainment committee." When delegates visited the San Jacinto Battlefield, "the colored delegates were escorted into the cave near the kitchen to partake of their entertainment"; at a rodeo, the blacks had a separate seating section.)

Randolph has been called "the conscience of the AFL" on racial matters. The son of a rural Florida Methodist minister, Randolph came to New York as a teen-ager, fell under the oratorical spell of Eugene V. Debs, embraced socialism, and launched veritably a one-man crusade against segregation and discrimination. A rangy, dignified man well over six feet tall, Randolph was a messianic orator (journalist John Herling once compared his basso-profundo voice to that of "De Lawd" in the play *Green Pastures*). He was also a patient organizer. In succession, in his youth, Randolph tried to start unions of elevator operators, maintenance men, and waiters on a pleasure boat. Each time he was fired. Finally, sleeping car porters employed by the Pullman Company sought him out. The struggle to win recognition took twelve years; in 1937 the railroads yielded and signed a contract that soon quadrupled the porters' wages. The AFL had given Randolph token financial help and took his all-black union into membership. But his major fights he waged on his own.

Soon after Pearl Harbor, Randolph told President Roosevelt that unless the government desegregated defense plants, he would lead a march of 100,000 Negroes on Washington to protest. Several intermediaries, including Mayor Fiorello La Guardia and Eleanor Roosevelt, sought to dissuade him. Randolph persisted, even in the face of personal pleas from the President. Roosevelt issued an executive order commanding war manufacturers to drop color barriers in their hiring. When the war ended, Randolph heard scores of returning black veterans complain of segregation in the armed forces. Randolph told President Truman he intended to tell young Negroes not to accept service in a segregated army. Truman ordered the military integrated.

But within the AFL Randolph was a lonely, unheeded figure. From his very first convention, in 1935, he asked for sanctions against international unions that did not admit colored members. Citing autonomy, the AFL refused to act. At times Randolph was abused. At the 1941 convention, venerable old John Frey attacked Randolph for being so bold as to document refusal of jobs to Negro painters at army bases and other defense installations. Randolph "has an advantage over every other delegate who is present," Frey declared. "He is the only one who has had the full advantage of an education in Harvard University.* He studied logic, he studied philosophy, he studied ethics, he studied the humanities and human nature as well. . . ." A delegate from the newsboys union interrupted. "Now, Mr. Chairman, if the colored boy went to college, that is no crime. I am only sorry I never had the opportunity." For years the opening words of a Randolph speech were a signal for delegates to begin a mass exodus from the convention floor to the nearest bar; seldom

---

* Wrong. Randolph studied at Cookman Institute, a Methodist school in Jacksonville, Florida, and took night courses at the City College of New York.

could he be heard over the hubbub of conversations. Benjamin F. Mc-Laurin, his long-time associate in the Brotherhood of Sleeping Car Porters, said, "Over the years there was an understanding on the part of our white friends in the federation that let Randolph talk and raise all the hell he wanted to raise. But after he got through talking, nobody would make a motion, and so it was just words in the convention record." On one occasion "a friend made the mistake of putting a motion in support of one of Randolph's resolutions. Well, this was not supposed to be done, and he caught a lot of hell as a result."

During the merger negotiations the AFL and the CIO put strong anti-discrimination language into the new constitution. A stated objective of the federation was "to encourage all workers without regard to race, creed, color, national origin or ancestry to share equally in the full benefits of union organization." It provided that "all workers whatever their race, color, creed, or national origin are entitled to share in the full benefits of trade union organization." It created a standing committee on civil rights (something the AFL had not had previously), "vested with the duty and responsibility to assist the executive council to bring about at the earliest possible date the effective implementation of the principle stated in the constitution of non-discrimination. . . ."

Explaining the antidiscrimination provisions to the Urban League in Milwaukee in September 1955, Meany declared: "This language is not inserted for lip service. . . . We want to make our movement free and to keep it free of any vestige of intolerance or discrimination, *and we propose to do it in the shortest possible time.*"

The strong language of the constitution, and AFL statements applauding the U.S. Supreme Court's 1954 ruling on school desegregation, "stymied and thwarted" organizing in the South for years. The school statement alone prompted some 10,000 letters to Meany from angry Southerners. "Every one of those letters had the same tone: 'We're Southerners, and we're going to stay Southerners, and if we can't stay Southerners, we are not going to stay in the trade union movement.'

"We never backed down. We answered, very patiently, every one of these letters. We sent people down there. Our main argument was, 'Look around. Find out who is heading up the white citizens' council. See if you don't find some familiar faces there—the same people who are on local boards of trades, the same people who are keeping unions out of those towns.' Sure enough, that's what they found—the same people who were setting up open shop and company union towns."

How, then, to implement the constitutional requirement on AFL-CIO unions and locals that remained segregated? Randolph wanted strict, immediate enforcement—unions that did not abide by the constitution should not be admitted to the AFL-CIO; those already in should comply or face expulsion. Violating the discrimination provisions was as grave as breaching the rules on corruption, Randolph said. He first raised the question in the executive council in August 1956 during debate on whether the Brotherhood of Locomotive Firemen and Engineers should be admitted prior to dropping of a color bar in its constitution. Randolph had fought this union for years. So long as locomotives were fired by coal, whites did not object to Negroes doing the sweltering, backbreaking fireman's work. Whites and Negroes formed engineer-firemen teams. The advent of the automatic coal stoker, and then the Diesel engine, made the fireman's job a featherbedding sinecure, whereupon the "brotherhood" turned on the blacks and staged "hate strikes" to force them from their jobs. Rednecks ambushed trains with shotguns and high-powered rifles, literally shooting black firemen—"Zulus," the Brotherhood called them—from locomotive cabs. During one four-year period in the 1930's at least ten Negro firemen were killed and twenty wounded in the Lower Mississippi Valley alone. In 1940 the Brotherhood coerced twenty-one Southern railroads to stop hiring blacks and to fire those already working (some with twenty years' seniority). Randolph's car porters union financed court suits that brought damage awards to the fired black firemen, and the Supreme Court in 1944 reversed the hiring ban. But when the firemen's brotherhood came before the AFL-CIO, seeking admittance, it remained segregated. "In good conscience," Randolph said, he could not vote for them. Benjamin F. McLaurin, Randolph's associate in the sleeping car porters, noted, "Since they were anxious to get in, here was an opportunity to get them to take the color bars out."

"Do you want to get rid of the color bar?" Meany asked.

"Yes, I do," Randolph said.

"Which is the best way to get rid of the color bar?" Meany demanded. "Do you want to do something for these people who are at a disadvantage because of the color bar, or do you want to raise this high moral flag? And if you do, why did you come into the AFL when that was loaded with people who had the color bar?" Meany was confident he could persuade the firemen to drop their color bar once they were in the AFL-CIO. "If you want to get rid of the color bar," he told Randolph, "this is the way to do it; otherwise, you won't."

Walter Reuther agreed with Meany. "Principle, in a vacuum, has no real value in the world in which you live." Meany, he said, "will have contact with them, can talk to them and persuade them." Reuther asked that Randolph not take the dispute outside the secrecy of the executive council. "It would be a very sad thing if the appearance was given that the executive council isolated you, and that we were doing the expedient thing, and you were defending moral principle." The council voted that the firemen be admitted, the color bar intact.

In Randolph's opinion, the AFL-CIO was unacceptably slow in going after color barriers, especially in the building trades. In isolated cases Meany applied the moral authority—and practical muscle—of his office against individual unions. One target was the International Union of Electrical Workers local in Washington, which came under heavy attack for using all-white work forces on federally financed projects in the heart of black ghettoes. "The federal government was raising cain about it," said Charles Zimmerman, the ILGWU vice-president who headed the AFL-CIO's civil rights committee at the time. Meany intervened, working through an Administration civil rights group chaired by Vice-President Nixon. The president of the union "was a very nice guy, but he wasn't going to have any Negroes in his union," said Meany. "And the electrical contractors in this town weren't going to have any Negroes. They defied the international union." According to Zimmerman, Meany "laid down the rule. He said the employers should hire black workers, nonunion or not. 'If the electricians strike, we will order the building trades workers to cross the picket lines. The hell with what the local president says; if he won't follow the law, we want nothing to do with him.' Meany carried it off, too. The union started taking black members —although there was absolutely not a word of publicity about what had happened."

But the electrical workers case was isolated. The Urban League, during a thirty-two-city survey in 1957, found few blacks in the skilled building trades unions. In Denver the operating engineers had not a single black, although an officer said Negroes would be admitted "if employers agree to hire them." Of 5,000 Denver carpenters, only five were black. There were no black electricians. Many unions would not accept transfer cards from blacks who belonged to out-of-town locals.

With the civil rights revolution increasing in intensity, Randolph's laments to AFL-CIO conventions began to take on new significance. How long must we rely upon gradualism and "education"? he asked Meany time and again. Had not the time come for the AFL-CIO to take affirmative action to cleanse its affiliates of racism?

Meany's capacity for accepting criticism was limited—especially on issues where he felt he was doing the right thing. On paper (though not in reality) the AFL-CIO's record was good: the constitution forbade discrimination; in time all unions would abide by it. Further, many civil rights groups accepted the rationale of Meany's gradualistic approach; the NAACP's Legal Defense and Educational Fund, for instance, gave him its Philip Murray Award in 1957 for his work against discrimination. Finally, at the 1959 AFL-CIO convention, after three confrontations with Randolph in a single day, Meany's patience snapped.

First, Randolph objected to readmitting the International Longshoremen's Association to AFL-CIO membership. Even though the ILA had purged corrupt elements, Randolph said, it remained a racist union in which blacks and Puerto Ricans received onerous work assignments. There were no minority-group workers among the 2,218 port watchmen or the 408 pier superintendents; when jobs were scarce, whites received first preference. Randolph recommended putting the ILA on probation until the next convention.

Retorting, Meany noted that Randolph was on the executive council and had attended three meetings where ILA reaffiliation was discussed. "That committee worked for eight months," Meany said. "Phil Randolph never came to that committee with any complaints. He never came to me with any complaints. . . . And to come at this late date, when he has an audience, and come up with this material, I just don't think is playing the game." Meany felt "it is time he [Randolph] joined the organized labor movement and became part and parcel of the AFL-CIO." He looked down at Randolph, still standing at a floor microphone: "Did you find out about it yesterday, Phil?"

"No," replied Randolph.

"All right," Meany snapped, "why discriminate against the members of the council . . . and withhold the information from them?" The convention voted overwhelmingly to readmit the ILA without any preconditions.

A few moments later Randolph was up again, with a resolution asking the expulsion of the firemen and trainmen unions within six months unless they dropped the color bars from their constitutions. Meany said he did not want a time limit; that the executive council was working on the problem—"as Phil Randolph well knows"—and would solve it. Officers of the two unions said the bars would be dropped at their next conventions.

Later in the afternoon Randolph attacked again, this time calling for a ban on all-black locals. Harry Bates of the bricklayers union said he would ignore such a ban even if one was enacted, because the locals "were long established" and eliminating them would violate union autonomy. Randolph persisted, asking, "What justification is there for Jim Crow locals?"

Meany had stood at the podium, listening to Randolph. Suddenly his face flushed and his shoulders tensed, and his angry voice crackled across the convention hall. "Who the hell appointed you the guardian of all the Negroes in America?" he shouted.

Stunned, Randolph stared up at Meany. "Brother President," he cried, "Brother President, let's not get emotional." Meany quickly brought himself under control and sat down, but the damage was done: he had lost his temper in public.

Benjamin McLaurin, Randolph's colleague, felt that Meany's outburst helped dramatize union discrimination, but not "because the newspapers had any love for the problems of the Negro worker. The truth of the matter is, they didn't have too much faith in the federation's program, and here was an opportunity to give the trade union movement a black eye." Randolph had been "making the same kind of rip-roaring speeches, presenting the same kind of solid resolutions," for thirty years. McLaurin continued, "If Meany hadn't made that statement, very few people would have known that Philip Randolph was at the convention." (Charles Zimmerman of the ILGWU dissented from the newspaper consensus that Meany had "insulted" Randolph. "Meany talked to him like an equal, one plumber to another," Zimmerman said. "If he had looked at Randolph as a 'Negro' and softened his words, that would have been racial. No, Meany looked at Randolph and saw a fellow unionist. Randolph understood that, too.")

Randolph left the convention in a slow burn. He did not question Meany's good faith in ending union discrimination. But he decided extraordinary pressures were needed to prod the AFL-CIO along. After several months' organizational work he announced the start of the Negro American Labor Council (NALC), and called a founding convention in Detroit in June 1960. The meeting attracted some one thousand black delegates from AFL-CIO and independent unions, including the Teamsters and United Mine Workers, chiefly lower-echelon officers and staff. Randolph wanted to make NALC a political force, not a separate labor organization. He outlined its purposes:

> We resent Jim Crow locals. We deplore the freezeout against Negroes in labor apprenticeship and training programs; we deplore the lack of upgrading and promotional opportunities for Negroes; we repudiate the lockout against Negroes by some unions. We, above all, reject tokenism, the thin veneer of acceptance masking as democracy.

In speeches and articles Randolph attacked racism in AFL-CIO unions, relying heavily upon Urban League data and studies by Herbert Hill, an intense young white lawyer who worked as a consultant for Representative Adam Clayton Powell (Dem., New York) and also as labor secretary for the National Association for the Advancement of Colored People.

Randolph and Meany stormed at one another in executive council meetings through 1961. In February Randolph called civil rights "germane to the future moral strength of the AFL-CIO." He complained the federation had "given greater urgency to fighting communism, corruption, and racketeering and completing the merger" than it had to civil rights. He felt the civil rights department was inadequate because "of its limited personnel." He did not understand criticisms, by Meany and others, of the Negro American Labor Council, comparing it with the Jewish Labor Committee, the Italian Chamber of Unions, and the Association of Catholic Trade Unionists, all respected labor groups. And Randolph asserted blacks had legitimate grievances: although Negroes comprised only ten percent of the U.S. work force, they represented twenty percent of the jobless. Less than one and a half percent of the apprentices in the building trades were black; hiring showed "no statistical movement whatsoever." Randolph proposed a sixteen-point program, ranging from a strong statement by Meany ("thereby giving hope and faith to the victims of discrimination") to "basic integration of Negroes in all apprenticeship programs and elimination of the policy and practice in many unions of accepting as apprentices only sons of present local union members." He asked for the appointment of a black as head of the civil rights department; for "a positive target date within the next six months for the desegregation of all racially segregated international and local unions"; and for a six-month limit for local unions to "discontinue their refusal to accept Negroes into their unions."

Meany responded by taking the offensive. He accused Randolph and the NALC of "harassing our affiliates" with public statements, many of them inaccurate. He referred specifically to a press release, in Randolph's name, accusing the International Molders and Foundry Workers Union of keeping Negroes from executive offices. Meany called in President William Lazzerini for rebuttal. Lazzerini said the molders' first constitution, written in 1859, had a nondiscrimination clause; that 27.8 percent of the membership was black, including eighty percent of a Chicago local, all officers of which were black; that the New York local was fifty percent black, with Negroes on the executive board; that three of the eleven overseers of the apprenticeship program were black. Meany refused to accede to any of Randolph's demands.

Randolph's attack so angered Charles Zimmerman that he resigned as chairman of the AFL-CIO's civil rights committee. Meany, too, was bitter, especially about the Negro American Labor Council. "We want to cooperate with them," he said, "but we just can't cooperate on the basis of broadside charges made on us and our affiliates without any hearings or any attempts to find out whether there's another side to the story. I hope Phil Randolph takes these words to heart." The council, in a formal resolution, urged teeth be put into government laws against discrimination in hiring, with enforcement to be directed against employers as well as unions. Kennedy did so several weeks later, acting through an executive order rather than waiting for legislation. He created the President's Committee on Equal Employment Opportunities, with Vice-

President Johnson as chairman. The commission was given authority to cancel government contracts if firms discriminated in hiring.

Beaten down twice by Meany, Randolph tried again, at the June executive council meeting. This time he protested plans of the Virginia AFL-CIO to hold a segregated convention. Letters of invitation listed separate facilities for black and white delegates:

> We are pleased to note . . . that the management of the Golden Triangle [restaurant] has promised to serve luncheon to our Negro delegates in a "private" dining room the three days of our convention. . . . The dance of the white delegates will be held in the Golden Triangle. Negro delegates will dance in the new and spacious air-conditioned hall of Longshoremen's Local 1248.

Randolph denounced the "god of white supremacy" and demanded that Meany tell the Virginia officers that if they proceeded with the segregated convention, their charter would be lifted. He wanted all Southern AFL-CIO councils, state and local, to end segregation within six months. "It is a matter of common knowledge that every one of the AFL-CIO state bodies in the South openly violates the constitution of the AFL-CIO by practicing discrimination in the housing and entertainment of Negro delegates," he said. Ending discrimination "will require positive, uncompromising, massive systematic and consistent attacks against all forms of race bias by the united high command of the AFL-CIO. And if the AFL-CIO loses this battle, it will lose the fight to organize the South."

Boris Shishkin, now director of the AFL-CIO civil rights department, defended the Virginia officers. He quoted the state president, Harold Boyd, as saying the arrangements were "the best that could be worked out under conditions prevailing in Virginia." Shishkin noted Boyd was chairman of the AFL-CIO Southern advisory committee on civil rights. Shishkin credited him with doing an "outstanding job . . . in furthering nondiscrimination."

The council ignored Randolph's demands for action against the state organizations. But he left with it for study a blockbuster which Meany well knew could blow the AFL-CIO into public turmoil over the race issue: a seventy-page memorandum detailing AFL-CIO "tokenism in civil rights," and charging a "crisis of confidence between the leaders of Negroes and labor." The memorandum demanded that the AFL-CIO and its affiliates use their existing authority to end segregation. It asked two conferences: a "summit" between Meany and blacks to map joint projects in such fields as voter registration, and a larger meeting to "give the leadership of the AFL-CIO the truth about the angry mood of Negro trade unionists, and Negro workers generally."

Meany realized he had lost the initiative to Randolph. He thoroughly disagreed with the charges in the report, but he was unwilling to have Randolph spread it before an AFL-CIO convention. Hence he moved deftly to cut the ground from under Randolph in a way that satisfied Randolph's demands, but also made Randolph the loser in terms of AFL-CIO politics.

First, Meany announced an entire day of the AFL-CIO convention would be turned over to discussion of civil rights matters, led by the Rev. Martin Luther King, Jr., and Randolph. The emphasis Meany gave the announcement signaled to AFL-CIO unions that he was serious about civil rights and that he wanted everyone to be on their best behavior. Next, Meany had the executive council fashion a club he could hold over Randolph's head to ensure he would not cause the AFL-CIO any embarrassment at the convention. On the eve of the convention a special three-man council subcommittee brought in a report resoundingly rebutting Randolph's "tokenism" memorandum and recommending that he be censured for his public castigations of the AFL-CIO. Boris Shishkin wrote the report—in effect, a report on the effectiveness of his own work. But the committee signing it had special moral authority because it included Jacob Potofsky of the Amalgamated Clothing Workers, one of labor's more renowned civil libertarians. The report offered pragmatic arguments against setting hard time limits for unions to comply with the AFL-CIO constitution:

> Mr. Randolph would have the AFL-CIO carry on its antidiscrimination program as a punitive program. But unlike the government which can enforce its laws through court-imposed penalties, a voluntary federation, such as the AFL-CIO, has only one form of punishment at hand to apply to an erring affiliate—namely, expulsion from its ranks.
>
> It is obvious, of course, that expulsion, as such, does not cure the offending practices. Put outside the ranks of the federation, the offending organization is left free to carry on its discriminatory practices—probably more stubbornly than ever. And, what is most important, once outside the federation, the membership of such an organization is no longer accessible to corrective influences from the parent body through education and persuasion.

The committee also attacked Randolph for remaining silent when critics made "false charges and unwarranted attacks" on the AFL-CIO. "Mr. Randolph did not choose to lift a finger against this deliberate defamation of the organized labor movement," the report said. "Actually, time and again he made statements and public comments derogating the AFL-CIO's positive drive for civil rights, belittling its advances and accomplishments and alienating the loyalty and devotion to the trade union movement among those dedicated to the cause of civil rights.

"The major share of the responsibility for the 'gap' that has developed between organized labor and the Negro community therefore falls upon Mr. Randolph himself."

Randolph called the report "distressing, innocuous, sterile and barren of any creative, broad-changing ideas that can give strength and force to civil rights within the AFL-CIO"; he said it was a "defense of a do-nothing policy." Potofsky, rebutting, said if the report was "trivial," it could be little else, "for the charges it dealt with were even more trivial."

Not a single council member spoke in support of Randolph. Meany pushed the censure motion to a vote, and only Randolph voted no.

Now that Meany had beaten down Randolph in private, he could be generous with him in public. Meany would decide whether the censure motion would be put before the convention or quietly buried within the secrecy of the executive council. A few days before the convention, Meany called in Randolph and other leaders of the Negro American Labor Council for two and a half hours of conversation. He said he was ready to cooperate in any "constructive" programs NALC developed, and that he would no longer consider it a vehicle for dual unionism. The next day he had a publicized luncheon with Randolph and Milton Webster, after which Randolph said he felt Meany had put the civil rights program on the "right track." The convention resolution called for "appropriate action" by the council against unions that persisted in discriminatory practices—"the best ever," in Randolph's opinion. The censure motion was never presented to the convention, nor was Shishkin's report circulated outside the executive council.

After muting Randolph's protests, Meany set about doing many of the things Randolph had requested. On his own initiative, Meany issued a directive barring state and local affiliates from holding conventions and other meetings in segregated facilities. He enlarged the civil rights committee, and put it under William Schnitzler, the secretary-treasurer. Meany leaned on his old friends in the New York building trades. He invoked the support of Whitney Young, Jr., executive director of the Urban League, who met with the executive council in November 1962. Young offered the league's help "in your effort to eliminate from the entire labor movement the last vestiges of segregation and discrimination." Young said his offer rested on the assumption that the AFL-CIO was sincere, and because of its "frank recognition that there still exist gaps between your public policies, your own personal convictions, and the practices within some local unions." Young was candid. "Make no mistake about it," he told the council. "The Urban League is not in business to help any institution segregate with more subtlety, or discriminate with more sophistication." The council accepted his offer.

At the same meeting (after Young left), Meany told of continuing problems with Herbert Hill, the NAACP labor secretary, who worked simultaneously as a consultant to Representative Adam Clayton Powell on the House Labor and Education Committee. Meany complained that Hill "was acting in an irresponsible manner that has brought harm to the labor movement." In one case, Meany said, Hill filed decertification petitions against an ILGWU local on the grounds of bias. David Dubinsky and David McDonald noted that since the NAACP executive board had endorsed Hill's actions, "criticism can be no longer confined to the actions of the labor secretary but becomes the responsibility of the entire organization." Meany wrote the NAACP a stern letter saying its "working relationship" with the AFL-CIO was in jeopardy, and that Hill had best be curbed.

The new campaign had only isolated success. Meany forced the Portsmouth, Virginia, local of the technical engineers union to drop its secret ballot on new members; nine Negroes were accepted. He suspended segregated locals of the United Federation of Postal Clerks in Jacksonville and New Orleans. The New York local of the painters union had nine blacks among the forty graduates of its apprenticeship program; 130 blacks and Puerto Ricans were among the 300 enrollees in training classes. The Florida and Arkansas state federations found integrated convention facilities. On November 15, 1962, a beaming Lyndon Johnson escorted presidents of almost 100 AFL-CIO affiliates into the White House to sign pacts pledging adherence to a "union program for fair practices." The unions agreed to accept all eligible applicants without regard to race, color, or national origins, and to refuse charters to segregated locals.

For all the surface activity, however, there was little positive accomplishment. "The sad fact of the matter was," said an AFL-CIO staff member active in civil rights, "many of the unions put together paper programs that meant nothing. George used to talk about how the federal government used a thousand troops and millions of dollars to get one Negro student [James Meredith] into Ole Miss. Hell, we had more than 60,000 local unions, and we didn't have any troops whatsoever."

In a New Year's statement in 1963, Meany called for a fair employment practices commission to put the force of law behind the AFL-CIO policy pronouncements. The civil rights revolution rose toward a heartsearing peak: in Birmingham ("the most thoroughly segregated big city in the U.S.," in Martin Luther King's words), mass arrests of more than 3,000 Negro men, women, and children; brutal assaults on nonviolent demonstrators by police armed with clubs, gas, and dogs led by the burly segregationist police commissioner T. E. "Bull" Connor; dynamite blasts in homes, schools, finally even a church, killing four small children on a Sunday morning. The revolution swept out of Birmingham into scores of other cities. "The fires of frustration and discord," President Kennedy said, "are burning in every city, north and south, where legal remedies are not at hand." On June 11, in a speech that Theodore Sorensen said "marked the beginning of the federal government's full-scale commitment to the fight against all discrimination," the President asked for legislation to make this "great change . . . peaceful and constructive for all. . . . We face a moral crisis as a country and as a people. . . . It cannot be left to increased demonstrations in the streets. It cannot be quieted by token moves or talks. . . ." Kennedy called a series of meetings to get ideas on specific legislation he could send to Congress.

Already pending was a rather perfunctory Administration measure, submitted in February, expanding the authority of the Civil Rights Commission and improving voting rights laws. Labor asked early in the year that a fair employment practices commission section be added, as Meany had requested in his New Year's Day message. "From then on those were orders," said Andrew Biemiller, the AFL-CIO lobbyist. "We went through the goddamnedest series of meetings you ever saw, with some of our congressmen friends [Representatives Richard Bolling (Dem., Missouri) and Frank Thompson (Dem., New Jersey)] and Nick Katzenbach [the deputy attorney general] trying to get something about employment in the bill. We told them, 'If this isn't in the bill, we lost a lot of interest in the bill'—meaning, we wouldn't work so hard for it. Why were we so set? Well, it was right, and we also *needed* it. There were a lot of howls in the executive council, but George had a majority with him, and he wouldn't budge."

After Kennedy's June 11 speech, the Leadership Conference on Civil Rights, a lobbying coalition embracing the NAACP, Americans for Democratic Action, Urban League, AFL-CIO, and other groups, met with Senator Hubert Humphrey (Dem., Minnesota) to discuss strategy. At Humphrey's request, Biemiller wrote a memo outlining labor's case for an FEPC. Administration leaders reacted coolly to the FEPC in preliminary talks.

Soon after, Biemiller said he had a "perfunctory meeting with Kennedy at the White House, and with malice aforethought I handed a copy of the Humphrey memo to Kenny O'Donnell [a key Kennedy assistant]. This was at noon, and I thought nothing more about it until about four in the afternoon, when Meany called me from Rome. He was over there for an International Labor Organization meeting, and had given me instructions on what our position was going to be on FEPC.

"He asked, 'What the hell kind of memo did you leave at the White House today? Jack Kennedy called me all upset. He says you are "trying to ruin my civil rights bill." ' I explained what had happened and Meany said, 'You are right, we're not quitting on this one.' Meany told me to get over to the White House and work it out, because they were counting on our support in Congress to help get it through."

Biemiller quickly arranged an appointment with the President and took along Lane Kirkland, Meany's administrative assistant, for moral support. "I've never seen Jack Kennedy so unsure of himself," Biemiller said. "He kept saying, 'You are going to ruin my bill, you are going to ruin the whole thing.' He kept quoting statistics about black unemployment and what great progress had been made. I told him, 'I'm sorry, but this is our line, and we are going to carry through on it.' " According to Theodore Sorensen, Kennedy omitted employment from the bill because he was "aware of the emotions surrounding the initials FEPC" and did not wish to drive away moderate support he needed for passage. Kennedy wanted "the best bill possible at the earliest time possible." Swift economic growth would provide more jobs than an FEPC, he felt. Kennedy submitted a bill with two main features:

—A ban on discrimination in places of public accommodation—hotels, restaurants, retail stores, places of amusement—that had a substantial effect on interstate commerce, and that had been the special targets of sit-in demonstrators in the South.

—Authority for the Attorney General to file suits for desegregation of public education on his own initiative, thereby relieving aggrieved parents or students of the dangerous requirement of suing racist local officials. In a message accompanying the civil rights package, the Administration endorsed FEPC in principle.

Testifying before the House Judiciary Committee on July 17, Meany said "the figures tell their own story" on discrimination in hiring—"a Negro unemployment rate at least twice that of whites; a pattern of Negro employment concentrated in the lowest-paid and most menial jobs." Meany said it would be easy "to point the finger at Southern industry, where genuinely integrated production forces are almost unknown. . . . It would be easy to say that the problem in northern cities stems to a considerable degree from the emigration of Southern Negroes who face a hopeless future in their home areas. All this is true, but it is not the whole truth, and the issue is too grave for hair-splitting. . . ." He continued:

> The plain fact is that Negro workers as a whole, north or south, do not enjoy anything approaching equal employment opportunity.
>
> We ask you now, as we have asked the Congress for many years, for effective enforceable legislation to correct this glaring injustice, which must be corrected in order to make the other aspects of a civil rights program effective.

We have a selfish reason; in fact, we have two of them.

First, we need the statutory support of the federal government to carry out the unanimously adopted principles of the AFL-CIO. . . .

Why is this so? Primarily because the labor movement is not what its enemies say it is—a monolithic, dictatorial, centralized body that imposes its will on the helpless dues payers. We operate in a democratic way, and we cannot dictate even in a good cause. . . .

Second, we want federal legislation because we are tired of being the whipping boy in this area.

We have never at any time tried to gloss over the shortcomings of unions on the subject of equal opportunity. Yes, some of our members take a wrongheaded view; I have just said so, I have said so before, and I repeat it again.

But we in the labor movement publicly deplore these few hold-outs against justice. We do our utmost to bring them around to the right side. And at the same time, the employers—who actually do the hiring—escape in many instances with no criticism whatever.

If there has been any widespread outcry from employers who want to hire Negroes but have been prevented from doing so by a union, it has not reached my ears.

Meany asked that penalties for violations be assessed against employers as well as unions. He urged that the jurisdiction of the President's Committee on Equal Employment Opportunity be extended to all employers, not just those with government contracts. And he argued against "superseniority" and hiring preferences for Negroes, as demanded by black groups:

First of all, superseniority would throw into the street white workers who were in no way responsible for the previous discrimination against Negroes. They would be deprived of their personal livelihood because of a community sin. It is possible, of course, that the ax might fall on a leader of the Ku Klux Klan. It is equally possible that the victim might be the long-abused chairman of the local union's civil rights committee.

It seems to me that our common goal is justice, not vengeance. This is especially true when vengeance would be exacted from those whose only guilt was the color of their skin. We are against that sort of thing for Negroes; we are against it for whites as well.

Second, the demand for special treatment for Negroes at any level misses the point. There is not much future in a program for sharing misery. Yes, Negroes have been held back, unfairly and unreasonably; to the extent that unions have been responsible, we accept our share of the blame. But the road ahead must be broad enough for all; not a bottleneck through which we squeeze people of one kind or another, leaving some of every kind looking in from the outside.

Meany said destruction of seniority violated a basic benefit of unionism. "If you destroy seniority in the hope of correcting racial injustice, you destroy it entirely. Those who might reap quick benefits could also be the first losers."

Congressman Richard Bolling, the pragmatic liberal from Kansas City, took responsibility for FEPC in the House. One of Biemiller's closest friends for almost two decades, Bolling understood why Meany needed FEPC. Labor, he said, "really had to force the Kennedys into the notion we had to have that goddamned FEPC. We had a hell of a time with both of the Kennedys, and with Nick Katzenbach. Katzenbach finally got the message, that the AFL-CIO had to have the umbrella of the law. We never would have passed the Civil Rights Act without labor. They had the muscle; the other civil rights groups did not."

At the same time labor lobbyists privately pushed the antidiscrimination legislation toward passage, Meany prevented AFL-CIO participation in the major "public" civil rights event of the year—the massive March on Washington climaxed by Dr. King's "I have a dream" speech at the Lincoln Memorial. Several black leaders delicately inquired whether labor could endorse the march without any direct involvement by Meany. One of them explained to Don Slaiman, of the AFL-CIO civil rights department, that Meany was anathema to many blacks, and that it might be "better" if he stayed away. The question, however, was moot. According to Slaiman, Reuther and David Dubinsky asked Meany about participating, but in such botched fashion that he would not have accepted even had he been so inclined. "We will do our work on the Hill," Meany said, referring to conventional lobbying. "Let them do what they want." In an executive council meeting on August 12, Reuther argued the AFL-CIO "must identify itself" with the march. He recognized the AFL-CIO "was not consulted prior to the announcing and setting of the date," but that "everyone was in somewhat of the same position." Reuther asked for a formal endorsement, a contribution of funds, and an appeal to members of affiliated unions to participate.

Meany did not like the idea. He did not want the AFL-CIO "to be identified with a public demonstration initiated by others and over which the AFL-CIO has no control." Instead, Meany got the council to pass— over Reuther's objection—a statement setting forth the AFL-CIO's position on civil rights; recognizing "the right of these organizations to go to Washington"; the "right" of affiliated unions to participate; and "the hope that the march will be helpful and peaceful." * Reuther snapped, "That resolution is so anemic it will need a transfusion to get to the mimeograph machine." Reuther and other UAW members helped plan the march and participated in it. "Marching isn't Meany's style," one of his staff people said. "For right or for wrong, he thinks demonstrations turn off congressmen who might otherwise go for controversial legislation. Meany prefers to work his own way, in the established channels."

The lobbying and hearings dragged through the summer and early fall, the Kennedy Administration finally swinging around to public support of a title on employment practices. The House Judiciary Committee voted out the bill on November 21, 1963.

In the fall of 1963 Meany looked forward to the 1964 elections as an opportunity to win the congressional majority needed to fulfill the promises of the New Frontier. He shared Kennedy's zest for the expected race against Senator Barry Goldwater. In November Kennedy paid an old debt of gratitude to Meany—and made an advance bid for support a year later—by coming to the AFL-CIO convention at the Commodore Hotel in New York. He was lavish in his praise: "I think that the AFL-CIO, at this convention, looking back over the years, over this country, can take pride in the actions it has taken, pride in the stand it has made, pride in the things it has done, not only for the American labor movement but for the United States as a whole." Meany sat beaming on the platform behind the young President; as Kennedy left, he said, "Let's get together when you're back in Washington."

* At the same meeting Secretary-treasurer Schnitzler reported the AFL-CIO was down to 172 segregated union locals out of 55,000.

# XIV

# Expansion at Home and Abroad

I N TERMS OF GROSS STRENGTH, the AFL-CIO went into
the Kennedy years with declining membership. The AFL-CIO had
12,622,000 members at merger; by 1961, the number was down to 12,-
553,000. The exodus of the Teamsters was one reason, for their expulsion cost the AFL-CIO 1.4 million members. But other factors contributed: automation; economic stagnation and the two recessions of the
second Eisenhower Administration; the decline in manufacturing employment and the upsurge in harder-to-organize white-collar workers; the
antiunion sentiment fostered by the unsavory findings of the McClellan
committee. As labor critic Thomas R. Brooks noted, blue-collar industrial unions suffered the most. The United Auto Workers, 1.4 million
strong in 1953, plummeted below the million mark in 1961 because of
automation and slumping auto production; the United Steel Workers fell
from 1.2 million in 1959 to 850,000 two years later; the International
Association of Machinists, from a million in 1958 to 800,000 in 1963.
Increasingly the industrial unions became more concerned with preserving existing jobs than in organizing new members. With the unemployment rate above the five percent mark, employers beat back organizing
drives with relative ease.

In gross percentages, the AFL-CIO represented less of the American
work force in the 1960's than it did at merger—22.5 percent versus 17.6
percent (in 1966). The AFL-CIO, while recognizing that the organized
share of the work force was woefully small, did question such "numbers-
manship." The executive council stated in a 1968 report:

. . . [T]he "civilian work force" figures are misleading as an
index of membership potential in a movement that has been based

essentially on full-time employment in the private economy. While the civilian labor force increased about 15 percent between 1955 and 1965, the total number of paid manhours—a measure of employment—in the private economy increased only 6½ percent. There was no real increase in paid manhours in the private sector until 1964.

From 1955 to 1963, the increase in employment and in manhours was in government (state and local) and in part-time work. . . . [T]here was some increase in private nonprofit institutions (such as hospitals, colleges, etc.). When one excludes these . . . institutions, there was stability or a decline of employment and manhours in the rest of the private economy.

Throughout the protracted argument over jurisdictions Walter Reuther had stormed at Meany for the AFL-CIO's lack of organizing vigor. Once the AFL-CIO solved the jurisdictions problem, Reuther said, it should get on with his oft-repeated goal of doubling membership (to 27 million persons). The 1961 convention, in effect, told Reuther to proceed. At the same time it approved the jurisdictions peace plan, it created a permanent standing committee on organization; Meany put Reuther at its helm as chairman. The committee was given constitutional authority to "develop programs and policies to assure a more effective and adequate effort in meeting the challenge of organizing the unorganized." The appointment in effect gave Reuther responsibility for AFL-CIO organizing thereafter (until he resigned from the executive council in February 1967).

Reuther made an interim report two months after the convention, at the February 1962 council meeting. He said the organizing climate had improved because of "a more friendly national administration," and changes in the National Labor Relations Board. His organizing committee had discussed plans to eliminate "fruitless competition" and to allocate organizing targets, but had no specific drives to recommend for the while.

In April Reuther presented a "draft proposal" for a pilot organizing drive in the Los Angeles area, concentrated in distributing and retail industries. Participating unions would be assigned specific plants to organize. Reuther wanted a Labor Day kickoff and participation of the 5,000 full-time labor officials in Los Angeles. He declared:

The task before us is to take the resolutions and the declarations of the AFL-CIO constitutions and to give the words meaning and substance by translating the words into practical trade union action on the organizational front. The longer we delay . . . the more difficult becomes the task and the greater is the jeopardy to our future.

The council approved Reuther's pilot project, and Meany scheduled a meeting for participating unions later in the summer. A key union objected. James Suffridge, president of the Retail Clerks International Association, noted his union was already dominant in the retail field in Los Angeles, and in fact was then engaged in organizing that was both "aggressive and productive." He saw no reason to throw the Retail Clerks' jurisdiction open to outside unions. By Reuther's account, Suffridge's opposition "cut the heart" out of the Los Angeles project; he fumed it was based upon a "possible jurisdictional claim." (The executive council, commenting on this squabble later in a report, noted that dismissing Suffridge's objection so lightly "is no more valid than would be the suggestion that the UAW's interest in automobile manufacturing in the Detroit area ought to be dismissed as just a 'possible jurisdictional claim.' ")

Lacking Suffridge's cooperation, and barred from retail organizing, the Los Angeles project proceeded, under the direction of John W. Livingston, the former UAW officer who now ran the AFL-CIO department of organizing. He reported progress periodically to the council over the next three years: at one time, in 1963, 162 staff people (four of them from the AFL-CIO national office) worked full time on the Los Angeles campaign. After four years, when it was turned over to international unions, the campaign had resulted in membership gains of 90,000 persons, including those signed through NLRB elections, voluntary recognitions, and organization of public employees. A similar campaign, on a smaller scale, won some 32,000 members in the Baltimore–Washington metropolitan area.

Reuther, however, displayed no further interest in the campaign after the tiff with Suffridge. Never again did he call a meeting of the committee on organizing, which he had sought for years. As the executive council commented later, the committee became "totally inactive." Livingston reported directly to the executive council on the Los Angeles and other campaigns.

Reuther was briefly active in another organizing campaign run under auspices of the Industrial Union Department. With sixty affiliated unions and the per capita tax from some six million members, the IUD had an ample money and jurisdictional base for organizing. In 1963 Reuther launched what he called a "comprehensive, cooperative, coordinated" organizing drive, and set up a special fund to receive contributions of cash and manpower from IUD affiliates. The IUD spent some $13 million over the next five years, and gained some 95,369 members for participating unions. But the final report (submitted by Reuther in 1968, just before the UAW left the AFL-CIO) told of the problems inherent in any multiunion organizing campaign:

The IUD program has gradually reduced its activity and is on the road to oblivion because of lack of participation by IUD affiliates. Soon after the program began, some of the unions looked at the score sheets to see how well they were doing in election victories. They did the arithmetic on the money and manpower they were putting into the program. If they saw that other unions were more successful, they concluded that if the same money and manpower were spent in their own independent effort they could do as well or better without IUD organizing assistance.

Meany frequently expressed disappointment at the lack of organizing gains. "I want to say very frankly to you that we are not moving as fast as we had hoped we would be able to move at the time of the merger," Meany told the UAW convention in March 1964. But he refused to take blame for the slow pace. His position was consistent from the time he became an AFL officer: international unions carry primary responsibility for organizing. The AFL-CIO would assist when needed and when asked, but unions are best able to organize persons in their separate jurisdictions. As the political spokesman for organized labor, the AFL-CIO's main task was providing a favorable economic and legal climate for organizing. For instance, largely at Meany's urging, President Kennedy in 1962 issued an executive order endorsing unions for federal employees. Kennedy said that "the efficient administration of the government and the well-being of employees require that orderly and constructive relationships be maintained between employee organizations and management." The American Federation of Government Employees, the chief union for federal workers, had 68,000 members when Kennedy issued the order. By 1967 it was up to 196,000; by 1970, almost a half million. The spill-over effect of legitimizing government unionism had dramatic impact on organizing elsewhere. The American Federation of State, County and Municipal Employees soared from 182,504 members in 1960 to well past half a million in 1972; its president, Jerry Wurf, saw an ultimate membership of two million—a goal toward which the union was rising at the rate of 1,000 new members a week. Meany called President Kennedy's executive order "the equivalent of a Wagner Act for public employees."

When the economy began to improve in 1963, AFL-CIO membership increased at about the same five percent rate as did paid man-hours worked in the private sector (labor's measure of the work force). Between June 1964 and January 1968 membership went from 12,717,000 to 14,951,000—fourteen percent in three and a half years. "Pretty good for an organization that is resting on dead center," Meany quipped to a building and construction trades department conference in 1968.

Chatting with President Kennedy in the White House a few days after the announcement of the Alliance for Progress, Meany expounded his views on what should be done in Latin America. The AFL-CIO was well along with its own plans for social action programs there, and Meany felt they might be intermeshed with the Alliance. Meany recollected, "We stressed very strongly that we were going to help the countries of Latin America and that the money that we were spending was not just to be channeled to the established societies of those countries—that would mean that the rich would get a little richer and there would be really no difference insofar as the conditions of the great mass of the workers in these countries were concerned. So we convinced him that we had a part to play, that instead of all of this money being channeled to business institutions or through banks or through governments, some of it should be channeled through trade unions, that trade unions should sponsor projects which are to be financed under the Alliance."

From that White House conversation grew a foreign policy operation that, in Meany's words, made an arm of the AFL-CIO "a working agency of the United States government, working with its expenses paid by AID [the Agency for International Development] under the Alliance to union-sponsored projects in Latin America." It also led, indirectly, to deep involvement by AFL-CIO affiliated unions in the spooky world of political warfare—one in which the Central Intelligence Agency used American unions and their officials as willing agents in jousts with Communist and other anti-American labor groups.

Several distinctions must be drawn. The American Institute for Free Labor Development (AIFLD), the AFL-CIO's chief operating arm in Latin America, drew most of its funds during the 1960's from AID—ranging from sixty-two percent in 1962 to ninety-two percent in 1967. Much of AIFLD's work paralleled activities in which the CIA had a deep interest. But Meany insisted firmly, both in public statements and private conversations, that AIFLD received "not . . . one cent from the CIA." Noting the millions of dollars a year AIFLD obtained from AID, Meany once quipped, "So when you get that kind of money, why do you have to run to the CIA?" Meany said he had a "natural ingrained opposition to spy activities as such. I think the CIA has a job to do, but I think they can do it without using the trade union movement."

Several AFL-CIO affiliates were not so discriminating. Between 1958 and 1964 the American Federation of State, County, and Municipal Employees (AFSCME), the American Newspaper Guild, and the International Oil, Chemical, and Atomic Workers used CIA money for international operations. Two CIA agents ran AFSCME's international affairs department and spent scores of thousands of dollars supporting a strike that helped topple Cheddi Jagan, the premier of British Guiana, the British crown colony on the northeast coast of the Latin American continent. The Newspaper Guild used its money to run seminars and training programs; the chemical workers, to provide logistical support for unions of Latin refinery workers. The funds went to the unions through bogus "philanthropic foundations" which the CIA created especially for use as conduits for covert funding. Meany insisted, however, that these activities should not be confused with those of the AFL-CIO or the AIFLD.

Finally, the fact that AID provided the bulk of the money for AIFLD and a sister operation, the African-American Labor Center (AALC), was kept deliberately fuzzy. An AID background memo on AALC said it should be described as a "private, nonprofit organization established by the American labor movement. This image should be preserved in Africa. However, there is no objection to indicating, if queried, that financial support comes from public as well as private sources." The AID man chosen to oversee AALC projects should "work with the AALC technician discreetly and tactfully to retain the union-to-union image. Site visits, when required, will be arranged with the AALC technician and will be as unobtrusive as possible." Similar guidelines covered AID contacts with AIFLD. Meany's public statements on financing were grossly misleading. Meany told the Chicago Executives' Club in 1963: "The institute is a three-way operation. It is supported, *in almost equal shares*, by industry, labor and the federal government." The AIFLD budget for 1963 was $1,252,000, of which AID paid seventy-six percent; labor, eleven percent; and business, thirteen percent. In 1967, during exposures of covert CIA funding of other labor programs, few critics would accept Meany's assertion that the AFL-CIO activities were financed by the AID rather than the CIA.

The AIFLD was conceived during 1959–60, when the U.S. government, and much of the public, saw Fidel Castro as a bearded Communist menace who well might carry out his stated intention of exporting the Cuban revolution throughout the continent. The AFL-CIO managed to offend Castro early on. The AFL-CIO long had a close relationship with Eusebio Mujal, the general secretary of the Confederation of Cuban Workers (CTC, by its Spanish initials). In May 1956 Mujal refused CTC support of a general strike Castro called in hopes of toppling dictator Fulgencio Batista. Serafino Romualdi, the AFL-CIO man in Latin America at the time, stated, "The rank and file were enjoying a relatively high purchasing power . . . and the trade union bureaucracy welcomed Batista's decree making compulsory the unions' dues checkoff. . . . The

daily preservation of the bread-and-butter function of the labor movement became the paramount preoccupation of the CTC leadership.
Everything they did until the ouster of Batista has to be viewed and
judged in terms of this main objective—the salvation of the CTC." If the
general strike failed—as the union leadership worried it would—Batista
would retaliate by crushing the CTC. But by not joining Castro in what
became a popular revolution, Mujal permanently tarnished CTC's reputation with the masses. The AFL-CIO, for its part, kept ORIT, the regional affiliate of the International Confederation of Free Trade Unions,
from publicly declaring its support of Castro's 26th of July Movement.
Castro's revolution triumphed on January 1, 1959. A month later the
CTC invited Meany to visit Cuba. He sent Romualdi as a "sort of advance scout to see what was going on and how things were shaping up,
reserving the option to go himself later if the circumstances were favorable. . . . Our position was that as long as there was an opportunity to
help steer the Cuban revolution along democratic lines, we should not
refuse to do our part in the field of our jurisdictions—organized labor."
A CTC reception committee escorted Romualdi to his hotel, where he
waited in vain for a meeting with the leadership. *Revolucion,* a Castro
journal, denounced Romualdi as a "gangster and millionaire" in a front-
page article, and he flew home. Romualdi said Meany "deeply resented
. . . the rebuff suffered by his personal representative." By April he
was warning Meany in letters that the new CTC leadership (Mujal had
fled into exile) was trying to persuade other Latin unions to withdraw
from ORIT, the ICFTU affiliate, and to break ties with the AFL-CIO.
"This is precisely the current Communist line," he wrote. In May 1960
the executive council called Castro's policies part of a well-planned strategy designed to make Cuba "an advanced outpost of the Soviet Union's
drive to infiltrate the New World."

Such was the AFL-CIO's thinking in August 1960 when Joseph
Beirne presented the council a proposal for a training program for Latin
union leaders. Meany liked the idea, and the council voted $20,000 for a
feasibility study. AIFLD was incorporated in August 1961, with Meany
as president and J. Peter Grace, president of W. R. Grace & Company,
the shipping firm, as board chairman; other businessmen were on the
board. Berent Friele, the Rockefeller family's house expert on Latin
America, served as vice-chairman. The business involvement raised
some eyebrows in the labor movement. Victor Reuther, head of the
United Auto Workers' international department, charged in a 1965
Voice of America broadcast: "Their presence on AIFLD's board seriously compromises its trade union training and educational role. Its
structure exposes it to the charge of conflict of interest and is a propaganda gift to the enemies of free trade unions who effectively character-

ize these businessmen as symbols of Yankee imperialism and enemies of social programs in Latin America."

"Well, we gave a lot of thought to this," Meany said of the business involvement. "The executive council finally decided unanimously that we should bring American business into this institution on the theory that they should have the same stake . . . in the building of free societies in Latin America as we do. They want to do business there, they certainly want to do business with countries that have viable economies." Meany felt "we have come a long way from the days of the banana republics, when American companies, out of necessity sometimes rather than of choice, made their deals with local tyrants, without regard for the welfare of the population. Mr. Grace and others like him are well aware that the choice today is between democracy and Castroism in Latin America; and that, if democracy is to win, it must meet the needs and the desires of the people, starting with a higher standard of living." Meany conceded that not all labor leaders shared his opinion. "Shortsightedness is not confined to any one segment of our society, or to any particular calling or profession," he said.

The AID/AIFLD link was mutually beneficial. To AID's advantage, use of AIFLD emphasized "union to union" contacts, and enabled U.S. officials to forgo the protocol of dealing with Latin labor ministries, notoriously corrupt and inefficient. The arrangement required minimum U.S. government involvement in the internecine politics of Latin labor.

For the AFL-CIO, the attractive feature was that the AID money enabled it to undertake projects far beyond the capacity of American labor. It also enabled the AFL-CIO to move further away from the ICFTU, an organization with which Meany slowly lost patience during the 1960's. The ICFTU complained of the AFL-CIO undercutting its work in Latin America and Africa, yet was unable to do anything there on its own. Meany complained at a press conference in early 1965: "Very frankly, it's not at this moment a very effective organization . . . very frankly, it's turned into a real bureaucracy—even to the fairies."

"My, my," exclaimed a reporter.

Meany told the executive council the same week that the ICFTU had squirreled away $4 million, half of it in unallocated "operations" funds unspent since 1961. The unused funds were "being placed in banks all over Europe, including $600,000 in an Austrian bank drawing six and a half percent interest, as well as large deposits in London and New York." At the ICFTU meeting in Brussels in midsummer Meany demanded the return of $818,000 to the AFL-CIO. He clashed with the ICFTU president, Arne Geijer of Sweden, who had complained AFL-CIO foreign activities "are only for aiding American foreign policy." The German labor federation newspaper, in an article printed during the

ICFTU meeting, called Meany a "terrible infant American," and its president termed the AFL-CIO "too anti-Communist." Reporting back to the executive council, Meany said he "felt keenly" the attacks, but that the ICFTU "had to be supported" lest the "world labor movement be left to the Communist WFTU" (World Federation of Trade Unions). All he had asked of the ICFTU was "honest financial reporting." The council agreed with Meany it should continue to work with the ICFTU, but guardedly, and not "succumb to the temptation to answer the many criticisms of which we are informed."

Because of these dissatisfactions, Meany looked more and more towards the AFL-CIO's own regional operations—the AIFLD in Latin America, the AALC in Africa.

AIFLD activities fell into two categories—worker education and social projects. Through the latter, it served, for all practical purposes, as the labor arm of the Alliance for Progress—financing housing projects, establishing farming cooperatives and credit unions, offering technical assistance. (Loans for housing projects came from U.S. unions, chiefly from welfare and pension funds; AID guaranteed the loans.) The education program, from which stemmed the controversy about labor "toppling governments," on the surface was simple. Latin unionists came to the AIFLD Center in the Shenandoah Valley for a three-month training period—first, in adult education techniques, then in techniques of running a trade union. After returning to their home countries, the unionists remained on the AIFLD payroll for nine months while they trained rank-and-file workers. During AIFLD's first five years more than 500 unionists went through the training program; Meany estimated they in turn trained another 60,000 "worker-students." AIFLD graduates often played roles far beyond that of union leader when they returned home. Some, in fact, were especially selected with specific postgraduation missions in mind.

One such instance involved Brazil. João Goulart, who succeeded to the Brazilian presidency in 1961 following the abdication of Juscelino Kubitschek, gave Communists an increasingly powerful role within his administration. He also talked of forming a new Latin regional federation independent of both the ICFTU and the Communist-dominated World Federation of Trade Unions. During a U.S. visit in 1962, Goulart met Meany, Secretary of Labor Arthur Goldberg, and Romualdi over breakfast in Blair House. Meany interrupted the rambling conversation to ask Goulart bluntly, "What is your stand, Mr. President, on cooperation with the free labor movement of the ICFTU, as opposed to dealing with the Communist-controlled WFTU?" Romualdi said Goulart gave an "ambiguous answer" which did not satisfy Meany.

On Meany's orders, Romualdi went to Brazil in 1963 to scout the political situation. Berent Friele, Governor Nelson Rockfeller's Latin expert, went with him. Romualdi stated, "I visited Governor Adhemar de Barros. He confided to us that plans were already under way to mobilize military and police contingents to counter any attempt by Goulart to establish dictatorial control by force." Romualdi brought Barros' statements to the attention of U.S. Ambassador Lincoln Gordon and labor attaché John Fishburn. Romualdi continued: "I knew that a substantial sector of labor's rank and file, particularly in São Paulo and Rio, was fed up with the Goulart regime and was ready to take to the streets, if need be, to bring it down. In the first three months of 1963, the AIFLD, of which I was the executive director, trained in Washington a special all-Brazilian class of thirty-three participants. Ten of these union leaders were later taken to West Europe and Israel under my personal supervision to learn more about the techniques and practices of democratic labor. When they returned to their country, some of the trainees were sent to the interior on internships to organize and conduct education seminars; others served their unions in Rio, São Paulo, Santo, and other industrial centers."

In March 1964 Goulart signed decrees on land expropriation and nationalization of all private petroleum refineries, overriding the Brazilian congress to do so. The Brazilian federation of labor, whose leaders were friendly to Goulart, called a general strike in his support. But the AIFLD-trained unionists had done their groundwork: few rank-and-file members responded and the general strike collapsed. "Later," Romualdi said, "the same democratic trade union leaders were among the organizers of the great mass demonstrations in the streets of Rio, São Paulo, Belo Horizonte, and other cities hailing the downfall of the hated, corrupt, incompetent, pro-Communist Goulart regime." William Doherty, Jr., another AIFLD officer (and Romualdi's successor as director) said the AIFLD group "became intimately involved in some of the clandestine operations of the revolution before it took place. . . . What happened in Brazil on April 1 [when Goulart fell] did not just happen—it was planned, and planned months in advance. Many of the trade union leaders—some of whom were actually trained in our institute—were involved in the revolution."

But unfortunately for Brazilian workers, the overthrow of a corrupt, pro-Communist leadership delivered the labor movement into the hands of an antiunion military junta. The generals imposed a repressive police state which took direct command of labor unions and gave short shrift to the "democratic trade union practices" the AIFLD trainees had sought.

Another capsulized case study: In July 1963, the New York *Times* carried an extraordinary letter to the editor from Dr. Cheddi Jagan, prime minister of British Guiana (since 1966, the independent nation of

Guyana). Jagan complained that "local trade unionists known to be hostile to the government—and none others—have been trained by the American Institute of Free Labor Development to overthrow my government. Serafino Romualdi, head of the institute, has declared his opposition to my government."

Romualdi cheerfully stated Jagan was absolutely correct. "I never tried to deny Dr. Jagan's charge. As a matter of fact, I publicly acknowledge the fact that, having become convinced of Dr. Jagan's subservience to the Communist movement since my first visit to British Guiana in 1951, I did everything in my power to strengthen the democratic trade union forces opposed to him and to expose Jagan's pro-Communist activities from the day he was elected prime minister. . . ." Romualdi's statement was remarkable for two reasons. Jagan's People's Progressive party won three successive elections (in 1953, 1957, and 1961)—even after the British government forcibly removed him from office on grounds he was attempting to set up a Communist state in the then-crown colony. Second, although President Kennedy acknowledged that Jagan was a Marxist, he stated in a 1961 interview that "the United States doesn't object because that choice was made by an honest election which he won." The United States recognized Jagan's government, and Jagan visited Kennedy in the White House.

Not too long afterward, however, both Kennedy and the AIFLD were plotting Jagan's overthrow—Kennedy with the use of the CIA, which in turn recruited AFL-CIO affiliates as partners; the AIFLD through its own programs. The CIA's chief partner was the American Federation of State, County and Municipal Employees. A CIA agent, Howard McCabe, went to British Guiana under the cover of "representative" of AFSCME and an international trade union secretariat, the Public Services International. The Man Power Citizens' Association, long the dominant union among sugar industry workers, ranked high in the Jagan opposition, and Jagan moved to break it in 1963. His wife, who had been active in the Young Communist League in Chicago before going to British Guiana in the 1940's, was made Minister of Labor. Jagan proposed legislation giving the Minister of Labor authority to decide which trade union should represent workers in collective bargaining, and compelling employers to deal only with the designated union. The Man Power Citizens' Association called a protest strike—one actually led by Howard McCabe of the CIA and Andrew C. McLelland, the AFL-CIO representative for Latin America. Romualdi said, "I simply put at the disposal of the strike committee the services of six graduates of the AIFLD . . . who were working as interns with various local unions." The CIA poured scores of thousands of dollars into British Guiana through its foundation conduits to support the strikers. When the turmoil quietened,

Jagan had been voted out of office, to be replaced by the moderate Forbes Burnham. The AIFLD gave his new administration a boost by agreeing to finance a housing project and to create a half-million-dollar industrial training center.

During a 1969 review of AIFLD by the Senate Foreign Relations Committee, Senator J. W. Fulbright (Dem., Arkansas) asserted the institute "undertakes to train" revolutionaries. "Oh, no, no," Meany rejoined. "That is completely wrong. . . . However, it is not surprising that a person who would be interested in a trade union would also be interested in establishing some kind of a free government in his own country. But we have no control over that. . . . After all, we can't get any pledge from them that they will not engage in politics in their own country. That would be completely ridiculous. . . . All we want to do is to give them a certain amount of knowledge as to how our economy operates, and how our trade unions operate, with the hope that they will be able to use that knowledge to advance the society and the conditions of the workers . . . where they live."

Fulbright persisted, "I think what a student does after his graduation often reflects, if the educational institution is effective at all, what he has been taught; either that, or your educational institution is a total failure."

"Mr. Chairman," Meany replied, "if what you say is true we would have to close all the universities in America. You say that an institution that trains them has got to be responsible for what they do after that? That is nonsense."

# XV

# All the Way with LBJ—to Vietnam, Too

G EORGE MEANY spent the weekend of President Kennedy's death in deep, brooding despair. "Washington is never going to be the same town again," he said. "I don't know if I want to keep on working here; is it really worth it?" Andrew Biemiller, who had worked with Meany for more than a decade, had never seen him so depressed. "Some of us really thought he might resign or something, he was that down."

The Tuesday morning after the assassination Biemiller came into his office and found a secretary eagerly awaiting him. "Mr. Meany wants you upstairs right away; he says it's important." President Johnson had called Meany at home before breakfast; he had had Meany come directly to The Elms, the Johnson home in northwest Washington, and ride downtown to the White House with him. En route Johnson told Meany he intended to "get the country busy again, right away, with some good legislation" and asked for labor support. He said he would give first priority to the civil rights bill, which seemed certain to clear the House but faced serious problems in the Senate. Meany went on to the White House with Johnson, spent a few minutes, and then returned to his own office, his "blue funk gone," in Biemiller's words, and ready for work.

Later in the morning, at Johnson's request, Meany brought the AFL-CIO executive council to the Cabinet Room to meet with the President. Labor's skeptical opinion of Johnson—as schemer, rather than leader —had mellowed during his three years as Vice-President. Labor and Johnson were thrown into close contact on the President's Committee on Equal Employment Opportunity and worked well together. Johnson grasped quickly Meany's thesis that business bore much of the blame for discriminatory hiring, and he was patient with Meany's attempts to cajole AFL-CIO unions. Johnson also succeeded in making peace with labor leaders who had vehemently opposed his nomination in Los Angeles three years earlier. A few weeks before the assassination Johnson went into the veritable epicenter of the leftist opposition as guest of honor at a Liberal party fete in New York, dining in back-slapping camaraderie with Alex Rose of the hatters union, the party chairman; and Jacob Potofsky of the Amalgamated Clothing Workers.

In the Cabinet Room meeting, Johnson told the AFL-CIO group, "You were always good warriors to President Kennedy. I need your help even more than he did because he had more talents than I have." Johnson had everyone stand a moment with bowed heads in tribute to Kennedy's memory.

Then he got down to specifics. He wanted "75 million jobs during my Administration" (about 45 million Americans were then working). "What is on labor's mind, George?" he asked. Meany listed approval of the civil rights bill, a tax cut, legislation to ameliorate unemployment, Medicare. "Education," chimed in Walter Reuther. Johnson talked about the civil rights bill, which had reached the House Rules Committee in its progress toward the floor; conservatives predicted it would go no further. Meany, however, was confident labor's lobbying could break it free. He said, "We've got everything going on the discharge petition," a parliamentary move whereby legislation is taken away from the Rules Committee and sent directly to the floor. (Meany's prediction was correct, the civil rights bill was voted out of the Rules Committee the next day.) Johnson took the labor contingent outside to pose for photographers. As they left, Johnson assured Meany, "The doors of this house are always open to you."

The Johnson presidency. A peculiarly symbiotic relationship, one that began in the shared agony of John F. Kennedy's death, continued through the shared glory of the Great Society, and ended, finally, in the shared isolation of siege—Johnson from a nation torn with debate over the Vietnam War, Meany from a labor movement ruptured by his confrontation with Walter Reuther. To both Johnson and Meany, the immediate post-Kennedy years were a reincarnation of the verve and excitement of the New Deal, both periods when moods of national tragedy produced a political majority that enthusiastically rushed to passage program after program. Meany compared Johnson's 1964–66 record with that of Governor Herbert Lehman during the 1930's. Later, as the Vietnam War discolored the national spirit, Johnson found Meany a wellspring of unqualified support and sympathy. Johnson's stubbornness in pursuing the war—the very stubbornness that alienated so much of the nation—made him all the more admirable to Meany, who believed (with a conviction surpassed perhaps only by Dean Rusk or Walt W. Rostow) that the President's course was correct.

Johnson courted Meany more fervently than had any President. Late one evening, soon after Johnson took office, Meany received a call at home from the President. Johnson said, in effect, "I wish you would drop over to the White House awhile; I don't have anything in particular to say, but I do wish you would come over." Meany long believed his working day ended when he crossed the threshold of his home. Hence he told the President a white lie: his car battery was dead, and he did not think he could locate the chauffeur of his AFL-CIO limousine so late in the day.

"Don't worry about that," Johnson said, "I'll have a White House car come out for you." He did, and Meany and Johnson sat in the President's bedroom until almost midnight, drinking root beer and talking—although, in fact, Meany told Virginia Tehas the next day, "Johnson did most of the talking." Johnson repeated the invitation time and again during his presidency, sometimes coupling the "invitation" with an aside, "A White House car is already on the way out for you." Meany would not say no to such a presidential request, but Johnson's performance at first puzzled and then saddened him. He saw the sessions as evidence of Johnson's insecurity, a need to be around a friendly listener, one who would break in to tell him what a great President he was. Seldom, if ever, did Johnson have a specific question for Meany. He would talk about the war, the Great Society, domestic politics, whatever issue happened to be current. Meany would sip his root beer and listen until the President yawned and said how nice it was that Mr. Meany could come over, and then he would leave.

Meany felt so comfortable with the President that he discouraged intermediaries. When Bill D. Moyers, an LBJ aide, asked cabinet members to solicit ideas for Johnson's first State of the Union address in January 1964, Secretary of Labor Wirtz told the White House in a memo: "Mr. Meany has decided to keep any questions he may have about the message for private conversation." Wirtz said Meany "seldom bothered with going through the Labor Department" on matters requiring White House decision.

The White House staff lacked any individual whom labor considered a trusted friend. The only person with labor-management experience, appointments secretary Marvin Watson, had been a labor relations executive for Lone Star Steel Company, a ferociously antiunion East Texas corporation. During the first years of his presidency, before Vietnam became an all-consuming issue, Johnson relied upon personal contacts with Meany and his chieftains, and avoided costly gaffes. But later, when he did not have time to keep himself current with labor thinking, an unsophisticated staff caused him repeated (and unavoidable) problems. Johnson let Kennedy's labor-management advisory committee lie dormant for two years, reviving it only after labor was publicly angry with the Administration because it was not being consulted on the wage-price guidelines. "Never before—with the exception of the Eisenhower Administration—has the White House staff been so alien, in knowledge and attitude, to organized labor," John Herling wrote in 1966. Johnson eventually learned to rely upon Willard Wirtz for guidance. A Wirtz memo to Johnson, written in July 1966, displayed Wirtz's recognition of Meany's sensitivity to protocol. Wirtz recommended that Johnson decline an invitation to speak to the bricklayers convention because "it is in Canada," but accept engagements with the Carpenters Union and International Brotherhood of Electrical Workers. Wirtz explained:

These are two of biggest and strongest building trades unions (about 800,000 members each).

These are "wavering" groups politically—and among the most upset about 14b* and the guideposts.

But the union officers (Gordon Freeman and Joe Keenan of the IBEW, and Maurice Hutcheson of the Carpenters) support you—and most Democrats.

Accepting these invitations—*after calls to George Meany* [emphasis in the original] and Joe Keenan—would effectively neutralize the feeling in some places that the Administration is closer to the old CIO unions (Reuther and Abel) than to the building trades.

These are good unions on international policy.

The Missouri delegation includes a lot of Democrats [he listed Senators Stuart Symington and Edward Long and eight Democratic representatives].

*One cautionary note:* Maurice Hutcheson (Carpenters' president) was convicted of embezzlement† and was pardoned by you—I think in 1964. But this isn't considered a typical "criminal case." If had to choose, do IBEW on basis 75th anniversary. But doing both—on the same day—would be *much* better.

The personal rapport between Meany and Johnson enabled the President to make demands upon labor that another, less sympathetic President would have found impossible. In 1967, after prolonged rail negotiations collapsed, Johnson asked for legislation putting bargaining into the hands of a special presidential commission whose findings would be

* Section 14b of the Taft-Hartley Act gave states authority to pass so-called right-to-work laws forbidding closed or union shops.

† Wirtz erred. The conviction Johnson set aside was for contempt of Congress.

binding through the end of 1968. Johnson and Wirtz carefully avoided use of the words "compulsory arbitration," anathema to labor. Johnson also persuaded Senator Wayne Morse, a labor friend, to take responsibility for the legislation. Labor opposed it vigorously. "We are told by the Secretary of Labor that this is not 'compulsory arbitration,'" Meany said. "This is just 'mediation to finality.' You try to buy that one. It is not compulsion! It . . . only affects 130,000 people and it does not say forever, it only says until January 1, 1969. . . . When you hear somebody say this is not antistrike or not compulsion, don't you believe it!" The bill passed, and Johnson promptly named Meany to the five-member arbitration board. "Despite the fact that I think it is a bad law," Meany said, "when I was asked to serve, I felt that I should do the best I can to protect the interests of our people." The rail unions received a contract far more favorable than the last management offer. On another controversial issue, the merger of the Labor and Commerce departments, Johnson backed down in the face of opposition by Meany. Johnson discussed the merger in his 1967 State of the Union address but, lacking any support whatsoever, never sent legislation to Congress. (The Labor Department's official history for the Johnson years noted laconically, "The last rites were performed quietly. The Bureau of the Budget task force prepared a final draft [of merger legislation] and filed it for future reference.")

Johnson's masterful occupancy of the presidency during the first months of 1964, and Congress' response to his demands for national unity, brought the flush of life to several labor-supported bills whose passage had been problematical in late 1963. Promises of compensating budget cuts persuaded Senate conservatives to approve a $10-billion tax cut. In a close vote in February, the House put Meany's fair employment practices section into the civil rights bill, and passed the entire package by the unexpectedly high margin of 290 to 130. Meany had feared Kennedy would trade off FEPC in the Senate if necessary to obtain the fair accommodations section, which the Administration felt was of more immediate importance, or to break a Southern filibuster. As a Southerner whose civil rights credentials remained suspect to many blacks, Johnson did not have comparable freedom of compromise. After the House vote, Johnson called in the captains of the Leadership Conference on Civil Rights—Biemiller of the AFL-CIO; Joseph Rauh of the ADA; Clarence Mitchell of the NAACP—and told them he "wanted the whole damned thing, intact, without a single thing deleted." Johnson said he would wring the act out of the Senate if he had to keep it in continuous session for the rest of the year. Opponents managed to keep a filibuster alive from March 26 through June 10. Then Senator Everett M. Dirksen

(Rep., Illinois), the minority leader, literally talked into exhaustion by Johnson, broke ranks and announced for cloture, taking enough Republican votes with him to end the filibuster.

Lauding passage of the act in a message to the NAACP convention in late June, Meany said equal employment rights were not enough. "The true goals of the civil rights bill will be attained only when the education and the income of Negro citizens are on a par with those of the community as a whole," he said. Meany convened a midsummer conference of heads of AFL-CIO affiliates and told them he expected each union to comply with the law. At Meany's behest, the executive council agreed to fund apprenticeship training programs through the specially created A. Philip Randolph Institute. As director he tapped Bayard Rustin, the long-time civil rights activist who had been over-all chairman of the 1963 March on Washington. A Communist during his youth, now mellowed to socialism and outspoken pacifism, Rustin was the archetype of the abrasive public personality Meany normally kept away from the AFL-CIO. According to Don Slaiman, "well-meaning friends" brought Meany dossiers on Rustin's radical background and unconventional personal life. (Another AFL-CIO source, not Slaiman, said these dossiers came from the Federal Bureau of Investigation, whose director, J. Edgar Hoover, was a Meany admirer.) "Meany doesn't care," Slaiman said. "He paid no attention to all that stuff. He judged Bayard on the basis of competence, not his public relations effect." The AFL-CIO hoped also that Rustin's reputation for militancy and his close relationship with Dr. King would give the apprenticeship program credence with blacks, an anticipation not entirely satisfied.

On other priority legislation the AFL-CIO decided to bide its time. After Kennedy's election, labor had continued lobbying for Medicare, working through a front group called the National Council of Senior Citizens, which the AFL-CIO funded. Residual public antagonism toward labor being what it was, Meany pragmatically decided that he had two choices: labor could either be the silent force behind Medicare, and win enactment of the legislation; or work for it publicly, with the distinct probability the legislation would lose. Legislation and no public credit, or public credit and no legislation? Labor chose the silent role.

The AFL-CIO quietly poured scores of thousands of dollars into the National Council of Senior Citizens, which did the more visible public relations for Medicare; Nelson Cruikshank "retired" from the AFL-CIO to become its director. What did labor spend on the campaign? "I wouldn't have any estimate," Cruikshank said, "and one of the reasons is that we never *wanted* an estimate." By the summer of 1964, the American Medical Association, the archfoe of Medicare, had been beaten down, and Cruikshank and Biemiller realized victory was within their reach. They tried to tack Medicare onto a bill increasing Social Security benefits by ten percent—a bill ordinarily sure of passage because of the imminence of the election. But Representative Wilbur Mills (Dem., Arkansas), chairman of the House Ways and Means Committee, remained opposed to Medicare. According to Biemiller, "We got into conference, and Wilbur wouldn't yield an inch. There were talks between Johnson, Meany, and me. Meany made a cold-blooded decision. He decided to take our chances on the 1964 election, and let the bill die. If we compromised and put through some half-assed form of Medicare, we'd take the steam out of our own campaign and lose chances for a better bill next session. Had it been anybody other than Goldwater running, this would have been a very dangerous decision, for it meant some old folks didn't get a ten percent increase in the Social Security for those months. But what the hell could Goldwater do—he was running *against* Social Security, and he wasn't about to say, 'Look how they stopped you from getting a Social Security raise!' Wilbur Mills then read the election results as well as we did, and he came around. The ratio on Ways and Means changed from fifteen–ten to seventeen–eight [Democratic–Republican] and this enabled us to write a better bill than had come out in 1964. As it turned out, the old folks didn't lose, either, because we put through the ten percent Social Security raise on a retroactive basis."

In 1964 Meany differed publicly from Johnson on only one major issue: the wage-price guidelines. Speaking to the 1964 convention of the United Auto Workers, Meany declared, "If we go down this road far enough, it leads to the end of free collective bargaining." The AFL-CIO executive council went on record as opposing the guidelines, saying "wage restraints without price and profit restraints are obviously neither workable nor equitable. . . . There can be no single national wage formula in a pluralistic economy." Johnson took the news in good humor. Soon after the vote Meany brought Ludwig Rosenberg of the German Federation of Trade Unions to the White House for an introduction. Johnson greeted Meany with a laugh. "I hear you fellows beat my brains out over there." Johnson professed not to be concerned at labor's attitude. "There is nothing mandatory about them," he said of the guidelines. "They don't have the compulsion of law. We hope they will be persuasive, and we think they will be."

That labor would support Johnson for election to a full term was a foregone conclusion by early 1964 (although Victor Borella, labor specialist for the Rockefeller family, brought Governor Nelson Rockefeller to the executive council's winter meeting for a just-in-case good-will session). Johnson made a busy swirl of convention speeches in the spring and summer, and he brought 280 union officials to the White House the week before the Democratic National Convention opened to tick off the "remaining business" he hoped to push through Congress the next year. Johnson's implication was clear: vote for me, and for Democratic congressional candidates, and this is the package we have waiting for you. Even before Johnson's nomination the United Auto Workers invited him to open his campaign with the traditional Labor Day speech in Cadillac Square in Detroit. Johnson's selection of a running mate delighted Meany. When the President asked him in the spring for the names of three men he would like to see as Vice-President, Meany replied he had only one, Hubert H. Humphrey.

*One night during the Democratic National Convention the AFL-CIO hosted a festive reception for delegates and other visitors. The biggest names of Democratic politics (and some lesser ones as well) assembled to pay homage to Meany—senators, governors, congressmen, assorted party professionals from every city and state, the 240 labor delegates. Leaning on his cane, Meany stood in a reception line for more than an hour shaking hands and chatting, enjoying his recognized eminence in the Democratic party.*

*Mrs. Meany stood with him for a while, then she tired, and someone brought her a folding chair. She sat and fanned herself and watched her husband; then she said to a friend, "You know, we didn't have to go through all this. Mayor La Guardia would have made George water commissioner of New York in 1937 for twenty thousand dollars a year. I don't know why in the world he didn't take it!"*

Immediately after the convention the AFL-CIO executive council voted the expected endorsement of Johnson-Humphrey. Meany noted no labor proposals were included in the Republican platform, whereas "almost every issue in which we are interested was included" by the Democrats. Goldwater, he told the council, had a "most unique record" of having voted wrong on fifty-three labor issues since entering Congress. "Even though President Johnson's record was not good before he became leader of the Senate, it improved during the time he was leader . . . and has improved considerably during the time he has been President."

Meany campaigned energetically for Johnson, concentrating on speeches to union groups. Meany did not doubt that Johnson would win; as did the President, he wanted as large a vote as possible to ensure a friendly Congress. Meany stressed two themes in his speeches: Johnson's legislative activism on behalf of labor (the current Congress, he said, had produced "the best record from the standpoint of labor since the days of Franklin Roosevelt"); and Goldwater's long antipathy to unions (the candidate of "union-hating extremists, racial bigots [and] woolly-minded seekers after visions of times long past"). Meany also put down any faint signs of labor discontent with Johnson. Peter Brennan, president of the New York Building and Construction Trades Council and an old friend of Meany's, planned a one-day strike of building tradesmen on the day of a Salute to the President rally at Madison Square Garden. Brennan wanted to "protest the use of nonunion labor on some federal construction projects and to call attention to growing unemployment in the trades." Wirtz hand-delivered a memo to the White House: "I discussed this today with George Meany. He has agreed to get in touch with Brennan to see what can be done to stop these plans, or at least change the date." Brennan called off the rally.

The AFL-CIO's Committee on Political Education spent well more than one million dollars ensuring Johnson's victory. Johnson, thoroughly enjoying the exhilaration of a can't-lose campaign, during a single week spoke to two union conventions live and to five others via closed-circuit television. Meany's role in the campaign was so conspicuous that Representative William Miller (Rep., New York), Goldwater's running mate, complained, "George Meany goes in and out of the back door of the White House at will. He is not a great leader of organized labor, he is a great leader of the Democratic party."

In November, three weeks after the election, Labor Secretary Wirtz met with the AFL-CIO executive council in Washington to express his appreciation for labor's support. In his opinion, Wirtz said, "the labor movement represented the strongest and most constructive political force in America." He viewed the Johnson landslide as a clear repudiation of the antiunion views Goldwater expressed during the campaign; the results "surely settled the beliefs that were introduced re the present against the past," Wirtz said. Looking toward the next congressional session, Wirtz went through a long list of priority items: "fully establishing full employment opportunities for every man and woman in the country"; "great strides in the elimination of poverty"; "full educational opportunities for every child through age twenty-one"; Medicare; updating Social Security; elimination of excise taxes; broadening unemployment insurance. He also pledged support for repeal of Section 14b of the Taft-Hartley Act.

Of all the items Wirtz listed, the council devoted most discussion to 14b. Meany said 14b had cost labor "millions of dollars and limitless time on the part of officers and individual workers." He did not "know of any other federal law quite like it," in that it permitted states to prohibit a type of union (the closed shop) otherwise legal under federal law. In Oklahoma alone, Meany said, the AFL-CIO spent $550,000 fighting right-to-work laws—not counting expenditures of state and local councils.

The Democratic platform, and Johnson in numerous campaign speeches, had promised to work for repeal of 14b. In Wirtz's presentation, however, Meany detected unmistakable signs that the Johnson Administration was not as eager as labor to put 14b repeal before Congress as a "must" item early in the session. Reporting to Johnson on December 1, Wirtz said he had held meetings with Meany, Reuther, and Biemiller in addition to the formal executive council presentation. "I have pressed strongly and bluntly at these meetings the position that the time of any Administration action regarding . . . 14b should and must be left *entirely* a matter of Presidential determination. This position has been accepted and meaningfully supported by Meany and Reuther. There are some—particularly Keenan and Biemiller—who continue to insist that an Administration bill and message on this subject be sent to Congress very early in the session. There is unquestionably a sharp division on this within the AFL-CIO council." Meany was disturbed enough to speak to Johnson about 14b. He then agreed, as Wirtz wrote Johnson in another memo on December 17, that "the time is not important and should be left entirely to you, but . . . the AFL-CIO must insist on (i) active and effective Administration support for repeal and (ii) action on this some time during the first session."

Administration waffling on 14b repeal was the first sobering signal to the AFL-CIO that its campaign ardor had been overdone. Labor so intertwined itself with Johnson that he took its loyalty and friendship for granted. The strain over 14b was the forerunner of a host of petty irritations that plagued labor's relations with the Johnson Administration thereafter—never to the point of acrimony, much less that of a formal break. And whatever Meany's pique with Administration spear carriers —specifically, W. Willard Wirtz—he did not criticize Johnson publicly, as he had Roosevelt, Truman, and Eisenhower.

Wirtz was another matter. Aloof, keenly intellectual, impressed with his own erudition and wit, Wirtz did not feel comfortable with Meany from his first days in office. Even during the euphoria of 1964, Meany frequently growled about "that blasted egghead" and complained of Wirtz's "damned superior attitude." Nelson Cruikshank witnessed one especially biting encounter:

Cruikshank and an AFL-CIO staff attorney were at the Labor Department discussing technical details of changes in an unemployment compensation law with Wirtz and several of his aides. "There was one point which appeared minor, but which actually would have far-reaching impact on the unemployed. I was pressing this point on Secretary Wirtz, and he looked at me and said, 'Are you really representing Mr. Meany on this, or is this your idea?'

"Jesus, I was furious. 'Mr. Secretary, if there is any question about that, there is no point in me staying here,' I said. I got up and walked out. What the hell—I've been working in this field for twenty years. To challenge my integrity at this point, and in a room full of people. I went right to Meany's office and reported what happened. He said I was right. He got Wirtz on the phone and said, 'I'd like to see you. When can you come over?' Then he told Virginia Tehas to 'let him sit out there in the outer office a little bit when he gets here.' "

When Wirtz was finally ushered into the office, Meany lectured him: "I understand you questioned whether Brother Nelson is representing me or not. I want to clear up any question there is on that. If I did not have confidence that he would represent me, I wouldn't have sent him in the first place. If there is ever any time when you think he is not, if you want to take it up with me, I'll let you know. Now is that understood?" Cruikshank said, "Now, here was a Secretary of Labor, mind you, in a sense a member of our own party (if we have a party), with me sitting right there. Now, all a cabinet officer needs to know is that a guy will back up his staff like that. Wirtz never questioned me again."

On another issue, that of an undersecretary of labor, Johnson sided with Meany in a confrontation with Wirtz. When Wirtz succeeded Arthur J. Goldberg he inherited John Henning, formerly an officer of the California State Federation of Labor, and a quiet power in the AFL-CIO's Building and Construction Trades Department. Henning was the top-ranking labor figure in government, and he had been appointed on direct recommendation of Meany. Henning and Wirtz wrangled quietly through most of 1964 over whether teen-agers working in the Neighborhood Youth Corps, a poverty program, should receive the $1.25 per hour minimum wage. Wirtz felt that since the jobs were only a step above welfare, participants should not expect regular wages. Henning, speaking for the AFL-CIO, maintained Wirtz was undercutting wage scales. Meany also intervened and talked with the President. In a heated intra-Administration argument, Wirtz had to back down.

Several weeks after the election, however, Wirtz told Johnson that as secretary he should be entitled to choose his own number-two man. Johnson acquiesced. But not wishing to make Henning's dismissal conspicuous, he attempted to conceal it in what the White House described as a general reshuffling of subcabinet officers. Meany realized exactly what was happening and raised such a clamor in the White House that Johnson and Wirtz yielded to him. The Minneapolis *Tribune* commented, "There is no reason why Wirtz should have to beg for Meany's permission to replace Henning and every reason why Wirtz should have a free hand in determining his assistant at that high policy level." (Henning finally went to New Zealand as ambassador in early 1967.)

But 14b remained the chief irritant between labor and the Administration. During the winter and early spring of 1965, Meany repeatedly reminded Johnson and Wirtz of the campaign promises. One complicating factor was a strike of dockworkers which began in late 1964 and dragged on into the next year. Wirtz told the executive council in February the Administration might hold back on 14b because of public backlash to the dock strike, but he "strongly felt" repeal would come during the 1965 session. Meany reported the President was "standing on his position on repeal," and that "we can expect his full support—the problem at the moment is the question of timing." Meany said Johnson "thought that Congress should settle down first and move ahead with what was left over from the 1964 legislative program" before plunging into 14b, which was bound to be controversial. Meany saw a "fairly good working margin" in the House for repeal but warned that "antilabor groups are extremely active in hiring prominent lawyers to further their cause." Further, Senator John McClellan was planning to revive his probe of "labor racketeering" to coincide with debate over repeal. When Johnson finally sent a labor message to Congress in May, he devoted one laconic paragraph to 14b, tagged onto the bottom.

By autumn labor was becoming restless, and its old suspicions about "Lying Down Lyndon" began to revive. Repeal passed the House handily and came out of the Senate Labor Committee with a comfortable twelve-to-three vote, only to run into the threat of a filibuster by Senator Dirksen. Although Dirksen did not claim to have enough support to kill repeal in a straight up and down vote, he said at least twenty Senators would filibuster—enough to deadlock the Senate indefinitely. The council put hard questions to Wirtz, who insisted 14b repeal remained at the "top of the Administration's legislative program." Meany would not accept the suggestion that repeal be put over for a year; failure to act "would be a terrific disappointment and would lead to substantial disillusionment among our members," he said.

At the AFL-CIO convention in December, Meany stripped criticism of the Administration from a resolution on 14b, although he did comment, "I find it hard to believe that a really determined majority cannot, if it has the will and leadership, overcome any tactics that a minority might pursue." But the fact was, as labor journalist John Herling wrote, "Organized labor has identified itself too intimately with the Johnson Administration to beat it about the head for the failure of the Democratic majority leadership" to achieve repeal.

When the repeal attempt revived in early 1966 Biemiller counted fifty-four votes for repeal, but not nearly enough for the two-thirds margin required to invoke cloture and break Dirksen's filibuster. "Meany and I visited Dirksen to see if we could find some way to break the jam," Biemiller said. "Meany loathed Dirksen and all those honey-toned speeches about 'issues of substantial national importance and overriding moral principle blah blah blah'; he would imitate him when we left. Anyway, Dirksen tried to make a deal with us. He said that if labor would not oppose his constitutional amendment overturning the Supreme Court's one-man, one-vote decision on legislative apportionment, he would stop fighting 14b. George told him that he would make no such deal." Meany also made Dirksen's offer public: "I hope the nation understands," he said, "that the filibuster is a punitive and coercive tactic. It is a cynical invitation to a deal. It is the crafty politician's way of saying, 'Come around to the back door. . . .' Well, as badly as we in the labor movement want 14b repealed, we do not want it that badly. And the Senate minority leader and all his antilabor stooges can filibuster until hell freezes over before I will agree to sell the people short for that kind of deal." Nor could Meany and Biemiller persuade Senator Mike Mansfield, the Democratic majority leader, to hold night sessions to break the filibuster. "Mansfield wouldn't say a damned thing when we talked to him, he'd just sit there and puff on that pipe," Biemiller said.

The most conspicuous absentee from the fight was the Johnson Administration. Despite its many promises to labor, the White House did not make the wholehearted campaign for 14b that told Congress the President was truly interested in an issue. Senators received calls from the White House asking support of Lady Bird Johnson's beautification program—not, however, on behalf of 14b repeal. The evidence suggests Johnson made no more than a *pro forma* battle either because he did not want to squander legislative credits over an issue that interested no one other than labor, or because he felt labor really did not care about 14b. Wirtz said he thought at the time "14b had more symbolic value to the AFL-CIO than anything else. Labor has trouble mobilizing the rank and file, getting them fired up for an election. Once they had done that with 14b, it lost any true meaning." Wirtz several years later denied any deliberate foot dragging by the Johnson Administration. "How do you define an 'all-out effort' anyway?" he asked. "There are gradations of campaigns, and I thought we pushed pretty hard on 14b."

Concurrently, labor became increasingly restive with the Johnson Administration's stated intention of holding wage increases within guidelines set by the Council of Economic Advisers. The CEA, continuing the anti-inflation strategy of President Kennedy, wanted to limit increases to around 3.2 percent, roughly the rate of productivity growth. The guidelines had worked well the first two years of the Kennedy Administration, a period of relative economic stability. In bargaining, unions settled for improvements in fringe benefits and job security, rather than increases in real wages. Steelworkers, for example, won a thirteen-week vacation for the top fifth of the work force each year for five years.

With the economic upswing of 1963, however, corporate profits began to soar. American Telephone & Telegraph Company went from $1.479

billion net earnings in 1963 to $1.796 billion in 1965; General Motors from $1.591 billion to $2.126 billion. With such riches in corporate bank accounts, neither business nor labor was in the mood for further restraints. The United Auto Workers, arguing that auto manufacturers could pay higher wages from profits without raising prices, won increases averaging 4.9 percent in 1964, followed shortly by large settlements in the steel and electrical goods industries. Corporate profits were rising twice as fast as the gross national product, almost twice as fast as wages. Yet the average worker was not winning increases even at the guideline level. Real hourly income rose by only 2.6 percent from 1961 to 1966, about $8 billion a year less than had pay scales matched the guidelines.

Even under normal conditions, the wage-profit disparity would have touched off inflation in the absence of controls. The fatal aggravating factor in 1965–66 was Vietnam. The sharp upswing in military spending in mid-1965, concurrent with the troop buildup, threw a kink into the American economy that was to last well into the 1970's.

The Johnson Administration faced two immediate questions in late 1965 and early 1966: whether the economy could support both the guns of the Vietnam War and the butter of the Great Society; and whether the wage-price guidelines should be maintained by the force of law or the iffiness of jawboning. The AFL-CIO early took the position that Vietnam spending should not disrupt social programs; that enough money was available for both guns and butter. Meany wrote the President in late 1965 he was "disturbed by numerous newspaper reports of impending slashes of the government's economic and social programs." Meany recognized the budgetary problems caused by Vietnam. "However, I do not believe that the burden of the war . . . should be borne by economic and social measures . . . such as the war on poverty and aid to education . . . the popular expectations [Great Society programs] have aroused should not be destroyed or undermined."

Meany told Wirtz during a private meeting in January that although labor officially opposed the guidelines, "if the President is going to hold prices in line, we have got to do our part" on wages. All he asked was evenhanded treatment. At Meany's direction, the executive council in February adopted a policy statement pledging:

If the President determines that the situation warrants extraordinary over-all stabilization measures, the AFL-CIO will cooperate so long as such restraints are equitably placed on all costs and incomes—including all prices, profits, dividends, rents, and executive compensation, as well as employees' wages and salaries.

But imposing wartime controls would be a tacit admission that Vietnam had blossomed into full-blown war—something Johnson was unwilling to do in 1966. Johnson was in the middle stages of graduated escalation, the war strategy intended to bring victory without full mobilization economically, militarily, or politically. AFL-CIO staff economists disagreed with the President; their opinion, relayed to the White House through Meany, was that the recovering economy would be thrown out of kilter by the heavy infusion of Vietnam spending and that controls should be brought into play early to prevent inflation. The AFL-CIO knew from past experience that wages never caught up with prices once a wartime inflation spiral began. After long debate, however, the Johnson Administration decided against mandatory controls. The evidence suggests Johnson felt he could control the economy through dint of personality alone; that his suasion of business and labor leaders would be sufficient.

As a result, Meany was considerably irked when the Administration attempted to use the guidelines as an excuse for opposing an increase in the minimum wage from $1.25 per hour to $1.60. Wirtz told the executive council at its winter 1966 meeting that the Administration felt the increase would be inflationary. Meany responded he would talk with the President. Later, back in Washington, Wirtz told newsmen privately of Meany's intentions and scoffed at them. "No one," he said, "engages in collective bargaining with the President of the United States." When the statement got back to Meany, he sent his own private message to Wirtz: "The day has long passed," he said in effect, "since the trade union movement approaches the President of the United States on bended knees." Meany made enough of his pique public to unsettle the Administration. At a press conference in early 1966 a reporter asked, "If the President comes out for smaller minimum wage [than the $1.60 asked by labor] what would be your reaction?"

"Our reaction would be to fight for what we think we should get," Meany replied.

"What is your general feeling toward the Council of Economic Advisers and the path it's taking?" another newsman asked.

"There's ladies present," Meany said. The minimum wage, he continued, "is a basic test of the good faith of the Great Society program."

Disturbed about labor's restiveness, Johnson called Meany and Reuther in for a long private talk in February. Meany told the President labor bore him "no personal animosity" on 14b but that he felt unions had legitimate complaints on the guidelines. Meany said he "didn't trust the mathematics" of the Council of Economic Advisers; that if it had been consistent, the "acceptable guidepost" should now be 3.6 percent, rather than 3.2 percent, because of productivity gains. He noted also that "if guidelines were to have any meaning, labor should be part of the formulating body. The guidelines were a political, not an economic, decision." Meany said he would no longer consider the CEA an impartial economic arbiter. Johnson said he "would work out something" on the minimum wage.

Andrew Biemiller picked up the story: "My phone rang one evening about seven o'clock, and it was the President. 'I've got Meany here,' he said, 'and he wants to talk with you.' Meany asked whether David Dubinsky and Jacob Potofsky 'would buy $1.40 the first year, $1.65 the second,' on the minimum wage. They were important because the garment workers rely upon the minimum wage as a sort of floor under their pay. I told him I though they would, and Johnson came back on the line. 'It's a deal,' he told me. I asked if he could keep his Council of Economic Advisers in line. He said, 'I'll have a letter on the Hill tomorrow from them saying the raise is not inflationary.'" Biemiller continued: "Now that is why we liked working with Lyndon Johnson."

By autumn the minimum wage decision and other breaches had bent the guidelines beyond recognition. In October, Gardner Ackley, chairman of the Council of Economic Advisers, all but admitted the guidelines no longer existed. "The guidepost* *arithmetic* doesn't change simply because prices have been going up," Ackley said in a CBS interview. "Perhaps the guidepost *politics* have changed in the sense that it becomes more difficult to ask labor to accept wage increases that are related to productivity gains." Johnson continued to give business and labor periodic lectures on the virtue of restraint. But his heart was not in it. At the 1967 AFL-CIO convention Johnson literally raced through the portion of his speech asking labor to hold back on its wage request, as if the plea were unpleasant but necessary business. The labor audience applauded Johnson thirty-five times during the speech, but not once when he was talking about wage restraint.

Throughout the spring of 1966 Meany played another trump card: the threat that labor would be indifferent to the 1966 congressional elections. No one in Meany's inner circle—nor in the White House—took Meany seriously. But Meany encouraged speculation about labor's political intentions "to put some backbone" in selected congressmen, in the words of one of his political advisers. Many first-term congressmen owed their election to the Johnson landslide; their continuing in office depended upon extraordinary outside support in 1966. Meany told the executive council in February, "It must be made known to the Democratic party that they cannot own us." Although Meany recognized that "President Johnson has done many good jobs . . . [he] has not done a good job on the repeal of Section 14b and minimum wages." But Meany had made the same threat so often, without fulfilling it, that he carried no credibility. AFL-CIO political activity was undiminished in the 1966

* Administration economists used the words "guidelines" and "guideposts" interchangeably.

campaigns. The Committee on Political Education concentrated on fifty-nine marginal districts where incumbent liberals had won in 1964 with less than fifty-five percent of the vote. According to COPE, on eleven key votes on major legislation in 1965 "these fifty-nine congressmen cast a total of 585 right votes, only forty wrong votes. . . . Not one piece of progressive legislation would have made it [without them]. . . . Many other districts, of course, are important, but these are make-or-break. They include some of the brightest, most imaginative, and most liberal members of Congress—the big hitters." COPE spent almost $1 million on political activity. Additionally, international unions detailed 140 men to work full time in state campaigns, and another 127 in congressional campaigns. Labor concentrated in Illinois, in an attempt to save Senator Paul Douglas, facing a strong challenge from Republican Charles Percy, and in California, where Governor Pat Brown was threatened by Ronald Reagan. Labor printed and mailed 2.5 million anti-Reagan brochures in California; 900,000 brochures in Illinois; 700,000 brochures in Pennsylvania (to help Milton Shapp, a Democrat running for the governorship).

The results were a disaster. Andrew Biemiller, surveying the new Congress for the executive council in November, found 181 "friends," compared with 223 the year before. Of the 59 "marginal" congressmen, only 29 won. Biemiller saw 232 "bad" congressmen. In the Senate, he counted 54 "good" members and five others who "might be friendly" on specific issues. But labor had no chance of passing 14b repeal in the Senate, even in the unlikely event it got through the House.

Alexander Barkan, national director of COPE, placed much of responsibility for the losses on the Democratic National Committee, which he said was "bankrupt in this campaign . . . and really not in existence." Factional fights abounded in the party, contributing to losses in California, Minnesota, Wisconsin, and New York. Barkan continued:

> Even so, many elections would have been won if the Democratic National Committee would have functioned. The unfortunate thing was that President Johnson, in spite of the best legislative record in history, suffers personal unpopularity, to which is added much frustration due to inflation, the farm program, and other matters, all of which add up to the tide which engulfed so many liberal legislators supported by COPE.
>
> The outcome . . . was frustrating for COPE because COPE had its best operations since merger, with more money, more manpower, more communication with members, better organization on registration and get-out-the-vote; more and better telephone banks, more and better ward and district organization.
>
> If there were any weaknesses in COPE, it might have been in the area of political understanding of our members.

Although Barkan made no formal recommendations, his implication was clear: labor could not rely upon the Democratic National Committee to take the lead in Lyndon Johnson's expected campaign for reelection.

The words "Great Society" vanished from the American political lexicon soon after the 1966 mid-term elections, as Johnson turned his nightotal attention to Vietnam.

Vietnam. The unbreakable bond. The issue on which Meany stood by Johnson even when the Democratic party—and much of the country— went elsewhere. Meany supported Johnson unflinchingly on Vietnam from the Gulf of Tonkin incident in August 1964, which took America over the threshold from adviser to warrior; through the graduated escalation of 1965–67; to the bloody Götterdämmerung of the Tet offensive of February 1968 and Johnson's abdication. "In adversity, the family always pulls a little closer together," Johnson said in November 1967 at a Jewish Labor Committee dinner honoring Meany, "and as the war clouds hover around us . . . I think it is good that we could be here and be in the same room together tonight." No nonofficial American clung closer to Johnson than did Meany. Meany spoke more on Vietnam than on perhaps any single issue during 1965–68. The executive council issued nine statements between August 1964 and February 1968 that dealt with Indochina in whole or in part; both conventions that met during the period issued ringing endorsements of Johnson's conduct of the war. Meany did not posture as an armchair general; American labor, he said, would not try to tell the generals where and if they should drop a single bomb. Several themes ran through Meany's speeches and the statements by the executive council (Jay Lovestone's language, but Meany's sentiments):

—*Loyalty to a friendly state.* "We have a commitment in Vietnam to help the people of South Vietnam maintain their freedom. . . . Suppose we stepped out of Vietnam. What would happen? Two million people would go into slavery immediately. . . ."

—*The war as continued Communist expansionism.* "Do you think the Communists would stop at South Vietnam? Well, of course they wouldn't. . . . I would rather fight the Communists in South Vietnam than fight them down here in the Chesapeake Bay, when they are landing on our own shores."

—*Scorn of war critics.* Meany quoted approvingly nineteenth-century humorist Josh Billings: "It's better to know nothing than to know what ain't so." He denounced "those elements [who] . . . would have the world believe that the war in Vietnam is President Johnson's war, that it is reactionary war and that America is seeking imperialist advantages and domination. I know of no more dangerous package of outright falsehoods. In many instances, these total lies have been prefabricated in Moscow and Peking." The executive council said in October 1965: ". . . *Slander of our country is not synonymous with study of its policies.* . . . Any organization or movement dedicated to breaking the law of the land (burning draft cards, stopping troop trains) can only be treated as a lawbreaking body."

—*Broad support of Johnson policies, both from labor and the public* ". . . I am quite sure that no matter what those college professors say, the great majority of the American people, if they know the facts . . . would be on the side of the President. . . . The American labor movement must lead now [August 1965] in letting all of the people know that they have a responsibility to support the Commander-in-Chief . . . because it is a war for us. . . . Labor has the organization, it has the knowledge, it has the courage, it has the strength to take this responsibility. We can't let these intellectual jitterbugs who preside over classes in some of our colleges—and God help us, God help our children if we don't do a little better with these fellows.

—*Opposition to total war.* Meany abhorred "the very very few in this country who would have the United States resort to a preventive war. The AFL-CIO does not buy this fatal fallacy. It is not our aim to kill Russians, Chinese, Albanians, or any other people. We want to see them live in peace and freedom."

Meany's Vietnam views were totally consistent with the anticommunism he had espoused publicly for three decades. Nonetheless they exacerbated his alienation from liberals and intellectuals long enraptured with their personal concepts of the labor movement. Vietnam stood as the *cause célèbre* of American intellectuals during the 1960's. That Meany, the voice of proletariat America, should take a position different from "the liberal mainstream," as the Vietnam critics fancied themselves, was idiocy of the rankest order. John Kenneth Galbraith, in his inaugural address as president of Americans for Democratic Action in April 1967, called labor leadership "aged, contented, and deeply somnambulant. . . . [O]n important issues of foreign policy its position is well to the rear of Gerald Ford [the Republican House minority leader from Michigan]."

In 1952, when French forces were on the brink of defeat, the executive council urged appointment of an "American deputy" to the French commander—an idea that, if heeded, could have hastened dispatch of U.S. troops to Indochina by almost a decade. The AFL's next policy statement, in a 1954 editorial Meany wrote for the *American Federationist,* offered an analysis of the pending Geneva peace conference. Inclusion of "Ho Chi Minh's Communist quisling regime" in the talks, Meany said, "will greatly increase the prestige of the Indochinese rebels among the people of Indochina and all Asia [and] . . . weaken the will of the Indochinese population to resist him and his terrorist bands." During the Geneva conference the AFL executive council proposed a plan calling for free elections under United Nations auspices; for the transfer of the "foreign investment in Indochina [about $300 million] to the Vietnamese people as aid to the reconstruction of their war-ravaged land"; for France and England "to break with their colonialist policies and practices . . . before the Communist agents of Soviet imperialism come into these areas [Indochina, Egypt, and North Africa] in full force to distort and destroy the national and democratic aspirations of these peoples"; and for a regional defense group, the "Pacific Alliance for Peace and Freedom," to stop further "Communist subversion."

The Geneva settlement—dividing Vietnam into two sectors pending elections—disgusted Meany, and in an *American Federationist* editorial he sounded disappointed that the United States had not intervened militarily. He said U.S. policy "has become confused, haphazard and chicken-hearted." Speaking to the American Legion convention in September, he said the Geneva agreement "has merely served to whet the appetite of the Communist conspiracy for further conquest. To put it bluntly, when the test came, our government lacked the courage to make a hard-and-fast decision and did nothing."

The AFL-CIO's next statement on Vietnam came almost exactly a decade later. The executive council was in session in Chicago during the Tonkin Gulf incidents of August 1964, and heartily approved Johnson's bombing of North Vietnam bases in retaliation for reported attacks on U.S. destroyers patrolling in the Gulf. Statements the next three years whisked through the executive council with minimum discussion and no dissent.

Prior to the 1965 convention Lovestone circulated drafts of resolutions on international affairs to members of the resolutions committee, which Reuther chaired. Reuther supported all of them save the one on Vietnam. "He didn't say that he was against it, only that he wanted to 'go over it more carefully,'" said Lovestone. "Days passed without comment. Then I forced the issue at a breakfast with Reuther, Meany, and George Harrison. Walter said he had no objection to the resolution, but he would like to have it shortened. Now, here I had him. When writing one of these resolutions, I always make it a little longer than necessary. If someone insists on 'change,' I can always find a harmless paragraph or two to delete, to let them think they are winning something—I 'give away one of the sleeves from my vest,' as the saying goes. So we cut out something or another and made Walter happy. Now, the resolution that came out, he had nothing to do with it except delay. Reuther spoke for it, however, and people thought it was his." The resolution said that "the

Communist enemy can never be defeated by military means alone." But it pledged AFL-CIO support "of *all measures the Administration might deem necessary* to halt Communist aggression and secure a just and lasting peace"—language broad enough to encompass any military adventure the U.S. might undertake. Reuther told friends later he succeeded in deleting some "overly militaristic" language and in emphasizing hopes for a negotiated settlement. Lovestone insisted this was not so.

But Vietnam debate did spill onto the floor of an AFL-CIO convention for the first time. Antiwar demonstrators interrupted Secretary of State Dean Rusk, a guest speaker, with chants and boos. Meany, from the rostrum, denounced them as "kooks." Emil Mazey, the UAW secretary-treasurer, attacked Administration war policy, only to be undercut immediately by a Reuther speech: "Lyndon Johnson is just as concerned about peace as was Jack Kennedy, because he too can understand that peace transcends every other question."

On the eve of the next AFL-CIO convention, in 1967, antiwar unionists held a "National Labor Leadership Conference for Peace" in Chicago and proposed that the AFL-CIO take no position on the war—an indirect means of withdrawing labor support from Johnson policies. The insurgent conference was caught up in the "Dump Johnson" antiwar fervor, and Senator Eugene J. McCarthy (Dem., Minnesota), who had just announced his candidacy for the Democratic nomination, was a featured speaker. The peace group's proposal was put before the AFL-CIO convention by Charles Cogen of the Teachers Union, supported by backbenchers from the retail and wholesale clerks union and the Colorado state federation. Their motion was overwhelmingly rejected, only six delegates of some 2,000 supporting it in a standing vote. Meany was scornful of the antiwar groups. Speaking on the basis of intelligence given him by the FBI, Meany charged that the Chicago meeting had been planned in Hanoi and that he had read "every line of the statement [it produced] in the *Sunday Worker* two weeks before" the conference began. Emil Mazey, who had participated in the conference, did not attend the AFL-CIO convention because the UAW was already in the process of withdrawing from the federation. But he angrily rebutted Meany, accusing him of telling "a deliberate lie . . . an outright lie." Mazey wrote: "I would like to believe that you were misinformed, but that is difficult since you twice claim personally to have read the resolution in the *Sunday Worker*. That is impossible, of course, because the resolution was not printed in that or any other paper before it was passed. Nor can I believe that you really thought that a group had gone to Hanoi to plan the meeting. If you had, you doubtless would have named the persons involved. . . . Your conduct in this matter raises serious questions as to your personal integrity and your capacity to lead in the American labor movement. The technique of the big lie, the use of character assassination, and the suppression of dissent must not become the hallmark of the American labor movement." Mazey demanded a retraction. Meany said he "absolutely" stood on his statement.

Besides making policy statements—valuable chiefly for public relations purposes—Meany helped the Johnson Administration in its relations with Vietnamese trade unions. The Confederation of Vietnamese Labor (CVT, by its French initials) was "one of the few free labor bodies in Asia" in the early 1960's, according to the veteran journalist Robert Shaplen. Its leader, Tran Quoc Buu, was in and out of favor with Saigon's swinging-door governments throughout the decade. He frequently visited the United States under State Department auspices, meeting each time with Meany or the executive council. Meany consistently maintained, in talks with Johnson and other Administration officials, that strong trade unions should be a part of any reconstructed South Vietnam. The AFL-CIO sent a steady flow of consultants and study groups to Vietnam. Thomas W. ("Teddy") Gleason, president of the International Longshoremen's Association, took responsibility for untangling logistical snarls in the port of Saigon and the mammoth U.S. supply base at Cam Ranh Bay. The AFL-CIO, using federal funds supplied through the Agency for International Development, created in 1968 the Asian-American Free Labor Institute to help guide the CVT. In its first three years, the AAFLI trained some 2,700 CVT leaders and financed CVT offices in fifteen Vietnamese provinces. The AFL-CIO bought such varied equipment as Lambretta buses, mimeograph machines, tractors, public address systems, and Vietnamese-keyboard typewriters. In turn, Johnson and his foreign policy advisers gave Meany and other labor leaders constant insider's information on the course of the war.

War opponents criticized Meany on several grounds for his continuing endorsement of Johnson's policies, especially after the wide revulsion following the Tet offensive of February 1968. They claimed, variously, that Meany was "out of touch with the rank and file" on the war and that Johnson "bought" his loyalty, by making federal funds available for AFL-CIO international operations. The existing data suggest otherwise. In January 1967 professional pollster John Kraft did a major study of attitudes of union members for the Committee on Political Education. He found that a "vast majority . . . support the President's conduct of the war there." In the fall of 1967 delegates were polled at conventions of ten state federations and three international unions. The results: 1,448 delegates endorsed the then-policy; 1,368 wanted to escalate; 471, to de-escalate; and 276 to withdraw.

Senator J. William Fulbright (Dem., Arkansas), chairman of the Senate Foreign Relations Committee, was among war critics who felt Meany and the AFL-CIO were overly enthusiastic about U.S. policy in Asia.

Questioning the $20 million in AID funds given the AFL-CIO's American Institute for Free Labor Development between 1960 and 1968, Fulbright asked, in 1969, "I have wondered if this represented the price we paid for Mr. Meany's support in Vietnam. He was a stalwart supporter of the previous Administration policies, but I should not think the new Administration would feel indebted to him." Fulbright made these remarks in connection with the release of a committee staff report which was highly critical of AIFLD's efficacy. Meany demanded an audience on the charges and during three hours of testimony (often shouted exchanges) forced Fulbright to back down partially. "It is a gratuitous insult on the American labor movement to accuse us of receiving a payoff for supporting the foreign policy of any administration," Meany told Fulbright. He asked if "you feel that anyone that disagrees with you on foreign policy must have an ulterior motive?" Meany went on sarcastically: "Who paid you when you voted to support their policy in Vietnam? Somebody pay you for that? I don't think so. But I have as much right to say that somebody paid you for voting for the Tonkin Gulf resolution as you have to say that Johnson was paying me for supporting him in Vietnam."

George Meany began 1968 ready to endorse Lyndon Johnson for reelection and to throw the full resources of labor into his campaign. Meany thought the Vietnam issue, which was tearing America asunder, was misused "by both 'liberal' appeasers and reactionary jingos as a weapon against domestic progress." Meany felt Johnson deserved reelection because of his record; that to oppose him because of Vietnam ("somebody else's war, and one he is trying to settle honorably") was cheap, shabby politics. Labor tried to discourage the "Dump Johnson" movement from its very beginning. Meany spoke bitingly of the union "woo-woos" who attended an anti-Johnson rally in Chicago in November. Gus Tyler, political director of the International Ladies' Garment Workers Union, called the Dump Johnson strategy "simple and suicidal." The "first victims . . . will be the representatives and senators in the 'peace wing' of Congress"—persons who generally supported labor on domestic issues.

The challenges to Johnson infuriated Meany, and he wanted labor to have no part of them. The 1967 AFL-CIO convention resolution supporting Johnson on Vietnam "left no doubt where union members stand," Meany said in a New Year's Day message, "and we are sure the convention spoke for the vast, silent majority* in the nation." When

* In November 1969 President Nixon said in a Vietnam speech over national TV: "And so—to you, the great *silent majority* of my fellow Americans—I ask for your support. . . ."

Americans for Democratic Action endorsed Senator Eugene McCarthy's campaign against Johnson for the Democratic nomination, I. W. Abel, president of the United Steel Workers, and Louis Stulberg, the ILGWU president, quit the board in protest.

On February 9—immediately after the disastrous Tet offensive— Meany moved to discourage any notion that swelling antiwar sentiment would sway labor away from Johnson. He called a conference of officers in affiliated unions, the fifty state central bodies of the AFL-CIO, and the major city central bodies, to meet in the Washington Hilton Hotel on March 29. Meany first intended the conference as the sort of perfunctory labor pep rally traditionally held at the beginning of a campaign year, one where orators warn about the "choice between liberalism and reaction," and about not permitting "a coalition of retreat to undermine gains we have already made" (phrases from Meany's letter of invitation) —speeches-for-all-ages usable in 1948 and 1958 as well as 1968. But the swift rush of early 1968 politics gave new urgency to the meeting. On March 12, Senator Eugene J. McCarthy (Dem., Minnesota), standard-bearer of the Dump Johnson movement, won an astoundingly high share of the New Hampshire Democratic primary vote, 42.2 percent compared with 49.4 percent for Johnson. Labor had worked hard for Johnson in New Hampshire, with the Committee on Political Education concentrating on blue-collar workers in the industrial section of Manchester. Despite these efforts, McCarthy received about one fourth of the vote in labor districts. More surprising, according to public opinion polls taken just before the primary vote, Senator Robert F. Kennedy, who was not even a candidate, drew almost as much support from union members as did Johnson—to the dismay and surprise of Meany. On March 16, after pained weeks of vacillation, Kennedy decided to make the race. He made a courtesy telephone call to Meany in advance, but did not ask—nor was he offered—labor support. At his announcement press conference, Kennedy was asked how much help he expected from labor. He replied, "Well, obviously, I'm going to need some support from members of labor organizations, or my effort will not be successful. I would hope that perhaps some of those labor leaders would support me. The indications have been from their public pronouncements and public statements that they are supporting Johnson and that I can understand."

McCarthy's New Hampshire performance and Kennedy's entry gave the Dump Johnson movement a momentum that Meany recognized could sweep an incumbent President from office. Hence Meany was somber when he faced some 5,000 unionists assembled in a ballroom of the Washington Hilton on March 29, a Friday. The thrust of his address was that you-never-had-it-so-good. He ticked off a catalogue of social legislation passed since 1964. He warned that "these guys trying to bust the party" would succeed only in electing a Republican President. As the *pièce de résistance,* the ballroom lights dimmed and the audience watched a film of a conversation between Meany and the President. Johnson earnestly swore that the economic demands of the Vietnam War would not diminish his commitment to the social and domestic programs sought by labor. Although no resolutions were offered, the conference was tantamount to a labor endorsement of Johnson—an advance convention for a major (if informal) wing of the Democratic party.

On Saturday, March 30, Meany went to New York to politic for Johnson before a dinner meeting of the ILGWU joint board. On Sunday evening, March 31, Meany settled down before the television set in the living room of his Bethesda home, awaiting a Johnson speech on Vietnam. The phone rang a few minutes before the speech began. It was Marvin Watson, calling from the White House. "The President wanted to tell you in advance," Watson said, "that . . ."

Looking through the debris of the Democratic party when he got to his office the morning of April 1, Meany saw two things that must be done: push Vice-President Hubert H. Humphrey into the race as swiftly as possible, as the legitimate heir to the Great Society; and dissuade any labor figures from bolting to Robert Kennedy.

Meany's early warm feelings about Robert Kennedy—a rapport as deep, in its own way, as that he had with John Kennedy—had begun to chill even while Robert was Attorney General. Kennedy came to Meany's office one day to ask AFL-CIO support for wire-tap legislation that was part of an omnibus crime control bill. Harking back to the days when management used phone taps to spy on union activities, Meany said that as a matter of principle he could not endorse wire tapping. "But this will help me in the Hoffa investigation," Kennedy exclaimed. "Jimmy Hoffa isn't that damned important," Meany responded. Later, after Kennedy left, Meany grumbled, "That kid ought to stop every once in a while and see where he's going." But when Kennedy ran for the Senate from New York in 1964, Meany helped consolidate his support in the New York State AFL-CIO. The incumbent, Senator Kenneth Keating, went before the convention and cited a voting record that was 80 percent "correct" by the AFL-CIO's continuing scorecard. He knew he faced a hopeless situation, and he tried to joke about it. "I don't think any baseball team would get rid of a man who batted .800," Keating said. "That's better than Babe Ruth or Mickey Mantle." But Meany had already spoken with Ray Corbett, the state federation president, and labor went with Kennedy.

But once in the Senate Kennedy accelerated his in-progress transition from conservative to reluctant liberal to what biographer David Halberstam called "a course of increasing radicalism—proffering more radical ideas and taking on, from people like [Allard] Lowenstein [the leader of the Dump Johnson movement], more radical advice. His course was not so much a consistent philosophy as it was the application of his puritanism (what one friend called his perpetual sense of outrage) to a changing America." Impatient with failure, both in men and in programs, Kennedy chafed at the glacial pace of conventional government —at the inequities and failures hidden behind grandiose, nonworking structures. Labor was one institution he felt was flawed. Speaking to an ADA dinner in early 1967, he resorted to the third person to say some things very much on his own mind:

> Labor has been in the forefront of many a great battle. But youth looks with other eyes, and their view is very different: they think of labor as grown sleek and bureaucratic with power, sometimes frankly discriminatory, occasionally even corrupt and exploitative; a force not for change but for the status quo, unwilling or unable to organize new groups of members, indifferent to the men who once worked the coal mines of Appalachia, a latecomer to the struggles of the grape pickers of California or the farm laborers of the Mississippi Delta.

Kennedy qualified this picture as perhaps "one-sided" but he concluded by saying that liberal groups, including labor, should not "ignore the need for change." Meany, who kept a close watch on what ADA and its followers were saying and doing, chiefly for political intelligence, was irritated enough by the speech to mention it to a staff member a few days later: "So I see Bobby's hired Walter Reuther as a speech writer." Later, as Kennedy attacked Johnson for letting Vietnam drag without resolution, Meany used a new epithet when referring to him in private conversations: "jitterbug." The word is one of Meany's favorites; defined loosely, it means anyone who is erratic and inconsistent in his thinking, and it is not complimentary. Meany, a man devoted to orderly procedures and consistency of thought, does not hearken to men subject to abrupt changes of philosophy. By 1968, when Kennedy entered the presidential race, Meany simply did not trust him enough to want him in the White House, either before or after Johnson's abdication.

In April 1968 Meany had no qualms whatsoever about Hubert H. Humphrey, a friend of two decades' standing and a champion of labor in Minnesota for even longer. Meany repeated with gusto a story dating to Humphrey's days as mayor of Minneapolis. "He was mayor just a very, very short time when they had a utility strike. The utility company, in keeping with long-time practice, brought in strikebreakers, set up a dormitory on their properties, set up kitchens, and so forth and so on. Then

Humphrey suddenly decided they didn't have a hotel license and he dumped the beds and the kitchen equipment out on the street and somehow or another that helped the strikers. I don't know whether he intended that to be, but that is the way it worked out." During Humphrey's sixteen years in the Senate, labor kept "right and wrong" voting records on 199 items. "Humphrey voted favorably from our point of view 199 times. He didn't have a single negative vote. That is amazing, because even the people who are deadly opposed to us once in a while have a favorable vote by accident, and you would think that a fellow who supported so much legislation would have at least one unfavorable vote, but that didn't happen." Civil rights, Medicare, aid to education—Humphrey worked in tandem with labor during his Senate tenure. His public devotion to Johnson's Vietnam policies matched, even surpassed, that of Meany.

Humphrey withheld a formal announcement for twenty-seven days after Johnson's abdication. He did not wish to be drawn into any primary confrontations with Kennedy or McCarthy; he considered them a waste of time and money, for delegates were to be had elsewhere—from the power brokers of the Democratic party. Humphrey spent an hour with Meany on April 3 and outlined his basic preconvention strategy: to line up a broad spectrum of endorsements, the consensus of Johnsonian politics; and to find as much hard cash as possible. Meany, wary of Kennedy, wanted Humphrey to announce immediately. But Humphrey was cautious. Once before, in 1960, he had gone forth to fight a Kennedy on an economy-class budget, and took a beating, psychic and political, that left him dazed for months. "Oh, hell, Hubert, get on with it," Meany told him. "No, no, let's do it right," Humphrey replied. Meany promised to do what he could in the interim. He called I. W. Abel, the president of the United Steel Workers, and arranged for Humphrey to address their convention in Pittsburgh two days later.

Later in the day, without even the formality of an executive council meeting, Meany put the AFL-CIO behind Humphrey's candidacy—one man, in effect, unilaterally speaking for more than thirteen million American union members. Meany issued the statement in his own name but used the pronoun "we" in promulgating labor's stand. The statement regretted Johnson's decision not to run again; it went on, "We looked forward to the opportunity to support his candidacy . . ." and tore into McCarthy, Kennedy, and other critics, although not by name.

We are convinced that the American people would have supported him [Johnson] despite the unfair, unremitting, unconscionable personal attacks upon him. No man—and certainly no President—should have been subjected to such a torrent of abuse from the press and from other politicians—including some in his own party upon whom he was entitled to rely for support, but who instead have cultivated and exploited division and disunity for their personal political advantage. . . . The American people must not be left with a choice only among candidates who themselves have symbolized the discord and disunity the President's actions sought to eliminate.

The statement next turned to Humphrey, with a broad suggestion that he run on the Johnsonian record:

To ensure that the issues will be fairly stated and the record adequately presented, defended, and advocated, there must be a presidential candidate as dedicated as the President himself to progress at home and freedom in the world, but who likewise places the welfare of the whole nation first and foremost.

We, therefore, strongly urge that Vice-President Hubert Humphrey declare himself now as a candidate for the presidency. . . .

When Humphrey announced his candidacy at a festive luncheon at the Sheraton Park Hotel on April 29, Meany sat on the dais as a member of "United Democrats for Humphrey." He assigned Al Barkan, the COPE director, to work full time on the Humphrey campaign, and he undercut attempts of Kennedy to win away labor support. Tom Consiglio, a California official of the United Steel Workers, declared for Kennedy, and his name went on the delegate slate for the Democratic primary. He called later, sheepishly, to say it must be removed. I. W. Abel and Meany would not permit him to "associate" the steelworkers with Kennedy. Jesse Unruh, the California legislator running Kennedy's campaign there, lamented, "We tried to get a labor committee going, but Meany said no. We tried desperately, but Meany's power was absolute." (Paul Schrade, state director of the United Auto Workers, was permitted to work for Kennedy, even though Walter Reuther and the UAW board leaned toward Humphrey; he was wounded in the fusillade of gunshots that killed Kennedy the night of the California primary.) John Gilligan, running for the Senate in Ohio with labor support, indiscreetly rode in Kennedy's car in a motorcade. When he went to Washington the next day for a scheduled meeting with Meany, he was snubbed. Not until late in the campaign did Gilligan begin to receive the sort of funding and manpower COPE had promised him. He lost.

Labor did not take the McCarthy candidacy—nor McCarthy, for that matter—seriously. In late 1967, when McCarthy first began to attract daily media attention, Meany remarked to a staff member, "That guy's got as much fuzz in his brains as he does in his mouth." McCarthy's pretense at political divinity, with his tacit assertion that the young and well-educated knew what was best for American, irked the practical-minded men of labor. One union officer told a reporter from the *Sunday Times* of London: "That sort of baloney is all very well for conning money out of rich women with baggy tits, but it just isn't politics!" The political brutality of the Pennsylvania primary illustrated why the Humphrey strategists could ignore McCarthy and concentrate on Kennedy, who played the old politics simultaneously with the new, hunting delegates simultaneously with charming crowds. McCarthy was the only candidate on the Pennsylvania primary ballot, and he received 428,259 votes. Kennedy got 65,430 write-ins; Johnson and Humphrey, another 73,263. With an eight to one lead, McCarthy presumably could expect all or most of Pennsylvania's 130 convention votes (spread among 160 delegates for patronage purposes). But because of an allotment system too bizarre for exploration here, Humphrey received 135 delegates, McCarthy 25. (Humphrey did not even announce his candidacy until four days after the Pennsylvania vote.)

Kennedy's assassination on June 6 ended any practical hope the Dump Johnson enthusiasts had of denying Humphrey the nomination. At the Democratic convention in August, Meany testified for the AFL-CIO before the platform committee and sat back to keep a cautious eye on the debate over the Vietnam plank, his presence a tacit reminder to Humphrey that if he repudiated Johnson's war policies, his candidacy could be one of the lonelier ventures in political history. On Monday, the first day of the convention, Meany hosted a luncheon for the 350-odd labor delegates and alternates, and strongly reminded them of their "duty" to stay with Humphrey. (Paul Schrade of the UAW drew less than fifty union people to a rival Labor-for-McCarthy lunch.) In the end, the shared self-interest of the old Democratic coalition—the white South, labor, northern Negroes, and the big city machines—prevailed, and the fact that McCarthy came to Chicago leading Humphrey in the final preconvention Gallup poll (McCarthy five points behind Nixon; the Vice-President, sixteen) mattered naught. Humphrey came to Chicago with something more important: 1,450 delegates committed even before the convention opened, comfortably above the 1,312 needed for nomination.

Meany's early prominence in the Humphrey coalition, and particularly his opposition to Bob Kennedy, excited the permanent enmity of the left wing of the Democratic party, the liberal intellectuals and doves who had wanted to purge the country of all vestiges of the Johnson Administration, and most certainly its Vice-President. Theodore Sorensen, who helped direct Senator George McGovern's game but foredoomed candidacy in Chicago, was mad enough two years later to fume, in print, at the "spectacle of Southern governors (who later switched to Wallace) and Wall Street bankers (who later switched to Nixon) teaming with George Meany" to oppose Kennedy's candidacy. Meany unreservedly embraced Mayor Richard Daley's handling of convention demonstrators. Speaking to a machinists' convention in Chicago several days after the Democrats dispersed, Meany declared: "I saw the invaders who came to this city. . . . I want to tell you quite frankly that I think the Chicago police did not overreact or whatever that means. What would you do if some group advertised that they were coming in here to prevent you from doing business as you have a right to do—prevent you from holding this convention? I know what you would do with this dirty-necked and dirty-mouthed group of kooks—to be very frank, I am afraid that you might overreact."

Meany's enthusiasm for Humphrey's candidacy, so obvious to the public and to union members who heard his fervent speeches for the Vice-President, was all the more remarkable because of a secret known only to the four or five people who formed the inner circle of the AFL-CIO bureaucracy: beginning in midsummer 1968, Meany had grave doubts as to whether Hubert Humphrey had the strength of character to be President of the United States. His doubts—ones that continued in 1972—came about in this fashion:

Humphrey began his campaign for the Democratic nomination with a Hydra-headed organization. The official campaign group, the United Democrats for Humphrey, was headed by Senators Fred Harris of Oklahoma and Walter F. Mondale of Minnesota, with Richard Maguire handling the money. Meany served on the honorific, nonfunctional steering committee of this group. Another group, Citizens for Humphrey, was built around a band of older Humphrey associates—Max M. Kampelman, David Ginsburg, and James H. Rowe, Jr., all seasoned politicians who had gone from government into lucrative careers as Washington lawyers. Humphrey's vice-presidential staff, headed by William Connell, also expected a big role in the campaign.

Al Barkan, the AFL-CIO's chief political operative, tried for several weeks in the summer to interface Humphrey's sprawling political structure with labor's Committee on Political Education. He had no success whatsoever. Citizens for Humphrey had one idea on how things should be done; United Democrats for Humphrey, another idea; the vice-presidential staff, yet another. Barkan brought in Andrew Biemiller, who knew most of the parties intimately through his lobbying experience. Biemiller threw up his hands after several days and told Barkan, "We'd better get George into this in a hurry." Each of the Humphrey cronies had a resounding title and prominent display on a letterhead, but little direct responsibility and even less penchant for work. "All chiefs and no

Indians, much less any squaws to clean the tepee," someone said of the Humphrey operation.

Barkan and Biemiller related the problem to Meany and arranged a meeting with Humphrey in the Vice-President's office. Meany told Humphrey that he should solidify his organization by appointing a single director, someone with decision-making authority, and clear out some of the bureaucratic underbrush. Humphrey listened politely, nodding his head affirmatively as Meany went through a long list of defects and irritations Barkan and Biemiller had compiled during the past weeks. Meany was blunt. "You'd better get it straightened out," he said, "or you are going to get your ass kicked off."

"George," Humphrey replied, "I know you are right, but these people are my *friends*. I just can't afford to hurt them by telling them to get out of the way. I promise you, we'll work it all out."

Meany went away in a mixture of rage, disbelief, and disgust. He declared he had "serious questions" about the presidential qualifications of a man who could not make unpopular decisions. Meany said that he could understand loyalty, especially when old friends were involved. But a President "must be able to say 'no' to his friends," Meany stormed.

Meany did not let even a hint of his displeasure seep out of his immediate inner circle. Thereafter, however, his private feelings about Humphrey's qualifications were at best lukewarm. His campaign statements for Humphrey during the late summer and early fall, according to one person in a position to know his thinking, resulted more from his deep antipathy toward Richard Nixon than from any desire to see Humphrey in the White House.

Based upon field reports from Al Barkan, Meany had warned President Johnson after the 1966 congressional elections that the Democratic National Committee was an organizational shambles and that it should be overhauled promptly if it was to have any value in 1968. The executive council, at its first postconvention meeting, on September 17, heard more bad news from Barkan. The national committee was more a mess than ever, "disorganized and in financial chaos," in Barkan's words. He worried that "the party cannot get its campaign off the ground with only six weeks remaining until election day." The cities of Philadelphia, Pittsburgh, and Chicago "have the only real political organization that we can count on," Barkan said. He compared the situation with 1960, when a crash voter-registration program by COPE enabled the Democrats to carry twelve of fourteen key targeted states. This time, Barkan said, COPE intended to run intensive registration campaigns in sixteen states, each under the direct supervision of an executive council member and funded by a special $300,000 budget. Barkan said he intended to continue to try to work with the Democratic National Committee, but omens were such that labor well might have to take charge of the Humphrey campaign.

Such proved to be the case, but enthusiasm for Hubert Humphrey was not the primary motive. The Nixon candidacy ensured Humphrey lesser-of-the-evils support. But even more frightening to Meany, according to one key figure on his staff, was the specter of George Wallace. Put most directly, Wallace succeeded in scaring labor into an all-out effort that otherwise might not have been made on Humphrey's behalf. Private polls commissioned by COPE suggested that Wallace could carry enough usually Democratic labor votes to throw Ohio, Pennsylvania, and possibly New Jersey to Nixon. Membership soundings by large international unions found Wallace with twenty-five percent of the union vote in Pennsylvania, thirty-two percent in Connecticut, almost thirty-seven percent in Maryland. In well-publicized straw votes, a UAW local in Flint, Michigan, gave Wallace forty-nine percent of the vote; Nixon and Humphrey split the remainder. Steelworker locals voted for Wallace in Baltimore, Gary, and western Pennsylvania. In some instances the Wallaceite sentiment related directly to attempts by dissidents to oust local union leaders; campaign literature circulated in a Pennsylvania union endorsed Wallace and demanded that the "coons' kissin' cuzzins" (the local officers) be voted out. Other internal analyses showed Humphrey and Nixon neck and neck outside the South, with Wallace's Dixie strength enough to put the election into the House of Representatives. Whatever Meany's reservations about Humphrey, he did not want the responsibility, direct or otherwise, for fragmenting the two-party system. The Louis Harris poll suggested that labor was overwrought. At Wallace's high-water mark in mid-September, according to Harris, only sixteen percent of the union members outside the South supported the Alabaman; Gallup gave him nineteen percent the same week. He faded rapidly thereafter. A postelection analysis by COPE gave him six and a half percent of the labor vote.

In attacking Wallace, COPE astutely outflanked him by circumventing a direct argument with him on the very issue that attracted blue-collar workers to his side: "law and order," a code word encompassing not only crime, but also anti-Negro, antidissident, and antiyouth feelings. "We were able to turn that around," Meany said. "We could concentrate on him and show just what his real attitude toward labor was." COPE went after Wallace on dollars-and-cents issues: that carpenters in anti-union Alabama earned $10 a day less than those in Maryland; that Birmingham schoolteachers received $2,000 to $4,000 a year less than those in the East. COPE assumed (correctly, as the election results proved) that economic self-interest moved blue-collar workers more than appeals to racial prejudice and frustration. Meany stressed Wallace's record as the governor "of a state known for low wages, poor working conditions, and weak unions." He declared, "The Wallace record is the record of Alabama—naked race discrimination, low wage rates, high crime rates, poor compensation for workers when they are unemployed or injured on the job, poor schools, little help for the poverty stricken, and high taxes for workers and low taxes for corporations." If Wallace were elected, Meany warned, he "would undertake to smash America's unions—for they stand as a firm bulwark against dictatorship and the only way Wallace could redeem his promises would be as a dictator." The AFL-CIO blanketed industrial districts with a flyer whose cover read: "George Wallace could cost you one thousand dollars a year."

The COPE campaign apparently succeeded, for Wallace support outside the South was whittled down to what labor considered to be an untouchable hard core; his highest identifiable union vote in the North was slightly less than ten percent (in Michigan, attributable to the bloody racial rioting of the previous summer in Detroit).

For labor, Richard Nixon was a politician indictable for complicity in antiunion legislation from the Taft-Hartley Act (Meany called him the act's "coauthor") to Landrum-Griffin ("he cast the deciding vote in a tie against us and as a result we got Landrum-Griffin"). Meany spent considerable oratorical time berating Nixon over such hoary issues, ones long forgotten by anyone outside labor. He ridiculed Nixon personally, calling him "Dicky" and "our friend Richard." He advised, "Think about the fellow who puts his two hands up and grins at you. It took three years of Hollywood training to develop that. But keep that in mind, that behind that grin is this same old 'Tricky Dick.' "

Oratory, however, seldom changes votes or persuades anyone to go to the polls. The important campaign work was done by COPE, which beginning in the middle of September ran what existed of the Humphrey campaign. Lane Kirkland, Meany's executive assistant (and, after 1969, AFL-CIO secretary-treasurer), stated, "We had to do what we did because the party was bankrupt intellectually and financially. I reached the point where I said I'd never go into Democratic headquarters. I'd go in feeling good and come out feeling terrible. The only useful thing they did was television, in the last couple of weeks, and beyond that they didn't do a goddamned thing except cry."

The COPE operation, at its core, was the time-honored labor stratagem of "register your friends, tell them the issues, then get them to the polls." The new factor was the computer. Volunteers put the names of union members on punch cards, the computers spewed out mailing lists and "walking lists" arranged by street numbers, to be used by personal canvassers, some 72,225 of them at one time or another. The Communications Workers of America, the major representative of Bell Telephone System employees, ran training courses for union volunteers who manned telephone banks—first, to get registration information and spread campaign information; next, to remind members to vote on election day. At the peak COPE had telephone banks in 638 cities, with 8,055 phones manned by 24,611 persons. In Michigan, a particular Wallace target, COPE registered 690,000 voters; in Pennsylvania, 492,000; in the nation as a whole 46 million persons—chiefly labor members and *Democrats.* COPE published a veritable blizzard of literature—55 million pieces under its own imprimatur, another 60 million from international unions and their locals. About a third of it consisted of anti-Wallace flyers. Reported COPE expenditures are meaningless because they do not take into account paid union officials who were detached for campaign duty. By one informed estimate, labor put a minimum of $10 million into the Humphrey campaign. Theodore H. White, the house historian of presidential politics, concluded after it was all over, "In the near-miracle of the Humphrey comeback in October, no single factor was more important than the army of organized labor, roused to the greatest political exertion of its history."

"I think if we had had another week," Meany said after the election, "we might have elected Hubert Humphrey. I think what beat Humphrey really was the lack of a party machine. They were split all over the lot and, despite that, I think that we were able to do a real job. We substituted to whatever extent we could. I have an idea that if Johnson had run, Johnson would have been elected."

During the last agonized days of his presidency, dissent and public rage imprisoned Lyndon Johnson in the White House. His public appearances were furtive, hurried affairs, to avoid the specter of assassination or the embarrassment of heckling. Military bases, a few hotel ballrooms hard by the White House, "controllable situations" carefully screened in advance by the secret service—such was the limited orbit of the President who only four years previously had enjoyed the greatest vote ever given a Chief Executive. In the end he even stopped going to labor conventions. Meany's friendship was one that did not fade as Johnson slowly sank to the status of political nonperson. In January 1969, a few days before he left office, Johnson told Meany, "I am going to invite myself to come over to your office. I don't think that I will break tradition or precedent because I would remind you that you have invited yourself to come to my office many times." On January 13 Johnson stood in the lobby of the AFL-CIO Building and toted up the record of five years. "I looked over my diary last night and I have met with Mr. Meany . . . forty-nine times, in personal meetings either in my office, the Oval Room, or in the Mansion. In addition to that, he has called me, or I have called him, eighty-two additional times." Johnson said the over-all goal of his Administration was "the greatest good for the greatest number." He continued: "I know of no living single group that I think has been more responsible for the advances that have been made in this field in the last five years than the AFL-CIO, headed by George Meany, and supported by millions of men and women throughout the country." Then Johnson presented Meany with a plaque containing pens used to sign 100 "landmark measures" passed during his Administration—in effect, a roster of Great Society legislation.

Meany had reason to feel empathy for the embattled President. He, too, spent most of 1967 and 1968 in a state of siege—in a climactic battle with Walter Reuther for control of the American labor movement.

# XVI

## Meany versus Reuther: Knockout

> *"Walter Reuther would rather be right than president."*
> *"There's a chance he'll be neither."*
> —Labor jest, *circa* 1966

SOMETHING NEW AND POSITIVE has happened to organized labor," columnist John Herling marveled in March 1965, immediately after the AFL-CIO executive council winter meeting. "It is fresh out of reasons for internal fights." After ten years of acrimonious marriage, the AFL and CIO finally appeared to care enough for one another to enjoy a honeymoon. The 1961 agreement on jurisdictional disputes had halted much of the strife between affiliated unions. Labor again had a friend in the White House, and it could strut pridefully at the legislative successes of the Great Society and its contribution to Lyndon Johnson's 1964 landslide. Wages had burst past the guidelines of the Council of Economic Advisers; the gush of defense and domestic spending steadily drove down the unemployment rate.

The peace, however, was deceptive. Walter Reuther still chafed under Meany's presidency. He was unable (or unwilling) to adapt himself to Meany's deliberate pace. He questioned Meany's close palship with Lyndon Johnson. Meany made a basic mistake in identifying labor with the Great Society program, Reuther mused to a friend: "When Lyndon gave us a list of what he wanted, we should have doubled it. Hell, you get a congressional majority like this once in a lifetime. Meany is pissing it away." But his long string of defeats dashed any thoughts Reuther had of overriding Meany through the executive council. Further, Reuther was fast losing what allies he had in the council. According to Jack Conway, Reuther's long-time assistant (and head of the Industrial Union Department after the merger), "the disintegration of the CIO unions worried the shit out of Reuther. The leadership was old, and many of these men accepted the complacency of the AFL. Meany made no demands on them, and they were willing to rock along with him. Soon Walter could count on only two persons for continuing support—Jim Carey, who was somewhat of a mixed blessing, erratic as he was; and Karl Feller [of the brewery workers], who was scared silly of the Teamsters."

In mid-1965 seven of the twenty-seven executive council members were no longer presidents of their international unions; two had been defeated, another five had retired. Meany privately tried to persuade the octogenarians to step down, but publicly he was indifferent. Asked about the "emeriti problem" in 1965 Meany said, "The custom has been that the people stay on the council as long as they feel like staying on the council, and as long as they get elected at the conventions. . . . There's nobody going to be asked to leave the council. . . . My opinion . . . is when they're elected to the council, they are elected. . . . The fact that they are 'out of power' . . . doesn't make any difference. Never has made any difference, so far as I can remember. I can point to cases where men stayed for many years after they had ceased to be active in their own organizations. The type of work we do here is of such a nature that you need all-around experience." One of Meany's friends said, "Because of his own age, George could hardly make a public campaign to retire Harry Bates [in his eighties] on the grounds of senility."

Reuther's declining influence with old CIO unions was graphically— and embarrassingly—revealed during a two-year hassle over a replacement on the council for L. S. Buckmaster, who retired as president of the United Rubber Workers in late 1961. Reuther wanted the council seat for Ralph Helstein, president of the Packinghouse Workers, a former CIO union. Meany objected on the grounds Helstein had not purged Communist influences from the union. Although Reuther had proposed four other names along with Helstein's, he decided to try to force the nomination through. Meany would not yield, and the vacancy continued in October 1963, when Reuther pressed for a showdown.

Reuther noted that at the time of merger, the AFL and CIO agreed there should be "balanced representation" on the council. The question, he said, was "whether or not the former CIO vice-presidents can select a representative from a former CIO union to fill the vacancy." Reuther said it was now up to the executive council to decide one way or another to honor the understanding as he understood it or to discontinue the agreement. If the council decided the "agreement" had ended, then the "vice-presidents from the former CIO will have no candidate and will abstain from voting. . . ."

Meany countered that no such agreement existed. Originally, he conceded, there was a gentlemen's agreement to maintain a seventeen–ten ratio on the council (AFL to CIO) through the 1959 convention. Whenever a "CIO vacancy" occurred, Meany said, he "always asked Reuther whom he would favor." But he denied that either the AFL or CIO had any right to pick who would fill the vacancies. And he also attacked Reuther's penchant for CIO caucuses: he said he had "never asked Reuther to caucus the former CIO vice-presidents on this or any other matters" and that he had never called an AFL caucus, although "on numerous occasions" AFL people had asked him to do so. His objection to Helstein, Meany said, represented only his opinion, and not the opinion of the executive council.

Then Meany unexpectedly cut the ground from beneath Reuther. He read a telegram from the absent David McDonald, nominating for the vacancy John J. Grogan, president of the Industrial Union of Marine and Shipbuilding Workers: "It is my viewpoint," McDonald said, "that this vacancy was permitted to exist too long and that action is imperative. The election of Brother Grogan would end conjecture in the nation's press with the attendant effort to create an impression that a factional split exists in the federation." Grogan was overwhelmingly elected. Reuther, Karl Feller, Emil Rieve, James Carey, and Jacob Potofsky, all heads of former CIO unions, abstained. "The meaning of this vote," said a CIO member, "was that Walter no longer could carry a majority of the CIO bloc. Dave cut him off at the knees, deliberately. No one was really unhappy about it, either."

Reuther's strength waned further in April 1965 when James Carey lost a hotly contested election for the presidency of his International Union of Electrical Workers. The union was the lineal descendant of the old United Electrical Workers which Carey had founded in 1936, when he was a few weeks past his twenty-fifth birthday. In the first count, Carey won over rival Paul Jennings by 2,193 votes. Jennings demanded a recount under provisions of the Landrum-Griffin Act. Labor Secretary Willard Wirtz issued an interim report giving Jennings a margin of 23,316 votes, and alleging "serious . . . misconduct" in the election proceedings. Meany immediately called a special session of the executive council—with "gleeful haste," one of Carey's friends stated—citing the ethical practices code provision that guaranteed "the integrity, honesty, and democracy of union elections." Carey announced the night before the council meeting he would not contest the recount, and resigned as IUE president. Meany went ahead with the meeting. He said the AFL-CIO should investigate "as we have some responsibility. Our enemies in the Congress have been openly saying that this election would have been stolen if it were not for the Landrum-Griffin Act and they are suggesting additional amendments." Carey retorted the council had no business intervening, in view of his resignation. He protested any action based upon Wirtz's preliminary report. The council appointed a subcommittee to investigate further; Carey remained on the council a few more months, then quietly resigned.

Reuther also gradually lost standing with erstwhile friends on the council. Stanley Ruttenberg, who was research director of the CIO and kept that position in the AFL-CIO, saw a "major flaw" in Reuther's tactics in dealing with Meany:

> Walter would force a confrontation, and then pull back without getting a vote. I differed with him on this strategy. I think his position in the federation could have been stronger, and Meany would have respected him more, if he would have taken a position and stayed with it. This would have increased his stature, even when he lost.
>
> As an example, at one stage Meany was distressed with the progress being made by Cesar Chavez [California farmworker organizer]. Meany had made the decision to cut off AFL-CIO support for Chavez, and it went before the council. Reuther came in vigorously, saying he was going to fight. Meany demanded support, and Reuther withdrew. As it worked out, the AFL-CIO had to resume support for Chavez a few years later anyway, but that isn't the point. Meany looked on Reuther as a man who kept chickening out; who would bring an issue up to the brink and back away.

Ruttenberg recognized there are times when it is politic to avoid being a perpetual loser.

> But here you are, the leader of the old CIO unions, and you announce in advance you are going to take an issue and push it hard, and you encourage your supporters to go along with you. But if you pull back and leave these fellows holding the bag—you do this a half dozen times, as Reuther did—you are no longer taking these people up there with you.

Meany reacted swiftly at any hint that Reuther was usurping his authority as president. In its early months the Kennedy Administration was considering new tax programs. Stanley Ruttenberg said, "Of course, the CIO had always been active and aggressive in the tax field. Meany was out of the country, and Kennedy asked Reuther for AFL-CIO views on what we considered to be appropriate tax policy. In Meany's absence we proceeded to put together a document on taxes for submission to the White House. I was acting as director of the tax policy committee, Walter as chairman. One of Meany's insiders—either Al Zack or Biemiller—got word to Meany that 'Reuther and the economic committee are putting together a set of proposals.' Meany called me from Europe—the only time he did this the entire time I was there, from the merger through 1963*—to say he didn't want the tax program presented to the Adminis- tration until he got back, and I should tell this to Walter Reuther. If Walter wanted to go to the White House with his ideas, 'Go as president of the UAW, or as chairman of the Industrial Union Department.' I was not to go with him as AFL-CIO staff.

"Now, this teed Reuther off no end. I tried to explain to Meany on the phone there was no difference of opinion; that what Reuther proposed taking to the White House was in line with what the executive council had already said in resolutions. But to Meany, it was a matter of proto- col."

Jack Conway had another explanation: "As time passed, Walter downgraded the importance of the AFL-CIO and his own participation in it, and upgraded the importance of the UAW. This distorted even further his judgment on what was feasible in the AFL-CIO." Conway felt Reuther would have been wasting his time in fighting Meany. "Simple inertia by Meany was enough to defeat Reuther on most of the things he wanted to accomplish. It takes leadership and effort to get people to do things; if you want to stop things, all you have to do is take no action. . . . It was not so much Meany outsmarting Reuther as Meany having all the power. The executive council was a bunch of old men—retired presidents who didn't even run their own unions, some sec- retary-treasurers, the number-two men. If they disagreed, Meany would go do what he wanted to do anyway. If presented a choice, these guys would vote for Meany, and then some would tell Reuther they agreed with him.

"Reuther was deluding himself in thinking he could work within the council, or that Meany would ever turn it over to him. There was never any true feeling between him and Meany at all, not even during the merger festivities. They just didn't mesh."

Reuther's verbosity being what it was, inevitably he said things pub- licly that infuriated Meany. On the NBC "Today Show" in December 1965, the day after a mostly harmonious convention adjourned, Reuther said there was "some truth" in the interviewer's statement about AFL- CIO leadership being "old and stagnant." Reuther hoped "we will con- tinue to move in the direction of getting younger, more vigorous leader- ship." Did rank-and-file members approve of Meany's raise from $45,000 to $70,000? "No," Reuther said, "my answer to that is I think they didn't think that they should. . . . I happen to believe that a labor leader doesn't need that much. I think if you want to get that much, you ought to work for General Motors, and then you'll get that much and a

* Ruttenberg resigned then to become Assistant Secretary of Labor for man- power.

great deal more if you're in the top leadership." Reuther said he did not vote against the pay raise (voted by the executive council over Meany's mild objections) because "I felt that that would be misunderstood. If Mr. Meany wants $70,000, I think we can afford to pay him that. . . . I don't think he took the initiative in this thing. I think other people did. But he has to live with his point of view and I live with my point of view."

In early 1966, Meany entered the Harkness Pavilion at Columbia Presbyterian Medical Center in New York for surgery on his hip. At age seventy-one, Meany faced grave danger undergoing the operation. The alternative, physicians told him, was agonizing pain the rest of his life, possibly even a wheel chair. The orthoplastic surgery, a new technique, involved cleansing his hip socket of minute pieces of bone and coating it and the ball with a plastic substance. The operation brought Meany almost instantaneous relief from the pain.

His visitors in the hospital included Walter and May Reuther. It was among the last face-to-face talks the men had, and one of the friendlier —a two-hour chat filled with reminiscences about past union battles and political personages, an effort at camaraderie: the sort of mutual respect, in fact, that Meany had hoped for at the time of merger.

Meany's physical rejuvenation after the operation was spectacular. He began exercising the hip while still abed, skateboard attached to his foot and pressed tightly against a vertical board at the end of the bed so he could swing his leg in an arc. James Suffridge, a long-time Meany friend and golfing companion, and head of the retail clerks union, said, "George came out of that hospital ten, fifteen years younger than he went in." Sheer physical courage helped. The doctor said, "Exercise, exercise." So each day Meany walked from his desk through a conference room and kitchenette to the vast executive council chamber on the east side of the AFL-CIO Building. He would close the door and remove his coat and start walking around the circular council table—a table large enough to seat thirty-four men in comfort. Around and around for an hour, wiping away the sweat and trying to ignore the protesting pangs from his recuperating hip, around and around and around, pausing to pant and sip a glass of bottled mineral water, then off again, trudging a lonely circle. The therapy worked. Meany continued to use his cane a few months, then said, "Let's forget this thing for a while." Thereafter he walked on his own—with an occasional limp or twinge of discomfort after he had been sitting for more than an hour—and he was back at the Columbia Country Club in Chevy Chase, striding over the golf course with Jim Suffridge and other labor pals.

And George Meany, when anyone asked, made plain he intended to remain as president of the AFL-CIO as long as he felt healthy enough to fill the job. In the spring of 1966, his robust appearance discouraged any speculation that Meany was about to step down.

Victor Reuther, from his vantage point as director of the UAW's international affairs department, seethed as Meany welded the AFL-CIO into tight support of Lyndon Johnson's Vietnam policy. The American Institute for Free Labor Development (AIFLD) was another irritant. Immediately after Johnson's intervention in the Dominican Republic in 1965, a union with which AIFLD had strong working ties (CONATRAL, by its Spanish initials) denounced the revolution as "Communist-inspired" and publicly thanked Washington for its dispatch of marines. Working closely with the U.S. Embassy, AIFLD and CONATRAL launched a crash program to win unionists away from the insurgent cause. Beginning in late 1965, a spate of newspaper and magazine articles criticized labor's Dominican activities, implying strongly the AFL-CIO was working in "counterrevolutionary" tandem with the Johnson Administration. After discreet detective work, Meany satisfied himself Victor Reuther was a major source—and in some instances, the inspiration—for the stories. Victor Reuther had some of them reprinted and distributed in UAW envelopes both in the United States and abroad. Meany groused to staff members that "he is undercutting us" but made no public complaint.

In May 1966, Reuther shed his anonymity and attacked the AFL-CIO directly and publicly. The occasion was the UAW convention in Long Beach, California. On May 21, a Saturday, the convention overwhelmingly approved resolutions calling for improved relations with Communist China and trade with Eastern European nations, positions directly contrary to those of the AFL-CIO. The Vietnam resolution supported Johnson but warned against escalation of the war—language Emil Mazey had wanted in the AFL-CIO convention the preceding December, but which Meany had rejected. The next afternoon Victor Reuther decided to tweak Meany's nose again, in interviews with labor reporters Patrick J. Owens of the Detroit *Free Press* and Harry Bernstein of the Los Angeles *Times*. Owens' story the next day began with the flat assertion, "The AFL-CIO and some of its affiliates have permitted themselves to be used by the CIA as a cover for clandestine operations abroad." According to Owens, Reuther called AFL-CIO foreign activities "retrogressive" and a "vest pocket operation" of Jay Lovestone. He accused Lovestone of running programs without consulting the executive council. Bernstein quoted him as saying Lovestone "seems to have brought into the labor movement the working habits and undercover techniques which he learned when he was in the highest echelons of the Communist Party."

I guess it's awfully hard to break those habits." Reuther gave only one specific example of "CIA activities" involving labor. He identified the labor group as the International Food and Drink Workers Federation, a secretariat of unions in that field headquartered in Geneva, Switzerland, and funded in part by the AFL-CIO. Reuther said "eight individuals in Panama alone" had posed as representatives of the federation. The general secretary "abolished" the Panama office when he learned of the deception.* Reuther also called the UAW resolutions on China and East-West trade "a major challenge" to the AFL-CIO. He thought they would "provoke considerable sympathy and understanding around the world, among the very nations we need understanding with, if we are to deal with the problems of underdeveloped nations."

Would the resolutions also provoke Lovestone? reporter Owens asked. "I would hope so," Reuther replied. Reuther was vague about details of labor links with the CIA, saying "a more appropriate time will come." He claimed he spoke as an individual, not for the UAW or his brother.

Meany called Walter Reuther immediately after the stories appeared and asked him, with icy sarcasm, whether it would be necessary in the future for the AFL-CIO to consult Victor rather than Walter Reuther "to ascertain the views of the UAW on international concerns of the AFL-CIO." According to Meany, Walter Reuther disavowed responsibility. He said he disagreed with the allegations made in the interview, and called it a "mistake" on Victor's part.† Meany decided to let the matter drop. Although Reuther in effect apologized for what his brother had said, Meany's call irritated him, according to one close associate, because "he felt Vic had the right to speak his mind without running to a convention or to Jay Lovestone for permission." Thus both Meany and Reuther were in somewhat belligerent moods over the episode. The next installment was not long in coming. The focal point again was a foreign affairs activity, the International Labor Organization (ILO), labor adjunct of the United Nations.

AFL-CIO relations with the ILO had been deteriorating for years.

* Actually, Joseph Beirne said later, the Panama office was closed as an economy measure—along with all others the federation had operated in Latin America. "There was no truth in this statement that they were closing their office in Panama because of collaboration between the . . . organization and the CIA," Meany told a press conference on August 22.

† For more than one reason. "Victor Reuther ought to be ashamed of himself," Thomas W. Braden, a former CIA official, wrote in the *Saturday Evening Post* later. Braden recounted that "at his request, I went to Detroit one morning and gave Walter $50,000 in $50 bills. Victor spent the money, mostly in West Germany, to bolster labor unions there. . . . In my opinion and that of my peers in the CIA he spent it with less than perfect wisdom, for the German unions he chose to help weren't seriously short of money and were already Communist." In the same article Braden told of the CIA money he had given to Irving Brown to help support AFL programs in Europe in the late 1940's. See Chapter VI.

Rudolph Faupl, the U.S. labor delegate* (appointed by President Johnson, on Meany's recommendation), gave a long account of the troubles at the April 1965 executive council meeting, which Reuther did not attend. Faupl said that ever since the Soviets entered the ILO in 1954, they had pressured the director-general, David Morse, for "posts and representations at all levels of the organization." Faupl felt the Soviets were more interested in political mischief than labor matters; that they did "not have the slightest intention of making any contributions which would further the principles for which the ILO was established." Soviet resolutions were consistently "slanted with political and ideological motives," Faupl complained. The increasing number of Third World nations in the ILO membership enhanced Communist strength in ILO bodies beginning in the early 1960's. The Kennedy Administration attempted to accommodate political reality. Its delegate, George Weaver of the Labor Department, supported a Soviet for the post of assistant director-general in 1961 over AFL-CIO objections. In February 1965 Weaver supported an increase in a key committee by eight nations— seven Communist countries and Indonesia—in fear the "ILO would collapse if the Communists didn't get what they wanted," in Faupl's opinion. Meany complained to Secretary of State Dean Rusk that the ILO should not be turned into a political forum, and that the AFL-CIO intended to speak for labor's interests, not necessarily those of the United States government. Meany told Rusk that should the ILO "further deteriorate by drifting into a largely intergovernmental institution and straying from its original purpose and structure, there would be no more place for it within the American labor movement." He wanted the U.S. government to develop "effective resistance" to the increasing Communist pressures. Otherwise, Meany said, the AFL-CIO would not submit labor nominees for the U.S. delegation to the 1965 ILO conference. Rusk assured Meany there would be more "consultation and coordination" between Weaver and the employer and labor representatives. Meany was satisfied, and so reported to the executive council in May 1965. The council gave Meany carte blanche to take whatever action he felt was necessary in continued dealings with the ILO.

In late 1965 Faupl learned that the Communist bloc countries were promoting the candidacy of Leon Chajn, an obscure Polish government official, for the presidency of the 1966 ILO conference. Faupl discussed the Chajn candidacy with other ILO delegates—Richard Wagner, the employer member; and Weaver and the State Department's Philip Delaney—and found them unanimous in opposition. "We all feared that the Communists would use the presidency of the conference as a stepping-

* Each ILO member nation has four delegates—two government, one labor, and one employer. United States delegates are appointed by the President.

stone in their attempt to increase Communist strength on the governing body," Faupl said. He thought it would be "insulting" to have a member of the Polish government chair a conference "dedicated and devoted to advancing the cause of human freedom and insuring workers the right to organize and bargain collectively." Faupl noted:

Not only does Polish law prohibit free association of workers in their own self-interest, but the Polish government has been formally censured by an ILO committee . . . for its denial of workers rights. For four successive years, Poland has been asked to bring its Trade Union Act of 1949 into conformity with the ILO's minimum standards of freedom. For just as many years, the Polish government has blandly replied that the ILO must adapt itself to the realities of the Communist system.

"Largely through the efforts of the U.S. government," Faupl said, M. J. Veldkamp, the Netherlands minister of social affairs and public health, agreed to oppose Chajn. The U.S. delegation campaigned vigorously for Veldkamp, but lost. Chajn, nominated by a Soviet official, won by a single vote, supported by the Communist bloc and Spain, Portugal, the Arab delegates, and a host of new African members.

Immediately after the vote, Faupl telephoned Meany to report what had happened. Faupl was neither an AFL-CIO officer or employee. As a worker delegate he had full decision-making authority in his own right, although as Meany has noted, consultation with AFL-CIO officers "is expected and practiced." Faupl said, "I advised him [Meany] that I could not, in good conscience, sit in the conference presided over by a representative of a totalitarian country and that 'I am withdrawing the delegation.' " Meany responded, "You are the delegate, you are in a position to weigh the situation. If I were in your position I would do the same thing, but don't do anything that would commit the AFL-CIO to withdrawing from the organization." That decision, Meany told Faupl, could be made only by the executive council. Faupl called the labor delegation together and it agreed unanimously to walk out, on June 1.

Because Faupl was a presidential appointee, Meany called Johnson immediately, told him what had happened, and asked for a meeting the next day. There Meany went through the entire matter, "including the Communist takeover of the ILO." Johnson suggested that Meany report also to Dean Rusk, in view of the fact that further ILO elections, those for governing board members, were due in a few days. Meany eventually located Rusk in Brussels. "Secretary Rusk never commented on the protest walkout," Meany said. Since Faupl was to be a candidate for reelection to the governing body, Rusk did suggest that he retain his seat. Meany so informed Faupl.

News of Faupl's walkout was reported in the Washington *Evening Star* on June 1 and in the Washington *Post* and the New York *Times* the next morning. Meany and Reuther spent most of June 3 together, discussing routine AFL-CIO business with other officers and staff members. Neither man mentioned the ILO incident.

At 7:00 P.M. on June 9 a reporter for the Washington *Post* called Meany at home and asked for comment on "the Reuther letter." Meany said he did not know what the man was talking about. The reporter said the letter had arrived via messenger late in the afternoon. Meany said that since he had not "seen or heard of such a letter" he would have no comment. The next morning he found out what the *Post* had been asking about; splashed over its front page was a story about a "major split" in the American trade union movement which threatened "the eleven-year merger of American labor."

Reuther's letter said the UAW international board, meeting on June 8, had "unanimously directed" him to "register the UAW's strongest objections to and sharp disagreement with" Faupl's walkout. He continued:

The board instructed me to protest with equal vigor the denial of the democratic process in the making of the decision to withdraw from the conference. A decision of such grave importance cannot properly be made except on the basis of a vote taken at the highest policy level of the AFL-CIO after thorough review and discussion of all relevant considerations. Neither the delegates to the conference nor any single officer has the right or the power to commit the AFL-CIO in a matter of such great significance. The action of the delegates in walking out . . . was unwise, undemocratic, contrary to established AFL-CIO policy, and unauthorized by any AFL-CIO body with authority to change that policy.

Reuther demanded that Meany direct "the AFL-CIO delegates . . . to resume their seats" at the conference.

The letter infuriated Meany—not so much because of the content, which he knew he could rebut, but because it was spread before the public. First, he sent a telegram to Reuther and other executive council members announcing a special meeting on June 16 to air both the ILO incident and "the slanderous attack made upon me" by Victor Reuther in the May 22 newspaper interviews. Next, he wrote a blistering reply to Reuther on "the deliberate publicity campaign used in connection with this letter." Meany said he did not "question the right of the UAW, or any other affiliate, to criticize any action of mine . . . but I seriously question the wisdom of giving widespread publicity to a matter which is surely an internal affair of the AFL-CIO. The challenge to the administrative conduct of any organization, by an affiliate of that organization, must be an internal matter, and should be pursued through the internal channels for the resolution of such charges and issues, at least before being made the subject matter of a publicity campaign."

Determination of whether Meany violated AFL-CIO policies "cannot be decided by any back-and-forth exchanges in the public press," he wrote. "Considering the over-all attitudes of the press in America in regard to the AFL-CIO and its activities, I am sure you must agree with me that they are more than happy to give wide coverage to any allegation which would indicate a major policy division in our organization." Meany noted newspaper stories placed "far greater stress on the idea of division and discord in the AFL-CIO than on the matter of any action taken in Geneva."

Meany did not release his letter to the press. And he opened the council meeting by chastising Reuther for airing "an internal matter in the press." A number of stories "indicated that the release had been accompanied by extensive background information." He cited articles that called him "the dictator of AFL-CIO foreign policy"; that said he was "heavy-handed in his dealings with associates and that he . . . had called the meeting of the executive council merely because he was certain he would have the majority of the votes." Meany also expressed irritation that he first learned of the UAW action through the newspapers. "Walter," he said, "don't you know there's such a thing as a telephone?"

Meany reviewed the process through which AFL-CIO foreign policy was formulated—"by conventions, not by Meany," he said. Some critics, Meany said, called labor foreign policy "unchanged, rigid, and frozen." Even if they were correct, Meany said, "it should not be taken as an indication that these policies should be changed." Meany noted other articles criticized him "personally" for disagreeing with President Johnson's policy of attempted rapport with Communist nations. "Our conventions make our policy—not President Johnson," he said.

Turning to Victor Reuther's May interviews, Meany said "emphatically" that the charge of connections between the AFL-CIO and the CIA "was not true." Meany outlined the relationship between the American Institute for Free Labor Development and the Agency for International Development. "This, however, has nothing to do with the CIA," he said.

Meany next brought in Rudolph Faupl, who gave a detailed account of the events leading up to his decision to walk out of the ILO conference. "I have acted in accordance with my own conscience," Faupl said, "without instructions from anyone and in accordance with the policy of this council as I have understood it, and in accordance with the will of the overwhelming majority of the American workers." Faupl said it would be a "sad day indeed if as mild a protest as this one, whose sole purpose was to focus world-wide attention on the struggle of the oppressed workers in Communist countries, is used as an occasion for the AFL-CIO to censure the American workers' delegate and condemn its principal elected officer." Meany told of his part in the ILO walkout—denying that either Johnson or Secretary Rusk had asked Faupl to return to the conference, as some news stories had stated (apparently on the basis of "background information" supplied by Victor Reuther). Reuther, in a lengthy reply, said he agreed with much of what Faupl said about conditions in the ILO, and that the dispute should not be considered a censure of either Faupl or Meany—but of a "major policy change" without council discussion. He noted that no worker delegates from other countries left with Faupl.

Recalling the two years he spent in the Soviet Union in the 1930's, Reuther said he was aware of how the Communists worked, and how they had penetrated the ILO. But labor couldn't fight Communists by "walking out," he said. He recollected that the AFL-CIO had roundly condemned employer delegates for walking out of the ILO during the 1950's. The United Auto Workers had a legitimate concern with world problems, Reuther said. "What good is the General Motors pension plan if the whole world is engulfed in nuclear or catastrophic war?"

Reuther said the ILO issue came up during a UAW board discussion of the World Automotive Council, a federation of autoworker unions. UAW board members were upset because they knew nothing of the walkout beyond what they had read in the papers. Reuther said he intended to send the protest to Meany by telegram but could not because of a Western Union strike; hence his use of a messenger. According to the minutes:

> He went on to say that this is not a personality fight and pointed out that neither President Meany nor himself has any control over the press of this country. He then said that he thought it was the policy of the AFL-CIO to fight the Communists from within and not to abdicate to them. If a motion were made for a vote of confidence for President Meany . . . Reuther said he would vote for it, but he will not, at any time, negotiate with anyone the right of the UAW to speak out on any matter with which they are concerned. They are deeply disturbed, he said, as to the direction in which the world is drifting, and he added that a number of people think there is a growing character in the AFL-CIO and it is not positive or constructive in its international affairs.

Reuther urged that the executive council hold a special meeting of three or four days' duration to discuss foreign policy in depth and review decisions made years in the past.

Council members counterattacked, using biting language in their denunciations of Reuther. Paul Hall, the gravelly-voiced president of the Seamen's International Union, said he "deeply resented that some people are being accused of being stool pigeons of the AFL-CIO" [*sic*]. Reuther's accusations were "totally irresponsible." If the UAW thought AFL-CIO policy was bad, "they should try to change it through constitutional channels." Other members joined the attack, shouting curses and pounding on the table.

Meany interrupted to read excerpts from a press release which Reuther's aides had distributed to reporters in the AFL-CIO foyer awaiting the results of the council meeting. The release was ostensibly the text of the statement Reuther was making to the council. An AFL-CIO staff member picked up a copy of the release and sent it in to Meany, who scanned it, and found some language that Reuther had not included in his oral statement. He read a paragraph to the council:

> In the last twenty-four hours the UAW has learned from authoritative sources that the boycott of the ILO by the AFL-CIO has been under consideration by the AFL-CIO headquarters for approximately a week prior to the walkout, and it is, therefore, evident that there was ample time for consultation and discussion with the leadership of the AFL-CIO before any final decision was taken.

Meany angrily demanded that Reuther identify the "authoritative source" who had supplied him with such information. He said the statement "was a complete and total falsehood," according to the council minutes. Another source said Meany was more direct, quoting him as saying "that is a damnable lie."

The debate raged for more than an hour. Roy Siemiller of the International Association of Machinists (Faupl's home union) agreed the UAW had the right to raise policy questions, but it was "morally wrong in the manner in which this was handled." Siemiller called it "a gross mistake!" Joseph Beirne of the Communications Workers of America said Reuther's release of the press statement while the council meeting was in progress was "destroying the very basis under which we are meeting." Only Jacob Potofsky of the hatters union defended Reuther's position— and even he said Reuther was "wrong in going to the press."

When the debate ended Siemiller presented a resolution saying the executive council "fully supports and endorses" Meany and Faupl in their ILO action. It said the protest was "the most effective means available" to dramatize "the reaction of the free workers of America" to the election of a "representative of a totalitarian regime" to the ILO presidency. The motion carried by a vote of eighteen to six, three former CIO presidents abandoning Reuther to side with Meany. (Five council members were absent.)

Having reaffirmed his solid council majority, Meany suggested that the council take up Reuther's suggestion that it review the foreign policy resolutions passed since the merger. He said the council "might want to consider the constant harassment" by Victor Reuther of AFL-CIO policies at the same time. A meeting was set for September. Reuther asked that the Latin American programs be aired at the regular council meeting in August, and that Joseph Beirne detail operations of the American Institute of Free Labor Development.

At a press conference immediately after the meeting someone asked Meany if he felt the episode raised any questions about Reuther's qualifications to succeed him. Meany grinned. "I haven't any great interest in that," he said, "because when that time comes, I won't be around." His audience guffawed. Round One had gone to Meany.

At the same meeting the council made what proved to be a public relations blunder of massive proportion. Meany said, "They [the council members] made a decision that if these things happened in the future—and everybody seemed to have a feeling that June 8, 1966, was only the beginning—that there would be no answer in the public press; that we would conduct the affairs of the AFL-CIO within the forums of the AFL-CIO." On strictly trade union grounds, the decision can be defended, for, as Meany has argued, "labor has enough enemies without our own people giving them material." In practice, however, silence meant that Reuther maintained the offensive for month after month, with devastating long-term damage to both Meany and the AFL-CIO. Close students of labor—including persons friendly to Reuther—realized many of his charges were distorted and based upon, at best, partial truths. But Meany refused to authorize the counterattack needed to blunt what became, for Reuther, an ongoing propaganda campaign.

Before the August council meeting, according to Jack Conway, Reuther came under strong pressure to let the Latin American matter drop without further discussion. "A strong effort was made to get this off the agenda—by the CIA, by Hubert Humphrey, by Robert Kennedy, and others. They made calls to Walter Reuther, to Victor Reuther, to Lane Kirkland [Meany's administrative assistant], and to me. A series of discussions was held, culminating in a meeting between Meany and Reuther in which it was agreed to take the issue off the agenda. When Reuther came back and reported this to me, I double-checked with Lane Kirkland and ensured he had the same information. Walter went to the meeting and it [the Latin American program] was the first thing on the agenda, raised by Joe Beirne. It was a disaster." (Meany denied that any such agreement was made.)

Beirne said he had requested council time "to tell the entire story" because of continuous attacks against the AIFLD, the AFL-CIO international affairs department, and the African-American Labor Center. He expressed concern with the "falsity of approach of various writers outside the labor movement," and said he observed "a crystallization of the attacks in April and May" when Reuther "joined in the attacks." Beirne continued: "When a responsible officer, such as Victor Reuther, who is known world-wide, joins in the attacks, then it must be of concern to the executive council because the confidence, honesty, and integrity of the AFL-CIO are being destroyed." He ticked off eight separate categories of charges that had been made against the AIFLD: that it was an "arm of the CIA"; the "labor arm of the State Department"; a "training ground for company unions"; that it was antidemocratic, antiworker, an intervener in affairs of foreign countries ("We invariably support dictators. We invariably repress democratic trade unions"); that it backed insignificant antidemocratic splinter groups; that it exploited Latin American workers "by charging excessive, exorbitant, business-dominated interest rates"; that it ignored policies established by AFL-CIO conventions; and that it insisted that "unions built or assisted by us must follow United States government policies and be submissive to the United States in foreign affairs."

Beirne said these charges "have been made by various individuals and organizations, including Moscow, and all follow the slanderous line of the Commies. The views of people outside the labor movement can be measured against their known background, but when the director of the international department of the UAW, Victor Reuther by name, joins in these false charges, it is time to review the whole subject."

Beirne's tough language put Reuther on the defensive. First, he complained that since the council was to discuss foreign policy in depth at its special meeting in September "this matter should have been presented to that meeting." Everyone in the labor movement understood freedom and tyranny, he said; "our big problem is how can the world free labor movement work more effectively." He did not "feel we can talk this matter out today because what Beirne said represents charges that should have been made known to the people accused, so they could be here to defend themselves."

Reuther continued, "Mistakes have been made, and Victor Reuther has made some, but others have made them as well, because Victor has no monopoly on mistakes." He thought Victor was "wrong in mentioning the Central Intelligence Agency as the CIA is something which you do not discuss publicly, and if it were to be discussed, it should be by a small subcommittee of the executive council." The newspaper stories based on Victor's May 22 interview, he said, did not link the AIFLD specifically to the CIA.

Concluding, Reuther said he thought "Beirne was right in feeling as strongly as he does about the attacks which have been made, but other people feel strongly about this as well."

After listening to Reuther, the council approved a resolution commending the AIFLD "for its work in carrying out the policies of the AFL-CIO in the international field." It rejected "the campaign of vilification" that had been waged against it. Reuther and Joseph Curran of the National Maritime Union voted no; Potofsky abstained. At Reuther's request, the council agreed to postpone the September foreign policy meeting until after the November elections.

According to Jack Conway, Reuther decided after the September meeting that he would take the UAW out of the AFL-CIO. The claimed breach of promise on discussing Latin America precipitated the decision. Conway said, "Reuther came back to the office afterward and said, 'You can't believe anything anyone tells you—I am through. When it gets to the point that two men make an agreement in a face-to-face meeting, and it isn't carried out, what's the use?' "

Reuther said nothing publicly about his decision to break away from the AFL-CIO. Conway said he "realized he first had to educate his own membership" on the reasons. To resign immediately on the heels of the disputes over the ILO and the AIFLD would create the public impression his differences with Meany concerned foreign policy alone. Actually, Conway pointed out, "his decision was the product of a long process of frustration." As Reuther told a UAW conference later, the dispute was more than a "personality fight between a plumber and a tool and die maker. If this were so, it wouldn't be worth five seconds of your time. . . . Our problem today is not that the plumber is the president and the tool and die maker wants to be president. The problem is that the American labor movement is paralyzed at dead center." Reuther put the UAW staff to work compiling position papers he intended to circulate to rank-and-file members detailing his grievances. He also told Meany he would not appear at the council meeting on foreign policy, which had been set for November 14 at his specific request. The stated reason was that the UAW international board had decided to hold a special meeting of its own on that date. The real reason, according to Conway, was that "Walter didn't see any point in wasting any more time with Meany; the outcome was foreordained, and nothing he said was going to change it." (Meany quipped later, "Now, maybe this is because we don't have TV cameras or radio transmitters in the executive council room.")

Meany, ever the devotee of procedural purity, went ahead with the meeting. Jay Lovestone compiled a massive loose-bound volume containing every foreign policy statement conventions and the executive council had adopted since merger, indexed and arranged by subject matter, and sent a copy to each council member for study in advance.

When Meany gaveled the meeting to order, Richard F. Walsh, of the theatrical workers union, complained that Reuther's absence made the discussion a waste of time, for it would have to be repeated later if he demanded another session. Meany retorted that the entire executive council had voted to hold the meeting, and there was no alternative.

The council spent four hours leafing through Lovestone's documents page by page, Meany insistent that each category be opened for discussion, from Africa to U.S. and International Economic Matters. A few minor questions arose. Jacob Potofsky wanted the council to drop its opposition to recognition of Communist China and its admission to the United Nations. Ralph Helstein wanted more emphasis on halting the nuclear arms race. Paul Hall wanted more meetings of the international affairs committee. Joseph Curran wanted a re-examination of foreign trade policies, and an updated statement on foreign investment policies of U.S. companies. At four-thirty in the afternoon, eyes bleary from skimming scores of thousands of Lovestone's words at a single sitting, the council approved a statement saying it believed the council's positions "have been sound and have been justified by events. We believe they have stood the test of time and therefore re-endorse them individually and collectively." Potofsky said he had "reservations" on the resolutions on East-West trade and recognition of Communist China; otherwise, the vote was unanimous. As the council was to note fourteen months later, when it broke its silence on the dispute, "If Mr. Reuther is in basic disagreement with any specific aspect of AFL-CIO policy as expressed in council and convention action, the council has yet to be advised as to what those disagreements are, or in what particular respects he would have changes made."

Reuther had no such inhibitions about complaints elsewhere as his campaign gradually escalated. Speaking on November 25 at the Wharton School of Finance and Commerce in Philadelphia, Reuther declared:

You read stories in the paper about a disagreement that I may have with a certain gentleman associated with the leadership of the labor movement and all the emphasis has been on foreign policy. Now, we do have differences on foreign policy. I happen to support the Test Ban Agreement. I happen to think we ought to negotiate a settlement in Vietnam. I happen to disagree with walking out of the ILO conference and a few other things like that. But that is only a small part of the basic disagreement with this gentleman.

Fundamentally, I disagreed because I believe that the American labor movement under his leadership is failing in the broad social responsibilities it has to the total community of America. I believe that the leaders, that the workers in the average union will respond to affirmative and constructive leadership and I believe that if they are given that leadership you can count upon their support.

After all, I'm a politician. I have to run for election and thus far I have been quite successful by this policy.

Actually, the 1963 convention had passed a resolution supporting the nuclear test ban, and Meany testified in favor of it before the Senate Foreign Relations Committee. Through both conventions and the executive council, the AFL-CIO favored a negotiated settlement of the Vietnam War. As the council commented later on this speech, "He sought to plant a contrary impression in the minds of his listeners."

Reuther also commenced a game of financial brinksmanship. Under the AFL-CIO constitution, any affiliate that is three months late in payment of its per capita taxes is automatically suspended. The payments due from the UAW in September were not received until December 8; each monthly payment thereafter came in two months late. The New York *Times,* quoting "sources close to Mr. Reuther," said the tactic was intended "to harass Mr. Meany." At a Washington press conference on December 8 Reuther said the UAW executive board had "made the decision to exert our independence on certain issues." He said, "Time will demonstrate what I mean by a more independent course" and that he would discuss his "very fundamental trade union differences with Mr. Meany" at the "appropriate time and place."

On December 28 the UAW issued the first of five Administrative Letters—its internal publications for officers and rank and file—devoted to the controversy, papers that ultimately were to total some 29,000 words over four months. The statements contained grandiose and sweeping general indictments but few specific charges. Two sentences give the thrust (and tone) of Reuther's case:

. . . [T]he AFL-CIO, as the parent body of the American labor movement, suffers from a sense of complacency and adherence to the status quo and is not fulfilling the basic aims and purposes which prompted the merger of the AFL and the CIO. The AFL-CIO lacks the social vision, the dynamic thrust, the crusading spirit that should characterize the progressive, modern labor movement which it can and must be if it is to be equal to the new challenges and the opportunities of our 20th century technological society.

The first letter listed eight areas of disagreement: organizing, including "exploited farm and migratory workers" and the "working poor"; the need for a "rational, responsible and equitable over-all national economic wage policy"; a collective bargaining program "to achieve equity for American wage earners"; new bargaining techniques in "critical and vital public service industries" without resort to strikes. It called also for more labor involvement in education, health programs, and programs for the elderly; in the war on poverty and equal rights; in conservation and "rebuilding our cities and rural areas"; and in developing "stronger ties with labor's historic and essential allies in the liberal intellectual and academic community and among America's young people." Reuther charged that "fundamental issues such as these are not subject to creative, frank and meaningful discussions within the highest councils of the AFL-CIO. The answer lies essentially in a willingness to permit in-depth discussion of issues, a willingness to evaluate new ideas with an open mind and . . . to share democratic leadership responsibility in the formulation of policies and programs and their implementation."

The UAW distributed the statement to its local unions, to the press, and to a wide mailing list outside the labor movement—not, however, to Meany and other AFL-CIO officers, who learned of it through the press. Meany refused to respond to the charges. Through various intermediaries, he let Reuther know he would be happy to "evaluate new ideas with an open mind" at the February 1967 council meeting.

In early February several council members heard reports Reuther was on the verge of resigning from the council. David Dubinsky, Reuther's friend since the 1930's, called him in Detroit and tried to arrange an appointment. "I hoped to get things worked out between him and George," Dubinsky said. "Walter said he didn't have time. I read in the papers the next morning that Reuther had already withdrawn, at the very time when I talked to him. He never mentioned it to me." In his telegram —sent February 3, seventeen days before the council meeting—Reuther told Meany the UAW executive board had "directed" him and other UAW officers to resign all their posts with the AFL-CIO. The same day, the UAW board called a special convention for April to "review" its relationship with the AFL-CIO. (Reuther's resignation from the executive council did not affect UAW membership in the AFL-CIO itself.)

In a statement accepting Reuther's resignation the council reminded him that the AFL-CIO constitution gave any dissatisfied affiliate "free and open internal channels . . . for the pursuit of its complaints and the advancement of its position. . . . As in any democratic order, they must be able to persuade the majority that their complaints are valid, that their proposals are sound and that their alternatives are preferable. Neither size, financial resources, nor extravagance of language can overcome or substitute for that simple basic requirement." The council declared its "complete readiness" to entertain "any complaint, charge, proposal or program—novel or ancient" at one of its own sessions or a special convention. "We are not, however, prepared to act upon the basis of a kaleidoscope of ever-changing allegations and demands, expressed through press releases, public speeches, or circular letters."

At one of his press conferences during the meeting, a reporter asked Meany if Reuther "contributes significantly to the brainstorming that goes on within the council when he's there." "You know," Meany replied, "we had a golf game a week or two ago and we had five and we were going to a course where only four were allowed. One fellow didn't show up. So when I met him I said that he made a great contribution to our game by not showing up." Meany also tried to put down newspaper talk about a "feud" with Reuther. "Let me make this crystal clear," he said: "I want to say to you gentlemen there is no feud between Walter Reuther and myself. I haven't had a cross word with Walter Reuther in five years with the exception of a discussion we had on the sixteenth of last June at a special meeting of the executive council on the ILO matter, and I have [had] nothing but the nicest relationship with him over the last five years."

Immediately prior to the UAW convention Reuther issued three more voluminous Administrative Letters outlining specific demands. He wanted a six-year, $90-million organizing drive, one third earmarked for farm workers and the "working poor," the balance for unorganized workers elsewhere. He wanted the committee system strengthened, and greater roles for the executive committee and the general board.* He wanted coordinated collective bargaining; a united defense fund; and an electronic data processing center "to facilitate the gathering and dissemination of factual information needed to assist union negotiations."

Reuther put his various proposals and charges into an omnibus resolution that he presented to the special UAW convention. He said he intended to circulate it "to the leadership of the AFL-CIO, to all of the affiliates, so they can study it." After the UAW finished its fall negotiating sessions with the auto companies, he said, "the leadership of your union will request a meeting of the executive council so that we can discuss this program and *we are going to fight for it."* † At Reuther's request, the convention passed a resolution directing the UAW board "to present these proposed programs and policies to the executive council of the AFL-CIO at an appropriate time after the completion of the 1967 UAW collective bargaining negotiations."

The UAW opened its negotiations in July 1967 and on September 6 struck the Ford Motor Company, settling on October 22. On November 2 Emil Mazey, the UAW secretary-treasurer, sent Reuther's omnibus

---

* The executive committee, composed of the president, secretary-treasurer, and six vice-presidents, was empowered to "advise and consult with the president and secretary-treasurer on policy matters." The general board, composed of presidents of affiliated unions, was to meet annually to discuss policy issues. Neither had any operational authority.

† Emphasis added.

resolution to the AFL-CIO for presentation at the convention opening on December 7. On November 30, however, Reuther wrote Meany that the UAW had set December 14 as a target date in negotiations with General Motors, and he and other officers could not attend the convention. He asked that the resolutions be withdrawn, and added that, when the negotiations ended, "It is our intention to request an opportunity to present our program to the executive council." Meany said later Reuther "contrived" the GM deadline—a date the UAW could control—as a means of dodging the convention. The AFL-CIO, at Mazey's request, meanwhile, waived three months of per capita taxes for the UAW because of its continuing strike expenses. Meany now prepared for a showdown with Reuther at the February executive council meeting in Bal Harbour, Florida.

None came. Several days before the council met, there was a spate of newspaper stories quoting "authoritative sources" in the UAW as saying Reuther would not appear. The Los Angeles *Times* reported on January 29 that "UAW leaders" wanted to "delay any confrontation with the AFL-CIO until after the elections" because "if liberal candidates lose and President Johnson is defeated, the UAW will be blamed, however wrongly, for having split the labor movement . . . on election eve." The story said Reuther would not go before the executive council because its meetings "are closed to the public and many UAW leaders felt the . . . members would just 'rubber stamp' decisions by Meany." (The AFL-CIO commented later that the supposed political concerns were "bizarre" in view of the fact the UAW had publicly announced in May 1967, through Mazey, it would give no further contributions to the Committee on Political Education.)

In his first Administrative Letter, on February 8, 1967, Reuther had said he decided not to seek allies because "to have done so would have opened us to the charge that we were building a power caucus within the AFL-CIO and that this is not a principled fight, but a political power drive. The UAW leadership is sufficiently sophisticated to know that if a political power drive is contemplated, it is essential to build a coalition of allies. Since we are not engaged in a power drive, we have taken no steps to create a caucus of allies and we have no intention of doing so in the future." Reuther changed his mind. The Los Angeles *Times* reported on January 29, "Now, though, Reuther has agreed to seek out other union leaders who may be sympathetic to his views, discuss the UAW plans with them, and get their understanding, if not support. . . ."

Reuther received conflicting advice. Jacob Potofsky, for one, counseled that he remain within the AFL-CIO and use the Industrial Union Department as a vehicle to promote his programs. Reuther did not think this was feasible. The unions that agreed with his programs, he said, would not make contributions because "available funds are being siphoned from the IUD into the AFL-CIO." David Dubinsky told Reuther, "You are wasting your time fighting Meany. If you go outside the AFL-CIO, you'll be lonelier than John L. Lewis." No one among the old CIO unions appeared anxious to follow Reuther out of the AFL-CIO. Nonetheless his decision remained the same: he would leave. The only questions were the route and the time.

On March 2 the UAW board initiated another exchange of letters. It asked for a special AFL-CIO convention in early December "for a sufficient number of days to facilitate a full and frank discussion of and action on the UAW's program." Should the convention not be called "the UAW will have no acceptable alternative but to disaffiliate from the AFL-CIO so [its] . . . full resources can be used to advance its program. . . ."

In March Reuther made a final desperate attempt to rally supporters. He tried to woo at least one AFL president with a veiled promise about "bringing back the Teamsters." During a single week Reuther held no less than eleven meetings with old CIO union presidents, singly and in groups. One of them recollected later, "Walter seemed to realize he had about run out the string. He got pretty damned personal in his attacks on Meany, and he used some language on his health and his 'character' that surprised even some of us who had listened to him for years." The thrust of Reuther's case was that labor would be more militant, both in its organizing and in its relations with government. With President Johnson's political support eroding rapidly because of the Vietnam War, Reuther turned on the "collaboration" between the AFL-CIO and the Administration. John W. Leslie, a Labor Department official, wrote Secretary Wirtz in a memo in March:

Al Zack [Albert J. Zack, Meany's public relations man] called to express the AFL-CIO's concern over rumors that the President was planning to attend the March 24 dinner here in Washington where Walter Reuther is being honored by having a professorial chair at the Weizmann Institute of Science in Israel named after him.

Zack went on to say that the President should know what Reuther has been telling the union people who have been attending the recent private meetings he has held.

Reuther is quoted as having attacked Meany for "kissing the President's ass." He is said to have stated that the only way to deal with Johnson is like John L. Lewis and Sidney Hillman dealt with Roosevelt, "by talking tough." He said that he, Reuther, called the President after the settlement at Chrysler to tell him the terms and when the President asked what it did to the guidelines, Reuther said he replied the terms "kicked the shit out of the guidelines."

Reuther is supposed to have thrown a book on the floor at the meetings and said that it represented the J. P. Stevens* contract and that if he were handling things he would throw the contract down in front of the President and tell him that he had one week to cancel that contract or he would lose the support of the labor movement.

In addition Zack says that the Ambassador from Israel is not planning to attend the dinner, unless the President attends.

I don't know the truth of any of this. Reuther this morning publicly said that labor solidarity in the election was critical and that he didn't want to do anything to jeopardize it. He also endorsed Johnson.

Wirtz forwarded the memo to Marvin Watson, one of Johnson's political advisers, with a note saying that "my best information (some of it from Reuther) is that [it is] at least 75 percent accurate." Johnson did not attend.

In his last round of caucuses, the weekend before the executive council meeting on Tuesday, Reuther made clear that if he was not satisfied with the actions of the special convention, he "could still walk out." He said there "must be massive and fundamental changes in the AFL-CIO constitution and policies," and indicated he would present even more proposals before the end of the year.

Meany opened the March 12 council meeting by announcing receipt of Reuther's letter requesting the special convention. He noted there had been a "constant barrage of publicity" against the AFL-CIO—"its officers and the executive council"—for twenty-one months. Meany reminded the council that he had said he "would not answer any allegations made in the public press, but that every opportunity would be given to the United Auto Workers to resolve these matters within the structure of the federation." Meany went through the chronology of meetings Reuther had requested, and the various reasons he had given for their postponement and his nonattendance.

The council minutes do not reflect any open support for Reuther. During several hours of discussion, members (not identified in the minutes) made these comments:

—Reuther was told of opposition by council members to the closed caucuses, and that whatever meetings he held should be open.

* The Stevens firm, a Southern textile company, had continued to receive government contracts despite its long defiance of NLRB rulings in an organizational dispute. President Johnson simply ignored several executive council members when they broached the subject at a luncheon in November 1967.

—Whoever goes to a special convention should abide by the decisions made there.

—"We resent being called tottering old men who do not know what we are doing."

—We are taking care of the welfare of all citizens through our legislative activities, not just AFL-CIO members.

—We do not like the ultimatum which was given; all matters should come to the executive council and not the press.

—"With what has happened in the past few days, we are on the road to a split in the labor movement."

—If the special convention did not make meaningful changes, the UAW would disaffiliate.

—"If you accept this ultimatum, you will live like Damocles with a sword constantly over your head."

—Neither the UAW nor any other international union would permit one of its local unions to say "Do it my way or else."

—We are all fed up with the propaganda that has appeared in the press; now is the time to show real unity.

—If we grant the request for a special convention without a commitment to abide by its decisions, we are only providing another platform for further abuse and propaganda.

—The "forces of reaction" are greater today than at any time in the past twelve years, and we need all the strength we can muster so we should take all unaffiliated unions back into the fold.

Meany, summarizing, said he agreed with Reuther that the "integrity of affiliates" must be retained. "And what about the integrity of the AFL-CIO?" he asked. To hold a special convention, at the cost of $1 million or more, would be an "exercise in futility" if the union requesting it refused to abide by the results. Meany asked that he be authorized to send a letter to the UAW stating:

> You can have a special convention on your charges and proposals—as soon as it is humanly possible to hold one, under these two conditions:
> 1. That you commit your organization without question to attend such a convention, if and when called.
> 2. That you further commit your organization to accept the democratically arrived at decisions of such a convention.

Reuther gave his answer the next day at a meeting of officers of the Industrial Union Department. "We are not willing to give anybody a loyalty oath," he said. Mazey read a UAW statement saying the council's condition "violates the spirit and the concepts of a voluntary association" and was "both improper and unacceptable." The UAW said it would try to get unions representing a majority of AFL-CIO members to sign petitions for a special convention without preconditions, as provided by the constitution. (Such an attempt was made, but it gained so little support Reuther dropped it.)

In May the UAW convention authorized Reuther to withhold any further per capita tax payments unless the AFL-CIO met his demand for a special convention. The council, on May 13, warned that withholding the payments was "an act tantamount to withdrawal from the federation." It warned Reuther that under the constitution the UAW faced automatic suspension unless per capita payments for February, March, and April 1968 were received by May 15. None came. On May 16 Meany sent Reuther a "dear sir and brother" letter telling him the UAW was suspended both from the AFL-CIO and subordinate state and local councils.

Reuther came back on July 1 (also using the "dear sir and brother" salutation) with a renewed complaint about the lack of a special convention, and a fresh one about Meany's suspension of the UAW "under a provision of the constitution never invoked previously in the more than sixty-year history of the American labor movement." He claimed UAW locals had been prepared to "continue to be active as part of the state and local labor movement." And he concluded that "to avoid any confusion or misunderstanding" as to the UAW's status, it "formally disaffiliated."

In a lengthy, often sarcastic reply, Meany told Reuther the AFL-CIO had given him repeated opportunities to present his case, and in effect accused him of running out on a fight—especially by not attending the 1967 convention.

> At the last minute you found one more excuse to refuse to confront your equals, many of whom know firsthand the actual facts about the matters which you have so flagrantly misrepresented to your own members and in the public press. If those issues were vital and urgent enough to warrant a subsequent demand for a special convention and the secession of the UAW from the main body of the trade union movement, surely they were urgent enough to warrant a day's recess in your talks with General Motors, prior to a deadline which you yourselves contrived.
>
> I give you the credit of believing that you can not have been in any real doubt as to the inevitable response of the AFL-CIO to the threats and ultimatums contained in your subsequent communications. Those tactics . . . represented a transparent attempt to set up the grounds and excuses to justify to your members your pre-

determined objective of withdrawal from this trade union movement.

That objective, I am convinced, stemmed in turn from a condition for which the AFL-CIO has no remedy—your apparent unwillingness to live in constructive harmony within an organization in which the rights, the interests and the views of other unions and other personalities are given equal consideration with those of the UAW and its president.

Three years after the UAW's break, a man who managed to remain close to both Reuther and Meany during the entire dispute mused about the reasons for Reuther's crushing defeat. "Had Walter kept his focus," this man said, "he could have moved around George and gotten pretty much what he wanted. On many liberal kinds of issues—free trade was a good example—I think Meany was ahead of most of the federation, and therefore not really averse to seeing fairly strong positions taken so long as those positions flowed through the organization. Meany could be pushed, no doubt about it. But it had to be done properly.

"Walter offended most of the council because he was so far off base with his charges. He said things people knew absolutely were not true. Also, you don't win any support by calling executive council members a bunch of worn out old farts, which is what he was doing in private. Hell, that could have applied even to some of his friends on the council."

Meany felt the Administrative Letters boomeranged on Reuther. Through them, he said, Reuther "gave the impression that he was fighting for these things inside the movement. There were twenty-nine men sitting there who know this wasn't true. In other words, if he said that he fought for this, that or the other, I have twenty-nine witnesses on that council to prove that that was not so. That includes everybody from the old CIO. After all, they are not going to falsify themselves just because they happened to belong to the old CIO."

*We have some loudmouth critics on our own side who say we are not doing too well.*

*The AFL-CIO is decadent, it is the custodian of the status quo, it is moribund. I looked that up. That means in the process of extinction. It is resting on dead center. It has failed to organize; and it has failed to display an adequate sense of social consciousness, whatever the hell that means.*

*—Meany to a legislative conference of the building and construction trades department, Washington, March 1968*

Reuther especially blundered by attacking Meany and the AFL-CIO for its role in the farmworkers organizing campaign which Cesar Chavez was leading in California. In February 1967 the Providence *Evening Bulletin* quoted a Reuther speech at the University of Rhode Island:

"How much money has the AFL-CIO put into supporting the grape strikers in Delano, California?" Mr. Reuther asked.

"Not a dime. The UAW has been the main support of the striking agricultural workers. . . ."

Reuther repeated this statement in one of his Administrative Letters, to a UAW skills trade conference, and again in March 1968 in his final report as president of the IUD: "To date, the AFL-CIO has made only a token contribution to organizing agricultural workers. Had it not been for the special and timely contribution of the IUD and the UAW, the Delano strike would have been lost and what progress has been made in organizing farmworkers would not have taken place." Reuther dramatized his support for Chavez by visiting the Delano strike headquarters with his wife (a trip Meany dismissed as "press agentry").

When the AFL-CIO finally got around to answering Reuther in April 1969 in a 98-page "white paper" entitled "To Clear the Record," it declared: "Nowhere has the mendacity of the UAW's propaganda campaign against the AFL-CIO been more blatant than in its repeated falsehoods concerning the role of the AFL-CIO, as compared to that of Mr. Reuther, in the organization of farmworkers in California." The farm strike warrants exploration in depth, because it is illustrative of the vast gap between rhetoric and reality in Reuther's broadsides of 1966–68.

The AFL-CIO began a pilot organizing project among California farmworkers in 1959, through the Agricultural Workers Organizing Committee (AWOC), which it wholly financed and staffed, with the help of the California state AFL-CIO. The AWOC, predominantly Filipino-Americans, won some basic improvements in wages and working conditions, but did not succeed in making itself viable and self-supporting, nor in attracting year-round membership. According to the AFL-CIO White Paper, "two major barriers to successful organization existed—first, the 'bracero' system, whereby employers were able to import Mexican nationals to displace and undercut domestic labor; and secondly, the exemption of farm operators from coverage under the National Labor Relations Act and the absence of any government-supervised system for the conduct of elections, union certification after the showing of a majority, or the enforcement of any requirement to bargain in good faith with unions of the workers' own choosing."

Immediately after President Kennedy's election, the AFL-CIO, in conjunction with other liberal groups, launched a lobbying campaign to terminate the bracero campaign. The AWOC went into limbo. The AFL-CIO worked with a National Advisory Committee on Farm Labor, including among its sponsors Norman Thomas, the long-time Socialist leader; Dr. Frank P. Graham, president of the University of North Carolina, and Meany's friend since their service on the National War Labor Board; A. Philip Randolph; and Mrs. Eleanor Roosevelt. The campaign succeeded in 1964 when Congress terminated the bracero program. The AFL-CIO resumed its organization drive and in May 1965 the revived AWOC won a strike in the Coachella Valley of California, increasing hourly wages from $1.20 to $1.40 and the box incentive from fifteen to twenty-five cents. Concurrently, the independent National Farm Workers Association, predominantly Mexican-American and led by Cesar Chavez, began a strike of its own against living conditions for grape pickers in the Delano areas. The AFL-CIO department of organization came to its assistance, along with the UAW and other interested unions, and Chavez won a landmark settlement with the vast DiGorgio Fruit Corporation, one of the nation's largest corporate farms. As the White Paper noted, DiGorgio "had defied organizational efforts for a generation." Chavez won a minimum wage of $1.75 per hour, a full union shop, a hiring hall, and arbitration of grievances. At the AFL-CIO's suggestion, the AWOC and the NFWA merged in 1966 into the United Farm Workers Organizing Committee (UFWOC). The White Paper toted up the record:

From March 1, 1959, to September 30, 1966, when AWOC was merged with the NFWA, the AFL-CIO paid virtually all of the costs of financing this operation, incurring direct expenses for the support of AWOC in excess of $1,400,000. . . .

There is no record of any UAW or IUD financial help in connection with this campaign until some time in 1966.

. . . Since October 1, 1966, . . . the AFL-CIO has contributed to UFWOC more than $400,000. In addition to substantial manpower assistance and other costs picked up by the federation, the AFL-CIO sends a regular cash contribution of at least $10,000 a month to the United Farm Workers Organizing Committee. All in all, since 1959, the California farmworker campaign has involved expenditures by the AFL-CIO of about $2 million. The AFL-CIO does not keep a penny of dues or per capita payments from these farmworker union members, turning back all per capita receipts to the committee. . . .

The only solid, tangible commitment made to the UFWOC by Mr. Reuther was a public pledge, announced in 1966, of $5,000 a month, to be split equally between the UAW and the IUD, with each pledging $2,500 a month.

Mr. Reuther, however, has not carried out the UAW side of that commitment as pledged. In 1966, according to its own financial reports, the UAW contributed $30,000 to UFWOC. The 1967 UAW financial report, however, shows a contribution to UFWOC of only $10,000 for the entire year. For 1968, UFWOC receipts show a contribution of only $5,000 from the UAW. UFWOC has received no contribution from the national UAW since early 1968.

The UAW did make a special grant of $50,000 in 1968 for the construction of a farmworkers' service center in Delano. Presumably, the UAW took this cost out of, or offset it against, its unmet pledges to UFWOC.

If the AFL-CIO's financial contributions to the farmworkers are, as Mr. Reuther charges, "minimal" or "token," how is the UAW contribution—from an organization with a 1967 net worth in excess of $80 million and an annual income in excess of $86 million —to be described?

In the White Paper the AFL-CIO compared the success of its California drive with a separate campaign Reuther launched in 1966 among farmworkers in Florida, through the IUD. The Florida venture began with a wave of publicity, the opening of field offices, and the dispatch of staff workers. The IUD spent $72,500 in Florida from mid-1966 to mid-1967, then abruptly halted the campaign and gave $20,000 to the Packinghouse Workers "for taking the remnants of the campaign off the hands of the IUD." As the White Paper commented, "the only thing now left of Mr. Reuther's own 'crusade' to organize Florida farmworkers is bitterness and resentment on the part of workers whose hopes were raised by the publicity and promises and then dashed to nothing. There is now* a residue of suspicion and distrust of unions by ministers and public-spirited citizens who wished to help in the Florida farm campaign, and who joined publicly in the effort, only to be left high and dry by the pullout."

The IUD also pulled organizers out of a farm campaign in the Rio Grande Valley of Texas. Three organizers who had been working there sent an emotional plea to the IUD, saying defeat was "handing our enemy the most effective weapon they can use in union busting."

Can you imagine the elation of the Chamber of Commerce, the Texas Merchants Association, the Slave Labor Minded Employers, the Anti-Union Press and all other antiunion factions of our population when news of the IUD's closing shop is released to the public? Worse yet, can you imagine the dejected workers whose

* April 1969.

only hope for a better life, for release from poverty . . . lay in the leadership, counsel, and direction of this benevolent arm of the AFL-CIO . . . ?

The IUD ignored the plea; the office was closed.

Within a month of his break with the AFL-CIO, Reuther joined with the International Brotherhood of Teamsters to form the Alliance for Labor Action (ALA). James R. Hoffa had finally gone to jail for jury tampering, and the Teamsters were in the hands of surrogate president Frank Fitzsimmons. With the two largest unions in the nation, the ALA claimed a membership of around four million, and it had the stated aim to "get the American labor movement on the march."

The AFL-CIO took a worried look at the alliance at its September 1968 meeting. There was soul-searching on whether the ALA offered something to American workers the AFL-CIO did not have, with one member commenting, "There is a surge in this country which we must study, as it may be possible that we are running blind in some areas." But the majority felt the ALA raised the specter of dual unionism, and that AFL-CIO affiliates must be warned away from it lest they "be misled." Meany commented, "It is clear that Reuther has his objectives and will use his influence to attain them, and we have the responsibility of warning others." With Jacob Potofsky and Joseph Curran voting no, the council warned that any affiliate joining "this UAW-Teamster combine" faced suspension or expulsion.

But the ALA had trouble "getting American labor on the march." A year passed before it had its first national conference in Washington; by then, it had picked up two new members, the International Chemical Workers, which the AFL-CIO immediately expelled, and the National Council of Distributive Workers, an independent union. At its founding convention the ALA took strong positions against the Vietnam War and the antiballistic missile; it adopted resolutions asking more spending on domestic problems, rather than military hardware, and advocating a national health insurance program. ALA also launched an organizing campaign in Atlanta with the goal of 25,000 members. What does this mean? someone asked Meany just before Labor Day 1969. "That would indicate he would have 200 more Atlantas to go to," Meany replied. "You know, he was setting up a national outlet, but that is organizing at the local level. That could have been done by the IUD. . . . If he finishes with Atlanta successfully, fine—what unions is he going to put them into? . . . He has three unions. . . . If he organizes these workers in Atlanta, where is he going to put them? In the Teamsters? In the Auto Workers? In the Chemical Workers?" Reuther reported to the UAW in

April 1970 that the Atlanta campaign had signed 2,000 workers, less than one tenth the goal.

But such comments were rare. After the split Meany and Reuther mostly ignored one another. In 1969 biographers Frank Cormier and William J. Eaton asked Reuther to comment upon the prevalent assumption in labor that he bolted because he despaired of Meany's ever retiring. Reuther laughed before he answered:

I never wanted Meany's job. What is Meany's job? It's got nothing to do with collective bargaining. I don't know whether he could lead a poverty crusade, or the fight [for] health care. I know I can lead these fights as president of the UAW, because our guys respond. I wouldn't want to hold the hand of reluctant labor politicians. I'm action-oriented and the UAW is the place where the action is. This is why I think I've got the best job in the American labor movement, and I'm very happy with it.

Meany did not accept this explanation. Chatting with a group of reporters in 1969, he said, "I think that he is interested only in being head of an organization. He would like it to be the whole thing. I think so." "He was head of the IUD," someone reminded Meany. "That wasn't the organization that he wanted to be head of," Meany replied.

Many observers noted a restlessness in Reuther. As a UAW convention opened in Atlantic City in April 1970, the *Wall Street Journal* opined that Reuther "faces his toughest year since he was first consolidating his power in the forties." Low profit margins for the auto manufacturers, soaring expectations of workers whose incomes had dropped by fifty percent because of slumps in overtime, a younger, more restive work force—"all these strains are surfacing," the *Journal* wrote. It quoted an "old friend" of Reuther's: "I have great admiration for Walter's resourcefulness. But I'm concerned about his boredom. He seems bored with the whole operation, kind of frustrated because there is not much place for him to go. He is boxed in politically by Meany. Legislatively, he is a creature of the thirties and forties, and those programs are already enacted. And he is stymied by the members who make more an hour than some guys did in a day when he started. How do you get worked up bargaining for those guys?"

*The UAW convention re-elected Reuther by an overwhelming majority. A few days later, on May 9, a Saturday, he and his wife flew to upstate Michigan to visit a UAW family recreation center under construction at isolate, intriguingly beautiful Black Lake. For four years Reuther had made the center a driving personal interest—a place of solitude where he could forget the strains of office. The chartered Lear jet neared Black Lake an hour after sunset, through rain and lightning. One and one-half miles short of the landing strip, unexplainedly low, it clipped the top of a fifty-foot elm tree, hurtled into a densely wooded area, and burst into flames. All six persons aboard died—the Reuthers; Philadelphia architect Oskar Stonorov, who had designed the center; Reuther's bodyguard (present at UAW insistence since a 1948 assassination attempt); and the two-man crew. Thus ended an era of American labor.*

# XVII

## Nixon One: Tricked by Dick

*Nixon. Labor has detested this man and fought this man for more than two decades, and now here he was in the White House. A man with absolutely nothing in common with George Meany, save for mutual enmity. Not even the old man's garrulity of Eisenhower, which permitted a semblance of rapport during those Republican years. Ike's simplistic views on labor Meany could blame on the flint-eyed businessmen who ran his Administration, not on any intrinsic meanness of Ike himself. But Nixon was different—an antilabor Republican politician who progressed from reactionary congressman to reactionary senator to reactionary Vice-President to Wall Street lawyer to President, imbued with that peculiar miserliness of the spirit so common in self-made men; the politician transformed into millionaire because of his friendship with monied America. "They say he was a poor boy," Meany said of Nixon during the campaign. "Well, let me tell you, he might have been a poor boy, but he has no poor friends any more."*

*The irony, even at the time, and especially now in retrospect, is how so many supposedly wise men, including the President himself, thought Meany and Nixon could be friends, even for political expediency. "Why the hell is it you can get along with Nelson Rockefeller, one of the richest Republicans in the world, and not with somebody like Nixon?" a friend once asked Meany. "Nelson is satisfied with his own share," Meany said, "and he don't try to keep the other feller from getting his. He doesn't have that mean streak you find in some of these Republican businessmen."*

*But oh how Nixon tried to woo Meany. He lunched Meany, and he golfed Meany, and he partied Meany, and he briefed Meany on matters*

*domestic and foreign. When Nixon sent U.S. troops into Cambodia in
May 1970, much of the nation crashed down upon his head with angry
protests. Good Soldier Meany did not protest; he saluted. "It is unmistakably clear," Meany said of the President, "that he made his decision on the
basis of his clear obligation as commander-in-chief to protect American
servicemen . . . he acted with courage and conviction . . . he should
have the full support of the American people. He certainly has ours."
Richard Nixon was so flattered he went to Meany's office, rather than
the other way around, which assuredly is not the way a President normally does things, and he took along maps of Indochina and a pointer
and gave the executive council a full-blown briefing on the war. A few
months later George Meany stood in the White House, on Labor Day
eve, and he said, in so many words,* Franklin D. Roosevelt was just as
tricky as you are, Dick. *And the men in the White House—which is to
say, Richard M. Nixon and the people who work for him, smart people
who are running the government—said to one another, Aha, with skilled
conmanship we are transforming this naïve old man from blood foe into
ally, and he and his hard-hats will march with us rather than the radic-
lib-peacenik Democrats.*

RICHARD NIXON'S BASIC ERROR with George Meany
was that he mistook politeness and respect for the office of the
President of the United States for political friendship. Meany is an old-
fashioned man, in the purest sense of the word. He loves his flag and his
country, and he thinks that a President deserves, ex officio, the civility of
the populace. As the titular leader of American workers, the AFL-CIO
president has an institutional responsibility to represent their cause before the federal government, regardless of the political complexion of the
Administration. Nixon saw in this cooperation during his first eighteen
months in office an opportunity to neutralize labor politically—even to
win away large chunks of a reflexively Democratic vote. When Meany
declined to be co-opted, because of deep reservations about the Administration's civil rights and economic policies, Nixon blundered into a second, even graver mistake: courtesy is a reciprocal quality. Meany felt
Nixon and a number of Administration officials treated him rudely, even
shabbily—deliberate personal slights, deeper than arguments over policy.

The Nixon-Meany relationship defies charting, for it was concurrently
antagonistic and cordial for months, depending upon the issue. From the

very beginning of his Administration, Nixon's course was politically erratic—he alternately courted and offended labor, his inconsistency gradually destroying his credibility.

Because of his strident partisanship in 1968, Meany neither deserved nor anticipated special treatment from Nixon. The morning after the election, he sent the President-elect a perfunctory telegram of congratulations, notable for its lack of warmth. Several days after the election Meany visited Nixon at his headquarters in the Hotel Pierre in New York—a stiffly polite ceremonial conversation devoted entirely to generalities. They discussed the position of Secretary of Labor, but not in terms of "any specific candidate," Meany said. A bit later Nixon selected George Shultz, dean of the University of Chicago Graduate School of Business. Shultz was chosen on the recommendation of Dr. Arthur Burns, the professor of economics from Columbia University who helped Nixon recruit the key figures of his Administration, and then himself accepted the position of counselor to the President. Meany remarked, "I think that I played a very important role in having Mr. Shultz appointed because Mr. Nixon asked me if I would prefer a businessman or somebody from the academic world. I said I would prefer a businessman and that did it."

To Meany's surprise, however, Shultz on close examination proved to be "a cut above the average professor," as he reported to his staff after an early meeting. Shultz subscribed wholeheartedly to the notion—shared by Meany—that excessive White House meddling in contract disputes is fatal to collective bargaining. He told Meany that during the Nixon Administration there would be no repeat of "Lyndon's television spectaculars"—referring to Johnson's live appearance on evening TV news shows to announce the settlement of a 1966 rail strike (one which, embarrassingly, blew up within hours when rank-and-file members would not ratify it).

With Nixon's approval, Shultz aborted a business fantasy that wafted into public view during the last days of the campaign. A coalition of thirty-five major business groups—the Chamber of Commerce of the United States, the National Association of Manufacturers, the American Retail Federation, among others—wanted to rewrite the Wagner Act to permit employers to refuse to engage in collective bargaining, and to abolish the National Labor Relations Board. The business combine raised a half-million-dollar campaign fund and hired Hill and Knowlton, one of the largest political public relations firms in the country, to coordinate the drive. The Republicans' failure to win Congress brought the campaign crashing to earth. A business delegation tried to interest Shultz in submitting the legislation anyway. He told them, in effect (and so reported to Meany), that "fighting that kind of losing fight is not worth the time and agitation."

In an alliance of convenience, the Nixon Administration worked closely with the AFL-CIO in passing the postal reorganization bill, which transformed the U. S. Post Office into an independent government corporation. In direct negotiations, Meany succeeded in obtaining from a supposedly hostile Administration sweeping concessions on bargaining rights of public employees which even President Kennedy had hesitated to give labor. His bargaining adversary was Postmaster General Winton Blount, a past president of the National Association of Manufacturers. Meany's interest was protecting members of seven AFL-CIO-affiliated postal unions. Blount agreed to a bill that authorized the postal unions to bargain for a closed shop—a power previously denied federal and other public employees. The postal reorganization law, passed in 1970, required "collective bargaining over all aspects of wages, hours, and working conditions . . . and *in general all matters that are subject to collective bargaining in the private sector."* The emphasized language, the *AFL-CIO News* commented later, constituted "a breakthrough, a new benchmark in labor relations." Meany was so happy about the settlement he declared that "in the field of government employees he [Nixon] has certainly been more liberal than any man in the White House before him." (The major labor concession was to accept final and binding arbitration of postal disputes.) President Kennedy, in his 1962 executive order on government unions, specifically protected workers who wished to "refrain" from joining unions. Arthur Goldberg, while Secretary of Labor, also opposed the closed shop. "But along came good old Winton Blount!" railed Reed Larson, of the National Right to Work Committee. "He became the determined and unswerving advocate of what George Meany had been advocating for years—that government workers should be stripped of all protection against compulsory unions." Larson "gagged at the spectacle" of a former NAM president negotiating final details of the bill at AFL-CIO headquarters and then announcing agreement with Meany at a White House press conference. (Agreement came against a backdrop of wildcat walkouts that snarled postal service throughout the country in March 1970 and prompted the White House to use troops to move the mail in New York City.)

The postal bill, however, was completely overshadowed by the Nixon Administration's first great confrontation with organized labor: the Philadelphia Plan controversy. Some brief background is in order before plunging into this dispute.

Inclusion of the equal employment opportunties section in the 1964 Civil Rights Act did not significantly increase the number of black apprentices in the building trades. Foot dragging by local unions was one factor, which Meany recognized in convention speeches after 1965. The Equal Employment Opportunity Commission, the enforcement agency created by the act, thought it could integrate the building trades locals by banning discrimination in the apprenticeship programs. "This was very simple," Meany said, "just get some regulations and ban discrimination. They [the EEOC] said the reason there were so few qualified journeymen was the minorities could not get into the apprenticeship programs, and there are some people in high places that have this same idea.

"Well, the AFL-CIO endorsed these regulations, and the building trades endorsed these regulations, but they found out that they did not bring any significant increase in minority group apprentices." Nor did "apprenticeship information centers" in black areas draw many applicants. "Whatever the reason," Meany said, "we found out that very few young Negroes who could qualify to enter existing apprenticeship programs were interested in entry. Now, what the reasons might be, I don't know. Maybe some of them just didn't believe that the doors were going to open to them."

Hence Meany changed AFL-CIO strategy. Since blacks wouldn't come to the unions, the unions would go to the blacks. Casting about for ideas with A. Philip Randolph and Bayard Rustin, among others, his attention fell upon a New York project that was having marked success in Local 28 of the Sheet Metal Workers Union in New York City.

This local had been notorious—it just wasn't going to take any black members. The New York State Commission for Human Rights secured a court ruling that the sheet metal workers' apprenticeship class was to be open to all applicants and that selections were to be made on an objective basis. The Workers Defense League, a human rights group long supported by the AFL-CIO, took on the task of helping Local 28 comply with the court order. Its first effort failed. WDL found twenty-eight black youngsters who agreed to take competitive tests to enter an apprentice class, and tutored them briefly. There were 340 applicants for 65 openings; the highest scorer among the WDL group ranked sixty-eighth; the next, ninety-seventh. Quite obviously, the WDL decided, merely supplying bodies would not produce results. Many of the youngsters did not know the simple techniques of taking tests and were unduly frightened by them. Hence the WDL began an intensive tutorial program, lasting from six to twelve weeks. Recruits practiced repeatedly on basic aptitude tests given by the WDL staff, concentrating on mathematics and reading comprehension. In the next test, WDL placed eleven black and Puerto Rican candidates in the class of thirty apprentices; eight of them eventually graduated and entered Local 28. Within four years more than twenty percent of Local 28's apprentices were from minority groups.* Meany saw

* Meany gives much of the credit for WDL's success to Ernest Green, director of the apprenticeship program. A quiet, studious man with a master's degree from the University of Michigan, Green was one of the "Little Rock Nine"—the Negro youngsters who braved Arkansas mobs to integrate Central High School there in 1957, under the protection of federal troops.

WDL's programs as a solution to his problem of finding a way to integrate the building trades unions without lowering apprentice standards or losing control of admittance policies. Committed as he was to racial equality, Meany was labor politician enough to know that unfair treatment of existing buildings trades members would only exacerbate their opposition to blacks. He explained:

> There are some of these do-gooders with official hats, or without official hats, who feel that the so-called minority groups should be provided a short cut to attaining the skills necessary to becoming skilled building trades mechanics.
>
> Well, you and I know there is no short cut, and we also know there is no place in today's highly competitive construction industry for those who are not fully capable of meeting whatever competition there is.
>
> To turn out half-trained mechanics would be a fraud and deceit on the industry, and a fraud and deceit on the trainees themselves.
>
> Handing out journeymen's cards without proper qualifications is no answer to the minority problem.
>
> There can be no basis for cooperation with so-called militant groups who pretend to represent these minority people, who threaten violence, nor can the training of skilled mechanics be turned over to people who are completely without competence in the industry.

At Meany's behest, the AFL-CIO, through front groups such as the A. Philip Randolph Institute, took tacit control of the WDL program. From his vantage point in Washington, Meany persuaded the obliging Labor Department to provide funds for its expansion throughout New York City, under the title of Operation Outreach. (The Taconic Foundation, one of the philanthropic arms of the Mellon family, had furnished most of the early money, in addition to that put up by the AFL-CIO.) Concurrently, with Whitney Young of the National Urban League, the AFL-CIO adopted WDL techniques into another apprenticeship project called Labor Education Advancement Program, or LEAP. Meany told the building and construction trades department 1967 convention that he would not permit Outreach or LEAP to lower standards. "How do you get colored boys into these highly skilled building trades? Well, you get them in the way you have always gotten them in . . . by the apprenticeship route. . . . There is no short cut. When we bring them in by the apprenticeship route, do we lower the standards? Do we compromise the standards? I say absolutely not!" By mid-1969 Outreach was operating in more than fifty cities, under federal grants of $3.8 million. Almost 4,000 apprentices had gone through Outreach programs to become apprentices. Meany was satisfied at the progress. According to the 1960 census, nonwhites comprised only 2.5 percent of the persons in apprenticeship programs. At the end of 1968, the percentage had increased fourfold—to 9.4 percent.

In June 1969 the Nixon Administration, through the Labor Department, tossed a bombshell into the building trades unions. It issued an order, the so-called Philadelphia Plan, requiring that on federal construction jobs involving more than $500,000, contractors had to agree to hire certain percentages from minority groups. The order aimed at seven trades: ironworkers; plumbers and pipefitters; steamfitters; sheet metal workers; electrical workers; roofers; and elevator construction workers. The Labor Department cited past findings of discrimination by the Philadelphia Commission on Human Relations and attempts by some unions to broaden apprenticeship programs. But it found that unions in those seven trades still had only about 1.6 percent minority group membership and that special measures were required to provide equal employment opportunity. The department claimed hundreds of qualified blacks were available for jobs, and it set goals for nonwhites of five percent in 1970 and fifteen percent in 1971.

Because of the building trades' historic lily-white complexion,* the Philadelphia Plan found immediate popularity with the press and a goodly number of civil rights leaders. Tom Wicker of the New York *Times* called it "remarkable" and was happy to see the Nixon Administration, noted for its "Southern strategy"—code words for gentlemanly racism—taking a strong and forthright position on union bias.

To Meany, the Philadelphia Plan was a "concoction and contrivance" that "would not bring a single minority worker into the area labor force." Contractors had no incentive to train new apprentices; they would meet the government quotas by transferring black workers to federal jobs—"checkerboarding," in Bayard Rustin's words. The Philadelphia Plan had another handicap as well: its statistical basis was phony. Labor Department publicity on the Philadelphia Plan stressed that minority workers "held less than two percent" of construction jobs in Philadelphia. "When that was checked by the unions involved," Meany related later, "we found out there was thirty percent of union members employed on unionized jobs within the jurisdiction of the Philadelphia trades that were black.

---

* Actually, the building trades had a better record than other industries. In mid-1969, 7.2 percent of the 90,000 persons in federally serviced construction apprentice programs were from minority groups. This compared with 4.3 percent in metal manufacturing ("including the great auto industry, if you please," Meany said in a sarcastic aside in a 1969 speech); 5.3 percent in nonmetal manufacturing; and 4.9 percent in public utilities and transportation. Nonetheless the building trades seem permanently cursed as the "last bastion of discrimination."

"Now, that is quite an error from two percent to thirty percent, and even taking the laborers out of the computation (because for some reason these spokesmen for the black militants say, 'We don't want to talk about the laborers,' all right, take them out), we find that the percentage for the other building trades of blacks in Philadelphia was twelve percent, which is still a long way from the two percent." Meany complained of another "misconception" about construction: that the few blacks who get jobs in the industry are given poorly paid and "dirty" work. "I don't know what they mean by poorly paid jobs. The lowest pay that I can find in the Philadelphia area . . . is $4.24 an hour, and that is the lowest-paid laborer. . . . As far as their being put on the dirty jobs, I don't know of any clean jobs in the construction industry, and I have been around quite a while—they are all dirty jobs."

The Iron Workers Union, one of those charged with discrimination, was said by the Administration to have only twelve blacks among 850 members in Philadelphia. Actually, it had 3,575 members in Philadelphia, 690 of whom were black (nineteen percent). Curious about the 302 blacks the Labor Department claimed were "qualified ironworkers" ready for employment, the international president wired Secretary Shultz for their names and addresses, pledging they would be "given every assistance in securing employment." Shultz replied two weeks later: "Because of the nature of the information-gathering techniques used by the Department of Labor arriving at specific numbers . . . it would be impractical to provide you with the names, addresses and work experience data which you request."

Denouncing the Philadelphia Plan in a speech to the National Press Club in January 1970, Meany charged it was designed to cover the Administration's tarnished civil rights record—"the softening on voters' rights, delayed desegregation of the schools in the South, the attempt to put Strom Thurmond's baby on the Supreme Court,* the cutting back of programs that could be helpful in the black community." Meany said "it would seem that this attempt to use the building trades as a whipping boy could be designed to give the Nixon Administration a few Brownie points to offset their shortcomings in the civil rights area as a whole." He called it a "Madison Avenue job."

The courts permitted the Philadelphia Plan to go into effect, over AFL-CIO protests, and the public—that is, the press—displayed no further interest in it. Eighteen months later, in a progress report, the Labor Department claimed that seventy-seven minority workers had been placed on federal construction jobs. The AFL-CIO civil rights department, suspicious of the Nixon Administration's arithmetic, found that workers who had been sent to more than one job were counted twice; the vast

* Clement Haynsworth, whose nomination was rejected by the Senate.

majority of them proved to be apprentices from the Outreach program. Outreach, meanwhile, had expanded into ninety cities, and had placed 9,953 minority members in the building trades.

The Philadelphia Plan related indirectly to another political strategy of the Nixon Administration which emerged later—to blame labor for inflation in construction costs. The *Wall Street Journal,* in a survey of contractors a few days after the plan was announced, found they welcomed it because it "might slow inflation in construction by increasing the supply of workers." Bayard Rustin noted that almost simultaneously with the Philadelphia Plan, Nixon ordered a seventy-five percent reduction in federal construction, "thereby reducing the number of jobs available in the industry and producing the twofold effect of exerting a deflationary pressure on wages and increasing competition over scarce jobs."

For all its furor, the Philadelphia Plan controversy did not shake the traditional civil rights lobbying coalition. The AFL-CIO played key but deliberately inconspicuous roles in the Senate rejections of Nixon's nominations of Judges Clement F. Haynsworth and G. Harrold Carswell. Indeed, a combination of luck and friendly persuasion by labor lobbyist Andy Biemiller started the chain of events that stopped Haynsworth's approval. After the nomination Biemiller did fast intelligence work with the Textile Workers Union in Haynsworth's native South Carolina and found him to be the prototype of the antilabor Southern judge. Seven labor-management cases had been appealed from Haynsworth's court to the U.S. Supreme Court; his decision was antilabor in each, and the high court reversed every one of them. Haynsworth's civil rights record left much to be desired. Biemiller checked with Meany, who said, "See if you can slow up the appointment while we find out what we can." Meany knew it would be difficult to stop Haynsworth simply because he had an antiunion record.

"I ran down the list of the Senate Judiciary Committee looking for someone to put a hold on Haynsworth," Biemiller said. "Vance Hartke was out because he had been such a supporter of Abe Fortas. Teddy Kennedy wouldn't do because this was too soon after Chappaquiddick. This left Birch Bayh, so I gave him a call. 'I'm leaving for Russia in an hour on a trip,' he said, 'I don't have the time to talk to you about it.' 'Okay,' I told him, 'just don't make any commitment until you get back.' Within ten minutes Senator Spessard Hollings (Dem., South Carolina) called and asked Bayh to declare for Haynsworth. "As a matter of courtesy," Biemiller said, "he normally would have said yes without thinking and been locked in. That would have assured Haynsworth's appointment."

The AFL-CIO next busied itself looking for allies. Meany called Clarence Mitchell, Washington director of the National Association for the

Advancement of Colored People, to tell him of labor's decision. Mitchell said Meany was wasting his time. "You'll never stop him," Mitchell said, "no one is going to line up with you on this one." Mitchell mentioned that the Senate had battered itself into exhaustion in the just-concluded fight over the antiballistic missile, and that no one wished another protracted conflict. Meany was insistent Haynsworth must be opposed on principle. He did not quarrel with Haynsworth's legal abilities, but felt he was hopelessly biased as a jurist.

During Bayh's absence, the Leadership Conference on Civil Rights and AFL-CIO political operatives and lawyers went over Haynsworth's record. The Textile Workers Union produced details of an intriguing incident in which Haynsworth served as an officer of a vending company that did $100,000 of business annually with a textile firm, simultaneous with his hearing a case involving the textile firm. A union member in Greenville, South Carolina, Haynsworth's home, suggested that the AFL-CIO check out the title on the judge's house. Sure enough, it had a restrictive covenant. The labor and civil rights lobbyists fed Bayh and other friendly senators a continuous flow of derogatory material on Haynsworth; the conflict-of-interest eventually beat him, fifty-five to forty-five.*

During these early skirmishes Nixon and Meany maintained a correct if not overly cordial relationship. When Meany had something to tell or ask the President, his phone calls went through within an hour, as they had with Kennedy and Johnson; when he wanted a personal meeting, one was arranged promptly. This is not to say, however, that Nixon followed Johnson's open-door policy for labor. Meany was informed of legislation, not consulted when it was being written. No longer did the White House limousine dart out to Bethesda in the evening to bring Meany to the President's private quarters for three hours of root beer and earnest listening. Meany's overriding impression of Nixon, during the first part of his Administration, was of a President without any guiding philosophy. Chatting with a group of reporters during 1969, Meany confessed, "I have been trying and trying, and waiting and waiting, and, up to the present time, I just can't size it up. He seems to come out with statements, he has a little bit for everybody, even if you are on opposite sides." Meany shook his head in bemusement.

And then, suddenly, Cambodia—at once the Nixon Administration's domestic equivalent of the Tet offensive, and an opportunity to test the politics of polarization, by melding Nixon's "silent majority" into a new Republican national majority. Kevin Phillips, a conservative Republican

* The last court nominee refused appointment was Judge John Parker of North Carolina; AFL lobbying played a major role in his defeat also.

theoretician, arguing that Americans had tired of liberalism, searched for a new conservative political doctrine, one tailored for the suburbs, the South, the "sunbelt" (from Florida through the Southwest to southern California), and ethnic Catholic workers. The Cambodian operation was revealed the evening of April 30; the next morning, campuses across the nation exploded with rage, with students occupying and burning buildings and calling protest strikes. The killing of four Kent State students by national guardsmen sent national emotions surging to a peak, and the polarization was swift and frightening: hardliners behind the President's Indochina policies, disgusted with "permissiveness" and welfare costs and a host of other problems, real and imagined; other Americans disgusted that the cancer of Vietnam had eaten even deeper into the soul of America.

The most conspicuous "labor" reaction was provided by construction workers who left their jobs in lower Manhattan on May 8 to pummel and beat antiwar marchers at City Hall. Three days later the hard-hats (so named because of their protective helmets) marched en masse through Wall Street, American flags on their work shirts, other flags hoisted aloft. Delighted at the support from a nominally Democratic sector, Nixon hurried twenty-two union leaders to the White House on May 26 for a handshake and an exchange of political pleasantries. The group included two Meany friends—Peter Brennan, president of the Building and Construction Trades Council of New York, and Thomas Gleason, president of the International Longshoremen's Association, and a member of the AFL-CIO executive council. Brennan gave Nixon a hard hat bearing the legend "Commander in Chief" (which the President accepted but declined to don for photographers).

Because of Meany's building trades background and his support of the President on the Cambodian incursion, the Nixon Administration decided in the early summer of 1970 that he could either be taken into the "emerging Republican majority" (Kevin Phillips' name for the new conservative coalition) or, at worst, neutralized. Meany's post-Cambodia speeches, to the Administration's glee, took on a hard-hat ring. Speaking to a clerks' convention in Florida on June 4 Meany surveyed the month of antiwar demonstrations:

> We have the young people blocking the highways, taking possession of administration buildings in the colleges throughout the country, we have them playfully throwing rocks. They say, "Oh, we only throw rocks, just a few rocks." Of course, in front of our building two weeks ago a policeman had his skull fractured by one of those rocks and they had to carry him off to the hospital.\* But these are boyish traits, this throwing rocks.

\* The target of this demonstration was not the AFL-CIO, but the White House, several hundred feet away across Lafayette Park.

I . . . contend that these nineteen- and twenty-year-old college kids who are rioting and breaking up buildings because they are dissatisfied . . . just don't know what they are dissatisfied about, and if they were given an opportunity to correct the situation I don't think they would know how to do it.

As the summer wore on Meany spoke bitingly of the "deterioration" of the Democratic party. Basic bread-and-butter unionism was among the issues. With unemployment continuing to rise, the AFL-CIO got behind the Nixon Administration's campaign for federal funding of the supersonic transport. The SST would provide tens of thousands of jobs for the aircraft industry, reeling because of cuts in defense spending. The International Association of Machinists, second largest in the AFL-CIO, with more than 900,000 members, was especially eager to obtain the SST. Yet the AFL-CIO found defeating the SST was the *cause célèbre* of Democratic liberals who normally supported labor pump-priming projects. Meany was also disgusted with Democratic senators who were "falling all over the ball park" in their attempts to find a safely fuzzy position on Vietnam. Meany felt the intellectual leadership of the Democratic party had succumbed to barn-burning nonsense. John Kenneth Galbraith, in a biting critique in *Harper's Magazine* in July 1970, asked "Who Needs the Democrats?" and said the remedy for the many ails of congressional Democrats was obvious: "If men suffer from having been too long in office, the answer is to end their suffering." Galbraith said union leadership was "geriatric" (Meany was seventy-five that summer) and "archaically hardline on communism, unapologetically for the Vietnam War and untroubled by the military power . . . [and] indifferent or hostile to what most concerns the younger party members." Meany [heard] the same refrain elsewhere in the Democratic party (from less articulate pens) and he growled over it for weeks privately. Finally his disgust rushed to the surface in a pre-Labor Day interview with a group of reporters who cover the AFL-CIO. One of the questioners opined that "rank-and-file workers may be more conservative than they used to be," and asked Meany whether he saw any labor swing to the Republicans. Meany agreed that political attitudes were changing:

"Not so much that our people are looking to the Republicans, but they are looking less to the Democrats because, actually, the Democratic party has disintegrated. It is not the so-called liberal party that it was a few years ago. It almost has become the party of the extremists insofar as these so-called liberals or new lefts, or whatever you want to call them, have taken over the Democratic party. . . . I think the Democratic party will finally get to the point where it will be of real concern and some character will come along and rebuild it. I don't see anyone there now. I think the party is in a shambles."

"The man on Pennsylvania Avenue knows that, too," a reporter commented.

"Oh, you bet your life he knows it," Meany replied.

Nixon certainly did. All that summer, as Labor Secretary George Shultz brought in reports of widening hard-hat discontent with the Democratic party, the Administration thought of ways of making political capital from blue-collar discontent. A Labor Department report, widely circulated in the Administration in 1970,* depicted the 70 million Americans who were members of lower-middle-class families ($5,000- to $10,000-a-year income) as "forgotten people" bypassed by New Frontier and Great Society programs. The blue-collars lived in proximity to the poor, often on wages only a notch above welfare payments, yet were excluded from social programs targeted at the disadvantaged (medical care, low-cost housing, job training, and legal aid). "As taxpayers they support these programs with no visible relief—no visible share . . . they are overripe for a political response to the pressing needs they feel so keenly."

Meany figured prominently in the Administration's political planning. With Meany in apparent revolt against the Democrats, converting his support of the President on Indochina into overt political friendship would be a political coup of no mean magnitude. Joseph Loftus, a former New York *Times* labor writer who had joined the Administration as a special assistant to Shultz, helped assemble the trap into which Meany was to be lured.

"We wanted some sort of ceremony on Labor Day involving participation of both the President and Meany," Loftus said. "We suggested a rally on the Ellipse, with invitations to the thousands of union representatives and workers in the Washington area. Meany wouldn't go for it." One of Meany's staff people said the AFL-CIO feared an "open" rally inevitably would attract war protesters, and the resultant confusion would "reflect poorly on labor and Meany." After suggestions back and forth between the AFL-CIO and the Administration, the President decided to hold a dinner Labor Day evening in the White House, hosting Meany and members of the executive council, and then to join other union representatives on the White House south lawn for a concert by the Marine Band.

Although less than two years previously Meany had been working vigorously to keep Nixon out of the White House, he cheerfully accepted the invitation to dine there, for two reasons. First, the invitation came to him not personally, but in his capacity as the leader of American union members. When a President asks a citizen to come to the White House,

* "The Problem of the Blue Collar Workers," by Jerome M. Rosow, Assistant Secretary of Labor for policy development and research.

Meany believes the citizen has the patriotic duty to respond, whatever their political differences. Secondly, Meany had no intention of taking labor away from the Democratic party, either in the November congressional elections or thereafter. The harsh language about the Democrats overshadowed something else Meany said in the Labor Day interview: although labor rank and file were alarmed about demonstrations and campus violence, "I still think that the biggest issue with our people is the economic issue." The AFL-CIO, even as he spoke, was preparing to help Democratic congressional candidates. Meany's criticisms of Democratic "extremists" was intended to nudge the presidential aspirants back toward the center of the party; they did not portend any endorsement of Nixon, whom Meany had already adjudged a failure as President because of his fumbling on the economy, the domestic issue of paramount importance to labor. But Meany realized his presence in the White House on Labor Day—a fete sure to be publicized by the Administration —would encourage speculation that labor was tilting toward the Republicans. Hence labor's work for the Democrats later in the fall would have maximum man-bites-dog impact.

The event was historic; never before, even in the halcyon days of Roosevelt, Kennedy, and Johnson, had a President honored American unions with a Labor Day dinner.

Nixon staged an extraordinary festive evening. To ensure that no one mistook it for a perfunctory breaking of bread, the President brought in five cabinet officers and his daughter Julie and her husband, David Eisenhower, grandson of the former president. The affair had the trappings of a full state dinner, replete with an armed forces string band playing softly just off the East Room, seven courses of fine food, and three wines. Mr. and Mrs. Meany sat at the head table and chatted with the Nixons during dinner. Finally, the President moved into the toasts. He spoke for almost half an hour and, after some genial small talk (Mrs. John Adams, he observed, "used to hang her wash out in this room"), he came tolerably close to claiming the political support of labor, in a sentence carefully festooned with disclaimers that he was so doing: "As a President of the United States, I have learned what it means for a President, be he a Republican or a Democrat, to have the solid support of the overwhelming majority of the leaders and the members of America's labor unions and of American labor generally for those policies and those programs which are above partisanship and beyond partisanship, but which are dedicated to preserving freedom in America and preserving and protecting freedom in the world."

Nixon said he did not suggest "that there are not times when Mr. Meany and I . . . have not agreed on some matters. That will always be the case where leaders of free independent organizations are involved with any government." He continued: "But I do know this: That this man has stood like a pillar in a storm—strong, full of character, devoted to his church, devoted to his family, devoted to his country, whether the President is a Republican or a Democrat, standing with that President and his country when he felt that that served . . . that kind of freedom which is so essential if a strong, free labor movement is to survive."

Responding, Meany reminisced about the Presidents he had known, and "the problems that are placed on his shoulders by virtue of his office." He said: "And one thing that I find in common that all of these men had, and that this man sitting on my left has in common with his predecessors, is that no matter how political they might have been—and let me tell you, Franklin Roosevelt, he was just as tricky a politician as anyone who bore the name of 'Tricky Dick' could be, and let me tell you, Lyndon was no slouch at politics. . . ."

Meany's sentence rambled on for another hundred words, concluding that all Presidents wanted "to be the best President that they possibly can be for the American people." Looking directly down at the President, and waving a big hand in his direction, Meany continued, "And this applies to this man here, and I may be bouncing on your head tomorrow morning, but this goes."

To much of labor the juxtaposition of Franklin D. Roosevelt with Nixon could not be tolerated. Edward Swayduck, a feistily outspoken officer of the lithographers union in New York City, called the statement "infamous," and declared, "For a fancy meal, the choice of three wines, and a little flattery, Meany paid off Richard Nixon. . . . It is a story to tell future generations of organized labor: Once upon a time George Meany and his Several Dwarfs ate at the White House and afterward they were all turned into toadies." Columnist John Herling commented, "It was somewhat as if some overenthusiastic cardinal had declared Khrushchev the equal in virtue of the late Pope John the XXIII." Joe Loftus of the Labor Department remembered reading the quotation the next morning and thinking, Well, he's put his foot in his mouth this time; FDR is a saint to an awful lot of working people in this country. A few days later Meany turned up at Burning Tree Country Club, a Republican retreat, in a foursome with President Nixon, Secretary of State William Rogers, and Attorney General John Mitchell (whom the AFL-CIO executive council had denounced the previous month for "persecuting" the Seafarers International Union, and its president, Paul Hall, with an indictment for allegedly corrupt campaign expenditures).*

Incredibly, Meany did not realize the gravity of the slip for several days. In fact, Albert Zack, his press agent, and others in Meany's circle thought the error lay elsewhere: "When I heard George say those words

* A federal court dismissed the indictments in June 1972.

'Tricky Dick' to Nixon's face, I almost fell on the floor," Zack said. "That isn't a nickname the President relishes, and I could see the head-lines the next morning: 'Meany Calls Nixon Tricky Dick.' " A heavy flow of mail from union rank and file the next few weeks informed Meany that whatever his strategy in "setting up" the Administration for an abrupt political turnabout in the congressional elections, he should not have spoken of FDR and Nixon in the same breath.

The Administration took Meany off an uncomfortable hook. Not content with the wide publicity immediately after the dinner, the Republican National Committee mailed out thousands of brochures reproducing the exchange of toasts between Meany and Nixon—implying, without saying so directly, that the AFL-CIO now considered the Republican Administration its friend. Meany considered this to be "exploitation." He complained, "I think this was crude and certainly not the way you handle a houseguest. You don't bring a houseguest to your home and have dinner with him and then use it politically in some way. It was a very shallow sort of thing." James Buckley, running for the Senate in New York on the Conservative party ticket (with Nixon's support against incumbent Republican Senator Charles Goodell), also tried to capitalize on the dinner and on some of the things Meany said in the Labor Day interview. He quoted the interview in campaign speeches and sent Meany a somewhat audacious two-page letter claiming their positions on many domestic issues were "almost parallel." "George got so mad he wouldn't even answer the letter," one of his staff people said.

Meany's answer was a blistering attack on Nixon's economic policies, delayed until the last two weeks of the campaign for maximum impact. Albert Zack said the speech had the desired surprise effect: "This was the sort of routine economic speech that normally would have been buried in the farther reaches of the newspapers, back beyond the comics," Zack said. "But because it was a 'turnabout' speech—or so the press thought, anyway—here George was, all over the front page." Meany recorded the speech with twenty-one different endings, each tailored to boost a particular candidate for Congress or a state legislature. The Committee on Political Education broadcast one version ninety-one times in a single Washington State senatorial district where the AFL-CIO wanted to unseat an antilabor incumbent (he lost).

When Nixon took office in January 1969, the problem of most immediate interest to labor was how he would carry out his avowed intention of stopping inflation without administering the economy a fatal shock. The economic troubles that culminated, eventually, in one of the angrier public brawls ever for an American President, had their genesis in the Johnson Administration.

Despite ninety months of sustained growth during the Kennedy-Johnson years, the economy that Nixon inherited on January 20, 1969, contained huge pockets of hot air. It was, in its own way, as dangerous a national problem as Vietnam. The pivotal fiscal error of the Johnson Administration was its failure to mobilize the economy for war. During the secretive early days of the war, Johnson made no pretense of giving either the Treasury Department or the Congress honest estimates of the duration or expected intensity of the fighting. In early 1966, as the Administration wrote its fiscal 1967 budget, the Pentagon portion was based upon the assumption the war would end by mid-1967, and that the 185,000 troops then in Vietnam would rise to only 250,000. Simultaneously, in another part of the White House, Johnson was approving a request from the field for 400,000 troops. Johnson's stubborn determination to prove he could fight a war and have a Great Society at the same time guaranteed economic disorder. Bogus budgetry got Johnson through the 1966 elections without asking for higher taxes—and Vietnam cost $20 billion in fiscal 1967, rather than the estimated $10 billion. Johnson asked Congress for surtaxes in January and August 1967, refusing each time, however, to cut domestic spending. Not until the spring of 1968, when ruinous inflation was well under way, did Congress find his requests credible enough to pass a ten percent surtax.

The Administration's sole attempt to slow inflation came in 1966, when the Federal Reserve Board tightened the money supply. The abrupt drop in housing starts produced a brief mini-recession, so the nervous board quickly turned on the money spigot again, and away inflation roared. Before-tax corporate earnings zoomed from $63.7 billion in 1964 to $83.7 billion in 1968. The cost-of-living increase, just under two percent in 1964, was above four percent in 1968. Wages spiraled upward with prices. Collective bargaining in 1964 brought wage settlements averaging 3.2 percent; by 1968, the increase was above 6 percent. But unchecked price inflation decimated these seeming wage gains. Average weekly pay for nonfarm workers increased $11 a week from 1965 to 1968, but considering inflation and higher Social Security deductions and income taxes, the worker's check bought less. Indeed, in terms of real income, he was two dollars worse off than in 1965. Mortgage interest rates, 5.8 percent in 1964, were above 7 percent in late 1968—"the highest since the Administration of Ulysses S. Grant," candidate Richard Nixon told the Republican platform committee.

In campaign speeches Nixon scoffed at the claims of Humphrey, Meany, and other Democratic orators that the Great Society had brought prosperity to Americans. "That's not prosperity—that's treadmill economics," he declared. Yet Nixon the candidate was vague in stating exactly what he intended to do about inflation, other than an "intelligent balancing of the economy over the business cycle." He was repeatedly specific about what he would not do: impose wage and price controls. And Nixon stridently attacked Hubert Humphrey for indicating he might do so if elected President. A Humphrey campaign task force reported that unless voluntary restraint was exercised by labor and management "a statutory approach will become unavoidable." Speaking over CBS radio on October 21, 1968, Nixon quoted the report and declared:

"In plain language that means the government will say 'Take what we give you—or else.' And Hubert Humphrey accepted that report and made it his own policy. If wage controls go in, the bargaining table will become a bureaucrat's desk—and there'll be no bargaining at all. It can happen, unless you do something about it this November."

In another CBS broadcast, this one in October 23, Nixon was more specific in his pledge about controls: "I do not believe the American people should be forced to choose between unemployment and un-American controls. There is a further choice: the American way of responsible fiscal policy. . . . If I am elected, I pledge that I will adopt this approach redressing the present imbalances without increasing unemployment or controls."

Candidate Nixon felt the "way to stop the inflation is to reverse the irresponsible fiscal policies which produce it."

Nixon's deep antipathy to controls dated to his brief, dreary tenure as a bottom-rung, $61-a-week lawyer ("a very low form of life") with the Office of Price Administration during the early months of World War II, before he entered the Navy. This fleeting exposure put the foundation of practical experience under what became a matter of dogmatic, ideological faith for Nixon: the government should not meddle in the private economic decisions of citizens, be they businessmen or workers. Indeed, he scorned even the voluntary guideposts and "jawboning" of Presidents Kennedy and Johnson. Business wanted to be left alone at a time of grandly richer profits, and candidate Nixon had told the corporations he did not intend to hector them about prices. At his first news conference after becoming President, Nixon was just as unequivocal:

"I do not go along with the suggestion that inflation can be effectively controlled by exhorting labor, management, and industry to follow certain guidelines. . . . [T]he leaders of labor and . . . management, much as they might personally want to do what is in the best interests of the nation, have to be guided by the interests of the organization they represent.

"So the primary responsibility for controlling inflation rests with the national administration and its handling of fiscal and monetary affairs."

Nixon's statement, in effect, told business and labor to do what they wished with prices and wages—that the government, by straightening its own finances, would solve the money problems of the rest of the nation. Speaking to a union convention later, Meany summarized a complex economic stratagem into language understandable to his blue-collar audience: "His policy for bringing down the inflation was quite simple: they were going to reduce the supply of money, cut the budget, and restrict business activity, and they were going to do it without causing more unemployment. That was the self-styled Game Plan*—the economic game plan—and it was the brainchild of a fellow by the name of Dr. Arthur Burns, one of these semiskilled intellectuals who play with other peoples' lives."

The classic formula for flattening a price spiral is simple, brutal, and effective: have a recession that will throw people out of work, cut the demand for goods and services, and increase the competition for sales and jobs. Whatever the economic morality of such a course, it works. But Nixon (as had Johnson) proclaimed that such medicine would be worse than the disease, and took the unprecedented route of attempting to slow down the economy's rate of growth just enough to discourage price and wage increases, but without causing any major hardship. Meany heard an outline of the Game Plan from Nixon, Arthur Burns, and Paul W. McCracken in January, and the President followed the briefing with a letter to the executive council.

> We must find ways to curb inflation, which robs working men and women and their families of hard-earned gains. And we must do this without asking the wage earners to pay for the cost of stability with their jobs.

Nixon failed. Nixon's Game Plan, within the space of a year, produced the economic phenomenon of simultaneous inflation and a complete halt in the growth of the economy. Interest rates soared to their highest mark in a century. The stock market panicked. The consumer price index marched steadily upward, from 4.2 percent in 1968 to 5.4 percent in 1969 and 7 percent in 1970. When Nixon took office, the unemployment rate was 3.4 percent, the lowest in fifteen years. By mid-1971 it had soared to 6.2 percent, with well over five million persons out of work, 1.3 million of them for fifteen weeks or more, half a million for twenty-seven weeks or more. The Nixon Administration blamed much of the unemployment on the cutbacks in the military, accompanying slow withdrawal from Vietnam.

A familiar pattern developed in statements from the Administration and from the AFL-CIO:

For two and one-half years Nixon made "light at the end of the tunnel" predictions about the expected imminent success of the Game Plan.

* So named because of the President's famed zest for football.

Nixon and his two economic braintrusters, Dr. Arthur Burns (first, White House counsel; next, chairman of the Federal Reserve Board) and Dr. Paul McCracken (chairman of the Council of Economic Advisers), steadfastly refused any broad wage and price controls. In mid-1970 Congress voted the President stand-by authority to invoke controls. On February 1, 1971, in his Economic Report to Congress, Nixon said, "I do not intend to impose wage and price controls . . . Neither do I intend to rely upon an elaborate façade that seems to be wage and price control but is not." On February 23, John Connally, the former Texas governor brought into the cabinet as Secretary of the Treasury, told the House Banking and Currency Committee: "We do not contemplate any circumstances—short of an all-out national emergency—in which the President would establish general wage-price controls without a further specific mandate from Congress."

The AFL-CIO repeatedly asserted its willingness to abide with any control system that applied equitably to all parts of the economy. It also pressed the Administration, unsuccessfully, to pour federal money into construction and public service projects to absorb some of the jobless.

When the Administration did move in the direction of controls it did so on a highly selective basis, in each instance aiming at wages rather than profits or prices. When the 1970 election returns ended his flirtation with the hard-hats, Nixon turned upon construction workers and said their "skyrocketing" wages were causing inflation in the housing market. He suspended the Davis-Bacon Act, which required that prevailing local wages (i.e., union rates) be paid workers on federal construction jobs, and asked state governments to do the same. (A majority of states with such laws refused to do so.) The President's action had surface plausibility, for he acted in the midst of well-publicized negotiations that were to increase construction wages by 11.9 percent. But as Meany quickly pointed out, the Davis-Bacon suspension was "decidedly one-sided," for it ignored four other components of housing costs—materials, land, financing, and profits. A study by the National Association of Home Builders—figures Meany recited from memory—showed that from 1949 to 1969, on-site labor costs fell from 33 percent of the price of a home to 18 percent. The builder's profit dropped from 15 to 13 percent; the cost of materials increased slightly, from 36 to 38 percent. The cost of land, however, nearly doubled, from 11 percent of the price to 21 percent. Financing charges went from 5 to 10 percent of the cost. Meany noted further that Nixon's tight-money policy pushed interest rates on new FHA-insured home mortgages from 7.13 percent in 1968 to 9.29 percent in March 1970 (the month after the Davis-Bacon suspension), a rise of about 30 percent. "And yet Dr. Arthur Burns looks down from his ivory tower and blames the housing mess on the workers," Meany commented tartly. Each one percent rise in the interest rate increased the homeowner's monthly payment by about ten percent. Realizing within a few weeks that Davis-Bacon suspension was accomplishing nothing, Nixon quietly reinstated the law and set up an independent commission to try to make sense of construction wages.

Another stratagem also proved short-lived. In June 1970 Nixon attempted a mild touch of jawbone restraint. He appointed a National Commission on Productivity—five Administration officials, plus eighteen members from labor, business, and the public—to issue "inflation alerts" on sharp price or wage movements. The President made Meany a labor member. Meany lasted one meeting. "The thing is open and shut. We sit down and we are told by the President that we are to release this first 'inflation alert.' We have never seen a draft of it. In comes McCracken and opens the thing up and, in effect, delivers it to us . . . and goes through a ten-minute or fifteen-minute résumé of what is in this document, which measures 188 pages. I thumbed through it very quickly and I found what I was looking for and what I was suspicious of—that this was a device of McCracken and others to put pressure on certain areas of the economy—either on the workers' side or on the employers' side. I looked and I immediately saw what I expected would be in there . . . a paragraph about construction workers.

"It was a very, very short paragraph . . . of about two or three sentences and it said the price of structures has gone up considerably in the last few years because, one, wages have gone up tremendously and, two, the construction industry doesn't seem to have any real plan for increasing production.

"And that was it. And, of course, I [challenged] McCracken on that because if he was going to come up with the answer to why the price of construction had increased, he would certainly have to look beyond wages."

After listening to McCracken, the Productivity Commission refused to issue the inflation alert in its own name. The commission's attitude, Meany said, was "Do what you want with it, but don't saddle us with it because we had nothing to do with it."

By midsummer 1971 economic conditions reached a crisis point, both domestically and in foreign trade. In the second quarter of the year, the United States ran a balance-of-payments deficit of a record $5.8 billion. Because of speculation against the dollar, U.S. gold reserves slumped to one-fourth the value of dollars held abroad. At home, unemployment and the cost of living continued to soar.

On August 9 the executive council, meeting in San Francisco, issued a resolution saying the country was in an "economic mess" because of "gross mismanagement" by the Nixon Administration. Secretary of

Labor James Hodgson, visiting with the council the next day, tried to allay labor's concern. According to Meany, "he said that they looked at the figures a little differently than we did, and that despite what we said, they felt that things were looking better." At no time did Hodgson mention controls. Nonetheless Meany was suspicious because of subtle ambiguities he had detected in statements by Ronald Ziegler, the White House press secretary, and other Administration figures. While in Denver in early August for the plumbers union convention, he taped a Labor Day television interview with the president of the Colorado AFL-CIO, Herrick Roth. Meany warned Roth "that stuff I said about controls" might have to be changed before September. And during the San Francisco council meeting, Meany remarked to Archie Robinson, the labor writer for U.S. News & World Report, that he felt controls were imminent. "Are you guys that sure?" Robinson asked. "Could he switch 180 degrees?" "Anyone who can switch from anticommunism to a visit to Peking can do anything," Meany replied.

On Saturday, August 14, the White House announced that Nixon was meeting with his economic advisers at Camp David. Early Sunday evening Hodgson began looking for Meany by telephone, and finally located him at the home of his son-in-law Ernest Lee (who works with Jay Lovestone in the AFL-CIO international affairs department). Hodgson asked Lee to inform Meany the President would be speaking to the nation on radio and TV later that night and suggested that he listen; Hodgson said nothing of the content of the speech. Meany wasn't impressed: "Anybody who's been listening to the radio today knows that Nixon is going to talk tonight; so what else is new?"

Considerable. "The time has come," the President said, "for a new economic policy* for the United States. Its targets are unemployment, inflation, and international speculation." He ordered a ninety-day freeze on all prices and wages—"action that will break the vicious circle of spiraling prices and costs." He created a Cost of Living Council, within the government, and directed it to meet with business and labor leaders "to set up the proper mechanism for achieving continued price and wage stability after the ninety-day freeze is over." He postponed pay increases due government workers and ordered a five-percent cut in the federal job force. He proposed repeal of the seven percent excise tax on autos, enactment of a ten percent investment tax credit for business (a "job development credit"). On foreign matters, he suspended the U.S. guarantee to redeem gold at $35 an ounce (to halt speculation in the dollar) and imposed a ten-percent surtax on most imports (an attempt to help the balance-of-payments problem).

* Also called the New Economic Plan in subsequent Administration statements, the more common usage.

Press reports the next week depicted Meany as springing from his chair in anger after the President finished and ordering a counteroffensive. Such was not the case. "I'd had a very pleasant dinner, with a couple of glasses of wine, and played with my grandchildren. Then I got into a very comfortable chair and watched the President. Ernie and I talked about it a few minutes when it ended, then I dozed off."

The next morning, however, Meany got down to business. He was mad for several reasons. The freeze was not even-handed; it did not curb prices, profits, interest rates, and other incomes. The freeze would deny workers pay and cost-of-living increases they had gained through collective bargaining. "Never in the history of this country, in peace or in war, has any other American President ever abrogated to himself the power to cancel contracts," Meany thundered. "And then, in addition, he ruled that while you lose this money during the ninety-day period, you cannot negotiate for it after the freeze." As he told a union convention ten days after the freeze, "It actually adds up to this: because of a presidential edict, the employer who sat at the bargaining table and reached a contract with you, now gets the money that you should get in your pay envelope as a result of deferred wage increases. . . . [I]t means that hundreds of thousands of workers throughout the country are being robbed of millions of dollars with this money turned over to their employer. This, by an edict, by an act of the President of the United States." The New Economic Plan contained tax breaks for business totaling around $4 billion a year—this atop $3 billion given corporations earlier in the year in an Administration decision permitting accelerated depreciation for tax purposes. Nixon provided no enforcement of price freezes—though as Meany said, "Every boss in the country will be happy to help freeze wages." Finally, Meany felt Nixon should have consulted business and labor before imposing any control system through the Cost of Living Council, as President Roosevelt had done in forming the National War Labor Board.

Meany spent the morning of August 16 preparing a statement with Lane Kirkland, the AFL-CIO secretary-treasurer; James Gildea, his personal assistant, and Al Zack, his press man. "I've never seen George so worked up," said Zack, who has worked for him since 1955. At midday Meany issued a statement calling the New Economic Plan "patently discriminatory" against workers, reiterating the AFL-CIO's willingness to cooperate with any program that placed equal restraints on all costs and incomes, and summoning the executive council into session later in the week to hear Administration officials explain the plan.

The White House felt Meany had spoken too quickly, that his opposition was reflexive and represented his own animosity toward Nixon, not the sentiment of organized labor. The White House's routine postspeech poll (conducted by phone by a private research firm) found overwhelming support for the freeze. So the Administration counterattacked, hoping to isolate Meany from labor rank and file. Secretary Connally insinuated Meany's opposition was political. "I used to think of M&M as . . . a chocolate-coated candy that doesn't get on your fingers. But I'm afraid M&M is about to take on a new meaning, the Muskie-Meany line." Meany, Connally said, "is not giving his workmen and his members credit for understanding their problems as well as they do." Hodgson chimed in that based on what he knew about rank-and-file sentiment, Meany was "sadly out of step with the needs and desires of America's working men and women." (Hodgson told reporters later the White House asked him to attack Meany for the purpose of "getting labor's attention.")

The executive council sat frigidly when Hodgson and George Shultz were ushered into the privacy of its conference room on the eighth floor of the AFL-CIO Building on August 19. Meany nodded curtly and told them to be seated. He ignored Hodgson ("a real minor leaguer," he had called the Secretary in private conversation that morning) and looked directly at Shultz. "I think a good place to start, George, would be to tell us why you gave up this wonderful plan that you first had and have been working on for the last two and one-half years. What happened?"

Shultz ignored his question and plunged directly into an explanation of Nixon's sudden action. Had Nixon permitted several months of debate, Shultz said, "you all know what would happen. Everything would escalate." Imposing controls during the Korean War took four months, he noted, "and during that four months everything went through the roof." He said there was a "need for something decisive and sort of instantaneous," especially because of international strains on the dollar. "That is why the President hit it the way he hit it."

Shultz claimed Nixon "deliberately kept his options wide open" on postfreeze programs "because he feels that it is vitally important to have discussion and to have available the ideas and the thoughts of leaders of labor, of industry, of agriculture, across-the-board on that. . . . We do want to sit down with you. The spirit is there . . . even if the flesh is weak."

Meany asked, "How in God's name can there be any confidence in the people, yourself included, to come up with a new 'game plan' when you gave us a game plan in February 1969 that has added two and a half million people to the unemployed rolls?" Meany would not accept Shultz's claim that immediate action was necessary. "I disagree completely," he said. "If you wanted the advice of somebody other than Arthur Burns and Paul McCracken and Mr. Connally, why could you not have put on a wage-and-price freeze and then called labor and other people into consultation while the . . . freeze was on, without doing these other . . . things that are completely unfair to the American worker?" He mentioned the tax and other boons for business. "Why couldn't we have had a chance to talk about that while the freeze was on? Why couldn't we have had a chance to talk about over a million federal employees who have their wage raises taken away from them? Where is the equity there? . . . In view of the record of complete and absolute failure [of the first game plan] which brought misery to millions of American families . . . you owed it to representatives of the people who were affected to at least talk to you before you did these other things." Meany's voice took on the rasp of exasperation. "George," he asked, "how in the name of common sense could we have confidence in the President after what he has done to us the last two and one-half years?"

Shultz replied, "Well, you will have your opportunity in about another year, and I assume from the way you speak you will—"

Meany interrupted. "Oh, this has nothing to do with it, George. This man is the President of the United States, and I respect that office very, very highly."

Shultz tried to defend other points of the New Economic Plan. Removing the auto excise tax would be a boon to Detroit, he said, because auto companies would not be able to sell at 1972 prices.

"You drive me to tears on the automobile industry," Meany said. "Poor old automobile industry."

Shultz tried cajolery. "The only time you would cry is when you would miss a three-foot putt, and I've never seen you miss one, so I know you've never cried." Shultz refused to answer questions on payments of retroactive wages once the freeze ended, and on the validity of existing contracts. "As everybody in town knows, the government leaks like a sieve." Until the government decided, he said, nothing would be said.

The discussion dragged on for an hour. As Schultz and Hodgson gathered their papers, Paul Hall, the old seaman, glared at them. "When you take your ass out of here," he told Shultz, "get measured for a pair of tin pants because you are going to need them."

"I would like to say that I admire the color with which you put these things," Shultz said.

A half hour later Meany went downstairs to a conference room packed with more than 100 reporters and broadcast technicians and read a lengthy council statement castigating the New Economic Plan. The statement contained two separate threats, either of which could do fatal damage to the plan:

Meany declared that the AFL-CIO had "absolutely no faith in the ability of President Nixon to successfully manage the economy of this nation," and asked Congress "to assert control over the economy," both by writing an equitable controls program and by rejecting Administration proposals "that would benefit only one sector of the economy at the expense of all others."

Meany rejected the Administration's contention it had the authority to bar strikes during the freeze period, and dropped a broad insinuation that unions could resort to that method if neessary to protect their rights. "We have never recommended and do not now recommend defiance of lawful orders," Meany said. "We do suggest and recommend to our affiliates that where, as a result of the President's action, contractual provisions are impaired and members suffer losses, that those contracts have been nullified by the President of the United States. Such contracts should be subject to renegotiations at the first opportunity."

Did Meany have any response to Hodgson's statement he was "out of step" with workers? "I don't pay too much attention to the Secretary," Meany replied. "He was there this morning, and I didn't even bother discussing it with him because, in the final analysis, if you have a problem with the landlord, you don't discuss it with the janitor." * How about Secretary Connally's criticisms? "Secretary Connally was not in on the original game plan—he is not an economist—but he is in on this one. I think what he is looking for is the field of enforcement. I think he wants the horsewhip concession so he can sell the horsewhips."

Meany also had harsh words about Dr. Arthur Burns. "I think a little word about this man is important," he said a few days later at a convention of the United Transportation Union. "He is an intellectual, supposed to be an economist. He pontificates at all gatherings. He looks down on people. He made no apology for the failure of his plan, no explanation as to why it failed. . . . [I]nstead of being chastised by the President for his failure, he was promoted and . . . made chairman of the Federal Reserve Board where he can, undoubtedly, do a great deal more mischief. If he was a Russian commissar with the sins of failure, he would have gone to Siberia." Meany congratulated the rail workers on winning a contract agreement just before the freeze, but added, "I don't know how much is going to be left of it when Tricky Dick gets through with it."

* The line was not spontaneous. Before the press conference Meany asked Al Zack: "Will anybody ask me about Hodgson? I have a good answer for a question about him."

# XVIII

## Nixon Two:
## The Battle of Bal Harbour

*Once again George Meany the business agent, bargaining as* de facto *spokesman for 20 million union members and their families; employing, on an unprecedently grand and audacious scale, the tactics he had learned in Local 463 of the Plumbers Union in the 1920's—heaping insulting jest and crude invective upon The Boss and his underlings, threatening at once the improbable and the possible and the certain, so intertwining intention and bluff that not even his followers, let alone his adversaries, could divine the next move. Meany transformed the media of the nation into a picket line which he posted around the Nixon Administration; in one week, in early September, his scowl and cigar glared at the President from the covers of* Time, Newsweek, *and* Business Week; *everywhere the President turned— "Meet the Press," "Issues and Answers," "Today," "The David Frost Show"—he faced electronic placards, with the Bronx voice growling "unfair to the workers."*

*One monologue shows Meany's penchant for insulting, debunking oratory.*

> *What happened after August 15 with the PR boys? They got real busy. They had polls taken, and, you know, you can arrange the polls. One of these pollsters came in to me some years ago, when we worried about something, and he said to me, "What is it that you want to prove?"*
>
> *So I said, "Well, if that's the way you do business, I don't want to prove anything."*
>
> *So they [the Administration] got real busy, and they announced overwhelming approval of the President's program, which the Presi-*

*dent named "The New Prosperity." There's one for you. The New Prosperity. Everything is new—new Fab, new Bon-Ami, now this. . . . Well, I don't know what is new about prosperity. I know 5½ million people who would like to have a little bit of prosperity, new, old, or any kind, by getting a job.*

*And what do the polls show? The polls show seventy-two percent of the people favored the President's program and we were told that the trade union members didn't agree with Mr. Meany, didn't agree with their leaders. They liked the President's game plan, too.*

*Well, when the people of this country heard that prices were going to be frozen, everybody said, "Well, it's about time this fellow [Nixon] got off his butt and did something about this situation."*

*So we checked out this one poll . . . [and] then when we got to the question—and what do you think the question was—and I am going to repeat it word for word: "Do you favor the Nixon program to provide more jobs and bring down prices?"*

*I can't understand why they only got seventy-two percent in favor of that. They should have gotten 99½ percent in favor on that one. In fact, I think the only people that really opposed that question are people who really just can't take Nixon in any shape, manner, or form.*

*Now, if the pollsters had asked, "Do you favor Mr. Nixon's plan to give big business $3 billion on top of the $3.7 billion you have already given them this year? Do you favor Mr. Nixon's action to take $1.3 billion out of the pockets of the federal employees, taking away increases already granted to them? Do you favor Mr. Nixon's action nullifying collective bargaining contracts, taking away hundreds of millions of dollars from members of unions?" I think if those questions had been asked, maybe the pollsters would have gotten a different answer.*

Good, roaring anti-Republican oratory, and with the enhancing grace of Irish wit; the jibes wearing potholes into Nixon's Madison Avenue economics; Meany simply reaching out and grabbing the mantle of opposition; and the Hydra-factioned Democratic party standing aside and staring, slack-jawed, at the new militant. Even long-time Meany critic A. H. Raskin conceded he "had suddenly become not only a tiger but a dynamo." Joseph Loftus, trying to devise an Administration counterstrategy from the Labor Department, was stunned by Meany's bustle. "He did better public relations for his people than ever before," Loftus said. "He got off his butt and made himself available for talk shows and private interviews and press conferences, he was all over town, and he was gaining ground. If his people were not in step with him, he was *damned well going to get them in step."*

*Meany spent six weeks, from mid-August through the end of Septem-
ber, softening Nixon. Finally George Meany, business agent, stuffed a
handful of fresh cigars into his coat pocket and rode around Lafayette
Park to the White House for a collective bargaining session with the
President of the United States.*

A S PROMISED, Nixon asked a labor delegation to the White
House to solicit ideas on how postfreeze controls should be
administered. With Meany went Leonard Woodcock, successor to Walter Reuther as president of the United Auto Workers, who had already
declared public unity with the AFL-CIO on the freeze; and Frank Fitzsimmons, president of the Teamsters, who was fast backing away from
an early declaration of support of the President. Sitting amidst a half
dozen of his chief economic advisers, Nixon began with what Meany
described later as "soothing words about wanting to tell labor of his long-
range plans." Meany raised his hand, palm outward, and stopped the
President. "If you are going down the route of government control,"
Meany said, "we'll fight you. We won't be a part of a sham window
dressing for government control." "We're one hundred percent with the
AFL-CIO," said Woodcock. "So are we," said Fitzsimmons of the
Teamsters.

"We told them we would suggest the establishment of an independent
voluntary agency free from government control, of a tripartite nature,
similar to the War Labor Board of World War II," Meany said. "We
urged him to study the history of the War Labor Board, the tripartite
setup, and the similar setup that was in existence for a short time during
the Korean conflict." Meany felt a voluntary approach would be best. He
considered a statutory wage-price control board, with decisions enforceable in the courts, as "the first step towards fascism, to me. My experience indicates that if government embarks on that road there will be no
turning back. . . . I don't think management wants that, and I don't
think labor wants that."

Several persons at the meeting said Nixon was apparently taken aback
by the strength of Meany's opposition to a statutory board. At one point
Herbert Stein, a member of the Council of Economic Advisers, produced
a sheaf of background papers which he said he "wanted" the labor men
to study. He put them on the table before Meany. Meany looked at them

and didn't move. "John," Nixon said to his treasury Secretary, "you haven't said anything yet."

Connally replied, "A wise old man in Texas once told me you never learned anything when you were talking. I have heard very little here today with which I would disagree." (Meany paid no mind to Connally's tone. "A snake oil salesman," he described him when he returned to his office.)

The Administration, meanwhile, put the temporary freeze under the Cost of Living Council, headed by Arnold Weber, a forty-two-year-old economist who had been a Shultz protégé at the University of Chicago. The President gave the CLC two roles: to draw up broad guidelines interpreting the freeze, which it issued through question-and-answer broadsides; and to assemble what the President called Phase Two machinery to run the freeze after the initial ninety-day period expired on November 13. Weber offended labor early on. "He said we couldn't get our money that was due to us under our contracts during the freeze," Meany said. "He said we could not negotiate for it after the freeze. Just think of that. He was not only going to control it during the freeze; he was going to tell us what we could do after the freeze." Weber's demeanor irritated many of the labor people. The son of a blue-collar family, he seemed anxious to "live down his working-class background, and show Connally and the rest of the wheels he could be as antiunion as them," in the words of a Meany staff member. The council, in its rulings, added heaping measures of confusion to the freeze. Hundreds of thousands of teachers had been due raises when schools opened in September, only to be caught by the freeze. But what if contracts had been signed before August 15, even though the teachers weren't working? "He [Weber] made seven or eight rulings on the teachers, and we kept a little box score on him," Meany said. "It was no, no, maybe, yes, no, yes, no. And I don't think he knows yet what those rulings were."

"And so then came the birth of Phase Two. Obstetricians, I think, would refer to it as a breech presentation. Surely it was a case of confusion compounded. October fifth came a bearer of good news, Brother Hodgson. The President had agreed to our plan for an independent voluntary agency. They wanted five, five, and five: five industry, five labor, and five public. They specified that two of the five labor, one would be Teamster, and one Auto. I said, 'Fine, that's okay with me.' I said, 'Jim, will you put this in the form of a memo? Because I would like to get these fellows together and let them see what this is. I think it is all right.' So he said yes, he would do that."

As the other AFL-CIO members of the new Pay Board Meany selected I. W. Abel of the United Steel Workers and Floyd (Red) Smith, of the International Association of Machinists, the two largest affiliated unions. Meany arranged for a breakfast on October 7 in the Hay Adams Hotel, several hours before Nixon was to announce the Phase Two format in a national telecast. Meany brought along Fitzsimmons, Woodcock, Smith, Abel, Lane Kirkland, and John H. Lyons of the International Association of Bridge, Structural and Ornamental Iron Workers, *de facto* spokesman for the AFL-CIO building trades unions.

Labor expected a detailed briefing, but Hodgson had only a single sheet of paper containing a bare description of the Pay Board. Hodgson said flatly the board would be "autonomous," with "liaison and review" with the Cost of Living Council, which would continue in existence. "There were a few words there that bothered us," Meany said. For instance, did the Pay Board have to submit its findings to the Cost of Living Council? He quoted Hodgson as replying, "No, no, no." " 'Well, how about that word review?' " 'No, it doesn't mean anything.' 'Well, can they veto the standards?' 'Oh, no.'

"Mr. Hodgson led us to believe that the standards were to be set by the Pay Board," Meany said. "They were not to be subject to review by the Cost of Living Council. He was very convincing." After a brief discussion Meany said, "Okay, we'll buy it." The other labor people nodded assent.

Hodgson then escorted Meany and his colleagues to the White House for another briefing, this one by George Shultz, on how the Cost of Living Council and the Price Commission would function. Shultz "gave us no cause for believing that Mr. Hodgson was wrong," Meany said. "When we left the White House we had to say amen, we are going along. We are going to try to help make this work. In fact, I told Mr. Shultz that, as this thing is laid out, I think there's no question we can go along. We went back to my office, had a very short meeting, and prepared a press release, which we would give to the press that evening after the President spoke." Al Zack and Nathaniel Goldfinger, director of research for the AFL-CIO, wrote the statement. But Meany cautioned them, "Don't put anything out until you hear from me, after the President speaks."

Nixon was midway through his speech that evening when Meany telephoned Zack. "Al," he said, "this doesn't smell right. I think a fast deal has been pulled on us." Nixon implied in his speech, without saying so directly, the Cost of Living Council would have supreme authority over both the Pay Board and the Price Commission. Meanwhile, the Associated Press and United Press International wires in the AFL-CIO press office moved stories based on background briefings by White House officials saying the Council would have veto power. So did postspeech analyses by the three television networks. Meany, angered, told Zack, "Tell everyone no comment. Something has gone wrong."

Instead of an expected labor endorsement the next morning, the Nixon Administration saw only, "No comment." Meany telephoned Shultz. "We tried desperately to get him to say do or do they not have a veto power. We thought we were talking to the head man, but we found out we weren't. He had evidently been demoted." Shultz suggested that Meany watch a televised news conference later that day (October 8) at which Connally would give more details. "So we watched the press conference and three times Mr. Connally was asked point blank to clear up the question about the Cost of Living Council's veto power over standards set by the Pay Board. But Mr. Connally did not clarify and did not answer the question."

Meany said he then told Shultz he would not serve on a Pay Board that gave the "façade" of independence. "We were not . . . going to be honorary pallbearers at our own funeral."

In his conversations with Meany, on October 8, Shultz claimed the misunderstanding was semantical. This explanation Meany would not accept. He and his staff concluded that one of three things happened (probably the latter):

—The White House, at the time of the Hodgson breakfast with labor, did not know what powers it intended the Cost of Living Council to exercise. (But Meany felt it unlikely that planning had progressed this far without the Administration's making such a basic decision. Shultz's White House briefings for the press came only a few hours later.)

—The White House, through Hodgson, deliberately lied, hoping to trap labor into an advance endorsement which it would be unable to abandon after Nixon's speech.

—Connally changed the order in late afternoon, just before the President's telecast, overruling Shultz and Hodgson.

Thoroughly angry at what he considered a "double cross" by the Administration, Meany issued a public call for a special meeting of the AFL-CIO executive council on Tuesday, October 12. He did not say labor intended to boycott the Pay Board—a threat the press readily made on his behalf in speculative stories. The Teamsters' Fitzsimmons was more direct in his anger. He telephoned Hodgson, called the labor Secretary a "goddamned prick," and charged flatly, "you lied to us." The hapless Hodgson continued to insist there was in fact no veto power, that although the Cost of Living Council would "approve or disapprove" of over-all pay standards set by the Pay Board, it would not question decisions in specific cases.

Shultz called Meany several times over the weekend, trying to make peace. Meany told him, in effect, "We've heard too many words, we cannot believe anything you people tell us." On the Monday evening before the executive council meeting, Shultz phoned Meany and asked if he and Hodgson could visit the next morning, before the session. Come ahead, Meany said.

Hodgson and Shultz brought with them an extraordinary document— one that tacitly acknowledged that the White House's spoken word was no longer acceptable to the AFL-CIO. The memo, bearing Richard M. Nixon's scrawled "OK RMN  10/11/71" at the bottom, outlined the "respective roles" of the Cost of Living Council, the Pay Board, and the Price Commission. It was a total surrender. Although the COLC would "serve as a policy review group for the postfreeze program," it would not "approve, disapprove, or serve as an appeal level for case decisions" by either the Pay Board or the Price Commission. Nor would it "approve, revise, veto, or revoke specific standards or criteria" of either the board or the commission. The board was given authority to establish "standards, criteria, and procedures" and to render "final decisions on individual cases."

Meany put the memo before the executive council, augmented by Woodcock and Fitzsimmons to display labor unity. The council agreed labor would serve on the Pay Board, "in light of the personal assurances we have received this morning from the President of the United States." Meany's statement was considerably less friendly than the original endorsement prepared (but never released) the preceding week. The original said the AFL-CIO would "cooperate with and support" the President in Phase Two. The second said it "will help try to make" Phase Two work. It also said the AFL-CIO "will establish our own watchdog units to monitor prices"—a roundabout way of saying the Administration could not be trusted to do so—and "continue to oppose the President's tax measures in the Congress." Neither point was in the original statement.

"Well," Meany said later, "I received a phone call of appreciation from the President that afternoon. Boy, I should have known better, that should have really made me suspicious."

On Saturday, October 16, Meany was dining with his wife and other family members at the Sir Walter Raleigh Inn, a favored restaurant near his Bethesda home, when Hodgson called him through the White House switchboard. ("Very impressive," Meany jibed later in a speech, "this business of the cabinet people using the White House. Somebody comes up and says, 'Mr. Meany, the White House is calling.' You think you are going to get the President, and you wind up with Hodgson.") According to Meany, Hodgson "asked me if I knew a judge by the name of Boldt out in the state of Washington." Meany didn't. Hodgson continued, "Well, try to get some information on him. He is being considered for chairman of the Pay Board." Meany replied that because of the weekend, he doubted that he could find any information before late Monday or early Tuesday. "That's okay," Hodgson replied, "there's no big rush."

On Monday the AFL-CIO staff, through phone calls to Seattle, assembled a brief dossier on U.S. District Court Judge George E. Boldt, sixty-seven years old, an Eisenhower appointee, on the bench since 1953. Boldt's record was solid if not spectacular. He had tried the income tax evasion case that sent Dave Beck, the disgraced Teamster president, to prison. He had tried the criminal cases of gang figures Mickey Cohen and Frankie Carbo. But the AFL-CIO could find little if any experience in labor-management relations, other than some routine injunctions in maritime and longshoremen strike cases. The Washington State AFL-CIO called him a "routine sort of judge" who had done nothing to offend or please labor. Even while the AFL-CIO did its research, however, Boldt was encountering problems elsewhere.

The Labor Department's Joseph Loftus, who worked with Hodgson in screening Boldt, said the appointment was the brainchild of John D. Ehrlichman, counsel to the President. "Boldt was urged to come here by Ehrlichman," Loftus said. "Their families are friends in Seattle, and Ehrlichman thought highly of him and recommended him for the job. Hodgson brought him in for a talk; after a very few minutes Hodgson knew he had no labor-management background, and that he would not do. Putting someone with no experience in such a position is a very risky business, despite his amiability.

"Hodgson sent him on to Weber and a few other people in the Administration, and they all concurred in his reaction—that a man without the proper background was not the man to be chairman of the board.

"Hodgson said—figuratively or literally, I don't know which he meant —'Put Judge Boldt on a plane back to Seattle.' "

On Tuesday morning Hodgson called Meany. By Meany's account (the essence of which Loftus substantiated), the conversation went as follows:

"He [Hodgson] said, 'You know that fellow Boldt?' I said, 'Yes.' He said, 'Forget him.' Then he said a rather odd thing. He said, 'He will be long gone in a short time. . . . he is totally and completely unfit for this job. He has absolutely no experience in this field and he just couldn't handle it at all. He knows nothing about it.'

"I thought, 'Well, that is the end of Boldt.' "

On Wednesday noon "a young man named Butler" in the office of White House press secretary Ronald Ziegler called Meany and told him to "report to the White House" at 10:30 A.M. Friday for the first Pay Board meeting. "It was the most arrogant telephone call I have ever received from a public official, especially a bush leaguer," Meany said. "I called Hodgson and asked, first, who the hell was Butler; and second, who the hell he thought he was, talking to people like he did." Hodgson told Meany to ignore the message; that he would call personally when something was definite about the Pay Board.

According to Loftus, "The problem was, time was running out, and the White House could not find another chairman." An economist at the University of Chicago refused the assignment. "After a while we were desperately shopping around." Other persons who declined included David Cole, a New Jersey attorney with long mediation experience, including jurisdictional disputes between AFL-CIO affiliates; Dr. Howard Johnson, the former president of the Massachusetts Institute of Technology; and Dean Sayres, of the University of Colorado.

Thursday evening Meany was Hodgson's guest at Blair House for a private party honoring a foreign visitor. Hodgson drew him aside and said, "By the way, George, the Pay Board meeting is for tomorrow morning at ten-thirty."

Surprised, Meany said, "But I thought you didn't have a chairman yet. That's what you told Kirkland just a few hours ago."

"Oh, sure we do," replied Hodgson, "we're going with Boldt."

The answer staggered Meany. "What the hell are you talking about? You told me this week that he was no good, that he was unqualified. He is going to be chairman after your description?"

Hodgson said, "Well, there are some people around there that don't agree with my estimate of his abilities, and besides, we couldn't get anybody else."

Hodgson then pulled a typed list of names from his pocket and told Meany they were the other members. The last in the column for public members was "A. Weber."

"What's that?" Meany asked.

"Oh, that's Arnie," Hodgson said.

"You mean Arnold Weber?" said Meany. "Hell, he's not public, he works for the government, he runs the Cost of Living Council."

Hodgson laughed heartily. "Yeah, that was today," he told Meany. "Tomorrow, he will be a public man. He is resigning from government to take this job." (Weber had been an Assistant Secretary of Labor before becoming director of the Cost of Living Council; his government service began in January 1969.)

When Meany got to his office the next morning, he declared, "That's a stacked deck, to hell with them." He did not attend the inaugural meeting of the Pay Board (which by labor's count had been scheduled and rescheduled no fewer than five times). Shultz, fearing the tenuous accord was about to explode again, called to attempt to mollify Meany. Meany responded he had wanted "hopefully knowledgeable neutrals" as the public members. He recalled the public members of the War Labor Board. The chairman, William Davis, had business connections through his practice as a patent attorney; nonetheless, Meany said, he was fair-minded. So, too, had been Wayne Morse and Frank Graham. In an acrimonious speech a month later at the AFL-CIO convention in Bal Harbour, Florida, Meany scathingly went through the list of "public" members of the Pay Board, beginning with Judge Boldt, the chairman:

. . . The Judge is on the federal payroll, and he certainly is neutral in the sense that he doesn't know a damn thing about labor and management. But he has someone right at his elbow who takes care of him and answers all the questions.

We were there for ten days with this guy [Boldt] and he answered no questions. Every time we asked him a question, in comes Mr. Weber. . . . He is the fellow that wrote the nice things that the Cost of Living Council got out. He is the hatchet man. He is the fellow that has been doing all the dirty work. He is on as a public member of the Pay Board.

Then we move to a gentleman, quite a nice man, by the name of [William] Caples. His whole life has been spent in industry—executive vice-president, Inland Steel Company; entire career spent on management's side of labor-management relations; a former vice-president of the National Association of Manufacturers. The last two years, however, he is the president of Kenyon College. He has retired from his business life.

This would be like taking one of our oldtimers who spent his whole life on the labor side and give him a title of emeritus and say now he is neutral, he can be a public member now. . . .

Then we have Mr. Kermit Gordon, who is from the Brookings Institution and the one-time Director of the Budget.*

Then we have Dr. Neal Jacoby, a conservative economist from the Council of Economic Advisers under Arthur Burns in the Eisenhower Administration, and he helped us to fashion those two recessions that we had in those days. For the past twelve years and up to the present moment a director of the Occidental Petroleum Company. How is that for neutral?

On the twenty-seventh of October, according to the Los Angeles *Times,* Dr. Jacoby said there was no need to control profits, that profits were not income to begin with, and there would be no need to control prices. Just keep wages down and that will take care of profits and prices.

So there are the public members of your Pay Board.

---

* Meany said nothing further of Gordon in the convention speech. In a private conversation a few days earlier, he called him "a flunky in the Kennedy-Johnson Administration" and noted he was the author of the wage-price guideline plan of the early 1960's.

Meany sulked for a week before attending his first Pay Board meeting, then plunged immediately into the fight over whether workers should receive retroactive pay for contract raises denied them during the freeze. Because of the "stacked deck" composition of the board he did not expect any success there. Thus the AFL-CIO opened a second front. At Meany's direction, Andrew Biemiller began a furious lobbying campaign in Congress to put payment of retroactive wages into the New Economic Plan legislation submitted by the Administration.

In the Pay Board, Meany wanted retroactive wages paid unless they were "unreasonably inconsistent" with wage stabilization. As he expected, however, the board voted labor down, ten to five. It approved a general policy statement saying that retroactive wages would be approved only if prices had been raised in anticipation of wage increases scheduled to occur during the freeze. For new contracts, the board laid down a general 5.5 percent limit on future pay increases (labor proposed six percent, employers five percent).

The next issue became the writing of specific regulations on retroactive pay—what Meany was to call "four days of complete frustration" in which public members "insulted and humiliated" the labor representatives, with Administration approval. In Meany's opinion the public members and at least two of the employer members deliberately tried to goad labor into walking off the board. As Andrew Biemiller explained, "Regardless of what happened, Nixon had labor in a bind. If labor stayed on the board and the economy straightened out, Nixon's plan got the credit. If the economic mess continued, labor's obstructionism was to blame. If we got mad and walked off the board—well, hell, we were un-American saboteurs." A steady flow of "private advisories"—some relayed by George Shultz—told Meany that labor "was going to win" on existing contracts. All the Administration wanted, the emissaries said, was to create the public impression that the wage hold-down was working. Unions would be given specific road maps around the Pay Board. "You'll be taken care of," was the message, repeated time and again.

Labor hoped to liberalize the retroactivity policy in the regulations. The bargaining was unproductive through mid-afternoon of November 5, a Friday, when labor suddenly found two unexpected allies among the employer members. Benjamin F. Biaggini, president of the Southern Pacific Company, and Rocco C. Siciliano, president of a Los Angeles title insurance company,* called Meany and asked for a meeting. Meany refused. He did not think private sessions proper. But his curiosity was whetted enough to suggest they talk with Lane Kirkland. Biaggini and Siciliano

---

* Siciliano had known Meany since 1953–57, when he served the Eisenhower Administration as Assistant Secretary of Labor; he was Undersecretary of Commerce during the Johnson Administration.

described themselves as "liberals" in the employer group ("true perhaps in the relative sense," said Biemiller) and said they wanted to try a compromise that would take the board off dead center. They offered language that would ensure equitable retroactivity to unions with "good cost of living and productivity arguments."

But Biaggini and Siciliano could not sell their compromise to the other employer members. In an early-morning caucus on Saturday labor found the employer position had changed again, away from retroactivity. When the formal board meeting began at 11:00 A.M., the labor representatives were the only ones present. "We were sitting in this room, all the labor members and the people working with us there," Meany said, "and the Old Judge [Meany's name for Boldt] stuck his nose in the door about a quarter after eleven and said, 'If you need me, I will be around.' Then he and the industry members went out to lunch and they didn't even tell us." The labor people ordered sandwiches and coffee from a drugstore. "We didn't see the judge again until four o'clock that afternoon. We just sat in this room. I think they were trying to goad us into walking out. When they [the employer and public members] finally got to the meeting at four that afternoon we requested a vote and we couldn't get it."

The board majority apparently felt it had Meany in a time bind, for he had been due to leave for Florida earlier in the week for meetings preliminary to the AFL-CIO convention. "We informed them that no matter how long they delayed [the vote] we were going to be there." Meany told them he was canceling part of his Florida schedule, "and I would stay until midnight on November 13 if that is what they wanted. I guess they understood they weren't going to force us to walk out." Boldt finally recessed the meeting until Monday evening to give the employer and public members time to continue working on a compromise.

Before the Monday evening meeting both labor and public members circulated new draft proposals. Meany yielded to the point of proposing that any retroactive pay increase of more than eight percent could be reviewed; all other increases would be automatically honored. The key point of the public proposal, section (c) 2 of a complex paper, was that retroactive increases would be approved if a wage agreement made after August 15 succeeded an agreement that had expired prior to August 16, and "retroactivity was an established practice or had been agreed to by the parties."

The Administration wanted unanimity, and its emissaries offered Meany some sweeteners if he would endorse the public proposals. Several hours before the Monday meeting, he said, "one of the public members came to me and said he could assure me, without putting it in the record, that they would not challenge any contract that was not over eight percent"—although the officially approved limit was 5.5 percent.

"He said, 'We can't put that in, but I can give you that assurance.' In other words he was going to give me a little under-the-table deal." The *quid pro quo* was labor support of the public position on retroactivity. Meany told the public member (whom he wouldn't identify) to "go to hell."

In the formal meeting that evening, the labor proposal was voted down, ten to five, and then the public proposal was approved by the same margin. Meany was curious about how the rules would be applied in several key negotiations then under way, many of them on contracts that had expired before the freeze began. It soon appeared that the Administration looked on (c) 2 as a valuable escape valve: "We had about half an hour of discussion asking Mr. Weber how this would work. And it was very, very interesting.

"He was sitting there with the proposal in front of him and we said, 'How is this going to affect the West Coast longshoremen?' He says, 'They will be taken care of under (c) 2.'

"How about the railroads? 'Oh, they will be taken care of under this, that, and the other thing.' And he went on down the line. Railroads, aerospace, me-too contracts."

Meany said Weber was trying to persuade the labor members to change their votes and make the approval unanimous. "What you are saying," he told Weber, "is that the big unions—the ones with the lawyers and the treasuries that let them fight—will win; they will get what they already have. You are saying, 'To hell with the little guy.' I'm not going to play that way."

After returning to his office Monday night Meany called in Biemiller and said, "We're not going to get anywhere with the board; I hope to hell you can persuade Congress to put up the retroactive pay." The next day Meany was off to the Americana Hotel in Bal Harbour, Florida, and meetings preliminary to the AFL-CIO convention, which was to open on November 18—thoroughly, irrevocably angry with the Nixon Administration, and eager to put the full story of the Pay Board controversy into the public domain.

Organized labor, among other failings, believes its own scare propaganda. Overstatement, the norm in collective bargaining, colors labor's interpretation of what it hears and says about itself; labor's permanent mood is collective paranoia.

Meany came to Bal Harbour convinced the Pay Board confrontation was but the beginning of a protracted struggle with antilabor forces. The nub of his fear was supportable by common sense and circumstantial evidence: a key political component of Nixon's New Economic Plan was to blame labor's wage demands for the runaway inflation racking the country, and to set up unions for the villain's role should the controls fail. The Nixon Administration had strewn clues all over the landscape. Dr. Burns, for instance, said in an early 1971 speech, "Our problems come because of the high wages demanded by the workers of this country." And Secretary Connally, in a background talk with Washington economic reporters (the substance of which was swiftly relayed to the AFL-CIO), said in early fall that "whether it [the NEP] works is up to the unions." The continuing string of fights over the Pay Board—its powers, its composition, the retroactivity dispute, the public sniping at Meany—were not isolated incidents. The White House was the silent mastermind, and the fight was far from finished.

Labor's analysis was not totally realistic. The Nixon Administration, if it wrecked the Pay Board, also wrecked the New Economic Plan—and, most probably, itself as well, in the 1972 elections. Labor cooperation is essential to any controls program. And at the time of the convention Nixon still clung to the notion that Meany did not speak for American labor—only for the bureaucrats who ran the AFL-CIO and the international unions. Some ostensibly wise men among his economic and labor advisers pushed this thesis upon the President: go around Meany, to the rank and file; look how the hard-hats responded to you last year. The members will buy a total freeze, even if Meany won't. He's griping over points so esoteric no one outside the immediate situation knows what the hell he's talking about. He's a petty, stubborn old man. But build a hot enough fire under him with the membership, one that will really scorch his old ass, and he'll *have* to cooperate with you. Go to Bal Harbour—talk *not* to the convention, but to the American workers who will watch you on TV, and read your speech in the newspapers. And if the convention is rude to you—well, so what? Nastiness to you, the President, will only point up what a surly bunch of bastards these union bums are. Rudeness is likely, too; remember St. Louis in 1953, Dick, when one of Meany's conventions guffawed at you when you tried to explain Eisenhower's flip-flop on Taft-Hartley and your bamboozlement of poor old Martin Durkin?

The idea of taking the battle into Meany's own convention entranced Nixon—think of it, going after that tough old man and his cigar, in front of his own people. Not everyone liked the idea. "George Shultz," one man said, "practically got down on his hands and knees and begged Nixon not to go. 'You'll just offend Meany all the more; we need him, and we can't drive him away,' Shultz said." But Nixon wouldn't listen.

On September 23 Meany had sent Nixon the AFL-CIO's customary invitation to speak at the convention. "No matter who the President is, he is the first man we invite to our convention," Meany said. "A few days later, I received a reply from George Shultz which said that the

President would consider this and look over his schedule and they would be in touch with us a little later. Well, seven weeks passed with no word of any kind."

The convention was to open on Thursday, November 18, with Meany delivering his keynote address in the morning—traditionally, a report on what happened to labor, politically and otherwise, in the previous two years. Wednesday evening Meany was having a snack in the coffee shop of the Americana Hotel when Schultz called. "He said the President wanted to address our convention at noon on Thursday. Now, to me it would seem that there was a little lack of courtesy there. He could have told us this and we would have been glad to work out something. But this was just twelve hours before the convention was to convene. So I told him it would be impossible to make that arrangement, that there was a council meeting set for twelve noon, but that I would be glad to have the President later in the afternoon or anytime he wanted on Friday." They agreed upon 10:30 A.M. Friday.

Meany realized that Nixon was not coming on any peace mission. "What this fellow intended to do was take the convention away from me," he groused to a staff member. "He wanted to get in his speech the day we opened, to steal the attention from our side of the argument." Meany retired to his suite late that night with a stack of five-by-seven cards to rough out notes for his speech—knowing he was going into direct oratorical competition with the President of the United States.

Meany's speech the next morning was a fifty-five-minute collage of factual exposition and grandstanding, the history of the New Economic Plan as witnessed and performed by George Meany, with ample ridicule for everyone in the Nixon Administration who had the slightest role in it, from the President on down. Here was Meany, arms spread and flapping —a rotund, elederly Irish duck suddenly gone berserk—imitating Hodgson's gestures as he answered labor questions about the Pay Board authority. "He reminded me," said Meany, "of a little league umpire I see around the neighborhood. He makes every decision with the same gesture. The trouble is, you can't tell whether one is safe or not." Here was Meany, relating, in deliciously indiscreet direct quotations, Hodgson's depiction of Judge Boldt as "totally and completely unfit" for the job of Pay Board chairman. Here was Meany deriding the competence and impartiality of other board members: Virgil Day, the high General Electric executive, an employer member, he dismissed as a "pip-squeak." Here was Meany relating attempts at "under the table deals" by employer members to split big and small unions. Here was Meany savaging Nixon for nullifying collective bargaining agreements, and Boldt for permitting him to do so, by refusing to approve retroactive pay. "The Old Judge is for the sanctity of contracts, but he says there is a vital principle involved here. And I said, 'What the hell is the vital principle?' He said, 'We've got to go along with the President.' In other words, the sanctity of contracts is not a principle. We have got to go along with the President; that is the principle."

With the two thousand unionists in the audience howling approval, Meany built to a climax. If the New Economic Plan did not succeed he forecast "more stringent and oppressive measures that could destroy our American institutions."

> If Phase Two fails, political expedience demands a scapegoat. The man in the White House never says, "It is my fault." No politician ever says it is his fault. . . . we have no explanation as to why the Nixon-Burns original economic game plan failed so miserably. There will be no explanation and no apology if Phase Two happens to fail. Harsher measures will be promulgated . . . against the nation's workers and their unions, and we can expect antistrike edicts and injunctions and all the other harassments that have been the lot of labor in the authoritarian countries in recent history.
>
> There is something ironic about this business. In the *Wall Street Journal* the other day there was a little quotation, "A highly placed Nixon Administration economist says, 'We have got labor just where we want them now. They either help in making the program work or get blamed for its failure.' " Well, whether we help or don't help, if it fails we get blamed anyway. . . .
>
> But it is ironic to note that . . . big business is applauding and promoting the President's crackdown on labor. It might be well for businessmen . . . to realize that the history of political domination of the means of production has in all cases eventually included business as well as labor.
>
> It is also ironic and interesting to note the new affinity of Mr. Nixon for totalitarian regimes from Peking to Moscow to Athens. The authoritarian mind in government trusts neither the people nor the free and voluntary institutions of the people. In defending the rights and the freedom of working people as they are constituted to do, the trade unions of America can expect to be objects of such attention and the targets of this type of power. . . .

The speech was the hard-line defiance of Nixon that the audience wanted, and Meany let the crowd yell for three minutes before rapping his gavel again. "For my first announcement," he said, "tomorrow morning put on your best bibs and tuckers; the President is going to address us at ten-thirty."

In a brief afternoon session the convention approved broad language giving Meany the effective authority to bolt the Pay Board at any time he desired. It said labor members should stay on the board "only so long as a reasonable hope exists" of getting existing contracts recognized, and of "achieving justice for working people generally." Commenting on the resolution, Meany said, "Now, if the President of the United States does not want our continued membership on these terms, he knows what he can do."

When the convention adjourned in late afternoon, Nixon's advance party, including security agents, moved into the Americana ballroom to make plans for the President's speech. Disputes developed immediately over points that made clear to Meany the President considered his primary audience to be not the AFL-CIO, but the television audience. The White House men wanted Meany to displace four tables of delegates immediately in front of the platform to make room for television cameras that could give live coverage. "I refused to grant that request. I said that this would upset the arrangements for eighty or ninety delegates." Videotape TV cameras were already mounted in the hall, "and I didn't feel that we should change that situation." Next, the White House wanted a microphone installed outside the Americana Hotel so that Nixon's arrival could be announced before he entered the convention hall. Meany declined. Guests had always been introduced from the platform by the AFL-CIO president, and he saw no reason to change precedent simply to dramatize Nixon's appearance. "Pure theater," he said.

It was finally agreed that Meany would leave the podium at 10:22, go to an offstage office with an escort committee, meet the President there, and accompany him to the platform. "Then I was asked would I have the orchestra play ruffles and flourishes as the President marched from the little door over to [the podium]. I said, 'We don't have an orchestra. We have what you might call some chamber music. I don't think you can play ruffles and flourishes on a violin. I could be wrong on that, but this is my impression.' "

Meany passed orders to leaders of the union delegations: he wanted the convention to be courteous to the President. "No boos, no heckling," he said. Meany said nothing on applause. But delegate comment the night before Nixon's arrival was consistent: "We won't need the air conditioning when that bastard is here."

The first part of the Nixon program went as planned on Friday. He and Meany met in the offstage office, chatted amiably a few moments about sailing and golf, and then walked out to a standing ovation. Nixon sat in the front row as Meany introduced him, saying simply, "Ladies and gentlemen, the President of the United States."

Nixon brought with him a prepared text (already distributed to the press) stuffed with self-praise about support of the Longshoremen's and

Harbor Workers' Compensation Act and the reorganization of the Man-power Administration in the Department of Labor—"the usual laundry list that the President of the United States is supposed to go over when he appears before the AFL-CIO or any other convention." Instead of using that text, he said, "I am going to do something that I believe President Meany will appreciate, and all the others here will appreciate. . . . You like it straight from the shoulder. I am going to talk to you about our differences, and I am also going to talk to you about some areas where we agree. . . ."

Nixon said both the press and "some of my own advisers in the White House" had asked why he decided to come to Bal Harbour. "Putting it quite bluntly . . . they said, 'You know a majority of those who are going to be at this great convention are against you politically. . . . Why do you go?' " He paused and smiled, and chuckled. The audience sat silently. "I will tell you why I came here: because while some of you are against me politically, and some of you are against my party, I know from the experience over the past three years that when the chips are down, organized labor is for America, and that is why I am here before this convention today."

The convention interrupted Nixon with warm, if brief, applause. Apparently thinking he had found a responsive chord he could strike at will, he tried again. He thanked labor for opposing unilateral disarmament. "The President can always count on labor for a strong national defense." He paused fleetingly, no applause came, and he continued. He said he appreciated labor's support on "hard decisions to protect America's fighting men." Pause. Silence. He talked about the Cambodia aftermath, when "a great majority of the members of the press and TV, a majority of America's businessmen, a majority of America's intellectual leaders, a majority of America's editorial writers" opposed him, "some very . . . violently." Nixon continued, "But I was not alone. One hundred fifty thousand [sic] American workers walked down Wall Street supporting the armed forces abroad and the commander-in-chief at home . . . that showed where American labor stood when the key issue of defending American lives was involved. . . ." But not even a salute to the hard-hats could stir the audience, which sat in glacial silence.

Nixon, his mannerisms now nervous, jerky, could coax only two more desultory responses in fifteen minutes of earnest oratory. Then, Phase Two, "prosperity without inflation," the freeze. Nixon stepped cautiously onto dangerous turf. "Now, I understand there's been some disagreement about whether that freeze worked. Well, let's look at the numbers. It was a remarkable success, because the figures are in." Scattered ooohs and ahhhs of disbelief began at scattered points in the ballroom, gradually rising in intensity and volume as Nixon pressed on. "The consumer price index, a rise of one tenth of one percent. That rise was the lowest in four years. And so it was worth doing." Flustered at the scoffing murmurs that several times appeared ready to burst into full-fledged laughter, Nixon jabbed back. "And if you don't think so," he snapped, "go home and ask your wives who go to the grocery store." An eruption of jeering, derisive laughter, apparently from about half the audience. "Go home and ask others," Nixon continued. "You will find that as far as prices are concerned, what they want rather than less action on the inflation front is more, and that is what we are going to provide. . . ."

As the audience quietened (some persons had risen to half crouches and muttered "hush, hush" to other delegates), Nixon said, "Now, I have noted that President Meany has had some things to say about Phase Two. As a matter of fact, it is a little hard not to note what he has had to say."

A roar of applause this time—but for Meany, not Nixon. "Just to be sure I didn't misquote him, I cut it out of the Washington *Post*. President Agnew* doesn't back this up, but nevertheless this is what it said." He quoted Meany's statement that "If the President of the United States doesn't want our membership on the Pay Board on our terms, he knows what he can do." Nixon made a half turn to his right, so that he faced Meany, and said, "Well, you know, President Meany is correct, I know exactly what I can do, and I'm going to do it." He said he would continue the controls program, hopefully with labor's participation. "But whether we get that participation or not it is my obligation as President to make this program . . . succeed. . . ."

When Nixon finished, to rising applause, Meany came to the microphone, said, "Thank you very much, Mr. President," and turned to escort him out of the hall, the arrangement that had been made with the White House advance party. Meany said, "I turned my head and he was gone. The escort committee was sitting right there and he just went right by them." Security agents had roped off the area to the right of the stage, where Nixon entered. As he came down the stairs, agents dropped the rope, and he plunged into the audience, trailed by a White House photographer with a motion picture camera and a technician with a portable klieg light. The President went about fifty feet deep into the crowd, shaking hands with delegates, throwing both arms high over his head in greeting.

Meany, watching from the platform, was infuriated. "This was planned, staged, all planned," he muttered.† "He'll be kissing babies

---

* A slip of the tongue the White House corrected in its transcript. The AFL-CIO proceedings let the error stand.

† The platform microphone remained live after Nixon finished speaking; the *sotto voce* comments appeared in the master tape recording of the convention proceedings.

next," said one of the executive council members standing with Meany. "What a show! What a show!" someone else exclaimed. "Look at that, he's all over the place," Meany said, voice heavy with disgust.

After three to four minutes delegates were swarming toward Nixon from all parts of the auditorium. Meany moved back to the lectern and stared down at the scene—Nixon in a cluster of delegates, obviously enjoying the attention, the glare of the klieg lights following him.

Meany rapped his gavel twice. "Will the delegates and guests kindly take their seats?" he commanded. The hubbub hushed momentarily, and there were titters of laughter, as if someone had said an indecent word in public. Nixon turned and walked slowly through the press of delegates, continuing to shake hands and exchange pleasantries; near the door he paused a full minute to autograph a convention program for a delegate. Meany stood with hand on hip, watching. When the President was out of the hall, he rapped his gavel again.

"We will now proceed with act two," he said. The audience sprang up with a cheer, and stood and applauded Meany for three minutes.

The Battle of Bal Harbour had ended. Meany went on with his convention. "The chair recognizes the chairman of the committee on resolutions," he said. . . .

Public relations battles, as the Nixon White House well realized, are won not at the scene, but in the communiqués. The Administration did its advance work. Its agent on the scene was Pasquale Juliano, a former officer of the Transport Workers Union in Philadelphia and a part-time political operative for the White House's Office of Emergency Preparedness (which, despite its name, is a political agency). George T. Bell, a special assistant to the President, recorded for his files a report of a phone conversation with Juliano:

> Mr. Juliano called at 9:30. He is at the AFL-CIO Convention. President Nixon is going to speak at 10:30 A.M. They will chastise him; and that will be the best thing that could happen. Geo. Meany will be trying to make himself look like a big deal; but the Am. people will see the spectacle; and decide for themselves on the merit of what Nixon is trying to do. Mr. Juliano will use the same experience he did when he invited Gov. Romney to an AFL-CIO meeting to speak B-4 he was elected Gov. of Michigan. It was televised and the labor group gave Romney a rough time of it. But in the end he won.
>
> Mr. Juliano will give Mr. Bell a full report upon his return from the meeting. He thinks it will make President Nixon look greater in the eyes of the Am. electorate.

Mr. Bell wants Mr. Juliano to call him after Nixon speaks and let him know how things went. Discreetly and indirectly to get the reaction of others.

Within an hour of Nixon's speech, Devan L. Shumway and Alvin Snyder, assistants to Herbert G. Klein, head of the White House public relations apparatus, received briefings from persons traveling with the President. They immediately began calling news service and television network bureau chiefs and friendly columnists in Washington to point up the "discourtesies" to the President. They cited the absence of a band, the cursory introduction, the laughter, and, finally, Meany's take-your-seats and act-two quips. They also said Meany had ordered delegates to "sit on their hands," hence the lack of friendly applause.

Over the weekend tons of critical headlines and comments fell upon Meany. "Never in our memory has a President of the United States received such loutish treatment from a domestic audience, even in the roughhouse of an election campaign," said the Miami *Herald*. The Washington *Star* complained of the "deliberate coolness" and "calculated discourtesies," and said, "A long and loud Bronx cheer, the sound of which George Meany might remember, is in order" for labor's performance. "George Meany is a crotchety and rude old man," said Senator William Saxbe (Rep., Ohio). Senator Barry Goldwater (Rep., Arizona) charged that Meany attempted to "intimidate the President . . . with the force of union power." Secretary Connally said Meany's actions "reflected an arrogance and a boorishness and a discourtesy that ill becomes a leader of the American labor movement. . . ."

Meany tried to set the record straight when the convention reassembled after a weekend recess. He detailed his negotiations with the White House advance party. He denied any discourtesies. And he swung back at the President. "He threw away his written text, and that corny act is as old as the Republic." Meany said he did not object to the speech ("pure political propaganda"). "But he did not discuss the . . . major basic issue that is disturbing the trade unions of America—do we have the right to sign a contract with our employers and see that contract observed?

"I have the impression the President did not come here to make a speech. He came here to contrive a situation under which he could claim that he had been unfairly treated. . . . I am proud of the conduct of the AFL-CIO. We respect the office, we respect the man that holds the office. . . . However, this doesn't mean that we have got to be subservient to the man who holds the office. This does not mean that our respect for the President and his office calls for us to submit to something that we consider unjust. . . . This is still a democracy. This is still not a monarchy. . . ."

The convention voted Meany a raise from $70,000 to $90,000 a year, re-elected him by acclamation, and adjourned.

*Letter to The Editor,* The Washington Post.
*December 5, 1971.*
*You have put a lot of cartoons of George Meany in your paper. Most of them I do not like. And some of them were very funny. The reason I wrote you was because I am George Meany's granddaughter. And he is a very nice man. And a very good grandfather.*

ELLEN LUTZ.

The evening the convention adjourned, Meany gathered old union chums for a nostalgic evening at an Italian restaurant where he attacked a double order of ravioli and a heaping side dish of spaghetti with trencherman gusto. Because of a hiatal hernia, Meany is supposed to avoid highly spiced foods. But the buoyancy of the convention swept him past caution, and he joked and gossiped until almost midnight. The next day he boarded a train for Washington with Andy Biemiller, Virginia Tehas, and other aides, and settled down for hours of gin rummy, interrupted only for a platter of corned beef and cabbage. After midnight a sleeping car porter rapped on Virginia Tehas' door. "That old man," he said, "something is bad wrong with him." Miss Tehas found Meany pacing the corridor, gasping and complaining of chest pains. She and Andy Biemiller had the conductor stop the train in Columbia, South Carolina. A physician diagnosed Meany's distress as gastric upset and gave him a sedative. Meany felt well enough the next morning to eat a hearty breakfast of eggs, ham, and hominy grits.

Back in Washington at noon, Meany went directly to his office and dictated a letter to Judge Boldt, informing him he had instructed the AFL-CIO comptroller not to put his or Kirkland's raises into effect until they were reviewed by the Pay Board. He delivered the letter personally to Boldt—neither man brought up Meany's public insults of "the Old Judge" of the previous week—and went home. (Meany did not receive the raise. A month later the board adopted guidelines saying the 5.5 percent limit on pay increases was ironclad for executives, regardless of the flexibility permitted for lower-rung workers.)

Meany had intended to spend Thanksgiving weekend with his sisters and other friends in New York. At three-thirty Thanksgiving morning, however, he awoke with severe chest pains—"the worst damned thing I've ever felt," he said later—and was rushed to George Washington University Hospital. Physicians at first feared a heart attack, and Meany was lodged in an intensive care cardiac unit. But electrocardiograms revealed no heart damage, and eventually his hiatal hernia was blamed—a combination of overwork and overeating. Meany stayed in the hospital ten days, out of range of the telephone and work, then was put under what he called house arrest at home for another month. "George wasn't a very good patient," Zack said. "He turned on an all-news radio station, and would call the office every hour all day long to make sure he wasn't missing anything." After Christmas the doctor gave Meany permission to travel, and he returned to Bal Harbour, and the Americana Hotel, for a month of rest in the sun—his whereabouts unannounced, a burly old man in a blazing blue sports jacket and double-knit slacks, one tourist among hundreds, inconspicuous in the very premises where only a month previously he and a President of the United States had hectored one another publicly.

Labor had the last say on retroactivity. On December 10 Congress ordered payment of virtually all wage and benefits increases that were denied workers during the ninety-day freeze. The legislation, an amendment tucked into Nixon's economic stabilization bill, gave labor basically what it had asked of the Pay Board—payment of all back wages unless the amount was "unreasonably inconsistent" with Pay Board standards. The vote was a swap-off between Democrats and Republicans, engineered by the deft hand of Andrew Biemiller. Labor put up a spirited but sham battle against the tax provisions of Nixon's New Economic Plan. The Republicans did the same against retroactivity. Then everyone stopped shouting, went into the privacy of a conference committee, and voted out both the tax breaks for business and the back pay for labor. "That little stint of 'collective bargaining,'" someone said of Biemiller's work, "was worth about $1.25 billion to people who had been caught by the freeze."

His illness, and the Florida recuperation, kept Meany away from the Pay Board for weeks. Judge Boldt proved as weak a chairman as Meany (and Hodgson) had feared. Unable to put together a cohesive majority, Boldt permitted the board to drift aimlessly its first months, baffling labor and business alike with contradictory decisions. The board permitted an 11.2 percent annual wage increase—twice the 5.5 percent limit—for soft coal miners in late November, with employer members siding with labor to avoid a certain strike. But a month later the employer members toughened and refused an 18 percent increase, over three years, for aerospace workers, because 12 percent came in the first year, and no cap was put on fringe benefits. The board, in an interim report given Congress in mid-March 1972, claimed that it had approved increases for 4.7 million workers which averaged, on a weighted basis, 4.13 percent, well within the 5.5 percent standard. To labor, however, the low average was statistical proof the board's standards were so chaotic as to be unfair, in view of the many high settlements.

After the Battle of Bal Harbour Meany rapped the Nixon Administration's shins with sufficient frequency and sharpness to let the President know labor had not been cowed by its adverse publicity from the convention. In December, AFL-CIO representatives withdrew from the planning committee for the White House Conference on the Industrial World —ostensibly to protest lack of meaningful participation; actually, to put labor a longer arm's length away from the Administration. In February, for the first time in its history, the AFL-CIO did not invite the Secretary of Labor to its executive council meeting in Bal Harbour. Meany said he snubbed Hodgson to retaliate for his "discourteous treatment of us" during the November convention. Hodgson had been invited to address the convention Friday, November 19, the day Nixon appeared. "He was due to speak at three o'clock. He was here until twelve noon on Friday and walked out and didn't have the decency to even come and tell me he wasn't coming back," Meany said. ("I think the 1972 campaign is on," a Hodgson aide told the press after the snub.) During the 1971 Christmas season Nixon sent a White House car to Meany's Bethesda home with a box of cigars and a get-well-soon note, and made a friendly phone call. Neither man mentioned the Bal Harbour confrontation, but neither made any pretense at anything other than surface civility.

Within the Pay Board, Nathaniel Goldfinger, the AFL-CIO research director who attended as Meany's alternate, used contemptuous language in rows with Boldt and other public members. During debate over exempting low-wage workers from controls Goldfinger called the majority proposal "a product of utter incompetency or maliciousness, or both." At another point Goldfinger turned to the dignified Kermit Gordon of the Brookings Institution, a public member, and inquired sweetly, "Why don't you tell us who you are trying to screw, Kermit?" Gordon became so mad he shouted, "Sit down and shut up, Goldfinger, we've heard enough of your damned bullying."

Labor was even unhappier with the Cost of Living Council, the key mechanism in the Administration's controls program. On January 19 the council lifted price controls from three quarters of all retail stores and nearly half the nation's rental units. The council's stated reason was that violation complaints were so numerous it was necessary to reduce the workload of the Internal Revenue Service, which had enforcement responsibility. Ten days later, the council ruled that only wages under $1.90 hourly would be exempt from controls. The AFL-CIO charged this ruling violated the Economic Stabilization Act of 1971, which said controls should not be imposed on wage increases of "any individual whose earnings are substandard or who is amongst the working poor." A wage of $1.90 produces annual earnings of $3,952—below the government's poverty line of $4,100 for a four-person family. As the AFL-CIO executive council noted, "It is about 44 percent less than the hourly earnings needed to reach the $7,000 annual income which is the Labor Department's lowest estimate of what it costs a family of four to live in an American city." Labor members had wanted to allow wages to go to $3.50 per hour without requiring board approval, for reasons of both equity and administrative efficiency.

Nor could labor find solace in the Price Commission. The AFL-CIO community services department set up a price monitoring program to supplement the commission's enforcement. According to Meany, "instead of encouragement, we received from the chairman [C. Grayson Jackson, Jr.] the statement that consumers had no way of telling if price increases were legitimate; from the Administration's consumer adviser [Mrs. Virginia Knauer], the charge that we were trying to sabotage price controls by reporting suspected violations; and from the Internal Revenue Service, nothing—no reply whatsoever concerning the suspected violations we reported." Meany felt the very composition of the Price Commission was "an affront to fairness." He complained, "There is not a single consumer representative on the Commission. Instead, there are so-called public members—all of whom have a history of corporate connections. The public is composed of consumers, not corporate consultants or directors or trustees. Would a Pay Board consisting of seven members, six with past union affiliations, be acceptable?" The commission made no effort at across-the-board price controls. It exempted retail establishments with less than $100,000 in annual sales, or 75 percent of all retail firms in the country. It imposed no controls on life insurance premiums, mortgage interest payments, or the price of land and homes. Nor were there controls on used cars, used furniture, or other used goods, "which are bought primarily by the poor," as Meany noted. The commission fretted for weeks over whether to require retailers to post base price lists. When the order was finally issued, most retailers ignored it; none was prosecuted. "Instead," said Meany, "those with less than $200,000 in annual sales, or most of the retail firms in the country, were told they didn't have to post the lists." Meany saw a double standard in procedures of the Pay Board and the Price Commission: "The Pay Board saw nothing wrong in revealing facts about labor-management contracts. For that matter, neither do we. But big business, on the other hand, screams bloody murder when someone wants to examine their contracts." Instead of controlling prices, he said, the Price Commission "is more concerned with profit margin maintenance and total profit expansion, no matter how large or profitable a company may be."

The AFL-CIO executive council, returning to Bal Harbour in February 1972 for its winter meeting, said "flagrant favoritism" in the controls program "is rapidly destroying public support" for it, and asked congressional intervention. In view of such dissatisfaction, Meany was asked on February 14, why did the AFL-CIO remain on the Pay Board? He replied: "Well, because we feel that no good would come at this time for us if we got off the Pay Board. There is a possibility that this whole business of controls—the way it is presently conducted by the Administration—would collapse, and . . . we would be loaded with the blame for the collapse of something that may collapse anyway." We don't know. The record on prices is bad—it is getting worse. Prices are not coming down and there is no attempt, as far as we can see, at enforcement. On the other hand there is, of course, pretty rigid enforcement on the Pay Board decisions." If public demands for action intensified, Meany said, "Then we will see the President go to that emergency thing that he has—where he breaks the glass and opens it up and there is the TV transmitter—and we may have a brand new policy. In other words, we may have another flip-flop."

Nixon brought Meany to the White House on March 10 to try to convince him the controls program was beginning to have effect, and that the early administrative snarls and inequities were being straightened. Meany was not impressed. He repeated his complaint that the board was not independent, and that the "public" members were in fact government flunkies. Nixon protested that no one in his Administration controlled the public members.

"That's a crock," Meany blurted. Meany told Nixon the $1.90 ruling especially disappointed him. He noted it was made by the Cost of Living Council, directly under White House control.

What Nixon sought, but did not receive, was an indication of what Meany would do if the Pay Board ruled against labor in a most complex pending case: the contract that in February had ended a 134-day strike on the West Coast docks. On its face, the longshoremen's contract was an unattractive case for labor to make into a *cause célèbre*. The contract called for increases in pay and fringe benefits totaling 21.5 percent, more than three times the Pay Board's basic limits. Ripple effects from the strike had harmed West Coast manufacturers and Midwest farmers, contributing to the first American balance-of-payments deficit of the twentieth century. The striking union, the International Longshoremen's and Warehousemen's Union, was not even an AFL-CIO affiliate. Meany loathed its long-time president, Harry Bridges, for his affinity to Communist causes. The CIO had expelled Bridges' union for communism in 1950, and Meany snorted disdainfully whenever he was asked whether it would be brought into the AFL-CIO.

However, Bridges had strong arguments for the justice of the contract. Over ten years' time, at the risk of alienating his membership, Bridges cooperated with stevedore companies in mechanizing dock operations, sharply reducing their per unit labor cost and increasing productivity by either 150 or 184 percent, depending upon whether one accepted management or labor figures. Forty-one longshoremen did work that formerly required 100 men. By union estimate, the stevedore companies cut their labor costs by $1 billion over the decade. The Pacific Maritime Association, the employer group, had grudgingly accepted the 21.5 percent increase under pressure from Congress, which in February created machinery for an imposed settlement if the parties did not reach their own agreement. The employers asked the Pay Board to accept the contract as noninflationary. Bridges, asking its approval on March 14, stressed "the right of *both* workers and employers to share in the savings of the machine." He noted the Pay Board's own policy guide that a raise would not be considered inflationary if it could be compensated for by increased productivity. The Pay Board's staff study recognized labor savings of more than $900 million from increased productivity in ten years.

The longshoremen lost. On March 16 Judge Boldt opened a Pay Board meeting by tossing a sheaf of papers onto the table in front of Nathaniel Goldfinger, sitting as Meany's alternate. "I think I can save you labor fellows some time," Boldt said, "by announcing at the outset that we already have ten votes for this decision. If you want to talk about it awhile, go ahead, but this is going to be the decision." The paper approved wage increases of 10 percent and fringe benefits of 4.9 percent, a total gain of 14.9 percent, about a third less than the negotiated contract. Goldfinger protested that the public and employer members should at least listen to labor before making such a decision. Goldfinger charged (and Boldt denied) that the Administration "dictated" the decision. Goldfinger thought it more than coincidental that the adverse ruling came at a time when the Senate Labor Committee had scheduled hearings on an Administration bill to impose compulsory arbitration on all transportation industries. If the ruling prompted a renewed longshoremen's strike, public and congressional pressures for arbitration would increase. Boldt did agree to postpone a final vote until the next morning, so labor members could study the document. On March 17, as labor expected, the public-management coalition approved the reduced contract—the vote was ten to five.

With the other four labor members, Meany joined in a statement charging the decision resulted from the "unholy alliance between public members and employer members" and said it "was not taken on any legitimate economic grounds. It is clearly a political maneuver. . . . The Pay Board is being used by the Nixon Administration in concert with some of the nation's largest employers to set the stage for permanent legislation robbing employees in all transportation industries of their right to free collective bargaining."

He called the executive council into session for March 22. During the days before the council meeting, Meany canvassed key members to see if they would support a bolt from the board. Meany said labor had made a good-faith effort, but that it was "silly to play Nixon's game any longer." Meany found some members wary of the political repercussions but not in serious opposition to his decision. An alarmed George Shultz, sensing Meany's mood, made a last futile attempt at conciliation on March 21. But Shultz had really nothing to offer. He said he would "try to get something done" for low-paid workers, possibly raising the $1.90 per hour limit for persons exempt from wage controls. Meany responded, "I've heard all of this before; you'll be hearing from us tomorrow."

Without dissenting voice, the council voted the next morning to take the three AFL-CIO members off the Pay Board—a direct challenge to the President of the United States, and not a step to be taken frivolously. Meany realized Nixon would accuse labor of wrecking the controls program and attempt to convert the walkout into a campaign issue. Hence the withdrawal statement was carefully drafted to cover the entire history of the controls program, and to emphasize that labor's resignation resulted from a series of affronts, not just the longshoremen's contract vote. (Meany skimmed over the longshoremen in one sentence of the 2,000-word statement, saying rejection of their contract "will mean an average loss of about $1,150 for each of the 15,000 workers on the docks in the 18 months of the contract and a $17 million windfall profit for the employers.") Meany's indictment contained two main points:

—The controls program was grossly one-sided, with freezes on wages but not on many prices. "In the guise of an anti-inflation policy," Meany said, "the American people are being gouged at the supermarket and squeezed in the paycheck." Corporate profits soared 19 percent in the second half of 1971 over the comparable period in 1970—"nearly three times faster than the 6.6 percent increase of total wage and salary payments of all the nation's employees."

—The Pay Board was not an independent tripartite agency but a tool of the Nixon Administration, "completely dominated and run, from the very start, by a coalition of the business and so-called public members. . . . The Pay Board represents government controls. It represents political and business interests."

If the wage stabilization program was to be government-controlled, Meany concluded, "let it be so, openly and clearly. Let the people who are exercising the power take the full responsibility for their decisions— without the façade of labor representation and the pretense of tripartitism."

Leonard Woodcock of the United Auto Workers resigned the next day, saying Nixon's controls system was an "abomination" and that the board had been "misused to rigidly control wages while prices and corporate profits soar." But the other non-AFL-CIO member, the Teamsters' Frank Fitzsimmons, decided to stay on the board, saying he could best speak for his two million members "by participating in Pay Board activities." (AFL-CIO staff members saw the Teamsters' decision as a *quid pro quo* for the Administration's parole, in late 1971, of former Teamster president James R. Hoffa.)

Next Nixon. In a terse televised statement, the President ignored Meany's substantive charges about inequities in the controls program, and talked as if Meany were mad only about the longshoremen's contract.

> When I announced our New Economic Policy on August 15 of last year, I said that fighting inflation must be everybody's job. Yesterday, George Meany walked off the job. His decision to walk out came after the ruling on the longshoremen's contract.
>
> While other American workers are being held to a 5½ percent wage increase, the Pay Board ruled against a twenty percent increase for the longshoremen. Mr. Meany supported the increase. The Pay Board was right. Mr. Meany was wrong.
>
> I respect Mr. Meany as a powerful spokesman for the nation's largest union organization, the AFL-CIO. But only seventeen percent of America's 80 million wage earners* belong to the AFL-CIO. It is my responsibility to act and speak for all the people, and I shall meet that responsibility.
>
> As President, I cannot permit any leader representing a special interest, no matter how powerful, to torpedo and sink a program which is needed to protect the public interest. . . .

Nixon cut the Pay Board to seven members and redesignated it a "single public unit." The Teamsters' Fitzsimmons thereupon became a "public" member. For balance, Nixon cut off four previous business members, leaving only Rocco Siciliano. Judge Boldt remained as chairman.

The same day the President denounced Meany, the Labor Department announced the sharpest monthly food price increase in fourteen years— 1.9 percent for the month of February. With or without Meany's cooperation, the Nixon Administration had staggering problems on its hands, and prominent among them was Meany's willingness to make the economy the prime issue in the 1972 presidential campaign.

*     *     *

* Nixon's definition of "wage earner" was broad. The eighty million figure, a Labor Department statistic, includes every employed American, from the president of General Motors to Wall Street executives and physicians and high-ranking government officials. By AFL-CIO computation, 27.4 percent of the "organizable" workers in America belong to unions.

Because of a combination of circumstances, George Meany was the most prominent among Nixon critics in the preliminary stages of the 1972 campaign. Initially Meany sought to keep the Pay Board dispute divorced from politics. In August 1971, during drafting of his statement criticizing the wage and price freeze, someone suggested language to the effect that the AFL-CIO "would hold the Nixon Administration accountable" for the program. Take it out, Meany said, we don't want a damned word in there that sounds like politics has anything to do with this. As the months passed, however, Meany's attacks on Nixon inevitably took on a political tone. The fragmentation of the Democratic party in the presidential primaries meant no effective, recognized party spokesman existed to challenge Nixon's economic programs. Thus Meany became *de facto* spokesman for the Opposition. In his public statements and press conferences, Meany carefully refrained from saying the AFL-CIO would oppose Nixon in 1972, a decision that could be made, constitutionally, only by the federation's general board. Meany even dropped broad hints he would look favorably upon Nixon if the Democrats nominated Mayor John Lindsay of New York,* Governor George Wallace of Alabama, or (perhaps) Senator George McGovern (Dem., South Dakota). But in private conversations Meany was unequivocal: he detested Richard M. Nixon as intensely as he did any man who had ever been in public life in the United States.

The maneuvering for the 1972 Democratic presidential nomination afforded graphic delineation of the bounds of labor's political power. Specifically, labor could not generate enough momentum to nominate its favored candidate—Senator Henry Jackson (Dem., Washington), a domestic liberal whose strong posture on defense satisfied Meany. Yet quiet frowns from Meany discouraged any meaningful union support for Senator Edmund Muskie (Dem., Maine), spoiling his attempt for a preconvention bandwagon. Meany said not a word publicly about either man. The political confusion of 1968 convinced him labor's best position would be to remain officially neutral and amass as large a delegate bloc as possible to the Democratic National Convention—hopefully 500 persons, versus 200 in 1968.

The *sub rosa* campaign for Jackson—one whose existence Meany would deny—began in December 1970, when the Senator called AFL-CIO headquarters and obtained an appointment. Jackson told Meany he intended to take soundings to see what support he could find for his

---

* Meany disliked Lindsay because he thought he was an incompetent mayor. Personal pique was also a factor. During his 1965 hospitalization for hip surgery, Lindsay sent Meany an effusive letter welcoming him to New York and expressing hopes they could meet. "Please have your secretary call my office to arrange a convenient time," Lindsay concluded. Meany thought the tone rude and threw the letter in the wastebasket.

candidacy. Jackson had little expectation of winning the nomination. "What I want to do," he told Meany, "is to bring some sense into this party." Meany was friendly but noncommittal. What he *did* do was to obtain invitations for Jackson to address union conventions throughout 1971. Not all unions were happy about Meany "selecting" a speaker for their programs. Louis Stulberg of the International Ladies Garment Workers Union was particularly unhappy—until he saw the reception his members gave Jackson. But Meany sought to keep his name off the Jackson build-up. One June 7, 1971, Joseph Alsop wrote a glowing column about the AFL-CIO's "serious effort" to make Jackson "organized labor's choice" at the Democratic convention. Alsop said Jackson's "impeccable record of domestic liberalism, plus his tough-mindedness about defense and foreign policy, adds up to just what the labor leaders want. And only Jackson offers that combination." Meany indeed liked Jackson for those reasons, but he did not wish to say so—or to have Alsop do so on his behalf. He read the column, detected the subtle hand of Jay Lovestone, an Alsop friend and sometime tipster, and sent down an order via Virginia Tehas: Keep your mouth shut about politics.

Nor would Meany be nudged by other candidates. In early 1971 David Broder of the Washington *Post* wrote that Senators McGovern, Muskie, and Harold Hughes (Dem., Iowa), all presidential aspirants, intended to visit the executive council's winter meeting in Bal Harbour. None had been invited, and Meany felt politicians owed him at least the courtesy of a phone call before they announced they would attend *his* meeting. Meany's retaliation was subtle. He told his staff to call Jackson and invite him to join everyone else in Bal Harbour—and also to address a meeting of the Committee on Political Education, a favor denied the other, overeager candidates.

Meany's antipathy to Muskie developed early in his candidacy and deepened as the campaign progressed. Soon after becoming an undeclared candidate, Muskie addressed a private dinner of Jewish establishment political and financial figures. During a question period he said, in effect, "The Arabs have some points on their side, too, and the Palestinian cause is not totally indefensible." Muskie, of course, was correct, but that he said the truth so bluntly to such an audience flabbergasted Meany. "How the hell can we go through that again—he's worse than Hubert Humphrey," Meany exclaimed. Meany grew increasingly disturbed at Muskie's ability to "caress an issue without grabbing it," and his overtures to the Democratic left he detested.

Chappaquiddick and youth dispatched Senator Edward Kennedy (Dem., Massachusetts). Meany dismissed McGovern as a "stalking-horse" for Kennedy and paid little attention to his campaign through the spring of 1972.

Which brings us to the saddest plight of any serious candidate—Hubert H. Humphrey. With the national Democrats in disarray in 1971, Humphrey was given an opportunity to re-establish himself with labor after his return to the Senate. Meany felt Humphrey's quavery behavior in the 1968 campaign could be dismissed as transient. Meany called Humphrey to his office in early 1971 and gave him a stern lecture about his new responsibilities in the Democratic party, and especially on the current controversy over continued funding for the supersonic transport. "You are titular head of the Democratic party, now that you are back in the Senate," Meany said, "and you owe it to the party to take the lead on the SST." For ninety minutes Meany, Biemiller, and researchers from the International Association of Machinists pumped Humphrey full of material on the SST. Jobs were a secondary argument. Meany said development of the plane was essential if the United States was to maintain its historical edge in aerospace technology.

Humphrey left the office enthusiastically in favor of the SST. "You can count on me, George," he said at the door. Humphrey even let his position leak to the press. The labor lobbyists felt they had made a major breakthrough in their campaign to save the SST.

Then, quiet indications that Humphrey was wobbling. A Humphrey staff man wrote a pro-SST speech for the Senator. Days passed, and it went undelivered. Humphrey said nothing directly to anyone at the AFL-CIO, but the weekend before the vote Biemiller heard he was wavering. Meany was unperturbed. He had Humphrey's promise, and no communication to the contrary.

Humphrey voted to kill SST funding. Meany was furious. He listened to Humphrey's phone call of explanation later in the day. "I'm sorry," Humphrey said, "but I was under so much pressure from the folks at home that I had to go against it. I hope you understand."

Meany didn't. That Humphrey went back on a promise was a political discourtesy, but that can be forgiven in time, especially among friends. Indeed, had Humphrey called Meany before the vote and begged off, Meany would not have tried to hold him to the pledge, for the labor count two days previously showed the SST to be dead. In such a situation Meany would not have expected Humphrey to cast a meaningless vote that would have hurt him with his constituents.

What Meany could not accept was further evidence of Humphrey's inability to risk unpopularity by voting for a controversial issue. Meany thereafter could not take Humphrey seriously as a presidential contender. He simply did not want a weak-willed man in the White House, regardless of his prolabor record over two decades. And one began to hear a politically fatal name Meany was using for Humphrey in private conversations. *Mush head.*

\*    \*    \*

*During the train ride back from the AFL-CIO convention, Andy Bie-miller mused aloud about whether John Connally would run with Nixon for Vice-President. Someone else said no, Connally would wait until 1976 and run for President on the Republican ticket.*

*Meany was sitting quietly in the corner of the compartment, reading over papers from the convention. After three or four minutes he took a long, deliberate puff on his cigar and said, "Well, I guess that gives me the incentive to stick around another four years."*

# EPILOGUE

He wouldn't quit, even after the scare of the Thanksgiving Day illness and the realization that when you are seventy-seven years old, the days end a few hours sooner, and it becomes harder to slough off the post-lunch tiredness. The constant references to his age bothered him—a sign, perhaps, that he recognized he *was* too old. He grumped privately when the newspapers called him "the seventy-seven-year-old labor leader," and he developed a keen distaste for the adjective "crusty," used so frequently it seemed a part of his name. Whenever the retirement speculation arose, at a press conference or elsewhere, he had a pat answer: So long as he considered himself healthy enough to act as president, he intended to remain in office.

No one dared suggest otherwise—especially no one on the executive council, whose thirty-three members had an average age of a few months under sixty-five.

He assiduously avoided pushing any favored successor toward stage center. Sam Gompers had tried to "rule from the grave" by promoting Matthew Woll as his successor, and Woll lost. "When I'm gone, let them decide," Meany would say. "It's none of my business." I asked eleven members of the AFL-CIO executive council whom they saw as a logical successor. I. W. Abel, of the United Steel Workers, largest in the AFL-CIO, with 1.2 million members at the end of 1971, was favored by three members. Lane Kirkland, Meany's secretary-treasurer, and John H. Lyons, of the Bridge, Structural and Ornamental Iron Workers, were mentioned by two members. But each of these men has drawbacks. Abel is from an old CIO union, and die-hard AFL people would not accept him. Erudition handicaps Kirkland: he can get through a complete sentence without slipping on a grammatical banana peel, and his acerbic tongue offends many council members. Lyons, an archetypical hard-hat, has the disconcerting habit of saying "nigger" at public meetings. One council member said, "John suffers from a native stupidity. He has all of Meany's bull-headed qualities, but only a smattering of his brains." Such are the parameters of the speculation. In early 1972 Byron E. Calame of the *Wall Street Journal* noted his paper had listed "four leading candidates" to succeed Meany in a 1963 story. "Today one is dead, two have retired as presidents of their unions, and the fourth has slipped from the ranks of front-runners," Calame wrote.

So Meany clung to office—to power, actually, which is really the important factor—with the determination of an old bull, the unchallenged leader of the American trade union movement. Power is the most transitory of qualities, especially in Washington, where a change of administration can drop the mighty into overnight obscurity. Meany outlasted them all, even the Southern mossbacks in Congress whose clout depends upon seniority, not ability. Meany's durability as a national figure was surpassed only by that of the redoubtable J. Edgar Hoover.* Meany so dominated the AFL-CIO executive council that the slightest murmur of dissent was magnified by outsiders into a major rebellion. At the winter 1972 meeting, for example, Paul Hall of the Seafarers International Union and Jerry Wurf of AFSCME swung a majority behind a resolution supporting construction of liquefied gas carrier ships by El Paso Natural Gas Company, to transport gas from Algerian fields. El Paso needed a favorable antitrust ruling to consummate the deal. Meany's initial position, developed by Andrew J. Biemiller, his lobbyist, opposed El Paso. Hall and Wurf argued that construction of the tankers would provide sorely needed jobs, and that AFL-CIO opposition to monopolistic mergers was impractical. They won, one of the few times in Meany's presidency that he retreated on an issue. Despite great excitement in the labor press, however, the issue did not diminish Meany's authority by one iota. When Hall also complained of AFL-CIO organizing lethargy, Meany replied, "OK, you run the organizing committee for the industrial union department. Get busy—nobody is stopping you from doing all the organizing you want."

One executive council member, speaking from the refuge of anonymity, asserted the unanimous votes reflect qualities more subtle than unflagging council support of Meany's positions. "Meany makes sure he has the votes before he puts an issue before the council," this member said. "Of the thirty-three men on the council, only a dozen or so really mean anything. The rest are ciphers who fill chairs and keep their mouths shut. If Meany smells any trouble in advance, he calls around and strikes a consensus. If he can't work it out, he simply lets the issue drop.

"Also, the council alliance is one of fear—fear of who might end up as president if Meany was put out of office. Meany doesn't make demands

---

* A Meany admirer. "George Meany is one of the finest men I know," Hoover told the Washington *Post* in a November 1970 interview. "There are no Communists in the AFL-CIO and he doesn't tolerate corruption. He's a fine man and the AFL-CIO is a fine organization."

on people, intellectually or otherwise, and he doesn't screw around with unions. One characteristic of conservatism is fear of the unknown. So a lot of these guys figure, 'Why start a fight with George? We might wind up with another Reuther.' "

Meany's total control of the AFL-CIO does not conceal some rather fundamental weaknesses of organized labor circa the 1970's.

Too many Americans look upon unions as yet another flawed institution—narrowly oriented, more concerned with material gains for their own members than with the over-all improvement of society; greedy at the bargaining table, to the detriment of the economy; afflicted by the dead hands of bureaucracy and the dead heads of geriatric leadership; unable to devise procedures for settling labor-management disputes that bring recurring discomfort, even economic disaster, to the public. Whether these shortcomings in fact are legitimate complaints or whether they are attributable to Meany's leadership is irrelevant; the tragedy of modern labor is that it has dissipated the mass public sympathy it once commanded in the United States.

Meany has argued that critics expect too much of labor. Whatever flaws labor has, he maintains, mirror the quality of American life. Meany goes about his work on the assumption—a correct one, according to the sparse evidence—that rank-and-file members want bread and butter, not crusades. Three statements of his trade union philosophy, made at decade intervals, reveal a consistency in organized labor's rationale during his years in power. In 1944, Meany described AFL members as "essentially conservative." The union member, he said

> is determined to secure the good things of life for himself and his family, and hopeful of accumulating enough to provide reasonable security. He believes in free enterprise and capitalism and wants to earn a piece of it. He believes in private property and wants to have some of it. He believes that everyone should work for what he gets. He is ready to help his colleagues get along, but he refuses to carry a slacker on his shoulder. . . .

Writing in *Fortune* in 1955, Meany elaborated on the same theme. "Our goals as trade unionists are modest," he said, "for we do not seek to recast American society in any particular doctrinaire or ideological image. We seek an ever-rising standard of living. Sam Gompers once put the matter succinctly. When asked what the labor movement wanted, he answered, 'More.' If by a better standard of living we mean not only more money but more leisure and a richer cultural life, the answer remains, 'More.' " And in 1966, after more than a decade as AFL-CIO president, Meany saw no reason to expand the role he had defined for labor in 1944:

The one word that best describes [the] day-to-day operation [of the labor movement] is "practical." We deal with one problem, or one set of problems at a time. We avoid preconceived notions, and we do not try to fit our program into some theoretical, all-embracing structure.

The bulk of union membership in the United States is now involuntary —workers in industries and trades where the closed shop and hiring practices make union affiliation a condition of employment. When the AFL and CIO merged in 1955, one of the declared aims of the new movement was promoting "the organization of the unorganized into unions of their own choosing for their mutual aid, protection, and advancement" (language from the AFL-CIO constitution). The 16,802,-000 union members represented 33.2 percent of the nonfarm work force; Walter Reuther (but not Meany) spoke of doubling membership within a decade. By 1971, 19,400,000 Americans belonged to unions—a numerical increase, but a proportionate decline to 27.4 percent of the labor force. Why is this so? Meany was asked in February 1972 by *U.S. News & World Report*.

"I don't know, I don't care," he replied. "We have never had a large proportion of the work force in this country—nothing like Britain, nothing like the Scandinavian countries, nothing like the Germans."

Well, would Meany prefer to have a large proportion of the work force unionized? "Not necessarily. We've done quite well without it. We've delivered more to the American worker than any labor movement that ever existed. . . . With all of our complaints, we have the highest standard of living in the world.

"Why should we worry about organizing groups of people who do not appear to want to be organized? If they prefer to have others speak for them and make the decisions which affect their lives, without effective participation on their part, that is their right."

Meany noted that labor made great gains under Sam Gompers, when the unionized percentage of the work force "was very tiny," compared with the present. "Frankly, I used to worry about the . . . size of the membership. But quite a few years ago I just stopped worrying about it, because to me it doesn't make any difference—and it's not just in legislation, it's anyplace." Meany maintained that the social legislation supported by labor improves the pay and working conditions of union and nonunion workers alike—in effect, an endorsement of "trickle-down unionism." The AFL-CIO legislative aims in fact *do* benefit millions of Americans outside organized labor. But some 11 million Americans— about one-seventh the work force—still do not benefit from the minimum wage law, an impoverished substratum of working America who are a collective blight on organized labor.

For more than a year I listened to various AFL-CIO bureaucrats tick off reasons why certain groups of workers could not be readily unionized. Southern textile workers are captives of reactionary local politicians and businessmen; organizers face the unflinching opposition of state and local governments. Insurance employees aspire to management positions and will not jeopardize promotion by joining a union. Technical and scientific personnel consider themselves professionals and feel unions are beneath their dignity. The turnover is so brisk among retail clerks, office workers, and hotel, laundry, and restaurant workers that unionization must be catch-as-catch-can. Persons in many service industries—appliance repairmen and service-station attendants, for instance—are split into so many minute economic units they cannot be reached by organizers. Each of these excuses has validity; failure can always be rationalized. Yet they are overshadowed by one central fact: American labor, as it is conducted in the 1970's, cannot persuade even a simple majority of the work force that their interests would be served by joining a union.

In terms of achieving his own goals, Meany's reign as AFL-CIO president was successful. He acquired the political and lobbying clout that made organized labor a permanent power bloc in Washington. Labor may not always win its battles; however, it has such residual strength, even under unfriendly Administrations, that it is able to veto any attempts to diminish the privileges it has acquired for itself over the years. Save for fringe operators, labor is tolerably free of corruption. The United Auto Workers, once they resolve grave financial troubles, will reaffiliate with the AFL-CIO; could they have afforded the $120,000 monthly per capita taxes, President Leonard Woodcock would have applied for readmission within a year of Walter Reuther's death. Through dint of personality, Meany succeeded in keeping American labor united during the period when the Reuther and Hoffa defections threatened to splinter the movement; indeed, he told me that his "greatest personal achievement" during his presidency was "keeping the boys together."

*This self-evaluation at first baffled me. After a public career spanning half a century, veritably one that parallels modern labor history, does George Meany truly feel that preserving the union bureaucracy is his most enduring contribution to American workers? I asked him the same question several months later, and received substantially the same answer. Then the reason came to me: George Meany, after all, had been an "organ-EYE-zation" man since those long Sunday afternoons in the Bronx at the turn of the century. The "organ-EYE-zation" is intact. George Meany is at peace with himself.*

# SOURCES AND ACKNOWLEDGMENTS

During the discouraging early weeks of this book I realized why several other writers had abandoned attempts at Meany biographies. One of the very first library items I read was a Meany profile from *American Labor* —which is friendly to its constituency—calling his personal life a "pretty closed book," and continuing, "When one tries to enter that private domain, the doors seem to shut. Few people are his close intimates and those who are respect his own desire for privacy. . . . It is one of the curious facets of his personality that he should have fought so fiercely to erect a thick wall."

I had to get over that wall. After three months of research, brisk but mostly nonproductive, I drew up a list of questions about obscure points in Meany's early career—the more esoteric the better, for my purposes —centered on the hopelessly convoluted politics of the plumbers union, and sent them to his office with the frank admission that they could not be answered from the existing record or the available witnesses. Meany's attitude changed dramatically within twenty-four hours. He never bothered to explain the reasons to me; I suspect, but cannot prove, that he decided any writer with enough tenacity (or so little sense) to spend weeks reading musty plumbers union journals should be brought inside for closer scrutiny. Meany did three things to facilitate this book. He opened a host of AFL-CIO records to me, including executive council proceedings dating to 1940, the year he came to Washington. Portions of the council minutes—especially for the years immediately after the merger—are in the form of verbatim transcripts; they are an invaluable record of the internal machinations leading to the expulsion of the Teamsters and other unions during the corruption probes, and of the bitter exchanges between Meany, Walter Reuther, and their assorted followers. Second, Meany let other labor people know he was interested in this book and that he would "be appreciative" if they would talk with me. Labor is not an open society, and his clearance took me through doors that otherwise would have remained closed. I ultimately talked with more than one hundred persons who have known and worked with Meany during his half-century career. Finally, and most important, Meany set aside many hours for me for private interviews. Much of the material gleaned from these talks is invaluable because it simply does not exist anywhere save in Meany's encyclopedic memory. Meany has assiduously avoided paper all his life. He does not keep a diary or write memos; he brings as few persons as possible into any discussion, and he demands discretion of those who work closely with him; he prefers the telephone to the letter as a means of communicating with people. Yet he remembers, and in incredible detail. If Meany says a certain date in August 1935 was a Friday, it was; and the titles and middle initials of the eight persons attending a conference are correct. When verifiable, so is his memory of what they said.

Further, Meany gave me this freedom to roam his career—along with a road map—without asking or attempting to invoke any controls. *Meany* is his story, but my book.

Most of my primary interview sources are named in the chapter notes below. Many persons asked anonymity. The presidents of some surprisingly large unions, supposedly fearless labor leaders, are frightened silly of offending Meany and would talk about him only in generalities or off the record. Hence I am not compiling the customary roster of names. Some people do deserve special mention. Miss Virginia Tehas, Meany's personal secretary since 1940, helped me find my way through a solid wall of documents in Meany's conference room files (referred to below as GM files), and pointed me toward some obscure sources who proved helpful. Other AFL-CIO staff people who were cooperative for months included Albert J. Zack, director of public relations; Jay Lovestone, of the international affairs department; Andrew J. Biemiller, of the legislative department; Boris Shishkin, now retired; Walter Davis, director of education; Don Slaiman, of the civil rights department; Nelson Cruikshank, retired; Peter McGavin, of the maritime trades department; Mrs. Jean Webber, the AFL-CIO librarian, and her associates, Mrs. Mary Louise McMillan and Mrs. Betty Hebb; and Saul Miller, of the *American Federationist*. Sid Brechner, the AFL-CIO sound engineer, played hours of tapes of Meany speeches and informal talks. M. S. Novik, longtime radio and television consultant to the AFL-CIO, and Meany's personal friend since the 1930's, was invaluable in gaining me entree to New York labor figures. There are many others who preferred not to be named.

Dr. Jonathan Grossman, historian of the Labor Department, obtained access for me to transcripts of executive sessions of the National War Labor Board, previously restricted although they dated back one and one-half wars. Dr. Grossman also read drafts of early chapters and helped me avoid gaffes in some obscure labor history. Other librarians who helped were Joseph Howardton, William E. Lind, and James Paulauskas, of the National Archives; James E. O'Neill, director, the Franklin D. Roosevelt Library; Louis M. Starr, director of the Oral History Research Office, Columbia University; Moreau Chambers, archivist of Catholic University; and Margaret F. Brickett, of the Labor Department library.

Some printed sources of continuing value were *Labor in America,* by Foster Rhea Dulles, Thomas Y. Crowell Company, New York, 1955; *A History of American Labor,* by Joseph G. Rayback, The Macmillan Company, New York, 1964; Philip Taft's two-volume history of the American Federation of Labor: *The AFL in the Time of Gompers* and *The AFL from the Death of Gompers to the Merger,* Harper and Brothers, New York, 1957, 1959. For ongoing coverage of labor news, *John Herling's Labor Letter* was enlightening for decades.

For reasons of conciseness, I have tried to hold chapter notes to a minimum. If a source is obvious in the text, I do not repeat it. If Meany said something at an AFL-CIO convention, his language comes from the printed proceedings. The quotations from his formal speeches elsewhere are from the textual file Miss Tehas maintains in his office. The quotations from our interviews are as spoken, edited only to rid them of such conversational debris as "now the next thing happened was" and "another thing I remember."

I am also indebted to Richard Kluger, who originally conceived of this book; to Herman Gollob, a fellow Texan who is both friend and editor; and to former Senator Ralph Yarborough of Texas, who gave an early endorsement which got me through a crucial first primary.

# Chapter One

Descriptions of life in the Meany home and his boyhood activities are from interviews with Meany and three of his sisters: Mrs. Anne Cassin, Mrs. Marie Tinsley, and Mrs. Helen Fitzpatrick. The early history of the plumbers union and its Bronx local was recounted to me by William Dodd, the international secretary-treasurer and a Bronx native; Eugene Murray, long a Local 463 officer and business agent; and David Holborn, also a former business agent. Other sources are as follows:

Page 7: "Organ-EYE-zation." Meany to executive board, United Steel Workers of America, March 2, 1955. (GM files)

Page 8: The Flynn quotations are from his *You're the Boss,* Viking Press, New York, 1947.

Page 8: The *North Side News* and J. A. Goulden quotations and the Bronx population figures are from *The Bronx and Its People,* by James L. Wells, Louis F. Haffer, and Josiah A. Briggs, Lewis Historical Publishing Company, Inc., New York, 1927.

Page 10: The Sack quotations are from his boyhood memoir published in *The Journal of the Bronx County Historical Society,* July 1966.

Page 11: "Official entry cards." "The Honest Plumber," by Merlyn S. Pitzele, *Saturday Evening Post,* November 20, 1943.

Page 12: The Segal quotations and background information on development of the plumbing industry are from his *The Rise of the United Association: National Unionism in the Pipe Trades, 1884–1924,* Harvard University Press, Cambridge, 1970.

Page 15: The building trades corruption under Brindell is described by John Hutchinson in *The Imperfect Unions,* E. P. Dutton & Company, Inc., New York, 1970. Trials of Brindell, Hettrick, Doran, and Chapman are reported in the New York *Times* of February 4, 8, and 24, 1921. Brindell's alliance with Hutcheson and the Carpenters Union is from *Men Who Lead Labor,* by Bruce Minton and John Stuart, Modern Age Books, Inc., New York, 1937.

# Chapter Two

The account of a plumbers union business agent's work came from interviews with Meany, Holborn, Dodd, and Murray. The early turmoil in Local Two is discussed in Martin Segal's *The Rise of the United Association, op. cit.;* the Segal quotations in this chapter come from that book. Dodd and Judge Edward A. Maguire were helpful, in interviews, with background on Meany's election to the state federation presidency.

Page 19: Local Two's 1886 landmark contract is described in proceedings of the United Association's 1889 convention, and by Segal.

Page 19: "Docilely accept." *Industrial Relations in the Building Industry,* by William Haber, Harvard University Press, Cambridge, 1930. Other Haber quotations are from this book.

Page 20: "My union was a closed union." Meany to the convention of the AFL-CIO Building and Construction Trades Department, Atlantic City, December 3, 1957. (GM files)

Page 20: "Strength of our organization." *United Association Journal,* Fall 1918.

Page 21: "The hell with sending superintendents." Meany in pre-Labor Day interview with labor press, August 28, 1969. (GM files)

Page 22: "For two or three years." Meany to convention of the Oil, Chemical and Atomic Workers International Union, New York, September 21, 1967.

Page 23: "Remained at a standstill." Final Report of the New York State Joint Legislative Committee on Housing, 1923, Legislative Document #48. The Kinney quotations are from this report as well.

Page 23: The arbitration awards are compiled in the *Handbook for 1930* of the Building Trades Employers' Association of the City of New York. The Local Two work rules are derived variously from Haber, Segal, the *United Association Journal,* and interviews.

Page 25: The 1927 plumbers strike was reported with varying thoroughness by the New York *Times* and the New York *Journal* between April and July 1927. The United Association was so piqued with Meany's tactics that its *Journal* did not once mention his name in its account of the strike, Fall issue 1927, giving credit for settlement to secretary-treasurer Burke.

Page 29: The Day statement is in the New York *Times*, March 14, 1933.

Page 30: The role of the CPLA in the drive for unemployment insurance, and the Budenz quotation, are from *Labor Age*, June–December 1930. The AFL's opposition is detailed in proceedings of its conventions from 1931–33.

Page 32: "Business agents were unable to find jobs." *Labor Age*, October 1932.

Page 32: "A number of members were in rather strong opposition." John P. Frey letter of December 12, 1932, in the Frey Papers at the Library of Congress.

Page 32: The national drive for unemployment insurance is discussed in *Survey of Labor Economics*, by Florence Peterson, Harper & Brothers, New York, 1947. The New York campaign is detailed in Meany speeches to the state federation conventions in 1933 and 1934.

Page 36: "Tammany Hall has been seeking my defeat." The Buffalo *Evening News*, August 29, 1934. Press coverage of Meany's election was scanty, and at least two New York City newspapers spelled his name "Meaney," an error the New York *Herald-Tribune* continued through 1937.

# Chapter Three

In addition to Meany, other interview sources on this chapter include Charles (Zacha) Zimmerman and David Dubinsky, on legislative activities and Meany's work with liberal unionists; Morris S. Novik, on Meany's relations with Lehman and La Guardia, and the formation of the American Labor party; Dan Ring, who was a personal assistant to General Johnson, on the prevailing wage and other WPA issues; and Bernard Tassler, on the 1937 mayoralty election and Meany's election as secretary-treasurer. Other anecdotal material came from Victor Borella, labor relations specialist for the Rockefeller interests, and Virginia Tehas and Boris Shishkin.

Page 38: "I worked hard." Meany in pre-Labor Day interview with labor press, August 28, 1969. (GM files)

Page 40: Labor's legislative platform and Meany's campaign speeches for Lehman are in the *State Federation Bulletin* in Fall issues, 1934.

Page 41: Daily details of the 1935 New York legislative session are from the Albany *Knickerbocker Press*, which although unfriendly to Lehman, even in its news columns, did give a tolerably intelligible account of what was happening. Meany gave thorough reports to the state fed membership via the *Bulletin* and his annual speeches to the state convention. A good over-all survey of the session is in *Herbert H. Lehman and His Era*, by Allan Nevins, Charles Scribner's Sons, New York, 1963.

Page 44: The fight over unemployment insurance is covered in a print of hearings on March 6, 1935, before a joint session of the Senate and Assembly committees on labor and industry (untitled).

Page 47–48: Accounts of post-1935 legislation are from the *Bulletin* and state federation convention proceedings.

Page 49: "Five dollars to cover an area." Meany to convention of International Union of Electrical, Radio and Machine Workers, New York, September 19, 1968. (GM files)

Page 51: The genesis of the public works program, and the Roosevelt quotes, are from *Roosevelt and Hopkins: An Intimate History*, by Robert E. Sherwood, Harper & Brothers, New York, 1948.

Page 52: "Colorful, vivid, and outspoken." *The Public Years*, by Bernard M. Baruch, Holt, Rinehart & Winston, New York, 1960.

Page 52–60: Meany gave accounts of the prevailing wage dispute to the 1935 and 1936 state federation conventions. The "public" statements in this chapter are from the New York *American* and the New York *Times* during the two-odd months the strike was in progress. Transcripts of the telephone conversations between Hopkins and Johnson are in the WPA section of the National Archives, in Washington, D.C., and in the Franklin D. Roosevelt Library, Hyde Park, New York.

Page 53: "Roosevelt in Retreat." *The Politics of Upheaval,* by Arthur M. Schlesinger, Jr., Houghton Mifflin Company, Boston, 1960. The mood of the Roosevelt Administration in mid-1935 is drawn from this book.

Page 55–57: The Meany and Johnson speeches were reported in the *American* and (less fully) the *Times.*

Page 59–60: The Hopkins-Branion transcript is in the WPA papers in the National Archives; the Meany letter to FDR, in the Roosevelt Library.

Page 60: "We are facing." *F.D.R.: His Personal Letters,* Volume I, Elliott Roosevelt (editor), Duell, Sloan and Pearce, New York, 1950. The political climate in 1935–36 is based on Schlesinger, *op. cit.;* and *Sidney Hillman: Statesman of American Labor,* by Matthew Josephson, Doubleday, Garden City, New York, 1952. Meany's campaign speeches are in the *State Federation Bulletin.*

Page 63–64: The attacks on Dubinsky and his responses are in newspaper clippings of imprecise dates and origin in Dubinsky's files.

Page 70–72: The 1930's mood within the AFL is based upon, in addition to interviews, Josephson, *op. cit.; Labor in America,* by Foster Rhea Dulles, Thomas Y. Crowell Company, New York, 1955 edition; *A History of American Labor,* by Joseph G. Rayback, The Macmillan Company, 1964; *Conflict Within the AFL: A Study of Craft Versus Industrial Unionism, 1901–1938,* by James O. Morris, Cornell University Press, Ithaca, New York, 1958; Minton and Stuart, *op. cit.;* and Taft's *The AFL in the Time of Gompers.*

# Chapter Four

Interview sources for this chapter included Meany, Virginia Tehas, Barnard Tassler, Nelson Cruikshank, and Jay Lovestone. The National Archives in Washington has transcripts of executive sessions of the National Defense Mediation Board, from which the quotations are taken. The NDMD's origin and work are discussed in the Termination Report of the National War Labor Board, its successor agency. Labor's prewar work is covered in *Juggernaut: American Labor in Action,* by Wellington Roe, J. B. Lippincott, Philadelphia, 1948; and *Labor Baron,* by James Wechsler, William Morrow Company, New York, 1944.

Page 91: The Gardner Jackson memorandum is in his papers in the Franklin D. Roosevelt Library.

Page 92: "Sounding board." Emspak transcript, Columbia Oral History Project, Columbia University (COHP hereafter).

# Chapter Five

The bulk of this chapter is drawn from transcripts of executive sessions of the National War Labor Board. Dr. George W. Taylor and former Senator Wayne Morse, who served on the board, gave me valuable interviews. The Byrnes quotes are from his *Speaking Frankly*, Harper and Brothers, New York, 1947. Meany spoke of the WLB's work at each AFL convention during the war years, and at most executive council meetings.

Page 93: "Not even the members of the War Labor Board." Meany in the *American Federationist*, April 1946.

Page 107: The Brophy letter is among his papers in the Catholic University archives.

Page 109: The Morse memo on the anti-Lewis publicity campaign is in the George Taylor papers, the National Archives.

Page 115: "Keep politicians out of the field." Meany in the *American Federationist*, April 1946.

# Chapter Six

Interview sources included Meany, Jay Lovestone, Nelson Cruikshank, David Dubinsky, James Carey, and Richard L.-G. Deverall. Deverall also gave me access to his voluminous papers in the Catholic University archives, consisting of his reports to Meany and Lovestone, and exchanges of correspondence with Lovestone. Labor's foreign programs in the immediate postwar years were expounded at length to AFL conventions. Of Meany's dozens of speeches on foreign programs, the best summation was to the Catholic Labor Alliance, March 13, 1951. *American Labor and United States Foreign Policy*, by Ronald Radosh, Random House, New York, 1970, is a revisionist study of labor abroad; it is useful, as Bernard De Voto once said in another context, if one wishes to grow paranoia from seed. Lovestone's early career in the Communist party and his break with Stalin are covered in *American Communism and Soviet Russia*, by Theodore Draper, Viking Press, New York, 1963. The Braden quotations are from his "I'm Glad the CIA Is Immoral," *Saturday Evening Post*, May 20, 1967.

Page 119: "Self-interest." Meany to Catholic Labor Alliance, March 13, 1951.

Page 127: "Untrustworthy political bastard." Carey letter to Meany, May 16, 1967.

Page 127: The Brophy quotations are from his papers in the Catholic University archives.

Page 128: Brown's letters to Woll are quoted in Radosh, *op. cit.*

Page 130: "Sufficiently strong." Meany to Catholic Labor Alliance.

Page 136: The Lens quotations are from his "American Labor Abroad: Lovestone Diplomacy," *The Nation*, July 5, 1965.

Page 137: "They don't turn the members into Communists." Meany to Bond Club of New York, March 19, 1964.

# Chapter Seven

Interview sources included Meany, Lovestone, Tehas, Tassler, Shishkin, and Joseph Keenan. Truman's postwar labor policies are in the second volume of his presidential memoirs, *Years of Trial and Hope*, Doubleday, New York, 1956. The CIO's struggle with Communists is detailed in Max M. Kampelman's essay, "Communists in the CIO," in *The Strategy of Deception*, Jeane J. Kirkpatrick (editor), Farrar, Straus and Company, New York, 1963.

Page 140: *Fortune* quotation, "The Labor Situation," December 1946.

Page 141: "It is no secret." Newton in the *Washington Evening Star*, January 27, 1946.

Page 141: "As concentrated capital is the chief asset." Green to International Association of Machinists, November 1, 1945.

Page 141: The Lewis *Collier's* quotations are in the issue of May 5, 1945.

Page 143: Rovere's description of Senator Taft is in his *The Eisenhower Years*, Farrar, Straus and Cudahy, New York, 1956.

Page 144: "May be simply stated." "The Taft-Hartley Act: A Favorable View," by Senator Robert A. Taft, in *Annals of the American Academy of Political and Social Science*, March 1951. "A Critical View" by William Green in the same issue outlines labor's objections.

Page 145: "The American wage earner." Meany on the Mutual Broadcasting Company, April 16, 1947.

Page 146: "Frightened men." Riesel in *Look*, June 24, 1947.

Page 147: "Inspires physical fear." James Wechsler in *PM*, March 28, 1943.

Page 149: The description of Lewis's speech dramatics is based upon the account of Nat Damien in "The AFL's Fighting Plumber," *Catholic Digest*, 1953.

Page 152: Riesel on Lewis' reaction, "Profile of George Meany," *New Leader*, June 15, 1953.

# Chapter Eight

Interview sources included Meany, Keenan, Carey, Eli Oliver, and Arthur J. Goldberg. Truman campaign quotations are from his memoirs, *op. cit.* Cabell Phillips' *The Truman Presidency*, The Macmillan Company, New York, 1967, is good for the politics of the Truman Administration, but has little to say about Korean War economic controls. I am also indebted to Eli Oliver for a private letter on the wage stabilization program and the United Labor Policy Committee.

Page 155: "Labor's estate." McDevitt in the *AFL News-Reporter*, September 11, 1953.

Page 157: "My name must have meant." Meany on ABC radio, September 2, 1947.

Page 159: "The sole test." Meany to 1948 AFL convention.

Page 159: The Clifford memo is quoted, among other places, in my *The Superlawyers*, Weybright & Talley, New York, 1972.

Page 162: "Was undoubtedly given too much credit." Meany to national committee meeting of Labor's League for Political Education, September 24, 1951.

Page 168: "American business, stated broadly." Business attitudes toward labor and labor's objections to persons working for Wilson are in "Labor Declares Wilson the Aggressor," by Claire Neikind, *The Reporter*, April 3, 1951.

Page 169: "In every key spot." Meany to the Academy of Political Science, May 1951.

Page 173: The GE management newsletters are quoted in Neikind, *op. cit.*

Page 173: "Haven't taken into consideration." Meany on Mutual Broadcasting System, March 7, 1951.

Page 175: "The new national board." The New York *Times*, April 8, 1951.

Page 176: "First time in the history of matrimony." Walter Reuther to 1953 convention of the United Auto Workers.

Page 177: "They want a president." Meany to City of Hope Dinner, New York, May 8, 1952.

# Chapter Nine

Interview sources included Meany, Jack Conway, James Carey, Lovestone, Arthur Goldberg, Maurice Hutcheson, David Dubinsky, Senator Wayne Morse, and Norman Van Buren. *Reuther,* by Frank Cormier and William J. Eaton, Prentice-Hall, Englewood Cliffs, N. J., 1970, is a friendly but objective study of the UAW president. A good secondary source on the ILA and the AFL's attitude toward corruption is Hutchinson, *op. cit.* The David McDonald quotes are from his *Union Man,* E. P. Dutton & Company, New York, 1969. Arthur J. Goldberg's account of the merger, *AFL-CIO: Labor United,* McGraw-Hill, New York, 1956, explains the evolution of each side's position, and is a good formal record. Persons from both the AFL and CIO, however, say Goldberg grossly overstated his own role in the merger. The best account of Meany's implementation of the no-raiding agreement is his speech in Proceedings of Conference of International Representatives, AFL, Chicago, May 14, 1954.

Page 183: "McDonald used Haywood." Reuther quoted in Cormier-Eaton.

Page 189: "One past association." Meany's visits to Fay and his past friendship are in the New York *Times,* October 4, 1953.

Page 196: "Good Lord." Meany in interview with *U.S. News & World Report,* November 6, 1953.

Page 200: "Dave realized the membership." Goldberg interview; other quotations are from his book.

Page 202: "Had to be a full-time operator." Brophy, in COHP.

Page 204: "There was no mood of history." Levey in the New York *Times,* December 2, 1955.

# Chapter Ten

President Eisenhower's side of the Durkin controversy is in his *Mandate for Change,* Doubleday, New York, 1963. Labor's role in the 1952 campaign is in *How to Cope with COPE,* by Terry Catchpole, Arlington House, New Rochelle, N. Y., 1968.

Page 207: Meany's account of his postelection meeting with Eisenhower was given to the executive council in January 1953. His campaign jibes at Eisenhower were at the 1952 AFL convention.

Page 208: Gray hurt because of Fay intervention. Guy Richard and Marvin Sleeper in the New York *Journal American,* October 15, 1953.

Page 209: The row with business representatives over Taft-Hartley changes is in proceedings of the Labor Department Advisory Committee on Taft-Hartley Reform, March 5–6, 1953, in the National Archives. The Meany quotations are from this transcript.

Page 210: Durkin's account of his problems with Eisenhower over Taft-Hartley are best summarized in his speech to the AFL convention in 1953. Ike's quotes are from *Mandate for Change.*

Page 220: "Most rabid anti-Communist in America." Meany on "The David Frost Show," Westinghouse Broadcasting Company, October 7, 1971.

Page 220: "Long cigar instead of an umbrella." Meany in *London Express,* July 7, 1953.

Page 220: "Just because Molotov." Meany to National Press Club, June 29, 1955.

Page 221: "We have never swallowed." Meany to League for Industrial Democracy, April 10, 1954.

Page 221: "Deadly drift into defeatism." Meany to American Legion convention, September 1, 1954.

Page 221: "The only acceptable assurance." Meany in *American Federationist,* April 1953.

Page 221: Meany's positions on various issues considered by the Labor Department's Trade Union Advisory Committee, and the CIA's interest in labor programs, are in Labor Department archives.

Page 224: "Destroy the railroad workers labor union." *My War with Communism,* by Miguel Ydígoras Fuentes, Prentice-Hall, Englewood Cliffs, N. J., 1963.

Page 224: A strong wave of anticommunism. Romualdi, *Presidents and Peons.*

Page 225: "Supporting the wrong people." The Mazey and Knight quotes are in Radosh, *op. cit.*

Page 227: "Preventive war." "George Meany, Top Man in the AFL-CIO," by Irvin Ross, the New York *Post,* December 8, 1955. The "sparks fly and hackles rise" quotes are also from this Ross profile.

# Chapter Eleven

Secondary sources for this chapter included *The Enemy Within,* by Robert F. Kennedy, Harper & Brothers, New York, 1960 (the Kennedy quotations are from this book); Hutchinson's *The Imperfect Unions; The Man in the Middle,* by Nathan W. Shafferman, Doubleday, New York, 1961; and *Crime Without Punishment,* by Senator John S. McClellan, Duell, Sloan and Pearce, New York, 1962. James P. Kelly, who worked under Kennedy as an investigator for the McClellan committee, had interesting insights on Kennedy's attitude toward Meany. The A. J. Hayes transcript in the Columbia Oral History Project was helpful.

Page 235: Three reasons for labor to worry about corruption. Meany to convention of AFL-CIO Industrial Union Department, 1957.

Page 244: "Meany says, 'You have got to get rid of Hoffa.'" English to Teamsters convention, 1961.

Page 245: "We can't depend upon the law." Meany to Labor Studies Center, November 8, 1969.

Page 251: The Hoffa quotation is from *The Trials of Jimmy Hoffa,* by James Riddle Hoffa, as told to Donald I. Rogers, Henry Regnery Company, Chicago, 1970.

Page 253: "Meany knows where to find me." Hoffa in the *Washington Evening Star,* February 19, 1959.

Page 253: "He's blocking us now." Hoffa in *Life,* May 25, 1961.

Page 256: "The particular policies adopted." "The Constitution and Government of the AFL-CIO," by John Hutchinson, *California Law Review,* December 1958.

Page 261: "We thought we knew a few things." Meany to IUD convention, 1957.

# Chapter Twelve

Reuther's objections to Meany's leadership are in the Cormier-Eaton biography. James Carey and Jack Conway, both long-time associates of Reuther, also discussed them with me at length. Albert Zack, who worked for Reuther as a press man before the merger, and then became Meany's public relations director, watched the feud as a nonobjective insider. Reuther was killed several months before I began this book. Hence Meany was reticent in talking about their differences. Peter McGavin was helpful on the internal disputes negotiations; Richard Deverall, on foreign programs; Joseph Loftus, on Meany's relations with outsiders, especially the press.

Page 266: "Abe Raskin's problem." Meany in 1970 Labor Day interview.

Page 267: The Sulzberger quotation is in his *Long Row of Candles,* The Macmillan Company, New York, 1969.

Page 273: Lovestone's plaints to Deverall are in the Deverall papers, Catholic University archives.

Page 277: "As far as Latin America was concerned." Romualdi, *op. cit.*

Page 278: The Wilkins memorandum is in the Labor Department archives.

Page 281: "Until he was eight months pregnant." Quoted in Cormier-Eaton.
Page 289: "Come on, let's get out of here." Quoted in Cormier-Eaton.

# Chapter Thirteen

Interview sources included Arthur Goldberg, W. Willard Wirtz, Joseph Keenan, Representative Richard Bolling, former Senator Joseph S. Clark, Boris Shishkin, Charles Zimmerman, Stanley Ruttenberg, and Don Slaiman. Meany discussed his relations with President Kennedy in an oral history interview for the Kennedy library with Goldberg. Unfortunately, there is almost as much Goldberg as Meany in the transcript. Meany's civil rights record is discussed by Benjamin F. McLaurin in a Columbia Oral History Project tape. Useful books were *Kennedy,* by Theodore Sorensen, Harper & Row, New York, 1965 (Sorensen's quotations on Kennedy's labor views while in the Senate are from this book); *A Thousand Days,* by Arthur M. Schlesinger, Jr., Houghton Mifflin, Boston, 1965; and *Power and Politics in Labor Legislation,* by Alan K. MacAdams, Columbia University Press, New York, 1964 (one of the most incisive books ever written on Congress).

Page 300: "Reuther did the job." Conway quoted in Cormier-Eaton.
Page 306: "There was a built-in prejudice." Meany on "Eternal Light," NBC radio, June 13, 1971.
Page 309: "We never backed down." Meany to AFL-CIO national civil rights conference, September 2, 1964.
Page 323: "That resolution is so anemic." Reuther quoted in Cormier-Eaton.

# Chapter Fourteen

Page 328: "Not . . . one cent from the CIA." Meany press conference, February 20, 1967.
Page 329: An AID background memo. "Policy and Procedure for AID-Supported African-American Labor Committee Programs and Projects," November 8, 1968.
Page 329: Romualdi's comments on Cuban labor, and his trip to Havana for Meany, are in *Presidents and Peons.*
Page 330: Victor Reuther's critical comments on the AIFLD are reprinted in *The Vista of American Labor,* published by the Voice of America in 1966.
Page 331: Meany on business role in AIFLD. Speech to Chicago Executives Club, September 20, 1963.

# Chapter Fifteen

Johnson's labor record prior to the White House is in *Sam Johnson's Boy,* by Alfred Steinberg, The Macmillan Company, New York, 1968. *Toil and Trouble,* by Thomas R. Brooks, Thomas Y. Crowell Company, New York, 1972 (second edition), discusses the labor policies of the Johnson Administration. Andrew Biemiller, Nelson Cruikshank, and Representative Bolling were helpful with Meany's legislative collaboration with the Johnson Administration. Willard Wirtz's papers for his years as labor Secretary are in the National Archives; unfortunately, much of the material he wrote for the White House was whisked away to the Lyndon B. Johnson Library in Austin, Texas, and is not available to researchers. The memos quoted in this chapter are from material left in the National Archives. The general tone of relations between Johnson and Meany is contained in dozens of laudatory speeches Meany made during 1964–68 on behalf of Administration programs.

Page 337: Johnson's postassassination meeting with Meany and other labor leaders is in a transcript issued by the White House press office.

Page 353: "We have a commitment." Meany to Virginia State AFL-CIO convention, August 19, 1965.

Page 353: "Do you think the Communists would stop?" Meany to American Legion convention, August 31, 1966.

Page 353: "I am quite sure." Meany to Virginia State AFL-CIO, *ibid.*

Page 355: "Confused, haphazard and chicken-hearted." Meany in the *American Federationist,* June 1954.

Page 357: Abbreviated findings of the Kraft poll were reported in the *American Federationist,* August 1967.

Page 358: The Fulbright hearings, formally, are "American Institute for Free Labor Development" hearings before Senate Foreign Relations Committee, August 1, 1969. These hearings contain a lengthy compendium of articles (strongly revisionist) on AFL-CIO foreign activities.

Page 360: Halberstam's biography of Kennedy is *The Unfinished Odyssey of Robert Kennedy,* Bantam Books, New York, 1969.

Page 361: Kennedy's ADA speech is quoted in Catchpole, *How to Cope with COPE, op. cit.*

Page 361: "He was mayor just a very, very short time." Meany to International Union of Electricians, September 19, 1968.

Page 363–64: The Unruh quote, the Gilligan episode, and the "rich women with baggy tits" remarks are from *An American Melodrama,* by Lewis Chester, Godfrey Hodgson, and Bruce Page, Viking Press, New York, 1969.

Page 365: "Spectacle of Southern governors." *The Kennedy Legacy,* by Theodore Sorensen, The Macmillan Company, New York, 1970.

Page 365: "I saw the invaders." Meany to International Association of Machinists, September 3, 1968.

Page 367: "We were able to turn that around." Meany in 1970 Labor Day interview.

Page 368: The Kirkland quote is from *The Making of the President 1968,* by Theodore H. White, Atheneum, New York, 1969.

# Chapter Sixteen

The Meany-Reuther feud is well documented in the broadsides from each camp. Meany's case is in "To Clear the Record," a 98-page report issued by the AFL-CIO executive council in March 1969. Reuther made his indictment in *UAW Administrative Letters* dated December 28, 1966, and February 8 and April 5, 20, and 21, 1967. Jack Conway, who is no longer in the labor movement, was most helpful in presenting Reuther's side of the case. UAW officers who spoke with me asked anonymity, apparently for fear of irritating Meany and disrupting chances for the UAW's re-entry into the AFL-CIO, which could be achieved by the time this book is printed.

Page 372: "The custom has been." Meany press conference, January 1965.

Page 385: "They made a decision." Meany to the Communications Workers of America, September 3, 1968.

Page 393: The Leslie memo quoting Albert Zack is in the Labor Department archives.

Page 402: "Only in being head of an organization." Meany in 1969 Labor Day interview.

# Chapter Seventeen

Meany's fury with Nixon erupted with full force a few months after I began working on this book; hence this chapter and the next are based substantially upon firsthand observation of their confrontation, over a period of more than one year. The evolution of Nixon's economic game plan is told in *Nixon in the White House*, by Rowland Evans and Robert Novak, Random House, New York, 1972. Meany's comments on the evolution of the AFL-CIO apprenticeship programs and the Philadelphia Plan are from talks to the building and construction trades department conventions in 1967 and 1969; to the Labor Studies Center, March 11, 1970; to the National Press Club, January 12, 1970; and to the 1969 AFL-CIO convention. Don Slaiman and the AFL-CIO civil rights department inundated me with material on Outreach and other apprenticeship programs. Joseph Loftus of the Labor Department assisted me in obtaining the Nixon Administration's side of several spats with the AFL-CIO.

Page 405: "It is unmistakably clear." Meany statement, May 1, 1970 (later endorsed by executive council).

Page 406: "I think that I played a very important role." Meany in 1969 Labor Day interview.

Page 407: "A breakthrough, a new benchmark." *AFL-CIO News*, April 11, 1970.

Page 407: "More liberal than any man in the White House." Meany in 1970 Labor Day interview.

Page 407: The Larson comments were in a speech to the Public Affairs Luncheon Club, Dallas, Texas, April 20, 1970.

Page 418: The Swayduck quotation is from the winter 1970 *Lithopinion,* journal of Local One of the Amalgamated Lithographers of America.

Page 419: "Exploitation." Meany press conference, February 15, 1971.

Page 421: "A very low form of life." Nixon to Treasury Department employees, February 9, 1969.

Page 422: "His policy for bringing down the inflation." Meany to United Transportation Union, August 24, 1971.

Page 424: "The thing is open and shut." Meany in 1970 Labor Day interview.

Page 426: "It actually adds up to this." Meany to United Transportation Union, *op. cit.*

Page 427: "M&M." Connally on "Today," NBC, August 17, 1971.

Page 429: "A little word about this man is important." Meany to United Transportation Union, *op. cit.*

# Chapter Eighteen

This chapter is based largely upon firsthand coverage of Meany before and after his confrontation with Nixon at Bal Harbour.

Page 431: "Not only a tiger but a dynamo." "George Meany: At War with That Man in the White House," by A. H. Raskin, the New York *Times Magazine,* January 23, 1972.

# INDEX

Abel, I. W., 200, 359, 362, 363, 433–434, 463
Ackley, Gardner, 351
Adams, K. C., 153–154
Adams, Sherman, 207
Aerospace workers, 452, 461
AFL. *See* American Federation of Labor
AFL-CIO. *See* American Federation of Labor-Congress of Industrial Organizations
*AFL News-Reporter*, 212, 216, 217, 226, 228, 263
Africa, labor interests in, 133, 221, 277, 278, 279, 331
African-American Labor Center (AALC), 329, 332, 386
Agency for International Development (AID), 328, 329, 331, 332, 357, 358, 382
Agricultural Workers Organizing Committee (AWOC), 398–399
Aircraft industry, 103–104, 415
Allen, Robert S., 98n.
Alliance for Labor Action (ALA), 401
Alliance for Progress, 328, 332
Alsop, Joseph, 460
Altmeyer, Arthur, 215
Amalgamated Clothing Workers, 36, 61, 202, 240, 316
American Communist party, 120, 121
American Federation of Government Employees, 327
American Federation of Labor (AFL), 70–73, 114, 141; anticommunist stance of, 119, 122, 123, 124–126, 128–132, 136, 147, 152, 177, 220–221, 223–225; beginnings and history of, 70–73; and Brindellism, 15, 27; building trades councils, 15, 27–28; charges of communism against, 56–57, 64; and Communist disclaimer oath, 147–153; and depression unemployment, 29–32; general conservatism of, Green quoted, 79; and ILA corruption, 186–194; and prevailing wage issue, 58, 67, 70; and racial discrimination, 305–309; Taft-Hartley opposed by, 144–146, 148; and unemployment insurance, 30–32,

139, 164; traditionally conservative on strikes, 40, 54, 58
**and CIO**, 70, 181–182, 199; as international rivals, 119, 124, 125, 126, 133, 227; cross-raiding, 70, 88, 184, 185, 194–195, 196–197, 199; jurisdictional disputes, 83–84, 95, 97, 194–195, 196, 197; Korean War ULPC collaboration, 170–172, 174–176, 182; no-raiding pact, 184, 195, 196–200; unity feelers (1946), 141; unity talks (1942), 88–92; unity talks (1953–55), 184–185, 186, 193, 194–205, 227, 275–276; World War II "harmony," 83, 87, 124–125, 138, 182
**conventions:** of 1931, 31; of 1932, 32; of 1935, 88, 308; of 1938, 48n., 117; of 1939, 70, 73–77, 117; of 1941, 308; of 1943, 100, 109; of 1944, 123; of 1947, 148–153, 155, 157, 306; of 1952, 177, 178; of 1953, 192, 211–212; of 1954, 195, 199, 222; of 1955, 204, 220; voting at, 73
**international involvements of**, 117–120, 123–137, 221–225; boycott of WFTU, 125–126; and BTUC, 117, 123–125, 126, 133; European free trade unions aided, 119, 123, 128–132, 135–136, 227, 228; foreign aid supported, 119, 134–135, 221–222; FTCU foreign arm of AFL, 119, 123, 127n., 129–130; funding, 128–130, 378n.; Guatemalan coup of 1954, 223–225; ICFTU member, 133–134, 176, 225–227; and IFTU, 123; and Indochina, 354–355
**in Korean War:** confrontation with Truman over economic stabilization, 166–176, 177; no-strike pledge offered, 167, 168
**and Lewis's UMWA:** readmission talks (1943), 109, 111; readmission (1946), 141–142; withdrawal (1947), 153–154
**organization**, 71–72; autonomy of affiliated unions, 184, 203–204, 265; federal unions, 148, 165, 209; financial problems, 166; internal politics, 73–74; internal structure,

American Federation of Labor (AFL)
(*continued*)
202, 203; organizational campaigns,
165–166, 209; presidency of, 81,
142, 153, 179–180; in states, 202
**political activity of,** 220; abstinence
of early decades, 36, 61–62, 63,
145, 156, 161n., 218; activist role
adopted, 138, 145, 155–166; congressional voting profiles published,
156, 159, 161, 164, 216; legislative
lobbying, 72, 77, 80–81, 144–146,
156, 212–215; LLPE, 153, 157–159,
161–166, 178, 217; in 1948 election, 158–163; in 1950 election,
164–165; in 1952 election, 177–
178; in 1954 election, 215–217;
Stevenson endorsed, 178, 218
**and wage controls:** Korean War, 167–
168, 171–172, 175; World War II,
102, 104, 105, 111–112, 139, 167
**in World War II:** in FDR's "labor
cabinet," 92; on National Defense
Mediation Board, 83–84, 85–86;
no-strike pledge, 87, 97, 98, 103,
107, 111, 139; and wage freeze,
102, 104, 105, 111–112, 167; War
Labor Board, 87, 91, 97, 102, 112
American Federation of Labor-Congress
of Industrial Organizations (AFL-
CIO), 4–5, 264–265, 463–467; and
ALA, 401; ethical practices code
of, 203, 234, 240, 248, 256, 268,
373; ethical practices committee,
193, 234–235, 244, 247, 258, 261;
expulsions from, 251, 256, 258,
316, 318, 401; factional rivalries,
264–265, 268–289, 291–292, 371–
401 (*see also* Reuther, Meany
and); headquarters, 220; Industrial
Union Department (IUD) of, 203,
274, 284, 326–327, 392–393, 399–
401; leadership criticized, 291–292,
372, 375, 387, 388–389, 401, 415;
organizing of farmworkers, 374,
398–401; organizing problems,
286–289, 309, 324–327, 464, 466–
467; UAW withdrawal from, 327,
356, 387–398
**anti-corruption drive of 1950's,** 233–
262, 283; expulsion of Teamsters,
247–252, 278, 324; policy on Fifth
Amendment use, 236–238, 240, 262
**civil rights struggle in,** 305–323; antidiscrimination clause, 202, 206,
309; antidiscriminattion enforcement, 309–318; Fair Employment
Practices Commission asked, 306,
318–323, 340; Meany's gradualism,

310–312, 316–318, 337; result
statistics, 323n.; WDL, Outreach,
LEAP programs, 408–410, 412
**conventions:** of 1955, 205–206; of
1957, 249–251, 258, 278; of 1959,
193, 280, 281, 287, 311–313; of
1961, 252–253, 287, 288, 302, 325;
of 1963, 323, 389; of 1965, 356; of
1967, 351, 356, 358, 392; of 1971,
439, 442–451
**and economic stabilization:** 1966
statement, 349; Nixon NEP, 426–
448, 453–458; withdrawal from
Pay Board, 457
**internal structure and workings,** 202–
204, 264, 381–382, 390, 391n.;
autonomy of affiliates, 5, 203, 234,
244, 265, 312; executive council,
203, 241, 243, 291–292, 372–373,
375, 464; jurisdictional disputes,
201, 271, 278, 282–289; jurisdictional peace plan, 289, 325, 371;
merger problems on state and local
level, 202–203, 282, 284–286
**international involvements,** 223, 228,
271–281, 328–335, 377; called "too
anti-Communist," 332, 415; foreign
programs put under ICFTU, 276,
278–279; funding, 278, 328–329,
331, 332, 334–335, 357–358; ILO,
378–384; Khrushchev visit, 280–
281; in Latin America, through
AIFLD, 328–335, 358, 377, 385–
387; Meany-Reuther differences,
227, 272–273, 275–281, 377–389;
policy formulation, 382, 383, 385,
387–388; Vietnam, 353–354, 355–
358, 389, 414, 415
**merger agreement,** 201–205, 227,
275–276; goals, 206, 466; name,
205; principles, 201–202, 309;
structure, 202–204, 273–274; on
top officers, 202, 285
**political activity,** 5, 220, 467; candidate endorsements, 459; COPE,
217, 219, 293, 301, 344, 352, 362,
365–369, 419; Humphrey endorsed,
362–367; Johnson endorsed, 342–
343, 360; Kennedy endorsed, 301,
legislative lobbying, 5, 229–232,
295–299, 304, 319–323, 341–342,
346–348, 466, 467; in 1956 election, 217–219; in 1958 election,
294; in 1960 election, 301; in 1964
election, 342–344; in 1966 election,
351–352; in 1968 election, 358–
369; in 1970 election, 417, 419; in
1972 election, 459–561; Stevenson
endorsed, 218–219

American Federation of Labor-Congress of Industrial Organizations (AFL-CIO) (*continued*)
  **statistical data:** membership, 4, 286, 324, 326–328; number of affiliated unions, 4
American Federation of State, County and Municipal Employees (AFSCME), 327, 328–329, 334, 464
*American Federationist, The,* 79–80, 115, 224, 354, 355
American Institute for Free Labor Development (AIFLD), 328–335, 358, 377, 382, 385–387
American Labor party (1936), 61–64
American Medical Association, 229, 230, 231–232, 341
American Newspaper Guild, 266, 328–329
American Retail Federation, 406
American Statistical Association, 113
American Telephone & Telegraph Co., 348
Americans for Democratic Action (ADA), 319, 340, 354, 359, 361
Anastasia, Albert, 187
Andrews, Elmer F., 32, 33, 45
Andrews, John B., 32
Annis, Edward, 231
A. Philip Randolph Institute, 341, 409
Apprentice and training programs, and Negroes, 313, 314, 318, 341, 407–412
Arbenz, Jacobo, 223, 224
Arbitration: compulsory, legislation on, 302, 339–340, 456; principle of voluntarism, 83, 86; wartime boards, 83, 86–87, 175–176. *See also* War Labor Board
Area Redevelopment Act, 304
Arévalo, José, 223
Armas, Carlos Castillo, 224–225
Asia, 136–137, 279; Communist guerilla activities, 132–133; FTUC and AFL interests in, 123, 127–128, 130. *See also* India, Vietnam
Asian-American Free Labor Institute (AAFLI), 357
Associated Industries of New York, 33, 41, 44
Association of Catholic Trade Unionists, 314
Auriol, Vincent, 221
Auto industry, 324, 402; minority employment, 410n.; strikes, 140, 141, 265, 391; unionization, 182; wage increases, 171, 175, 349
Automation, 30, 324, 456

Autonomy of affiliated unions, 5, 66, 127, 184, 203–204, 244, 265, 296; and corruption cases, 187–189, 190–192, 234; invoked as excuse for civil rights gradualism, 308, 312

Baker, Jacob, 54
Bakery and Confectionary International Union of America, 256–259
Balance-of-payments deficit, 424, 455
Barbash, Jack, 206
Barkan, Alexander, 352–353, 363, 365–366
Barkley, Alben W., 178, 216
Barros, Adhemar de, 333
Barry, James, 59
Baruch, Bernard, 52, 220–221
Bates, Harry, 74–75, 78, 237, 240, 248, 267, 271, 289, 312, 372
Batista, Fulgencio, 329–330
Bayh, Birch, 412–413
Beck, Dave, 193, 196, 198, 199, 204, 235–244, 246, 247–248, 251, 267, 294, 437; corruption exposed, 233–235, 239–240, 241–242; and Fifth Amendment, 236–238, 239–240, 262; pension of, 248; suspension of, 240–243; in rival federation plot, 195–196, 198
Beck, Dave, Jr., 239, 241
Becu, Omer, 226
Beha, James, 43, 44
Beirne, Joseph, 246, 249, 254, 289, 291, 303, 330, 378n., 384, 385–386
Bell, George T., 449–450
Bellino, Carmine, 234
Berger, Henry W., 136
Berlin, 280; JFK and Meany in, 304–305
Bernstein, Harry, 377
Berry, George L., 63
Betheran, Robert, 128
Biaggini, Benjamin F., 440
Biemiller, Andrew J., 213–214, 231, 235, 295, 296, 297, 319–320, 322, 336, 340–342, 345, 347–348, 351, 352, 365–366, 412, 440–442, 451, 452, 461, 462, 464
Bittner, Van, 104
Black, Hugo, 30
Black, Robert, 94
Blount, Winton, 407
Boldt, George E., 437–439, 441, 444, 452–453, 456, 458
Bolling, Richard, 298, 299, 319, 322
Bonnet, Henri, 221
Borella, Victor, 342
Boyd, Harold, 315

Bracero program, 398–399
Braden, Thomas W., 129–130, 378n.
Bradley, William, 193
Brandeis, Louis D., 32
Branion, R. C., 60
Brazil, AIFLD operations in, 332–333
Brennan, Peter, 344, 414
Brennan, Sidney, 248
Brewery Workers Union, 195, 372
Brewster, Frank, 240, 246, 248
Bricker, John, 207
Bricklayers union, 73, 74, 251, 289, 339;
    segregated locals, 312
Bridges, Harry, 152, 455–456
Brindell, Robert P., 15–16, 27
Brisbane, Arthur, 58
British colonies, 132–133, 134, 221
British Guiana, 329, 333–334
British press, on Meany and Reuther,
    225, 226
British Trades Union Congress
    (BTUC), 117, 123–125, 126, 132,
    133
Broder, David, 460
Brooks, Thomas R., 325
Brophy, John, 107, 127, 202
Brotherhood of Locomotive Firemen
    and Engineers, 206n., 310, 312
Brotherhood of Railroad Trainmen,
    206n., 312
Brotherhood of Sleeping Car Porters,
    206, 252, 301, 307, 308, 309, 310
Brown, George, 185, 276
Brown, Irving, 127, 128–130, 131, 136,
    227, 278, 378n.
Brown, Pat, 352
Brownell, Herbert, 208
Brownlow, James, 235
Buckley, James, 419
Buckmaster, L. S., 269, 372
Budenz, Louis, 30
Building Service Employees Interna-
    tional Union, 48, 252
Building trades councils of AFL, 15,
    27–28, 56, 198; New York, 29, 344,
    414
Building trades unions, 15, 18–27, 48,
    54, 67, 88, 240, 251, 296; jurisdic-
    tional disputes, 22, 70, 88, 97, 196–
    197, 278, 282–285, 287, 288, 289;
    oppose WPA "security" wage, 51–
    60, 67–68; prehire contracts, 209,
    299; racial discrimination in 311,
    313, 314, 317, 407–412. See also
    Construction industry
Bulganin, Nikolai, 272, 277–278
Bureau of Labor Statistics, 94, 112–114
Burke, Admiral Arleigh, 281
Burke, Thomas, 26–27

Burnham, Forbes, 335
Burns, Arthur, 406, 422, 423, 427, 429,
    439, 443
Business: AFL-CIO cooperation with,
    in Latin American programs, 330–
    331; antiunion activity cloaked by
    wartime "patriotism," 82, 115;
    attitudes toward unions, 168; "big,"
    Meany's contempt for, 49, 145, 173–
    174, 445; and closed-shop issue,
    82, 87, 96; coalition to rewrite
    Wagner Act, 406; discriminatory
    hiring, 321, 336–337; favored in
    New Economic Plan, 426, 428,
    445, 453–454, 456–459; hostile to
    fringe benefits, 173; Kennedy's
    show of force with, 302; Korean
    War economic stabilization ma-
    chinery controlled by, 167, 168–
    170, 173–176; and National De-
    fense Mediation Board, 83; post-
    World War II stance, 138, 139, 140,
    144–145, 157, 287; and Taft-Hartley
    revision, 209–210, 211; and War
    Labor Board, 93, 95–96, 98, 100.
    See also Profits
Business agents, 20–27
Business unionism, 28
Byrne, William T., 45, 47
Byrnes, James F., 101–103, 111, 131

Calame, Byron E., 463–464
California farmworkers, 398–400
Cambodian invasion, 405, 413–414, 447
Campaign contributions, by labor, 63,
    144, 156, 162
Caples, William, 439
Captive coal mines strike (1941), 85,
    86
Carey, James B., 84, 88, 91, 120, 127,
    135, 155, 169, 194, 199, 301, 372;
    and AFL-CIO postmerger disputes,
    268–269, 270–271, 274, 281, 288,
    373; ULPC member, 172, 176–177
Carlough, Edward, 251
Carpenters Union, 15, 23, 28, 73, 148,
    196–199, 251, 339; jurisdictional
    disputes, 286, 287, 288
Carswell, G. Harrold, 412
Castro, Fidel, 329–330
Catchpole, Terry, 220
Cenerazzo, Walter, 147
Central Intelligence Agency (CIA),
    118–119; connection with AFL-
    CIO aired, 377–378, 382, 385–386;
    funding of labor programs by, 129–
    130, 328–329, 334; Latin American
    involvements, 223–224, 328–329,
    334

Central Trades and Labor Council of N.Y., 28, 49–50, 118, 125, 187; and La Guardia, 65; WPA strike, 52, 53, 55–57

Chajn, Leon, 379–380

Chamberlain, Joseph P., 32

Chapman, William H., 16

Chavez, Cesar, 374, 398, 399

Chemical workers, jurisdictional disputes, 286, 287–288

Child labor, 115; legislation, 47, 48–49

Ching, Cyrus S., 168, 209

Churchill, Judge Thomas, 26–27

Churchill, Sir Winston, 220

CIO. See Congress of Industrial Organizations

Citrine, Walter, 123–125

Civil rights, 301, 306–323; AFL and fair employment, 177, 306; AFL antidiscrimination clause, 306; AFL-CIO clause, 202, 206, 309; AFL-CIO "gradualistic" approach to, 310–312, 316–318; AFL-CIO lobbying, 318–323; issue of superseniority and hiring preferences for Negroes, 321–322; labor's bad record, 305–306, 308, 310–315, 321. See also Discrimination

Civil Rights Act of 1964, 337, 340–341, 407; AFL-CIO asks equal employment section, 318–323

Civil Rights Commission, 319

Civilian Conservation Corps, 40, 55

Clark, Joseph, 293

Clay, General Lucius D., 131, 169, 172

Clifford, Clark M., 159, 169

Closed-shop issue, 82, 86, 87, 96, 176, 466; in "captive coal mines," 85–86; "elective plan," 96; "maintenance of membership" plan, 96; public employees, 407; Taft-Hartley, 144, 209, 210, 344

Coal mining industry: "captive mines" closed-shop issue, 85–86; conditions, 107; portal-to-portal pay, 110; strikes, 40, 85, 86, 93, 107, 108–111, 142; wage increase, Phase Two, 452

Coefield, John, 23, 74, 75–76

Cogen, Charles, 356

Cohen, Ben, 103, 108

Cohen, Ray, 255

Cohen, Wilbur, 215

Cohn, Lee, 271

Colby, Bainbridge, 46

Cole, David, 438

Collective bargaining, 86, 95, 140, 168, 287, 406, 407, 420, 421; internal union discipline needed, 296;

limited by Kennedy wage-price guidelines, 302, 342; limited by Nixon NEP, 426, 429, 431, 432, 433, 444, 456; limited by wartime controls, 95, 99, 115, 171, 175; right to, 38n. See also Arbitration

Collier's magazine, 80n., 141

Colonialism, 132–133, 134, 221

Colorado State AFL-CIO, 356

Cominform, 127, 132

Committee on Industrial Organization, 182

Committee on Political Education (COPE), 217, 219, 293, 301, 344, 352, 357, 359, 362, 365–369, 392, 419, 460

Communications Workers of America (CWA), 246, 254, 289, 296, 368–369

Communism: AFL-CIO principle against, 202; charges of, against unions, 56–57, 63–64; cold war stance of AFL (AFL-CIO) against, 119, 122, 124–126, 128–132, 136, 177, 332, 415; in Guatemala, 223–224; influence in ILO, 379–380, 383; Meany and, 57, 119, 120, 122–123, 125–126, 129, 135–137, 220–221, 223–228, 267, 272, 354, 355; union infiltration by, 57, 121, 122, 132, 133, 140, 148, 152, 185

Communist China, recognition, 377, 388

Communist disclaimer oath, Taft-Hartley, 144, 146, 147–153

Compulsory arbitration. See Arbitration

Condon, William F., 190

Conference for Progressive Labor Action (CPLA), 30, 32, 36, 45

Congress: AFL-CIO legislative lobbying, 5, 229–232, 295–299, 304, 319–323, 341–342, 346–348; AFL legislative inefficiency, 72, 155–156; AFL legislative lobbying, 77, 80–81, 144–146, 156, 212–215; anti-labor moods, 67–70, 83, 85, 86, 95, 108, 138, 143–145; control gained by Republicans (1946), 143, 145, 155–156; control regained by Democrats (1948), 162; Democratic gains of 1958, 231, 294; Landrum-Griffin Act, 296–299; and New Deal legislation, 46–47, 51, 67–68; Republican/Southern Democrat coalition in, 156, 163, 169, 181, 214, 217; seniority system, 218; voting records published by AFL, 156, 159, 161, 164, 216; Taft-Hartley Act, 144–146, 155–

Congress (*continued*)
156, 163, 214–215. *See also* Congressional elections

Congress of Industrial Organizations (CIO), 70, 72, 111, 126, 181–205, 220, 374; beginnings of, 182; Communist infiltration, 121, 122, 132, 133, 140, 148, 152, 185, 455; *de facto* labor wing of Democratic party, 156; in FDR's "labor cabinet," 92; internal structure, 202–203; on National Defense Mediation Board, 83–84, 86; and 1948 campaign, 161; Political Action Committee, 156, 165, 217; postwar strikes, 141; Reuther succeeds Murray, 180–184; state organization, 202–203; Taft-Hartley opposed, 146; in United Labor Policy Committee, 170–172, 174–176; and War Labor Board, 87, 91

**and AFL,** 70, 181–182, 199; CIO demand for AFL expungement of corruption, 186, 193, 234; cross raiding, 70, 88, 184, 185, 194–195, 196–197, 199; as international rivals, 119, 124, 125, 126, 133; jurisdictional disputes, 83–84, 95, 97, 194–195, 196, 197; Korean War ULPC cooperation, 170–172, 174–176, 182; no-raiding pact, 184, 195, 196–200; unity feelers to CIO unions by AFL (1946), 141; unity talks (1942), 88–92; unity talks (1953–55), 184–185, 186, 193, 194–205, 227, 275–276; World War II "coexistence," 83, 87, 124–125, 138, 182

**international involvements,** 126, 133, 225, 227; foreign aid supported, 132, 135; ICFTU member, 133, 176, 227; IFTU member, 124; WFTU member, 125–127, 132, 133

Congressional elections: of 1946, 143, 157; of 1948, 157–159, 162–163; of 1950, 164–165; of 1952, 178; of 1954, 215–217; of 1958, 294; of 1966, 351–352; of 1970, 417, 419

Connally, John, 423, 427, 429, 433, 435, 443, 450, 462

Connell, William, 365

Consiglio, Tom, 363

Construction industry: boom, 284; costs, 412, 423–424; Brindell scandal, 15–16; depression unemployment, 29; interstate highway program, 219–220; New York City, 25–27, 29, 49; strikes and picketing, 25; wages, 423–424. *See also* Building trades

Consumer price index rise: 1945–1950, 171; 1945–1952, 219; 1952–1955, 219; 1968–1970, 422; 1971 freeze, 448

Contracts nullified by wage freeze, 426, 428, 429, 431, 433, 444–445; and retroactive wages, 433, 440–442, 444, 452

Conway, Jack, 300, 304, 371, 375, 385, 387

Cooper, John Sherman, 280

Corbett, Ray, 360

Cormier, Frank, 206, 304, 402

Cost of Living Council, 425, 426, 433–436, 438, 439, 453, 455

Cost-of-living index, 100, 102, 112, 115, 172, 420; Meany's attack on, 112–114

Coughlin, Charles E., 54, 61

Council of Economic Advisers, 348, 350–351, 371, 423, 439

Craft severance, 185

Craft unionism, 182, 185, 201

Croizat, Ambroise, 155

Cross, James, 256–259

Cruikshank, Nelson, 118, 189, 190, 215, 229–231, 260, 292, 341, 345–346

Cuban revolution, 329–330

Cullen family, 7–8, 14

Curran, Joseph, 193, 252, 253, 269, 387, 388, 401


Daley, Richard, 365

Daly, Mark, 33, 41, 43, 44

Damien, Nat, 150

Davis, William H., 83, 88, 94, 97, 99, 100, 102–104, 106–107, 109, 110, 112, 438

Davis-Bacon Act, 173, 423–424

Day, Albert F., 29

Deakin, Arthur, 132, 133

Debs, Eugene V., 308

Delaney, Philip, 379

Democratic party: CIO the *de facto* labor wing of, 156; "Dump Johnson" movement, 356, 358–359, 361, 364; labor and, 36, 40, 60–65, 68, 69, 156, 177–178, 220, 294–299, 302; labor alienation, 415–417; National Committee criticized, 352–353, 366; in New York, 40–42, 46, 47; in 1936 election, 60–64; in 1948 election, 162; in 1952 election, 178; in 1954 election, 217; in 1958 election, 231, 294; in 1966 election, 352; 1968 National Con-

Democratic party (*continued*)
vention, 364–365; 1972 presidential
contenders, 459–461
Denham, Robert N., 146, 148
DeNille, J. Lawrence, 54
Department of Health, Education and
Welfare (HEW), 215, 229, 230–
231
Department of Labor, 112, 208, 222–
223, 303, 338, 340, 409–410, 416,
447, 454, 458. *See also* Durkin,
Martin; Goldberg, Arthur; Hodg-
son, James; Mitchell, James; Perkins, Frances; Schultz, George;
Tobin, James; Wirtz, Willard
Depression unemployment, 29–30, 40,
45, 60, 70
Detroit *Free Press,* 377
Deverall, Richard L.-G., 127–128, 130,
132, 134, 136, 273, 276, 278–280
Dewey, Thomas E., 160, 161, 187, 188
Dirksen, Everett M., 340–341, 347–348
DiSalle, Michael V., 168, 171
Discrimination, racial: AFL clause
against, 305; AFL laxness, 305–
306, 308; AFL-CIO clause against,
202, 206, 309; AFL-CIO "gradualistic" approach to, 310–312, 316–
318; all-black locals, 312; in
apprenticeship programs, 313, 314,
318, 407–412; in empoyment, 320–
321, 336–337, 410–411; on federally financed projects, 311, 315;
at labor conventions, 307, 315, 317,
318; labor union record, 305–306,
308, 310–315, 321; union autonomy cited as labor excuse for
inaction, 308, 313
DiVittorio, Giuseppe, 130, 132
Dodd, William, 13, 16
Doherty, William C., 248, 269, 270
Doherty, William, Jr., 333
Dominican Republic, intervention in,
377
Doran, William L., 16
Douglas, Paul, 163, 216, 297, 352
Dreier, Mary, 32
Dual unionism, 128, 152, 258, 296, 317,
401
Dubinsky, David, 36, 61, 62, 63–64, 90–
91, 122, 197, 198, 226, 267–268,
276, 351; and civil rights, 318, 322;
FTUV member, 123, 136, 278; and
foreign affairs, 118, 120, 121,
127n., 131, 277; quoted on Meany,
66–67, 118; political activist, 156,
158, 164; and Reuther, 390, 393;
and Teamster corruption, 240, 243

Dulles, Allen, 129, 223
Dulles, Florence Rhea, 141
Dulles, John Foster, 222, 267
Dunnigan, John J., 41, 42
Durkin, Martin, 208–212, 216, 220, **443**

Eaton, William J., 206, 304, 402
Economic growth: Eisenhower years,
304; Johnson years, 348–349, 420;
Kennedy years, 302, 420; Nixon's
effect, 422
Economic stabilization programs:
Korean War, 166–176, 427; Nixon,
*see* New Economic Plan; Vietnam
War years' failure, 349–351, 420;
World War II, 98–105, 111–114
Economic Stabilization Act (1971),
452, 453
Economic Stabilization Agency (1950),
168
Edwards, Frank, 166
Ehrlichman, John D., 437
Eisenhower, Dwight D., 46, 178, 179,
181, 215, 216, 217, 219–220, 228–
232, 339; economic recessions and
unemployment, 216–217, 270, 304,
324; foreign affairs, 220, 221, 222,
223, 225, 227, 280, 281; and
Landrum-Griffin, 298; Meany and,
207–208, 212, 219–220, 228–229,
232, 345, 404; and Taft-Hartley,
178, 208–212
El Paso Natural Gas Company, 464
Elections. *See* Congressional elections;
Presidential elections
Electrical industry, 349; strikes, 140
Electrical workers, 50, 92, 152, 173; job
discrimination, 311, 410. *See also*
International Brotherhood of Electrical Workers; International Union
of Electrical Workers; United
Electrical Workers
Emspak, Julius, 87, 92, 152
English, John F., 240, 243–246, 251
Epstein, Abraham, 32, 33
Equal Employment Opportunity, Presi-
dent's Committee on, 314–315,
321, 336
Equal Employment Opportunity Com-
mission (EEOC), 407–408
Escalator clauses, 173
Ethical practices code of AFL-CIO, 203,
213, 234, 240, 248, 256, 373
Europe: AFL field work for free trade
unions, 119, 123, 128–132, 135–
136, 227, 228, 378n.; Marshall aid
to, 135
Excess profits tax, World War II, 140

Fair employment practices legislation, 214, 340, 407; labor demands for, 177, 306, 318–323, 340

Farley, James A., 42, 60, 61–62

Farmworkers, 374, 389, 391, 398–401

Faupl, Rudolph, 379–381, 382–384

Fay, Joseph, 189–190, 208

Fearon, George R., 42

Featherbedding, 302, 310

Federal Bureau of Investigation (FBI), 341, 356

Federal employees, 327, 407, 425

Federal Reserve Board, 420, 423, 429

Federal Shipbuilding and Dry Dock Co., 83

Federal unions, 148, 151, 165–166, 209

Federally financed projects: and job discrimination, 311, 315; Philadelphia Plan, 410–412; prevailing wage issue, 51–60, 67–68, 423

Feller, Karl, 372, 373

Ferguson, Joseph, 165

Fifth Amendment privilege, AFL-CIO policy on, 236–238, 240, 262

Financial reporting by unions, 295–296

Fishburn, John, 333

Fitzsimmons, Frank, 255, 401, 432, 434–436, 458

Flemming, Arthur, 231

Flight Engineers Union, 302

Florida farmworkers, 400

Flynn, Edward J., 8

Folsom, Marion B., 46

Ford, Gerald, 354

Ford Motor Company, 391

Foreign aid, 119, 133, 134, 135, 221–222

Foreign Operations Administration, 221–222

Foreign policy, labor, 117–137, 328–335; AIFLD programs in Latin America, 328–335, 358, 377, 382, 385–387; AFL-CIO programs transferred to ICFTU, 276, 278–279; AFL criticized for, 135–137, 228; anticommunism of AFL, 119, 122, 123, 124–126, 128–132, 136, 220–221, 223–225; basic postwar goals, 118–119, 134, 137; CIO, 126, 132, 133, 135, 225, 227; differences of factions after AFL-CIO merger, 272–273, 275–281, 377–389; foreign aid supported, 119, 132, 134–135, 221–222; FTUC as arm of, 119, 123, 136, 276; funding of programs, 128–130, 278, 328–329, 331, 332, 334–335, 357–358, 378n.; in Guatemalan coup of 1954, 223–225; ILO, 378–384;

isolationism of 1930's, 117, 119; labor attaché system, 134–135, 136–137, 222–223; postwar European unionism aided, 119, 123, 128–132, 135–136, 227, 228, 378n.; Vietnam issue, 353–358, 389, 401, 414

Foreign trade, 377, 388, 397, 424, 425

Fortas, Abe, 412

*Fortune,* 140, 465

Fowler, Henry, 32

France, 135; AFL involvement in, 128–130, 135–136; and Tunisia, 221

Free Trade Union Committee (FTUC), 119, 123, 127n., 136, 137, 275–278; funding, 128–130; Reuther opposed, 275–276

Freedman, Monroe, 297

Freeman, Gordon, 339

Frey, John P., 32, 308

Friele, Berent, 330, 333

Fringe benefits, 115, 173, 348

Fuentes, Miguel Ydígoras, 223

Fulbright, J. William, 335, 357–358

Furniture industry, jurisdictional disputes, 286, 288

Galbraith, John Kenneth, 354, 415

Garment industry, 36, 40, 47; jurisdictional dispute, 286; wages, 351

Garner, John Nance, 62, 63

Geijer, Arne, 331

General Electric Company, 80, 83, 168; "Manifesto," 173

General Motors Corporation, 141, 168, 171, 183, 265, 287, 349, 392

Geneva conferences: on Indochina (1954), 354–355; summit (1955), 220, 227

Germany, 61, 125, 134, 144, 227, 280, 378n.; AFL field work in, 127, 130, 131–132, 135–136, 169

Gildea, James, 426

Gillette, Guy, 216

Gilligan, John, 363

Ginsburg, David, 365

Gleason, Thomas W. ("Teddy"), 357, 414

Goldberg, Arthur, 170, 172, 177, 200, 201, 258, 300, 303; as Secretary of Labor, 302, 303, 332, 346, 407

Golden, Clint, 135

Goldfinger, Nathaniel, 434, 453, 456

Goldwater, Barry, 229, 298, 323, 342–344, 450

Gompers, Samuel, 15, 31, 34, 61, 63, 71, 72, 156, 161n., 188, 463, 465, 466

Goodell, Charles, 419

Gordon, Kermit, 439, 453

Gordon, Lincoln, 333

Gorman, Patrick E., 249, 250, 251

Goulden, Joseph A., 8

Goulart, João, 332–333

Government employees, 325, 327, 407, 425

Government role, in labor relations, 30–33, 39, 48, 86, 115, 139–140, 295; under New Economic Plan, 425, 432, 457–458; Nixon's early view, 421; wartime, 83, 86, 99, 101–104, 139. *See also* Pay Board; War Labor Board

Grace, J. Peter, 330, 331

Graham, Frank P., 87–88, 95, 399, 439

Gray, Herman, 32

Gray, Richard J., 198, 208, 235, 284–285, 288

Green, Ernest, 408n.

Green, William, 30–32, 36, 40, 63, 65, 68, 87, 92, 158, 160, 164, 167–168, 190, 197, 259; AFL president, 71–74, 88, 97; background and characterization, 71–72; and CIO, 176, 182; failing health and death of, 177–179; and international affiliations of AFL, 124, 133; leaves foreign affairs to Meany, 116, 118, 123, 137; and Lewis's AFL-CIO unity scheme, 88–90; and Lewis's ascendancy, 142, 146–147; and Meany, at AFL, 76–77, 78–81, 92, 114, 116, 139, 212; on National Defense Mediation Board, 83, 85; at 1947 convention, 149, 150, 152–153; in prevailing wage issue, 58, 67, 70; quoted, on AFL conservatism, 79; and racial discrimination, 305; ULPC member, 171, 174–177; and UMWA readmission question, 109, 141

Grill, Joseph E., 62

Grogan, John J., 373

Guatemalan coup of 1954, 223–225

Gutierrez, Victor Manuel, 223


Haber, William, 19, 21, 27, 28

Haggerty, C. J., 288

Halberstam, David, 360–361

Hall, Paul, 253, 254, 384, 388, 418, 428, 464

Hard-hat demonstrations, 414, 416, 447

*Harper's Magazine*, 415

Harriman, Averell, 135, 217, 301

Harris, Fred, 365

Harris, Thomas, 297

Harrison, George H., 157, 158, 161, 163, 165, 175, 179, 243, 270, 285, 289, 303, 355

Hartke, Vance, 412

Hartley, Fred, 143–144, 283

Hartnett, Al, 254

Hatters Union, 64, 251

Hayes, A. J., 195, 234–235, 288–289, 303

Haynsworth, Clement F., 411n., 412–413

Haywood, Allan S., 170, 183, 185, 194

Hedlund, Don, 241–242

Helstein, Ralph, 372, 373, 388

Henderson, Leon, 102

Henning, John, 346

Herling, John, 292, 308, 339, 347, 371, 418

Herzog, Lester, 59–60

Hettrick, James T., 15–16

Hill, Herbert, 313, 318

Hill, Lister, 214

Hillman, Sidney, 36, 61–64, 70, 156, 393

Hinrichs, A. Ford, 113, 114

Hitler, Adolf, 61, 124, 144, 228, 307

Hobby, Oveta Culp, 215, 231

Hodgson, James, 425, 427–429, 433–438, 444, 452, 453

Hodson, William, 40, 67

Hoffa, James R., 193, 244–256, 259, 283, 294–295, 360; charges against, 244, 245, 250; elected Teamsters president, 247–248; expulsion by AFL-CIO, 248–254; imprisonment, 255, 401; paroled, 255, 458; pension of, 255–256; relatives on payroll, 255; trials of, 250, 254

Hoffmann, Sol, 251

Holborn, David, 20, 21, 23, 24

Hollings, Spessard, 412

Hoover, Herbert, 36

Hoover, J. Edgar, 341, 464

Hopkins, Harry, 51–54, 57–60

"Hot cargo" contracts, ban on, 298, 299

Hughes, Harold, 460

Humphrey, Hubert H., 163, 231, 297, 300, 319, 342, 361–367, 385; labor record, 362; Meany's doubts about, 365–366, 460, 461; Meany's support for, 362–369; presidential candidate in 1968, 362–369, 420–421, 461; in 1972, 461

Hungarian uprising of 1956, 277, 280

Hunt, Lester C., 163

Hushing, W. C., 165, 213

Hutcheson, Maurice, 197, 198–199, 208, 253n., 261–262, 339

Hutcheson, William, 15, 28, 36, 71, 72–74, 81, 139, 148, 153, 156; and

Hutcheson, William (*continued*)
  Lewis's schemes, 88–91, 109, 196–199
Hutchinson, John, 15, 91, 256

Ickes, Harold, 108–109, 110
India, 132; Meany-Reuther dispute over, 272–273, 275
Indochina agreement of 1954, 355
Industrial Union of Marine and Ship-building Workers, 373
Industrial unionism, 27, 70, 88, 138, 141, 206, 287; losses and organizing drive, 324, 326–327; versus craft unions, 182, 185, 201
Inflation: Johnson and, 348–350, 419–420; Kennedy's measures against, 302, 348; Korean War, 167; 1945–1950, 143, 171; Nixon's "Game Plan" and, 421–424; and Nixon's NEP, 447–448, 457–458; wage increases blamed for, 442–443; World War II, 99, 102–103. *See also* Cost-of-living index
Injunctions, in labor disputes, 26–27, 38, 50, 142; Taft-Hartley rule, 144
Interest rates, 422, 423; uncurbed, 426
Internal Revenue Service, 453, 454
International affairs. *See* Foreign policy
International Association of Machinists, 73, 103, 182, 195, 228, 288, 296, 384, 433, 461; color bar, 306; membership figures, 324, 415
International Brotherhood of Electrical Workers, 339
International Brotherhood of Long-shoremen (IBL), 192–193, 263
International Brotherhood of Teamsters (IBT). *See* Teamsters Union
International Chemical Workers, 401
International Confederation of Free Trade Unions (ICFTU), 133–134, 136, 176, 184, 225–227, 276–280, 331–332; AFL-CIO programs transferred to, 276, 278–279, 282; Hungarian revolt, aid of, 276–277; in Latin America, 330, 331
International Federation of Trade Unions (IFTU), 123, 124
International Harvester Company, 98
International Labor Organization (ILO), 117, 378–384, 387, 388
International Ladies Garment Workers Union (ILGWU), 14–15, 30, 61, 67, 127n., 217, 318, 358, 359, 460; foreign programs of, 18, 120, 121, 123, 128, 130
International Longshoremen's Association (ILA), 28, 31, 187–194, 357,

414; corruption, 181, 187–189, 190–192, 233, 234; expulsion from AFL, 192; readmission to AFL-CIO, 193–194, 311–312; representation elections against IBL, 192–193, 263; "shapeup" hiring, 187, 188, 190, 191
International Longshoremen's and Warehousemen's Union, 152, 455–458
International Molders and Foundry Workers Union, 314
International Oil, Chemical, and Atomic Workers, 329
International Typographical Union, 69, 105, 203, 251
International Union of Electrical Workers, 254, 373; color bar, 311
Investment tax credit, 304, 425
Iron Workers Union, 410–411
Isolationism, 117, 119
Israel, 226
Italian Chamber of Unions, 314
Italy, 120, 135; AFL involvement in, 129, 130–131; Meany in, 226–227
Ives, Irving, 42, 214

Jackson, C. Grayson, Jr., 454
Jackson, Gardner, 91
Jackson, Henry, 239, 300, 459–461
Jacobs, Joseph, 260
Jacoby, Neal, 439
Jagan, Cheddi, 329, 333–335
Japan, right-wing labor movement, 136
Jennings, Paul, 373
Jewish Labor Committee, 314
Johnson, Howard, 438
Johnson, General Hugh, 52–59, 67
Johnson, Lyndon B., 262, 290, 336–362, 366, 369–370, 371, 379, 380, 382–383, 392, 393–394, 406; domestic legislative achievements, 229, 340–342, 359–360, 370; "Dump Johnson" movement, 356, 358–359, 361, 364; economic conditions under, 348–351, 419–420; labor record as President, 340, 343, 345–348, 351, 359; Meany and, 300–301, 336–340, 343, 345, 350–351, 353, 358–360, 369–370, 413; as senator, and labor legislation, 213, 214, 294, 295, 297–298; as vice-president, 300–301, 315, 318, 336; and Vietnam War, 337–338, 349–350, 353, 355–358, 360, 361, 377
Johnston, Eric, 168, 171
Jones, David, 266
Jouhaux, Léon, 128

Juliano, Pasquale, 449–450
Jurisdictional disputes, 22, 83–84, 95, 97, 165, 194–195, 196, 197; after AFL-CIO merger, 201, 271, 278, 282–289, 325; Miami Agreement (1959), 287; in organizing, 109, 201, 286–289, 325; peace plan, 289, 325, 371; strikes barred by Taft-Hartley, 144. *See also* Raiding

Kadar, Janos, 276
Kaminsky, George, 42
Kampelman, Max M., 365
Katzenbach, Nicholas, 319, 322
Keating, Kenneth, 360
Keenan, Joseph D., 132, 155, 156, 167, 169–170, 213, 297, 303, 339, 345; head of LLPE, 158–159, 161, 164–165
Kefauver, Estes, 178, 218
Kelly, James P., 245
Kempton, Murray, 239
Kennedy, Edward M., 413, 460
Kennedy, John F., 281, 290, 293, 302–306, 327, 336, 337, 360, 379, 398; AFL-CIO endorsement of, 301; in Berlin, 304–305; civil rights efforts of, 314, 319–323, 340; labor record as president, 302, 304, 322–323, 340, 407; and Landrum-Griffin, 293, 294–296, 299; Latin American policies, 328, 334; Meany and, 290, 293, 299–301, 303–305, 323; and Medicare, 229, 231, 232, 301, 341; wage-price guidelines, 302, 348, 421
Kennedy, Robert F., 259, 293–294, 298, 322, 360–361, 385; investigation of Beck and Teamsters, 233–234, 239, 242; investigation of Hoffa, 245, 252, 360; presidential candidate, 359–365
Kennedy, Thomas, 83, 149
Kenya Federation of Labor, 279
Kethley, Anna, 281
Khrushchev, Nikita, 221, 272, 280–281
King, Martin Luther, Jr., 316, 318, 322, 341
Kinney, Patrick F., 23
Kirkland, Lane, 320, 368, 385, 426, 434, 438, 440, 451, 463
Klein, Herbert G., 450
Klenert, Lloyd, 259–260
Knauer, Virginia, 454
Knight, John, 41
Knight, O. A., 225, 281
Knights of Labor, 18, 71
Knowland, William, 205, 214
Knudsen, William S., 97

Korean War, economic stabilization program, 166–176, 177, 427
Koveleski, Emanuel, 34, 35–36
Kraft, John, 357
Krane, Jay, 279
Kroll, Jack, 161, 202, 217
Kubitschek, Juscelino, 332

Labor attaché system, 134–135, 136–137, 222–223
"Labor cabinet," FDR's, 92, 102, 116
Labor corruption, 16, 66, 231–233, 260–262, 467; AFL-CIO constitutional bar, 202, 234, 240, 248; Brindellism, 15–16; Cross' Bakers Union, 256–259; ILA, 181, 187–189, 190–192, 233, 234; Meany's methods of handling, 256; Teamsters Union, Beck, 233–243; Teamsters Union, Hoffa, 244–256; UTWA, 259–260
Labor Education Advancement Program (LEAP), 409
Labor legislation, 38, 50, 70, 466; under Johnson, 340–342; under Kennedy, 302, 304; New York State, 38–39, 40, 41–48; under Truman, 143–145, 164. *See also* Landrum-Griffin Act; Right-to-work laws; Social Security; Taft-Hartley Act; Unemployment insurance
Labor's League for Political Action, 63
Labor's League for Political Education (LLPE), 153, 157–159, 161–166, 167, 178, 217
La Follette, Robert, 158, 161n.
La Guardia, Fiorello, 50, 61, 62, 64, 68–69, 308, 343; labor support, 65–66, 187
Landon, Alfred M., 61, 64
Landrum, Phil, 298
Landrum-Griffin Act of 1959, 261, 296–299, 303, 368, 373; "bill of rights" amendment to, 296–297; Kennedy's original bill, 293, 294–296
Lapham, Roger, 96, 100, 105
Larson, Reed, 407
Latin America, labor interests in, 117, 118, 123, 128, 223–225, 277, 279; AIFLD, 328–335, 358, 377, 382, 385–387
Laundry Workers International Union, 260
Lazzerini, William, 314
Leadership Conference on Civil Rights, 319, 340, 413
League of Nations, 117
*League Reporter, The,* 164
Lee, Ernest, 292, 425
Leheney, Ray, 241

Lehman, Herbert L., 33, 34, 40, 62, 64, 187, 337; labor legislation of, 38–39, 41–42, 43–48; Meany and, 38–39, 41, 43–45, 47, 70; as senator, 214

Lemke, William (Liberty Bill), 61

Lens, Sidney, 136

Leslie, John W., 393

Levey, Stanley, 204

Lewis, John L., 63, 71, 72, 84–92, 138, 170, 185, 202, 221, 283, 292, 392; as CIO leader, 70, 72, 84–85, 182; calls "captive coal mines" strike, 85, 86; causes 1943 coal strike, 107–111; Communist disclaimer oath refused by, 148–153; and National Defense Mediation Board, 84, 85–86; party orientation, 156; and postwar UMWA strikes, 142, 160; and Roosevelt, 36, 63, 84–86, 88, 107–111, 141–142; and War Labor Board, 87, 88, 107, 108–111

**and AFL,** 146–154; his AFL-CIO unity scheme, 88–92; ask readmission of UMWA (1943), 109, 111; gains readmission (1946), 141–142; presidency coveted, 142, 146–147, 153; rival federation plot of 1954, 195–196, 198, 200; withdrawal of UMWA, 153–154

Liberal party, New York, 64n., 163, 337

Liberals, Meany's views on, 272, 354, 358, 364–365

Lincoln, Murray, 164

Lindsay, John V., 459

Lippmann, Walter, 172

Little Steel companies, unionization, 84

Little Steel Formula (LSF), 100–101, 103–104, 112, 115, 139

Livingston, John W., 264, 286–287, 326

Lobbying: AFL, in Washington, 77, 80–81, 144–146, 156, 212–215; AFL-CIO, 5, 229–232, 295–299, 304, 319–323, 341–342, 346–348, 467; individual union autonomy in, 203; Meany, in New York, 38–39, 40, 41, 42–49, 70, 159; at state level, 159

Lodge, Henry Cabot, 281

Loftus, Joseph A., 266, 416, 418, 431, 437, 438

Long, Breckinridge, 61

Long, Edward, 339

Long, Huey P., 42, 53

Los Angeles *Times,* 377, 392, 439

Lovestone, Jay, 127, 128–131, 134–135, 149, 153, 186, 205, 226, 227, 273, 275–282, 292, 460; background, 120–123; FTUC director, 119, 123, 136, 276–278; the Reuthers and, 121, 275–278, 281, 377–378, 387–388; Vietnam statements, 353–354, 355–356

Low-cost housing, 48, 177, 216

Lowenstein, Allard, 361

Luciano, Lucky, 187

Lutz, John, 292

Lynch, George, 251

Lyons, John H., 434, 463

Lyons, Thomas, 82

MacAdams, Alan K., 296, 297, 299

MacArthur, General Douglas, 128, 168

McCabe, Howard, 334

McCarran, Pat, 51

McCarthy, Eugene, 356, 359, 362, 363–364

McCarthy, Joseph R., 207

McClellan, John, 233, 235, 246, 251, 296–297, 347

McClellan Committee, 256, 257, 258, 260, 261–262, 287, 293, 294; Beck investigation, 233–237, 239–240, 242; Hoffa investigation, 244, 245, 248n., 250, 252

McCormack, John, 217, 218

McCracken, Paul W., 422, 423, 424, 427

McCurdy, Joseph, 251

McDevitt, James L., 155–156, 158–159, 217

McDonald, David J., 183, 185–186, 199, 200–201, 203, 206, 277, 291, 296, 318, 373; and Hoffa, 252; in rival federation plot, 195–196, 198, 200

McFetridge, W. C., 179

McFetridge, William L., 252

McGavin, Peter, 260, 285–286

McGinnies, Joe, 41

McGovern, George, 364, 459, 460

MacGowan, Charles J., 170

McGrady, Edward F., 52–53, 57

Machinists, 73, 103, 182, 306. *See also* International Association of Machinists

McInerney, Joseph A., 48

McLaurin, Benjamin F., 309, 310

McLelland, Andrew C., 334

McMillan, E. J., 95, 97

McNamara, Pat, 216

Maguire, Edward, 29, 33

Maguire, Richard, 365

Mahoney, Jeremiah T., 65–66

"Maintenance-of-membership" plan, 96

Mansfield, Mike, 348

Marchitto, Anthony (Tony Cheese), 187

Marín, Luis Muñoz, 269

Marshall, George C., 135

Marshall Plan, 119, 129, 130, 132, 135
Martin, Homer, 121
Massachusetts Federation of Labor, 33
*Masses, The*, 192
Mayer, Robert, 250, 292
Mazey, Emil, 225, 356–357, 377, 391–392, 395
Mboya, Tom, 279
Mead, James, 158
Meany, Eugenia McMahon (wife), 4, 14–15, 39, 75, 81, 267, 290, 301
Meany, George: on AFL/CIO split, 181–182; and AFL/CIO unity talks, 184–185, 186, 194–195, 197, 199–205, 213, 227, 275–276; and AFL president Green, 76–77, 79–81, 92, 114, 116, 137, 139, 182; anticommunism of, 57, 119, 120, 122–123, 125–126, 129, 135–137, 220–221, 223–228, 267, 272, 354, 355; autonomy of unions respected, 66, 187–188, 190, 191, 203, 234, 265; British press on, 225, 226; and charges of communism, 56–57; and Charles E. Wilson, 168–169, 172–174; and closed-shop issue, 86, 87, 96; and Communist disclaimer oath, 147, 149, 151–153; his contempt for big business, 49, 145, 173–174, 445; cost-of-living index attacked by, 111–114; Democratic party criticized by, 415, 417; distrust of press, 265–266, 291; in FDR's "labor cabinet," 92, 116; and Gov. Lehman, 38–39, 41, 43–45, 47, 70; and Haynsworth nomination, 412–413; and La Guardia, 50, 65–66; and Landrum-Griffin Act, 295–299; and LLPE, 157–158, 161–162, 164–166; and minimum wages, 31, 47–48; National Defense Mediation Board member, 83, 84, 85–86; NEP Pay Board member, 433–442, 448, 453–458; nepotism, 292; "never conducted a strike" charge against, 25, 51, 253; at 1939 AFL convention, 73–77; and Nixon's Commission on Productivity, 424; plumbers union membership, 13, 15, 16, 20n.; in plumbers strike (N.Y., 1927), 25–27; and prevailing-wage issue and WPA strike, 51–60, 67–68, 69; Reuther and, *see* Reuther, Meany and; and Robert Kennedy, 360–365; "strong defense" posture, 221, 227–228, 459; successor, speculations on, 463–464; and ULPC, 170–172, 174–176; and unemploy-ment insurance, 30, 31, 32–33, 44–46, 139; War Labor Board member, 87, 94–115, 116, 138, 140
  career of, 28–29, 138; AFL-CIO president, 5, 202, 230; AFL president, 179–180, 212–213, 463–465; AFL secretary-treasurer, 74–77, 78–82, 177, 179–180, 188, 189; building trades council secretary, 27–28; business agent, 16, 20–27; campaign for presidency of N.Y. State F of L, 33–35; National attention gained, 25, 27, 33, 46; N.Y. State F of L president, 35–37, 38–49, 66–70, 76, 78–79, 159, 187–188; N. Y. State F of L vice-president, 28; plumber, 13–14, 16; switch to career as union official, 16–17
  and corrupt unions, 66, 234, 256–262; bakers, 256–259; Brindellism, 16; ILA, 187–194; Teamsters (Beck), 233–243; Teamsters (Hoffa), 244–256; textile workers (UTWA), 259–260
  foreign affairs interests of, 116–117, 118–119, 122–126, 129, 131–132, 133–134, 137, 220–228, 328; AIFLD president, 330–332, 335; anti-Soviet stance, 119, 122, 125–126, 136, 220–221, 225–227, 272, 280–281; CIA subsidies denied, 129, 130, 328–329, 382; colonialism criticized, 221; disagreements with Reuther, 227, 272–273, 275–281, 377–389; foreign aid supported, 119, 135, 221–222; FTUC member, 123, 127n., 137, 278; Guatemalan coup of 1954, 223–225; and ICFTU, 133–134, 225–227, 277–280; speeches, 125–126, 134, 221, 226, 272; Vietnam War views, 337–338, 353–358
  as labor lobbyist: in Albany, 38–39, 40, 41, 42–49, 70, 159; spokesman against Taft-Hartley, 144–146, 159, 163; in Washington, 77, 80–81, 212–214, 229–230, 295–299, 320–322, 341, 342, 347–348
  and labor politics, 36, 39, 40, 42, 49, 218; endorsement of presidential candidates, 177–178, 217–219, 301, 343, 360, 362–367; enters national politics, 60–65, 138, 145, 155–166; in 1948 campaign, 161–162; in 1972 campaign, 458–461
  Lewis and, 147, 149, 152–153, 182; "Lew-McBeck" plan, 195–198; Meany caught in Lewis's AFL-CIO

Meany, George (*continued*)
    unity scheme, 88–92; UMW re-
    admission requests, 109, 141
  **the man:** characterization, 4–5, 39,
    267, 268–269, 291, 292–293; life
    style, 267, 292; mental astuteness,
    23, 29, 33; moral convictions, 256,
    260–261; personal integrity, 189–
    190; physical appearance, 3, 291;
    public behavior and image, 4, 266–
    267, 291; religiousness, 266
  **modus operandi of,** 4–5, 49, 230, 268,
    430; delegating ability, 161, 229;
    getting his way, 292, 375
  **personal data:** background, 7–8; in
    baseball, 10–11; birth date, 8;
    childhood, 7–11; children, 39, 81,
    292; choice of occupation, 11–13;
    education, 9–10, 11, 12–13; family
    and home, 4, 39, 81, 292; health
    problems, 267, 290–291, 376, 451–
    452; marriage, 14–15; salary, 5, 69,
    74, 267, 375–376, 451
  **and racial discrimination,** 306–307,
    309–323, 407–411; apprentice
    training programs, 407–410; gradu-
    alist approach, 310–312, 316–318,
    337; Philadelphia Plan, 410–411;
    quoted on equal employment, 320–
    321, 341
  **relations with U.S. Presidents:** Eisen-
    hower, 207–208, 212, 219–220,
    228–229, 232, 345, 404; Johnson,
    300–301, 336–340, 343, 345, 350–
    351, 353, 358–360, 369–370, 413;
    Kennedy, 290, 293, 299–301, 303–
    305, 323; Nixon, 366, 368, 404–
    407, 413–419, 426–427, 432–433,
    443–450, 453, 458–459; Roosevelt,
    60, 61–62, 63, 68–69, 111, 113–
    114, 116, 345; Truman, 161, 166–
    168, 174–175, 345
  **trade union philosophy of,** 465–466;
    early traditionalism, 18, 36–37, 40,
    47–48; move toward progressivism,
    67
  **and wage stabilization:** Korean War,
    167–168, 170–175; New Economic
    Plan, 426–433, 440, 451, 452, 454,
    456–458; 1960's failure, 349–351;
    World War II, 99–105, 111–112,
    114, 115
Meany, Michael Joseph (father), 7, 8,
    11, 12, 14, 16
Meatcutters Union, 251
Medicare, 342; labor goal, 177, 229–
    232, 337, 341–342; 1960 campaign
    issue, 229, 300, 301
Merrill, Lewis, 152

Meskimen, John J., 222
Metalworkers Union, 251, 278
Metcalf, Lee, 298
Meyer, Cord, Jr., 223
Meyer, Eugene, 83
Miami *Herald,* 450
Mikoyan, Anastas, 280
Millard, Charles, 277
Miller, William, 344
Mills, Wilbur, 232, 342
Minneapolis *Tribune,* 346
Minton, Bruce, 72
Mitchell, Clarence, 340, 412–413
Mitchell, James P., 216–217, 220, 223,
    278
Mitchell, John N., 418
Mohn, Einar, 234, 237, 248, 249, 251
Mondale, Walter F., 365
Morrison, Frank, 72–77, 78, 81
Morse, David, 379
Morse, Wayne, 87, 94–97, 105, 106,
    109–111, 439; as senator, 212, 217,
    340
Moses, Harry, 209
Moses, Robert, 40
Moyers, Bill D., 338
Mujal, Eusebio, 329–330
Mullaney, Joseph A., 76
Murphy, Charles S., 174
Murray, Eugene, 22
Murray, James E., 163, 214, 297
Murray, Philip, 83, 84, 85, 87, 88, 127,
    132, 152, 170, 183, 196, 202; death
    of, 178–179; in FDR's "labor cab-
    inet," 92; and Lewis's AFL-CIO
    unity scheme, 88–91; Taft-Hartley
    opposed by, 146; ULPC member,
    171, 174–176
Murrow, Edward R., 192
Muskie, Edmund, 459, 460
Muste, A. J., 30

National Association for the Advance-
    ment of Colored People
    (NAACP), 311, 313, 318, 319,
    340, 341, 412–413
National Association of Home Builders,
    423
National Association of Manufacturers,
    95, 96, 139, 140, 167, 210, 294,
    298, 406
National Commission on Productivity,
    424
National Council of Distributive Work-
    ers, 401
National Council of Senior Citizens,
    341
National Defense Mediation Board, 83–
    84, 85–86, 88

National Farm Workers Association, 399

National Industrial Recovery Act, 46, 52

National Labor Leadership Conference for Peace, 356–357

National Labor Relations (Wagner) Act, 63, 72, 86, 140, 144, 398, 406

National Labor Relations Board, 144, 166, 185, 192, 209, 214, 325, 406; on Communist disclaimer oath, 146, 148–149; representation cases, 194, 195, 209, 287

National Maritime Union, 193, 252, 387

National Recovery Administration (NRA), 52, 63

National Right-to-Work Committee, 283n., 407

Neely, Matthew M., 163

Negro American Labor Council (NALC), 313, 314, 317

Negroes: in AFL-CIO high office, 206; in apprenticeship and training programs, 313, 314, 318, 341, 407–412; job discrimination, 320–321, 336–337, 410–411; unemployment rate, 314, 320. See also Civil rights; Discrimination

Nehru, Jawaharlal, 272

Neikind, Claire, 170

Nelson, Donald, 168

Neuberger, Richard L., 216

New Deal, 37, 40, 46, 51–53, 60, 61, 69

New Economic Plan: freeze, Phase One, 425–433, 447–448; lack of profit controls, 426, 439, 454, 457–458; nullification of contracts, 426, 428, 429, 431, 433, 444–445; Phase Two, 433–442, 452–458 (see also Pay Board); price controls ineffective, 436, 439, 453–455, 457–458; retroactive wages issue, 433, 440–442, 444, 452; tax provisions, 425, 426, 452; wage increase limit, 440, 451, 452

New Hampshire primary, 1968, 359

New York American, 52, 55, 57, 58

New York City: building trades council, 15, 27–28, 29; building trades strikes against WPA, 51, 52–59, 67–68; construction industry, 15–16, 25–27, 29, 49; labor and La Guardia, 50, 65–66; hard-hats' march, 414; 1937 mayoral election, 65–66; 1934 welfare rolls, 40; WDL program, 408. See also Central Trades and Labor Council

New York Herald Tribune, 172

New York Post, 228

New York State: labor legislation, 38–39, 40, 41–48; legislature, 33, 39–47, 159; 1934 elections in, 40–41; in 1936 national elections, 61–64; unemployment insurance, 31–33, 38, 40, 44–46; workmen's compensation, 38, 42–44

New York State Federation of Labor, 28, 29, 62, 81–82, 118, 145; La Guardia endorsed by, 66; Lehman endorsed by, 40; legislative program of, 40, 41, 42–47, 48; Meany a vice-president, 28; Meany campaign for presidency of, 35–37; Meany president of, 35–37, 38–49, 66–70, 76, 78–79, 159; membership, 39, 73; 1934 convention, 33, 34–36; 1939 convention, 68–69; 1940 convention, 69; and prevailing wages, 60, 68; and unemployment insurance, 32, 33

New York Times, 26, 66, 68, 89, 91, 143, 175, 266, 272, 333, 381, 389, 410

Newsweek, 163, 189, 297

Newton, James Y., 141

Nixon, Richard M., 265, 404–429; at AFL-CIO 1971 convention, 443–444, 446–450; civil rights record of, 405, 411; and communism, 220, 425; Hoffa parole, 255, 458; labor record of, 219, 368, 407; and Landrum-Griffin, 297, 368; Meany and, 366, 368, 404–407, 413–419, 426–427, 432–433, 443–450, 453, 458–459; and Taft-Hartley, 211–212, 368; as vice-president, 211–212, 219, 297, 311; and Vietnam, 413–414

economic policies of, 4, 255, 405, 417, 419–458; Game Plan, 422–424, 445; wage and price controls, 420–421, 423, 425–429, 457–458. See also New Economic Plan

presidential candidacies: of 1960, 301; of 1968, 364, 366, 367, 368, 420–421; of 1972, 459

No-raid pact, 184, 195, 196–199, 288–289

No-strike pledge, World War II, 87, 97, 98, 103, 107, 111, 139; ends with war, 139–140; offered in 1950 by AFL, 167, 168

Norris-La Guardia Act, 26, 38, 50

North American Aviation Company, 83

Novik, Morris S., 50, 61, 62

Nuclear test ban, 388–389

O'Donnell, Kenneth, 319

Office of Defense Mobilization, 168
Office of Economic Stabilization, 101–102
Office of Price Administration (OPA), 113, 114, 143, 421
Office of Price Stabilization, 168, 169
Office of Production Management, 97
Office of Strategic Services (OSS), 118, 120, 123
O'Hanlon, John, 34, 42, 43
Olander, Victor, 31
Oldenbroek, J. H., 134, 227
Oliver, Eli L., 170, 176
One-man, one-vote rule, 348
Organizing, 464, 466–467; AFL, 165; AFL federal unions, 165–166, 209; AFL-CIO drive of 1960's, 324–327; costs, 165–166; of farmworkers, 374, 389, 391, 398–401; industrial, 70, 182, 324; jurisdictional problems, AFL-CIO, 201, 286–289; picketing for, 298; problems in South, 309, 466; right to, 38n.; staff, 166, 286; white-collar workers, 286, 324, 467. See also Jurisdictional disputes; Raiding
Outreach program, 409, 412
Overtime pay, 138, 164
Owens, Patrick J., 377–378

Pacific Maritime Association, 456
Packard Motor Company, 282
Packinghouse workers, 140, 175, 372, 400
Panto, Pete, 187
Parker, John, 413n.
Pay Board, Nixon's NEP, 433–443, 448, 453–458; AFL-CIO withdrawal from, 457; authority of, 434–436; chairman, 436–439, 444, 458; employer members, 440, 444, 456–458; initial tripartite set-up, 432, 433, 457; labor members, 433, 457–458; limit on pay increases, 440, 451, 452; and longshoremen's contract, 455–458; public members, 439, 440, 455–458; reconstituted "all-public," 458; retroactive wages decision of, 440–442, 444–445
Pearl, Philip, 85, 226, 273
Pearson, Drew, 98n.
Pegler, Westbrook, 189
Pension funds, union, corrupt use, 295
Percy, Charles, 352
Perkins, Frances, 71, 108, 169
Perkins, John A., 230–231
Peterson, Florence, 93, 139
Philadelphia Plan, 407, 410–412
Phillips, Kevin, 413–414

Picketing: building sites, 25; organizational, 298
Pitzele, Merlyn S., 116
Pizer, Morris, 288
Plumbers union, 208, 410. See also United Association
Poletti, Charles, 41
Political Action Committee (PAC) of CIO, 156, 165, 217
Politics, labor and, 36, 39, 49, 60–65, 158–159, 467; CIO, 156; endorsement of candidates, 36, 40, 62–63, 65–66, 69, 161n., 178, 217–219, 301, 343, 360, 362–367, 459; individual union autonomy in, 203; campaign financing, 63, 144, 156, 162. See also American Federation of Labor, political activity of; American Federation of Labor-Congress of Industrial Organizations, political activity of; Lobbying; Vote, labor
Possehl, John, 76
Postal reorganization bill, 407
Potofsky, Jacob, 240, 316–317, 337, 351, 373, 384, 387, 388, 392, 401
Powell, Adam Clayton, 313, 318
Pre-hire contract, 209, 299
Presidential Advisory Committee on Labor-Management Policy, 303
Presidential elections: of 1936, 60–64; of 1940, 69, 84–85; of 1944, 156; of 1948, 158, 159–163; of 1952, 177–178; of 1956, 217–219; of 1960, 300–301; of 1964, 342–344; of 1968, 358–369; of 1972, 459–461
Prevailing-wage issue, 51–60, 67–68, 69, 70, 423
Price, Harry, 73
Price Commission, NEP, 434, 436, 454
Price stabilization, 422; Kennedy/Johnson guidelines, 302, 342, 348–349, 421; Korean War, 167, 171–172, 175, 427; post-World War II failures, 143, 145, 171, 174; Vietnam War years failure, 349–351, 420
Nixon: his early views, 420–421, 423; NEP freeze, 425–426, 433, 447–448; NEP Phase Two, 434, 436, 439, 453–455, 457–458
World War II, 99, 101, 102–104; lack of success, 111–114, 115
Printing Pressmen's Union, 63
Profits, corporate: NEP lack of curb on, 426, 439, 454, 457–458; post-World War II, 143; restraints demanded, for economic stabilization,

Profits, corporate (*continued*)
167–168, 342; soaring in mid-to-late 1960's, 348–349, 420, 421; tax, World War II, 140

Public employees, 325, 327, 407, 425

Public opinion, on labor, 138, 142, 143, 341, 465; effect of union corruption on, 231, 235–236, 243, 246, 324

Quill, Michael J., 64, 152, 204–205, 252–253

Race relations. *See* Civil rights; Discrimination; Negroes

Raiding: between AFL and CIO, 70, 88, 184, 185, 194–195, 196–197, 199, 259; intra-AFL, 195; no-raid pact, 184, 195, 196–199, 288–289; Teamster attempts after ouster, 254. *See also* Jurisdictional disputes

Railroad unions, 125; compulsory arbitration laws, 302, 339–340; racial discrimination, 206, 310, 312; strikes, 142, 302, 406

Randolph, A. Philip, 206, 252, 301, 307–317, 341, 399, 408

Randolph, T. K., 251

Randolph, Woodruff, 203–204

Rarick, Donald C., 296

Raskin, A. H., 89–90, 91, 266, 431

Rauh, Joseph, 340

Rayburn, Sam, 218, 231, 294, 295, 297, 298

Reagan, Ronald, 352

Recessions, 1950's, 216–217, 270, 287, 324

Reed, James A., 63

Republican party: business-oriented, 145, 157, 177, 181; gains Congress in 1946, 143, 145, 155–156; labor friends of, 84, 156; in N.Y. State, 33, 40, 42, 46, 47; in 1936 election, 60, 61, 63–64

Reston, James, 266

Retail Clerks International Association, 326, 376

Retail, Wholesale and Department Store Union, 185, 356

Reuther, Victor, 264, 273–274, 275, 330, 377–378, 381–383, 385–386

Reuther, Walter, 92n., 121, 140, 225n., 253, 254, 303, 337, 345, 351, 432; AFL-CIO organizing drive headed by, 325–327; and AFL/CIO unity talks, 184–185, 186, 194–196, 199–205, 227, 275–276; aid to UFWOC, 399–400; austere life style of, 267–268, 269; characterization, 265, 374, 375; CIO president, 182–184,

199, 200, 206; and civil rights issue, 310, 322–323; death of, 402–403; decides on UAW withdrawal from AFL-CIO, 387, 393; decline of influence of, 371–375; demands made of AFL-CIO before UAW withdrawal, 389–392; and foreign affairs, 221, 227, 272–273, 275–281, 377–389; head of Industrial Union Dept., 203, 274, 326–327, 392–393, 400, 402; joins with Teamsters in ALA, 401; Lovestone and, 121, 275–278, 281; pro-Humphrey, 363; pro-Kennedy, 300–301, 304; pro-Stevenson, 217–218, 219; relations with press, 265; resignation from AFL-CIO executive council, 390; and Teamster corruption, 239, 240, 243; ULPC member, 176–177; and Vietnam, 355–356

**Meany and,** 263–289, 291, 304, 361, 371–402; confrontations, 264, 269–271, 300–301, 372–374, 381–385; differences in personality and attitudes, 264–269; distrust, 264; foreign policy disagreements, 227, 272–273, 275–281, 377–389; in jurisdictional disputes, 282–283, 287–289; M. comments on Reuther's withdrawal, 396–397, 402; Reuther quoted, 199, 402

Rickert, T. A., 71, 74

Riesel, Victor, 146, 152

Rieve, Emil, 278, 281, 373

Right-to-work laws, 158, 210, 339n.; 14b repeal sought, 344, 346–348, 352; National Committee, 283–284

Robinson, Archie, 425

Rockefeller, Nelson, 118, 215, 301, 333, 342, 404

Rogers, William, 418

Romney, George, 449

Romualdi, Serafino, 120, 128, 224–225, 277, 329–330, 332–334

Roosevelt, Eleanor, 272, 308, 399

Roosevelt, Franklin D., 33, 36, 70, 71, 77, 126, 156, 182, 306, 308, 343, 405, 418; as Governor of N.Y., 31, 42, 187; and Hillman, 36, 63, 71, 156, 393; labor endorsements of, 62–64, 69, 218; and Lewis, 36, 63, 84–86, 88, 107–111, 141–142, 182, 393; and Lewis's AFL-CIO unity scheme, 90–92; and Meany, 60, 63, 68–69, 111, 116; Meany's public criticism of, 111, 113–114, 345; and WPA, 51, 53; WPA wages, 57, 58, 59–60, 67–68, 69

Roosevelt, Franklin D. (*continued*)
   **his re-election bids:** of 1936, 60–64;
   of 1940, 69, 84–85; of 1944, 156
   **and World War II,** 69, 82, 83, 86,
   125; fight for economic stabiliza-
   tion, 98–99, 101, 102, 104; "labor
   cabinet," 92, 116; 1943 coal strike,
   108–111; War Labor Board, 86–88,
   93, 99, 102, 104, 109–110, 426
Rose, Alex, 64, 251, 337
Rosenberg, Anna, 90, 170
Rosenberg, Ludwig, 342
Ross, Michael, 134, 278
Rostow, Walt W., 338
Roth, Herrick, 425
Rovere, Richard, 143
Rowe, James H., Jr., 365
R. R. Donnelly & Sons, 105–106
Rubber workers, 141, 182, 372
Rusk, Dean, 338, 356, 379, 380, 383
Rustin, Bayard, 341, 408, 410, 412
Ruttenberg, Stanley, 230, 374–375
Rutz, Henry, 127, 131
Ryan, Joseph P., 28, 31, 50, 56, 57, 64,
   65–66, 76, 193; background of,
   187; ILA corruption under, 187–
   188, 190–192

Saillant, Louis, 127, 132
Santo, John, 205
Sarnoff, David, 281
*Saturday Evening Post,* 116, 378n.
Saxbe, William, 450
Sayres, Dean, 438
Schlesinger, Arthur, Jr., 53
Schnitzler, William, 180, 202, 204, 213,
   215, 256, 258, 270, 271, 278, 288,
   317, 323n.
Schoemann, Peter, 289, 301
Scholle, Gus, 286
Schrade, Paul, 363, 364
Seafarers International Union, 253, 418
Secondary boycotts, 144
"Security wage," WPA, 52–60, 67–68,
   69
Segal, Martin, 12, 18, 25
Seniority issue, in Negro hiring, 321–
   322
Shaplen, Robert, 357
Shapp, Milton, 352
Sheet Metal Workers Union, 351, 408,
   410
Shefferman, Nathan, 234, 239, 240
Shelley, John, 298
Shipyard industry, 175
Shishkin, Boris, 78–79, 80, 135, 153,
   177, 178, 215, 227, 315–317
Shultz, George, 406, 411, 416, 427–428,
   434–436, 438, 440, 443–444, 457

Shumway, Devan L., 450
Siciliano, Rocco C., 440, 458
Siemiller, Roy, 384
Sims, Curtis, 256–258
Slaiman, Don, 322, 341
Sloan, Alfred P., 281
Slum clearance, 48, 304
Smith, Alfred, 36, 40, 41, 42, 61, 187
Smith, Floyd (Red), 433–434
Smith, Margaret Chase, 213
Smith, Walter Bedell, 222
Snyder, Alvin, 450
Snyder, John W., 143, 169
Social Security: Act of 1935, 30, 44,
   45, 46–47; Administration, 215;
   disability benefits, 229; increases,
   164, 304, 342; and Medicare, 177,
   230, 342
Socialist party of New York, 61, 63
Sorensen, Theodore, 299, 302, 305, 319,
   320, 364
South Vietnam, labor unions, 357
Soviet Union: in ILO, 379–380, 383;
   Meany's attitude toward, 119, 122,
   124–126, 136, 220–221, 225–227,
   272, 280–281; and 1956 Hungarian
   uprising, 276, 280; trade unions of,
   123, 125–126, 136; WFTU dominated by, 126–127, 132
Spicer Manufacturing Company, 97
SST plane, 415, 461
Stalin, Joseph, 121, 127, 135, 225, 228
Stassen, Harold, 221–222
*State Federation Bulletin* (N.Y. F of
   L), 47, 48, 66
States: AFL and CIO merger problems,
   282, 284–286; AFL versus CIO
   organization in, 202–203; legisla-
   tive election campaigns and labor,
   158, 159; prevailing wage laws,
   423; right-to-work laws, 158, 210,
   344; unemployment insurance, 30,
   31–33, 44, 46, 164
Steamfitters union, 22–23, 410
Steel industry: closed shop, 176; juris-
   dictional disputes, 287; strikes, 140;
   unionization, 84, 182; wage in-
   creases, 176, 348
Steel Workers Organizing Committee of
   CIO, 84
Steelman, John, 86, 169
Stein, Herbert, 432
Steingut, Irwin, 42
Stevenson, Adlai E., 178, 217–219, 290,
   303
Stevenson, Coke, 297
Stonorov, Oskar, 403
Strikers, Taft-Hartley disenfranchise-
   ment of, 208–210

Strikes: AFL view of, 40, 54; auto workers, 140, 141, 265, 391; barred during NEP freeze period, 429; Eisenhower years, 219; jurisdictional, 83–84, 144; coal miners, 40, 85, 86, 93, 107, 108–111, 142; dock workers, 40, 347, 455–456; Kennedy years, 302; Meany's involvement in, 25–27, 51–59; of 1934, 40; of 1940–1941, 82–83; post-World War II, 138, 140–141, 142, 143; prewar mediation efforts, 83–84, 85–86; railroads, 142, 302, 406; Taft-Hartley rules on, 144; use of injunctions in, 26–27, 38, 50, 142, 144; World War II, 93–94, 95–96, 103, 107 (see also No-strike pledge); against WPA, New York City, 51, 52–59, 67–68
Stroller, Anthony (Tony Bender), 187
Stuart, George, 256–257
Stuart, John, 72
Stulberg, Louis, 359, 460
Suffridge, James, 292, 303, 326, 376
Sullivan, Francis X., 41, 42, 43, 65, 66
Sullivan, John, 28, 34
Sulzberger, C. L., 267
Summerfield, Arthur, 294
Swayduck, Edward, 418
Swope, Gerard, 83
Symington, Stuart, 170, 231, 290, 339

Taft, Robert A., 143–144, 164–165, 167, 207–211, 212
Taft-Hartley Act of 1947, 143–145, 155–156, 160, 165, 298, 368; ban on political use of union funds, 144, 162; Communist disclaimer oath of, 144, 146, 147–153; Eisenhower and, 178, 208–212; labor opposition to, 144–146, 148, 159, 161, 177, 208–209, 216; 1949 repeal effort, 163; provisions of, 144, 158, 184, 208–209; repeal endorsed by Stevenson, 178; revision attempts, 165, 209–212, 214–215; Section 14b, 210, 339n., 344, 346–348, 352
Tammany Hall, 28, 36, 46, 50, 61, 62, 64, 65, 187
Tassler, Bernard, 65–66, 80
Taylor, George, 88, 93, 95, 96, 97, 98, 99, 100, 103, 107, 110, 114–115, 175
Taylor, Myron, 86
Teachers Union, 356
Teamsters Union, 28, 29, 72, 73, 88, 95, 147, 148, 151, 178, 195, 196, 199, 204, 231–232, 285, 296, 393; corruption under Beck, 233–243, 294; corruption under Hoffa, 244–256, 294–295; expulsion from AFL-CIO, 247–254, 278, 324; joins UAW in ALA, 401; loan offer to ILA, 193; membership figures, 254, 324; and NALC, 313; on Pay Board, 432, 433, 458; raiding by, 256; reaffiliation efforts, 252–253
Tehas, Virginia, 4, 118, 179, 250, 258, 264, 292, 338, 346, 451, 460
Telephone workers, 140
Tewson, Sir Vincent, 133, 176, 225–226, 227, 276–277, 279
Texas farmworkers, 400–401
Texas Federation of Labor, 295, 297
Textile industry, 307, 467; jurisdictional disputes, 259, 286; 1934 strike, 40
Textile Workers Union of America, 259, 412–413
Thomas, Elmer, 87
Thomas, Norman, 61, 63, 399
Thomas, R. J., 92, 97, 100, 112, 114, 121, 285–286
Thompson, Frank, 319
Thorne, Florence, 79, 80, 114
Thurmond, Strom, 411
Tile layers union, 23
Tobey, Charles W., 191
Tobin, Daniel, 28, 31, 36, 63, 68, 72, 148, 193, 196, 197, 243, 251; and AFL-CIO unity efforts, 89–92; and AFL presidency, 179–180; and Communist disclaimer oath, 147–149, 151; and Lewis, 109, 147, 149; and Meany's move to AFL job, 72–77, 78, 81
Tobin, James, 163
Townsend, Francis E., 61
Townsend, Willard S., 206
Towr, Ray, 59
Trade Union Unity League, 152
Transport Workers Union, 64, 152, 204–205, 252
Transportation industries, 410n.; compulsory arbitration, 456
Truman, Harry S, 131, 134–135, 140, 178, 217, 308, 345; confrontation with labor, 142–143, 166–175, 177; and Korean War economic stabilization, 167–170, 172, 174–175; labor legislation under, 144, 164; lectured by Meany, 174–175; re-election campaign, 158, 159–162; Taft-Hartley veto of, 146, 155–156
Tunisia, 221
Turco, Anthony, 149
Two-party system, Meany on, 163–164
Tyler, Gus, 358

Udall, Morris, 298
Unemployment, 45, 82, 324, 371, 421–
    422; black-to-white ratio, 314, 320;
    depression, 29–30, 40, 45, 60, 70;
    Eisenhower recessions, 216–217,
    271, 304; Nixon years, 415, 422,
    423, 424, 427; post-World War II,
    140; relieved by Kennedy pro-
    grams, 304
Unemployment insurance, 139, 164,
    304; AFL stance, early depression,
    30–32; N.Y. State, 31–33, 38, 40,
    44–46; Social Security Act, 30, 44,
    46; state programs, 30, 31–32, 44,
    46, 164
Union party (1936), 61
Union shop, 176, 209, 210. See also
    Closed-shop issue; Right-to-work
    laws
Unions, unionism: business, 28; ethnic,
    racial and religious groupings, 314;
    federal versus national, interna-
    tional, 148, 165; craft versus
    industrial, 182, 185, 201; officials'
    power, 24; secretiveness, 49; self-
    perpetuation of bureaucracies, 24;
    use of injunction by, 26–27
    **membership statistics:** U.S. total, 1940
    versus 1945, 115; U.S. total in
    1971, 466; U.S. total as percentage
    of labor force, 458n., 466
United Association (plumbers union),
    13, 18–27, 48, 52, 73, 208; and
    Brindell scandal, 15–16; full title,
    13; Local One, 25; Local Two, 7,
    18–20; Local 463, 18, 20–26, 29,
    189, 306; Meany a member, 13, 15,
    16, 20n.; Meany's father in, 7, 16;
    1927 strike, 25–27
*United Association Journal*, 20, 211
United Auto Workers (UAW), 92, 112,
    121, 140, 141, 171, 183, 217, 323,
    342–343, 375, 467; in ALA with
    Teamsters, 401; convention of
    1967, 390, 391; of 1968, 396; of
    1970, 402; and farmworker union-
    ization, 389, 391, 398–400; foreign
    affairs statements (1966) 377, 381,
    383–384, 386; jurisdictional dis-
    putes, 97, 195, 278, 282–283, 288;
    membership figures, 324; in 1968
    election, 363, 364, 367; on Pay
    Board, 432, 434, 457; pay increases,
    171, 175, 349; strikes, 140, 141,
    265, 391; ultimatum to AFL-CIO
    (Administrative Letters), 389–392,
    397–398; withdrawal from AFL-
    CIO, 327, 356, 387–398

United Construction Workers Organ-
    izing Committee, 70, 88, 109, 111
United Electrical Workers, 199, 373
United Farm Workers Organizing Com-
    mittee (UFWOC), 399–400
United Federation of Postal Clerks, 318
United Garment Workers, 71, 74, 251
United Labor Policy Committee
    (ULPC), 170–172, 174–176
United Mine Workers of America
    (UMWA), 36, 63, 71, 83, 84, 87,
    149, 152, 265; construction organ-
    izing committee, 88, 109, 111;
    District 50, 109, 111, 142; and
    NALC, 313; plea for readmission
    to AFL (1943), 109, 111; re-
    admission to AFL (1946), 141–
    142; in rival federation plot with
    USW, 196; strikes, 85–86, 108–111,
    142; withdrawal (1947) from AFL,
    153–154; in WFTU, 125
United Nations, 125, 134, 223, 276–277,
    378
United Rubber Workers, 141, 372
United Steel Workers of America, 100,
    183, 186, 246, 252, 277, 296, 303,
    433; AFL reaffiliation feelers to,
    141; membership figures, 324, 463;
    1962 contract, 302; and 1968 elec-
    tion, 359, 362, 363, 367; rival
    federation plot with UMW, 196,
    200; 1954 convention of, 200–201
United Textile Workers of America,
    259–260
United Transport Service Employees,
    206
Unruh, Jesse, 363
Upholsterers union, 251, 286
Urban League, 305, 309, 311, 313, 317,
    319, 409
U.S. Chamber of Commerce, 96, 167,
    168, 298, 406
*U.S. News & World Report*, 425, 466
U.S. Steel Corporation, 85, 86, 302
U.S. Supreme Court, 53, 348; civil rights
    decisions, 309, 310; and NIRA, 46,
    52; Nixon nominations to, 411,
    412–413; and Taft-Hartley, 162

Valente, Anthony, 259–260
Van Arsdale, Harry, 50
Veldkamp, M. J., 380
Velie, Lester, 269
Viereck, George Sylvester, 158
Vietnam War, 337–338, 349–350, 353–
    361, 377, 415; AFL-CIO position,
    353–354, 389; ALA stand, 401;
    Cambodia, 413–414, 447; economic

Vietnam War (continued)
  effects of, 349, 420, 422; labor
    attitudes study by COPE, 357;
    Meany's views, 353–358, 364
Villatoro, Rubén, 224
Vinson, Fred, 111
Virginia State AFL-CIO, 315
Voice of America, 273, 330
Vorse, Mary, 192
Vote, labor: education programs, 157–
    162, 164, 166, 367–369; labor
    participation, 157, 164; in 1968,
    367; registration drives, 159, 164,
    178, 301, 352, 365, 368–369

Wage-profit disparity, 349
Wage stabilization, 115, 422; Kennedy/
    Johnson guidelines, 302, 342, 348–
    351; Korean War, 167–168, 171–
    172, 175–176, 427; post-World War
    II, 114, 139–140, 143; Vietnam
    War years failure, 349–351, 371
  Nixon: early views, 420–421, 423;
    NEP freeze, 425–429, 433; NEP
    Phase Two, 433–436, 440, 451,
    452, 455–457. See also Pay Board
  World War II, 98–101, 102–105, 111–
    112, 114, 139; disregarded in coal
    strike case, 110–111; FDR's hold-
    the-line order, 104; Little Steel
    Formula (LSF), 100–101, 103–
    104, 112, 115, 139
Wage Stabilization Board, 114, 168,
    171, 175
Wages: level exempt from NEP control,
    453–454; overtime, 138, 164; "pre-
    vailing" versus "security," 51–60,
    67–68, 69, 70
  increases: blamed for inflation, 442–
    443; construction industry, 423;
    industrial, World War II, 82, 115,
    139; Korean War, 171, 175–176;
    1953–1956, 219; of 1960's, 302,
    348–349, 371, 420; post-World War
    II, 141; under PhaseTwo of NEP,
    452, 455–456
  minimum, 177, 300, 346, 350–351;
    circumvention of, 40; increases in,
    164, 304; Meany's early opposition
    to, 31, 47–48; not-covered workers,
    466
Wagner, Richard, 379
Wagner, Robert F., 30, 46
Wagner Act. See National Labor Re-
    lations Act
Waldrop, Frank, 110
Wall Street Journal, 211, 402, 412, 445,
    463

Wallace, George C., 365, 367–368, 369,
    459
Wallace, Henry A., 162
Walsh, Richard F., 388
Walsh-Healy Act, 173
War Labor Board, 87–88, 91, 93–115,
    116, 140, 182, 426, 432; change in
    voluntary, independent status of,
    101–105, 107, 111; and closed-shop
    issue, 87, 96; members of, 87–88,
    94, 95, 438–439; and 1943 coal
    strike, 108, 109–111; record of,
    114; and wage controls, 98–101,
    102, 103–105, 111, 115
Washington, March on, (1963), 322,
    341
Washington Evening Star, 189, 271, 381
Washington Merry-Go-Round column,
    98n.
Washington Post, 263, 381, 448, 460,
    464n.
Washington Star, 141, 450
Watson, Marvin, 338, 360, 394
Watt, Robert J., 105, 116
Weaver, George, 379
Weber, Arnold, 433, 437–439, 442
Webster, Milton, 307, 317
Wechsler, James A., 84, 147
Weeks, Sinclair, 211
Weinberg, Sidney, 169, 172
Welfare rolls, depression year 1934, 40
West Coast dock strike, 1971–72, 455–
    456
Wharton, Arthur, 182
Wheeler, Burton K., 158
Wheeler, George, 131
White, James E., 223
White, Theodore H., 369
White-collar workers, 286, 324, 467
Wickens, Mrs. A. J., 113, 114
Wicker, Tom, 410
Wilkins, J. Ernest, 278
Williams, Cy, 10
Willkie, Wendell, 69, 84
Wilson, Charles E. ("Electric Charlie"
    of GE), 168–169, 171n., 172–176
Wilson, Charles E. ("Engine Charlie"
    of GM), 171, 216
Wilson, Woodrow, 46
Winter, Herman, 258
Wire tapping, 360
Wirtz, W. Willard, 303, 338, 339, 340,
    344–350, 373–374, 393–394
Woll, J. Albert, 201, 234, 237–239, 303
Woll, Matthew, 65, 66, 68, 71, 87, 90,
    91, 106, 179–180, 198, 201, 204,
    463; and foreign affairs, 120, 123,
    127n., 128, 131
Women's labor legislation, 47

Woodcock, Leonard, 255, 432, 434, 436, 457, 467
Work Relief Act, 51, 55
Work week, 30, 139, 302; New York, 47
Workers Defense League (WDL), 408–409
Workmen's compensation, 38, 42–44
Works Progress Administration (WPA), 51–60, 67–68, 69n.; N.Y. building trades strikes, 55–59, 67–68
World Federation of Trade Unions (WFTU), 125–127, 131, 132, 332; split, 132–133

World War II, 69, 82; AFL stance during, 118, 119, 167; veterans, 139, 140. *See also* War Labor Board
Wurf, Jerry, 327, 464
Wyzanski, Charles, 83

Yellow dog contract, 38, 47
Young, Whitney, Jr., 317–318, 409

Zack, Albert J., 266, 393–394, 418–419, 426, 429n., 434, 452
Zaritsky, Max, 64, 158
Ziegler, Ronald, 425, 437
Zimmerman, Charles, 67, 311, 313, 314

# Joseph C. Goulden

Joseph C. Goulden was born and educated in Texas. He wrote for the Dallas *News* from 1958 to 1961, and for the Philadelphia *Inquirer,* first as an investigative reporter and then as Washington correspondent, from 1961 to 1968. He spent the year 1966 in Guatemala and Mexico as an Alicia Patterson Fund Fellow, writing on divergent forms of Latin nationalism. Goulden's earlier books were *The Curtis Caper,* on the *Saturday Evening Post* debacle; *Monopoly,* a muckraking study of AT&T; *Truth Is the First Casualty,* on the Gulf of Tonkin incidents; *The Money Givers,* on philanthropic foundations; and *The Superlawyers,* on high-powered Washington attorneys. Goulden is a contributing editor of *Audience* and has written for *Harper's, Ramparts, Washingtonian, Earth,* and *Vista;* he is a frequent contributor to *The Nation.* Goulden lives in Arlington, Virginia, with his wife, Jody, also a journalist, and sons Trey and Jim Craig.